COLLECTION

ELI, ELI, LAMMA SABACTHANI?[1]

By
Atila Sinke Guimarães

---

[1] See explanation for the choice of this title § 14 of the General Introduction.

"The Council is like a spring that becomes a river. The river's current follows us even though its spring may be far away. One may say that the Council leaves itself as a legacy to the Church that held it. The Council does not oblige us so much to look back at the act of its convening, but it does oblige us to take into account the inheritance we have received, which is present and will remain present in the future. What is this inheritance?"[2]

---

[2] PAUL VI, General Audience of January 12, 1966, in *Insegnamenti di Paolo VI*, Tipografia Poliglotta Vaticana, vol. IV, p. 698.

ERRATA

Page 139, line 16: John XXIII in place of John XXII

Page 157, fotnote 86 b, line 9: William in place of Willian

Page 187, line 29: static condition in place of state

Page 190, line 15; page 192, lines 1 and 21: *substratum* in place of *substractum*

Page 217, footnote 5, line 11: John XXIII in place of John XIII

Page 272, line 28: bring in place of brings

Page 280, line 16: Council in place of Concil

Page 283, line 13, came from in place of come from

Page 306, line 20; page 307, lines 22, 26: Petrine in place of Petrian

Page 307, line 34: papolatry in place of papalatry

Page 323, line 21: Haerlem in place of Haarlen

Page 325, line 5: Pederborn in place of Padernborn; line 13, Casey in place of Case

Page 325, line 13: Casey in place of Case

Page 429, Line 12, Under KUNG: *Veracidade* in place of See*acidade*

TABLE OF CONTENTS

1st phase * The conservatives arrive at the Council not organized among themselves but confident that the dogmatic schemata prepared in the pre-Council will be approved.

  * The progressivists arrive very well organized and ready to make their best efforts, but uncertain of victory.

2nd phase * Right at the opening of Vatican II, by declaring that the Council was to be predominantly pastoral and relegating dogmatic questions based on the traditional teaching to a secondary plane, John XXIII disorients the conservatives.

  * With the withdrawal of the schema *De fontibus Revelationis* by the express desire of John XXIII, nearly all the remaining schemata of the pre-Council are dropped from the agenda.

* The conservatives show discouragement and resignation.

3rd phase
* Alleging pastoral attitudes, the progressivists introduce into the schemata ideas of adaptation to the world and different religions.

* The conservatives protest against some of them.

* Paul VI, directly or indirectly, uses his authority to silence the conservatives and give the victory to progressivists.

* Faced by contradictions with traditional doctrine, the conservatives accept them only by force of the pontifical authority and under the allegation that they are pastoral attitudes.

* This tatic is used until the end of the Council.

4th phase
* Once Vatican II is over and victory clearly won by the progressivists, they gradually begin to say that the Council was not only pastoral, but also dogmatic.

* Their tendency is to accentuate the doctrinal aspect of the victories obtained.

5th phase
* The conservatives, on the contrary, once Vatican II is over, begin to stress its pastoral aspect.

* Their apology seeks to demonstrate that, since the Council was pastoral, it does not require obedience as dogmatic ones do.

6th phase
* In the post-conciliar period, when the possibility of a conservative reaction arises, the Vatican leadership uses its power and prestige to try to destroy the reaction by alleging that the Council was dogmatic.

7th phase
* When, in the post-conciliar era, the progressivists have problems with their grassroots who complain about Vatican II's ambiguity, the leadership call to mind the dogmatic victories in the Council and stress the need for making them more explicit in the future.

---

[3] *Ardito, arditi* = Italian for hothead, hotheads.

*   *   *

Foreground: Atila Sinke Guimarães, author of the Collection
Eli, Eli, Lamma Sabacthani?

Right: Atila Sinke Guimarães reviews *In the Murky Waters of
Vatican II* with his mentor, Professor Plinio Corrêa de Oliveira in
Serra Negra, Brazil in May of 1987.

SPECIAL FOREWORD
by Dr. Malachi Martin

This first volume of *The Collection: Eli, Eli, Lamma Sabacthani?* establishes the author Atila Sinke Guimarães as one of the best informed latter-day students of that epochal event, the Second Vatican Council. Up to this moment, the most encyclopedic and detailedly informed examination of the Council was provided by Professor Amerio in his *Iota Unum*. Guimarães' *Collection* bids fair to replace *Iota Unum* as the best all-purpose source-book about the Council; and it is not hazardous or rash to predict that this work of Guimarães will be a standard reference work on the subject and well into the 21st century.

The title of this first volume, *The Murky Waters of Vatican Council II*, tells exactly what the contents are. All of us who lived through the years of Vatican Two (1962-1965) and have had to deal with the consequences can recognize immediately the pinpoint accuracy of this first volume: the ambiguity, cultivated and, as it were, perfected in the composition of the sixteen main documents of the Council, is now seen as the most skillful means devised to undo the essential Roman-ness and Catholicism of the Roman Catholic Church, and to deliver that entire one-billion member institutional organization into the ready and eager hands of those for whom the existence of the traditional papacy and hierarchical organization has long been anathema. One reads in this volume with a certain sickening feeling the unified way in which the Church's own theologians and prelates conspired willingly to bring about the present trend to the de-Romanization and de-Catholicizing of the once monolithic institution.

9/25/97

*

FOREWORD

To shed light where before there was obscurity, to
bring order to mayhem is a great charity that can be done
by one man for another not only in the realm of things,
but also in that of events and ideas. For the last three
decades, a controversy regarding Vatican Council II has
engaged "conservatives" and "liberals" inside the Catholic
Church, with the former group performing every form of
intellectual gymnastics in order to comprehensively fit the
"spirit" and the "letter" of the Council into the traditional
Magisterium of the Church. At the same time, the
progressives and neo-modernists have pushed increasingly
radical reforms based on this "spirit" and "letter" of the
Council. The debate has been further confused by certain
ecclesiastics, who show amazing tolerance toward
heresies, yet lose their ecumenical spirit of tolerance when
dealing with those who stand for tradition.

It is a great intellectual *tour de force* of Atila Sinke
Guimarães to have prepared this eleven-volume collection
with unprecedented documentation entitled *Eli, Eli,
lamma sabacthani?* in order to clarify and analyze with a
scholarly and objective study the letter, spirit, thinking,
and fruits of the Second Vatican Council. Doing so, he
provides us with a most important tool for the defense of
the Holy Catholic Church against progressivist currents,
such as the *We Are Church movement*, which is now
calling for a Third Vatican Council "to finish the work
begun at Vatican Council II." For years, faithful Catholics
have struggled with the avowed ambiguities present in the
Conciliar documents. Using an inductive method, Atila S.
Guimarães has delimited and documented these ambiguities, their historical roots, and their consequences in
the impressive analysis entitled *In the Murky Waters of
Vatican II.*

The polemics over the letter and spirit of Vatican
Council II has been at the center of Church life over the
last three decades and raises great passion on all sides of
the religious/ideological spectrum. It takes great care, as

well as rare courage, to stand up and speak frankly about what the Council mentors intended when hitherto there have been veiled allusions or undocumented accusations. As we reach the threshold of the new millenium with all the events and promises it portends in the ecclesiastical sphere, the work of Atila Sinke Guimarães takes on a new urgency and importance.

These last thirty years the Church has been afflicted by a particularly strange phenomenon – the fear of any comprehensive, objective critique of a controversial Council. Fear of being labeled "integrist," narrow-minded, close-minded, or out of synch with the Vatican has set unwritten, but predetermined, limits to this debate. This one-sided fear – for there is no fear on the side of the progressives to draw ever more radical consequences from Conciliar ambiguities – has only proven its protagonists to have a profound lack of objectivity.

"Do not hold back a word when it can be wholesome." (Ecc 4:28) Failure to define, clarify, and then arrest doctrinal and spiritual ambiguity ultimately has been the vehicle used by the progressives to neutralize opponents and to give free reign to dissent and heterodoxy – with all the multiform evils that this represents for the Church and, consequently, temporal society. Silence and submissiveness in the name of respect for authority and obedience does not take into account that all disciplinary authority and all obedience presupposes the clear and unequivocal doctrinal teaching of the Holy Church.

It is significant that the spirit of the author of *In the Murky Waters of Vatican II* is not that of a dissident, hostile to Papacy or authority, but one of humility, love, obedience, and fidelity to the Holy Catholic Church, the Successor of Peter, and the ordinary and extraordinary teachings of the Magisterium, in whose defense he undertook this great effort. For this reason, this work deserves the careful reading and reflection of bishops, priests, scholars, historians, and the faithful.

Atila S. Guimarães undertook this endeavor at the request of Prof. Plinio Corrêa de Oliveira, a great Catholic thinker and man of action who commissioned and directed the study, desired this work to be published, and never feared public opinion more than God. Prof. Plinio viewed the Council not as an isolated event that ignited a great crisis, but placed it within its historical perspective. Already in 1943, Prof. Corrêa de Oliveira perceived the re-emergence of the Modernist errors in his prophetic work *In Defense of Catholic Action* and denounced these trends that contended for control of the Second Vatican Council.

Time has only confirmed these early perceptions, making more opportune than ever this important analysis by Sinke Guimarães. Already in 1991, Prof. Corrêa de Oliveira sent these words of encouragement to the author: "An enormous effort of both intelligence and will enabled the author to achieve this work for the glory of Our Lady, the Holy Church, and Christian Civilization. When published, it will constitute an irreparable blow to the forces of the Revolution that have infiltrated the Holy Church in this phase of self-demolition and the internal expansion of the smoke of Satan."

Thus, it seems opportune for *Tradition in Action* to avail itself of the opportunity to bring this unique study before the American public. In tribute to Prof. Plinio Corrêa de Oliveira and his spirit of obedience to and love for the Holy Catholic Church, *Tradition In Action* publishes this study.

Marian T. Horvat, Ph.D.
President, *Tradition In Action,*
Center for Christian Culture and Apologetics

*

HOMAGE AND GRATITUDE

I wish the first lines of the Collection *Eli, Eli, lamma sabacthani?* to be of homage and gratitude to the outstanding paladin of the Holy Catholic Church and Christian Civilization, Professor Plinio Corrêa de Oliveira. To him I owe the spiritual and intellectual formation which, since 1964, I was honored to receive in daily contact with him, his words and works, in the ranks of the Brazilian Society for the Defense of Tradition, Family and Property (TFP).[1] By him I was given the task — kindly presented as an invitation but respectfully accepted as a duty — to analyze Ecumenical Council Vatican II.

His example of dedication and courage gave me strength to undertake this work. His unshakable faith, untiring hope and edifying charity were the mainstays that supported me at a crucial moment when these virtues vacillate all over the world. To his penetrating discernment, unique global view, and inexhaustible culture I had recourse in every difficulty. To him, therefore, as Author of the idea of this Collection and my mentor, I want to offer a most respectful and filial homage of gratitude.

> "You and the words you spoke have moved my heart
> With such desire to continue onward
> That now I have attained my first purpose.
> Let us start, for both our wills, joined now, are one.
> You are my guide, you are my lord and teacher."[2]

To this homage, after his death on October 3rd, 1995, I add my profound sadness at his absence and growing nostalgia for the noble bonds that increasingly united us during the 31 years I was privileged to share with him.

My sincere thanks also to my dear TFP brothers in the ideal who most especially helped me put together this Collection:

Mr. Wilson Gabriel da Silva, an intellectual contributor to this work from beginning to end, who assisted in the research and updating, as well as in the revision of texts and translations contained in the whole Collection;

---

[1] About the TFP, see Notes 12 and 16 in the General Introduction.

[2] "Tu m'hai con disiderio il cor disposto / si al venir con le parole tue, / ch'i' son tornato nel primo proposto. / Or va, ch'un sol volere è d'ambedue: / tu duca, tu segnore e tu maestro." (DANTE, La Divina Commedia, Inf. II, 136-140).

Mr. Renato Murta de Vasconcelos, who worked until 1991 on complementary research of documents of the Catholic Magisterium, the verification and completion of the historic data mentioned and the documentation used, and checking of translations. To him is due a considerable part of the research in German language texts.

Mr. José Coutinho, who helped with preliminary readings and complementary research to this work, and is responsible for most of the translations from Latin;

Mr. Paulo Roberto Carriello Rosa, who has performed the general revision of this Collection and has helped with updating readings and also with translations from Latin and German;

Mr. Paulo Hideo Moriyama, who has been my secretary in my studies for about 20 years and taken care of typesetting and other computer-related tasks.

My thanks go also to my TFP friends for their help: Juan Gonzalo Larrain Campbell, Rodrigo Antonio Guerreiro Dantas, Leo Nino Foscolo Danielle.

With regard to the English edition of this work, I thank the following counter-revolutionary friends:

Mr. Leo A. Horvat, a member of the American TFP who worked for eight years with the Brazilian TFP, and to whom both organizations owe important intellectual contributions. His encouragement to have this English version published, his countless personal contacts and concrete initiatives that he undertook to reach this goal have played a vital role.

Mr. José A. Schelini, a longtime friend and interpreter who kindly translated this whole Collection into English.

Dr. Marian T. Horvat, Ph.D., the articulate and dynamic president of Tradition in Action, Inc. (TIA). To her selfless dedication to the Catholic Cause, I owe a thorough and accurate revision of the English text. Because of this careful and enriching revision, I could perhaps consider her as co-translator of this present volume.

Dr. Remi E. Amelunxen, Ph.D., a scholarly and responsible editor both from the doctrinal and linguistic standpoints. Along with Dr. Horvat, he made the necessary contacts to facilitate the publication.

Dr. William H. Mitchell, M.D., who revised the English text and effectively contributed, with Dr. Horvat and Dr. Amelunxen, to make this initiative successful.

Dr. John P. Mitchell, Ph.D., whose unfailing generosity and technical assistance were an invaluable help.

*   *   *

GENERAL INFORMATION

§ 1   The collection *Eli, Eli, lamma sabacthani?* contains, at the time of the publication of volume I, approximately 14,000 quotations from around 900 authors.

§ 2   Various quotations appear in more than one place in the eleven volumes of this collection. If it is a merely informative quotation, it will simply be repeated for the reader's convenience. If it is a doctrinal quotation, it may be repeated for an analysis from a different viewpoint or to give the subject the emphasis that we deem necessary. Repetitions, however, are not frequent.

§ 3   The Church publications that were regularly followed as this study was written are: *L'Osservatore Romano, La Civiltà Cattolica, Concilium, Il Regno, 30 Giorni, Adista.* Religious sections of lay periodicals routinely monitored were those from *Corriere della Sera, Avvenire, La Repubblica, Time, Newsweek, Folha de S. Paulo, O Estado de S. Paulo.* Other news items were taken from publications we receive occasionally or were drawn from the well-organized documentation service of the Brazilian TFP's Readers Commission.

§ 4   Seeking to delve deeply into conciliar thought and the tactics used at the Council, as well as to assemble a more select bibliography to grasp the spirit of the Council, the author of this collection traveled to seven European countries in the beginning of 1983 to interview personages, some of them major ones, who participated in the Council, wrote about it, or helped to implement it. Such interviews will be cited as required. Tapes of the interviews can be found in the author's file.

§ 5   For Portuguese-language quotations of conciliar documents in this book, we have used the work, *Documentos do Vaticano II - Constituições, decretos e declarações,* introduction and analytical index by Fr. Boaventura Kloppenburg, OFM, general coordination by Fr. Frederico Vier, OFM (Vozes, Petrópolis, 1966); bilingual edition with the Portuguese text reviewed by sub-secretaries of the National Conference of Brazilian Bishops. For English-language quotations, we have used *Vatican Council II – The Conciliar and Post-Conciliar Documents,* ed. Austin Flannery, OP (Collegeville, MN: Liturgical Press, 1975).

§ 6   Following the reforms by John XXIII and Paul VI in the Roman Curia, John Paul II carried out yet more reforms with the apostolic Constitution *Pastor Bonus* (June 28, 1988). The latter caused name changes in various Dicasteries, for example, in the three main ecumenical Secretariats: The Secretariat for the Union of Christians, established by John XXIII on July 5, 1960, came to be called the Pontifical Council for the Union of Christians; the Secretariat for Non-Christians, founded by Paul VI on May 19, 1964, was changed to the Pontifical Council for Inter-Religious Dialogue; the Secretariat for Non-Believers, established by Paul VI on April 9, 1965, is now called the Pontifical Council for Dialogue with Non-Believers.

Such changes caused a minor problem to our work regarding references. Should we replace the names of the ancient Secretariats with their current designations each time they appear? We thought it better to keep their names as they appear in the documentation. Warned about the name changes, our reader will know what we are referring to as they appear.

§ 7   Since this collection cites documents from about 900 authors, it became quite difficult to accompany — for the entire time span during which this study was put together — the itinerary of the ecclesiastical and intellectual careers of contemporary authors in order to update their titles. Thus, although we have made an effort to update such data, it is unlikely that it has been carried out to the extent we would have liked.

§ 8   The collection was written in Portuguese and has been translated into English. At this time, the author is not planning for a Portuguese edition. The English edition of volume I is the first of the works in the Collection to be published.

§ 9   The author clarifies that while he has been a member of the Brazilian TFP since 1964, the publication of this collection is not intended as an official or unofficial position taken by the Brazilian, American, or any other TFP. The author, therefore, assumes full and exclusive responsibility for what has been written.

The references to the TFP contained in volume I were revised by Prof. Plinio Corrêa de Oliveira, who is unfortunately no longer with us. The author publishes them only as a homage to that great Catholic combatant and as a token of admiration for the organization to which he dedicated his life.

*   *   *

ABBREVIATIONS

1. The Books of the *Bible*:

Abd	Abdias	**Jude**	Jude
Acts	The Acts of the Apostles	**1 Kg**	1 Kings
Apoc	Apocalypse	**2 Kg**	2 Kings
Bar	Baruch	**Lam**	Lamentations
Cant	Canticle of Canticles	**Lev**	Leviticus
Col	Colossians	**Lk**	Luke
Dan	Daniel	**1 Macc**	1 Maccabees
Dt	Deuteronomy	**2 Macc**	2 Maccabees
Ec	Ecclesiastes	**Mal**	Malachi
Eccl	Ecclesiasticus	**Mic**	Micah
Eph	Ephesians	**Mk**	Mark
Esd	Esdras	**Mt**	Matthew
Est	Esther	**Nah**	Nahum
Ex	Exodus	**Neh**	Nehemiah
Ezel	Ezekiel	**Num**	Numbers
Gal	Galatians	**Ob**	Obadiah (Abdias)
Gen	Genesis	**Os**	Osee (Hosea)
Hab	Habakkuk	**1 Paralip**	1 Paralipomenon
Hag	Haggai (Aggeus)	**2 Paralip**	2 Paralipomenon
Heb	Hebrews	**1 Pet**	1 Peter
Hos	Hosea (Osee)	**2 Pet**	2 Peter
Is	Isaiah	**Phil**	Philippians
Jas	James	**Pr**	Proverbs
Jdt	Judith	**Ps**	Psalms
Jer	Jeremiah	**Rom**	Romans
Jg	Judges	**Ru**	Ruth
Jl	Joel	**Soph**	Sophoniah
Jn	John (Gospel)	**1 Th**	1 Thessalonians
1 Jn	1 John (Epistle)	**2 Th**	2 Thessalonians
2 Jn	2 John (Epistle)	**1 Tim**	1 Timothy
3 Jn	3 John (Epistle)	**2 Tim**	2 Timothy
Job	Job	**Tit**	Titus
Jon	Jonas	**Tob**	Tobias
Jos	Joshua	**Zech**	Zechariah

We do not adopt the abbreviations 1 Sam (1 *Samuel*) and 2 Sam to refer to the 1st and 2nd *Book of Kings*; 1 Chron (*1 Chronicles*) and 2 Chron to designate the 1st and 2nd *Book of Paralipomenon*; Sir (*Sirach*) to replace reference to the *Ecclesiasticus*. When such abbreviations appear in the documents used in this collection, they are replaced with their traditional designation.

2. The Conciliar Documents:

LG   *Lumen gentium*: The Dogmatic Constitution on the Church
DV   *Dei Verbum*: The Dogmatic Constitution on Divine Revelation
GS   *Gaudium et spes*: The Pastoral Constitution on the Church in the Modern World
SC   *Sacrosanctum Concilium*: The Constitution on the Sacred Liturgy
UR   *Unitatis redintegratio*: The Decree on Ecumenism
OE   *Orientalium Ecclesiarum*: The Decree on the Catholic Oriental Churches
AG   *Ad gentes*: The Decree on the Church's Missionary Activity
CD   *Christus Dominus*: The Decree on Bishops
PO   *Presbyterorum ordinis*: The Decree on Priests
PC   *Perfectae caritatis*: The Decree on Religious Life
OT   *Optatam totius*: The Decree on the Training of Priests
AA   *Apostolicam actuositatem*: The Decree on the Apostolate of the Laity
IM   *Inter mirifica*: The Decree on the Means of Social Communication
GE   *Gravissimum educationis*: The Declaration on Christian Education
DH   *Dignitatis humanae*: The Declaration on Religious Liberty
NA   *Nostra aetate*: The Declaration on the Church's Relations with non-Christian Religions

3. Abbreviation of references:

a.	article	**n.**	number
aa.	articles	**nn.**	numbers
bk.	book	**op. cit.**	*opus citatus*
chap.	chapter	**P.**	Part
chaps.	chapters	**p.**	page
can.	canon	**pp.**	pages
cans.	canons	**q.**	question
cf.	confer	**qq.**	questions
col.	column	**s.**	solution
cols.	columns	**sec.**	section
d.	distinction	**ses.**	session
dd.	distinctions	**sol.**	solution
disp.	*disputatio*	**t.**	tome
f.	the following page	**tt.**	tomes
ff.	the following pages	**th.**	thesis
i.e.	*id est*	**V.A.**	various authors
lec.	*lectio*	**v.gr.**	*verbi gratia*
lect.	*lectura*	**vol.**	volume
		vols.	volumes

4. Bibliographic Abbreviations:

CSEO Monthly review of the Centro Studi per l'Europa Orientale.

D Henricus DENZINGER, *Enchiridion Symbolorum* - a collection of the most important excerpts of the Magisterium, put together by the German priest Heinrik Joseph Denzinger (1819-1883) first published in 1854.

DB Henricus DENZINGER - Clemens BANWART - Denzinger's collection updated by Banwart between 1908 and 1921.

DR Henricus DENZINGER - Carolus RAHNER - idem, updated by Rahner between 1946 and 1954.

DS Henricus DENZINGER - Adolphus SCHOENMETZER - idem, updated by Schönmetzer between 1955 and 1965.

DTC *Dictionnaire de théologie catholique*, published under the responsibility of Alfred VACANT - Eugène MANGENOT between 1923 and 1972.

ICI *Informations Catholiques Internationales.*

LThK *Lexikon für Theologie und Kirche.*

NRTh *Nouvelle Revue Théologique.*

MüThZ *Münchener Theologische Zeitschrift.*

PG *Patrologie grecque-latine* (PG), 217 vols., more than 3 indexes, published by Paul Migne.

PL *Patrologie latine* (PL), 161 vols. more than 1 index, idem.

REB *Revista Eclesiástica Brasileira.*

Rev. Th. Louv. *Revue Théologique de Louvain.*

SEDOC *Serviço de Documentação.*

TS *Theological Studies.*

5. Abbreviations of Names of Religious Orders and Congregations:

CMF *Cordis Mariae Filii.*

CSSR *Congregatio Sanctissimi Redemptoris.*

MM U.S. Society for Foreign Missions (Maryknoll).

OC *Ordo Carmelitarum.*

OCD *Ordo Carmelitarum Descalciatorum.*

OFM *Ordo Fratrum Minorum.*

OP *Ordo Praedicatorum.*

OSB *Ordo Sancti Benedicti.*

SI or **SJ** *Societas Iesu.*

SVD *Societas Verbi Divini.*

* * *

NOTES ON STYLE

§ *1* Due to the large number of authors and works quoted and commented upon in this Collection, as well as to the frequent references to other Volumes of the Collection, when we refer to books, works, or volumes by other authors, we use lower case; when referring to this Collection, we capitalize the first letter: Collection, Work, Study, Volume, Chapter, Author, etc. Likewise, we capitalize the first letter when referring to our Reader to distinguish him from readers of other authors.

§ *2* For the sake of uniformity in our presentation, we take the following liberties in relation to the transcribed texts:

* When the author being quoted puts any word, expression, or phrase in bold, we put it in italics.

* All foreign words used by the authors are not translated but simply italicized by us regardless of the criterion used by the author.

* Book, newspaper, and magazine titles are italicized, thus rendering uniform the various criteria used by the authors quoted.

* When an author places a bibliographical reference in parenthesis in his own text, we place it into a footnote that stands out from the others by adding an asterisk; for example, if, in the text you have **4***, in the footnote you find also **4***.

§ *3* Bold texts are always our responsibility;

§ *4* In the texts cited, comments between parentheses are by their authors, and those between brackets are ours.

*   *   *

GENERAL INTRODUCTION
TO THE COLLECTION
ELI, ELI, LAMMA SABACTHANI?

§ *1*   The **primary goal** of this Collection is to analyze Vatican Council II. This analysis will include the conciliar documents as such, the spirit of the Council, its underlying thought, and the fruits it has generated. Its **secondary goal** is to study the unity that these elements present among themselves.

§ *2*   The **criterion of analysis** is twofold. *First*, it is traditional Catholic doctrine as known by a layman endowed with a general culture and who studies sociological, historical, philosophical and theological matters related directly to Christian Civilization and indirectly to the Holy Catholic Church. *Second*, it is the *sensus fidelium* [1], that is, common sense in matters of Faith and Morals.

---

[1] a. The expression *sensus fidelium* is used here according to the doctrine of Saint VINCENT OF LÉRINS in his *Commonitorium* (PL 50, 670), in the sense that a faith that was believed *semper, ubique, ab omnibus* in the Holy Church is the true Faith thanks to a special protection the Holy Spirit gives the ensemble of the faithful along the centuries.

b. Even before Saint Vincent of Lérins, TERTULLIAN wrote about this characteristic of the faith of all faithful: "Will the Spirit of truth let the churches believe something other than that which Christ preached?" (*De praescriptionibus adversus haereticos 28*, in PL 2, 40). Saint GREGORY NAZIENZENUS also appealed to the faith of the martyrs and Bishops: "If this is not true, our faith is vain; in vain have the martyrs died, in vain have the Bishops governed the peoples" (*Epistula 102, 2 ad Cledon*, in PG 37, 200). But perhaps no one was more conscious of this fact than Saint AUGUSTINE as he invoked the Church's faith in the non-repetition of the baptism for heretics (*De baptismo contra Donatistas*, lib. 2, chap. 9, n. 14, in PL 43, 135); on the necessity of grace attested to by the meaning that the faithful attach to prayer (*De dono perseverantiae*, chap. 23, n. 63, in PL 45, 1031); on the need for, and efficacy of, the baptism for the salvation of all, especially of children (*Sermo 294*, chap. 17, in PL 38, 1346, in Vicente PROAÑO GIL, "Infalibilidad," in *Gran Enciclopedia*, Madrid: Ed. Rialp S/A, 1971-1976, vol. XII, p. 683).

c. The *sensus fidelium* (sense of the faithful) comes from the *sensus Fidei* (sense of Faith) and is the universal adherence of the faithful to the teachings in matters of Faith and morals. "What does the expression [*sensus Fidei*] mean? In the opinion of theologians, it is a gift of God which has to do with the subjective reality of the Faith and gives the whole Church the assurance of an indefectible Faith. It is a strength, an almost instinctive power to know the truth revealed by God, adhere to it, discern it and penetrate it in all of its amplitude. It certainly is not a religious sentiment of a modernist type; it is a knowledge by assimilation, adaptation, conformity or co-naturalness" (Ibid., pp. 683f.). To this definition we would add, in the spirit of Saint Vincent of Lérins, that it also is a special affinity with everything that Holy Church has taught over the centuries in a uniform and consistent manner and which has always stirred up enthusiasm in the best that could be found among the faithful.

d. Based on the well-known work by Melchior Cano, *De locis theologicis*, Fr. Claudio Garcia Extremeño, OP, professor of Dogmatics at the Dominican Faculty of Theology in Madrid, studied the field in which the *sensus fidelium* is applied and its limitations: "Naturally, the sense of the faithful will be exerted upon matters of faith and morals, but not the subtleties and explanations proper to theologians. 'Demanding an opinion of the people [about such matters] is so absurd that it would not occur to the wise, let alone the fool'" (M. CANO, *De locis theologicis*, lib. IV, chaps. IV, VI, Rome, 1890, in C. GARCIA EXTREMEÑO, "El sentido de la Fe, criterio de la Tradición," in *La Ciencia Tomista,* Salamanca, July-December, 1960, p. 576). CANO adds: "There are two kinds of things that, as we said, are believed by the Church. One, the things that have to do with everyone equally .... and in this case it is not very difficult to know the faith and the sense of everyone .... Another kind is the things whose knowledge is not of interest to the simple and unscholarly, but to the experienced and learned. Asking the people to pronounce themselves about matters of this second type would be tantamount to calling upon a blind man to distinguish between colors" (Ibid., Note 25).

e. Garcia Extremeño studies the *sensus fidei* and enumerates related expressions used to designate the faith of the faithful as a whole, namely: *sensus Ecclesiae, sensus catholicus, sensus* or *consensus fidelium, sensus socialis Ecclesiae, christiani populi fides* and *communis Ecclesiae fides*. He also studies the nature of the *sensus Fidei*, its subjective principles — the virtue of Faith, the gift of knowledge, science and wisdom, its objective principles and the relation between the *sensus Fidei* and the teaching of the Ecclesiastical Magisterium (Ibid., pp. 569-605).

f. According to the Spanish Dominican, "The Holy Spirit watches over the twofold reality of the faith, objective and subjective, in order to keep the former always intact and give the faithful Christian a nearly instinctive power of faith to adhere to its object in order to perceive it and discern it" (Ibid., p. 572). This assistance of the Holy Spirit to the *sensus fidelium* gives it an authority that often contributed decisively to guarantee orthodoxy and push ahead the progress of Dogmatics. "Thus, for example, take the definition of the real presence of the Body and Blood of Christ under the sacramental species of bread and wine, against Berengario; the truth of the immediate vision of God by the souls without need to wait for the Last Judgment; the introduction of the *Filioque* in the Creed of the Mass and, finally, the mysteries of Mary" (Ibid., p. 585).

g. Of the innumerable cases of accurate judgment by the *sensus fidelium* in the course of History, we would like to point out two among the most expressive.

The *first one* is related to the generalized defection of the Episcopate during the Arian crisis in the 4th century. John Henry Cardinal Newman is very forceful about it: "What I sustain is that, at that time of great confusion, the sublime dogma of the divinity of Our Lord was proclaimed, strengthened, defended and (humanly speaking) guaranteed far more by the Church *discens* than by the Church *docens*; that in general, the Episcopate as a body were unfaithful to their office, while the laity as a body remained faithful to their baptismal grace" (J. H. NEWMAN, "On consulting the faithful in matters of doctrine," in *The Rambler*, 1859, p. 217, in C. GARCIA EXTREMEÑO, op. cit., p. 602).

Writing about this topic, theologian Joseph Ratzinger also evokes the example of the Arian crisis: "In the universal Church there is something like an infallibility' of faith by virtue of which this universal Church can never let herself fall into error as a Church, in its totality. This is the laity's share in infallibility. That this share can at times take on an extremely active meaning, can be seen in the Arian crisis, during which at times it appeared as though the whole hierarchy had fallen prey to the Arianizing tendencies of mediation and only the firm position of the faithful ensured the victory of faith in Nicea .... for truth is not a privilege of the hierarchs, but a gift made to the Spouse of Christ as a whole" (J. RATZINGER, *Il nuovo popolo di Dio*, Brescia: Queriniana, 1971, pp. 164f., in J. M. GONZALEZ RUIZ, "Lettera aperta al Cardinale Ratzinger - Le 'verità' del Cardinale prima e dopo il S. Ufficio," in *Adista*, Rome, 1/19-21/1987, pp. 4f.).

h. In some way the *second case* is even more grave than the first, since it entailed 'resistance' to the doctrine taught by a Sovereign Pontiff: "In 1332, Pope John XXII, in Avignon preached with his private authority that the souls of the just would not enjoy beatific vision until after the resurrection of the dead and the last judgment. Gérard Eudes, Superior General of the Franciscans, made this opinion his own and spread it, preaching it publicly in Paris. Upon hearing it, *magnum murmur inter scholas auditum est*. As the matter was examined, professors of the University of Paris and the King, impelled by the common feeling of the people, asked the Pope to define the truth 'in the sense it was always defended by the piety of the Christian people.' It was solemnly defined by Benedict XII on January 29, 1336" (DS 530s.; Xavier-Marie

LE BACHELET, *Benoît XII*, in V.A., *Dictionnaire de Théologie Catholique* eds. A. VACANT - E. MANGENOT, vol. II, Paris: Letouzey & Ané, 1923-1972, cols. 657-696; DENIFLE-CHATELAIN, *Chartularium Universitatis Parisiensis*, Paris, 1851, II, nn. 970-987, in C. GARCIA EXTREMEÑO, op. cit., pp. 599f.).

i. Among the famous people who wrote about the *sensus fidelium*, its premises and consequences, several others, in addition to those already mentioned, stand out: Saint BASIL, *Adversus Eunomium*, 3, 1 in PG 29, 654; Saint JEROME, *Contra Vigilantium*, 5 in PL 23, 343; Saint AUGUSTINE, *Contra Julianum*, 1, 7, 31 in PL 44, 662; *De duabus animabus contra manichaeos*, chap. 11 in PL 42, 105; CASSIANUS, *De Incarnatione Christi contra Nestorium haericutum*, I, 6 in PL 50, 30, in C. GARCIA EXTREMEÑO, op. cit., p. 573, note 14. According to the same author, in various places Saint THOMAS AQUINAS dealt with knowledge through co-naturalness, a premise of the *sensus fidelium*, notably in the *Summa theologiae*, I, q.1, a.6 ad 3; *III Sententiarum*, d. 24, q.1, a.2, sol. 2; d. 23, q. 3, sol. 2, ad 2. The Angelic Doctor also considers the gifts of the Holy Spirit as characterizing an 'instinct' and a 'motion' that should complete the contribution of reason (*Summa theologiae*, I.II: q.68, a.8 *sed contra*; a.2). Saint Thomas deals with the gift of understanding, which according to the scholars is present in the *sensus fidelium*, in *III Sententiarum*, d. 25, q. 2, a. 2, sol. 1; *Summa theologiae*, II.II: q.8, aa. 1 ad 3; 2, 4 ad 2, 6, 7; q.49, a.2 ad 2; q.9, a.1. As for the gift of knowledge, in connection with this subject, see: idem, q.9, a.1; ad 2; q.8, a.6; q.9, a.3. In relation to the gift of wisdom, see idem, q.45; q.9, a.2 ad 1; ad 2; q.45, a.2; q.8, a.5.

j. On the importance of the *sensus fidelium* as a testimony to the indefectible Faith of the Church, G. Extremeño cites, among others: F. SUAREZ, *De Christo*, q. 27, d. 3, s. 6, n. 4; J. M. de RIPALDA, *De Fide*, d. 8, s. 2, n. 24; J. de LUGO, *De Fide*, d. 1, s. 13, n. 277, Saint Robert BELLARMINE, *De Verbo Dei*, 1.1, chap. 10, ad 2 (Garcia EXTREMEÑO, op. cit., p. 596).

k. Some contemporary authors — whose theories should be viewed with reservations — attribute to the *sensus fidelium* an even greater amplitude as they designate it with expressions such as 'inerrancy *in credendo*' (Herbert VORGRIMLER, "Dal 'sensus fidei' al 'consensus fidelium'," in *Concilium*, 1986/4, p. 17), 'infallibility *in credendo*' (A. GRILLMEIER, LThK, K I, 189, in Hans WALDENFELS, "Autorità e conoscenza," in *Concilium*, 1985/4, p. 62) or the 'passive infallibility' of the faithful (Heinrich FRIES, *C'è un magistero dei fedeli?*, Ibid., p. 115, based on F. van der Horst, E. J. De Smedt, B. van Leeuwen); or when they attribute to the 'experience' of the *sensus fidei* a profundity that could approach the experience of an interior 'revelation' of a modernist bent (Zoltán ALSZEGHY, *Sens de la Foi*, in V.A., *Vatican II: Bilan et perspectives, vingt-cinq ans après,* ed. R. LATOURELLE, Montreal/Paris:Bellarmin-Cerf, 1988, vol. I, pp. 162f.).

§ *2*   The **prism of the analysis** adopted here is an overall view of the Council. Having studied the conciliar documents, the Author noticed they were dissonant in a certain number of points with the ordinary and universal teaching of the Magisterium of the Church, and also clashed, at some other points, with the *sensus fidelium*. Asking himself what could be the underlying unity that would explain such points, as well as the post-conciliar fruits they bore, the Author put together an overall picture that sheds some light on so much confusion. Thus, in addition to analyzing each part in itself, the Work strives to discern in each one its most profound foundation and the relationships of the various parts among themselves in order to arrive at a unitary conception of Vatican Council II and its fruits.

§ *3*   The **method** used is inductive. Aware of his small authority, the Author will let the facts speak for themselves as much as possible; and when dealing with doctrine rather than fact, he will cite the opinions of renowned specialists in the matter.

In the face of certain groups of facts or opinions, the Author will ask himself whether there are enough proofs or clues to present a plan of conduct or to describe a current of opinion in the case of doctrinal matters. He will present conclusions on a level of either certainty or hypothesis, according to the usual rules of the inductive method. Exceptionally, when the matter dealt with is clearly opposed to Catholic Doctrine or gravely offends

---

Others, founded on *Lumen gentium* (n. 12) go as far as to uphold a generic infallibility of the believers, "overturning the fatal distinction between the passive and active infallibility of the Magisterium" (H. VORGRIMLER, op. cit., p. 18).

The goal pursued by the most advanced progressivists is well-defined by the comment of French Dominican Christian Duquoc, professor at the Faculty of Theology of Lyon and member of the boards of directors of the magazines *Lumière et Vie* and *Concilium*: "The Constitution *Lumen gentium*, subverting the relationship between the hierarchy and the people, bears a good witness to this need for a rupture with the model born out of the Counter-Reformation, in which the people was practically nothing and the hierarchy made decisions unsupervised" (C. DUQUOC, "Il popolo di Dio, soggetto attivo della fede nella chiesa," in *Concilium*, 1985/4, pp. 102f.).

I. Obviously, we will not consider the *sensus fidelium* from this progressivist perspective. Quite on the contrary, this Work is intended to reflect it in a harmonious and submissive consonance with the perennial teachings of the hierarchical Magisterium through whose voice the Holy Spirit has directed the Church along the centuries.

against the *sensus fidelium*, he will use the deductive method, starting out from the truths that were transgressed.

The use of the inductive method will be conditioned by this factor: Since the authors who deal with the Council often use hermetic language or refer only fragmentarily to concepts not expressed in their works, it will be necessary at times to present views that explain the thinking implicit in their language and the unexpressed unity of the fragments so that the analysis may be accessible to Readers presumably not specialized in the subject. Such explanatory overall views, presented as hypotheses, always refer to the places in the Collection where the matter is proved by induction. They are, therefore, necessary anticipations to overcome obstacles rather than preconceptions contrary to the method adopted.

§ 4   This collection's **plan** is designed to analyze the Council by stages. An ideal plan for the Work was made on the basis of the documents chosen prior to the writing.

In practice, however, the ideal plan underwent some changes that turned into the actual completed work. Let us say an explanatory word about each part of this Collection so as to clarify how they relate to one another.

The **ideal plan** called for analyzing first the letter of the conciliar documents, then the spirit according to which the doubtful points of its letter should be understood; next, the concrete fruits produced by the Council in the institutional and doctrinal spheres by virtue of its principles and dynamism; and finally, the underlying thought that would provide a unity to the letter, spirit and fruits.

Since the writing started, however, the plan was adapted according to the probating value of the documents used. In fact, the latter very often inductively proved more than the specific point we wanted to make. For example, as we analyze the spirit of Vatican II, we will collaterally bring forth to the Reader innumerable fruits of the Council, as well as several facets of its thought. Thus, when the analysis of the spirit is over, the Reader will already have an approximate notion of the fruits of the Council and a sketch of its thought. Likewise, as the fruits are analyzed later in the work, the great panoramas of conciliar thought collaterally become evident.

For this reason, that is, the cumulative character of the proofs, the actual plan of the Collection is an imperfect rendition of the ideal plan, albeit as close to it as possible.

Concretely, the **actual plan** of the present Collection is:

* analysis of the letter of the conciliar documents (Volume I);
* analysis of the spirit of the Council (Volumes II, III, IV, and V);
* analysis of the fruits of Vatican II (in addition to those treated in previous Volumes), especially Vols. VI, VII, IX, X and XI;
* the analysis of conciliar thought is made parallel to the study of its fruits: Volume VIII and parts of Volumes VI, VII, IX, X and XI.

§ 5   The **limits** of the Work are inherent to the multiple topics dealt with, the method adopted, and the probating character to which it aspires.

In view of the multiplicity of topics covered and the inductive method adopted, this Collection could go on indefinitely piling up proofs and arguments about each topic. The Author selected only those he found more expressive of each subject and conducive to an overall view of the Council as a whole.

The probating character of the Collection is made up of unequal parts. Many times the proofs presented will lead to certainty, at other times to a mere hypothesis. This nuance can be apprehended in the course of the expositions and, more characteristically, in the conclusions.

Even the unitary conception that comes across in the analysis as a whole, does not have the character of an absolute certainty. It is a consistent, explanatory, comprehensive hypothesis that takes on, for the Author, the characteristics of a moral certainty. Nevertheless, he does not lay aside the possibility that some aspects of the general architecture unifying the letter, spirit, and thought of the Council may have escaped his perception. Nor does he exclude that there may exist a more profound and complete conception to explain the Council and what has followed it. If that should be the case, he would be grateful for any correction enabling him to know the unitary reality he so earnestly sought.

6   The **credentials** permitting the Author to make such an analysis do not go beyond those of a Catholic layman.

Indeed, Natural Law entitles a Catholic to speak about his Faith as long as he is moved by love of the Church and does so according to the dogmatic and moral precepts taught by Her, with due respect for the members of the Hierarchy and, above all, the Sovereign Pontiff. However, when one takes into account that Pope Paul VI characterized the present situation in the Church as a process of 'auto-demolition,'[2] and that such process cannot take place without the participation of many Prelates, that which for a Catholic was only a right becomes a duty. This duty is not only to talk about points of the Faith, but also to question those responsible for the deviation regarding those points of the Faith.[3] This

---

[2] In his Allocution to the Students of the Lombard Seminary on December 7, 1968, the Pontiff said: "Today the Church is going through a moment of disquiet. **Some practice self-criticism, one would even say auto-demolition. It is like an inner, acute and complex disturbance such as no one would have expected after the Council.** People thought of a flourishing, a serene expansion of the concepts that matured in the great conciliar assembly. This one aspect, of flourishing, does still exist in the Church. But since *bonum ex integra causa, malum ex quocumque defectu*, attention falls especially on the painful aspect. **The Church is struck also by those who are part of it**" (*Insegnamenti di Paolo VI*, vol. VI, p. 1092).

[3] a. The doctrine on the right of the faithful, even the most simple ones, to resist decisions by the ecclesiastical authority that are dangerous to the Faith and objectively erroneous, was expounded by Fathers and Doctors of the Church as well as by theologians and canonists, some of whom were elevated to the altars.

b. Saint THOMAS AQUINAS, in many passages of his works, upholds the principle that the faithful can question and admonish Prelates. For example: "There being an imminent danger for the faith, prelates must be questioned, even publicly, by their subjects. Thus, Saint Paul, who was a subject of Saint Peter, questioned him publicly on account of an imminent danger of scandal in a matter of Faith. And, as the *Glosa* of Saint Augustine puts it (*Ad Galatas 2,14*), 'Saint Peter himself gave the example to those who govern so that if sometime they stray from the right way, they will not reject a correction as unworthy even if it comes from their subjects'" (*Summa theologiae,* Taurini/Romae: Marietti, 1948, II.II, q.33, a.4).

Referring to the same episode, in which Saint Paul resisted Saint Peter 'to his face,' Saint Thomas teaches: "The reprehension was just and useful, and the reason for it was not light: there was a danger for the preservation of evangelical truth .... The way it took place was appropriate, since it was public and manifest. For this reason, Saint Paul writes: 'I spoke to Cephas,' that is, Peter, 'before everyone,' since the simulation practiced by Saint Peter was fraught with danger to everyone. In 1 Tim 5:20, we read: 'Admonish those who sin before everyone.' This should be understood to refer to manifest sins, not hidden ones, since in these cases one should proceed according to the rules proper to fraternal correction" (*Super Epistulas S. Pauli, Ad Galatas*, 2, 11-14, lec. III, Taurini/Romae: Marietti, 1953, nn. 83f.).

The Angelic Doctor also shows how this passage of the *Scriptures* contains teachings not only for Hierarchs but for the faithful as well: "To the Prelates [was given an example] of humility so that they do not refuse to accept reprehensions from their inferiors and subjects; and to the subjects, an example of zeal and liberty so they will not fear to correct their Prelates, above all when the crime is public and entails a danger for many" (Ibid., n. 77).

In his *Comments on the Sentences of Peter Lombard*, Saint Thomas teaches how respectfully correcting a Prelate who sins is a work of mercy all the greater as the Hierarch's position is higher: "Fraternal correction, being a spiritual alms, is a work of mercy. But mercy is due mainly to the Prelate since he runs the greatest danger. Hence Saint Augustine says in *Regula* (n. 11, PL 32, 1384): 'Have pity not only on yourselves, but on them as well,' that is, on the Prelates 'among you who run a danger as high as the position they occupy.' Therefore, fraternal correction extends also to the Prelates.

"Furthermore, Eccl. XVII, 12, says that God 'imposed on each one duties toward his neighbor.' Now, a Prelate is our neighbor. Therefore, we must correct him when he sins. .... Some say that fraternal correction does not extend to the Prelates either because man should not raise his voice against heaven, or because the Prelates are easily scandalized if corrected by their subjects. However, this does not happen, since when they sin, the Prelates do not represent heaven and, therefore, must be corrected. And those who correct them charitably do not raise their voices against them, but in their favor, since the admonishment is for their own sake. .... For this reason, according to other [authors], the precept of fraternal correction extends also to the Prelates, so that they may be corrected by their subjects" (*IV Sententiarum*, d. 19, q.2, a.2).

In addition to Saint Thomas Aquinas, other prominent Saints and Doctors have also pronounced on the right of the faithful to resist, in grave circumstances. For example:

c. Saint AUGUSTINE thus comments on the episode of Saint Paul's public resistance to Saint Peter: "Peter accepted with holy and pious humility the useful observation Saint Paul had made, inspired by the freedom of love, thus leaving for posterity a rare example for them not to despise being corrected by their inferiors whenever they have strayed from the right way" (*Epistula 82*, n. 22, in PL 33, 285f.).

d. Fr. Francisco de VITORIA, OP: "Caietano, in the same work defending the superiority of the Pope over the Council, says in chap. 27: 'Therefore, a Pope must be resisted who publicly destroys the Church, for example, by refusing to give ecclesiastical benefits other than money or in exchange for services; and with all obedience and respect, the possession of such benefits must be denied to those who bought them.' And Silvestre (Prierias), in the entry Pope, § 4, asks: 'What should be done when the Pope, because of his bad customs, destroys the Church?'. And in § 15: 'What should be done if the Pope wanted, without reason, to abrogate Positive Law?' To which he answers: 'He would certainly sin; he should neither be permitted to act in such fashion nor should he be obeyed in what was evil; but he should be resisted with a courteous reprehension.'

"Consequently, if he wished to give away the whole treasure of the Church or the patrimony of Saint Peter to his relatives, if he wanted to destroy the Church or the like, he should not be permitted to act in that fashion, but one would be obliged to resist him. The reason for this is that he does not have the power to destroy; therefore, if there is evidence that he is doing it, it is licit to resist him. The result of all this is that if the Pope destroys the Church by his orders and acts, he can be resisted and the execution of his mandates prevented ....

"Second proof of the thesis. By Natural Law it is licit to repel violence with violence. Now then, with such orders and dispensations the Pope exerts violence, since he acts against the Law, as we have proven. Therefore, it is licit to resist him. As Caietano observes, we do not affirm all this in the sense that someone could have competence to judge the Pope or have authority over him, but meaning that it is licit to defend oneself. Indeed, anyone has the right to resist an unjust act, to try to prevent it and to defend himself" (*Obras de Francisco de Vitória*, Madrid: BAC, 1960, pp. 486f.).

e. Fr. Francisco SUAREZ, SJ: "If [the Pope] gives an order contrary to good customs, he should not be obeyed; if he attempts to do something manifestly opposed to justice and the common good, it will be licit to resist him; if he attacks by force, by force he can be repelled, with a moderation appropriate to a just defense" (*De Fide*, disp. X, sec. VI, n. 16, in *Opera omnia*, Paris: Vivès, 1958, vol. XII, in A. V. XAVIER DA SILVEIRA, *La nouvelle Messe de Paul VI: Qu'en penser?*, Chiré-en-Montreuil: Diffusion de la Pensée Française, 1975, pp. 323f.).

f. Saint ROBERT BELLARMINE, the great paladin of the Counter-Reformation, maintains: "Just as it is licit to resist to the Pontiff that aggresses the body, it is also licit to resist the one who aggresses the souls or who disturbs civil order, or, above all, who attempts to destroy the Church. I say that it is licit to resist him by not doing what he orders and preventing his will from being executed; it is not licit, however, to judge, punish or depose him, since these are acts proper to a superior" (*De Romano Pontifice*, lib. II, chap. 29, in *Opera omnia*, Neapoli/Panormi/Paris: Pedone Lauriel, 1871, vol. I, p. 418).

g. Fr. Cornelius a LAPIDE, SJ, shows that Saint Augustine, Saint Ambrose, Saint Bede, Saint Anselm and other Fathers teach that Saint Paul resisted Saint Peter publicly "so that the public scandal given by Saint Peter was amended by a likewise public reprehension" (*Commentaria in Scripturam Sacram, Ad Galatas* 2:11, Paris: Ludovicus Vivès, 1876, vol. XVIII, p. 528).

Later on, a Lapide argues that "superiors can be, with humble charity, reprehended by their inferiors in the defense of truth; that is what Saint Augustine (*Epistula 19*), Saint Cyprian, Saint Gregory, Saint Thomas and others cited above declare about this passage (Gal. 2:11). They clearly teach that Saint Peter, being a superior, was reprehended by Saint Paul. .... With good reason, therefore, Saint Gregory said (*Homilia 18 in Ezechielem*): 'Peter kept quiet so that, being first in the apostolic hierarchy, he would also be first in humility.' And Saint Augustine wrote (*Epistula 19 ad Hieronymum*): 'By teaching that superiors should not refuse to be reprehended by inferiors, Saint Peter gave posterity an example more rare and holier than that of Saint Paul as he taught that, in the defense of truth and with charity, inferiors may have the audacity to resist superiors without fear'" (Ibid.).

h. Dom Prosper GUÉRANGER, Abbot of Solesmes, notes: "When the shepherd turns into a wolf, it behooves the flock to defend itself in the first place. Doctrine normally flows from the Bishops down to the faithful people, and subjects should not judge their chiefs. But, in the treasure of Revelation, there are certain points that every Christian necessarily knows and must obligatorily defend" (*L'année liturgique - Le temps de la septuagesime*, Tours: Maison Mame, 1932, pp. 340f.).

i. Francisco Xavier WERNZ and Pedro VIDAL, theologians of the beginning of the 20th Century, citing Suarez, admit the licitness of resisting a bad Pope: "The just means to be employed against a bad Pope are, according to Suarez (*Defensio Fidei Catholicae*, lib. IV, cap. 6, nn. 17-18), a more abundant help from the grace of God, the special protection of one's Guardian Angel, the prayer of the Universal Church, admonishment or fraternal correction in private or even in public, as well as the legitimate self-defense against aggression, whether physical or moral" (*Ius canonicum*, Rome: Aedes Universitatis Gregorianae, 1927, vol. II, p. 436).

j. Antonio PEINADOR, CMF, a contemporary Spanish theologian, adopts the sentences of those who preceded him: "'Also a subject may be obliged to fraternally correct his superior' (*Summa theologiae*, II.II, q.33, a.4). For also a superior can be spiritually indigent, and nothing prevents him from being liberated from such indigence by his subjects. Nevertheless, 'in the correction in which subjects reprehend their prelates, they must act in a proper manner, that is, without insolence and harshness but with meekness and reverence' (ad 2)" (*Cursus brevior Theologiae Moralis*, Madrid: Coculsa, 1946, vol. I, p. 287).

k. More details about the circumstances in which it is licit for the faithful to resist their Prelates can be found in F. SUAREZ, *De legibus*, lib. IX, chap. XX, nn. I9-29; *Defensio Fidei catholicae*, lib. IV, chap. VI, nn. 14-18; Anacletus REIFFENSTUEL, *Theologia Moralis*, Venice: Bortoli, 1704, tract. IV, d. VI, q.5, nn. 51-54, pp. 162f.; Joannes Petrus GURY - Antonius BALLERINI, *Compendium Theologiae Moralis*, vol. I, pp. 222-227; Camillus MAZELLA, *De Religione et Ecclesia*, pp. 747f.; Teofilo URDANOZ, *Commentaire sur les 'Relecciones teologicas de Francisco Vitoria,'* Rome: Tip. Polygl., 1880, pp. 426-429, in A. V. XAVIER DA SILVEIRA, *La nouvelle Messe*).

duty is all the more cogent since failure to fulfill it would amount to a sin known as *peccatum taciturnitatis* [the sin of omission].[4] For these reasons, the Author believes he has the right and the

---

[4] Dealing with the *peccatum taciturnitatis* (sin of omission) in general, Vincent de BEAUVAIS thus explains this grave moral fault: "Next we should consider taciturnity. For one must know that just as an excess of loquaciousness is vicious, so also is, at times, excessive taciturnity. Indeed, 'There is a time to keep quiet and a time to speak' (Ecc. III, 7); [Saint] Isidore: 'The tongue must be watched, but not inflexibly arrested.' For it is a vice, by keeping quiet, to allow someone unworthy or unfit to be chosen for promotions and honors, or permit someone worthy to lose his dignity, goods, or honor. The same can be said if, in meetings of the council, you keep quiet out of ignorance or malice and thus withhold the truth from the other advisers. Likewise, during a court hearing, if you see someone make a fraudulent accusation or be unjustly condemned, you will sin. And if you fail to reprehend the detractors in conversations defaming others, by neither excusing nor praising the person defamed, if you keep quiet, you will sin. Likewise, when you perceive that a word to edify, instruct, exhort or correct someone is necessary, you commit a delict if you withhold that wholesome advice. Hence Isaiah exclaimed: 'Woe betide me, who kept quiet' (6:5). The same is said in *Ecclesiasticus*: 'Do not hold back a word when it can be wholesome' (4:28)" (*Speculum quadruplex sive speculum maius*, Graz, Akademische Druck-Verlagsanstalt, 1964, col. 1228).

This command is directed primarily to the Hierarchs and clerks who keep quiet. Nevertheless, their defection obliges all laymen to speak up, since Vincent de Beauvais, cited below, uses the adverb **especially** when referring to the Prelates, which means that those who are not vested with priestly dignity have an analogous duty.

"This is obligatory **especially** for prelates and all those who direct or take care of souls. This is clearly stated in *Exodus:* 28, whose precept called for placing little bells alternating with pomegranates hanging from the priestly chasubles so that the priest would be heard as he entered or left the sanctuary and thus would not die. [Saint] Gregory explains this by saying: 'The priest who enters will die if the sound is not heard, for he will attract for himself the wrath of the Eternal Judge if the sound of preaching does not come from him.' Likewise, *Ezechiel*, 33:6: 'If the sentinel sees the sword coming and fails to sound his trumpet so that the people does not take refuge in a safe place, and the sword comes and takes the life of one of them; this one certainly was surprised in his iniquity, and I will ask the sentinel to account for his blood'" (Ibid.).

Furthermore, failure to exercise this duty of the laymen to speak up when Prelates defect also implies a sin. The Church's ancient Codes of Law defined the *peccatum taciturnitatis* incurred by the faithful who failed to warn Prelates who deviated from their mission (B. KLOPPEN-BURG, *A Eclesiologia do Vaticano II*, Petrópolis: Vozes, 1971, p. 53).

duty to analyze the Council. His *first credential* is, therefore, the fact that he is a Catholic.

§ 7   The Author's *second credential* is his condition as a lay-man. Council Vatican II itself so exalted the mission of the laity [5]

---

[5] a. On the mission of the laity stemming from the Council it is opportune to see the synthesis presented by Fr. Boaventura Kloppenburg, a conciliar expert, chronicler of Vatican II, member of the International Theological Commission and Bishop of Novo Hamburgo, in which he consistently enumerates the various conciliar documents exalting the laity to such a point that he states: "The theology of the laity appears to have placed the theology of the priest into a crisis. Having been abundantly instructed by Vatican Council II about the lay people, we now know that a true equality reigns among all the baptized in regard to the dignity and action common to all faithful in building the Body of Christ (LG 32c); that everyone participates in the mission of the whole Christian people in the Church and the world (LG 31a); that all play an active role in the life and action of the Church (AA 10a); that the lay people are now 'brothers' of their shepherds (LG 32c, 37a); that absolutely everyone (*quicumque sunt*) is called by the Lord to the fostering and perennial sanctification of the Church (LG 33a; AA 2a); that everyone (*omnes omnino christifideles*) is destined by the Lord himself to the apostolate (LG 33c); that all laymen have the noble burden of working to make the divine plan of salvation reach increasingly all men at all times and in all places (LG 33d), that all who have been baptized participate in the priestly, prophetic and royal mission of Christ (LG 31a; AA 2b, 10a); that the Supreme and Eternal Priest wants to continue his testimony and his service also through the lay people (LG 34a), by granting them, in part, his priestly charge (LG 34b); that the Great Prophet exerts his prophetic mission not only through the Hierarchy but through the laity as well (LG 35a), having, for this reason, made them into witnesses and embellished them with the sense of faith and the grace of the word (Ibid.); that also the lay people play an active role in the eucharistic action, during which they should also offer up themselves and 'not only through the hands of the priest' (SC 48).

"All this generous conciliar doctrine on the nature of lay people and their place and action in the Church has caused many to ask themselves about the meaning and reason for being of ministers in the Church, and precisely to what degree they are distinct from those who hold the common priesthood" (B. KLOPPENBURG, op. cit., pp. 203f.).

b. Should laymen, in this great participation opened by the Council, passively accept everything their Shepherds propose to them, or would it be possible for them to disagree when faced with serious and well-weighed reasons? It would seem that the orientation of Vatican II gives lay people a freedom of analysis that few would dare to advocate some years ago. This can be deduced from the comments of the above cited Franciscan theologian, whose notion of contestation would deserve, it seems to us, certain qualifications:

that, of themselves, such documents would suffice to place the Author entirely at ease to analyze the Council.

§ 8   Furthermore, in the post-Council there was no lack of exhortations in the same sense, which can be found, for example, in the *Code of Canon Law* [6] and in the conclusions of the Extraordi-

---

"On principle, an attitude of contestation in the Church is possible and can be legitimate and necessary. It is perfectly possible to love the Church, identify with her, live in her and for her, and at the same time to want her to become more consistent with herself, holier and more immaculate, without stains or wrinkles. For, according to the Council, in fact the Church is 'at the same time holy and always in need of purifying herself' (LG 8d); and as a human and earthly institution she is 'in need of constant reform' (UR 6a). For this reason, as Mother, 'she exhorts her children to purification and renewal so that the sign of Christ may shine brighter on the face of the Church' (LG 15). These words, 'renewal' and 'purification' frequently reappear in the documents of Vatican II and invite us to take an attitude of criticism and contestation. .... The Council goes so far as to invite the faithful to 'examine with a sincere and attentive mind that which must be renewed and accomplished inside the Catholic family itself, so as to give a more faithful and luminous testimony of the doctrine and teachings received from Christ through the Apostles' (UR 4e). It is an authentic invitation to contestation, especially if the word is understood in its etymological and positive meaning, that includes the idea of bearing witness to.

"The Council asks laymen to 'manifest to shepherds their needs and wishes with the freedom and trust becoming children of God and brethren in Christ. According to their knowledge, competence, and ability, they have a right and at times even a duty to express their opinion about things related to the good of the Church' (LG 37a). And the Council asks that 'the just freedom of investigation and of thought of the faithful, clergy, or laity, be recognized, as well as their just freedom to express their ideas with humility and firmness in matters of their competence' (GS 62g). The old collection of ecclesiastical law spoke of *peccatum taciturnitatis*, the sin of those who failed to freely warn prelates when they were harming the Church. A good contestant exerts the function of a prophet. But a prophet is not always pleasant. In the history of the Church there have been powerful contestants, some of whom have even been canonized; but before being canonized, they were burned..." (B. KLOPPENBURG, op. cit., pp. 52f.).

[6] Canons 224-231. On the emphasis given in the new *Code* to the role of the laity in the Church, Fr. Jesus S. HORTAL, commentator, writes: "One of the complaints about the 1917 *Code* was that it paid little attention to the laity, dedicating only one canon to them (# 682), since the others found in Part II of Book II spoke about associations of the *faithful*, which also included the clergy. Now, in addition to the canons of Title I, common to all faithful, are also laid down the obligations and rights of those who make up the immense majority in the Church: the lay people" (*Comments*, in JOHN PAUL II, *Código de Direito Canônico*, pp. 98f.).

nary Synod convened by the Holy Father John Paul II in 1985 to review Vatican Council II, analyze its consequences, and relive its spirit. In the *Message to the People of God*, the final document of the meeting, the Synod's Fathers recommended that everyone strive to study Vatican II in depth: "We invite you to know Vatican Council II in a better and more complete way, intensify and deepen your study of it, and better understand the unity and riches of all its Constitutions, Decrees and Declarations."[7]

John Paul II gave a homily endorsing the message of the Synod.[8]

§ 9

In October 1987, a Synod of Bishops was held in Rome to study the role of the laity in the Church and temporal society. In the homily closing the Synod, John Paul II expressed his satisfaction not only with the participation of lay people in the works of the Synod but also with the more profound understanding of the importance of the laity in the present day: "Today, the last day of the Synod's assembly, we wish to thank the Good Shepherd for bringing us together from all peoples in order to give us a new heart and bring upon us a new spirit (Ez. 36:24-26). This 'Spirit' .... manifested itself with new clarity and strength in the teaching of Vatican Council II about the life and vocation of the laity in the Church and in the world. .... We are thankful for the fact that during the Synod we were able to rejoice not only in the participation of laymen (male and female attendants), but also because the development of the Synod's discussions enabled us to listen to the voices of those invited, representatives of the laity

---

[7] EXTRAORDINARY SYNOD OF BISHOPS, "Mensagem ao povo de Deus," in *L'Osservatore Romano* (Portuguese edition), 12/15/1985, p. 1.

[8] "The Synod has attained the goals for which it has been convened: to celebrate, evaluate, and promote the Council. As we leave this Synod, it is our desire to intensify pastoral efforts to make Vatican Council II more widely and profoundly known; so that the orientation and guidelines it has given us may be assimilated in the depth of hearts and translated into the lives and behavior of all members of the People of God, with consistency and love. ....

"At the end of this eucharistic celebration, the *Message* the Synod's Fathers want to address the Church and the world will be proclaimed in various languages. Would that it touches [people's] hearts, reinforcing the commitment of everyone to generously and consistently put in practice the teachings and guidelines of Vatican Council II" (JOHN PAUL II, Homily at the Mass Closing the Synod, in *L'Osservatore Romano*, "Solene encerramento do Sínodo extraordinário dos Bispos - O Sínodo projeta o Concílio para o terceiro milênio," 12/15/1985, n. 7).

coming from all around the world from various countries, who allowed us to take advantage of their experience, advice, and suggestions springing from their love of the common cause. In a certain sense, this synodal experience is unprecedented, and we hope it may become a 'model,' a point of reference for the future .... The synod endeavored to deepen [the understanding of] the figure of the faithful lay person, bringing to light his extraordinary importance in today's world. The starting point was the teaching of the Council on the Church in her reality as a 'Mystery' of 'communion' and 'mission.'"[9]

§ 10   Since the Synod, there has been no lack of exhortations in all ecclesiastical echelons about the mission of laymen in the Church and today's world. This stimulates us to speak out in public.

§ 11   *Tempora mutantur!* In the past, the great Saint Ignatius of Loyola — when still a mere layman — confronted several times the tribunals of the Inquisition, accused by church personalities who claimed he had no right to speak about the great problems of the Church and highest concerns of the Faith, since he had no titles or courses that permitted him to do so.[10] Admonished eight times in juridical proceedings by the Inquisition and imprisoned twice (one time for 42 days and the other for 22), the indomitable Saint did not lose heart. He was honored to be able to wear "the mantle of Our Lord Jesus Christ, which is that of opprobrium, false testimonies, and all other insults."[11] What an heroic, fiery example! It should be imitated by those faithful who feel they have a duty to raise their voices in defense of the Catholic Faith and Christian Civilization.

Would Saint Ignatius, the outstanding paladin of the fight against Protestants, encounter similar problems today? Consistent

---

[9] JOHN PAUL II, Homilia na concelebração final da Assembléia sinodal, in *L'Osservatore Romano*, (Portuguese edition), 10/30/1987.

[10] Saint IGNATIUS OF LOYOLA himself explains this to the King of Portugal, Dom João III, in a letter sent from Rome on March 15, 1545: "And if Your Highness wishes to be informed why there was so much indignation and inquisition against me, know that it was not for something having to do with schismatics, Lutherans, or the illuminated, since I have never met them or talked with them; but it was because people were surprised, mainly in Spain, that I, not a graduate in letters, would speak and converse at such great length about spiritual matters" (*Obras Completas*, Madrid: BAC, 1952, p. 701).

[11] Ibid., p. 702.

with the pattern of behavior of innumerable church authorities, the Saint should be able to speak freely about all the problems of the Faith and the world without any constraint from some new Inquisition.

§ 12

The *third credential* of the Author is that, since 1964, he has had the honor of being a disciple of Plinio Corrêa de Oliveira and a member of the Brazilian Society for the Defense of Tradition, Family and Property - TFP.[12]

Indeed, the struggle that Plinio Corrêa de Oliveira — a Crusader of the 20th Century[13] — has been waging for more than half a century as a Catholic layman[14], is an example of how fi-

---

[12] Working in the temporal sphere in defense of the perennial values of Christian Civilization - tradition, family and property - against the wily infiltration of socialism and the brutal attacks of communism, the TFPs base their civic action on the Social Doctrine of the Church and undertake it according to the principles of Catholic morality.

The Brazilian Society for the Defense of Tradition, Family and Property was founded in São Paulo in 1960 by Prof. Plinio Corrêa de Oliveira. It was the starting point for the formation of 26 other autonomous and kindred organizations that exist on four continents.

[13] Prof. Corrêa de Oliveira indisputably stood out among the most outstanding Catholic personalities in contemporary Brazil. His thinking has become ever more known and appreciated. His renown as an intellectual and a man of action has made him the subject of dissertation studies.

The writings of the founder of the Brazilian TFP number over 2,300 published titles, including books and articles, and were the object of a graduation thesis, (1984) at the University of São Paulo, by Prof. Lizânias de SOUZA LIMA, titled *Plinio Corrêa de Oliveira, a Crusader of the 20th Century* (about this thesis, see article by Gregório LOPES under the same title in *Catolicismo*, September 1985).

Two quite controversial Ph.D. papers also dealt with relevant episodes of the public action of Plinio Corrêa de Oliveira. The *first*, presented in 1971 at the Columbia University College of Political Sciences by Prof. Margaret Patrice TODARO, was titled *Pastors, Prophets and Politicians: A Study of the Brazilian Catholic Church, 1916-1945*, University of Columbia, 1971, pp. 180, 192, 225, 238, 318s., 321, 449s., 503-506; the *second*, presented in 1981 by Fr. José Ariovaldo da SILVA, OFM, at the Anselmianum's Liturgical Institute in Rome: *O movimento litúrgico no Brasil - Estudo histórico* (Petrópolis: Editora Vozes, 1983).

[14] About the action of Plinio Corrêa de Oliveira over more than fifty years, the Reader may consult *A Half Century of Epic Anticommunism*

delity to the traditional teaching of the Magisterium and the *sensus fidelium* can be employed by a layman to analyze questions related to the Church and Christian Civilization.

To speak of books alone, leaving aside the inestimable public action that he has been carrying out since 1928 in this struggle, the following works are especially noteworthy:

Works related to the Church:

* In Defense of Catholic Action (1943);

* Agreement With the Communist Regime - For the Church, Hope or Self-Destruction?, originally published under the title The Freedom of the Church in the Communist State (1963);

* Unperceived Ideological Transshipment and Dialogue (1965);

* The Church Faced With the Escalation of the Communist Threat - Appeal to the Silent Bishops (1976);

* Indigenous Tribalism: A 'Communist-Missionary' Ideal for Brazil in the 21st Century (1977);

* At the "Sandinista Night," 'Christian' Sandinistas Incite the Catholic Left in Brazil and Hispanic America to Wage Guerrila Warfare (1980);

* The BCCs... Much Talked About But Little Known - The TFP Describes Them as They Are; in collaboration with Gustavo Antonio Solimeo and Luís Sérgio Solimeo (1982).

Works related to Christian Civilization and, indirectly, to the Church:

* *Revolution and Counter-Revolution* (1959 update in 1977 and 1992);

(New York: The Foundation for a Christian Civilization, Inc., 1980); *Um homem, uma obra, uma gesta - Homenagem das TFPs a Plinio Corrêa de Oliveira*, (São Paulo: Edições Brasil de Amanhã, 1989); Comisión de Estudios de las TFPs, *Tradición, Familia, Propiedad - Un ideal, un lema, una gesta - La Cruzada del siglo XX* (São Paulo: Artpress, 1990).

* *Agrarian Reform, a Question of Conscience*; in collaboration with Msgr. A. Castro Mayer, Msgr. G. de Proença Sigaud and L. Mendonça de Freitas (1961);

* *The Morro Alto Declaration*; in collaboration with Msgr. A. Castro Mayer, Msgr. G. de Proença Sigaud and L. Mendonça de Freitas (1964);

* *Self-Managing Socialism: In Regard to Communism, a Barrier? Or a Bridgehead?* (1981);

* *As a Catholic, May I Oppose Land Reform?*, in collaboration with Carlos del Campo (1981);

* *Private Property and Free Enterprise in the Hurricane of Land Reform in collaboration with Carlos del Campo* (1985);

* *Warriors of the Virgin: The Response of Authenticity - The TFP Without Secrets* (1985);

* *In Brazil, Land Reform Takes Misery to Countryside and City - The TFP Informs, Analyzes, Alerts* (1986);

* *Projected New Constitution Anguishes the Country* (1987);

* *Is Communism Dead? And Anticommunism as well?* (1989);

* *Communism and Anticommunism in the Fringe of the Last Decade of the Millenium* (1990);

* *Nobility and Traditional Elites in the Allocutions of Pius XII to the Roman Patriciate and Nobility* (1993).

In these works the author analyzes delicate contemporary problems of the Church, especially from the standpoint of their repercussions in temporal society. Along with a remarkably penetrating analysis of today's problems and the vigorous logic of his thinking, his language reflects a deep-rooted *sensus fidelium* or *sensus Fidei*.[15]

---

[15] The qualities of Prof. Plinio Corrêa de Oliveira were described by the Holy See itself in two honorable letters of praise that it sent him.

The *first*, written in the name of Pius XII by the then Substitute of the Secretary of State, Msgr. Giovanni Baptista MONTINI, later Paul VI, conveys the applause of that Pontiff to the Brazilian thinker for his book *In Defense of Catholic Action*, with a preface by the Apostolic Nuncio in Brazil, Msgr. Bento Aloisio MASELLA, later Cardinal. Dated February

To the same effect, much could be said about the civic action of the TFPs, now established in 26 countries, inspired by principles of the traditional doctrine of the Church and in the *sensus fidelium*. But this would unduly prolong the present Introduction.

Being a TFP member, therefore, is the Author's third credential.

§ 13   Having thus dealt with the credentials that allow the Author to analyze the Council, a word should be said about the **supplementary nature** of this Study. Indeed, since the holding of Vatican II, the TFP has requested several Hierarchs and ecclesiastics of a high intellectual caliber to analyze it in depth from the standpoint of perennial Catholic Doctrine. The TFP proposed to make great sacrifices in order to facilitate such a study. But for various reasons that do not need to be pursued here, these initiatives proved to have been in vain. Thus, facing the imperative of conscience to analyze Vatican Council II, Prof. Plinio Corrêa de Oliveira decided vicariously to take up the task that others refused. And so he invited the Author to carry out that task. Ecclesiastical preparation and theological erudition, therefore, should not be required of him, but only a level of competence normal to a layman not specialized in theological studies.

26, 1949, the letter is published in the second edition of the book, celebrating the 40th anniversary of its publication (São Paulo: Artpress, 1983, p. 3).

The *second* refers to the essay, *The Freedom of the Church in the Communist State*, which Prof. Corrêa de Oliveira wrote during the Second Vatican Council and had distributed to the Conciliar Fathers. In this letter, signed by Cardinal Giuseppe PIZZARDO and Msgr. Dino STAFFA, prefect and secretary of the Dicastery respectively, the Sacred Congregation of Seminaries and Universities congratulates the "scholarly author, deservedly celebrated for his philosophical, historical, and sociological science," and deems his work "a most faithful echo of the Documents of the supreme Magisterium of the Church."

This letter is dated December 2, 1964 and appears in the essay's several editions. In it, these high Prelates augur "the widest possible distribution of the significant booklet." The book had ten editions in Portuguese, eleven in Spanish, five in French, four in English, three in Italian, two in Polish, one in German, one in Hungarian, one in Ukrainian and one in Vietnamese, for a total of 171,000 copies. It was also transcribed by 39 newspapers or magazines in 13 countries.

§ 14   The **words of the title of this Collection** *"Eli, Eli, lamma sabacthani?"* [Father, Father, why hast Thou forsaken me?] were the words Our Lord Jesus Christ pronounced on the height of the Cross. These words seem to signify the supreme affliction and perplexity in which Catholics, including the Author of these lines, find themselves vis-a-vis the enigmatic silence and the surprising 'unconcern' of the Sovereign Pontiffs and the Catholic Hierarchy in regard to the disarray, unprecedented in History, that has become installed in the bosom of Holy Church and in the treasure of Catholic Doctrine since the conciliar winds began to blow.

The TFP (founded in 1960), and prior to that, the Group gathered around the monthly *Catolicismo* (founded in 1951), as well as the staff of the weekly *Legionário* (1933-1947), under the leadership of Plinio Corrêa de Oliveira, had recourse innumerable times to the Holy See. Curiously, however, after the elevation of John XXIII to the pontifical throne, he and the conciliar Popes who followed appeared to be deaf to the clamors of these Catholics.[16]

---

[16] a. It is not within the goals of this Collection to enumerate the several instances in which this lay family of souls had recourse to the Apostolic See and the Sovereign Pontiffs. We mention only two initiatives of the TFPs, of gigantic proportions, addressed to Paul VI and which had the most complete silence for an answer:

In 1968, denouncing leftist infiltration in Catholic circles, the Brazilian TFP organized a petition drive in support of a message that it sent Paul VI, asking that efficacious measures be taken against such an infiltration. The campaign to collect signatures was held in 229 cities and towns all over the country. In only 58 days, 1,600,368 Brazilians had signed. A similar campaign was carried out in Argentina, Chile and Uruguay on the iniative of the local TFPs. The number of signatures in the four countries reached the impressive grand total of 2,038,112. Microfilms of the petition - the largest in Latin America's history - were delivered to the Vatican on November 7, 1969. Nevertheless, this appeal to the Supreme Shepherd from millions of children of Holy Mother Church only drew from Paul VI an inexplicable silence.

Greater details about this document can be found in *Catolicismo*, August-October 1968, and in the articles by Plinio CORRÊA DE OLIVEIRA, "Das páginas da imprensa para as da História-I", and "SOS de Milhões – A mala pequena – 'Tudo normal'", in *Folha de S. Paulo*, 8/17/1968 and 11/30/1969 respectively.

b. In 1974, the TFPs published in papers all over the world of a manifesto of resistance to the Vatican *Ostpolitik* undertaken during the Council and continued by Paul VI. The policy of *Ostpolitik* consisted of a gradual "relaxation of tensions" between the Holy See and the communist regimes.

Significant milestones in this policy included the audience John XXIII granted Alexis Adjubei, chief-editor of *Izvestia* and Nikita Kruschev's son-in-law, and the audience that Paul VI granted Nicolai Podgorny, president of Soviet Russia. Nevertheless, this new road to *rapprochement* was impassable without removing certain obstacles. One of these was Cardinal Mindszenty, the hero of Hungary's Catholic anticommunist struggle. As the policy of Paul VI required, the Prelate was demoted from his Primate Seat of Esztergom and obliged to leave his exile in the American Embassy in Budapest. In his Memoirs, the Cardinal himself describes the episodes of this tragedy, involving a whole nation with a venerable history (József MINDSZENTY, *Erinnerungen*, Frankfurt: Ullstein, 1974, pp. 410ff.). Another event profoundly troubling for Catholics was the visit to Russia by Cardinal Willebrands, president of the Secretariat for the Union of Christians, to attend the installation ceremony of Pimen, a notorious puppet of the Kremlin's bosses, as new 'patriarch' of the schismatic church. During the Bishop's Synod of 1971, statements by Cardinal Josyf Slipyj, Archbishop of the Ukrainians, revealed details hitherto unknown about the negotiations of the Holy See with communist regimes. Furthermore, the frequent travels of Msgr. Casaroli — then Secretary of the Vatican Council for Public Affairs — to 'Iron Curtain' countries were disquieting because of his cordiality toward communist leaders. Most disconcerting were his statements after a visit to the island-prison of the Caribbean: "Catholics living in Cuba are happy with the communist regime" (see list of the highlights of the Vatican *Ostpolitik* in Vol. V, *Animus delendi-II*, Appendix II).

Such attitudes could only cause perplexity among faithful followers of the true social teaching of the Church. Indeed, especially in the Encyclicals of Leo XIII, Pius XI, and Pius XII, She had condemned communism as a complete subversion of the natural order (see Chap. I, Note 14c). At the same time, such attitudes placed anticommunist Catholics in a disturbing situation, since their position became inexplicable to public opinion.

Thus, pressed by the successive advances of Vatican *détente*, the TFP declared itself in **state of resistance** to the *Ostpolitik* of Paul VI. It made known its stand in the manifesto, *The Vatican Policy of Detente With Communist Governments. For the TFP: To Do Nothing? Or to Resist?*

In Brazil, the document was published in its entirety in 37 newspapers around the country, namely: *Catolicismo*, April 1974; *Folha de S. Paulo*, 4/10/1974; *Folha da Tarde*, São Paulo, 4/10/1974; *Diário da Noite*, São Paulo (SP), 4/10/1974; *Correio do Ceará*, Fortaleza (CE), 4/11/1974; *Estado de Minas*, Belo Horizonte (MG), 4/16/1974; *Novo Jornal*, Londrina (PR), 4/21/1974; *A Tribuna*, Santos (SP), 4/21/1974; *O Globo*, Rio de Janeiro (RJ), 4/23/1974; *Folha de Londrina*, Londrina (PR), 4/23/1974; *Correio do Povo*, Porto Alegre (RS), 4/23/1974; *A Tribuna*, São Carlos (SP), 4/23/1974; *Jornal de Santa Catarina*, Blumenau (SC), 4/27/1974; *Jornal da Manhã*, Ponta Grossa (PR), 4/27/1974; *Diário de*

Natal, Natal (RN), 4/27/1974; *Jornal de Hoje*, Maceió (AL), 4/28/1974; *Diário da Região*, São José do Rio Preto (SP), 4/28/1974; *A Cidade*, Ribeirão Preto (SP), 4/28/1974; *Diário da Manhã*, Recife (PE), 4/29/1974; *O Estado do Paraná*, Curitiba (PR), 4/30/1974; *Jornal dos Municípios Brasileiros*, Rio de Janeiro (RJ), April 1974, *Diário de Aracaju*, Aracaju (SE), 5/3/6/1974; *A Tarde*, Salvador (BA), 5/4/1974; *Diário de Pernambuco*, Recife (PE), 5/5/1974; *O Popular*, Goiânia (GO), 5/8/10/1974; *Jornal da Cidade*, Olímpia (SP), 5/11/1974; *A União*, João Pessoa (PB), 5/12/1974; *A Província do Pará*, Belém (PA), 5/12/1974; *Comércio de Franca*, Franca (SP), 5/28/1974; *Diário de Borborema*, Campina Grande (PB), 5/28/1974; *O Jornal*, Manaus (AM), 5/30, 6/1/2/5/1974; *Centro Sul*, Barra do Piraí (RJ), 6/1/1974; *Jornal da Paraíba*, Campina Grande (PB), 6/2/1974; *O Estado do Maranhão*, São Luís (MA), 6/19/1974; *Jornal Pequeno*, São Luís (MA), 6/22/1974; *A Gazeta*, Vitória (ES), 8/7/1974; *Correio Braziliense*, Brasília (DF), 9/10/1974.

Summaries were published in *Folha do Comércio*, Campos (RJ), 4/14/1974; *Correio do Povo*, Porto Alegre (RS), 4/16/1974; *A Cidade*, Campos (RJ), 4/16/1974; *Tribuna do Ceará*, Fortaleza (CE), 4/17/1974; *Unitário*, Fortaleza (CE), 4/18/1974; *A Nação*, Blumenau (SC), 4/21/1974; *Correio do Sul*, Cachoeira do Itapemirim (ES), 4/26/1974; *O Social Democrata*, Cuiabá (MT), 5/1/1974.

It was also published by 21 periodicals in ten countries. In Argentina, *La Nación*, of Buenos Aires and *Voz del Interior*, of Córdoba; in Bolívia, *El Diario* of La Paz; in Canada, *Speak Up* of Toronto; in Chile, *La Tercera*, of Santiago, *El Sur* of Concepción, *El Diario Austral* of Temuco and *La Prensa* of Osorno; in Colombia, *El Tiempo* and *El Espectador* of Bogotá; in Ecuador, *El Comercio* of Quito; in Spain, *Hoja del Lunes* and *Fuerza Nueva* of Madrid, and *Región* of Oviedo; in the United States, *The National Educator* of Fullerton, California; in Uruguay, *El País* of Montevideo; and in Venezuela, *El Universal*, *El Nacional*, *Ultimas Notícias*, *El Mundo* and *2001* of Caracas.

The Declaration of Resistance was also published by the following organs of the TFPs: *Tradición, Familia, Propiedad* of the Argentine TFP; *Fiducia* of the Chilean TFP; *Cristiandad* of the Young Bolivians for a Christian Civilization; *Reconquista* of the Ecuadorian TFP; *Cruzada* of the Colombian TFP; *Covadonga* of the Venezuelan TFP; and *Crusade for a Christian Civilization* of the American TFP. In Spain, the Covadonga Cultural Society distributed 300,000 copies of the manifesto in the streets of Madrid and other cities. The Bureau Tradition, Famille, Propriété distributed it in France and also among German Catholic circles in a booklet titled *TFP - der Kreuzzug des 20. Jahrhunderts*.

To this gigantic initiative the Holy See did not deign to give any answer whatsoever.

Thus, the cry of Our Lord Jesus Christ on the Cross, *"Eli, Eli, lamma sabacthani?,"* forsaken by His own Eternal Father, appears as an adequate expression for the situation of the innumerable faithful who, though loving and obedient children of Holy Church and of the Vicar of Christ, see themselves abandoned and knowing of no one else to have recourse to.

The title of this Collection is also, and above all, a prayer to Almighty God, through the intercession of Mary Most Holy, to protect and restore the Holy Catholic Church.

We beseech Him to shorten the days of agony His Church is going through and make Her rise again from the present crisis even stronger, more beautiful and perfect than ever. This is also a plea that He may bring to completion, in History, the entire implantation of His Kingdom through the triumph of the Immaculate Heart of Mary, so that as many souls as possible will be saved, according to the initial design of Divine Wisdom for the Church Militant and the Church Triumphant.

§ *15*   **To whom is** this Collection **addressed**?

First of all, to the Shepherd of Shepherds, so that he may receive our analysis as a homage to the only one true Church, the Holy Roman Catholic and Apostolic Church, Mystical Body of Christ, upon whom the gates of Hell shall never prevail, and of which he, as Sovereign Pontiff, is the visible Head. May he deign to consider what we expound here as an expression of our love and obedience to the perennial teaching of the Ecclesiastical Magisterium, and orient us in this regard. If we are wrong, let him offer us the charity of pointing out where we have strayed from the infallible path of truth. His correction will be considered an honor and a gift, and will be received with an open heart. If we are right, let him save the Bark of Peter from the storm in which it appears to be going asunder and thus acquire, in the eyes of God and of History, the angelic stature of a Saint Gregory VII that would be reserved for him.

It is also addressed to the ensemble of Hierarchs, successors of the Apostles, Princes of the Church, guardians of Faith and Morals, and to theologians as a whole. To all of these, we renew our above request to the Sovereign Pontiff.

Finally, it is addressed to the faithful so that they may consider this ensemble of events and send us their opinions and suggestions on what should be corrected or perfected.

We hope that the present Collection will serve to enlighten those who do not see the whole picture of what is happening and act as a cry of alert to those who see and do nothing.

§ *16*   Therefore, the **state of mind** of the Author is one of love, obedience, and fidelity to the Holy Catholic Church, the Successor of Peter, the ordinary and extraordinary teaching of the Ecclesiastical Magisterium, the *sensus fidelium*.

From first line to last, this Collection has been written with the most sincere dispositions of faith, hope, and charity. Our dispositions have not been altered even by the profound perplexity that took hold in our mind as we noted in the documents, spirit, and fruits of the Council an apparent or real installation of a new conception different from the Catholic one.

As we present our dispositions of veneration and obedience to the Sovereign Pontiff, it is well to say a word advising the Reader about the **style** we will use in this Collection when referring to the Popes.

In a study of an analytical type such as this, it did not seem feasible for us to combine the reverence we would like to display with the coldness proper to this method of exposition. If renewed at every mention, the reverential manifestations of our obedience would even further increase the size of this Work, which, due to the method adopted, is already quite large. We had to choose a style. And although lamenting that it prevents us from always paying the homages we would like, we chose brevity.

As a general rule, references to the Holy Pontiffs will be simple and bereft of adjectives. Our analyses of their words will seek to get to the bottom of the matters raised. And if, at one time or another, the thinking of one of the recent Popes apparently disagrees with the perennial teaching of the Magisterium of the Church, we will say so in the hope that, if we are wrong, we will be paternally corrected. And for this, as we have said, we are ready *toto corde*.

No arrogance dwells in our hearts as sons. And if we analyze, among several excerpts from other authors, the thinking and action of the conciliar Pontiffs, it is out of duty of conscience and following venerable examples from Saints who acted likewise without the least prejudice to their zeal for the Papacy or their love of the Church. Even in extreme cases, no one was ever branded as arrogant for having analyzed the attitude of a Pope in an upright manner to fulfil an imperative of conscience. This is what one learns from the life of Saint Augustine. Faced with the attitude of Pope Zozimus, "praising as true and Catholic the faith of Pelagius and his accomplice, Celestius,"[17] he did not fear to raise his voice in a vigorous *obtestatio*[18] addressed to Rome.[19] In it the great Bishop of Hippo, along with Saint Aurelius, Bishop of Carthage, and other African Bishops, stated that the previous judgment of the Church, opposed to Zozimus' opinion, remained in force.[20] Later, the future Saint Zozimus, realizing that he had been deceived by Pelagius and his accomplice, agreed with Saint Augustine and the African Bishops.[21] In a long document titled *Tractoria*, he demonstrated the Pelagian errors and expressed his gratitude for the service rendered by his African children.[22]

---

[17] FACUNDUS Hermianensis: "They will find blessed Zozimus, Bishop of the Apostolic See, praising as true and Catholic the faith of the same Pelagius and of his accomplice Celestius, against the sentence of Saint Innocent, his predecessor, who had condemned the Pelagian heresy .... and also censuring the African Bishops for considering the two of them as heretics" (*Liber VII*, chap. 3, in PL 45, 1723; *Pro defensione trium capitulorum*, in PL 67, 687).

Among the works of Pope Zozimus, see the letter *Postquam nobis*, of September 21, 417; Joannes Dominicus MANSI, *Sacrorum Conciliorum nova et amplissima collectio*, Venice, 1759, vol. VI, col. 353; JAFFÉ-WATTEMBACH, *Regesta Pontificum Romanorum*, Leipzig, 1885, 330; cited by G. de PLINVAL, *Les luttes pélagiennes*, in V.A., *Histoire de l'Eglise depuis les origines jusqu'à nos jours*, ed. A. FLICHE - V. MARTIN (Paris: Bloud & Gay, 1945), vol. IV, p. 108.

See also, by the same Pontiff, Letter *Magnus pondus*; J. D. MANSI, op. cit., vol. IV, col. 350; JAFFÉ-WATTEMBACH, op. cit., vol. IV, 329, in G. de PLINVAL, Ibid.

[18] *Obtestatio* = an oath that takes God as witness.

[19] G. de PLINVAL, Ibid.

[20] Here is the text of the *obtestatio* referred to by Saint PROSPER OF AQUITAINE: "We declare before God that the sentence pronounced from the See of most blessed Peter by the venerable Bishop Innocent, against Pelagius and Celestius, stands until they profess, most clearly, that we are helped by the grace of God, coming from Our Lord Jesus Christ, not only to know justice but also to put it into practice in each of our actions, for without it we can have, think, and do nothing with a true and holy piety" (*Liber contra Collatorem*, in PL 45, 1808).

[21] G. de PLINVAL, op. cit., p. 109.

[22] Saint AUGUSTINE, *De gratia Christi et peccato originali*, II.XXIV, apud G. de PLINVAL, Ibid.

This Collection's particular aim, however, is not to analyze the position of this or that conciliar or post-conciliar Pontiff. Their thoughts will come into the analysis of Vatican II in conditions analogous to those of the other authors cited.

Having thus explained our position of veneration for the Papacy and the methodological necessity of using a cold, nearly scientific language, we close this part of the General Introduction that sets the premises to the Collection *Eli, Eli, lamma sabacthani?*

*

§ 17

The Author finds it opportune to add to these introductory remarks a **brief history** of how this Collection took shape. This will certainly help the Reader understand the actual plan that we presented above.

Having received from Prof. Plinio Corrêa de Oliveira an invitation to do this work, we dedicated ourselves to studying the texts of the official documents of Vatican II.

After some time of analysis and reflection, we reached the conclusion that it is difficult to harmonize the conciliar texts among themselves. They present a fundamental dicotomy of language in which one can perceive, behind the most important concepts, a clash between two currents of thought. For the most part, conciliar language appeared to us to have been written so that it could be interpreted either from the standpoint of sound and traditional Catholic Doctrine, or, surprisingly enough, of the doctrines of the neo-modernist current, which has billeted itself into so many key positions of the contemporary Church. Such language appears to be a masterpiece of linguistic wordsmith. Woven like precious Flemish lace, with the inestimable threads of the traditional doctrine's vocabulary, it nevertheless appears to reveal the specter of another mentality. Thus, progressivism [23]

---

[23] Asked by the Author in a Paris interview on February 16, 1983 how he would define the current of thought to which he belongs and which prevailed in Vatican II (Vol. I, *In the Murky Waters of Vatican II*, Chap. VI), Fr. Yves CONGAR stated that it can be defined as *progressiste* or better, *progressante*.

In our view, this current took on the name progressivist in order to avoid the label modernist, since Modernism had been vigorously condemned by Saint Pius X in the Encyclical *Pascendi Dominici gregis*. But progressivism is essentially the same as modernism, as we will see entered the official documents of the Magisterium with its head covered by the laced veil of the old traditional language.

As we advanced in our present study, we verified that analysts of great standing and renown had reached the same conclusions that we had, even though their position was quite opposed to ours. So we dedicated the first Volume of this Collection to expound this initial difficulty we faced: the ambiguities in the documents of Vatican II.

---

during this Collection. Incidentally, even though this is not so well-known, the very modernists at times called themselves progressivists (Antonio FOGAZZARO, *Il Santo*, no publisher mentioned, Milan, 1907, pp. 121, 124, 223; Th. DELMONT, *Modernisme et modernistes*, Paris: P. Lethielleux, 1909, pp. 24f., 103); Emmanuel BARBIER, *Histoire du Catholicisme libéral et du Catholisme social en France - Du Concile du Vatican à l'avènement de S.S. Benoît XV*, Bordeaux: Imp. Y. Cadoret, 1924, vol. III, p. 191). That makes sense, since both modernists and progressivists profess an unlimited adherence to modern progress under its various facets: historical, sociological, psychological, technical, etc. They also profess the same desire of reforming the institution and doctrine of the Church in order to adapt them to modern progress.

After the Encyclical *Humani generis* by Pius XII, cautioning against certain errors of that current, the word 'progressivism' (which soon became widely used to designate that set of errors, even though it was not used in the Encyclical) took on a suspect connotation. With the advent of John XXIII, that connotation disappeared from official Vatican circles and was kept only in traditionalist milieus.

Nevertheless, in the post-conciliar period, due to a muted but considerable reaction that sprung up in the Catholic 'silent majority' in regard to the Council's innovations (Vol. I, *In the Murky Waters of Vatican II*, Chap. X.1-4), the term was taken up by some theologians representing the Holy See's official line in order to distinguish their own moderate positions from those of theologians eager to draw every last consequence from the Council. These people the moderates call 'progressivists,' but using the expression in such a way that it has lost the heterodox connotation that the *Humani generis* had given it. It now sounds more like a synonym of 'advanced' or, at worst, 'imprudent.'

In this Collection the expressions 'progressivism' and 'progressivist current' will be used with the suspect connotations, from the standpoint of orthodoxy, which stemmed from *Humani generis*. The French expression *progressante* undoubtedly conveys with greater cogency the ongoing evolutionism professed by this current. But even though Congar used it during our conversation, it is not habitually employed, so we will not use it to designate this current.

An immediate consequence of such ambiguities is to make an analysis of the conciliar texts sterile and fruitless. Indeed, since they are ambiguous, they can be used to a greater or lesser degree by any of the currents — conservative or progressivist — in order to draw as much advantage for its own camp as possible. And any discussion based on the letter of the conciliar documents will be doomed to wear itself out for lack of unity among doctrinal points of reference.

*

18   Since there are difficulties with the letter, one must seek in the spirit of the Council the elements required to interpret it correctly.

What is the spirit of the Council?

Usually one has recourse to the spirit of a Code or a Constitution as an element to elucidate the letter of a law or norm that can lend itself to confusion. This is done by searching for the general line of thinking that oriented the legislator as he wrote the ensemble of laws in question. The thinking of an author is normally supposed to have a unity, hence the possibility of using such a recourse to clarify points in doubt.

Therefore, in its current expression, spirit is synonymous with an unexpressed unity of thinking.

Now then, as we prepared to apply this criterion to Vatican II, we ran into yet another difficulty. Since the letter of the conciliar documents is ambiguous because of the clash between the thinking of two currents, the documents as a whole are not susceptible to be understood as having a unity of thought. It is difficult, therefore, to define what is the spirit of the Council in the current meaning of the word. Logic dictates that since the writing of the documents obeyed two opposed conceptions, the only fitting definition would be that the spirit of Vatican II is a spirit of conflict. This definition, however, helps little to clarify the equivocal points in the conciliar documents.

Having thus eliminated the usual meaning of spirit to determine the spirit of Vatican II, we strove to define other meanings in which the expression could be understood.

19   As one considers the ambiguity of conciliar texts, one verifies that it was due mainly to the introduction of new concepts of a progressivist substractum. In fact, everyone knows that

the perennial thinking of the Church, as well as her spirit, is habitually crystalline, most holy and upright. If there is ambiguity in the documents of Vatican II, it was not due to the current of conciliar Fathers who adhered to the clarity and uprightness traditionally found in the documents of the Church. Therefore, it can only have resulted from the action of individuals who desired ambiguity and perhaps were co-natural with it. Such action is fraught with harmful results, since it soils the pure waters of the Church documents and gives the progressivists a convenient 'right of citizenship.' When one wants to delve into the actual composition of murky waters, one does not argue about its composition when the water was crystalline — that has already been established. What is necessary is to determine the nature and makeup of the new element that has soiled it.

So it becomes indispensable to determine the thinking of the progressivist current of the conciliar Fathers in order to analyze if it has filtered — and to what degree — into conciliar ambiguity.

During our writing, we found that the expression, the spirit of the Council, can be legitimately understood as the spirit of the progressivist current. In this case one can really find an unexpressed unity of thought that explains many ambiguities contained in the texts. It is, therefore, a valid and consistent meaning for the 'spirit of the Council.'

In this sense, the search for the spirit of Vatican II coincides with the search for the unity of the progressivist thinking. It is from this standpoint that the letter of the conciliar documents should be understood.

§ 20　　　　Another meaning of the spirit of the Council that we frequently encountered is one whereby the spirit of the Council coincides with the dispositions of soul and the purposes of those who convened it. Therefore, the 'spirit of the Council' would be the effusive manifestations of goodness on the part of John XXIII, who gave the Council an impulse and a direction to which Vatican II was meticulously faithful to the end.[24] Thus, the un-

---

[24] These are the words of JOHN XXIII at the Council's solemn *Opening Speech* on October 11, 1962: "As the Ecumenical Vatican Council II begins, it becomes more evident than ever that the truth of the Lord remains eternally. Indeed, as one epoch succeeds another, we see that men's opinions also succeed each other, excluding one another. .... The Church has always opposed these errors; many times She has even condemned them with the greatest severity. In our days, however, **the Spouse of Christ prefers to use the remedy of mercy more** than that of severity: She deems to better satisfy today's needs by showing

derlying intention of the Council would be a particularly broad mercy toward the world and the false religions so that the resulting thaw would cause the militant character of the Church to deteriorate as much as possible. Therefore, such a spirit would be characterized by tolerance toward the world and the false religions and opposition to Catholic militancy. And every writing interpreted under this prism would reveal the underlying unity of the conciliar documents.

In our view these are the two most widely employed meanings for the expression the spirit of the Council, even though only seldom are they recognized clearly. The second meaning — the spirit of tolerance — usually prevails over the first — the unity of the progressivist thinking. The reason for this ascendancy is that the second appears much nicer and more attractive to many people, whereas the first, when confronted with traditional Catholic thinking, has the drawback of suggesting that there must have been some progressivist plot to dominate the Council and the Church.

After making this analysis of the meanings of the spirit of the Council, we found that the first meaning is so comprehensive that studying it would be tantamount to expounding the whole matter contained in this Collection. In other words, there would be no real distinction between the spirit of the Council and the thinking of the progressivist current that inspired it. We believe that to do this would introduce an element of confusion in a Work whose goal is to clarify.

For this reason, we adopted the second meaning to analyze the spirit of the Council.[25]

As we endeavored to delve deeply into the much-trumpeted kindness and mercy toward the world and the false

---

the validity of her doctrine than by condemning errors .... The Catholic Church, raising by means of this Ecumenical Council the torch of religious truth, **wishes to show herself as the loving mother of all, benign, patient, full of mercy and kindness .... The Church ....** through her children, also **extends everywhere the amplitude of Christian charity**, which is the best aid to eliminate the seeds of discord; and nothing is more efficacious to foment concord, a just peace, and the fraternal union of all" (JOHN XXIII, *Opening Speech*, in B. KLOPPEN-BURG, *Concílio Vaticano II*, Petrópolis: Vozes, 1963, vol. II, pp. 310f.).

[25] The Reader can find a more detailed examination of the expression the "spirit of the Council" and the reasons why we have adopted the second meaning, in Vol. II, *Animus injuriandi-I*, Introduction.

religions, we found in innumerable authors a veritable apology of tolerance and an utter aversion for the militant, sacral, and hierarchical character of Holy Church. Their attitudes were so categorical and loaded with hatred that, in our view, far from reflecting a 'constructive' and disinterested mercy, they constitute a real *animus injuriandi* [propensity to insult] toward the Catholic Church and Religion. As a matter of fact, their hostility goes so far as to characterize an *animus delendi* [propensity to destroy]. Thus, the *animus injuriandi* and *animus delendi*, shown by innumerable and important exponents of conciliar theology, would reveal the other side of the coin of the conciliar spirit, usually presented with its rosy side.

It is to expound the impressive roll of such offenses and self-destructive designs, inasmuch as they express the spirit of the Council, that we dedicated Volumes II to V of this Collection.

§ 23   What is the underlying thinking of the Council? How to determine it?

Two possible ways came to our mind to determine the thinking of Vatican II.

The *first* consists in examining the key concepts of the conciliar documents — the Church as mystery, as Spouse, as People of God, as Sinning Church; the concept of pastoral, world, man, history, evolution, etc. — trying to analyze them and draw from each concept all that is implicit in it both in the field of ideas and of tendencies, as did Prof. Plinio Corrêa de Oliveira with the word, dialogue. In his work *Unperceived Ideological Transshipment and Dialogue,* [26] he draws from the 'talisman-word' dialogue all the consequences it carries in its bosom. He shows how it presents the peculiar characteristic of luring those who hear or use it into a dialectical game and of eliciting a series of psychological reactions, sympathy, and connivance that turn the one who dialogs into the victim of a subtle process of *psy war.* [27] Without perceiving it, the victim who goes through the

---

[26] Plinio CORRÊA DE OLIVEIRA, *Unperceived Ideological Transshipment and Dialogue*, in Crusade for a Christian Civilization, New York, Vol. 12, n. 4, Oct.-Dec. 1982.

[27] a. The expression *psychological warfare*, or *psy war* for short, has been used more and more frequently. We believe it can be applied not only to specifically military battles, even though its primary analogical sense is that of a confrontation between armies. Thus, the communist offensive to conquer the West is to a large extent a *psy war*. By analogy, we apply the expression to the progressivist expansion. Here are

various stages of this process will end up by tendentially adhering to Hegelian dialectics and will even acquire a propensity to accept the socialist and communist ideas that he once fought.

As for the progressivist offensive, there are many proofs and indications that *psy war* has been used in its development, based on certain concepts. For example, 'Church Mystery' favors conceptions of modernist pneumatology; 'Spouse Church' induces a new theology with certain erotic connotations of a Freudian kind; 'people of God' paves the way for democracy in Church government, common ownership of property and a structuralist tribalism; 'Sinning Church' pays tribute to Protestant *kenosis*, which in turn ends up in the theology of the death of

---

some testimonies by specialists corroborating the wider concept of warfare contained in the expression, *psy war.*

b. Russian Marshall Nikolay BULGANIN states: "Modern war is a psychological war in which the Armed Forces must serve only to stave off armed attack or, eventually, to occupy territory conquered through a psychological action" (in Hermes de ARAÚJO OLIVEIRA, *Guerra revolucionária*, Rio de Janeiro: Bibliex, 1965, p. 60).

Terence H. QUALTER, from the University of Waterloo (Iowa, USA), observes: "Originally psychological warfare was designed as a preliminary to military action, demoralizing the enemy soldiers before the attack was launched, or as an aid to military action, hastening and cutting the cost of victory. Today it has become a substitute for military action. .... A defeat in the Cold War could be as real and as final as a military defeat and, certainly, it would be followed by military defeat" (*Propaganda and Psychological Warfare*, New York: Random House, 1962, pp. XIIs.).

French specialist Maurice MÉGRET explains that "from Clausewitz to Lenin, technological evolution and the progress in the psychological sciences have conspired to give psychological warfare the quasi magical powers of an 'art of subversion'" (*La guerra psicologica*, Buenos Aires: Paidós, 1959, p. 31).

Another well-known French scholar, Roger MUCCHIELI, notes with special lucidity: "The classic conception [of warfare] viewed subversion and psychological warfare as one war tool among others, employed during hostilities only. Modern day States, immobilized by this archaic distinction, have failed to understand that psychological warfare pulverizes the classic distinction between war and peace. It is not a conventional war flying in the face of the norms of International Law and the known rules of war; it is a total war that disconcerts jurists and pursues its goals under the protection of its own [law] codes .... Modern warfare is above all psychological, and its relation with classic arms has been inverted" (*La subversión*, Paris: Bordas, 1972, pp. 26f.).

God, a remote daughter of Nietzsche; 'pastoral' leads to existentialism, etc.

A demonstration of this matter would lead us to describe a method of the progressivist current of thought and how it determines the goals it has in mind. If it were proven that the accomplishment of this project were the intention of the progressivist wing in Vatican II, we would have gone a long way toward determining what their thinking was.

§ 24   The *second* way would consist in studying the thinking of the principal theologians who idealized and applied the Council, and in trying to determine their system of thinking: its substractum, methods and goals.

After a symposium in which we expounded to Prof. Corrêa de Oliveira the advantages we found in each of the two ways, it was decided to opt for the second.

So we put ourselves to it.

§ 25   A trip to Europe, during which we were kindly received by prominent people who inspired or wrote various of the Council's documents, and by other personalities now highly placed in the theological world, enabled us to clarify various points of their thinking, learn some details about the history of their action in the Council, and collect a select bibliography. This also saved us years of study, giving us the advantage of a navigator who possesses a precise map as opposed to one who sails at random.

Upon our return, we carefully organized the knowledge thus gathered, and, following the compass of Catholic sense that assists a common faithful, set out to read and study.

Progressivist thought as a whole, with its foundations and ultimate goals, as well as the fruits of the Council, will be presented beginning in Volume VI; Volume VIII will be especially dedicated to it. Incidentally, several characteristics of this thought are outlined in Volumes II to V as we analyze the spirit of the Council.

*

§ 26   Among progressivist authors, especially the most prominent ones, we found a vigorous unity of thought and habitual coordination in action.

Nevertheless, the yet unachieved part of their ideological yearnings and practical goals explicably casts, to a certain degree, a shadow of uncertainty upon their very followers. Such uncertainty generates differences in methods and even, at times, in the understanding of final goals.

For minds less inclined to grand overall visions and more prone to advancing safely, in a reasoned fashion, from stage to stage, it could seem that small differences in methods or disagreement over ultimate goals among progressivists, would generate profound and irreconcilable divergencies. For example, it would seem that various army corps attacking a given fortress could not have different methods of attack and varying intentions on how to maintain the citadel and take the most strategic advantage from it once it was conquered. These minds perceive neither clearly nor immediately all that unites the progressivists and the next-to-nothing that divides them. They would begin by classifying them in schools, and then divide these in sub-schools. In little time, the risk rises of fragmenting the unitary vision of the progressivist current's underlying thinking. As a consequence, such people would be led to doubt the accuracy of the underlying unity in the progressivist current that this Work presents.

In order to save Readers who have this legitimate way of reasoning from embarrassment, we suggest they read the Volumes of this Collection in which we analyze the unity of thought, taking into account the diversities among the schools of conciliar progressivism.[28]

Normally, however, we will address the progressivist current as a whole, without excessive concern about real or fictitious differences that many of its components present among themselves.[29] While consciously paying tribute to a certain impreci-

---

[28] Vol. IV, *Animus delendi-I*, Chap. III.1.A, C-E; Vol. V, *Animus delendi-II*, Part II, Chap. V.B; Vol. VI, *Inveniet fidem?*, Chaps. III.2,5, V.6; Vol. VII, *Destructio Dei*, Chaps. II, III; Vol. VIII, *Fumus Satanae*, passim; Vol. IX, *Creatio*, Chaps. I.1, IV.3; Vol. X, *Peccatum-Redemptio*, Chaps. V, VI.2, VII.

[29] About the harmonization between an overall view of a historic phenomenon — whether it be social, political or religious — and its nuances, one can certainly apply to the conciliar reform carried out by progressivists the principles made explicit by Prof. Plinio CORRÊA DE OLIVEIRA in this brilliant page commenting on the *Allocution* of Pius VI of June 17, 1793 about the French Revolution and the beheading of Louis XVI:

"The revolutionary phenomenon is seen here in its ensemble: ideology, impulse, countless multitudes filling streets and squares, impious and unseen plotters, the radical goals that attracted the revolutionaries from the outset to the outcome. In this terrible outcome could be seen, behind the initial and at times mild formulas, the radical goals toward which, more and more openly, the Revolution marched as a whole.

"This way of seeing the Revolution does not ignore the existence of nuances in the revolutionary phenomenon.

"Thus, one cannot equate the *feuillants* of the early stage of the Revolution with the Girondins. The first were liberal monarchists who, compared with the unconditional enthusiasts of the Ancien Régime, were to a certain extent revolutionary figures; the latter were for the most part republicans hostile to the clergy and nobility but favorable to the conservation of a liberal socioeconomic regime that spared free enterprise, private property, and the like from the revolutionary hurricane. The Girondin position had all the elements to appear radically revolutionary not only to the manifest counter-revolutionaries (*émigrés*, *chouans*, and other royalist guerrillas) but also to the *feuillants*. Yet it enraged the ultra-radicals of the Mountain, who besides demanding the abolition of royalty and the radical and bloody persecution of the clergy and nobility, frequently cast threatening glances upon the great fortunes of the bourgeois class.

"Having observed this succession of nuances, from the *feuillants* to the members of the Committee of Public Safety and their throngs of admirers, one perceives that each nuance or stage of the revolutionary march seems markedly leftist when compared to the preceding nuance or stage, and ultra-conservative in relation to the subsequent one. This continues until the Revolution's last breath, exhaled as it lay dying in 1795. This gasp was the communist revolution of Babeuf, to whose left one can conceive nothing save chaos and void, and to whose right a Babeufist would consign everything that preceded it.

"A view of the Revolution that distinguishes its nuances, implicitly or explicitly, presupposes the need to take into account that even the most moderate analysts of the Revolution manifested, along with their moderate designs, an inexplicable and contradictory indulgence toward and at times outright sympathy for the crimes and criminals of the Revolution.

"The simultaneous presence of moderate inclinations and revolutionary connivances in the minds of 'moderates' throughout the Revolution's stages led one of the most fervent apologists of the revolutionary phenomenon — Clemenceau — to dodge the accusation of contradiction by the summary assertion that 'la Révolution est un bloc' (in François Furet - Mona Ozouf, *Dictionnaire critique de la* sion, such generalization appears to us the only way to analyze the current's unity of thought. We thus follow the example of Saint Pius X, who, in the Encyclical *Pascendi*, did not delve into accidental distinctions between schools and authors, but instead presented a synthesis of modernist thought in that which was most essential and general about it.

*

27

The research we carried out to determine the thinking of the Council also enabled us to find many of its fruits.

To us such fruits appear indisputable, since they are consequences of Vatican II that are found in the realm of actual facts and are thus susceptible to an unimpeded comprehension.

Révolution Française, Paris: Flammarion, 1988, p. 980), **in which cracks and contradictions are only apparent**.

"In other words, the Revolution — the consequence of a miscellanea of propensities, doctrines, and agendas — cannot be praised or censured when identified with only one of its nuances or stages. It must be considered in the light of all of this evident miscellanea.

"**Clemenceau's expression** may appear attractive to many minds; nevertheless, it **is still an insufficient description of the historical reality**.

"In fact, **in this apparent miscellanea, one notices an ordering principle of primary importance. From the outset, almost until Babeuf, each stage of the Revolution sought to destroy something and, at the same time, retain something of the old socio-politico-economic edifice.** This may and must be admitted, but without ignoring that **at each stage the destructive ferment acted with more efficacy, self-assurance, and victorious impetus than the conservative tendency did. In fact, the latter always appeared intimidated, insecure, and minimalist in what it wished to preserve and readily compliant in what it consented to sacrifice.**

"**In other words, from beginning to end, the same ferment was active in each of these nuances or stages, making each stage a fleeting marker in the march toward global surrender. Consequently, the Revolution was already entirely present in its ferment, just as a tree is entirely present in its seed**" (*Nobility and Analogous Traditional Elites in the Allocutions of Pius XII*, York, PA: The American Society for the Defense of Tradition, Family and Property - TFP, 1993, pp. 411f.).

§ 28   At first we planned to analyze the fruits of the Council in Dogmatics, Morals, and Liturgy, and to dedicate a minutely detailed study to ecumenism and secularization (understood as the desacralization of the Church and the abolition of Christendom).[30] Finally, we intended to present the various models of "Church" that are outlined for the future.[31] Although we had the necessary material to do this, in order to save time, we thought it better to deal, for the time being, only with the fruits in Dogmatics (Volumes VI to XI). So the possibility of continuing the analysis of the fruits of the Council, if need be, remains open.

§ 29   Having analyzed the letter, spirit, thought, and fruits of the Second Ecumenical Vatican Council, we hope to have fulfilled our duty as *miles Christi* by providing elements for the defense of Holy Church. In other words, such analysis resulted in an exposition of the situation of the Catholic Church and Doctrine facing the onslaught of the progressivist current, so that those who have eyes may see and those who have power may judge.

*

This is the history of the present Study.

*   *   *

---

[30] Ecumenism and secularization are analyzed *en raccourci* in Vol. V, *Animus delendi-II* in light of the spirit of the Council.

[31] A rather brief summary of this matter is found in Chap. VII of Vol. IV, *Animus delendi-I*.

COLLECTION
ELI, ELI, LAMMA SABACTHANI?

VOLUME I

IN THE MURKY WATERS OF VATICAN II

*

CLARIFICATION

The title of this Volume, *In the Murky Waters of Vatican II*, could appear as a disrespectful accusation hurled at the Council, right in the beginning of a Collection that seeks to analyze it impartially.

However, the 'murky waters' image that refers to Vatican II is not ours. It was used by Msgr. Philippe Delhaye, professor emeritus at the University of Louvain-la-Neuve and secretary general of the International Theological Commission (1973 to 1988). Indeed, Msgr. Delhaye says: "Vatican II was an apex in Church life which contributed movements of ideas such as the liturgical movement; an apex from which flow and will continue to flow torrents of living water for the Church. **At the moment these waters are** at times **murky**; certain deviations occur; but what will occur with this Council is what has happened with others: it will take years for its effects to be seen."[1]

Cardinal Leo Józef Suenens, the late retired Archbishop of Malines, one of the four moderators who directed the Council and certainly one of the most influential personages at the conciliar assembly, also employs the metaphor of turbulent waters. He says: "In a few words, a work remains to be done: that of harmonizing two viewpoints and leading them back into a perfect synthesis. There is in Ireland a place well-known to tourists, called the meeting of the waters. It is **a valley in which two rivers impetuously clash against each other to form, downstream, only one river of calm waters**. I offer you this metaphor as an invitation to carry out, in a fraternal dialogue, the marvelous symphony — unfortunately incomplete, like all human creation — of *Lumen gentium*."[2]

Referring to the same conflict of tendencies, this time in the post-conciliar phase of the pontificate of Paul VI, Msgr. Suenens also employs the 'murky waters' metaphor: "**Paul VI had to steer the bark of Peter between opposing currents that made**

---

[1] Philippe DELHAYE, *In caritate non ficta*, Louvain-la-Neuve: Centre Cerfaux-Lefort, p. 108, in Eliodoro MARIANI, "La morale cristiana di fronte ai problemi degli uomini d'oggi," in *L'Osservatore Romano*, 1/5/1984.

[2] Leo Józef SUENENS, "Discorso ufficiale d'apertura - Alcuni compite della teologia oggi," in V.A., *L'avvenire della Chiesa - Il libro del Congresso*, Brescia: Queriniana, 1970, p. 48 (Congress of the magazine *Concilium* in Brussels, September 1970).

the waters murky. For some, in Rome itself, he too strongly welcomed the majority [progressivist] tendencies, and the reforms carried out met strong local opposition. Meanwhile, outside of Rome, sluggishness and hesitation [toward reform] became accentuated."[3]

§ 4   One thus sees that the image of murky and turbulent waters did not originate in this Work. The reason we used the "murky waters" metaphor employed by Msgr. Delhaye and Msgr. Suenens as the title to this Volume, is that we believe it expresses the actual reality.

        Any disrespectful intent, therefore, is far removed from our motives.

*   *   *

---

[3] L. J. SUENENS, *Souvenirs et espérances*, Paris: Fayard, 1991, p. 253.

INTRODUCTION TO VOLUME I

1

In this Volume we endeavor to show the ambiguity of the Council's documents. We say show, rather than demonstrate, because the number of authors who take the *chiaroscuro* [a mixture of clarity and obscurity, in other words, ambiguity] of such documents as a premise to their analyses is so large as to make any demonstration practically superfluous.

Nevertheless, the Volume follows the logical order of a demonstration.

2

Before asking any question, we give the Reader, as a few samples of many that could be cited, some examples of the Council's ambiguous or contradictory texts (Chapter I). We then bring to the fore a whole array of questions so as to help him orient himself amidst the several hypotheses that could explain the use of ambiguity, whether it be fortuitous or not (Chapter II). We then assemble the testimony of well-respected authors who affirm that there is ambiguity in the texts of Vatican Council II (Chapter III). Couldn't the *chiaroscuro* of Vatican II have been the result of a strategy? In Chapter IV we cite for the Reader several famous authors who state that this was indeed the case. Consistent with that strategy, once the Council was over, the progressive current began to draw from that *chiaroscuro* a new stimulus for its adherents (Chapter V). In addition, the Council's ambiguity reflects a temporary equilibrium of forces between the two opposing currents of thought, the conservative and the progressivist, which we demonstrate in Chapter VI. Now then, if two opposing currents clash over basic concepts, would there be, latent in the ambiguity, a new doctrine different from Catholic Doctrine? This is what we strive to answer in Chapter VII. In Chapter VIII we point out how, in addition to clear ambiguities, there are also omissions that favor progressivist concepts.

At that point it will have become clear to a Reader endowed with simple Catholic sense or even mere common sense, without the need for an elaborate theological formation, that the lack of clarity in the Council's documents is an indisputable reality.

3

Having attained this level of certainty about the ambiguity of the Council — which is what we try to demonstrate in this first Volume — we begin to draw the chief consequences from that conclusion. The first consequence, of a doctrinal order, is that the very *chiaroscuro* of the conciliar documents entails grave concessions to other religions and to the modern world, implying a virtual destruction of the Faith and a modification of the concept of

the Catholic Church. To this we dedicate Chapter IX. Other consequences are the crises of Faith and discipline among the faithful. We show how the Council's ambiguity brought about a crisis
in Church unity. Progressivist and conservative currents interpret
the ambiguous texts each in its own way and with its own criteria,
tearing apart the unity which bound them together. In addition to
this ominous consequence, the authority of the Bishops and even
that of the Pope began to be brought into question in view of such
ambiguous positions. Finally, we deal with the crisis that affected
the secular Clergy and religious Orders as a consequence of the
Council. Chapter X studies this problem.

§ 4   Although much could be concluded from the exposition
contained in the ten Chapters of this Volume, we will restrict ourselves to saying the undeniable: the Council's texts are ambiguous. Some scholar or Reader may understandably wish to draw
from this Volume conclusions other than those stated herein. We
have no objections provided that they are guided by the same
spirit of Faith and love of the Church that inspires these lines.

                                   *

§ 5   The first Chapters of this Volume will be very brief.

         Someone might imagine that we found only a few quota-
tions to prove the theses of these Chapters. That would be an error. Practically all the texts which corroborate the theses expounded throughout the Work could also be cited in the first few
Chapters. It was difficult to find a criterion of selection to put in
proper order a number of texts that were not only meaningful but
proved several things at the same time. Further on we will say a
word about this criterion. In later Chapters, as we repeat some
quotations that show ambiguity in language, ambiguity as a
method, and so on, the theses expounded in the first Chapters will
take on added strength in the Reader's mind.

         The method of exposition, which we chose from among
several, is of a psychological type, born of our own experience. It
is aimed at a Catholic reader who, like ourselves before carrying
out this study, would be inclined not to admit that there could be
the slightest shadow of ambiguity in documents of the Catholic
Church such as those of Vatican Council II, whether the ambiguity arose from contradiction or any factor of the sort. We first
endeavor to open the Reader's eyes to become accustomed to the
possibility of ambiguity, then to its probability, then to its certainty and, once this certainty has been established, we draw vari-

ous conclusions that flow naturally from the analyzed documents. This criterion is aimed to show the painful situation of the Church in our days in a gradual and objective manner.

*

§ *6*   Another objection that could be raised, and to which we would like to answer *avant la lettre*, is that we fail to expound our thinking with the elegant concision that has come to be increasingly appreciated in certain intellectual circles and that we quote a large number of long texts, making the exposition heavy.

We were actually not especially concerned with elegance. In this Volume, as in the whole Collection *Eli, Eli, lamma sabacthani?,* we follow the inductive method, which requires that a sufficient number of texts be cited before each conclusion is drawn. In truth, this method might not be elegant.

However, who in his right mind would criticize a sailor for failing to act elegantly as he attempts to plug up a gaping hole in a sinking ship's hull?

Is Holy Mother Church not immersed in a 'mysterious process of autodemolition'? Does the Bark of Peter not seem to be sinking? Is the 'smoke of Satan' not penetrating everywhere? The hour, therefore, is not one calling especially for elegance, but rather for dedication and courage.[1]

*   *   *

---

[1] To corroborate the need for courage in face of the present crisis in the Church, we could cite the words of PAUL VI in the Audience for the participants of the International Thomistic Congress (September 12, 1970): "Do we not see an excess of Christian-ideas-gone-awry drag in their unrestrained tumult the most well-founded certainties and the most secure beliefs? What an admirable work you can and must carry out, in this hour that calls, more than ever, for the 'courage of truth'!" (*Insegnamenti di Paolo VI*, vol. VIII, p. 865; Allocution to the Sacred College of May 18, 1970, Ibid., pp. 585f.).

CHAPTER I

AMBIGUITY IN THE TEXTS OF VATICAN II'S OFFICIAL DOCUMENTS

If someone gifted with an average Catholic culture and moved by his love for the Church were to read the documents of Vatican Council II, his mind would gradually be filled with questions as he progressed in his study.

Right in the first Chapter of the Dogmatic Constitution *Lumen gentium*, he would be in for a surprise: "This .... sole Church of Christ which in the Creed we profess to be one, holy, catholic and apostolic .... constituted and organized as a society in the present world, **subsists in** the Catholic Church, which is governed by the successor of Peter .... Nevertheless, many elements of sanctification and of truth are found outside its visible confines [sic]. Since these are gifts belonging to the Church of Christ, they are forces impelling towards Catholic unity" (LG 8b).

This passage would have been clear if it had stated that the Church of Christ is the Catholic Church or that the Church of Christ **exists exclusively in** the Catholic Church. The way it has been written, it implicitly affirms that there are two distinct realities — the Church of Christ and the Catholic Church — and that the latter, which is more restricted, receives its life from the former, more universal and more noble.[1]

What "Church of Christ" would this be, different from and nobler than the Catholic Church, which receives its very life from it? Could this 'church' contain the 'elements of sanctification and truth' that are found 'outside' the visible Catholic structure? As he searches for an explanation, the Reader ends up in an even

---

[1] The progressivists base themselves on the supposed distinction between the Catholic Church and the "Church of Christ" to promote ecumenism with heretical and schismatic confessions. The Reader can find more about this matter in Vol. V, *Animus delendi-II*, Part II.

greater confusion: Could there be, then, habitually, 'sanctification and truth' outside the sacred bosom of the Catholic Church?

This statement implying the existence of two different churches clashes both with the perennial teaching of the Magisterium and the Catholic sense of the faithful, who has always nourished himself, as a child with his mother's milk, with the idea that the Catholic Church is the sole Church of Christ.[2] Desirous to

---

[2] a. In his Allocution *Ubi primum*, of December 17, 1848, PIUS IX recalls the traditional doctrine that the Church of Christ is the Catholic Church: "Let those, therefore, who wish to be saved, come to this column, this foundation of the truth which is the Church. **Let them come to the true Church of Christ which, in her Bishops and in the Roman Pontiff, supreme chief of all, possesses the uninterrupted succession of apostolic authority**, which has desired more than anything to preach, preserve and defend the doctrine announced by the Apostles, fulfilling the command of Jesus Christ. [The Church] which, since the times of the Apostles, grew amidst all kinds of difficulties and, radiant with the luster of miracles, multiplied by the blood of Martyrs, ennobled by the virtues of the Confessors and Virgins, fortified by the testimonies and sage writings of the Fathers, **laid roots and flourished in all countries of the earth, and shines through the perfect unity of faith in the same sacraments and the same spiritual regime. We who**, in spite of Our indignity, occupy the supreme Chair of the Apostle Peter, upon which Our Lord Jesus Christ established the foundation of his Church, **have never spared effort nor work to bring back to this sole way of truth and salvation**, by the grace of the same Jesus Christ, **those who are in ignorance in error. And let all those who are Our adversaries remember** that though heaven and earth shall pass, none of the words of Christ can pass; **that nothing can be changed in the doctrine that the Catholic Church received from Jesus Christ to preserve, defend, and preach**" (In V.A., *Recueil des allocutions consistoriales, encycliques et autres lettres apostoliques des Souverains Pontifes Clement XII, Benoît XIV, Pie VI, Pie VII, Léon XII, Grégoire XVI et Pie IX. Citées dans l'Encyclique et le Syllabus du 8 décembre 1864, suivi du Concordat de 1801 et de divers autres documents*, Paris: Adrien le Clere, 1865, p. 207).

b. Thus says LEO XIII in the Encyclical *Parvenu*, of March 19, 1902: "Returning to Christianity will not be a real and efficacious medicine if it does not mean returning to and loving the one, holy, Catholic and apostolic Church. Indeed, **Christianity acts through and identifies with the Catholic Church**, a sovereignly spiritual and perfect society **that is the Mystical Body of Jesus Christ** and whose visible Chief is the Roman Pontiff, the Successor of the Prince of Apostles. It is she who continues the mission of the Saviour, daughter and heiress of His Redemption; she it was who propagated the Gospel all over the earth, spreading it at the cost of her blood; and it is she who, according to the promise of divine assistance and immortality, never compromising with error, carries out the mission of preserving in its fullness the doctrine of Christ till the end of time" (Petrópolis: Vozes, 1960, n. 26).

c. In the Encyclical *Satis cognitum*, of June 29, 1896, the same Pontiff teaches: **"We say,** therefore, **that the Catholic Church is unique in its essence, in its origin, and in its excellence...** Furthermore, **the eminence of the Church arises from its unity,** as the principle of its constitution – a unity surpassing all else, and **having nothing like unto it or equal to it**" (S. Clemens ALEXANDRINUS, *Stromatum*, lib. VIII, chap. 17). For this reason **Christ, speaking of the mystical edifice, mentions only one Church, which he calls His own:** 'I will build my Church;' **any other church except this one,** since it has not been founded by Christ, **cannot be the true Church"** (Petrópolis: Vozes, 1960, n. 7).

And later on, quoting Saint OPTATUS DE MILEVIS: "Explaining this passage, Optatus de Milevis says: 'It is written in the prophet Isaias: 'From Sion the law shall go forth and the word of the Lord from Jerusalem.' For it is not on Mount Sion that Isaias sees the valley, but on the holy mountain, that is, the Church, which has raised itself conspicuously throughout the entire Roman world under the whole heavens .... **The Church is, therefore, the spiritual Sion in which Christ has been constituted King by God the Father, and which exists throughout the entire earth, on which there is but one Catholic Church'** (*Libri septem de schismate Donatistarum*, lib. III, n. 2)" (n. 9; nn. 10, 18).

d. In his Encyclical *Mortalium animos*, of January 6, 1928, PIUS XI equally identifies the Church of Christ with the Catholic Church: **"In this sole Church of Christ, no one is found nor does anyone remain unless he recognizes and accepts, in obedience, the authority and power of Peter and of his legitimate successors. ....** Unfortunately there have been children who deserted the paternal home .... **Let them hear the voice of Lactancius** exclaiming: **'Only .... the Catholic Church** preserves the true worship. **It is the source of truth, the dwelling place of faith, the temple of God. He who does not enter it, or he who leaves it, loses all hope of life and salvation.** Let no one allow himself to be carried away by recalcitrant contestations. This is a matter of life and salvation. If one is not attentively and prudently vigilant, it is perdition and death' (*Lactantii divinarum institutionum libri septem IV*, 30, 11f.)" (*Actes de S.S. Pie XI*, Paris: Bonne Presse, vol. IV, p. 80).

e. In the beginning of the Encyclical *Mystici Corporis Christi*, of June 29, 1943, PIUS XII is peremptory: **"In order to define and describe this true Church of Christ — which is the Holy, Catholic and Apostolic Roman Church** (Council Vatican I, *Constitutio dogmatica de Fide catholica*, c. 1), **there is nothing more noble, excellent or more divine than the concept expressed in the designation 'Mystical Body of Jesus Christ.'"** (Petrópolis: Vozes, 1960, nn. 9, 103).

find a respectful solution to such an awkward statement, the faithful is led to ask himself whether the expression *subsistit in* was used inadequately.

The impression of ambiguity becomes even more striking when, after the consideration above, one returns to the text to see whether it could be interpreted in a benign but consistent manner.

"The sole Church of Christ which in the Creed we profess to be .... Catholic .... **subsists in** the Catholic Church governed by the successor of Peter."

If the intention was to state that the Catholic Church is the Church of Christ, as it has always been taught, why cast a doubt in the mind of the faithful? Why this ambiguity of the *subsistit in*? [3]

---

[3] a. Here is an astonishing statement by Cardinal Yves Congar, OP, one of the most authoritative theologians on Vatican II: "It is said [in LG 8b] that the Church of Christ and of the Apostles *subsistit in*, is found in the Catholic Church 'even though many elements of sanctification and truth are found outside [sic] its structure.' Therefore, there is not a strict, *that is, exclusive*, identification between the Church Body of Christ and the Catholic Church. Deep down, Vatican II admits that non-Catholic Christians are members of the Mystical Body and not merely *ordinati ad*. The categories used in the decree on ecumenism and also in a number of documents and speeches of H.H. Paul VI, are: fully belonging to the sole Church through baptism [but having] an imperfect subsequent communion" (Yves M. J. CONGAR, *Le Concile du Vatican II - Son Eglise, peuple de Dieu et Corps du Christ*, Paris: Beauchesne, 1984, pp. 160f.).

b. For his part, Msgr. Christopher Basil Butler, General Abbot of the Benedictines in England and later Auxiliary Bishop of Westminster, a member of the Congregation for the Doctrine of the Faith and Customs during the Council who participated in the writing of *Lumen gentium*, believes that the *subsistit in* marks an 'advance': "Here we can gauge the advance of the Constitution *[Lumen gentium]* over *Mystici Corporis*, [and we have] the basis for the Decree on Ecumenism and other elements of the Council's teaching and proposals. An exclusive material identification of the Church with Roman Catholic communion is carefully avoided" (C. B. BUTLER, *The Theology of Vatican II*, London, 1967, p. 70, in Y. CONGAR, op. cit., p. 160).

c. Fr. Avery DULLES, a well-known American Jesuit theologian, draws some consequences from this general principle: "The Church of Jesus Christ does not exclusively identify with the Roman Catholic Church. It certainly subsists in Roman Catholicism, but is also present, in various ways and in diverse degrees, in other Christian communities

Taking a brief look at the beginning of chapter II of the same dogmatic Constitution, a Catholic mind could not fail to raise, with concern, several questions about whether it would be opportune to replace the notion of a hierarchical and sacral Church with the notion of the 'people of God.' We would like to say a word about its context, leaving the analysis of the text for later.[4]

---

inasmuch as they are faithful to that which God started with Jesus and obey the inspirations of the Spirit of Christ.

"As a result of their common participation in the reality of the only Church, the various Christian communities already have among themselves a real, though imperfect, communion. Relations among churches, therefore, are not simply 'external relations' that can exist between distinct sovereign states, but 'domestic relations' analogous to those that exist between groups inside an individual political society. Under certain aspects the relationship is also a more intimate one, because all Christians are incorporated into the single body of Christ, animated by his Spirit. Intimacy among all Christian groups, which is a divine gift, makes more imperative the restoration of full communion among all" ("Ecumenismo: problemi e possibilità per il futuro," in V.A., *Verso la Chiesa del terzo millennio*, Brescia: Queriniana, 1979, pp. 108f.).

d. Other renowned theologians around the world, in addition to the three cited above, comment that the *subsist in* represents an important opening toward recognizing the existence of an ecclesial reality that extends beyond the borders of the Catholic Church. They are pointed out by Francis A. SULLIVAN, SJ, in his article "Le sens et l'importance de la décision de Vatican II de dire, à propos de l'Eglise du Christ, non pas qu'elle 'est' mais qu'elle 'subsiste dans' l'Eglise Catholique Romaine," in V.A., *Vatican II - Bilan et perspectives*, vol. II, p. 302: G. PHILIPS, *L'Eglise et son mystère au deuxième concile du Vatican*, vol. I, p. 119; J. FEINER, untitled, in V.A., *Commentary on the Documents of Vatican II*, Herder, vol. II, p. 69; A. GRILLMEIER, untitled, Ibid., vol. I, p. 150; E. FISCHER, *Kirche und Kirchen nach dem Vatikanum II*, München, 1967, pp. 79f.; H. FRIES, *Eglise et Eglises*, in V.A., *Problèmes et perspectives de théologie fondamentale*, ed. R. LATOURELLE, Paris-Tournai-Montreal: G. O'Collins, 1982, p. 418; A. DULLES, *The Church, the churches and the Catholic Church*, in T.S., 33, 1972, p. 211; A. de HALLEUX, "Les principes catholiques de l'oecumenisme," *Revue Théologique Louvain*, 16, 1985, pp. 320ff.

e. Quite different from the interpretation these authors present to explain this controversial passage of *Lumen gentium* is the teaching of the traditional Magisterium, which has always identified the Church of Christ **exclusively** with the Catholic Church.

---

[4] The progressivist notion of the 'people of God' is analyzed in Vol. IV, *Animus delendi-I*, Chap. IV, in caput; Vol. XI, *Ecclesia*, Chap. II.

Even though the expression, people of God, of itself can be legitimately applied to the Holy Church, a Catholic could ask whether, in a world devastated by a tendency to abolish all superiority, contaminated by the errors of Illuminism and the French Revolution and profoundly undermined by the virulent germs of Communism,[5] it was opportune to present the structure of the Church predominantly as a people and no longer as a hierarchy.[6] Is this not opening a door to that egalitarian tendency?[7]

---

[5] Plinio CORRÊA DE OLIVEIRA, *Revolution and Counter-Revolution*, York, PA: The American Society for the Defense of Tradition, Family and Property, 1993, Part I, chap. III.5.C,D.

[6] Within the context of the conciliar document, we refer especially to these excerpts:

* "Christ the Lord .... made the new people 'a kingdom of priests to God, his Father' (Apoc 1:6; cf. 5:9-10). The baptized, by regeneration and the anointing of the Holy Spirit, are consecrated to be a spiritual house and a holy priesthood, that through all the works of Christian men they may offer spiritual sacrifices and proclaim the perfection of him who has called them out of darkness into his marvelous light (1 Pet. 2:4-10)" (LG 10a).

* "All men are called to belong to the New People of God. This People therefore, whilst remaining one and only one, is to be spread throughout the whole world and to all ages in order that the design of God may be fulfilled" (LG 13a).

* "The one People of God is accordingly present in all the nations of the earth, since its citizens, who are taken from all nations, are of a kingdom whose nature is not earthly but heavenly" (LG 13b).

* "This character of universality which adorns the People of God is a gift from the Lord himself whereby the Catholic ceaselessly and efficaciously seeks for the return of all humanity and all its goods under Christ the Head in the unity of his Spirit" (LG 13b).

* "Hence it is that the People of God is not only an assembly of various peoples, but in itself is made up of different ranks" (LG 13c).

[7] a. This egalitarian tendency inspires movements such as the Basic Christian Communities (BCCs) and 'small groups' struggling to institutionalize a type of participatory democracy in the Church. Such a tendency has found support, for example, in the expression 'communion' or *koinonia*, that should exist in the 'people of God,' used in several documents of the Council (LG 4, 7b, 9b, 13a, 15; GS 32d; UR 2d). This enabled one of the conciliar *periti* [experts], Bishop Boaventura KLOPPENBURG, to state that "strictly speaking there are no 'superiors' and

'inferiors' or 'subjects' in the Church. One must read this and take it seriously (Mt 23:8-11; Lc 22:25-27): 'All you are brethren' (Mt 23:8) — brethren in only one large Family which has no special 'dignitaries.' The Church is and must be a fraternity, a *koikonia*, a communion. It is certain that even though all are brethren and equal in dignity, there must be diversity in *services* or ministries so that the People of God may believe .... That is why the Church is a *communio hierarchica*. But the word 'hierarchical' is an adjective and should not be turned into a noun so as to identify with the Church" (*A eclesiologia do Vaticano II*, p. 127).

Further on, comparing the Church with democracy, the theologian writes: "Drawing from the non-democratic nature of the Church an argument against the people's active participation in designating candidates for ecclesiastical posts would be a simple fallacy. That which is most praised in Democracy — liberty, fraternity, equality, co-responsibility — will perfectly have its place in *koinonia*. By means of a government of love (*per gubernationem in dilectione*), the fraternal concord of the family of God will be attained (UR 2d). Neither Democracy nor, even less, Monarchy, but rather *koinonia*, through which 'there reigns a true equality between all with regard to the dignity and to the activity which is common to all the faithful in the building up of the Body of Christ' (LG 32c). This concept must be taken seriously and put into practice" (op. cit., p. 128).

b. For his part, Spanish theologian Joaquim Losada, commenting on the fundamental lines of the Council's conception of the Church, writes: "The doctrinal assertion that *all* members of the people of God, each in his own way, participate in the threefold function of Christ, implies recognizing the ministerial character of the whole Church. .... This recognition opens the way for a real participation of everyone in the life of the Church, which can find concrete forms in the models offered by modern democratic society. From here onward, based on the Council's ecclesiology, it is necessary to speak of the urgency of a process of *democratization of the Church*" (Joaquim LOSADA, *El posconcilio: el problema de la transformación de la Iglesia*, in V.A., *Desafios cristianos*, Madrid: Loguez Ediciones, 1990, p. 89).

c. One can see that as B. Kloppenburg and J. Losada understand it, when the Council's documents speak of communion, of *koinonia* in the 'people of God,' they are speaking for the immediate establishment of a representative democracy in the Church, to be later replaced by the kind of participatory democracy so fiercely proposed by BCCs leaders.

d. In this regard, Leonardo BOFF's explanation of the Basic Christian Communities as a new 'manner of being Church' is quite meaningful: "The principal characteristic of this new manner of being Church is community and fraternity [sic]. All are effectively brethren, everyone participates, everyone takes up his own task. This is the first commandment. Afterward comes the incipient structure of leadership and coordination. Though all are essentially equal, not everyone does the same job. Thus there are the coordinators, who are often times women

In this context, dosn't the affirmation of the common priesthood of the faithful [8] act to stimulate Rousseau's myth of the people's sovereignty? Is this not a revival of the old errors of Catholic Action,[9] which called for the laity to participate in the hierarchical *munus*?

---

responsible for maintaining order, for presiding over celebrations and for the sacramental aspect of the community. We know that in the first centuries the Church was known mainly as *communitas fidelium*, a community of the faithful, with a great participation of the people in everything. After the year 1,000 there was a greater and greater imposition of a hierarchical Church. The sacred power came to be considered the structuring element, and not so much the community *(koinonia)*. This way of organizing the Church certainly was due to an historical necessity, but it did not facilitate the responsible participation of everyone. The Basic [Christian] Community opens up the possibility of a greater participation and equilibrium among the various Church functions" (*Igreja - Carisma e poder - Ensaio de eclesiologia militante*, Petrópolis: Vozes, 1982, p. 200).

[8] The excerpts of *Lumen gentium* especially in question are:

* "Though they differ essentially and not only in degree, the common priesthood of the faithful and the ministerial or hierarchical priesthood are nonetheless ordered one to another; each in its own proper way shares in the one priesthood of Christ. The ministerial priest, by the sacred power that he has, forms and rules the priestly people; in the person of Christ he effects the eucharistic sacrifice and offers it to God in the name of all the people. The faithful indeed, by virtue of their royal priesthood, participate in the offering of the Eucharist. They exercise that priesthood, too, by the reception of the sacraments, prayer and thanksgiving, the witness of a holy life, abnegation, and active charity" (LG 10b).

* "The sacred nature and organic structure of the priestly community is brought into operation through the sacraments and the exercise of virtues" (LG 11a).

* "The holy People of God shares also in Christ's prophetic office [*munus*]: it spreads abroad a living witness to him, especially by a life of faith and love and by offering to God a sacrifice of praise, the fruit of lips praising his name (Heb. 13:15)" (LG 12a).

[9] Plinio CORRÊA DE OLIVEIRA, *Em Defesa da Ação Católica*, São Paulo: Ave-Maria, 1943, especially Part. I, pp. 54-106.

After the Council approved such singular notions, apparently to the detriment of the Church's hierarchical constitution, how could one avoid excesses such as those of Leonardo Boff [10] and Fr. Edward Schillebeeckx,[11] who call for an egalitarian church? In the long run, what can be the efficacy of the laudable admonishments that Cardinal Ratzinger has made to those authors,[12] who actually feel protected by the ambiguity in the text and context of *Lumen gentium*?

As far as the ecclesiological notion of the 'people of God' is concerned, ambiguity is found not only in incidental passages. It pervades the whole context in which the Church appears to adapt herself to the errors of Illuminism, the French Revolution and, indirectly, of Communism,[13] all of which She had fought up until then.[14]

---

[10] Especially in *Igreja: Carisma e poder*, pp. 204-219.

[11] See for example, E. SCHILLEBEECKX, *Le Ministère dans l'Eglise*, Cerf, Paris, 1981, pp. 108-116. See also his contribution "Funcionamento da autoridade na Igreja," in V.A., *Cinco problemas que desafiam a Igreja de hoje*, São Paulo: Herder, pp. 39-54.

[12] "Notification de la Congrégation pour la Doctrine de la Foi à propos du livre de L. Boff: '*Église: Charisme et pouvoir*,'" in *La Documentation Catholique*, 5/5/1985, pp. 484ff; see also the "Lettera della Congregazione per la Dottrina della Fede a P. Schillebeeckx" of June 13, 1984, published in *L'Osservatore Romano*, 1/11/1985.

In spite of the censure by the Congregation for the Doctrine of the Faith, the former Franciscan from Brazil was offered the solidarity of 115 Capitulary priests of his Order, including its Superior General, and by 108 European theologians, in different petitions. He was clearly supported by the leadership of the National Conference of Brazilian Bishops (CNBB). In addition, about twenty bishops publicly came out in his support against the Roman Congregation (*Roma locuta - Documentário sobre o livro 'Igreja: Carisma e poder - Ensaios de eclesiologia militante' de Frei Leonardo Boff, OFM*, Petrópolis: Vozes, 1985, pp. 58f., 61, 71ff.).

[13] a. We are not the only ones to consider the ecclesiology of the People of God under this prism. Henri FESQUET, a well-known French journalist and chronicler of Vatican II, concludes his work about the Council with the expressive subtitle: *Liberté, égalité, fraternité*. He explains: "This liberation of Catholic thinking, for long a prisoner of the negative current of the Counter-Reformation, makes it possible somehow to operate a junction with the trilogy of the French Revolution .... 'Liberty, equality, fraternity': this glorious motto that was, in short, that of Vatican II, as Hans Küng has recently suggested" (*Le journal du Concile*, Folcalquier: Robert Morel, 1966, p. 1127).

Indeed, Fr. Hans KÜNG, a conciliar *perito* [expert], defends the idea that the Church must become more democratic in accordance with the revolutionary trilogy, which, in his view, is a Christian motto. Thus, the first chapter of his book *Prêtre, pour quoi faire?* (Paris: Cerf, 1971, pp. 19-32) is titled: *The Church, Communion in Liberty, Equality and Fraternity.*

b. On the support of conciliar Popes, Bishops and famed theologians to the ideals of the French Revolution, see Vol. IV, *Animus delendi-I*, Chap. IV.1.

c. Also in regard to the affinity between the ecclesiological ideas of the Council and communist yearnings, it is opportune to transcribe here the euphoric finding of the Italian Communist Party (PCI) referred to by Msgr. Rudolf Graber, Bishop of Regensburg. During its 1964 congress, the Italian Communist Party (PCI) published a special issue of the magazine *Propaganda*, dedicated to 'dialogue with Catholics,' in which it states: "The extraordinary eruption of the Council, justly compared to the General Assemblies of 1789, has demonstrated to the whole world that the old political-religious Bastille is shaken in its foundations. A new situation has thus been produced which we must face with proportionate means. Thus, there appears an unheard-of opportunity for us to draw closer to the final victory by means of an adequate maneuver" ("Statements on Dialogue With Catholics," in *Propaganda*, in R. GRABER, *Athanasius und die Kirche unserer Zeit*, Arensburg: Josef Kral, 1973, p. 69).

Another paragraph in the same communist magazine, subtitled *Arguments*, quoted by the Bishop of Regensburg, concludes: "Thus, the Council itself gratuitously places at our disposal the best resources to reach the Catholic public" (Ibid., p. 70).

This part of the PCI magazine's commentary on the matter closes with the words: "Never has the situation been so favorable to us."

[14] The Popes have been fighting the nefarious errors of Illuminism, the French Revolution, liberalism, religious indifferentism, as well as Socialism and Communism, since the end of the 18th century. Here is a list of the main pontifical documents condemning those errors:

a. Against the Principles of the French Revolution:

Pius VI: Letter-Decree to the Cardinal de La Rochefoucauld and the Archbishop of Aix-en-Provence, of March 10, 1791, in *Pii VI Pontificis Maximi Acta* (Rome: Typis S. Congreg. de Propaganda Fide, 1871), vol. II, pp. 70f; Allocution in the Secret Consistory, of June 17, 1793 confirming the words of the Encyclical *Inscrutabile Divinae Sapientiae*, of December 25, 1775, Ibid., vol. I, pp. 26f; Bull *Auctorem Fidei*, of August 28, 1794.

b. Against Liberalism, Naturalism, and Religious Indifferentism:

Gregory XVI: Encyclical *Mirari vos*, of August 15, 1832, in V.A. *Les enseignements pontificaux - La paix intérieure des nations*, ed. MONKS OF SOLESMES (Tournai: Desclée & Cie., 1952), nn. 24f.

Pius IX: Encyclical *Qui pluribus*, of November 9, 1846; in DS 2785; (Petrópolis: Vozes, 1960), n. 8; Allocution *Ubi primum*, of December 17, 1847, in V.A. *Recueil des allocutions*, pp. 205, 207; Encyclical *Nostis et nobiscum*, of December 8, 1849, Ibid., p. 243; Letter *Multiplices inter*, of June 10, 1851, Ibid., p. 287; Allocution *Acerbissimum*, of September 27, 1852, Ibid., p. 325; Allocution *Singulari quadam*, of December 9, 1852, in D 1642; Alocution *Nemo vestrum*, of July 26, 1855, Ibid., pp. 351-355; Encyclical *Singulari quidem*, of March 17, 1856, Ibid., pp. 365, 367, 369; Allocution *Nunquam fore*, of December 15, 1856, Ibid., p. 387; Allocution *Iamdudum cernimus*, of March 18, 1861, Ibid., pp. 435, 437, 439; Allocution *Maxima quidem*, of June 9, 1862, Ibid., pp. 455, 457, 459; Letter *Gravissimas inter* to the Archbishop of Munich-Freising, of December 22, 1862, in DS 2850-2861; Encyclical *Quanto conficiamur*, of August 10, 1863, in DS 2865ff.; V.A., *Recueil des allocutions*, p. 477; Letter *Tuas libenter* to the Archbishop of Munich-Freising, of December 21, 1863, in DS 2875.

Saint Pius X: Apostolic Letter *Notre charge apostolique,* of August 25, 1910 (Petrópolis: Vozes, 1953), nn. 12, 20.

c. Against Socialism and Communism:

Pius IX: Encyclical *Nostis et nobiscum,* of December 8, 1849, in V.A., *Les enseignements pontificaux*, n. 36; Encyclical *Quanta cura*, in DS 2890; (Petrópolis: Vozes, 1951), nn. 5, 7; *Syllabus,* of December 8, 1864, in DS 2902, 2915-2918, 2977-2980, § 4.

Leo XIII: Encyclicals *Quod apostolici muneris,* of December 28, 1878, in DS 3133; V.A., *Les enseignements pontificaux*, nn. 62ff., 71, 77, 81, 83f.; *Diuturnum illud,* of June 28, 1881, Ibid, n. 105; *Auspicatum concessum,* of September 17, 1882 (Petrópolis: Vozes, 1953), n. 24; *Humanum genus,* of April 20, 1884 (Petrópolis: Vozes, 1960), n. 23; *Immortale Dei,* of November 1, 1885 (Petrópolis: Vozes, 1953), nn. 32, 38; *Libertas praestantissimum,* of June 20, 1888, in V.A., *Les enseignements pontificaux*, n. 195; *Rerum novarum,* of May 15, 1891 (Petrópolis: Vozes, 1954), nn. 7, 9, 22; *Laetitiae sanctae,* of September 8, 1893 (Petrópolis: Vozes, 1953), n. 5; *Graves de communi,* of January 18, 1901 (Petrópolis: Vozes, 1956), nn. 2, 6, 27; *Parvenu,* of March 19, 1902 (Petrópolis: Vozes, 1960), n. 19.

A person who analyzes the ensemble of the Council's documents beginning with *Lumen gentium* enjoys a moment of calm as he reaches Chapter II. Indeed, it reads: "Hence they cannot be saved who, knowing that the Catholic Church was founded by God through Christ as a necessary institution, would nonetheless refuse either to enter it, or to persevere in it" (LG 14a).

In fact, we are facing here the perennial axiom of dogmatic teaching: *Extra ecclesiam nulla salus*.

In this passage, the consistency of the thinking of Vatican II with the whole Tradition of the Church gives the person studying it a feeling of security, confidence, and hope that the ambiguities cited previously can be resolved by a crystal clear explanation.

Nevertheless, such hopeful and filial sentiments are shattered like a wave dashing against a rock when the person reaches the text of the Decree on Ecumenism, *Unitatis redintegratio*; and further on, the Declaration on Religious Liberty, *Dignitatis hu-*

St. **Pius X:** *Motu propio* about the Catholic Popular Action, of December 18, 1903, in *Lettres apostoliques de S. Pie X* (Paris: Bonne Presse, 1926), pp. 109ff.

Benedict XV: Encyclical *Ad beatissime,* of November 1, 1914, in V.A., *Les enseignements pontificaux*, nn. 479ff.; Encyclical *Soliti nos,* of March 11, 1920, Ibid., n. 496.

Pius XI: Encyclical *Quadragesimo anno*, of March 15, 1931, in DS 3742ff.; (Paris: Ed. Spes, 1954), nn. 2, 11, 16, 34, 51, 61ff., 105, 119-139; Encyclical *Divini Redemptoris,* of March 19, 1937, in DS 3773; (Buenos Aires: Ed. Roma, n.d.), nn. 8-24, 57f.

Pius XII: Christmas Radiomessage 1944 (Petrópolis: Vozes, 1951), n. 28; Speech at the 9th International Conference of Catholic Associations, May 7, 1949, in Discorsi e radiomessaggi, vol. XI, pp. 63f.; Decree of the Sacred Congregation of the Holy Office Against Communism, June 1, 1949, in AAS, vol. XLI, p. 334; Speech to the International Congress of Social Studies and the International Christian Association, June 3, 1950, in Discorsi e radiomessaggi, vol. XII, pp. 100f.; Speech to the First International Congress on the Problems of Rural Life, July 2, 1951, Ibid., vol. XIII, pp. 199f; Radiomessage to the Katholikentag of Vienna, September 14, 1952, Ibid., vol. XIV, p. 314; Letter to the 41st Social Week of France, July 14, 1954, Ibid., vol. XVI, pp. 465f.; Speech to the 7th Congress of Italy's Christian Union of Corporate Leaders and Managers, March 7, 1957, Ibid., vol. XIX, p. 30.

manae, and finally, the Declaration on Relations with Non-Christian Religions, *Nostra aetate*.

Let us consider, for example, the Decree *Unitatis redintegratio*, which reads: "Large communities became separated from full communion with the Catholic Church. .... However, **one cannot charge with the sin of separation** those who at present are born into these communities and in them are brought up in the faith of Christ, and the Catholic Church accepts them with respect and affection as brothers. .... Moreover, some, even **very many of the most significant elements** and endowments **which go together to build up and give life to the Church itself, can exist outside the visible boundaries of the Catholic Church**: the written Word of God; **the life of grace; faith, hope, and charity** with the other interior gifts of the Holy Spirit, as well as visible elements. .... The brethren divided from us also carry out many liturgical actions of the Christian religion. .... These .... **can aptly give access to the communion of salvation**" (UR 3a,b,c).

In this case we no longer appear to be dealing with ambiguities; one would say that we are faced with inconsistency and contradiction. How could one not see a contradiction between what has been said here and the above quotation from *Lumen gentium*?

*

Here are three examples of ambiguity and contradiction taken from only two of sixteen final documents of Vatican Council II.

How much would have to be written in order to make a complete analysis only of the ambiguous, contradictory, and incomplete points in the documents of Vatican II...

*   *   *

CHAPTER II

WHY THE AMBIGUITY?

§ 1   Ambiguous is defined as that which has more than one meaning, that which is equivocal, uncertain, hesitant.

As a means of expression, the deliberate use of ambiguity can be seen today in several instances:

§ 2   * In a propaganda campaign, it is used to persuade people to accept that which they would reject if it were stated clearly. For example, ambiguity can be used to canvass legislators discussing the approval of a bill or to confuse public opinion, which will later be presented with a ready-approved bill.

§ 3   * Ambiguity conceivably could also be used by two opposing currents of equal strength each of which, desiring a truce that provides some temporary respite, accepts an ambiguous formula that gives victory to neither current.

§ 4   * One can also imagine someone with debatable sanity who sees ambiguity as the expression of an ideal doctrine. He believes nothing should be expounded clearly because everything is mysterious. There should not be distinct manifestations of good and evil, truth and error, light and darkness. Such unequivocal expressions, if stated expressly, should be condemned as manifestations of 'Manichaeanism;' if spoken spontaneously, they should be condemned as an outburst of sinful pride.

5   * Finally, ambiguity can be understood merely as a transitional phase of an ascending or descending process. Thus, an adolescent (in the case of an ascending organic process) has certain ambiguous characteristics, which at times show some adult traits and, at other times, reveals the child who is still there. In a process of decay, something analogous takes place, as in the case of a man who is leaving maturity and entering old age.

*

Contrary to what it might seem, listing such possibilities for the use of ambiguity is not superfluous. In the following Chapters we will see how a large number of celebrated and widely read authors have recourse to one or more of the types of ambiguity we have mentioned as they attempt to explain and justify ambiguities in the documents of Vatican II.

*

§ 6
We know from history that the modernist movement largely employed indefinition and ambiguity on the pretext that its inspiration in ecclesiastical matters is so profound that it could hardly be made explicit. When it took a powerful blow with the publication of the Encyclical *Pascendi*, its defense was to take refuge in the shadows of a pretended "intermediary phase" between the all-encompassing tendencies it fancied to possess and the still embryonic tenets it had managed to make explicit. After the most acute phase of the Holy See's official antimodernist reaction had passed, the modernists continued to resort to indefinition and confusion to carry on their work.

Let us consider some excerpts by Fr. Ernesto Buonaiuti, perhaps the main exponent of modernism in Italy, which attest to this fact.

In the first excerpt, the author is very clear about the doctrinal fluidity in which his movement was deliberately placed: "The distinctive character of modernism is the indefinition of its first program. In it, modernism does not stick to a given point of official dogmatics; it does not rise up against a disciplinary rule .... Actually, modernism is something other than taking a stand about one single problem of Catholic dogmatics. In the process of development of modern spirituality, it is essentially a new and original orientation tending to draw, from the different tendencies of speculation, a more powerful and objective representation of religious experience, and to obtain, from the moral crisis of our time, a clearer and purer adhesion to the innovative Message of the New Testament's preaching."[1]

Seeking to defend the movement from the condemnations of the Decree *Lamentabili*, Buonaiuti again presents theological fluidity and a confused yearning for change as the characteristic traits of modernism. Indeed, he says: "A vast, collective and

---

[1] Ernesto BUONAIUTI, *Le modernisme catholique* (Paris: Ed. Rieder, 1927), pp. 28f.

multiform movement of believing consciences, modernism was, especially in the beginning, like an incandescent matter that could not be poured into the narrow molds of theological speculation without completely changing its nature. A confused aspiration to a full rebirth of the evangelical spirit beyond all dry formulas and conventional disciplines, it could represent a force whose direction and development should have been followed by men of faith, instead of blocked without pity."[2]

Further on, the author boasts that modernism escaped the condemnations of *Pascendi* precisely because of its undefined nature, which derived from an ardent and vague empathy with the achievements of modern times. Buonaiuti writes: "At the Holy Office one must have had the impression that the encyclical *Pascendi*, in spite of the solemn and severe controls that it demanded, in spite of its relentless application in dioceses of the Catholic world, had still been unable to extirpate the 'poison' of modernist tendencies from the hearts and minds of the young clergy. Not being a defined system, representing above all a disposition of soul ready to complacently view and to ardently desire all the conquests of modern times in the realm of culture and social progress, the movement, struck by the brutal measures of the Curia, could not be stamped out by an imprecise doctrinal exposition and a series of police measures. It kept resurfacing in the minds of young churchmen who were necessarily in contact with the procedures of modern critique and speculation; it continued to permeate the enthusiasm of their vocations and, imperceptibly, to gain proselytes. Two years of arduous persecution .... should have shown that the roots of modernism and its capacities for conquest were more solid than the theologians of the opposed party had imagined."[3]

We can thus see that modernism deliberately employed indefinition, confusion and, consequently, ambiguity, as an efficient strategy to introduce the movement and to defend it against the attacks of Saint Pius X, or as a means to survive all the condemnations of which it was the object.

Therefore, it does not appear inopportune to focus our attention on certain aspects of ambiguity in the progressivist movement, the heir and perpetuator of modernism. We might also ask ourselves whether or not ambiguity, to the degree that its in-

---

[2] Ibid., p. 46.

[3] Ibid., p. 62.

fluence was present in conciliar documents, was also employed for strategic purposes.

By pointing out this historic precedent, we do not intend to pre-judge the Council. By reading the following chapters the Reader will have elements to gauge, with equity, to what point the progressivist movement was present in Vatican II.

Let us now go on to study testimonies on ambiguity in conciliar documents.

*   *   *

CHAPTER III

THE LANGUAGE OF VATICAN II IS AMBIGUOUS: AUTHORITATIVE TESTIMONIES

§ 1

A person analyzing the documents of Vatican II will be able to find out, without much difficulty, that the Council deliberately abandoned the rigor of Thomistic language. Incidentally, this fact is clearly avowed by several theologians cited in this Collection,[1] who express their satisfaction with the end of what they call the 'era of theological cloistering,' a fruit of Scholasticism.

§ 2

Scholasticism, of which Thomism is the supreme expression, is nothing but the apex of a long process of perfecting theological and philosophical language, a process unleashed by the polemics between the Fathers and Catholic doctors, and the heresies and errors that sprung up during the first twelve centuries of the Christian era. Indeed, in the battles waged in favor of orthodoxy, nothing was more indispensable than a systemization of these two disciplines and the elaboration of a highly precise technical language placed at their service. This prevented the infiltration of ambiguous expressions that could favor the promoters of error. So great was the effort made to clearly express theological and philosophical concepts that finding precise terms and formulas that left no shadow of doubt about a controversial doctrinal point was like discovering a treasure.

Thus, in 1588, explaining the origin, nature and excellence of Scholastic doctrine, Pope Sixtus V stated: "By the divine generosity of Him Who alone imparts the spirit of wisdom and, along the ages and according to necessity, ceases not to enrich his Church with new benefits and endow her with new defenses, our

---

[1] In addition to the testimonies contained in this Chapter, the Reader will find this subject dealt with in more detail and with sufficient proofs in Vol. VI, *Inveniet fidem?*, Chap. IV.2,3.

forefathers, men of profound science, invented Scholastic theology. Above all, however, it was the two glorious Doctors, the angelic Saint Thomas and the seraphic Saint Bonaventure, both illustrious professors .... who, with their incomparable talent, assiduous zeal, great works and vigils, cultivated this science, enriched it and gave it as a legacy to future generations, organized in perfect order, amply and admirably developed. Undoubtedly the knowledge and habit of such a wholesome science, which emanates from the most fecund sources of the Sacred Scriptures, the holy Fathers and the Councils, has been an invaluable help to the Church at all times, whether to facilitate a wholesome comprehension and true interpretation of the Scriptures, to read and explain the Fathers with greater assurance and usefulness, or to unmask and refute the several errors and heresies; but these latter days, which have brought us the critical times predicted by the Apostle, in which blasphemous, proud and seductive men make progress in evil, erring themselves and leading others into error, the science of which we speak is more than ever necessary to confirm the dogmas of the Catholic faith and refute heresies."[2]

Thus, Scholastic Theology and Philosophy gradually built over the centuries an invulnerable wall protecting Revelation and the Magisterium from the insidious attacks of adversaries. That is why they deserved such high praise from Sixtus V, who saw in them "this tight and perfect cohesion between cause and effect, this symmetry and order resembling those of an army in battle array, these luminous definitions and distinctions, this solidity of argumentation and subtlety in controversy by means of which light is separated from darkness, truth distinguished from error and the lies of heresy, deprived of the prestige and fictions enveloping them, are unveiled and laid bare."[3]

§ 3   Nevertheless, the language adopted by Vatican II despised that "tight and perfect cohesion between cause and effect," those "luminous definitions and distinctions," that "solidity in argumentation" typical of Scholastic language in favor of texts that were 'patched up,' 'worked over,' 'incoherent,' 'promiscuous,' more appropriate to a 'Babel' and its 'confusion of languages.'[4]

---

[2] SIXTUS V, Bull *Triumphantis*, 1588, in LEO XIII, Encyclical *Aeterni Patris*, August 4, 1879 (Petrópolis: Vozes, 1960), n. 28.

[3] Ibid., n. 23.

[4] These various expressions are used by renowned theologians, as the Reader can see in the following texts.

That which the Thomists of old feared was thus achieved: the entrance of ambiguity into the expression of theological thinking.

*

§ 4   In this Chapter we will bring to the Reader's attention a selection of texts by famed theologians who acknowledge the existence of ambiguity in conciliar documents.

First we will present texts regarding the Council's documents as a whole; later, some texts relating to the most important documents.

§ 5   Msgr. Luigi Sartori, President of the Italian Theological Association (ATI), professor of theology and a consultant to the Secretariat for Non-Christians, comments on the texts of the Council *in genere*: **"Different, not to say opposed interpretations, are given of the Council; everyone pulls toward his own side. Worse, not a small part of responsibility for the mixups and confusions arising today out of the Council, is attributed to the Council itself. Some go as far as to speak, with irritation, of 'Babel' and the 'confusion of languages'"**[5]

Msgr. Sartori goes on to say: **"With Vatican II comes an end to the era of 'cloistering', of the defensive belt, of the** internal (esoteric) [sic] **technical language, of uniformity**. The foundations have been laid for the catholicity of Church language. **In order to attain that**, Vatican II committed itself to the arduous work of achieving a synthesis that seemed impossible. In a large number of cases **it was necessary to resort to compromise, as always happens with texts prepared in collegiality.**

"The difficulty in reading, the obstacle created by the evident promiscuity of language, find a clear **explanation** in the three reasons mentioned above [6] .... Nonetheless, all of the

---

[5] L. SARTORI, "Il linguaggio del Vaticano II," in V.A., *Il linguaggio teologico oggi,* ed. Associazione Teologica Italiana (Milan: Ancora, 1970), p. 236.

[6] The three reasons for this mentioned by SARTORI are: "1) The clash of the 'scholastic' mentality with the so-called 'open' mentality; 2) the specialized literature and language of the 'cultural movements' formed in the pre-conciliar period such as the biblical movement, the liturgical movement, the apostolate of the laity; 3) the role played by the different 'cultural areas' from which the Council Fathers had come. The latter were further influenced by the presence of Protestants and schismatics,

Council's Fathers and all the experts worked with the conviction that they were preparing a synthesis that only at the end would be revealed clearly. This synthesis, or fundamental structure of Vatican II, was therefore sought in spite of the **strong impressions of disequilibrium, discontinuity, excessive variety of languages. Therefore, in the language of Vatican II one should expect a desired, intentional and conscious plurality.**"[7]

Sartori also says: "Here is the new fact. **The Council has preferred the imperfection of patched-up, worked over, incoherent, promiscuous texts** in spite of initiating this attempt at achieving a superior synthesis of diverse perspectives."[8]

§ 6   Fr. Alfredo Marranzini, SJ, was professor of Dogmatic Theology and Rector of the Regional Seminary of Reggio Calabria from 1951 to 1961. From there he went on to teach at the San Luigi Faculty of Theology; he wrote for *L'Osservatore Romano, La Civiltà Cattolica, Concilium* and other theological journals and was secretary of the Italian Theological Association and a consultant to the Secretariat for the Unity of Christians. In the introduction to a work about current theological language, Fr. Marranzini remarks: "**A Council that,** in living contact with tradition and the thinking of the past, **wished to lead the whole Church toward a greater communication with all men today, should necessarily use a polyvalent language.**"[9]

§ 7   Fr. René Laurentin, a conciliar *perito*, one of the best known chroniclers of Vatican II and a journalist of *La Croix*, dedicates a special item of his work *L'enjeu et le bilan du Concile* to the various ambiguities of Vatican II and gives some examples: "**Another ambiguity**" — Laurentin says — "**went through the whole Council itself: the one involving the word 'pastoral.' This adjective, launched by John XXIII, was a success. .... Its usage remained vague** and pragmatic **during the first session. But, beginning in the second session, some fell into the trap of understanding 'pastoral' as unrelated to 'doctrinal',** as if, for instance, collegiality in matters of hierarchy and love in matters of marriage had to do with 'pastoral' and not 'doctrinal.' **The**

---

of representatives of the laity and women, and by the constant reference to the 'voice of public opinion' (Ibid., pp. 244ff.).

[7] Ibid., pp. 246f.

[8] Ibid., p. 252.

[9] Alfredo MARRANZINI, Introduzione, in V.A., *Il linguaggio teologico oggi*, p. 24.

wish was to find a solution for opposing tendencies: That which was 'pastoral' escaped the requirement for rigor that is posed by doctrine. .... Right from the beginning of the fourth session Cardinal Silva was surprised that such a principle had found its way even into the official explanation for the amendments to the *Schema XIII.*"[10]

§ 8   Writing on conciliar production as a whole, Fr. Angel Antón, SJ, notes: "On essential points **this Council attained a compromise** not **related** to contents but **only to formal enunciations. Hence such divergent positions adopted to interpret the texts of the Council,** absent a compromise on contents, **remained necessarily ambiguous.**"[11]

§ 9   Further on, writing on the dispute over papal primacy versus episcopal collegiality, Antón reaffirms: "Once again **one must recognize that Vatican II reached nothing but a compromise on the formulas about this theme, whereas in relation to its content, a tendency to equivocation prevailed among the majority and the minority** at the conciliar assembly."[12]

10   Fr. Brian Harrison, of Rome's Nepomucene College, draws a conclusion worthy of attention as he writes about ambiguity in the Council's language and its relation with the current crisis in the clergy: "In the crisis of the contemporary Church we are faced with an extraordinary fact: the two contending parties [conservatives and progressivists] claim to be the authentic interpreters of Vatican II. We find nothing like this in the history of the Church and in the Councils of Florence, Trent, and Vatican I. The teaching of these Councils did not lend itself to different and opposing interpretations. He who did not accept these teachings knew he was placing himself outside [the Church]. The unity and vitality of the Church were not threatened.

"It seems to me essential for the leaders of the Church to honestly recognize the *ambiguities* we have inherited from the Council. It frequently happened, in the Council, that a traditional, orthodox **proposal would be approved with modified language** or placed in the footnotes **because of the strong**

---

[10] René LAURENTIN, *L'enjeu et le bilan du Concile - Bilan de la quatrième session* (Paris: Seuil, 1966), pp. 359f.

[11] Angel ANTÓN, "L'ecclésiologie postconciliaire - Les attentes, les résultats et les perspectives pour l'avenir," in V.A., *Vatican II: Bilan et perspectives*, vol. I, p. 428.

[12] Ibid., p. 432.

resistance from the liberals. With this, **the conciliar Church issued an uncertain call** about practical matters, **achieving the result predicted by the Apostle Paul: 'For if the trumpet give an uncertain sound, who shall prepare himself to the battle?'** (I Cor 14:8)."[13]

§ 11   Bishop Gérard Philips of Louvain, who acted in the Council under several titles, stood out as the main writer of *Lumen gentium*.[14] No one, therefore, could be more qualified to assess the degree of precision to be found in the language of the conciliar documents. Speaking generally, Msgr. Philips makes this apology: **"No one is trying to say that the texts promulgated are perfect.** But the perspective of time will help discover what was the openness of mind and heart that Vatican Council II has inaugurated in history."[15]

*

§ 12   Let us now see some comments about the most important documents.

    About *Lumen gentium*, Msgr. Philips states: "The first phrase, [LG 37a] which begins, 'Like all Christians, the laity,' **is the example of a declaration that can be read with very different sentiments and interpreted in contradictory ways.**"[16]

§ 13   Fr. René Laurentin also comments on *Lumen gentium*: **"In some** difficult **cases, solutions went only half-way,** or even less. **Formulas were wisely calculated to leave the road open to opposing opinions. Hence a certain fluctuation [in the texts].** Thus, a theologian who is well-known for his preoccupation with doctrinal integrity was able to deem himself authorized to publish, several months after the promulgation of the Constitution On

---

[13] Brian HARRISON, "Se a trompa emite um som confuso...," in *30 Giorni* (Portuguese edition), July 1989, p. 82.

[14] Y. CONGAR, "À guisa de conclusão," in V.A., *A Igreja do Vaticano II*, ed. G. BARAÚNA (Petrópolis: Vozes, 1965), p. 1289.

[15] Gérard PHILIPS, *La Chiesa e il suo mistero nel Concilio Vaticano II - Storia, testo e commento della Costituzione Lumen gentium* (Milan: Jaca Book, 1975), pp. 13f.

[16] Ibid., p. 380.

the Church, a thesis claiming that 'the doctrine of collegiality is false.'"[17]

§ 14

In a critique of *Lumen gentium*, Fr. Antón says: **"If the post-conciliar Church does not show considerable progress in this participation of the laity in respective directive organs in the Church, one must also look for the cause of this in the** *doctrinal ambiguity* **of the Council's decrees on important points** of theology on the laity.

"a) We find this ambiguity in the purely descriptive notion of lay person that LG left us after having refused to present an *ontological definition,* taking a position on points already discussed about ecclesiology and canon Law. ....

"b) Vatican II showed the same lack of precision when called upon to decide whether to classify, as part of the hierarchy, a lay person who takes part in certain ecclesiastical offices *(munera)*, **or who replaces ministers in certain sacred functions** *(officia sacra)* **or,** finally, **who is called by the bishop to consecrate himself entirely to apostolic tasks.**"[18]

§ 15

Testimonies by highly authoritative Fathers of the Council can be cited about the deliberate risk of assuming ambiguities in *Gaudium et spes*. Such testimonies were drawn from the discussions held during the 132nd and 133rd general congregations of the Council.[19]

Therefore, the following testimonies by five Cardinals do not deal with the definitive text of *Gaudium et spes*. We cite them mainly to demonstrate that the Council's Fathers already had a clear awareness of the risk that ambiguity would bring. Furthermore, some of the objections were manifestly not heeded, such as those about the title, pastoral Constitution, and the methodology adopted. At least in these cases, criticisms of the project can be applied to the definitive text.

---

[17] R. LAURENTIN, op. cit., p. 357.

[18] A. ANTÓN, op. cit., pp. 433f.

[19] *Schema XIII*, which later became *Gaudium et spes*, was debated up until the 153rd session, when the text was delivered to the commission in charge of presenting the definitive writing. This final text was voted upon in the 161st, 162nd and 163rd sessions, with some amendments (B. KLOPPENBURG, *Concílio Vaticano II*, vol. V, p. 324).

§ 16   Cardinal Bea, of the Secretariat for the Union of Christians, admits that "**it is necessary to perfect the text afterwards.**" He criticizes the **presence of "improper terms joined with rather obscure expressions.**" "**The ambiguity,**" he adds, "**derives from the effort to use classic Latin**" and "**in some points it was necessary to resort to French in order to understand the Latin.**"[20]

§ 17   Speaking on behalf of 91 German-language Fathers, including some from Scandinavian countries, Cardinal Döpfner implicitly recognizes flaws in the text of *Schema XIII* and proposes that its final writing be postponed until 'after the Council': "Finally," states the then Archbishop of Munich, "**since it seems impossible,** in such a new subject, **to arrive at a perfect exposition,** it will be good to recognize it with simplicity and consider the text as the beginning of a dialogue that shall be prolonged after the Council and allow the Church to progressively cast, upon the problems of a world in evolution, the treasures of her own doctrine."[21]

§ 18   The Archbishop of Palermo at the time, Cardinal Ruffini, says: **The language employed in the schema** "**is such that it cannot even be called Latin and is unworthy of a conciliar document; it contains several expressions so obscure and confusing as to become unintelligible and presents, furthermore, some rather inexact, not to say false, statements!**"[22]

§ 19   Cardinal Silva Henríquez of Santiago, Chile, notes: "**It is necessary to make precise the meaning** and the value **of the schema, beginning with its title. The expression, 'Pastoral Constitution,' should be suppressed because it is ambiguous.**"[23]

§ 20   Cardinal Landázuri Ricketts, then Archbishop of Lima, warns: "**By adopting the two methods** [philosophical and hu-

---

[20] Augustin BEA, "Comments on the 13th Schema in the Conciliar Assembly," in Giovanni CAPRILE, "Il Concilio Vaticano II" (Rome: La Civiltà Cattolica, 1969), vol. V, p. 70.

[21] Julius DÖPFNER, "Comments on the 13th Schema in the Conciliar Assembly," Ibid., p. 74.

[22] Ernesto RUFFINI, "Comments on the 13th Schema in the Conciliar Assembly," Ibid., p. 71.

[23] Raul SILVA HENRIQUEZ, "Comments on the 13th Schema in the Conciliar Assembly," Ibid., p. 69.

manist] **at the same time, the schema runs the risk of satisfy-
ing neither the expectations of the faithful nor those of the
non-Christians.**"[24]

§ 21   The celebrated Fr. Henri de Lubac, SJ, a conciliar expert
honored in 1983 by John Paul II with the Cardinal's purple, referring not to the schema of *Gaudium et spes* but to its definitive
text, points out the ambiguity: "**The title of the first part,** even
more so in French than in Latin, **has an ambiguous tone, and
undoubtedly this ambiguity was necessary** in order to enable it
to cover the whole field of the exposition. 'Human vocation' here
is the vocation of man (*vocatio hominis*). Now, this vocation of
man — everything that follows shows it — is not only human,
but divine."[25]

22   Fr. Giuseppe Dossetti, who during the Council had been
secretary to the four Moderators and in some way a spokesman
for them, tries to reflect a general opinion about the pastoral Constitution. He says: "All of these fathers spoke in the sense of fin-
ishing up the schema and tying it nicely together; to the point that
**one may now say, as is almost unanimously recognized, that
the doctrine expressed in the *Gaudium et spes* is a doctrine *in
fieri*, requiring further development.**"[26]

23   Fr. Laurentin provides a few more examples of ambiguity
in the text of *Gaudium et spes* as he examines the following formulation in the chapter on matrimony: "'Love is profaned by
illicit customs against conception.' Should it be understood that
all the customs against conception are illicit (something that
would settle the case of certain 'pills' still under discussion) or
that the Council condemns only those that are illicit but admits
the lawfulness of some others? One can say the same about the
wording of note 14 of the same chapter about the doctrine of Pius
XI and Pius XII: '*Sic stante doctrina Magisterii*'. Should it be
understood as: 'The doctrine of the Magisterium remains stable,
unshakable'?" "**Here and there,**" Laurentin continues, "**ambiguity was cultivated as an escape from inextricable oppositions. One could lengthen the list of such wordings encompassing opposing tendencies, because they could be looked at**

---

[24] Juan LANDAZURI RICKETTS, "Comments on the 13th Schema in
the Conciliar Assembly," Ibid.

[25] Henri de LUBAC, *Athéisme et sens de l'homme - Une double requête
de 'Gaudium et spes'* (Paris: Cerf, 1968), p. 92.

[26] Giuseppe DOSSETTI, "Vaticano II: Quale recezione," in *Il Regno*,
12/1/1991, p. 706.

from both sides just like those photographic tricks whereby you see two different people in the same picture depending on the angle you look at it. For this reason, Vatican II already has given, and will continue to give rise to many controversies."[27]

§ 24

Commenting on one of the Council's most important documents, the Constitution *Dei Verbum*, in his *dissertatio ad lauream* in Theology at the Gregorian University, recommended to the author of this work by a highly placed Vatican personality, Fr. Alberto Franzini, SJ, notes: **"The concept of Tradition in the Constitution [*Dei Verbum*] is understood with different meanings not always clearly specified or even intelligible, thus giving rise to confusions** that theological reflection, based on good textual hermeneutics, should attempt to eliminate. .... Regarding the first criticism, the *Dei Verbum* **can hardly escape the accusation that a certain 'semantic sleight-of-hand' has taken place. Until the various meanings of the term 'Tradition' are clarified, it will be difficult** even **to agree upon the precise meanings that,** at times, **it may take on**. .... In Number 8 of *Dei Verbum* are seen fundamentally two concepts of Tradition which are constantly interchanged: a concept which is broader in some contexts and more restricted in others."[28]

A little further, Franzini concludes: **"The semantic uncertainty found in *Dei Verbum* is perhaps the sign of a more profound uncertainty** regarding the complexity of the reality of Tradition."[29]

§ 25

The various texts cited in this Chapter speak for themselves.

The general opinion about the existence of ambiguities in the language of the final documents of Vatican II is, therefore, an indisputable finding.

*

---

[27] R. LAURENTIN, op. cit., p. 357.

[28] Alberto FRANZINI, *Tradizione e Scrittura - Il contributo del Concilio Vaticano II* (Brescia: Morcelliana, 1978), pp. 241ff.

[29] Ibid., p. 243.

Once the pervasive lack of clarity in the texts of Vatican II has been verified, a question naturally arises: Why this ambiguity? Is it for tactical reasons? Because of an evolutionary method? A clash between currents? Ideological dictates?

The following Chapters strive to help the Reader see more clearly on this ambiguous panorama.

*   *   *

CHAPTER IV

STRATEGIES THAT LED TO AMBIGUITY DURING THE COUNCIL

§ 1   Two currents of thought confronted each other in Vatican II.[1]

§ 2   The *first* current, called conservative, was based mainly on the perennial teachings of the Councils of Trent and Vatican I. Pius IX and Saint Pius X were the two Pontiffs who best represented this thinking in the Tridentine era over the last two centuries for their overt action against the errors of the modern world, their fearless proclamation of the anti-egalitarian, monarchic and sacral nature of the Church, and their struggle against Modernism. For this reason, they have become symbols of the conservative thinking and movement. At the time of Pius XII, the echoes of Trent and Vatican I and the reflections of these two great Pontiffs' personalities still held strong sway over the conservatives who, in large numbers, took part in the Council's Preparatory Commissions. So this current had a significant influence on the preparation of the projects that were to be presented at Vatican II. It can be said without any doubt that, as a whole, the schemata presented by the Preparatory Commissions were an indication of the orientation the conservatives wanted to impart at the August Assembly.

That program, nevertheless, was condemned by the progressivist current right at the beginning of the Council and eliminated by the authority of Pope John XXIII.[2]

---

[1] We deal with this confrontation in more detail, though not exhaustively, in Chap. VI.1.

[2] On November 22, 1962, John XXIII rejected the schema *De fontibus Revelationis* and with it nearly all the schemata of the pre-conciliar Theological Commission. In his chronicle, B. KLOPPENBURG comments: "Thus came to a close, in a melancholy way, the discussion on

§ *3*   The *second* current, called progressivist, is a direct heir to the old romanticist school of Tübingen — particularly in regard to ecclesiology — whose main proponent was Fr. Johann Adam Möhler (1796-1838). In the philosophical field it is an indirect heir to German idealism, notably of Kant, Schelling, Hegel, above all Schleiermacher and, more recently, of Husserl, Scheler, and Heidegger.[3]

---

the text prepared by the Pre-Conciliar Theological Commission: *rejected.* Yesterday's vote still gave its proponents a glimmer of hope. The absolute majority, however, clearly had already given its *non placet.* Indeed, it would have been useless to go on discussing a text practically already rejected, since it would never be approved by two-thirds [of the Assembly] as required by the rules. Thus the Pope decided to give it the *coup de grace.* And it died" (*Concílio Vaticano II*, vol. II, p. 193). It was perhaps due to this fact that Henri FESQUET called the first conciliar session the 'demolition session' (Op. cit., p. 1031).

For more about the role of John XXIII in the rejection of the pre-conciliar schemata, see Chap. VI.4.§§ 49-56 and in § 83 the comment Fr. Chenu made to the Author of this work.

[3]   a. For the sake of brevity, this view is necessarily simplified. Let us point out some other sources of the progressivist current: the religious influence of the movements for biblical, patristic and liturgical renewal of the missionary and lay apostolate. "Indeed, Vatican II is not interpreted as an episode which erupted abruptly, but as a terminal point that completes a prior evolution and maturation of an ecclesial conscience that inherited and perfected those movements which, since the middle of our century, had prepared biblical, patristic, liturgical, and pastoral renewal through study and experiences." (*La Civiltà Cattolica*, Editorial: "Concilio, post-Concilio, para-Concilio," 1/5/85). Such movements were fruits of the work of the Dominicans from Le Saulchoir, the Jesuits from Innsbruck, the Faculties of Theology of Louvain, Paris, Lyons, and the Biblical School of Jerusalem (Joseph COMBLIN, "La théologie catholique depuis la fin du pontificat de Pie XII," in V.A., *Bilan de la théologie au XXe. siècle*, eds. R. VANDER GUCHT - H. VORGRIMLER, Tournai-Paris: Casterman, 1970, vol. I, pp. 479-495).

b. We also emphasize the philosophical influence of the Danish philosopher Sören Kierkegaard and the French philosophers Maurice Blondel and Henri Bergson, among various thinkers worthy of note (On the philosophical origin of the progressivist current, see Vol. VI, *Inveniet fidem?*, Chap. III, passim).

Therefore, when this Work refers mainly to Möhler and German idealism as the basis for the progressivist current's ecclesiology and philosophy, it defines the picture by its key note, rather than its entire composition.

Möhler's followers were the defeated wing during Vatican Council I.[4] Later, Saint Pius X condemned many of their ideas as part of Modernist thought.[5]

---

[4] The confirmation of this assertion is found in Chap. VI, 1,§§ 4-15.

[5] a. On the influence of *Möhler's* ideas in French Modernism (Loisy and Le Roy) and English Modernism (Newman and Tyrrel), see Edmond VERMEIL, *Jean-Adam Möhler et l'Ecole Catholique de Tubingue* (Paris: Armand Colin, 1913), pp. 451-473.

b. Independent of progressivism's historical genesis, it is worthwhile to note some basic ideas of the professor from Tübingen that later became the patrimony of modernism and today are adopted by progressivism. Here are some excerpts from and comments on the works of Möhler found in the entry *Moehler* by A. Nicolas FONCK, in DTC, vol. X:

c. **Concept of faith:** "'According to the doctrine of the primitive Church, the true faith, the true knowledge of religion could not exist without the Holy Spirit, who could not be received if the person was not linked to the Church. But if we are attentively to examine how this doctrine was understood, we will obtain the following result: Each individual should, through an immediate impression, gather in himself the holy life diffused in the Church; he should, through an immediate contemplation, transform the experience of the Church into his own experience; he should rouse in himself pious sentiments and a holy conduct, and from the depths of his sanctified soul he should develop the knowledge of religion' (*Unity in the Church*, p. 8). Every Christian should, therefore, be a mystic. This is full-blown Schleiermacherism: faith begins with sentiment, with religious experience" (col. 2057).

"Love engenders faith: 'Love is the source of truth; the faith of a Christian is formed by the rays of his holy love which rise from his soul, are captured by his spirit, are reflected and transformed into ideas' (*Unity*, p. 18)" (Ibid.). "Who does not see the relationship between the origins of the faith and that which the Encyclical *Pascendi* encounters in the modernists? (Ibid)

d. **Concept of dogmatic teaching:** "'Just as each one in particular receives the principle of life and the interior faith only from the community, ... so also the true expression of the interior faith and the true doctrine cannot be determined and preserved except by the community' (*Unity*, p. 26)" (col. 2058).

"'The same Holy Spirit that animated the Church while these holy men were alive (the preceding Fathers), animating it always, in like manner manifests itself in him (the Catholic man of these times) as he had in them; for this reason, he (the Catholic) believes that which Christians had always believed before him: his faith is **not** a faith of authority ....; his concordance with the faith of all time is a necessary sequence of the special character of Christianity' (*Unity*, pp. 36f.)" (col. 2058).

We do not intend to deal here with the genesis of this school and its appearance in Vatican II. References made to it in this Work are general and, therefore, relatively superficial.[6]

---

e. **Concept of tradition:** "Definitively, and to speak clearly, tradition would be nothing else but interior faith, still not formulated as doctrine, which the Holy Spirit constantly preserves and renews in the Church; it is an 'intimate sense,' a symbolic 'conscience' (*Symbolik*, t. I, pp. 36-39) that enables the Church to discern Christian truth intuitively and infallibly, or better, that contains this truth in such a way that the Church needs only to fall into itself to know true Christianity .... Vermeil warns us that this Möhlerian conception of tradition is no other than Schleiermacher's (Ibid., p. 139) and his disciple Neander's (Ibid., p. 152, note 5)" (col. 2059).

f. **Evolution from natural to supernatural:** "Möhler arrives at 'a kind of *sui generis* transformism which takes pleasure in seeing religious conscience as a living being and making it evolve under the action and with the help of divine grace' (Vermeil, p. 46). *Similarity with God*, that is, with the supernatural, is nothing but a 'development' of the *image of God*, that is, of our natural 'spiritual faculties' (*Symbolik*, t. I, p. 15)" (col. 2061).

g. **Concept of Church:** "For Möhler, the spiritual powers of the Church have a 'charismatic' origin. 'Ordination, as it presents itself exteriorly, is a recognition by the whole Church that its spirit is found in a certain faithful, enabling him to represent the love of a certain number of faithful and unite them with the whole Church: thus, the Holy Spirit is not communicated only in the ordination, but one recognizes that He had *already* communicated *in advance* a certain gift to the one being ordained' (*Unity*, p. 217). Read in annex XIII (Ibid., pp. 283-295) the curious theories of Möhler on 'the participation of all Christian in the vocation of churchmen,' particularly in the power of forgiving sins" (col. 2062).

[6] In addition to the previously cited book by Edmond Vermeil, here are some bibliographical data on where to find more information about the genesis of this school:

V.A., *Bilan de la théologie du XXe. Siècle,* eds. R. VANDER GUCHT - H. VORGRIMLER, (Tournai/Paris: Casterman, 1970); the collaborations of: R. AUBERT, *La théologie catholique au milieu du XXe. siècle*, vol. I, pp. 437, 444; J. COMBLIN, *La théologie catholique depuis la fin du pontificat de Pie XII*, vol. I, pp. 479, 484; R. MARLE, *Méthodes historiques et problèmes théologiques*, vol. II, p. 53; WERNER-KÜMMEL, *Les recherches exégetiques sur le Nouveau Testament*, vol. II, pp. 190, 193; G. COLOMBO, *La création*, vol. II, p. 272; J. FRISQUE, *L'ecclésiologie au XXe siècle*, vol. II, pp. 415f.., 440; J. BEUMER, *Histoire de la théologie et des dogmes*, vol. II, pp. 654, 657; V.A., *L'ecclésiologie au XIXe. Siècle* (Paris: Cerf, 1960), especially the writ-

§ 4   The pontificates of John XXIII and Paul VI and Vatican II
crowned the great counter-offensive launched by this wing.[7]

---

ings by R. AUBERT, *La géographie ecclésiologique au XIXe. siècle*, pp.
25-35; W. BARTZ, *Le Magistère de l'Eglise d'après Scheeben*, pp. 309-
327; A. CHAVASSE, *L'ecclésiologie au Concile du Vatican -
L'infaillibilité de l'Eglise*, pp. 233-245; Y. CONGAR, *L'ecclésiologie, de
la Révolution Française au Concile du Vatican, sous le signe de
l'affirmation de l'autorité*, pp. 100-114; H. F. DAVIS, *Le rôle et
l'apostolat de la Hiérarchie et du laïcat dans la théologie de l'Eglise
chez Newman*, pp. 329-349; B. D. DUPUY, *Schisme et primauté chez
J. A. Möhler*, pp. 197-231; J. R. GEISELMANN, *Les variations de la
définition de l'Eglise chez J. A. Möhler*, pp. 141-195; O. ROUSSEAU,
Les attitudes de pensée concernant l'unité chrétienne au XIXe. siècle,
pp. 351-373; V.A., *Nouvelle Histoire de l'Eglise*, eds. R. AUBERT - M.
D. KNOWLES - L. J. ROGIER (Paris: Seuil, 1975), vol. V, pp. 581-689;
A. ACERBI, *Due ecclesiologie - Ecclesiologia giuridica ed ecclesiologia
di communione nella 'Lumen gentium'* (Bologna: Dehoniane, 1975), pp.
9, 19, 330, 361, 406, 422; K. ADAM, Die *Katholische Tübingen Schule*,
in *Gesammelte Aufsätze* (Augsburg, 1936), pp. 389-412; H. U. von
BALTHASAR, *El complejo antirromano - Integración del papado en la
Iglesia universal* (Madrid: BAC, 1981), chaps. II, IV, passim; *Love
Alone: The Way of Revelation* (London/Dublin: Sheed & Ward, 1982),
pp. 25-42. Y. CONGAR, *Le Concile de Vatican II*, pp. 124, 148-152; J.
R. GEISELMANN, Introduction to the critical edition of *Die Einheit*
(Kölh-Olten, 1956); *Der Wandel des Kirchenbewusstseins und der Kir-
chlichkeit in der Theologie J. A. Möhlers* (Freiburg, 1961), pp. 531-675;
S. JAKI, *Les tendances nouvelles de l'ecclésiologie* (Rome: Herder,
1957), pp. 24-35, 57f., 61f., 84, 148f., 156, 174, 202; J. PINSK, "La
situation actuelle de la théologie catholique en Allemagne," in V.A.,
Catholicisme allemand (Paris: Cerf, 1956), pp. 343ff.; O. ROUSSEAU,
"A Constituição no quadro dos movimentos renovadores de teologia e
de pastoral das últimas décadas," in V.A., *A Igreja do Vaticano II*, pp.
115-134.

See following footnote.

[7] a. An editorial in *La Civiltà Cattolica* (Rome) entitled "Dalla 'società
perfetta' alla Chiesa 'mistero,'" 1/19/1985, p. 111, describing the genesis and history of the new ecclesiology, says: "Thus, just as the movement started by Bellarmine led to the definition of papal primacy and
infallibility in Vatican I, so also the movement begun by Möhler culminated with the Encyclical *Mystici Corporis* (June 29, 1943) of Pius XII
and with Vatican II."

b. Angel ANTÓN concurs with this summary statement: "That which
in Vatican I was the ecclesiology of a minority became [the ecclesiology
of] a majority in Vatican II, whereas the minority in Vatican II was the
majority in Vatican I" (Op. cit., p. 427).

c. To prove what we just said, no words could be more explicit than these by Hans Küng: "**How could we have arrived, with regard to Vatican II, to this turnaround .... if there had not been a long preparation before the Council, a sort of hibernation? John XXIII, a charismatic in the Seat of Peter, was the wick ....** How could he **have unleashed this process if, long before the Council, there had not been people both known and anonymous who gathered the material that made the spark become a flame? ....** We have every reason to bow with respect and gratitude before the Christian commitment of these silent heroes of the struggle for a renewed truthfulness. **....** Suspected, impeached, discredited, branded as heretics, persecuted and exiled by their brethren, shepherds, and theologians in the Church, they carried on their work as best they could! **Singled out as dangerous, extremists, ultra-radicals, heretics, revolutionaries, they always advanced** as far as they were allowed to, and, at times, even beyond. **.... Many times only after decades, other times only after death, was there a gesture of gratitude shown toward them; some of them were rehabilitated only by Vatican Council II. .... That which a few started** with modesty and insignificance, **that which only slowly succeeded in taking hold amidst great efforts, has now developed and multiplied many times over: in the renewal of liturgy, of church life in general. ....** It has been proven that those harbingers were not people on the fringe, **lonely outsiders, but rather the vanguard of an army which, though undoubtedly slow, had strongly determined to forge ahead, an army to which some official representatives of theology and the Church leadership have shown that they actually were a rear guard**" (H. KÜNG, *Veracidade - O futuro da Igreja,* São Paulo: Herder, 1969, pp. 161f.).

d. Already at the inception of the modernist crisis, Italian senator Antonio FOGAZZARO, in his romance *Il santo,* placed on the *Index* by order of Saint Pius X, mentioned the existence of modernist groups — apparently the 'slow army' to which Küng refers — that wanted reforms in the Church like those carried out during and after the Council: "**We are a good number of Catholics**," says Giovanni Selva, a personage in the cited romance, "**in Italy and outside of Italy, ecclesiastics and laity, who desire a reform in the Church. We want it without rebellion, carried out by the legitimate authority. We want reforms in the religious teaching, reforms in the liturgy, reforms in the discipline of the clergy, and reforms also in the supreme government of the Church. In order to achieve that, we need to create a public opinion that will lead the authorities to act according to our opinions, even if this takes twenty, thirty, or fifty years.** We do not know each other, except for the few who publish books. Very likely, **there is in the Catholic world an enormous number of religious and cultured people who think as we do.**" (*Il santo,* Milan: s.p., 1907, p. 38).

Fogazzaro makes more explicit the tenor of such reforms in the advice that Benedetto, "*il santo*" in the romance, offers the Pope: "Holy Father .... the Church is ill. Four evil spirits have entered her body to wage war against the Holy Spirit. One is the spirit of the lie. .... Today, few Christians know that religion is not mainly an adhesion of the intelligence to formulas of truth, but it is principally to act and live according to this truth. .... And **those who know this are fiercely combated, defamed as heretics, reduced to silence, all through the work of the spirit of the lie which for centuries has installed in the Church a tradition of deceit ....** Holy Father .... **Honor before the whole Church some of these men, some of these priests combated by the spirit of lie. Elevate some of them to the episcopate, to the Sacred College!** And also this, Holy Father! Advise exegetes and theologians, if necessary, to advance with prudence, ... but **permit not the *Index* and the Holy Office, on account of some excessive audacity, to remove men who are the honor of the Church.**

"[The second evil spirit] is the spirit of domination by the clergy. The priests imbued with the spirit of domination are not pleased that souls communicate directly and normally with God to ask Him advice and orientation. .... He [the evil one] has suppressed the ancient and holy Catholic liberty. He attempts to make obedience, even when not required by law, into the first of virtues; he would want to impose non-obligatory submissions, retractions of one's conscience .... Do not give in, Holy Father! .... Take on public advisers, let the bishops gather frequently in national councils, and **allow the people to participate in electing the bishops .... and let the bishops mix with the people ....**

"The third evil spirit .... is the spirit of greed .... The spirit of poverty is not taught there [in the Church] as Christ taught it. .... Enjoying pomp and the honors of riches, adhering with their whole souls to the comforts of wealth appears licit to many preachers of Christ's word and example. .... It is not one day's work, but **let the day be prepared in which the priests of Christ may give the example of real poverty ....**

"The fourth evil spirit .... is the spirit of immobility. All **clergymen,** Your Holiness, **above all those who are today adversaries of progressivist Catholicism, would have crucified Christ**, in good faith, in the name of Moses. **They are idolaters of the past, they would want to keep everything in the Church immutable from the forms of pontifical language all the way to the *flabelli*"** (Ibid., pp. 219-223).

e. Already in the '20s, Ernesto BUONAIUTI, an expressive figure of Italian modernism, made the following assessment of his movement, apparently foreseeing Vatican II: "In fact, one finds that **if the repression meticulously commanded by the Encyclical *Pascendi* stopped modernism as an organized *movement*, nevertheless something of the methodological and intellectual tendencies that it defended remained** .... After a long and tiresome circulation in clandestine, the problems of critique and exegesis that modernism timidly raised are reappearing in the conscience of the Catholic clergy .... **However little one may know about the secret tendencies of a part of the Italian clergy, one may say that, despite this cold disciplinary uniformity** imposed by the Encyclical *Pascendi*, **latent forces lie**

dormant, ready to provoke a new explosion. **The day they become active, modernism will be able to look back and contemplate without repentance its long wait and anxious suffering**" (*Le modernisme catholique*, pp. 176f.).

f. Regarding this phase of "disciplinary uniformity," the modernists were fully aware that they were the forerunners of a change in the Church. Such a premonition is clear in the words with which the anonymous editors of a modernist Roman magazine, *Nova et Vetera*, responded to a polemic: "And who knows if, even as we are writing, in some seminary in Italy, deep in some faraway monastery, the soul predestined to accomplish all this that we have merely prepared is already throbbing and praying? May God permit it! Each one of us is ready to say with joy: *Me oportet minui, illum autem crescere* [I must diminish, that he may grow]" (Ibid., p. 125).

g. The modernist dream of changing the ecclesiastical institution and eventually obtaining a Pope favorable to it coincides with masonic aspirations in relation to the Church. Indeed, the well-known antimodernist and antimasonic author, Fr. Barbier, transcribes authoritative documents originally published by Copin Albancelli, Crétineau-Joly, and Delassus. In one of these documents dated April 3, 1844, a high-ranking leader of Italian secret forces, called Nubius, commented in a letter to another highly-placed mason: "Now then, in order to ensure a pope in the required proportions, we must first of all prepare a generation worthy of the kingdom of which we dream.

"Cast aside the old and men of a mature age; go to the youth, and if possible, even to children... It is to the youth that we must go, it is the youth that we must lead, unperceived by them, under the flag of the secret societies. In order to advance with prudent steps on this dangerous but sure way, two things are absolutely necessary. You must have the simplicity of doves and the prudence of the serpent... Never pronounce before them a word of impiety or impurity: *Maxima debetur puero reverentia* .... Once your reputation has been established in colleges, high schools, universities, and seminaries, once you have gained the confidence of professors and students, make sure that especially those who enter the ranks of the clergy be pleased with your meetings ....

"Such reputation will give your doctrine access to the young clergy and to convents. In a few years, this clergy will naturally have invaded all functions: they will govern, administer, judge, form the Sovereign's council, be called to choose the Pontiff who must reign; and this Pontiff, like most of his contemporaries, will be more or less imbued with Italian and humanitarian principles that we will start placing in circulation .... **Let the clergy move forward under your standard always believing they are advancing under the banner of the apostolic Keys. Cast your net like Simon Bar Jonas; spread it to the bottom of sacristies, seminaries, and convents**, rather than casting it to the bottom of the sea; **if you do not precipitate anything, we promise you a catch [even] more miracu-**

§ 5   Among the thinkers of this current who were active in
Vatican II stand out Frs. Karl Rahner, SJ; Yves Congar, OP;
Henri de Lubac, SJ; Marie-Dominique Chenu, OP; Edward
Schillebeeckx, OP, and Hans Küng. Influential even without
having participated in the Council were Frs. Hans Urs von
Balthasar and Pierre Teilhard de Chardin, SJ.[8]

§ 6   At the Council's assembly this current had spokesmen of
great prestige such as Cardinals Giovanni Battista Montini, Archbishop of Milan and later Paul VI; Leo Jozef Suenens, Archbishop of Malines and Brussels, Primate of Belgium; Julius
Döpfner, Archbishop of Munich; Giacomo Lercaro, Archbishop
of Bologna; Augustin Bea, president of the Secretariat for the
Union of Christians, former confessor of Pius XII and a close
friend of John XXIII; Joseph Frings, Archbishop of Colon and
leader of the German episcopate; Achille Liénart, Bishop of Lille
and president of the French Bishops Conference; Bernard Alfrink, Archbishop of Utrecht.[9] Beginning in the second session,
Cardinals Suenens, Döpfner, and Lercaro directed the Council as
Moderators.

---

lous than his .... **You will have fished a revolution dressed in [the
Pope's] triple crown and cape, carrying the cross and the flag, a
revolution that will need only a small stimulus to set fire to the
four corners of the earth"** (NUBIUS, *Secret Instructions on the Conquest of the Church*, in Emmanuel BARBIER, *Les infiltrations maçoniques dans l'Eglise*, Paris/Brussels: Desclée de Brouwer, 1901, p. 5).

[8] These names are among the ten greatest ones of Catholic Theology
in our time, according to Fr. Battista MONDIN (*Os grandes teólogos do
século XX*, São Paulo: Paulinas; 1979, vol. I). Although the name of
Hans Küng does not appear in this study, in a more recent work Mondin
placed him among the greatest theologians of the day (*Introduzione alla
teologia*, Milan: Massimo, 1983, pp. 372, 375f.).

Küng, for his part, already enjoyed great notoriety in his capacity as
official expert of the Council on account of the 'frankness' with which he
expounded his bold doctrinal positions. As Henri FESQUET puts it, "his
writings acquire considerable importance and exert as much influence"
(*Le journal du Concile*, pp. 548f.).

[9] This list includes the progressivist *aile marchante* of what Fr. Ralph
Wiltgen called the 'European Alliance,' made up of bishops from ten
nations but also widely supported by non-Europeans. About the 'European Alliance' and the Fulda Conference, interesting details are to be
found in R. WILTGEN, *The Rhine Flows Into the Tiber* (Devon, England: Augustine, 1978), pp. 15ff., 78ff.

§ 7   The situation between the two wings was one of confrontation. However, the enthusiasm of the conservatives was soon dampened as the schemata drawn up by the Council's Preparatory Commission were withdrawn and the opposition of John XXIII became manifest, while the progressivists became triumphant, especially after Cardinal Montini ascended to the papal throne.

The conservatives counted on an enormous latent force made up mainly of the consistency of their thinking with the past of the Church, the peaceful support of that thinking by a majority of Catholic public opinion and by the implicit adherence of a large part of the Council's Fathers. In addition, the conservatives could easily have brandished against the progressivists the weapon of innumerable condemnations by previous Pontiffs against the liberal-modernist-progressivist current. This enormous force could have been used at any moment during the Council.

The progressivists enjoyed the considerable advantage of surprise, intelligent and shrewd organization, and the great force represented by the support of John XXIII and later of Paul VI, as will be shown in this Collection.

That precarious balance of forces imposed a delicate strategy on the progressivists as they gained ground. Above all, they had to prevent the conservatives from waking up from their lethargy and consequently making use of the tactical potential at their disposal, as explained above.

The concern of the progressivist current was, therefore, understandable: avoid dissension and achieve unanimity. The price to be paid would be that of ambiguity.

1. Ambiguity to Achieve Unanimity

§ 8   **"Paul VI achieved**, therefore, **this unanimity he so earnestly worked for. The consequence is that we are only halfway there. We could not go farther without causing ruptures,"** explains Fr. Yves Congar in a book-interview.[10]

---

[10] *Jean Puyo interroge le Père Congar - Une vie pour la verité* (Paris: Centurion, 1975), p. 149.

§ 9   The justification given by Cardinal Suenens at Toronto's international theological congress two years after the Council ended has a similar tenor.

The Belgian prelate stated: "**Another obstacle to the full flowering of the Council**, astonishing as this may seem at first glance, **was the quest for this unanimity.** It is both the glory and the weakness of a Council to strive to win the assent of all its members to the proposed texts and decrees. .... In fact, the important votes were for the most part nearly unanimous.

"**This unanimity, however, had its price. It can happen**, in the course of debate with the interplay of numerous amendments .... **that certain texts lose their point, or at least their forcefulness.** Historians of the future will have to disentangle here and there the central affirmation from the interpolations and embellishments. The quest for a 'common denominator' does not always do full justice to the underlying thought of the majority, and it is not easy to bring into synthesis elements that have originated in quite divergent currents of thought. **Hence the texts are sometimes far richer in what they imply than in what they openly affirm.**

"**In the conciliar texts there are some formulas whose aim was to counterbalance other assertions or win wider assent;** in some cases, like temporary stopping places in a long climb."[11]

10   Fr. Rahner roughly concurs: "Naturally, here or there, **the unity of all** in liberty **was diligently sought and obtained in this Council through the tactic of leaving questions unsolved or by other means which**, at first sight, **may appear as an unfortunate compromise.** But even in these cases, true unity was attained in a climate of authentic freedom."[12]

11   Equally elucidating is a concrete example described in great detail by Msgr. Philips, the main writer of *Lumen gentium*;

---

[11] Leo Józef SUENENS, "Co-responsibility: Dominating Idea of the Council and its Pastoral Consequences," in V.A., *Theology of Renewal - Renewal of Religious Thought* (Montreal: Palm Publishers, 1968), vol. II, p. 10.

[12] Karl RAHNER, *Vaticano II: Um começo de renovação* (São Paulo: Herder, 1966), p. 12.

its final lamentation is particularly expressive. It is the vote on collegiality.

Msgr. Philips says: "One hundred and ninety-one Fathers voted *non placet* against the institution of the college of twelve Apostles; 322 Fathers opposed the existence of the college of Bishops; 325 refused to admit that a bishop's consecration imparts the threefold sacred function in the Church. The number of opponents was a record for the 2,247 ballots cast. These voting rounds took place from September 21 to 30, 1964. One year earlier, on October 30, 1963, the number of opponents totaled 408. Therefore, this group appeared to shrink rather than grow; finally, it was almost entirely absorbed by the general current.

"In order to achieve this result the majority agreed to insert, in the exposition about the college, a certain number of subordinate propositions, emphasizing each time that the pontifical primacy remained intact. Now, it is certain that these additions made the text heavy to read. To gauge this effect, it suffices to put them between parentheses. **The multiplication of these safety measures pacified a certain number of Western Fathers;** on the other hand, especially the Eastern Fathers, who insisted that episcopal dignity be frankly recognized, were disappointed by so many restrictions marked by mistrust. How difficult it is to satisfy even one's own friends when in opposing fields!"[13]

*

2. Ambiguity to Prepare the Future[14]

§ 12   The fact that ambiguity was owed to this strategic need to carry a near-unanimity does not exclude — on the contrary, it even presupposes — that such ambiguity would be adroitly inoculated with the thinking of the progressivist current.

§ 13   Cardinal Suenens had insinuated that in the text cited above when he said: **"The texts are sometimes far richer in what they imply than in what they openly affirm."**

§ 14

---

[13] G. PHILIPS, *La chiesa e il suo mistero nel Concilio Vaticano II*, p. 53.

[14] In this Item we present only two texts to corroborate the statement in our subtitle, since Chapter V will take up mostly the same subject.

Fr. Schillebeeckx gives an even clearer testimony as he states that **"a few intended to adopt formulas with double meaning so that the field would be open to their interpretation of 'papal collegiality.'"**[15]

15   The same tactics can be noticed in the declaration of Fr. Giovanni Caprile, editor of the famous Jesuit magazine *La Civiltà Cattolica* and author of a highly regarded chronicle of Vatican II: **"The Council opened some doors. Other doors it left ajar because it saw that the times were still not ripe; however, it did not close them. It only left them ajar, saying: he who comes after me will do it."**[16]

*

16   Here we conclude this Chapter with the notion that ambiguity in the language of the Council obeyed strategic designs to facilitate handling the conservative reaction in the Assembly. But it also served to pave the way for future and more explicit developments in the thought of the progressivist current.

*   *   *

---

[15] Edward SCHILLEBEECKX, "Wij denken gepassioneerd en in cliche's," in *De Bazuin*, January 1965, in A. ACERBI, op. cit., p. 472.

[16] G. CAPRILE, Interview with the Author - Rome, February 3, 1983.

CHAPTER V

ONCE THE COUNCIL IS OVER, AMBIGUITY STIMULATES PROGRESSIVISTS TO DRAW EVEN MORE RADICAL CONSEQUENCES FROM IT

§ 1   The leaders of conciliar and post-conciliar thought, consistent with their strategy, started emphasizing the fact that the Council, rather than saying everything that it had desired, had stopped half-way. Taking advantage of the texts' purposeful ambiguity (some of which had been proposed by the very authors who commented on them), those leaders encouraged interpretations that drew even more radical consequences.

2   Cardinal Suenens, quoting Paul VI, comments: "For his part, Pope Paul VI wrote these far-reaching words that engage the future: **The Council's decrees, more than a point of arrival, are a point of departure toward new goals.** The Spirit and the renewing wind of the Council must continue to penetrate deeply into the life of the Church. **The germs of life sown by the Council in Church soil must reach their full maturity.**"[1]

3   Cardinal Döpfner, another Moderator of the Council, speaks along the same lines: "There is something unusual in the Church that has emerged in the work of the Council: this openness, this readiness, this willingness to change, this departure from a rigidly delimited vital space to a vastness which it had long ignored. No, the **closure of the Council did not mark an end, but an inception, the beginning of a new way.** In truth, the words with which the Pope addressed the conciliar theologians in the audience he granted them on the second to last day of the

---

[1] L. J. SUENENS, Discorso ufficiale d'apertura, in V.A., L'avvenire della Chiesa, p. 46.

Council are valid for each member of the Church, whether bishop, theologian, or lay person, each in his own way: **'Go on doing research and work; it is absolutely necessary!'"**[2]

§ 4   Also symptomatic is a statement by Fr. Schillebeeckx: "We say things in a *diplomatic* way, but after the Council we will draw the implicit conclusions."[3]

§ 5   Equally meaningful is a small discrepancy in opinion between Fr. Hans Küng and Fr. Congar, narrated by the latter in a book containing some of his memoirs: "**[Küng] certainly recognized that the Council had done a very good job** [4], but... **one day I told him**: 'It's the story of the half-full and half-empty bottle. **You say it's half empty; I say it's half full; it's not that bad.**'"[5] "Indeed, I believe **the Council** has done a very good job. But it is true that **in numerous questions,** it **has stopped halfway.** It started a work that it did not finish, whether you're talking about collegiality, the role of lay people, the missions, and even ecumenism."[6]

§ 6   In an interview to Vatican Radio about the expectations for the 1985 Synod of Bishops, Cardinal Suenens said: "**If we were looking at an elevator at the tenth floor of a 20-story building, we would say it's already on the tenth floor; but if we were looking at it from above, we would say that it was still at the tenth floor. This is more or less what happened with the Council.**"[7]

---

[2] Julius DÖPFNER, *La Chiesa vivente oggi* (Bari: Paoline, 1972), pp. 14f.

[3] In Romano AMERIO, "*Sob a cúpula, o vazio,*" in *30 Dias* (Rome/São Paulo), January 1991, p. 25.

[4] In his book, *Veracidade - O futuro da Igreja* (p. 130), Hans Küng presents a list of the reforms undertaken by Vatican II and adds: "True, **the Council has not done everything it could have — from today's perspective. But it has done more than one would have dared expect of it back then.**"

[5] Here Fr. Congar is probably referring to the German adage: "*Der Pessimist: Die Flasche ist schon halb leer... / Der Optimist: O nein! Sie ist noch halb voll!*". ["The pessimist: The bottle is already half empty... / The optimist: Oh no! It's still half full!"]

[6] Jean Puyo interroge le Père Congar, p. 131.

[7] Statement to Vatican Radio, transmission for Brazil, 11/7/1985.

§ 7   On December 12, 1965, four days after the closing of the
Council, Karl Rahner gave a lecture in Munich on how that great
ecclesiastical event should be seen. The lecture's title, *Vatican II:
A Beginning of Renewal*, reflects well its thesis. In various parts
this thesis comes to the surface in very clear words. For example:
"In fact, Vatican II established a beginning of *aggiornamento*
[updating], an inception of renewal. It took steps of penance and
conversion, always fruitful, by the way. But **this is only the beginning of a beginning.** It is very important, undoubtedly. **But it
is nothing more than the start of a beginning. Everything,
almost everything, is still only on paper. And written paper
(Constitutions, Decrees) can be transformed into spirit and
life,** service, faith, and hope. **Not, however, automatically.**"[8]

§ 8   Rahner adds some facts that corroborate his thesis: "**Much
still has to be done in order that,** starting from this beginning of
a beginning, **a true and real advance toward the future may
materialize. We will even say that nearly everything remains
to be done.** Indeed, the determinations of the Constitution on the
Liturgy still need to be transformed into concrete liturgical forms
so that they can be later inserted into the life of prayer of the
Church as a true prayer to God in spirit and truth. Now it is necessary to start a generous, humble, persevering, optimistic, and
intelligent ecumenical dialogue. We still do not have Deacons,
for whose existence the Council opened new possibilities. The
Council of Bishops [Synod] must now prove that it can, through
new and living attitudes, make the principle of a personal and
collegial government in the Church a reality. The promised reforms of the Roman Curia are still to be minutely codified so that

---

The text of Suenen's statement reached our hands in typed form, sent
by the TFP radio monitoring service. A few months later, we asked the
Ufficio Tradizione, Famiglia, Proprietà of Rome to contact Radio Vatican to ask for a copy of the recording. Unfortunately, however, the
magnetic tape had already been erased.

Mr. Wilson Gabriel da Silva, a collaborator of this Work, wrote Cardinal
Suenens asking him to confirm his statement. The Prelate kindly did so
and offered one of his works in which the same metaphor is used in
analogous terms (L. J. SUENENS, *Souvenirs et espérances*, p. 128).

The statement is also found in the Cardinal's comments to an Italian
newspaper (L. J. SUENENS, "Un nuovo battesimo per la Cristianità - I
grandi testimoni del Vaticano II/2," interview granted to Silvano
STRACCA, in *Avvenire*, 10/23/1992, p. 15).

[8] K. RAHNER, Vaticano II: Um começo de renovação, p. 24.

it can be truly revitalized. We will still have to wait for a long time until the Code of Canon Law is restructured so that it corresponds to the spirit and letter of Vatican II."[9]

§ 9

He continues: "The Directory related to ecumenical work still has to be concluded. The Statutes of the Bishops' Conferences are still to be written. The Decree on the formation of future priests awaits its adaptation to different regional conditions to be made by the Bishops .... The work of codification of Eastern Canon Law, already begun by Pius XII, still has to be adjusted to the Council's line."[10]

§ 10

Further on, Rahner says: "This is why Vatican II is no more than the beginning of a beginning. Undoubtedly, this is already a lot. However, **a severe judgment will weigh upon all of us**, shepherds and sheep, **if we limit ourselves to words without putting them into action, if we accommodate ourselves to the beginning of the road without trying to reach its end.**"[11]

§ 11

Suenens draws consequences of the Council's ecumenism in his speech to 223 theologians from around the world gathered in Brussels in September 1970 to celebrate the fifth anniversary of the magazine *Concilium*. The Primate of Belgium refers with ardent enthusiasm to a possible Vatican Council III or a Jerusalem Council II, as well as to the pan-religious unity he already foresees: "You have before you, theologians and brothers in the Faith, a magnificent mission: **giving Vatican II its full continuation and preparing the next chapter in the history of the Church.** How will the future be? We do not know. But **we may expect that Vatican II was but a prologue, and that one day an Ecumenical Council bringing together representatives of all the world's Christians will be able to reestablish and proclaim the visible unity of all the Lord's disciples.** .... If the signs of the times do not deceive us, we may believe that the hour for Christians to return to unity is drawing near.

"The star that guided the Magi Kings to Bethlehem already shines in the sky of ecumenism. Pilgrims of unity have set out again; the road is continuously filled with stones and the ways are uncertain; we are still crossing the desert. But, unlike the Magi Kings whose names come to us from the legends, today's

---

[9] Ibid., pp. 26f.

[10] Ibid., pp. 29f.

[11] Ibid., p. 41.

pilgrims have well-known names .... they are called Paul VI, Athenagoras, Ramsey. .... I know neither where nor when the decisive meeting will take place. **Will it be a Vatican III?** Perhaps.

"But since in a dream you can overcome all obstacles, **why couldn't the final meeting be in the same place that was the cradle of Christianity? Why would the Council of reconciliation not be a Second Council of Jerusalem?** This return of all of the Lord's disciples to the starting point, Jerusalem, seems to me to have been finely prefigured in these verses which I leave to you as a hope and an invitation:

> "We shall not cease from exploration
> and the end of all our exploring
> will be to arrive where we started
> and know the place for the first time" (T. S. Elliot)[12]

12   Defending Vatican II from the attacks of certain radicals who deem conciliar concessions to pneumatology to be too small, Msgr. Walter Kasper, Bishop of Stuttgart-Rottenburg, says that the Council is only a starting point: "Y. Congar demonstrated that this censure is not true insofar as one-sidedness is concerned. H. Mühlen, G. Philips, Ch. Möhler, H. Cazelles, and A. M. Charrue, among others, have investigated the pneumatological statements of the Council. However, the malaise persists. On this, as on many other questions, one finds that **the texts of the Council are an impulse and a starting point rather than a conclusion and a complete answer.**"[13]

13   Concurring with statements that Vatican II is but a beginning is the testimony of Cardinal Ratzinger, the present Prefect of the Congregation for the Doctrine of the Faith: "Now, after the refusals of the last hundred years, the Council has taken the initiative to start the process of accepting this positive encounter to coordinate the Church and the modern world. .... **The fight of the conciliar Fathers over *Schema XIII* [*Gaudium et spes*] can be nothing but the beginning of a movement that continues.**"[14]

---

[12] L. J. SUENENS, "Discorso ufficiale d'apertura," in V.A., *L'avvenire della Chiesa*, pp. 55-58.

[13] Walter KASPER, "Espírito-Cristo-Igreja," in V.A., *A experiência do Espírito Santo* (Petrópolis: Vozes, 1979), p. 73.

[14] Joseph RATZINGER, *Problemi e risultati del Concilio Vaticano II* (Brescia: Queriniana, 1967), pp. 10f.

§ 14   Many and dangerous are the consequences that these Prelates encourage us to draw from the 'half-way' mark at which Vatican II halted. For example, let us look at a quotation from Nicola Colaianni, a Catholic professor who writes for the magazine *Concilium* and is a member of the editorial body of the magazine *Il Tetto* of Naples:

"Such criticism [made by Liberation Theology] is not outlandish... It **represents a consistent development of many of the achievements .... in which .... the Council had stopped 'half-way.' ....** Indeed, **it is on the dogmatic level that the Council stopped 'half-way,' looking for compromise solutions not only .... in regard to contents but also to formulas, dogmatic** *enunciations*, precisely **because they could be interpreted with diverse and conflicting meanings.**"[15]

§ 15   For his part, Msgr. Philips confirms: "*Lumen gentium* **did not say the last word about the priestly ministry**, but outlined an authentic and sincere explanation."[16]

§ 16   Let us see what are the immediate consequences of *Lumen gentium*'s failure to say the last word about ministry.

Fr. François Houtart, author of the introduction to *Gaudium et spes*, professor at the University of Louvain and Secretary General of the International Federation of Institutes for Social and Socio-Religious Research, states: **"One may say that the Vatican II is but a beginning in the institutional transformation of the Catholic Church. The future will undoubtedly see a much wider distribution of ministries, a much greater participation in the way the people in charge are designated,** more numerous communications shaped by a public opinion [inside the Church], **a less precise and less centrally organized system of norms, a very wide variety of liturgical expressions and also of theological formulations.**"[17]

§ 17   Also bearing witness to the ambiguity of Vatican II, Cardinal Ratzinger agrees that the moral climate of dogmatic tolerance was established with the Council: "Under many aspects ....

---

[15] Nicola COLAIANNI, "Crítica ao Vaticano II na literatura atual," in *Concilium*, 1983/7, p. 127.

[16] G. PHILIPS, op. cit., p. 325.

[17] François HOUTART, "Les religions comme réalités sociales," in V.A. *Bilan de la théologie du XXe. siècle*, vol. I, pp. 72f.

almost more important than the solutions offered by the text [of *Gaudium et spes*] is the '*ethos*' behind it, which produced a new kind of ecclesiastical language: the courage of approving **an open document that does not intend to be a concluding definition but rather a beginning that must continue.** This fundamental feeling contributed to make the Council rediscover its unity after its early difficulties, **notwithstanding many particular statements that remained insufficient.**"[18]

*

[18]

      Finally, there are also those who, for strategic reasons, admitting an evolutionist conception and having drawn nearly all the possible consequences from the ambiguity of the Council, as time went by began to consider it outdated and to prepare the minds of their followers for new changes. Several of the greatest theologians of the day are found among these. Here are only a few samples of their thinking, two by Fr. Congar, one by Fr. Rahner, and other by Fr. Huizing.

[19]

      Fr. Congar: "One cannot seek a 're-launching' of Vatican II without recognizing that, from certain standpoints, we have moved beyond it, and that however rich and fecund it may be, **the Council cannot be treated only as a point of arrival,** a vast warehouse that it would suffice to exploit. So, giving ourselves time to digest Vatican II (a Vatican III or Jerusalem II? Not so quickly!!!), **we must realize that yet something else is needed.**"[19]

      On a different occasion, Congar says: "**The Council,** being a moment in the life of the Church, **is absolutely not a definitive revelation.** One can see that in relation to many facts **the Council is already outdated.** There were things that it failed to perceive and others that it didn't. For example, the revolt of the youth, the fact that young people have broken with tradition. This the Council did not see!"[20]

---

[18] J. RATZINGER, op. cit., p. 125.

[19] Y. CONGAR, Le Concile de Vatican II, p. 107.

[20] Y. CONGAR, Interview with the Author - Paris, February 19, 1983.

§ 20   In a dialogue with one of his disciples, Johann Baptist Metz, who formulated a controversial political theology,[21] Karl Rahner gives an idea of what may be the famous 'starting point' or 'half-way' point that progressivists talk about so much but whose final goal they fail to disclose. In that dialogue both theologians deem the achievements of Vatican II so timid as to be insufficient starting points to solve modern-day problems.

K. Rahner: "**The topics** explicitly **dealt with in Vatican Council II are not** properly **the central problems of the post-conciliar Church.** Except perhaps for the pastoral decree [sic] on the Church in today's world and the problems related to this subject, it seems to me that **all the** purely **conciliar problems** which have to do with the Church as such **are essentially secondary if compared to the urgent current problems in the Church.** With this **I am not criticizing the Church as if she had dealt only with unimportant things in Vatican II. I am only** relating this simple **finding** about something entirely justified: **The Church must subject herself to a certain *aggiornamento*, she needs to prepare herself before tackling the problems .... that are presented today.** Inasmuch as this work of preparation can depend on a Council, the Church carried it out in Vatican II. But **now the moment has come .... for the Church to face the really central problems ....** Do you agree .... ?

Metz: "I agree. I also believe that **the problems** explicitly **treated in the Council cannot serve as a starting point for us to determine the problems of the post-conciliar Church."**[22]

---

[21] a. Ralph WILTGEN shows the leadership role the conciliar Fathers from the Rhine Valley played in Vatican II. Among them, the German Episcopate played a decisive role, and its main theologian was none other than Karl Rahner, who authored a large number of the schemata accepted by the Council (Op. cit., pp. 78ff.).

During the second Session of Vatican II the Archbishop of Freiburg im Breisgau introduced the Jesuit theologian to Paul VI, who praised both his work as a scholar and his theological work (Antoine WENGER, *Vatican II - Chronique de la deuxième session*, Paris: Centurion, 1964, p. 254; H. FESQUET, op. cit., p. 313). And at the end of Vatican II Paul VI called Rahner to thank him for his contribution to the conciliar work (B. MONDIN, *Os grandes teólogos do século vinte*, vol. I, p. 98).

b. As for Metz, many consider his political theology as the main source of inspiration for the so-called Theologies of Liberation, notwithstanding the efforts of a certain media to bestow an aura of originality on several South American theologians.

[22] Karl RAHNER in a dialogue with Johann Baptist METZ, in V.A., *Cinco problemas que desafiam a Igreja hoje*, pp. 149f.

§ 21   Fr. Peter Huizing, SJ, professor of Law and History at the University of Nijmegen and consultant to the Commission for the Revision of the Code of Canon Law, goes so far as to speak about the "bankruptcy of Vatican II" and to ask for a Vatican III. He says: **"Council Vatican II did not translate its doctrine into the institutions of the church. The declarations** on the collegiality of bishops, the responsibility of the laity, the nature of Christian marriage, and so on **are useless if not anchored in institutions of the Church. This is the main reason for the bankruptcy of Vatican II. Vatican III should fill this gap."**[23]

*

§ 22   As a whole, these quotations shed light on something we just broached in the previous Chapter: While greatly necessary to achieve the unanimous support of the conciliar Fathers, the ambiguity in the Council's texts carried in its bosom a series of developments which, once Vatican II was over, would be stimulated and applied. Hence, important theologians, some of whom were great mentors of the Council, raised their voices in unison to say that the texts of Vatican II stopped 'half-way' and were only 'a starting point.'

*

23   Once again it becomes clear, in this Chapter, that ambiguity in the documents of the Council was 'desired, intentional and conscious.'[24] Further, this strategically served to stimulate the development of more radical positions in the post-conciliar period.

*   *   *

---

[23] P. HUIZING, "Vaticano III: una costituzione sulla Chiesa," in V.A., *Verso la Chiesa del terzo millenio*, p. 167.

[24] L. SARTORI, op. cit., p. 247; see above Chap. III, § 5.

CHAPTER VI

AMBIGUITY: FRUIT OF THE CLASH BETWEEN TWO OPPOSING THOUGHTS

§ 1

Until now, our analysis and examples dealt only with the wording of the texts and the progressivist current's strategic interest in exploiting ambiguity.

We will now see how ambiguity in the Council's documents resulted from the clash of two opposing thoughts, two concepts of the Church confronting each other.[1] The texts of Vatican II are, as it were, a picture of the final phase of this battle in which one of the combatants (the progressivist current) was winning and the other (the group of conservatives) was being defeated. The texts recorded, at that moment, all the maneuvers of attack and defense by the contenders. In the next stage — that is, after the Council — the struggle may present the analyst with a quite different picture.

1. Two Concepts of the Church Confront Each Other

2

The progressivist current, as we said, inherits the thought of J. A. Möhler,[2] to whom are attributed the foundation of the ecclesiology that triumphed in Vatican II. That ecclesiology aimed at replacing the centuries-old conception of the Church as *societas perfecta* that descended coming from her Tradition and was made explicit by the Council of Trent and by Saint Robert Bellarmine.

---

[1] In footnotes to Chap. IV, we indicate some intellectual foundations of the progressivist current.

[2] Chap. IV, §§ 3, 4.

§ 3   Traditional ecclesiastical thinking is expressed by Saint Robert Bellarmine in his work, *Disputationes de controversiis christianae Fidei.*

"Our sentence," says the Saint, "is that there is only one Church, not two; and that the only one true Church is the community of men united by the profession of the true Christian faith and the communion of the same sacraments, under the government of legitimate shepherds and above all, of the sole Vicar of Christ on earth, the Roman Pontiff." From this definition one can easily see who belongs to the Church and who does not belong to her. Indeed, this definition is made up of three parts: profession of the true faith, communion of the sacraments and submission to the legitimate shepherd, the Roman Pontiff. The first part excludes all infidels, those who were never in the Church such as the Jews, Turks, and pagans, or those who once were in it and later fell away, like the heretics and apostates. The second part excludes the catechumens and excommunicated, since the former are not admitted to the sacraments and the latter are excluded from them. The third part excludes the schismatics, who have the Faith and the sacraments but are do not submit to the legitimate shepherd. .... All others are included, even if they are reprobates, delinquent and impious."[3]

The spirit of a Catholic faithful joyfully exults upon reading this sentence, so holy, consistent, limpid and secure. In contrast, it is filled with suspicion at the vagueness of Möhler's notion of Church, which we will see a little later.

Saint Robert Bellarmine continues: "Between our sentence and the others there is this one difference: all the others require interior virtue to declare that someone is a member of the Church, and thereby make the true Church invisible. We, on the contrary, believe with certainty that in the Church are found all the virtues, Faith, Hope, Charity and the others; however, we do not believe that any interior virtue is required to be able to say that someone is somehow part of the true Church, of which the Scriptures speak, but only the external profession of Faith and the communion of the sacraments, which can be perceived by the senses. Indeed, the Church is as visible and palpable a community

---

[3] Saint ROBERT BELLARMINE, *Disputationes de controversiis christianae Fidei adversus huius temporis haereticus* (1586-1593), (Venice, 1721), 53, in *La Civiltà Cattolica*, Editorial: "Dalla 'società perfetta' alla Chiesa 'mistero'," 1/l9/l985, p. 107.

of men as the community of the Roman people, the Kingdom of France, or the Republic of Venice."[4]

Commenting on this passage, *La Civiltà Cattolica* — from which we have taken the quotation above — says: "At this point Bellarmine notes that in the Church there is soul and body. The soul is the gifts of the Holy Spirit, the theological virtues, etc.; the body is the external profession of Faith and the communion in the sacraments. It so happens that some belong to the soul and others to the body of the Church (the members who are alive to Faith and Charity), others belong to the soul but not to the body, like the catechumens and the excommunicated, if — as it can happen — they have Faith and Charity; still others belong to the body but not to the soul of the Church, such as those who have no interior virtue but nevertheless, out of hope or some temporal fear, profess the Faith and participate in the sacraments under the government of the shepherds; these are 'like the hairs or nails or the bad humors of the human body'[5*]."[6]

§ 4   *La Civiltà Cattolica* goes on to emphasize the contrast between the concepts of Saint Robert Bellarmine and those of Möhler: "A change in perspective took place in the first decades of the nineteenth century when, under the influence of Romanticism .... there arose a desire to emphasize the vital, organic and mystical aspect of the Church. In this, the contribution by Johann Adam Möhler, author of two famous works, *Unity in the Church* and *Symbolik*,[7] played a decisive role."

"He conceives the Church as an organic unity of all faithful, produced by the presence in them of the Holy Spirit who makes use of her to communicate divine life. This organism is visible because the Holy Spirit tends to form his own body for himself. For this reason, the Holy Spirit is linked as much to the visible Church as to his own body. But where does the Hierarchy stand? Möhler answers: The Holy Spirit is the soul of the Church; just as the soul replaces its organs, so also the Spirit regenerates

---

[4] Ibid.

[5*] Saint ROBERT BELLARMINE, Ibid.

[6] *La Civiltà Cattolica*, Ibid.

[7] Original titles: *Die Einheit in der Kirche oder das Prinzip des Katholizismus dargestellt im Geiste der Kirchenväter der drei ersten Jahrhunderte* (Tübingen, 1825); *Symbolik, oder Darstellung der dogmatischen Gegensätze der Katholiken und Protestanten nach ihren Öffentlichen Bekenntnisschriften* (Mainz, 1832).

the organs of his activity. These are the ecclesiastical ministries. However, the action of the people also counts in making up the ecclesiastical hierarchy: as a community of love inspired by the Holy Spirit, this tends to reproduce in the Hierarchy the model of the apostolic college just as Jesus indicated, giving it a living image. This is the extent to which the functions of the hierarchy are a living expression of charity, given by the Holy Spirit to the totality of faithful.

"This view of the Church .... leaves little room for the visible and hierarchical element in the Church," admits the well-known Jesuit magazine, adding: "This is why Möhler himself, in *Symbolik*, abandons the pneumaticism of his book *Unity in the Church* in order to better establish the Church upon Christ by showing that the Hierarchy carries on Jesus' authority and that the visible side of the Church continues, in turn, the mediation of Christ's humanity. He adds, however, that in the Church the interior element is more important than the exterior one: 'We are not living members of the exterior Church unless we belong to the interior Church'[8]*."[9]

§ 5   The notion of the Church as the body of the Holy Spirit, as Möhler conceives it in *Unity of the Church*, causes astonishment and suspicion. The egalitarian presentation of the people as the source of the Hierarchy approximates the romanticism of Rousseau and the myths of Illuminism and the French Revolution. The appearance of Christ in his second work, replacing the Holy Spirit in the first, judging from the context of the editorial in *La Civiltà Cattolica*, appears to be due more to a reshuffling in the nomenclature caused by adverse reactions than to a real change in concepts. This impression is strengthened by his final statement, cited by the magazine, that entirely confirms his first idea that only those who participate in the interior Church are members of the Church. This is thoroughly opposed to the notion of visible Church since, as Saint Robert Bellarmine says, and we quote again, "Between our sentence and the others there is this one difference: all the others require interior virtue to declare that someone is a member of the Church, and thereby make the true Church invisible."

§ 6   Edmond Vermeil and A. Nicolas Fonck confirm the fact that the same conceptions found in *Unity* remained in *Symbolik*: "Vermeil believes that 'at depth, the master ideas remained the

---

[8]* *Symbolik*, 2nd ed., § 48.

[9] *La Civiltà Cattolica*, Ibid., pp. 108f.

same.' It seems to me that he is totally right .... Möhler made of Christianity a conception inspired by the theories of Schleiermacher, which one sees he has not abandoned. One does not even conceive he could abandon them, to such a point were they in agreement with his mystical temperament; by this token, one may say that Möhler was an unconscious precursor of Catholic modernism."[10]

*

§ 7   These are, basically, the two conceptions of the Church that confronted each other in Vatican I and, a century later, in Vatican II. Vatican I was the glorification of the limpid and masterly conception made explicit by Saint Robert Bellarmine. Vatican II, as we have pointed out, was the success of Möhler's conception.

*

§ 8   But how did Möhler's concept make it to our days?

La Civiltà Cattolica says that "J. A. Möhler died prematurely at age 38,[11] but his ideas had an enormous influence on later theology; by means of Fr. G. Perrone, a professor in the Roman College, they were passed on to his disciples, Passaglia, Schrader, and Franzelin.

"It is thus understandable that Schrader and Franzelin, who were in charge of writing the Constitutio de Ecclesia to offer the Fathers of Council Vatican I a schema for discussion, entitled its first chapter, The Church Is the Mystical Body of Christ. This is because, they say, if you want to define the Church you must start by examining her intimate nature .... so that people will not believe that the whole truth of the Church is reduced to her exterior and sensible aspect. Unfortunately, the Council was unable to debate this schema for lack of time .... only an excerpt of it was discussed — chapter XI, which dealt with papal primacy and infallibility. However, one may suppose that the schema was in some trouble with the Fathers, either because many of them were

---

[10] A. N. FONCK, Moehler, in DTC, vol. X, col. 2063.

[11] There seems to have been a small discrepancy with the calculation of Möhler's age by the writer of Civiltà Cattolica. In fact, he died just before turning 42 (May 6, 1796 to April 12, 1838). (A. N. FONCK, op. cit., cols. 2049f.).

used to defining the Church by her exterior aspects, or because the expression 'mystical body' was suspect since it had been misused and misinterpreted by the Synod of Pistoia."[12]

§ 9   Skipping over the era of modernism, during which Möhler's ideas had a great influence, we arrive at the end of World War I. The two currents continued to oppose each other during this time. Przywara writes, "The '*Corpus Christi mysticum*' has become the central idea in Catholic Germany in opposition to the *ecclesia militans* and to the Church as a juridical formation, society, organization, institution."[13]

§ 10   In a lecture in the capital of Peru in July of 1986, Cardinal Joseph Ratzinger provides data that corroborate and further develop the words of Przywara. Ratzinger comments on Romano Guardini's statement that the Church 'is a living reality' and not simply an organization. The following excerpt holds our attention: "It is difficult to communicate the enthusiasm, the joy that took place with this raising of awareness. During the time of liberal thought, including up until the first World War, the Catholic Church was seen as a fossilized bureaucratic apparatus which tenaciously opposed the achievements of the modern era. Theology presented the question of the primacy as a central issue to such a degree that it made the Church appear essentially as an institution organized in a centralist way. It became a question tenaciously defended in the face of which, however, everyone placed himself from the outside. Now it once again became clear that the Church is much more, that all of us make it vitally advance in the faith, just as it makes us progress.

"It became clear that the Church follows an organic growth over the centuries, which continues today. Likewise, in it the mystery of Incarnation remains current: Christ still marches on through the times. If we ask ourselves what are the elements acquired at this starting point which later reappeared in Vatican II, we can answer: the first aspect was the Christological definition of the concept of Church. J. A. Möhler, the great regenerator of Catholic theology after the desolation of Illuminism, said: 'A certain erroneous theology could be caricatured in this phrase: 'In the beginning, Christ founded the hierarchy and thus sufficiently provided for the Church until the end of time.' But in counterpo-

---

[12] *La Civiltà Cattolica*, Ibid., p. 109.

[13] Erich PRZYWARA, "Corpus Christi mysticum. Eine Bilanz," in *Zeitschrift für Aszese und Mystik*, 15 (1940), p. 197, in A. ACERBI, *Due ecclesiologie*, p. 38.

sition to this is the fact that the Church is a mystical Body, that is, that Christ Himself is always her new foundation and that He is never a past in her, but He is always, and above all, her present and future. .... She lives because of this: Christ is present in our hearts. Hence He forms his Church. Consequently, the first word of the Church is Christ and not herself; she remains whole to the degree that all of her attention is directed to Him.' Vatican II emphasized this conception so strongly as the apex of its considerations that the fundamental text on the Church begins precisely with the words: *Lumen gentium cum sit Christus*. ....

"Secondly, ... one must establish the aspect of interiority and the character of the communion of the Church. She grows from the inside out, and not vice-versa. The Church means first of all the most intimate communion with Christ; she is formed in the life of prayer, in sacramental life, in the fundamental attitudes of faith, hope, and love .... The Church grows from the inside: this is what the expression 'Body of Christ' means.[14]

The notion of 'Mystical Body' has taken on different names. Sometimes it returned to Möhler's radical pneumatology in *Unity of the Church*, receiving the title 'Church of the Spirit;' other times it was called 'ongoing Incarnation,' 'Church as mystery,' 'mystical Person,' 'Church Sacrament,' or 'Sacrament of Salvation.' Whatever the designation, the same latent conception was there, opposing the Church as *societas perfecta, inaequalis, hierarchica*.

Under the guise of criticism, Fr. Congar makes an indirect defense of the 'Church Sacrament' and the 'Church as ongoing Incarnation,' which reveals his opposition to the *societas perfecta* and his support of Möhler. The French Dominican writes: "We can understand .... the insufficiency of presenting the Church as 'sacrament,' a presentation which, in its own time and context, was itself a way of overcoming a wholly juridical and, in the final analysis, quite naturalistic conception of the Church. It is the presentation of the Church as the continuation of Incarnation or ongoing Incarnation. It was dear to Möhler, in *Symbolik*, and, after him, to the Roman School. It is still found in numerous contemporary expositions. What makes it seductive is that it translates the structure of the Church as a visible and invisible reality at the same time, hence its analogy, under this standpoint, to the Christological mystery. But this still suffers from an excessively static view of the Church. Other criticisms can be made to

---

[14] J. RATZINGER, "La eclesiología del Vaticano," in *Iglesia-Mundo* (Madrid), October 1986, pp. 13f.

the theme 'ongoing incarnation,' as applied to the Church as Body of Christ."[15]

§ *13*   In the text below, Congar emphasizes the difference be-tween the two conceptions: "Until the ecclesiological renewal of the last forty years, a renewal consecrated by the Council, the view of the Church commonly spread in manuals was dominated by the idea of a *societas inaequalis hierarchica*, instead of a community or people of God. The Mystical Body doctrine at times opened a breach in the clerical tower, but it was itself inter-preted in a context of unequal or hierarchical society... People spontaneously had a clerical perspective of the Church."[16]

§ *14*   The clash of currents dealt with in this Chapter also be-comes clear in another statement by Fr. Congar in which he dis-closes the plans of Vatican II in this regard: "The idea of Church sacrament .... was, on the part of the Council, a means to emerge from a predominantly juridical vision."[17]

*

§ *15*   Thus, beginning with Möhler, we arrive at Vatican II. The unity of thought indicates a current that wishes to destroy the notion of the Church as *societas perfecta, inaequalis, hierar-chica*.

*

---

[15] Y. CONGAR, *Un peuple messianique* (Paris: Cerf, 1975), pp. 40f.

[16] Y. CONGAR, *Ministeri e communione ecclesiale* (Bologna, 1973), p. 34, in Piero Antonio BONNET, "Le 'fidèle' récupéré comme protago-niste humain dans l'Eglise," in V.A., *Vatican II: Bilan et perspectives*, vol. I, p. 539.

[17] Y. CONGAR, *Un peuple messianique*, p. 38.

2. In the Murky Waters of Vatican II, a Meeting of Two Rivers

§ 16

With great lucidity, Fr. Raymond Schwager, SJ, in an interview with the Author,[18] let it be known that in order for Vatican II to be well understood, it must be considered as a meeting of the waters of Vatican I with those of a future Vatican III. It is no wonder that Vatican II is confused: as time goes by, the more radical perspective of a future Vatican III will explain it.

The simple metaphor of the meeting of rivers easily explains the confusion and ambiguity that prevail in the texts of Vatican II, fruits of a clash between the two opposing currents.

The sequence of texts below is aimed at giving the reader elements to make his own judgment of the Council's ambiguity as a result of the struggle between two opposing ecclesiological conceptions.

17

The first text, by Cardinal Suenens, evokes the same metaphor. At the inaugural speech of the Congress of the magazine *Concilium* in 1970, after analyzing the 'heated argument' about the collegiality of Bishops in regard to *Lumen gentium*, the prelate says: "In a few words, **a job remains to be done: that of harmonizing two viewpoints and leading them to a perfect synthesis. There is in Ireland a place** well known to tourists **called** *the meeting of the waters.* **It is a valley in which two rivers impetuously throw themselves against each other to form,** a little farther down, **only one river with calm waters. I offer you this image as an invitation to bring to completion,** in a fraternal dialogue, **the marvelous symphony — unfortunately as incomplete as any human creation — of** *Lumen gentium.*"[19]

---

[18] Fr. Karl Rahner set an appointment for an interview with the Author in Innsbruck. Unfortunately, on the eve of the interview, he was rushed to a Munich hospital where he remained interned with grave heart problems. Fr. Rahner's secretariat asked Fr. Raymond Schwager, SJ, a director of and professor at the Faculty of Theology of Innsbruck University, to replace him at the interview. Fr. Schwager kindly received the Author for two conversations, totaling four hours, on February 11, 1983.

[19] L. J. SUENENS, "Discorso ufficiale d'apertura," in V.A., *L'avvenire della Chiesa,* p. 48.

§ *18*   Msgr. Luigi Sartori also describes the confrontation between the two currents present at the Council: "Considering the protagonists, **I believe that the factors of the Council's plurality of language can be grouped** in at least three ways: **First of all, the most radical difference that was** lived and suffered was **that of the shocking clash between a** predominantly **scholastic mentality .... and the mentality** that we can generally call **open** ....

"**The first 'impasse' of the Council was**, in fact, ascertaining and **verifying this coexistence (historic condensation?) between different generations.** *The Church's today should sew together yesterday with tomorrow.* True, **the first schemata** presented to the conciliar Fathers were withdrawn, because in fact they **were too openly linked with the outlook and language of the preceding scholastic theology** (accused of juridical formalism, manualism). Now this is something that did not happen, for example, in the Councils of Trent or Vatican I. Nevertheless, **one could not break totally with the past, even more so since the people with a scholastic formation remained alive and functioning**. (How many were they? A few? Many? I am tempted to suppose that they were a majority. But that would need verification.)

"**The texts should** *also* **know how to speak the old language**, now more, now less, **so that they could be** understood and **approved by readers who had inherited the preceding formation. It is no wonder that the Church today faces the inconvenience of two different readings of the same texts**: concentrating one's attention on aspects of consonance and greater need can prevent or hinder a global and complete penetration."[20]

§ *19*   Fr. Cipriano Vagaggini, OSB, a conciliar *perito,* an important member of the International Theological Commission and a professor at Rome's Pontifical Atheneum of Saint Anselm, in the preface to Antonio Acerbi's work, *Due ecclesiologie,* says: "**This work demonstrates that the obligatory starting point for a later deepening** [of theoretical-practical problems] **in the present development of the life of the Church is the manner and the state in which such problems appear in the Council** itself. **Both manner and state are not always simple nor limpid**.

"Indeed, **the Council raised, broached upon, or implicitly outlined these problems, but only solved them partially and not always with maximum clarity and consistency; when it did more or less solve them, it was very far from drawing**

---

[20] L. SARTORI, op. cit., p. 244.

all their consequences either on the theoretical or practical levels. As for the rest, reading the book makes it obvious that **it could not have been otherwise given the ideas and currents that confronted each other in the Council** — and continue to do so in the post-Conciliar era — **as well as in the unfolding of the Council itself. The fact that arriving at a harmonization of the two viewpoints was often laborious is inevitably reflected in the texts themselves."**[21]

§ 20   Another author who confirms the double ecclesiology in the Council's texts is Fr. Gustave Martelet, SJ, a conciliar *perito* and professor at the well-known Faculty of Theology of Lyons-Fourvière, of the French Jesuits: **Vatican II "must reconcile a twofold requirement that leads some to say that it remains subservient to a double ecclesiology. The first would truly be 'communal,'** as it has been called since then: in it appears the grandeur of Christians and their fundamental equality in the mystery of Christ; **the other ecclesiology would properly be 'juridical' and unduly reinstate a 'hierarchical' dependence of the faithful on a ministry that would govern them from the outside** and thereby compromise the free expression of their authentic grandeur! **Nobody will truly deny, and the Council less than anybody else, that it is difficult to achieve a synthesis of these two aspects, often opposed,** at the discretion of their mutual distortions, **because of the very mystery that it must express."**[22]

§ 21   Fr. Angel Antón, SJ, says: **"The dynamics of the confrontation between the socio-juridical, abstract, and apologetic** ecclesiology that prevailed since the Counter-reformation, **and the new ecclesiology, historic and communal,** founded on Scripture and on the Fathers, which eventually imposed itself on the Council, **did not permit the desired synthesis to be achieved. It is necessary to recognize that the ecclesiology of Vatican II .... presents a certain *juxtaposition* of the two ecclesiological tendencies,** as is easy to verify by comparing chapters I and II of LG with chapters III and IV."[23]

---

[21] Cipriano VAGAGGINI, *Presentazione*, in A. ACERBI, op. cit., p. 6.

[22] Gustave MARTELET, *Deux mille ans d'Eglise en question - Crise de la foi; crise du prêtre* (Paris: Cerf, 1984), p. 59.

[23] A. ANTÓN, "L'ecclesiologie postconciliaire," in V.A., *Vatican II: Bilan et perspectives*, vol. I, p. 419, pp. 426f.; for analogous observations on the role of sin in the world in the text of *Gaudium et spes*, p. 436.

§ 22   One of the most typical points of contention in the struggle between these two currents was the dispute on episcopal collegiality *versus* pontifical primacy. After giving ground in relation to most topics under discussion, the conservatives reacted a
little more strongly when *Lumen gentium* dealt with episcopal
collegiality. In the manner it was written, it paves the way for a
more or less rapid erosion of papal primacy and the abolition of
the monarchical principle inside the Church.

So the conservatives sought and obtained a *Preliminary
Explanatory Note* 'by superior authority,' which was to be attached to *Lumen gentium* saying in what sense chapter III on
collegiality should be interpreted. The Note clearly defends papal
primacy. The text, and especially the context, of chapter III defend the bishops' collegiality to the detriment of papal primacy.
How is it possible to read one part under the prism of the other
when both wish the opposite as far as the primacy of the Pope is
concerned? Nevertheless, the conservatives, who could have condemned the document as a whole or at least chapter III, contented
themselves with the Pyrrus victory of the *Preliminary Note*.

§ 23   This did not prevent Fr. Congar from considering them
allies, since conservative complaints obliged the progressivist
current to take special care and be prudent with the final writing.
Without such prudence this important point in the progressivist
advance would have been left more exposed and vulnerable.[24]

§ 24   Cardinal Ratzinger, speaking out about this *Note* and its
writing, makes ambiguity stand out as a fruit of the confrontation

---

[24] Indeed, addressing the conservatives, CONGAR says: "Brethren, let
us work together! The very rigor of your demands can be beneficial to
us. If the Council's Theological Commission was able to do a quite
notable work as a whole, it owes this in part to a tenacious minority
which obliged it to be more precise. See, for example, the explanatory
note preceding chapter III of *Lumen gentium*" (*La crisi nella Chiesa e
Mons. Lefebvre*, Brescia: Queriniana, 1976, pp. 80f.).

On another occasion Fr. CONGAR explained what he meant by
'working together' with conservatives: "The Council's preparation had
been carried out under the domination — not only the influence, but
domination — of the men from the Curia and the Holy Office .... They
held the reins of things; they knew their *métier*. The whole thing consisted, practically speaking, in leaving them in a minority, for they were
nothing but a minority. .... I don't blame them. They have rendered us a
great service by obliging us to make our thinking more precise and to
lay the foundations of our reasonings" (*Jean Puyo interroge le Père
Congar*, pp. 140f.).

between the two currents and does not hide his sympathy for the progressivist thought.[25]

---

[25] a. The sympathy for progressivism that the present Prefect of the Sacred Congregation for the Doctrine of the Faith nurtured during the Council reveals itself in his poor reception of the *Preliminary Note*. As for the 'bitter flavor' in the last meetings of the Third Session to which he refers, it appears to have been due to the fact that progressivists had expected to advance to the end of the road without encountering obstacles. In this regard, here is an interesting report about one of his *Tischgespräch* during the Council:

"Fr. Ratzinger, personal theologian of Cardinal Frings, said one day over lunch with a group, that after obtaining a majority in the Commissions, the progressivists thought they would have a free hand in the Council. Nevertheless, in the speeches and votes in the Assembly, he said, they began to note some resistance to their proposals, and the Commissions had to take this into consideration when revising the schemata" (R. WILTGEN, op. cit., p. 150).

b. If someone were to cast into doubt Cardinal Joseph RATZINGER's affiliation with the progressivist current, he could find the prelate's own acquiescence to this designation in the book-interview in which journalist Vittorio Messori calls him a 'balanced progressivist' and points to him as one of the founders of the magazine *Concilium*, a meeting place for the so-called 'progressivist wing' of theology" (*Rapporto sulla Fede - Vittorio Messori a coloquio con Joseph Ratzinger*, Rome: Paoline, 1985, p. 14).

c. Ratzinger's statements to the same journalist, published by the magazine *Jesus*, are even clearer. He thus presents the Cardinal: "Perhaps what is most annoying is the fact that the supposed 'guardian of the faith' in reality has not only the stature of a great theologian .... but also of an open, modern theologian, open to the signs of the times. A *perito* of the German episcopate at Vatican II, he is later found among the founders of *Concilium*,'an international magazine that brings together the so-called 'progressivist wing' of Catholic theology.

"'Was it a sin of youth, your Eminence, this engagement with *Concilium*?' I ask him, joshing. 'Absolutely not,' he answered. 'I did not change; they changed'" (J. RATZINGER, interview with Vittorio MESSORI, "Ecco perché la fede è in crisi," in *Jesus*, November 1984, p. 69).

d. During a visit to Brazil in 1990, the Cardinal spoke to the press about the same subject:

Question: "What are the most marked differences between the Ratzinger of Council Vatican II and the Ratzinger of today? Who has changed more, you or the Church?

Answer: "I do not see a real, profound difference between my work in Vatican Council II and my present work. On preparing this course for

"The *Preliminary Explanatory Note*, as it is known, has helped to give a somewhat bitter flavor to the final journeys, filled with bold hopes, of the Council's third session. We would go too far if we wanted to analyze here in a precise fashion this very complicated text. Its result — to which we will limit ourselves — would be the recognition that this does not create a substantially new situation, but in principle continues the same dialectics,"

The resulting ambiguity, as far as the actual competence of the episcopal college is concerned, is already inserted in the conciliar text itself. Undoubtedly, this dialectics was later aggravated [sic] in favor of the pole for the primacy. But the text, under the impulse of this tendency in each enunciation, reintroduces on the side another enunciation and re-establishes the equilibrium, making it possible to interpret the whole both in the sense of the 'primacy' and in relation to the principle of collegiality. Therefore, one can easily speak of a certain intrinsic disharmony in the *Note*'s text, which reflects the disharmony among those who wrote it and attempted to reconcile conflicting tendencies. If

---

bishops, I reviewed a course of ecclesiology that I gave for the first time in 1956. Naturally, I found elements that need to be analyzed. But with respect to the fundamental vision, I found a profound identity, and what I proposed to the bishops in Rio de Janeiro was the same fundamental vision that I put together then" (J. RATZINGER, interview to Walter FALCETA, "Ratzinger reafirma identidade católica," in *O Estado de S. Paulo,* 7/29/1990).

e. Answering a journalist's question, the Cardinal confirms: "In my history as theologian I see no fracture, but a development" (J. RATZINGER, "Um passado que não lhes diz respeito", in *30 Dias*, January 1994, p. 72).

f. A renowned Protestant theologian bears testimony about the position of the Cardinal-Prefect of the Congregation for the Doctrine of the Faith. He says:

Question: "How do you explain this dialogue with a personality who many Catholics see as reactionary and an enemy of ecumenical dialogue?

Answer. "I do not understand. It is an erroneous opinion. I met Ratzinger thirty years ago, at Vatican Council II. He was the best of the so-called expert theologians, or *periti*, with a reputation for being a radical progressivist" (Oscar CULLMANN, "O filho de Lutero e Ratzinger," interview with Lucio BRUNELLI and Alfred LABHART, in *30 Dias,* March 1993, p. 13).

the resulting text gives an impression of disharmony, this is a sign that a complete harmonization was not attained, nor was it possible."[26]

*

The testimonies of these highly qualified theologians thus testify that the murky waters of Vatican II are the meeting point of two rivers: the progressivist and the conservative currents.

*

3. Synthesis: A Name Given to Ambiguity In Order to Favor Progressivism

Once it has become clear that in the Council there was a confrontation between progressivists and conservatives that is reflected in its final texts, it appears opportune to focus, albeit in passing, on a new maneuver apparently adopted to try to dampen conservative reaction after the Council. This was an attempt to present conciliar texts not as ambiguous, but rather as though they had been written with the academic intent of seeking a transcendent, elevated, and serene synthesis.

This tactic, it seems to us, is meant to divert attention from conciliar ambiguity and the clash of ideas to imply that opposed interpretations are nothing but a temperamental confrontation between the hotheads on both sides. This clash of opposing views can then be viewed as mere 'mischief-making' by fervent partisans on either side. Therefore, the solution would be to leave the final word to the 'moderates,' who would supposedly have enough balance to find the *juste milieu*, the *via del mezzo,* the middle ground. This 'middle of the road' position is presented as always being the ideal, sensible, and impartial one. This is as if to say that if one were presented with two glasses of water, one with poisoned, murky water and the other with pure, crystalline water, the right thing to do would be to drink out of a third glass with a mixture of the poisoned water and the pure water!

---

[26] J. RATZINGER, *Problemi e risultati del Vaticano II*, pp. 64f.

In fact, the defenders of this position want to legitimize progressivist victories in the Council and prevent a return to the *statu quo ante*.

The argumentation of this position's proponents appears to us doctrinally inconsistent and easily destructible. Nevertheless, it is a dangerous position because its adherents seek to catalyze in its favor the mentalities of the pseudo-moderates — those who dislike disputes and desire above all the petty comfort of their private lives.

In the excerpts that follow, we will seek to bring to the fore two things: *First*, they confirm what we have been dealing with in this Chapter, the existence of two opposing currents; *second*, they imply that the Council's ambiguity should not be understood as a victory of the progressivist wing (which it clearly was), but rather as a scholarly, elevated, and balanced position.

§ 27

Which of the two currents the Council's ambiguity favored becomes obvious when we consider the statements by A. Acerbi in his work, *Due ecclesiologie*. He confirms what we said in the beginning of this Chapter and defends the eclectic position: "*Lumen gentium* often brings to the mind of an attentive reader the image of Moses who, after a long journey, gazes from the top of a hill at the land he will not enter. The Constitution is a frontier document, which hails from afar and is faced with new horizons, unable to explore them in depth.

"The starting point was the societal vision, whose guiding principle was that the Church's spiritual dimension has no bearing upon how she is understood by people; an adequate ecclesiology could and should emphasize only the societal dimension of the Church. ....

"The theology of the mystical body was a reaction against this vision. In fact, between the two [world] wars, the 'mystical body' indicated .... the most significant and essential reality for understanding the nature of the Church, which is not just a 'means' (an institution of salvation) in view of an end that is extrinsic to her (the salvation of souls). But she herself is the sanctification and communion of life with God in Christ. We know how this reaction, albeit just, brought with it the risk of subverting the affirmations of the societal tendency, without contradicting its logic of separation."[27]

---

[27] A. ACERBI, op. cit., p. 551.

After upholding the idea that even long before the Council, a synthetic school had integrated the two currents and inspired Pius XII's Encyclical, *Mystici Corporis Christi*,[28] Acerbi continues: "*Lumen gentium* welcomed the data of this theological reflection [of the supposed synthetic school], validating it with the authority of the magisterium. But it attempted to do even more. By presenting the Church as the mystery of the divine action of salvation sacramentally manifested by means of the people of God, it upheld both the prevalence of the communion of life with God in Christ in the constitution of the Church, and the union of the social structure with the mystical side; at the same time, it endeavored to show the tension that exists in the Church between *res* and *sacramentum*. Even though the two are united, in the Church's present condition as pilgrim they no longer harmonize perfectly. Furthermore, the communion of divine life is historically symbolized and accomplished not by means of a structure of authority, but rather by a communion of the mission and services, nonetheless directed by an authority which holds itself as a ministry among ministries."[29]

The attempt to legitimize the Council's ambiguity by striving to present it as an elevated synthesis that superseded and integrated the two currents has already been implicitly refuted. As we have seen in the previous Chapter, a number of highly placed personalities involved in the Council testify, without the shadow of a doubt, that at the very root of the confusion in the Council's texts was a 'meeting of waters,' to use the expression of Cardinal

---

[28] a. With no desire to enter into a polemics about Acerbi's claim that a doctrinal synthesis between the two ecclesiologies would be possible, we would like to emphasize, in opposition to that, the statement by Msgr. G. Philips that the Encyclical *Mystici Corporis* represented an opening for the progressivist theological thought that prevailed in Vatican II: "Between the two [world] wars, many Catholics rediscovered, so to speak, the doctrine of the Church as Mystical Body. Pius XII's Encyclical, *Mystici Corporis*, published in the midst of the world conflict, places this theme under his aegis against some conservative or fearful theologians. But there is more: this encyclical concentrates attention on the spiritual element that reveals to the ecclesial community its full meaning: The professional theologians have contributed to this progress, stimulated by the progress in biblical studies, impelled by the liturgical movement and moved by the profound ecumenical aspirations that would show themselves a short time later" (G. PHILIPS, op. cit., p. 12).

b. Msgr. Philips's belief is corroborated by the fore-cited editorial in *La Civiltà Cattolica*: "The movement initiated by Möhler culminated with the Encyclical *Mystici Corporis* (June 29, 1943) of Pius XII and Vatican II."

[29] A. ACERBI, op. cit., p. 552.

Suenens, a clash of thoughts, a strategic measure dictated by concrete situations rather than a serene academic harmonization.

This notwithstanding, we will go on to present one more apology of the pretended conciliar synthesis as a means of transcending the two mentioned currents. Afterward, in order to reinforce the certainty that this position is untenable, we will cite another unequivocal statement by Cardinal Suenens.

§ 30
    The following text is by the then Archbishop of Cracow, Msgr. Karol Wojtyla, followed by a commentary of Rocco Buttiglione, a professor at Lateran University and a scholar disciple of Karol Wojtyla at international congresses.[30] Buttiglione is also the philosopher of the movement *Communione e Liberazione*, which is said to be partly inspired by Cardinal Ratzinger. Summarizing the thinking of Msgr. Wojtyla, he says: "'Integration means .... an organic cohesion that acts simultaneously on both the thinking and acting of the Church as a community of believers. *That is, it acts in such a way that on one hand we find and, so to speak, 're-read' the magisterium of the latest Council in the whole prior Magisterium of the Church;* on the other hand, we again find the whole preceding magisterium in the magisterium of the last Council, in whose context we somehow re-read it.'[31]* This principle of integrating novelty and tradition, which has constituted the Church's identity and her unity, is what leads directly beyond the controversy between integrists and neo-modernists on the way to understanding the Council's new synthesis."[32]

§ 31
    Among the men who were privy to the most subtle aspects of the Council's intentions, it is difficult to find someone with stronger credentials to speak out than Cardinal Suenens. We recall here only three important facts regarding the Belgian Prelate's relevance: it was he who proposed the general plan adopted by Vatican II;[33] he exerted a great influence on the preparation of

---

[30] In 1985 Buttiglione went to Brazil, where he gave a lecture at the International Congress promoted by the Archdiocese of Rio de Janeiro to study the thinking of John Paul II.

[31]* *Alle fonti del rinnovamento*, p. 39.

[32] Rocco BUTTIGLIONE, *Il pensiero di Karol Wojtyla* (Milan: Jaca Book, 1982), pp. 235f.

[33] The plan is transcribed *ipsis verbis* by the Cardinal in one of his works. L. J. SUENENS, *Souvenirs et espérances*, pp. 72-79.

the Dogmatic Constitution *Lumen gentium*,[34] whose title, incidentally, came from one of his early speeches;[35] and he presented the proposal for the writing of *Gaudium et spes*, the boldest of all the documents of Vatican II.[36]

In order to forestall any 'temptation toward synthesis' that could come to the Reader's mind as he reads the following paragraph by Cardinal Wojtyla, commented upon by Prof. Buttiglione, we go on to add other statements by Cardinal Suenens.

What he says about the current that won in the Council, and how it opposes the idea of a synthesis defended by Acerbi and by the text from Wojtyla-Buttiglione, is noteworthy: **"The Second Vatican Council"** — says Suenens — **"marked the end of an epoch, or even of several epochs, depending on one's historical perspective. It brought to a close the Constantinian era, the era of 'Christendom'** in the medieval sense, **the era of the Counter-Reformation and the era of Vatican I. With regard to that past, it marks a turning point in the history of the Church.**

"However, with regard to a more immediate past — namely, the first half of this century — **we see it** not as an end but **as a culmination, as the heir and beneficiary of those great currents of renewal which were and are at the very heart of the contemporary Church: scriptural, liturgical, patristic, theological, and pastoral renewal. The Council caught and

---

[34] In his book, *La Chiesa e il suo mistero* (p. 25), Msgr. Gerard PHILIPS, writer of the final version of *Lumen gentium*, says that Cardinal Suenens proposed an amendment changing 'the very skeleton of the [document's] schema.' That proposal was accepted without objection by the coordinating commission (see also L. J. SUENENS, op. cit., pp. 33, 84).

[35] G. PHILIPS, op. cit., p. 19.

[36] Fr. Chenu thus describes the action undertaken by the Belgian Cardinal in favor of *Schema XIII*: "Everyone remembers the intervention of Cardinal Suenens at the end of the first session (December 4, 1962), immediately accepted by Cardinals Frings and Montini. Out of a confused agenda he extracted the decisive line of the Council: the Church has to define herself within herself, but also outside herself in a 'dialogue' with the world. This was the launching of the famous *Schema XIII*, a charismatic shock from which emanates the whole theology of renewal" (Marie-Dominique CHENU, "The History of Salvation and the Historicity of Man," in V.A., *Theology of Renewal*, vol. I, p. 155; L. J. SUENENS, op. cit., pp. 63, 84f., 111; Antoine WENGER, *Chronique de la deuxième session*, p. 242).

channeled the waters of these streams, which had grown stronger and stronger under the influence of the Holy Spirit, and **it resolutely directed them towards the open sea** which was their goal."[37]

In a more recent work, Suenens corroborates that opinion with respect to Vatican II: "**We were to live at the end of an epoch which inherited a long past: from Constantine** (fourth century) **to the Council of Trent** (sixteenth century), **and from Trent to Vatican I** (nineteenth century). Undoubtedly, [there was] a fundamental continuity, but also **a new perspective that would raise to a primary plane a vision of the Church enriched by a return to its sources. The theologians who had been a cause of concern for the Holy Office (Congar, Danielou, de Lubac, Rahner...)** would, as periti, **help to rescue that vision, a fact that constituted one more paradox**."[38]

§ 32

Given the clarity of the Belgian Prelate's words and what has been said so far in this Volume, how could someone reading texts such as these by Acerbi and Wojtyla-Buttiglione (among so many others that could be cited) [39] not have the impression that the preaching of that alleged synthesis in fact favors progressivist expansion in this post-conciliar age and staves off a possible awakening by the conservatives?

*

4. Pastoral Council? Dogmatic Council? *Chassé croisé* of Interpretations. Who Profits From the Confusion?

§ 33

While we are dealing with the opposition between these two currents that generated the conciliar ambiguity, it is oppor-

---

[37] L. J. SUENENS, "Co-responsibility: Dominating Idea of the Council and its Pastoral Consequences," in V.A., *Theology of Renewal*, vol. II, p. 7.

[38] L. J. SUENENS, *Souvenirs et espérances*, pp. 63f.

[39] For example, Cardinal Alfonso LOPEZ TRUJILLO, *A los veinte años del Concilio* (Department of Publications of the Archdiocese of Medellin, 1985), pp. 18f.

tune to analyze one of the greatest ambiguities that to this day has not been entirely ascertained.

Was the Council a pastoral one? Or was it dogmatic? [40]

A. Theological Qualification of Vatican II

§ 34

Confusion still reigns about the Council's theological qualification. Some say it was pastoral. As such, they understand in principle a Council primarily turned to the good of souls and the conversion of peoples. Dogmatic questions dealt with are supposedly mere repetitions of the teachings of the Ordinary and Extraordinary Magisterium of the Church. In this case, it did not bring about doctrinal changes, but merely new doctrinal approaches in view of its pastoral goal. Others, on the contrary,

---

[40] Some hermeneutic clarifications on this matter:

a. *Pastoral* - a word relating to the missionary effort of the Church to convert peoples by employing tactics and strategies which, without modifying the deposit of Faith, strives for the most efficient way of proselytizing.

b. *Doctrinal* – 1) a term concerning matters of Faith and Morals of the ordinary and extraordinary ecclesiastical Magisterium which supposes some infallibility and which commands, in various degrees, the obedience of the faithful (Adolphus TANQUEREY, *Synopsis Theologiae Dogmaticae*, Tournai: Desclée, 1937, vol. I, nn. 953-957, pp. 637-640). 2) a general term referring to the ensemble of non-theological theoretical principles that should orient the liturgical, canonical, exegetic, social, pastoral, etc. spheres.

c. The *pastoral* or *dogmatic* alternative, which usually arises when one seeks the theological qualification of the Council, could perhaps be better expressed by *pastoral* and *doctrinal* (first meaning); so that the Council would be generally related to Dogmatic Theology and Moral Theology. However, classifying a Council as *doctrinal* is less precise than it would appear at first sight, since there are several types of non-theological doctrine that do not directly require obedience from the faithful, for example, considerable parts of liturgical, canonical, exegetic, social, pastoral doctrine (second meaning).

Therefore, we believe it is better to use *pastoral* or *dogmatic and moral*, or simply *pastoral* or *dogmatic*, supposing the moral content of the dogmatic questions that orient the Council.

deem it a dogmatic Council since, in fact, the subject matter dealt with has to do with topics directly related to the Faith.

Adding to the confusion, others say it was at times pastoral, at times dogmatic.

Faced with this picture, some conservatives allege that there is no need to obey Vatican Council II since the doctrine contained therein was intended to be nothing but pastoral.

However, there are progressivists, and a large number of them, who try with ever greater emphasis to present Vatican II as binding on all Catholics, assuming it *ipso facto* dogmatic.[41]

Faced with all these positions, it seems to us opportune to present some distinctions to try to clarify the confusion.

a) In the History of the Councils the Two Qualifications — Dogmatic and Pastoral — Do Not Exclude Each Other

§ 35

An overview of the history of ecumenical councils suffices to show that they were not convened to deal with the subjects of interest to the Church in each epoch from only one standpoint.

The near totality of ecumenical councils dealt primarily with dogmatic and moral topics. [42] However, in doing, so the councils concomitantly issued disciplinary norms on ecclesiastical life, liturgy, and exegetics,[43] expressed pastoral intentions[44]

---

[41] Section B, 4th and 6th phases.

[42] Exceptions are, although not entirely, the First Council of Lyons (1245), which discussed mainly the deposition of Emperor Frederic II, and the Council of Vienna (1311-1312), which dealt primarily with the Order of the Temple and the Holy Land (V.A., *Conciliorum oecumenicorum decreta*, eds. G. ALBERIGO - P. JOANNOU - C. LEONARDI - P. PRODI - Freiburg im Breisgau: Herder, 1962, pp. 286f.).

[43] Ibid., passim.

[44] For example, the Council of Basel-Ferrara-Florence-Rome (1431-1445), in Sessions XIX and XXV in Basel, sought the union of the

and laid down socio-political orientations.[45] In reviewing the history of ecumenical councils, it is clear that the application of the ensemble of their teachings was never limited exclusively to one field. Their teachings are simultaneously dogmatic, moral, disciplinary, pastoral, socio-political, depending on the matter dealt with, for the good of the Church.

§ 36   Therefore, Vatican II could very well address both pastoral and dogmatic matters since they do not exclude each other.

In order to determine how the Council should be qualified, it is necessary first of all to see what matters it addressed.

*

Greek schismatic Church with the Catholic Church (Ibid., pp. 454-458, 486ff.); also in Session XIX the Council dealt with those who want to convert to the Catholic Faith (Ibid., p. 460); in Session VIII, in Florence, was issued a Bull for the union of Armenians with Holy Church (Ibid., p. 510); in Session XI was issued a Bull for the union of the Copts (Ibid., p. 543); Session XIII, held in Rome, another Bull was issued for the union of the Syrians (Ibid., pp. 562ff.) and in Session XIV, a bull was issued for the union of the Chaldeans and the Moors from Cyprus (Ibid., pp. 565ff.).

[45] Thus, for instance:

* The Fourth Lateran Council (1215) addressed the question of whether duels could be fought by clergymen (Ibid., p. 220), the limits of secular and ecclesiastical justice (Ibid., p. 229) and the subject of usury and the Jews (Ibid., p. 241);

* The First Council of Lyons (1245) dealt with usury in general (Ibid., pp. 269ff.), financial help for the liberation of the Empire of Constantinople (Ibid., pp. 271f.), and the Crusades to the Holy Land (Ibid., pp. 273-277);

* The Second Council of Lyons (1274) dealt with extorsion of the faithful by Church delegates (Ibid., p. 303);

* The Fifth Lateran Council (1512-1517) stimulated the reestablishment of peace between Catholic and heretical princes (Ibid., pp. 582ff.); issued a Bull containing the Concordat between the Roman Pontiff and Francis I, King of France, on the abrogation of the pragmatic sanction (Ibid., pp. 614-621).

b) According to the Subject Matter It Dealt With, Vatican II Is Simultaneously Dogmatic and Pastoral

§ 37

Two of the four Constitutions promulgated by the Council, *Lumen gentium* and *Dei Verbum*, are officially entitled Dogmatic Constitutions. This title is appropriate, since the first one addresses the doctrinal foundations of ecclesiology. Its topics are dogmatic from beginning to end. The second one deals primarily with divine Revelation and secondarily provides guidelines for exegesis and makes an exhortation to read the Sacred Scriptures. Therefore, the topics covered by the two documents are principally dogmatic.

§ 38

In addition to pastoral matters, the Constitution *Gaudium et spes*, entitled a Pastoral Constitution, also covers innumerable points involving dogmatics and morals. *Verbi gratia*: "P.I, C.I [Part I, Chapter I]: Man as the image of God; Sin; Dignity of moral conscience; The mystery of death; The attitude of the Church towards atheism; Christ, the new man. C.II: Communitarian nature of man's vocation in God's plan; Respect and love for enemies; Essential equality of all men: Social justice; Need to transcend an individualistic morality; The Word made flesh and human solidarity. C.III: Human activity infected by sin; Human activity: its fulfillment in the paschal mystery. C.IV: What the Church receives from the modern world; Christ: Alpha and Omega. P.II, C.I: Marriage and the family in today's world; Holiness of marriage and the family; Married love; The fruitfulness of marriage; Married love and respect for human life; Fostering marriage and the family: a duty for all. C.II, 2nd section: Faith and culture; Multiple relations between culture and the Good News of Christ.

These subtitles represent a little more than one-fourth of all subtitles in the document.

Even though the other problems addressed by *Gaudium et spes* are not primarily dogmatic or moral, they involve delicate points which make up part of the Church's social doctrine but have serious dogmatic and moral implications. *Verbi gratia*: P.II, C.III: Co-Responsibility in enterprise and in the economic system as a whole; Labor disputes; Earthly goods destined for all men; Ownership, private property, large estates. C.IV: Nature and purpose of the political community; The political community and the Church. C.V: Nature of peace; First section: Avoidance of war; Curbing the savagery of war; Total warfare; The arms race; Total outlawing of war: International action to prevent war; second section: Establishment of an international community; The community of nations and international organizations; Effective presence of the Church in the international community.

§ 39   The Constitution *Sacrosanctum Concilium*, which addresses the reform of the liturgy, focuses on important dogmatic or closely dogmatic-related topics. *Verbi gratia*: C.I: The work of Salvation, willed by God, is fulfilled in Christ; The work of Christ continues in the Church and is crowned in the liturgy; The presence of Christ in the liturgy; earthly liturgy and celestial liturgy; Liturgy does not exhaust all the Church's action; The Sacrifice of the Eucharist is source of life in the Church. C.II: The most sacred mystery of the Eucharist; reform of the Rite of the Mass, of the readings, the homily and common prayer; concelebration. C.III: The other sacraments and the sacramentals; reform of the rites of all sacraments.

§ 40   The Decree on Ecumenism, *Unitatis redintegratio*, tackles primarily dogmatic topics, to wit: C.I: The unity and oneness of the Church; Relation of the heretics with the Catholic Church; Ecumenism. C.II: The practice of ecumenism; Church renewal; Conversion of the heart, The way of expressing and expounding the doctrine of Faith; Cooperation with heretics.

41   The Decree *Orientalium Ecclesiarum* refers to an important dogmatic subject as it discusses the relations of the Catholic Church with schismatics (nn. 26-28).

42   The Decree *Ad gentes,* about the missionary activities of the Church, presents in C.I the missions of the Three Divine Persons as the foundation of the mission of the Church, a fundamentally dogmatic theme.

43   The five decrees that follow: *Christus Dominus*, on the mission of Bishops; *Presbyterorum ordinis*, on the ministry and life of priests; *Perfectae caritatis*, on the updating of religious; *Optatam totius,* on priestly formation; and *Apostolicam actuositatem*, on the lay apostolate, are moral, ecclesiastical, disciplinary, pastoral, educational and social norms founded upon the dogmatic points covered in the previous Constitutions and Decrees.

44   The Decree *Inter mirifica*, on the means of social communication, is quite original as a conciliar document. It is, in fact, an exaltation of modern technology. The press, radio, television, cinema, and other media are presented as tools for the pastoral action of the Church. There is nothing directly dogmatic in it.

§ 45   The Declaration on Christian Education, *Gravissimum educationis*, presents important moral and social questions, though not directly dogmatic.

§ 46   But the Declaration on Religious Liberty, *Dignitatis humanae*, is wholly based on a new concept of Faith and Morals, to wit: I: On the right of the person and communities to social and civil liberty in religious matters; The object and foundation of religious freedom; Religious freedom and the relation of man with God; Freedom of the religious communities; Fostering religious freedom. II: Religious freedom in the light of Revelation; The doctrine of religious freedom is rooted in Revelation; Freedom of the act of faith; The conduct of Christ and the Apostles; The Church follows in the footsteps of Christ and the Apostles; Freedom in the Church; The obligation of the Church.

§ 47   Finally, the Declaration on the Relation of the Church to Non-Christian Religions, *Nostra aetate*, is the dogmatic approach to relations with any of the false religions, especially the Muslim and Jewish ones.

§ 48   Thus having enumerated the subjects covered by Vatican II, *à vol d'oiseau* and as a whole, we can conclude that it discussed dogmatic topics at length and in depth. In addition, let it be stressed, it also addressed moral, ecclesiastical, liturgical, disciplinary, pastoral, educational, and social topics.

    Therefore, judging from the subject matter it dealt with, Vatican II covered topics of which the most important were dogmatic. Thus, it is stretching matters to conclude that it was an exclusively pastoral council.

    As expounded here, the question of the theological qualification of Vatican II appears, up until now, quite clear.

*

c) Reasons Making It Convenient to Qualify Vatican II As Pastoral

§ 49   Before continuing to analyze the remaining elements that will enable us to qualify the Council, let us look at two reasons why the pastoral aspect of the Council was emphasized. We present these reasons as working hypotheses to help understand the pronouncements of John XXIII and Paul VI presented in Section d.

§ 50   The *first* concerns the convenience of using the material put together in the preparatory phase of the Council — the pre-Council. The *second* refers to taking advantage of the documents of Vatican II in the post-conciliar age.

On November 22, 1962, John XXIII rejected the schema *De fontibus Revelationis* and with it nearly all other schemata of the pre-conciliar Theological Commission.[46] Now, the material presented in the phase preceding Vatican II was essentially dogmatic,[47] seeking to present the errors opposed to Catholic Doctrine in today's world and condemn them according to the teachings of Vatican I.

It seems that even earlier, in the Council's *Opening Speech* on October 11, 1962, John XXIII was already preparing to reject the pre-conciliar schemata, which he did, as we will see in Section d. On that occasion, for the first time, he tried to avoid

---

[46] Chap. IV, Note 2.

[47] Bishop Boaventura KLOPPENBURG, who participated in the preparatory works of the Council as a consultant to the Theological Commission, mentions some of the topics studied: "All questions of a purely doctrinal nature suggested by the Bishops (in the 15 volumes of the pre-preparatory documents) to be dealt with in the Council, were sent to our Commission. Once this basic material was gathered, it was first divided into five groups of different subjects, thus giving rise to the formation of five sub-commissions: 1) On the Church (ecclesiological questions left over from Vatican I and new ones that rose later, which, by the way, are not few; 2) On the sources of Revelation (questions of exegesis, some extremely delicate, and tradition); 3) On the complete custody of the deposit of Faith (with doctrines nowadays cast into doubt or denied by some); 4) On the moral order; 5) On the social order. Each of these sub-commissions was assigned between 7 and 12 members (there being no strict difference between 'member' and 'consultant'), one of them as its president.

"I was part of the third sub-commission (complete custody of the faith), who was charged with preparing schemata on: 1) Human reason and the truths of the faith; 2) The existence of God; 3) Creation and evolution; 4) Revelation and faith; 5) Progress in doctrine ('evolution of the dogmas'); 6) Natural and supernatural order; 7) Spiritism, reincarnation and the four last things; 8) Monogeneanism; 9) Original sin; 10) Destiny of children who die without baptism; 11) Vicarious redemption" (*Concílio Vaticano II*, vol. I, pp. 157f.).

calling the Council dogmatic and presented it as 'predominantly pastoral.'[48]

It seems to us that for strategic reasons it was more convenient to John XXIII to impose the rejection of the pre-conciliar schemata in the name of pastoral necessity rather than claim dogmatic principles. If, from the outset, he were to have presented the dogmatic ensemble that Vatican II actually approved, he would have run the risk of setting off a serious polemic and blocking the Assembly's work from moving in the direction he wanted it to go.

In our judgment, this was the first reason of convenience to emphasize the pastoral aspect of the Council.

§ 51 The *second* reason, also of a strategic nature, has to do with taking future advantage of the documents approved by the Council.

The dogmatic teaching of any ecumenical Council requires the obedience of all Catholics. Now then, as a whole and in a large number of its points, the dogmatic teaching of Vatican II is opposed to the traditional doctrine of the Ecclesiastical Magisterium, as we intend to make clear in this Collection and especially beginning in Volume VI. If, soon after Vatican II, emphasis had been placed on the dogmatic aspect and the demands of obedience, this would probably have given rise to a reaction and people would have compared the Council's doctrine with the previous dogmatic doctrine. Such a reaction could have thwarted the advantages expected to be drawn from the approved documents.

Thus, we believe that the emphasis given to the pastoral aspect in the post-conciliar era and the failure to immediately demand obedience greatly served the designs of those who conceived Vatican II and steered its application, by avoiding a reaction and assuring the ripening of its fruits.[49]

*

---

[48] Text in § 52.

[49] These reasons, which we present here only to facilitate the understanding of the possible intentions of John XXIII and Paul VI, which we will analyze now, are dealt with in more detail and with due proof in Section B.

d) The Emphasis Given by John XXIII and Paul VI to the Pastoral Aspect of the Council Does Not Exclude Its Dogmatic Qualification

§ 52

In the *Opening Speech* (October 11, 1962), John XXIII thus indicated the Council's pastoral orientation:

"**The *punctum saliens* of this Council is not .... discussing one or the other article of the fundamental doctrine of the Church,** repeating and proclaiming the teaching of the ancient and modern Fathers and Theologians, which, we suppose, is quite present on and familiar to our minds.

"There would be no need of a Council for that. But from the renewed, serene and tranquil adhesion to the whole teaching of the Church in its integrity and exactness, as it shines in the Conciliar Acts from Trent to Vatican I, **the Christian,** Catholic and apostolic **spirit** in the whole world **expects progress in the doctrinal penetration and formation of consciences in a more perfect correspondence with and fidelity to the authentic doctrine; but also that this be studied and expounded through the means of the investigation and literary formulation of modern thought. One is the substance of the ancient doctrine, the *depositum fidei*,** and **another is the formulation encasing it; and this is what we must** — with patience, if necessary — **take very much into account, measuring everything in the forms and proportions of a predominantly pastoral magisterium.**"[50]

---

[50] In B. KLOPPENBURG, *Concílio Vaticano II*, vol. II, p. 310.

Some observations on this translation of John XXIII's speech:

* The text by Kloppenburg that we transcribe is a faithful translation, verified by us, of the speech published in Italian by *L'Osservatore Romano* of 10/12/1962, p. 3. The speech was also distributed on October 10 to journalists stationed at the Holy See by the Vatican Press Service, linked to the Secretariat of State, to be part of the next day's news coverage and make possible a simultaneous translation of the Pope's speech (A. WENGER, *Chronique de la première session,* p. 47).

* This is why the same version is found in whole or in part in various of the main chronicles of the Council (G. CAPRILE, *Il Concilio Vaticano II,* vol. II, pp. 2-7; René LAURENTIN, *Bilan de la première session*, pp. 12-15; Henri FESQUET, *Le journal du Concile,* pp. 27f.; A. WENGER, op. cit., p. 42).

Let us analyze this fundamental excerpt.

In the first paragraph John XXIII states that doctrinal discussion based on the traditional teaching of the Church will not be the keynote of the Council. This seems to be a first salvo against the conservatives. With it he appears to be preparing for the rejection of the pre-conciliar schemata, which he will do a little later. His language, however, is skillful: it does not definitely exclude traditional doctrine from the discussion but says it will not be the *punctum saliens*. A door is thus left open either for a concession or a retreat of a conservative nature if John XXIII's program is not accepted by everyone.

He goes on to say that the "Christian spirit .... expects progress in the doctrinal penetration and formation of consciences in a more perfect correspondence and with fidelity to the authentic doctrine." A goal of the Council would be to fulfill that expectation. Now then, presenting "progress in the doctrinal penetration and formation of consciences" as a goal does not exclude dogmatic and moral topics but rather presupposes them as one of the Council's goals.

John XXIII then provides the prism from which doctrine will be considered. It is that "this be studied and expounded through the means of investigation and literary formulation of modern thought." Here we are faced with the first imprecise generalization: What are the means of investigation of modern

---

* However, this unofficial version of Vatican II's opening speech is a relatively free translation of the official Latin text (JOHN XXIII, *Discorsi, messaggi, colloqui del Santo Padre Giovanni XXIII*, Tipografia Poliglotta Vaticana, 1963, vol. IV, pp. 578-590; *L'Osservatore Romano*, 10/12/1962, pp. 1f.). There are, therefore, certain differences between the two texts.

* Such differences have caused polemics (Jean MADIRAN, "Autour du Concile," in *Itinéraires*, Paris, December 1962, pp. 10-26; February 1963, pp. 100-106, in A. WENGER, op. cit., pp. 46-50).

* But such polemics appear to have been resolved by the sheer weight of an argument of authority, since on December 23, 1962, responding in Italian to the wishes of Cardinal Tisserant, JOHN XXIII employed the same terms of the unofficial Italian version when he described the meaning of the Council (*L'Osservatore Romano*, 12/24-25/1962, in A. WENGER, op. cit., p. 48).

We therefore believe the translation we have used is sufficiently authoritative.

thought? Could they be, perchance, Kant's criticisms of reason, Nietzsche's of God, Darwin's of creation, Marx's of property, Freud's of morality? All these are outstanding authors of modern thought. John XXIII does not indicate clearly what modern thought is, and, as a consequence, one cannot know for sure what are the means of investigation and literary formulation with which he proposes to 'study and expound' Catholic doctrine. The fundamental criterion is ambiguous.

Nevertheless, John XXIII goes on to explain: "One is the substance of the ancient doctrine .... and another is the formulation encasing it." Compared to the statement preceding it, that Catholic doctrine must be expounded by means of the literary formulation of modern thought, this sounds like a justification. It would therefore be possible to modify the very formulation of dogmatic truth according to the patterns of modern thought. Was this what John XXII stated? As we go back to the text we verify that what he says is only that there is a difference between the substance of the Faith and its formulation. That, of itself, is entirely true. Therefore, there is in the context a tendency that does not exist in the statement as such, taken separately. Once again it seems to us that we are faced with the use of ambiguity. One does not know for sure to what degree Catholic doctrine should be reformulated.

Once the Council's goals have been established: 1) progress in doctrinal penetration; 2) progress in the formation of consciences; 3) the study of doctrine through the means of the investigation of modern thought; 4) expounding doctrine according to the literary formulation of modern thought — the first, third and fourth being dogmatic goals, and the second a moral one — John XXIII tells in what way such goals should be attained: "And this is what we must take very much into account, measuring everything in the forms and proportions of a predominantly pastoral magisterium."

This phrase has a curious twist that calls one's attention. Taken in combination with the other excerpts of John XXIII's speech cited above, it can be understood either as an encouragement to progressivists or, on the contrary, as a warning to them of a conservative tone.

Some will interpret it as meaning: "to proceed earnestly with the study, exposition and reformulation of aspects of the Faith according to the criteria of modern thought, since such goals may be considered as included in the ambit of the pastoral magisterium." Others will take it as a word of caution: "Be very careful not to understand, reformulate, and expound the Faith according to modern thought except in accordance with the criteria and limits of the pastoral magisterium." In our view, the possibility of giving rise to opposed interpretations configures the essential ambiguity of the phrase.[51]

If we analyze its ambiguous expressions, we will find:

* **Take very much into account** - can be understood as 'take very earnestly' or 'take great caution.'

* **everything** - can refer either to modern thought or the reformulation of the *depositum fidei*.

* **measuring** - if the direct object is modern thought, it can be understood as 'considering:' considering modern thought **included** in the forms etc.; or it can be taken as 'judging:' judging modern thought **according** to the forms etc. If the direct object is the reform of the *depositum fidei*, 'measuring' can be understood as 'adapting:' adapting the reformulation of the *depositum fidei* **only** in the forms etc. In addition to the verb's ambiguity, the omission in the sentence of each and all the expressions emphasized in this paragraph makes the action being recommended even more ambiguous.

* **in the forms and proportions** - this expression can be understood as 'in the ambit' or as synonymous with 'according to the criteria and limits.' Now since this expression is the point of reference for the action to be carried out, and since it is ambiguous, the whole action being recommended is left without direction, independent of the other ambiguities.

* **predominantly pastoral magisterium** - the adverb, 'predominantly,' can be taken as synonymous with: 'nearly exclusively,' thereby reflecting a great emphasis; 'mainly,' thus showing a smaller emphasis; and 'preferentially,' an even lesser emphasis. None of the meanings, however, excludes the dogmatic aspect of the ecclesiastical Magisterium as the ambit in which the Council will take place.

We have thus analyzed the ambiguities contained in the sentence in which John XXIII announced the goal of Vatican II. They are so numerous as to permit several other interpretations, with new combinations of meanings. However, we believe that

---

[51] Although we present only two interpretations, there would be others which we left out in order not to complicate the understanding of the subject.

the two mentioned above — one progressivist and the other conservative — are landmarks between which are to be found the most likely interpretations.

§ 56   The analysis of ambiguities notwithstanding, we have seen that calling the Council "predominantly pastoral" does not preclude the fact that it may deal with dogmatic topics.

*

§ 57   In an Audience given to the participants of the Week of Pastoral Updating on September 6, 1963, Paul VI also stresses the role of 'pastoral' in the Council: "**We must** also **welcome another expression** that qualifies the activity of which you are promoters and disciples: **the word 'pastoral.' Nowadays this glorious word constitutes a whole program. As everyone knows, the Ecumenical Council has made it its own, polarizing in it its goals of reform and renewal.**"[52]

The text adds nothing essential to the speech of John XXIII, but confirms it. The statement that the word pastoral 'polarizes the Council's goals of reform and renewal' does not seem to exclude its dogmatic aspect.

58   A little later, referring to John XIII in the *Opening Speech* of the Council's Second Session, Paul VI says: "You have called your brethren, the successors of the Apostles, not only for them to continue the doctrinal study interrupted (by Vatican I) and the legislative work that had been suspended, but also that they may feel united to the Pope in the same Body and receive support and guidance from him so that the 'sacred deposit of Christian doctrine be better preserved and presented in a more efficacious manner.'[53]* Nevertheless, even while **pointing out** in this way **the most elevated objective of the Council, you added to it another goal, more urgent and at present of a more beneficial nature, the pastoral goal .... We shall not forget the norms that you yourself** [John XXIII], the first Father of the Council .... **drew up for it and We are pleased to repeat: 'one will have recourse to a manner of presenting things that better corresponds to a teaching, above all, of a pastoral character'**[54]*."[55]

---

[52] PAUL VI, "Audience to the Members of the13th Pastoral Actualization Week," September 6, 1963, in B. KLOPPENBURG, *Concílio Vaticano II*, vol. III, p. 501.

[53]* AAS, 1962, p. 790.

[54]* Ibid., pp. 791f.

Stating that "one will have recourse to a manner of presenting things that better corresponds to a teaching, above all, of a pastoral character" adds nothing essential to what was said by John XXIII.

§ 59　　The same can be noted in the Brief *In Spiritu Sancto*, with which Paul VI closed Vatican II. In it he says: "**Council Vatican II** .... must undoubtedly be considered one of the great events in the Church. Indeed, it was the largest as far as the number of Fathers who came to the Seat of Peter is concerned .... the richest one in topics .... finally, it was the most opportune, because having in mind the needs of the present time, **it confronted above all the pastoral necessities**."[56] The statement that the Council 'confronted above all the pastoral necessities' seems to confirm that the dogmatic aspect was not excluded.

*

e) The Dogmatic Tone Is Accentuated in the Promulgation of the Documents

§ 60　　In the solemn manner that Paul VI promulgates each conciliar document, the keynote is of a dogmatic teaching. Indeed, it even appears to fulfill the conditions characterizing the Extraordinary Magisterium of the Pope.[57]

---

[55] In B. KLOPPENBURG, op. cit., vol. III, pp. 510f.

[56] Ibid., vol. V, p. 516.

[57] Studying the conditions for an *ex cathedra* pontifical pronouncement to take place, A. V. XAVIER DA SILVEIRA summarizes the thought of Diekamp, Billot, Choupin, Hervé, Journet, Nau, Salaverri, and Cartechini, and points out four conditions: "1) That the Pope speak in his capacity as universal Doctor and Shepherd; 2) that he use the fullness of his apostolic authority; 3) that he manifest a will to define; 4) that he deal with a matter of Faith or Morals" ("Qual a autoridade doutrinária dos documentos pontifícios e conciliares?," in *Catolicismo,* October 1967).

He then notes: "The crucial point of the question is in the third condition: that he manifest a will to define. How is that intention manifested? Is it by employing the expression '*we define*'? Is it by excommunicating whoever says the opposite? Is it by the juridical nature of the docu-

The Pope calls upon the representation of Christ and the assistance of the Holy Spirit with such great solemnity that one wonders whether he is making use of Papal Infallibility. In fact, he declares: "The whole ensemble and each of the points that have been enunciated in this Dogmatic Constitution appeared sound to the Fathers of the Sacrosanct Council. And **We, by the Apostolic Power entrusted to us by Christ,** together with the Venerable Fathers, **in the Holy Spirit, approve it, decree it, and enact it.** And **We order that what** has thus been decided in the Council **be promulgated** for the greater glory of God."[58]

Imperative characteristics that usually follow official dogmatic and moral declarations by the Extraordinary Magisterium of the Church are also used in the Brief *In Spiritu Sancto*, which closed the Council: **"With Our Apostolic Authority .... We order and command ....** that all that was established by the Synod **be religiously observed by all faithful ....** These things **we have sanctioned and established, decreeing that the present letters be permanent** and continue firm, valid and efficacious, **that they be fulfilled and attain full and complete effects, and that they be fully validated by those on whom it will or may behoove in the future. Thus it must be judged and defined. And all that is done contrary to this by any individ-**

---

ment? None of these signs is apodictic" (Sisto CARTECHINI, "Dall'opinione al domma," Rome: La Civiltà Cattolica, 1953, pp. 29, 31, 36, 54). The fundamental thing is that it be clear, in any way whatsoever, that the Pope wants to define a dogma.

"Thus it is that, **in solemn definitions, the Holy Pontiffs use a number of verbs to make their intention unmistakable: We '*promulgate, decree, define, declare, proclaim,*'** etc. In other cases, while such verbs may be absent, the circumstances surrounding the document will show that there was a will to define. This is what happens when the Pope imposes on the whole Church the acceptance of a formula of faith." (A. V. XAVIER DA SILVEIRA, Ibid.).

[58] These words are the formula of promulgation of *Lumen gentium*. A similar formula — only one or the other word having been replaced, as well as the title (Dogmatic Constitution with Pastoral Constitution, Constitution, Decree or Declaration) — was used for promulgating the other documents (V.A., *Documentos do Vaticano II - Constituições, decretos e declarações,* eds. B. KLOPPENBURG - F. VIER; Portuguese edition reviewed by the undersecretaries of the National Conference of Brazilian Bishops, Petrópolis: Vozes, 1966, pp. 133, 252, 299, 327, 342, 394, 429, 475, 496, 517, 557, 573, 592, 611, 621).

ual or authority, consciously or out of ignorance, **must be considered, from this moment onward, null and void.**"[59]

One can see, therefore, that the tone is imperative and solemn, typical of the most important dogmatic documents and appropriate to oblige acceptance by all Catholics.[60]

*

f) The Pastoral Characteristic Is Stressed in the *Preliminary Notes*

§ *61*

When the schema *De Ecclesia*, which would come to be the Dogmatic Constitution *Lumen gentium*, was discussed, there was a serious polemic about episcopal collegiality. Many conservatives saw in it an attempt to undermine the monarchic and absolute power of the Sovereign Pontiff. So the *Preliminary Explanatory Note*, which safeguards traditional doctrine on the matter, was written.[61] The *Announcement*[62] that precedes the

---

[59] Brief *In Spiritu Sancto*, December 7, 1965, in B. KLOPPENBURG, *Concílio Vaticano II*, vol. V, p. 516.

[60] A precise analysis of the scope of the application of such formulas and the manifestation of such intentions from the standpoint of Canon Law and the tradition of the Pontifical Magisterium goes beyond the bounds of the present Collection. On reading the above cited promulgations and the *Brief*, we limit ourselves to stating the opinion of Catholics based primarily on the *sensus fidelium*.

[61] On the disagreements that arose about this matter, see Section B, 3rd phase, §§ 100-102.

[62] Here is the full text of the *Announcement* made by the Secretary General of the Council in the 123rd General Assembly on November 16, 1964:

"A query has been made as to what is the *theological qualification* of the doctrine expounded in the schema *De Ecclesia*, on which a vote is to be taken.

"The doctrinal commission has thus replied to this query in appraising the *modi* proposed for the third chapter of the schema *De Ecclesia*:

"'As is evident, a conciliar text should always be interpreted in harmony with the general rules known to everyone.'

Preliminary Explanatory Note to *Lumen gentium* says: "Taking into account conciliar practice and the pastoral purpose of the present council, the sacred synod has defined as binding on the Church only those matters of faith and morals which it has expressly put forward as such."

One could say, therefore, that this pronouncement exempts Vatican II as a whole from any dogmatic responsibility and *ipso facto* does not oblige any faithful to accept it.

§ 62   Nevertheless, the second and seventh paragraphs of the *Announcement* appear to indicate that such an exemption from responsibility refers exclusively to chapter III of *Lumen gentium*, which deals with the subject of collegiality. Except for that, what is said in the third paragraph seems to prevail, to wit:

"As is self-evident, the conciliar text is to be interpreted in accordance with the general rules which are known to all."

Therefore, there is an imprecision about the limits for applying the criteria mentioned: is it the Council as a whole or only chapter III of *Lumen gentium*? This imprecision will necessarily generate ambiguity in the interpretation of the *Announcement* and, consequently, in the theological qualification of Vatican II.

Taken in their broader sense, the intentions stated in the fifth paragraph of the *Announcement* seem to clash with the words of promulgation Paul VI used to enact the contents of *Lu-*

"In this regard, the Doctrinal Commission calls attention to its *Declaration* of 6 March, 1964, whose text we transcribe below:

"'Taking into account conciliar practice and the pastoral purpose of Council Vatican II, this Sacred Synod intends to issue, in matters of faith and morals, only the definitions it openly declares as such.

"'Everything else that the Council proposes as doctrine of the Supreme Magisterium of the Church is to be acknowledged and accepted by each and every member of the faithful according to the mind of the Council which is clear from the subject matter and its formulation, following the norms of theological interpretation.'

"'By superior authority, a previous explanatory note on the *modi* presented in regard to chapter III of the schema *De Ecclesia* has been communicated to the Fathers. The doctrine expounded in this chapter III should be explained and understood according to the spirit and meaning of this note" (Pericle FELICI, "Notificações," November 16, 1964, in V.A., *Atas do Concílio Ecumênico Vaticano II*, in V.A., *Documentos do Vaticano II*, pp. 108f.).

men gentium and the other conciliar documents. For as we have seen above, he used the normal formulas of the Extraordinary Magisterium of the Pope.

In order to avoid such a clash, the intentions under scrutiny should be understood as restricted to chapter III of *Lumen gentium*.

We point out that this *Announcement*, interpreted in its broadest meaning, is the only document that could be claimed to argue that the Council was not simultaneously dogmatic and pastoral.

§ 63   In the initial *Note* referring to the title of *Gaudium et spes*, even though it affirms the prevalence of the pastoral aspect in this Constitution, the usual interpretation of councils that are both dogmatic and pastoral already appears. It says: "Although it consists of two parts, the Pastoral Constitution 'The Church in the World Today' constitutes an organic unity. The Constitution is called 'pastoral' because, while resting on doctrinal principles, it seeks to set forth the relation of the Church to the world and to the men of today. In Part I, therefore, the pastoral emphasis is not overlooked, nor is the doctrinal emphasis overlooked in Part II."[63]

The initial *Note* of *Gaudium et spes* is such as to confirm our interpretation of the Council — that it is both dogmatic and pastoral — and therefore appears to restrict the explanations of the *Announcement* to the *Preliminary Explanatory Note* to *Lumen gentium* only to chapter III of that Dogmatic Constitution.

*

§ 64   On ending the analysis about the theological qualification of the Council, we may conclude this Section A by saying that it was at the same time dogmatic and pastoral. Fundamental ambiguities remain, however, on how the Council's proposed goals should be achieved, namely the adaptation of dogmatics to modern thought, and how cogent the Council's dogmatic characteristics are. To be consistent with Catholic Doctrine and the tradition of the councils, such characteristics should demand acceptance by all Catholics and, should any point diverge from Catholic Dogma, it should be judged by traditional doctrine.

---

[63] "Constituição pastoral Gaudium et spes sobre a Igreja no mundo de hoje", footnote regarding the title in V.A., Documentos do Vaticano II, p. 137.

In our view, this analysis reduces as much as possible, but does not eliminate, the Council's ambiguity from the standpoint of its theological qualification.

*

B. A Practical Consideration: Ambiguity in Theological Qualification Serves As a Tool of Progressivist Victory

§ 65   A complete ambiguity generally hovers over the theological qualification of the Council, independent of the above analysis. When conservatives say it is dogmatic so they can judge it according to traditional Catholic doctrine, progressivists contend it is pastoral; when the former agree it is pastoral and consequently refuse to obey it, the latter, in flagrant contradiction to what they had maintained, say that the Council is dogmatic and requires obedience. Thus, what happens in practice is that the progressivists methodically use ambiguity regarding Vatican II's theological qualification in order to obtain advantages for their current.

§ 66   Now we will attempt to clarify this method by presenting to the Reader, as an hypothesis, a concatenation of phases showing the oscillation in the meanings the progressivists use to qualify the Council. This concatenation is based on observation and founded on facts and texts by various authors.

§ 67   Someone could object that it is not licit to attribute to the progressivist current such an underhanded maneuver based on the alternate employment of the dogmatic or pastoral nature of the Council, since, contrary to Church practice, that would entail judging intentions.

To this we would answer:

* Several progressivist authors of great renown have stated — as we have already documented [64] — that ambiguity in the conciliar texts was due to a strategic maneuver to attain unanimity and to prepare the future.

---

[64] Chaps. IV, V, VI.2,3.

  * The modernists — whose successors are the progressivists[65] — are known to have frequently resorted to such tricks in order to deceive the unwary.[66]

  * The employment of ambiguity to define the Council gives the progressivists elements to carry out a maneuver similar to those they avowedly have used in the past and to the ones employed by their modernist ancestors.

  * Therefore, it seems to us entirely licit to suppose that they are the ones carrying out this maneuver. To deny such a supposition, we believe, would be unforgivable naivete.

  Nevertheless, on raising an hypothesis about this maneuver, we do not intend to go beyond the bounds of conjecture. We lack the data and information necessary to affirm this with certainty; such information is perhaps accessible only to those more closely involved with the strategic and doctrinal plans of progressivism.

*

§ 68
  As one analyzes the use of ambiguity in the theological qualification of the Council, one can distinguish in the confrontation between progressivists and conservatives the following intertwining of chronological strategic phases:

§ 69
1st phase * **The conservatives arrive at the Council not organized among themselves but confident that the dogmatic schemata prepared in the pre-Council will be approved.**

    * **The progressivists arrive very well organized and ready to make their best efforts, but uncertain of victory.**

§ 70
2nd phase * **Right at the opening of Vatican II, by declaring that the Council was to be predominantly pastoral and relegating dogmatic questions based on the traditional teaching to a secondary plane, John XXIII disorients the conservatives.**

---

[65] Chap. VI.1.

[66] *Pascendi Dominici gregis*, n. 4.

* With the withdrawal of the schema *De fontibus Revelationis* by the express desire of John XXIII, nearly all the remaining schemata of the pre-Council are dropped from the agenda.

* The conservatives show discouragement and resignation.

§ 71   3rd phase   * Alleging pastoral attitudes, the progressivists introduce into the schemata ideas of adaptation to the world and different religions.

* The conservatives protest against some of them.

* Paul VI, directly or indirectly, uses his authority to silence the conservatives and give the victory to progressivists.

* Faced with contradictions with traditional doctrine, the conservatives accept them only by force of the pontifical authority and under the allegation that they are pastoral attitudes.

* This tactic is used until the end of the Council.

§ 72   4th phase   * Once Vatican II is over and victory clearly won by the progressivists, they gradually begin to say that the Council was not only pastoral, but also dogmatic.

* Their tendency is to accentuate the doctrinal aspect of the victories obtained.

§ 73   5th phase   * The conservatives, on the contrary, once Vatican II is over, begin to stress its pastoral aspect.

* Their apology seeks to demonstrate that, since the Council was pastoral, it does not require obedience like dogmatic ones.

§ 74   6th phase   * In the post-conciliar period, when the possibility of a conservative reaction arises, the Vatican leadership uses its power and prestige to try to destroy the reaction by alleging that the Council was dogmatic.

§ 75   7th phase   * When, in the post-conciliar era, the progressivists have problems with their grassroots who complain about Vatican II's ambiguity, the leadership call to mind the dogmatic victories in the Council and

stress the need for making them more explicit in the future.

*

We now present documents to corroborate these phases of a hypothetical progressivist maneuver.

1st phase   * **The conservatives arrive at the Council not organized among themselves but confident that the dogmatic schemata prepared in the pre-Council will be approved.**

                        * **The progressivists arrive very well organized and ready to make their best efforts, but uncertain of victory.**

§ 76   With respect to the disorganization and consequent unpreparedness of some episcopates, especially from more conservative countries, these words by Msgr. Guglielmo Montolese, Archbishop Emeritus of Taranto, appear expressive of the **1st phase**: **"We Italian bishops *in genere* were not very prepared, unlike those of France, Germany and the other countries of Central Europe.** Along with four other Italian bishops, I was part of a work group that included several French prelates. We would meet at Rome's French college to compare each other's positions. Suddenly, I realized the difference in preparedness."[67]

§ 77   His opinion is somewhat confirmed by Msgr. Aurelio Sorrentino, Archbishop of Reggio Calabria, who says: **"I must honestly recognize that I, like, I believe, many others, arrived at the Council absolutely unprepared both with respect to the themes to be discussed as well as the method to be followed."**[68]

§ 78   Cardinal Suenens tells how early in the Council he was assigned by John XXIII to "clear up" the schemata which had been written *grosso modo* by conservatives. He confirms progressivist articulation in this **1st phase** as follows: **"During an audi-**

---

[67] Guglielmo MONTOLESE, "La Chiesa, compagna di viaggio dell'uomo - I grandi testimoni del Vaticano II/7," interview with Silvano STRACCA, in *Avvenire*, 11/27/1992.

[68] Aurelio SORRENTINO, "La Chiesa, compagna di viaggio dell'uomo," Ibid.

ence in March 1962, I complained to Pope John XXIII about what I felt was **the abusive number of schemata prepared** for the coming conciliar discussion. There were 70, I believe, of very unequal value and in any case of an excessive weight, preventing *a priori* a fruitful and valid work in the Council. **John XXIII asked me to clear the way and make him a project** based on these schemata. **After studying these documents I sent John XXIII a preliminary note aimed at uncluttering the council** and placing it into a true pastoral perspective .... **The preliminary note was intended to remove excessively juridical conceptions away from the council. It fully suited the views of John XXIII, who gave it his personal approval."**[69]

Suenens, after transcribing his note continues to explain how he prepared the plan that would be adopted by the Council by organizing his political contacts, partly under the orientation of John XXIII himself: **"The road having been thus cleared, I worked to prepare a project. At the end of April 1962 the plan was ready.** In it I inserted, as much as possible, the themes that were dear to me, with the constant concern of promoting the pastoral adaptations I deemed of first importance. **The confidential document remained strictly personal until the moment I found it useful to communicate it to some cardinal friends, among whom was Cardinal Montini.** In my files I find a letter from cardinal Liénart, dated June 14, 1962: **'Your project is fully satisfactory to me** and I do not want to wait until evening to tell you this in a mere phone call. **I fully approve** the apostolic spirit with which you conceived [the project], the disposition of its parts as you outlined them, and the broadness of the perspectives that you opened.' **Other cardinals reacted,** orally, **in the same sense. For his part,** on May 19, 1962 **Cardinal Cicognani**, the Secretary of State, **by order of John XXIII, sent photocopies of this plan to a certain number of cardinals,** so that they might be informed of it.

"John XXIII wanted to gain the adhesion of some influential cardinals to this project so that, at the opportune moment, he would be able to present it under their collective sponsorship. Toward this end, he asked me to go to some whom he himself indicated."[70]

After naming Cardinals with whom he met and who supported him — Montini, Döpfner, Liénart, Siri — the Belgian

---

[69] L. J. SUENENS, *Souvenirs et espérances*, pp. 65f.

[70] Ibid., p. 69.

prelate alludes to the Pontiff's tacit endorsement of his plan: **"John XXIII**, for his part, **adopted it in its major parts as its own. One can read this between the lines in his memorable radiomessage of September 12, 1962, announcing and presenting the council** to be inaugurated a few weeks later. .... **The Holy Father's speech explicitly adopted the proposed distinction between the Church** *ad intra* **and the Church** *ad extra*, **which was the mainstay of the plan."**[71]

These testimonies show without a doubt how the progressivist current, in its most high-ranking members, arrived at the Council entirely organized.

§ 79   Fr. Bernard Häring, CSSR, describes the role he played before the beginning of the Council to sound out reactions and arrange for the rejection of the conservative schemata: **"Cardinals Suenens and Döpfner charged me, after the closure of the preparatory works, to survey the largest possible number of bishops and cardinals about the positions they would take at the Council regarding the 72 previous schemata.** Shortly before the opening of the Council, I explained to some of our friendly Cardinals that, **based on all these contacts, it was certain that only the schema on liturgical reform would have some probability of being accepted** and discussed. **For certain, more than one-third of the votes would be against the other 71 schemata. My friends and I took advantage of every possibility to explain our assessment of these schemata to the largest possible number of bishops** and to linguistic groups."[72]

§ 80   Confirming the **1st phase**, the group presided over by Cardinal Gerlier of Lyons displays a typical example of the progressivists' close-knit organization. The well-informed Fr. Chenu writes: "About fifty bishops and thirty *periti* .... had gathered at the Belgian College on October 26, 1962. .... **This commission,** which held private sessions in its workings, **was in constant relation with Council officials.** In the first place, it was **efficaciously presided over by Cardinal Gerlier,** archbishop of Lyons; furthermore, **it would never fail to keep Cardinal Lercaro, who informed the Pope, abreast of events. The intervention by various of its members in the Assembly opened up its debates to the [conciliar] experiences, analyses, doctrines, and projects. Various documents of great scope came out of this**

---

[71] Ibid., p. 70.

[72] Bernard HÄRING, "Minha participação no Concílio Vaticano II," in *Revista Eclesiástica Brasileira*, June 1994, p. 382.

group, which, incidentally, **had imposed extreme discretion on itself as a duty.**"[73]

§ 81   Fr. Schillebeeckx, a *perito* of the Dutch episcopate and the author of many of Cardinal Alfrink's interventions, gives a meaningful testimony on the well-organized progressivist scheme, which continued until the end of the Council: "**Undoubtedly Alfrink played a great role in the council. He was not alone. He would always meet with other cardinals: Liénart, Döpfner, König. They formed a small college and discussed above all the strategy to be adopted. The idea of collegiality was taken ahead by Alfrink. It was he who proposed to establish** the synod, which he then described as the crown's council."[74]

§ 82   As to the uncertainties of victory on the part of the progressivists, Hans Küng himself testifies: "**The Council** did not do everything .... But **it did more than one would have dared expect of it back then.**"[75]

2nd phase   * **Right at the opening of Vatican II, by declaring that the Council was to be predominantly pastoral and relegating dogmatic questions based on the traditional teaching to a secondary plane, John XXIII disorients the conservatives.**

              * **With the withdrawal of the schema *De fontibus Revelationis* by the express desire of John XXIII, nearly all the remaining schemata of the pre-Council are dropped from the agenda.**

              * **The conservatives show discouragement and resignation.**

83   We have thus analyzed the Council's *Opening Speech*, in which John XXIII states the predominantly pastoral goal of Vatican II and relegates traditional dogmatic teaching to a secondary plane.[76]

---

[73] M. D. CHENU, "A Igreja dos pobres no Vaticano II," in *Concilium*, 1977/4, p. 64.

[74] Edward SCHILLEBEECKX, "Dio è un dono non una garanzia," interview with Francesco STRAZZARI, in *Il Regno*, 6/15/1990, p. 332.

[75] H. KÜNG, *Veracidade*, p. 130.

[76] Item 4.A.d, §§ 52-56.

In an interview with the Author, Fr. Chenu confirms the **2nd phase** as he describes the surprise and disconcertment the Council's *Opening Speech* caused among conservatives: "Adaptation to the needs of the times is indeed a principle of the Council, according to **John XXIII**, who **made an *opening speech* saying that the Church must look at the world in order to adapt herself to it. It is the opposite of what had been prepared.** You know that there was a preparatory commission that had written the schemata. And on the opening day the Pope said the opposite. I was there in Rome. **Traditional theologians were disconcerted.**"[77]

The following excerpt by Fr. Chenu depicts the impasse in which the speech of John XXIII left the conservatives: "On the one hand, there was John XXIII's opening speech defining the reasons for convening [the Council] and, on the other, an interview by Cardinal Siri, Archbishop of Genoa, published in the Italian weekly *Oggi*. 'A Council,' said the latter, '**is being held to reinvigorate the truth that finds itself threatened; therefore, it is above all dogmatic.**' .... **In opposition** to the doctrinally-oriented people of the Siri type, **John XXIII spoke of a 'pastoral' attitude.**"[78]

§ 84   In addition, to confirm this **2nd phase** is John XXIII's typical interference in closing the debate on the sources of Revelation, which was the object of great rows between conservatives and progressivists. After successive discussions, the vote was held on November 21, 1962. Out of 2,211 voters, 1,368 opposed keeping the schema for discussion; 822 voted for its normal course to proceed. The progressivists had failed to muster the two-third majority needed for the schema to be definitively rejected. So, in this very strict sense, the conservatives were holding the upper hand. But the following day, the Secretary General, Msgr. Pericle Felice, on behalf of the Secretary of State, Cardinal Amleto Cicognani, transmitted to the Assembly a pontifical communique withdrawing the matter from debate and entrusting it to a Special Commission charged with rewriting it.[79]

---

[77] M. D. CHENU, Interview with the Author - Paris, February 20, 1983.

[78] *Jacques Duquesne interroge le Père Chenu* (Paris: Centurion, 1975), p. 175.

[79] B. KLOPPENBURG, *Concílio Vaticano II*, vol. II, p. 190; R. LAURENTIN, *Bilan de la première session*, pp. 44f.; H. FESQUET, op. cit., pp. 114-119.

Thus, the victory that the conservatives — even though a minority — were about to celebrate was turned into a defeat.

3rd phase   * **Alleging pastoral attitudes, the progressivists introduce into the schemata ideas of adaptation to the world and different religions.**

* **The conservatives protest against some of them.**

* **Paul VI, directly or indirectly, uses his authority to silence the conservatives and give the victory to progressivists.**

* **Faced with contradictions with traditional doctrine, the conservatives accept them only by force of the pontifical authority and under the allegation that they are pastoral attitudes.**

* **This tactic is used until the end of the Council.**

§ 85   Corroborating what we said about the **3rd phase**, perhaps the most typical boycott carried out against the conservative wing was the one of a petition asking for the condemnation of communism and socialism. Here is a summary of what happened.[80]

On December 3, 1963, as the Second Session was coming to an end, Msgr. Castro Mayer, Bishop of Campos, Brazil, delivered to the Secretary of State, Amleto Cardinal Cicognani, a petition signed by 213 Fathers of the Council from 54 countries asking the following of Paul VI: That he might deign to "order the study and preparation of a schema of a conciliar constitution in which: 1) Catholic social doctrine would be expounded with great clarity and the errors of Marxism, socialism and communism from the philosophical, sociological and economic standpoints would be condemned; 2) the errors and mentality that prepare the minds of Catholics to accept socialism and communism and give them a propensity to the latter would be eradicated."[81]

---

[80] See the report by Henrique CHAVES, "Desfazendo manobras astuciosas de Moscou, duzentos Padres conciliares pedem nova condenação do comunismo e do socialismo," in *Catolicismo,* January 1964.

[81] The full text of the petition was published by the monthly journal on religion and culture, *Catolicismo,* January 1964.

§ 86   The text of this petition — in support of which two Brazilian Bishops worked — takes a stand against the great process of the de-Christianization of the West — the Revolution — expounded in the essay, *Revolution and Counter-Revolution*, by Plinio Corrêa de Oliveira. It also presents a close logical connection with his study, *The Freedom of the Church in the Communist State*, in which the Catholic thinker demonstrates the unfeasibility of setting up a *modus vivendi* between the Church and the communist regimes. This timely essay by Prof. Corrêa de Oliveira was sent to all the conciliar Fathers [82] and, along with the petition, undoubtedly played an important role [83] in creating the favorable climate that later enabled important Prelates to feel at ease as they questioned, in the Plenary assembly, the reasons for the ominous refusal of tackling the question of communism.

§ 87   By his silence, Paul VI rejected the request of the 213 conciliar Fathers.[84] A few months later, shortly before the start of the Third Session, in the Encyclical *Ecclesiam Suam*, he spoke of a 'dialogue of salvation' in which he did not rule out the hypothesis of including the communists.[85]

§ 88   As the Third Session began on October 20, 1964, *Schema XIII* on 'the presence of the Church in the modern world' came up for discussion. At that meeting and subsequent ones, the conciliar Fathers debated at length about the part of the schema dealing with atheism, but carefully avoided the word commu-

---

[82] A. WENGER, *Chronique de la deuxième session*, p. 240.

[83] The petition by the 213 conciliar Fathers and the distribution of *The Freedom of the Church in the Communist State* had ample repercussion in the Italian press. The following newspapers published reports about the matter:

Il Tempo; Il Messagero; Il Secolo; Daily American (of the American community) of Rome; *Corriere della Sera;* the magazine *Il Borghese,* of Milan; the daily *Roma, Il Mattutino,* of Naples; *Il Resto del Carlino,* of Bologne; *La Nazione,* of Florence; *Arena,* of Verona; *Il Giornale,* of Vicenza; *Alto Adige,* of Bolzano; *Il Giornale del Popolo,* of Bergamo; *La Provinzia,* of Cremona; *Messaggero-Veneto,* of Udine; *Gazetta,* of Mantua; *Gazetta,* of Reggio Emilia; *Gazetta Emiliana,* of Modena; *Gazetta Padana,* of Ferrara; *Gazetta di Parma; Tribuna del Mezzogiorno,* of Messina; and *Il Giornale di Sicilia,* of Palermo.

[84] R. WILTGEN, op. cit., p. 273.

[85] Encyclical *Ecclesiam suam*, August 6, 1964, in *Insegnamenti di Paolo VI*, 1963-1970, Encicliche, pp. 45-48.

nism. Several prelates, both orally and in writing, lamented such an omission.[86]

_____

[86] a. Msgr. Luigi CARLI, Bishop of Segni, in a collaboration entitled "Il comunismo e il Concilio Vaticano II" for the book by G. SCANTAM-BURLO, *Perché il Concilio no ha condannato il comunismo* (Rome: L'Appennino Ed., 1967), presents a collection of the main interventions by conciliar Fathers criticizing *Schema XIII's* failure to mention communism. Here are some of the most significant criticisms:

b. Msgr. (later Cardinal) Willian CONWAY, Archbishop of Armagh, Ireland: "The schema .... does not speak of the persecution of the Church in certain countries. One may object that this silence is intentional, in order not to hinder the dialogue with atheism, but truth and sincerity are essential conditions of any dialogue" (in L. CARLI, op. cit., pp. 201f.).

c. Msgr. Maximo HERMANIUK, Ukrainian Archbishop of Winnipeg, Canada: "It is necessary .... to show clearly what is the vocation of man that atheist Marxism wants to reduce to a mere force of production.... It would be deplorable to forget the testimony of the martyrs and confessors of the faith" (Ibid., p. 202).

d. Msgr. Joseph STIMPFLE, Bishop of Augsburg, Germany: "The schema should speak openly about the militant atheism spread in so many countries which has caused so much harm to the Church and contemporary humanity. How can one keep a tranquil conscience if one fails to speak about and even mention the Marxist phenomenon, the real and gravest danger to humanity today, a humanity of which the Council claims to want to take pastoral care?" (Ibid.).

e. Msgr. Raffaele BARBIERI, Bishop of Cassano all'Ionio, Italy: "The principal goal of this Council is pastoral .... but it would be a scandal for many faithful if the Council gave the impression that it was afraid to condemn the greatest crime of our time, scientific and practical atheism, which is worse than the atomic bomb itself because of its consequences in the moral and spiritual planes" (Ibid., pp. 202f.).

f. Cardinal YU PIN, Archbishop of Nankin (China), speaking in the name of 70 conciliar Fathers: "The schema puts a great enphasis on the signs of times, but appears to ignore that communism and Marxist materialism are the greatest and saddest characteristic signs of our times. A declaration about this point is necessary in order to defend the truth, since communism, materialism, and militant atheism comprise the apex of all heresies. We must also remember that wherever communism exists, there is no lack of bloody or at least destructive persecution. Likewise, the doctrine of peaceful coexistence, the policy of the extended hand, and the concept of the so-called Catholic communism are sources of dangerous confusions. In order to fulfill the expectations of peoples, especially those who suffer and groan under the communist yoke; in order to give the schema a greater balance and correspondence to the present situation in the world, it would be necessary to

§ 89   On April 7, 1965, during the recess between the Third and Fourth Sessions and while *Schema XIII* (which gave rise to the Pastoral Constitution *Gaudium et spes*) was being revised, Paul VI created the Secretariat for Unbelievers, with the aim of fomenting dialogue with atheists.

§ 90   The second version of *Schema XIII*, sent to be examined by the conciliar Fathers on May 27, 1965, also omitted any explicit reference to communism. Thus, in the Fourth Session, when the schema was debated in the assembly, there were criticisms of the document and requests that Communism be condemned.[87]

§ 91   On September 29, 1965, faced with such a flagrant and repeated omission, 25 Bishops from various countries took up an initiative by Coetus Internationalis Patrum[88] and sent the conciliar Fathers a circular letter expounding a series of reasons why it was indispensable that "after paragraph n. 19 of the schema on atheism, *The Church In the Modern World*, a new and adequate paragraph dealing expressly with the problem of communism should be added."[89] This exposition,[90] initially supported by 334, and

---

complete it with a chapter dedicated exclusively to Marxist ideology and its political expression, communism, accompanied with an explicit condemnation" (Ibid., pp. 203f.).

g. Also speaking at the conciliar assembly along these same lines were Msgr. S. Garcia de Sierra, Archbishop of Burgos (Spain); Msgr. G. Bolatti, Archbishop of Rosario (Argentina); Msgr. J. Pogacnik, Archbishop of Liubliana (Yugoslavia); Msgr. J. Wright, Bishop of Pittsburgh, Penn. (USA) (Ibid., pp. 204ff.). Msgr. Luigi Carli himself should also be included in his list.

[87] A. WENGER, *Chronique de la quatrième session*, pp. 156ff., 159ff., 164ff.; R. LAURENTIN, *Bilan de la quatrième session*, pp. 117, 166f.; H. FESQUET, op. cit., pp. 1012f.

[88] This International Group of Fathers was set up at the beginning of the Council on the initiative of some conservative Bishops, among them Msgrs. Luigi Carli, Marcel Lefebvre, Geraldo P. Sigaud, Antonio C. Mayer. Its goal was to disseminate and defend viewpoints of traditional Catholic doctrine. In addition to coordinating the activities of its members in the conciliar assembly, it promoted contacts with influential personalities of the Hierarchy, sponsored public lectures, issued press releases, and so on.

More information on the action of the Coetus can be found in R. WILTGEN, op. cit., pp. 148ff., 231, 235f., 240, 247ff., 274.

[89] Giovanni CAPRILE, *Il Concilio Vaticano II*, vol. V, p. 119.

later 435 conciliar Fathers,[91] was accompanied by a proposed addition to *Schema XIII*.[92]

In this circular letter, Coetus warned, "Tomorrow the Council will be blamed — and quite justly so — for its silence in regard to communism, a silence that will be taken as a sign of cowardice and connivance."[93]

On October 9, within the required deadline, the text of the amendment to *Schema XIII* and its formal preamble, with the 334 signatures gathered by Coetus supporting the proposal, were delivered to the General Secretariat of the Council by Archbishops Geraldo Sigaud and Marcel Lefebvre.

§ 92

Nevertheless, the third version of the *Schema,* distributed on November 13, again failed to make any reference to communism. There is more. In the official report presented by Msgr. Garrone, the Commission in charge of reviewing the text did not mention the amendment proposed by the 435 conciliar Fathers; it only said that "two Fathers asked that atheism be called by its proper name. But the Commission was not of this opinion."[94] This was a flagrant violation of the *Procedural Rules*, which mandated that all proposed amendments be made known to the plenary assembly, even if introduced by only one Father.[95]

Invoking papal authority to justify that refusal, Msgr. Garrone explained: "It seemed to the Commission that this manner of proceeding agrees very well both with the pastoral ordination of

---

[90] Ibid., pp. 119ff.

[91] R. WILTGEN, op. cit., p. 277.

[92] Full text in L. CARLI, *Il comunismo e il Concilio Vaticano II*, in G. SCANTAMBURLO, op. cit., pp. 217ff. It was also published by the magazine 30 DIAS, "A petição 'desaparecida,'" August-September 1989, pp. 54f.

[93] R. WILTGEN, op. cit., p. 274.

[94] *Schema constitutionis pastoralis de Ecclesia in mundo huius temporis. Textus recognitus et relationis*, Pars I (sub-secreto), Typ. Polygl. Vat. MCMLXV, p. 24, in L. CARLI, op. cit., p. 228.

[95] Ibid.

the Council and the **express will of Popes John and Paul**."[96] Soon thereafter, Fr. Caprile, of *La Civiltà Cattolica*, commented: "This part of the report contained .... an indirect but clear answer to those who proposed an explicit mention of communism; this measure, as has been insinuated, was also ruled out by the prudent and qualified advisors of a specialized Secretariat; the path chosen by the Commission was in line with the pastoral guidelines given to the Council by John XXIII and also corresponded to the wishes of Paul VI."[97]

§ 93   Conservative conciliar Fathers were left perplexed. On that same day, Msgr. Luigi Carli filed an appeal with the Council's Presidency. Voting on the *Schema* would take place on Monday the 15th. So Coetus members still had the option of re-introducing the amendment as a *modus*. However, Luigi Carli comments: "The battle was already lost. In fact, at least 700 votes would be needed to have the Commission reexamine the *Schema*; unfortunately, it was not humanly possible to collect them in an Assembly that had ignored not only the text but even the amendment about communism."[98] So the collection had to be made that very Monday at the entrance of St. Peter's Basilica. Even then, 220 conciliar Fathers introduced the *modi* to the text of the third version.

§ 94   The whole case was widely reported by the "Divine Word News Service."[99] The Italian press commented on it *per longum*

---

[96] In a footnote, Giovani Caprile reports that Cardinal Garrone had been received in an audience by Paul VI in the first weeks of November 1965. In order to lay out clearly the position of Paul VI, opposed to that of the conservative Fathers, he cites Fr. Tucci, a member of the Commission in charge of reviewing *Schema XIII*: "We have good reasons to believe that Msgr. Garrone covered this matter with the Holy Father .... This seems to be confirmed by the spoken statements added at this point of the exposition" (Roberto TUCCI, "Introduzione storico-dottrinale alla costituzione pastorale Gaudium et spes," in *La Costituzione pastorale sulla Chiesa nel mondo contemporaneo,* Turin, 1966, p. 116, note 111, in G. CAPRILE, op. cit., vol. V, p. 403).

[97] G. CAPRILE, Ibid.

[98] L. CARLI, op. cit., p. 230.

[99] "Divine Word News Service," a news agency set up in Rome by the Congregation of the Divine Word, was headed during the Council's sessions by Fr. Ralph M. Wiltgen, SVD. This Catholic agency, whose dispatches were sent to 3,000 subscribers in 97 countries (including all international news agencies), rendered a great assistance to Coetus Internationalis Patrum, reporting on its actions and disseminating its documents (which a certain media generally relegated to a secondary

et latum, making a considerable impact on Catholic public opinion.[100]

§ 95   Fr. Roberto Tucci, SJ, a *peritit* on the Revision Commission and later coordinator of John Paul II's trips,[101] said in a press conference that the amendment had not come to the knowledge of his Commission's members perhaps because it had been barred by a 'red light.' In view of the general disconcertion created by the case, Cardinal Tisserant decided to set up an inquiry to clarify irregularities. It was found that the 'red light' had been the work of Msgr. Achille Glorieux, Secretary of the Commission for Revising the Schema on the Church in the World, Secretary of the Commission for the Apostolate of the Laity, and also a holder of other Vatican posts. Although the amendment had been delivered to the General Secretariat on time, the Secretary of the Revision Commission had 'shelved it,' preventing it from reaching the hands of other Commission members[102]. There is no news of any sanction ever having been given the French churchman for this arbitrary action so beneficial to pro-communist designs.

§ 96   Fr. Häring also played a salient role in the '*veto*' of the Bishops' request: "In a recently published book-interview, German theologian Bernhard Häring, who was secretary-coordinator of the committee in charge of writing *Gaudium et spes*, recounts: 'When about two hundred bishops asked for a solemn condemnation of Communism, Monsignor Glorieux, secretary of the commission for the apostolate of the laity and of the mixed commission, and I, in particular, were accused as scapegoats. I have no reason to deny that I did everything possible to avoid this con-

---

plane or simply boycotted). When Vatican II ended, Fr. Wiltgen became famous by publishing his book, *The Rhine Flows Into the Tiber*, revealing the intimate cohesion among the prelates of the 'European alliance,' whose progressivist orientation prevailed in the Council.

[100] Fr. Wiltgen's agency contributed to that end by carrying in its bulletin unpublished news on the efforts of Coetus and the sabotage to which the conservatives were subject. Such news made front-page headlines in the Italian newspapers *Il Giornale d'Italia, Il Messaggero, Il Tempo, Il Popolo, Il Secolo, L' Avennire d'Italia*, and was published on inside pages of *Il Giorno, La Stampa, Paese Sera, Corriere della Sera*, and the Communist Party daily, *L'Unità* (R. WILTGEN, op. cit., pp. 275f.).

[101] Lucio BRUNELLI, *1994* - "Ao som de Bill e da família," in *30 Dias*, December 1993, p. 10.

[102] R. WILTGEN, op. cit., p. 276; Tommaso RICCI, "A 'distração' do Concílio," in *30 Dias*, August/September 1989, pp. 53f.

demnation, which clearly resounded as a political condemnation. I knew that John XXIII had promised the Moscow authorities that the Council would not condemn Communism in order to make possible the participation of observers from the Russian Orthodox Church."[103]

§ 97   On December 2, the definitive text was distributed to the Fathers. Its section on atheism said not even a word about communism. According to the official report, "It is not advisable to mention communism since this word includes political and economic concepts that are not dealt with here. Furthermore, strictly speaking, 'Marxism' constitutes a philosophical system that would require a long exposition. For this reason, it is better that the word not be employed."[104]

§ 98   The epilogue is that the petition for a special schema condemning communism and socialism was turned down and the proposed amendment to the Constitution *Gaudium et spes* did not even come up for consideration. Nor were the votes modifying those documents taken into account. As a "consolation prize" for defeated conservatives, a footnote was inserted in the fourth and definitive version of the Schema making a brief mention of documents by previous Pontiffs that referred to communism. Here again the forbidden word 'Communism' was not mentioned,[105] and the conservative wing was thus defeated by an action that could not but have been known and approved by Paul VI.

§ 99   A telltale sign of the effort to shackle the action by conservative Bishops that we are studying in the **3rd phase** is a letter that the Vatican Secretary of State, Cardinal Cicognani — presumably under instructions from Paul VI — sent to Msgr. Luigi Carli, coordinator of Coetus Internationalis Patrum. In it the Cardinal expressed surprise that the Bishops of Coetus share similar viewpoints in theological and pastoral matters and claims that they provoke the 'accentuation of tendencies and divisions among the conciliar Fathers.' He finishes by advising that Coetus be closed down. Here is the full text of Cardinal Cicognani's letter:

---

[103] Bernhard HÄRING, *Statement*, in T. RICCI, "O mistério do pacto Roma-Moscou," *30 Dias*, October 1989, p. 55.

[104] *Schema constitutionis pastoralis de Ecclesia in mundo huius temporis*, p. 76, in L. CARLI, op. cit., p. 234.

[105] Pastoral Constitution *Gaudium et spes*, P.I, chap. I, n. 21 (Relation of the Church with atheism), note 16, in V.A., *Documentos do Vaticano II*, p. 157.

"Most Reverend Excellency: The letter which, as the IV session of the Ecumenical Council Vatican II approached, Your Excellency, along with other conciliar Fathers, sent to the Holy Pontiff to present some requests in order to make the work of this Session more agile and fruitful, has recently come into my hands. It was my duty to refer its contents to His Holiness, who paid careful attention to the proposals suggested.

"However, I must tell Your Excellency that a certain surprise was caused by the fact that the request was presented in the name of a *Coetus Internationalis Patrum, idem in re theologica ac pastorali sententium*, that is, of a particular group in the bosom of the Council. This initiative could authorize the official appearance of other 'alliances' to the detriment of the Conciliar Assembly, something which, in fact, as Your Excellency understands, hampers the Fathers' liberty of judgment and choice that must be guaranteed above all private interest, and accentuates tendencies and divisions among the Fathers themselves whereas every measure should be taken to attenuate them in favor of serenity and concord, for the success of the Council and the honor of the Church. This initiative cannot, therefore, be approved, and it is advisable for the said *Coetus* not to function as an organ representing the positions of the Fathers affiliated with it. As for the proposed suggestions, offered with a desire for a fecund progress of the works in the coming Session, they will be examined with all diligence in view of the high goal at which they must aim.

"Upon expressing my heartfelt thanks for Your solicitude and attention, I am pleased to take advantage of this circumstance to manifest my distinctly courteous sentiments.

To Your Most Reverend Excellency
Most devoted *in Domino*, Antonio Cardinal Cicognani."[106]

*

Another pontifical interference directly aimed against the conservatives took place in regard to the discussion about collegiality in chapter III of *Lumen gentium*. Such interference also shows the difficulties encountered by the conservatives in accepting conciliar doctrine, pointed out in the **3rd phase**.

---

[106] From *Corrispondenza Romana*, Agenzia di Informazioni per la Stampa, 3/28/1990.

John XXIII was succeeded by Cardinal Montini, who had been one of the most ardent progressivist leaders in the defense of collegiality to the detriment of pontifical primacy. He went so far as to send, even as Pope, several suggestions on collegiality to the theological commission.[107]

§ 101

Nevertheless, Paul VI's direct interference to disarm conservatives did not stop at this.

On the day following the opening of the Third Session, Msgr. Dino Staffa, then secretary of the Congregation for Seminaries and Universities, asked to speak to the Assembly before the vote on the subject was taken. His request was based on the *Procedural Rules*[108] and was further supported by the signatures of 70 conciliar Fathers who thought as he did. His request was turned down by the Council's Presidency, and the subcommittee in charge of reviewing the text on collegiality ignored his objections.

Msgr. Staffa wrote the Pope a long letter dated November 7, 1964, expressing his problem of conscience with accepting collegiality, which was opposed to the traditional teaching of the Church. He said that he felt obliged to vote against it. He added that the action of the Moderators (whom the Pontiff had personally chosen as his representatives and vested with full authority) forbidding him to speak had been illegal.

Paul VI asked for an investigation to examine the votes of Procedure and forwarded Msgr. Staffa's observations of a theological nature to the Theological Commission. Msgr. Staffa was not given the opportunity to speak.[109]

§ 102

Also corroborating the **3rd phase**, 35 Cardinals and five superiors of large religious orders wrote the Pope saying that the text on collegiality was ambiguous and that, after the Council, it would certainly be interpreted according to the tenets of the extreme progressivist current.

Paul VI wrote Cardinal Arcadio Larraona, whose name Fr. Wiltgen does not mention in his chronicle, criticizing the arguments that had been presented. The Cardinal went to talk to Paul

---

[107] R. WILTGEN, op. cit., p. 230.

[108] a. 57, sec. 6, *Procedural Rules*.

[109] R. WILTGEN, op. cit., pp. 230f.

VI in the name of the group to explain their suspicions. Paul VI did nothing.[110]

The Cardinal also suggested that a debate involving theologians be held in the presence of the Pope. Paul VI did not accept this suggestion.

It was at that point that a progressivist representative boasted, in writing, of the ambiguity of the texts on collegiality and indicated how his partisans would interpret it after the Council. This document came to the knowledge of the wary group of Cardinals and religious superiors. Thus, faced with a clear progressivist admission of how they would take advantage of this ambiguity, the Cardinal, who represented these 34 prelates and the five superior generals, went again for an interview with Paul VI.

It was only then that, as a consequence of an imprudence by a progressivist hothead, Paul VI ordered the famous *Preliminary Explanatory Note* to be written. Even so, he did not want it incorporated into the text of the document.[111]

103

We conclude our comments on this **3rd phase** with the words of Henri Fesquet on the confrontation between progressivists and conservatives and the tenacious papal action opposed to the latter. He gives his opinion at the beginning of the fourth session: "Conciliar mechanics — as is normal after functioning for four years — has come a long way. The [progressivist] majority has become aware of its youthful energy, formerly unimagined. It learned to avoid clashes with the minority. It discovered less onerous methods to gain ground. For its part, the minority became aware of its true limitations. Facing harsh realities, it learned how to draw consequences from its failures. It has less of a pretention of being the custodian of orthodoxy after having perceived that the two last popes, though remaining above the fray, not only failed automatically to support it, but also untiringly incited it to carry out its own *aggiornamento*."[112]

*

---

[110] Ibid., pp. 231f. As for the Cardinal's name, Andrea TORNIELLI, "O timoneiro do Concílio," in *30 Dias*, July 1992, p. 38.

[111] R. WILTGEN, op. cit., pp. 231ff.; see this Volume, Chap. VI, 4.A.f.

[112] H. FESQUET, op. cit., pp. 860f.

§ 104

Perhaps it would not be superfluous to point out the final defeat of conservatives, who, led by Cardinal Ottaviani, head of the Holy Office at the time, made their *ralliement* with progressivism by signing the documents they had opposed.

§ 105

Indeed, as rumors circulated about the imminent reform of the Holy Office, Cardinal Ottaviani gave an interview in which he said: "I am the soldier who watches over the gold reserve. Do you think I would fulfill my duty by arguing, abandoning my post, turning a blind eye? My son, seventy-five years are seventy-five years! I lived them defending certain principles and certain laws. If you tell the old soldier that the laws are going to change, it is obvious that .... he will do everything so they will not change. But, if they nonetheless change, God will certainly give him the strength to place himself in the defense of a new treasure in which he believes. Once the new laws become the treasure of the Church, an enrichment of the gold reserve, no more than one principle counts: to serve the Church. And this service means to be faithful to her laws."[113]

In addition to Cardinal Ottaviani, another lamentable example of *ralliement* was made by Cardinal Pietro Parente, another exponent of the Holy Office and a model of "conservatism." Referring to his action in the Council, he says: "Inspired by God, John XXIII carried out Vatican Council II, which suffers from the crisis [of the *nouvelle théologie*] but is able to contain it. I actively participated in this magnificent 'ecumenical assembly' and remember two interventions of mine: on collegiality and on Mary's mediation. I strongly fought in favor of the former .... Some people were surprised at my stand because of my position as an aide to the Holy Office. But collegiality was approved unanimously: only five no's out of 2,156 Fathers! The rumor spread that I was the cause."[114]

§ 106

Regarding the general defection of the conservative conciliar Fathers, the journalist of *Le Monde* comments: "Attached to a past that has just died, despising the present world whose grandeurs and advantages the last two popes have striven to make them see, the opposition Fathers (from fifty to three-hundred?) finally adhered, not without grandeur of soul [sic!], to the sche-

---

[113] Alfredo OTTAVIANI, interview with *Corriere della Sera*, 10/28/1965, in H. FESQUET, op. cit., p. 1019.

[114] Pietro PARENTE, "Cristo, Maria, la Chiesa: i punti nevralgici della mia ricerca teologica," interview with Gino CONCETTI, in *L'Osservatore Romano*, 12/19/1985.

mata that prickle their sensibilities and transform their mental habits."[115]

§ 107   It is no wonder that the post-conciliar conservative opposition was profoundly affected by such attitudes hardly compatible with Catholic heroism.

4th phase   * **Once Vatican II is over and victory clearly won by the progressivists, they gradually begin to say that the Council was not only pastoral, but also dogmatic.**

             * **Their tendency is to accentuate the doctrinal aspect of the victories obtained.**

§ 108   These words by Paul VI, a few months after the end of Vatican II, are characteristic of this **4th phase**: "There are those who ask what authority, what theological qualification the Council intended to give to its teachings, knowing that it avoided issuing solemn dogmatic definitions engaging the infallibility of the ecclesiastical magisterium. The answer is known by whoever remembers the conciliar declaration of March 6, 1964, repeated on November 16, 1964: given the Council's pastoral character, it avoided pronouncing, in an extraordinary manner, dogmas endowed with the note of infallibility. However, **it gave its teachings the authority of the supreme ordinary magisterium, which, [being] the ordinary magisterium and, thereby, manifestly authentic, must be docilely and sincerely accepted by all the faithful according to the Council's intention with respect to the nature and ends of each of the documents.**"[116]

109   In 1966, Fr. Umberto Betti, OFM, professor of Fundamental Theology at Rome's Antonianum, wrote about Vatican II, confirming what has been said about this **4th phase**: "**Even if its infallibility and,** consequently, **its irreformability were not explicitly declared, one must not, thereby, think it does not exist. Indeed, just as an infallible definition always expresses the conviction of the universal Church, so also the conviction**

---

[115] H. FESQUET, op. cit., p. 1033.

[116] PAUL VI, General Audience of January 12, 1966, in *Insegnamenti di Paolo VI*, vol. IV, p. 700.

of the universal Church indicates the doctrine that is its infallible object."[117]

§ 110   The statements by Fr. Karl Rahner, two years after the end
of the Council (1967), confirm the **4th phase:** "*What form* must
the Church give today to this legitimate influence in face of a
secular world? .... How must the Church herself be presented in
her concrete structure and in the mentality of her members if she,
in fact, wants to exercise an influence such as this on secular society? To begin to answer the first question, it would be advisable
first of all to reflect a little on a distinctive trait of certain encyclicals of John XXIII (*Mater et Magistra, Pacem in terris*), of Paul
VI's encyclical *Populorum progressio,* and especially of the
pastoral constitution *Gaudium et spes* of Vatican II. What is characteristic of these documents?

"**They contain**, to be sure, **a good number of fundamental, theoretical, and ever valid 'doctrinal' truths (with good
reason, it must be said, and necessarily)**, but the salient point of
these texts, **what in them is stimulating and 'shocking' for the
pure theoretician**, rests in their intention, which can be described first of all (in the terminology of Vatican II) as 'pastoral.'
Nevertheless, **one would underestimate and misconstrue this
'pastoral' element in its essence by understanding it as a series of purely practical consequences** whose certain and com-
pelling deduction from general principles the merest glance at the
actual situation of the world would suffice to bring about. **The
intent of these documents is clearly present in 'imperatives,'
in emphases**, in an historical program that calls the world to decision."[118]

§ 111   Even though this item is not intended to analyze the doctrine underlying the notion of 'pastoral,'[119] it would be well to
point out in passing that behind the Council's pastoral approach,
often presented merely as an overflowing of its mercy for the
world, is a doctrinal background.

§ 112   The following remarks by Fr. Chenu also confirm the
characteristics of the **4th phase**, as they began to stress the Coun-

---

[117] Umberto BETTI, "Qualification théologique de la Constitution," in
V.A., *L'Eglise de Vatican II*, vol. II, p. 217.

[118] Karl RAHNER, "Theological Reflections on the Problem of Secularization," in V.A., *Theology of Renewal*, vol. I, pp. 179f.

[119] Chap. VII.

cil's doctrinal character: "**The *demarche* by the Council has been very significant. This Council, while retaining the two words [pastoral and dogmatic], prepared** .... **a double constitution, one said to be 'dogmatic,' and the other 'pastoral,'** but both of them true 'constitutions' **without, however, effecting a formal dogmatization.** A preliminary explanatory note to the constitution *Gaudium et spes* would later clarify the ambiguity that still remained in people's minds and express in an excellent fashion the organizational unity that commanded the proceedings. **But in the beginning and during the writing of *Gaudium et spes*, with all its vicissitudes, a certain indetermination would still persist even in regard to the objective of the Council.**"[120]

13   Also supporting the **4th phase** is a statement by Msgr. Clemente Riva, then Auxiliary Bishop of Rome and commentator of the document on religious liberty, along with Cardinal Jean-Jérôme Hamer, later Prefect of the Congregation for Religious: "First of all, **we cannot fail to recognize the *doctrinal* importance the Declaration [*Dignitatis humanae*] takes on in the progress of Catholic doctrine.** The problem of freedom of conscience and religious liberty, coupled with the duty of the apostolate and evangelization, offers a very broad visualization to the thinking and action of Christians. .... **Applying this theological consideration, not only to the truth's idealistic-objective values but also to real-personal values, cannot fail to give theological doctrine itself a vaster panorama and a possibility for greater depth.** .... **This conciliar document** .... also **represents a stimulus and a basis for deepening a doctrine open to immense theological, juridical**, sociological and practical developments."[121]

14   This excerpt by Msgr. Philips also corroborates the **4th phase** of the hypothesis raised above at the beginning of Section B: "For certain one can loyally recognize that the Council did not proclaim any new thesis as *de fide definita*. But **to state that the Fathers limited themselves to giving practical guidelines and taking merely disciplinary measures is to wish to deny the brightness of the sun** .... Fr. Semmelroth touches the crux of the matter when he writes that **the Council, even though it did not promulgate definitions of faith strictly speaking, did resolve various more or less disputed questions. Although these 'deci-**

---

[120] *Jacques Duquesne interroge le Père Chenu*, pp. 175f.

[121] Jérôme HAMER - Clemente RIVA, *La libertà religiosa nel Vaticano II* (Turin: Elle Di Ci, 1967), pp. 260, 262.

sions' are valid, the magisterium that published them did not
want to say the last word since the Fathers were quite conscious of the progressive nature of the knowledge of truth that
the People of God acquire along their pilgrimage. This explains the dynamic character the Council deliberately imparted on its sentences.** It is not advisable to burn the stages [by
moving too fast]; but, on the other hand, it is not worthwhile to
convene an ecumenical Council only to tread once again an already beaten path."[122]

§ 115   The remarks of Fernand Dumont, professor of Sociological Theology at Laval University, Canada, on the new conception
of Pastoral Theology and its opposition to Dogmatic Theology,
also apply to progressivist longings about Vatican II and confirm
this **4th phase**: "In a Church that wishes to be both missionary
and concerned with her own reform, **it was inevitable that in
recent decades there should have been great activity in pastoral theology. It is considered less and less as a heteroclite
ensemble of practices and prescriptions on the fringe of the
main body of doctrine and has become, progressively, a comprehensive vision of the Church in its project of perpetual
edification. One can** even **think**, as we have suggested elsewhere, [123]* **that .... pastoral theology is soon going to question
the most profound bases of systematic theology. .... If pastoral
theology and theological anthropology continue to develop
along the lines indicated thus far**, it is unlikely that they will
limit themselves to adding new tracts to the *corpus* of theology.
**They will suggest new, comprehensive perspectives to all of
theology**, an as yet badly defined opening to the concrete historical situation of man."[124]

§ 116   Fr. Raymond Schwager, SJ, in a dialogue with the Author
of these lines, expressed his opinion about the dogmatic character
of Vatican II in this way: "It is a manner of interpreting the
Council to say: 'All this is solely pastoral.' In the end, **the document on the Church, *Lumen gentium*, is not a pastoral document but a very dogmatic document. There are people who
wish to diminish the scope of this document by saying that it**

---

[122] G. PHILIPS, op. cit., p. 603.

[123]* Fernand DUMONT, *Pour la conversion de la pensée chrétienne*,
1964, pp. 205ff.

[124] F. DUMONT, "The Sociology of Religion and the Renewal of Theology," in V.A., *Theology of Renewal*, vol. II, pp. 271f.

is only pastoral, but this is already a strategy. It is a strategy to reduce the document's scope."[125]

§ 117   The year 1988 saw the publication of an important collection about the Council, *Vatican II: Bilan et perspectives, vingt-cinq ans après (1962-1987)*. It came out under the auspices of Rome's Gregorian University, Biblical Institute and Eastern Institute and under the direction of Fr. René Latourelle, SJ. In the *Introduction* to the three-volume work, Fr. Latourelle makes an apology of Vatican II. His exposition, which compares Vatican II to other milestone councils outstanding for their dogmatic importance, is useful to show the growing doctrinal role being attributed to Vatican II. Thus confirming the **4th phase,** Latourelle says: "**Vatican II is undoubtedly the most vast operation of reform ever undertaken in the Church,** not only on account of the number of conciliar Fathers .... but **above all because of the breadth of the topics covered: revelation, the Church** (its nature, constitution, members, pastoral and missionary activity), **the liturgy, the sacraments,** the other Christian communities and the other religions, the laity, religious life, the reform of ecclesiastical studies, **religious liberty, relations between faith and culture,** the means of social communication.

Vatican II represents an Event of a *unique originality.* For the most part, the previous Councils were provoked by heresies or particular, that is, regional, deviations. Even the Council of Trent evolved within clearly limited doctrinal borders: the relation between the Scripture and Traditions, original sin, justification, the sacraments. **In Vatican II, you have an operation that affects the universal Church at all levels and under all aspects** .... In 1987 twenty-five years will have gone by since the beginning of the Council (1962). The Church has gone .... from a past which still has not disappeared to a future that is only beginning. **The Council of Trent gave its name to a 400-year period. Now, Vatican II marks a much more profound change. .... Vatican II is a planetary and simultaneous event,** but one must not forget that it is also a *great sign* in history."[126]

---

[125] Raymond SCHWAGER, interview granted to the Author, Innsbruck, February 11, 1983.

[126] René LATOURELLE, Introduction, in V.A., *Vatican II - Bilan et perspectives,* vol. I, pp. 7f.

About the doctrinal content of the texts, Latourelle notes: "**The texts are presented** not as dogmatic definitions, but **as broad doctrinal expositions** with a pastoral visualization."[127]

§ *118*

And Msgr. Philippe Delhaye, confirming the **4th phase**, categorically declares: Our research "is sufficient to show that, **on a certain number of doctrinal points, Vatican II wanted to bear witness to the faith of the Church with authority. Such authority is, more explicitly than in the past, based on fidelity to revelation, continuity of the magisterium**, but also on the consciousness of being able to express itself on points that complement the knowledge of the mystery of Christ and of the Church. **To speak only about points of doctrine that have never been established, let us cite, for example, the sacramentality of the episcopate, and the collegial character of the authority of bishops** gathered around the pope. **These texts of Vatican II certainly oblige as much as the constitutions of Vatican I**, which at times they imitate."[128]

§ *119*

Perhaps one of the most categorical confirmations that the Vatican strives to present the Council as dogmatic comes from Cardinal Willebrands, then President of the Secretariat for the Union of Christians, in a speech to the Jews about authority in the Declaration *Nostra aetate*. In the excerpt below, the Cardinal appears to defend the infallibility of this conciliar document by saying it was supported by the assistance of the Holy Spirit. His words are important inasmuch as they reflect an intention to present Vatican II under a light different from the initial, preponderantly 'pastoral,' one. As such, they indirectly confirm the **4th phase**.

"If the Jews," says Willebrands, "over the last years have come to better appreciate the novelty and **the** practically **unique character of the text of *Nostra aetate*, we Catholics have realized** better **how it is** really **in accordance** with a more profound layer of our tradition and even **with the Word of God in the two Testaments. It could not have been otherwise, since this would be approved by an Ecumenical Council. The conciliar documents**, I am sure that you all know this, in traditional Catholic teaching **are considered as having** ultimately **issued from the Holy Spirit, who assists, illuminates and,** if necessary, **corrects the human process of reflection and decision-**

---

[127] Ibid., p. 17.

[128] Philippe DELHAYE, "Vatican II: Autorité des textes conciliaires," in DTC, Tables, vol. III, col. 4335.

making. **Therefore, if God is behind the text of** *Nostra aetate* **and also behind** *Lumen gentium* **(n. 16) .... then the new relations with Judaism are not a matter of practical [pastoral] decision,** however noble and great the alleged reasons may be. **It is for us, as Catholics, a question of fidelity to our own vocation, one part of our response to God."**[129]

5th phase   * **The conservatives, on the contrary, once Vatican II is over, begin to stress its pastoral aspect.**

             * **Their apology seeks to demonstrate that, since the Council was pastoral, it does not require obedience like dogmatic ones.**

120

     Fr. Congar corroborates the **5th phase** as he castigates the 'unacceptable attitude' of those who, by regarding the Council merely as 'pastoral,' deem themselves not obliged to follow its teaching:[130] **"Vatican II was doctrinal. The fact that it did not 'define' new dogmas takes nothing from its doctrinal value,** according to the qualifications classic theology gives in various degrees to the documents that it promulgated. "Some are 'dogmatic,' expressing common doctrine. They would be comparable to the great doctrinal encyclicals .... Such is the case of *Lumen gentium*, of the doctrinal parts of *Dei Verbum*, of the Constitution on the liturgy and *Gaudium et spes*, but also of various 'decrees' and the declaration *Dignitatis humanae personae*.

"Other texts or parts of these same documents are of a purely 'pastoral' nature, that is, they provide practical guidelines in accordance with the supernatural prudence of the shepherds gathered in the Council. .... In these parts of a 'pastoral' character of the conciliar teaching, based more or less directly on Revelation, there is a content that goes beyond the development of the deposit of faith as such, which does not come from a pure deduction of the articles in that deposit. It is what the Body of Shepherds, gathered in prayer and reflection, dares to say about historical situations which traditional Faith must clarify beyond its classically acquired propositions .... **It is, we believe, precisely this aspect of openness, of induction, of guidelines given ac-**

---

[129] Jan WILLEBRANDS, "Allocution au Comité International de liaison du dialogue judéo-chrétien," in *La Documentation Catholique* (Paris), *Bilan du dialogue judéo-chrétien*, 1/19/1986, p. 122.

[130] Congar's document also confirms that **4th phase** we have just analyzed.

cording to the circumstances, that certain spirits refuse. Since then, these men have said: this Council was nothing but 'pastoral,' and did not intend to be anything but that. Therefore, it does not oblige, it remains debatable and free [to be obeyed or not]. This is an unacceptable attitude: what we have just said shows it well."[131]

§ 121 Msgr. Marcel Lefebvre shows a sense of irony as he defends the pastoral character of the Council in opposition to the 'dogmatism' of 'liberal' theologians who want to impose acceptance of Vatican II: "I believe you have noticed in Maritain, Yves Congar and their likes, the perversity of historic-doctrinal relativism. We are dealing with people who have no notion of the truth, no idea of what an immutable truth may be. It is strange to learn that **these same relativist liberals, who were the real authors of Vatican II, now end up by dogmatizing this Council which,** nevertheless, **they used to call pastoral, and by seeking to impose conciliar novelties upon us as definitive and untouchable doctrines.**"[132]

§ 122 The first successor to Msgr. Lefebvre, Fr. Schmidberger, emphasizes the pastoral aspect of the Council: "**Council Vatican II is not a super dogma, but, by the manifest will of two conciliar popes, John XXIII and Paul VI, is a simple pastoral council** that expressly renounced condemnations and new definitions. This is a completely new fact in the history of the Church. **For this reason, it is not the Council that guarantees infallibility**, but the conformity of each of its texts with the doctrine of the Church."[133]

§ 123 Lay author Anne Roche Muggeridge also corroborates the **5th phase** as she alludes to the conservative position while referring to the progressivist maneuver we describe here: "Only two of the documents of Vatican II, the Dogmatic Constitution on the Church, *Lumen gentium*, and Divine Revelation, *Dei Verbum*, were termed 'dogmatic.' The others were described as 'pastoral,' a distinction upon which both radicals and conservatives seized, the radicals 'in order to obtain the passage of certain formulations with a modern tendency,' as Edward Schillebeeckx, a leading

---

[131] Y. CONGAR, *Le Concile de Vatican II*, pp. 64f.

[132] M. LEFEBVRE, *Ils l'ont découronné - Du libéralisme à l'apostasie - La tragédie conciliare* (Escurolles: Fideliter, 1987), p. 136.

[133] Franz SCHMIDBERGER, "Mas eu respondo a König," interview to Stefano PACCI, in *30 Dias*, November 1992, p. 60.

radical theologian at the Council, admits; **the conservatives to discredit these new departures as 'merely pastoral,' not having the force of doctrine.** 'This gap between *doctrinal* and *pastoral*, which was used as a pawn, will continue to have a bearing on the interpretation of the council and is, in my opinion, one of the most important shadows cast on the council debates ....'[134]* Schillebeeckx is right. The double voice of the Council has been a major cause of post-Conciliar confusion in the Church."[135]

124   Bishop Rudolf Graber, a typical leader of the 'conciliar right,' says that the keynote of conciliar documents is pastoral, even though he admits to an 'opalescent ambivalence' in the goal of the topics covered: "It is still early to formulate a definitive judgment of the Council. But the terrible thing is that events as grand as this one touch several levels and develop on different planes. The texts certainly are entirely orthodox [sic], and some passages are formulated in a classic fashion. It will be our task, for a long time, to struggle with the Council's words in order to prevent it from being distorted, especially by the famous 'spirit' of the Council. However, **since the Council aimed, above all, at a pastoral orientation and, therefore, stopped short of promulgating dogmatically definitive sentences and from dissociating itself from errors and false doctrines by issuing clear anathemas, many questions have taken on an opalescent ambivalence, which has given a certain credence to those who speak about the spirit of the Council.** Furthermore, as we have seen, a series of concepts arose, such as collegiality, ecumenism, religious liberty, which may undoubtedly have been well-founded but have also had a boomerang effect."[136]

6th phase   * **In the post-conciliar period, when the possibility of a conservative reaction arises, the Vatican leadership uses its power and prestige to try to destroy the reaction by alleging that the Council was dogmatic.**

125   Substantiating the 6th phase is the categorical statement by Paul VI in a letter to Msgr. Lefebvre on June 29, 1975, that

---

[134]* E. SCHILLEBEECKX, *The Real Achievement of Vatican II* (New York: Herder and Herder, 1967), pp. 84f.

[135] A. R. MUGGERIDGE, *The Desolate City - Revolution in the Catholic Church* (San Francisco: Harper & Row, 1990), p. 56.

[136] R. GRABER, *Athanasius und die Kirche unserer Zeit*, pp. 70f.

Vatican Council II "is no less authoritative, and under certain aspects is even more important, than that of Nicea."[137]

§ 126   John Paul II speaks out in the same vein: **"We nourish the profound conviction that the Spirit of truth that speaks to the Church** (Apc 2:7; 11; 17 et allii) **spoke in a particularly solemn and authoritative way through Vatican Council II**, preparing the Church to enter the third millennium after Christ."[138]

§ 127   Cardinal Ratzinger, speaking about conservative criticisms of the doctrine of collegiality, also establishes that **"Vatican II is sustained by the same authority as Vatican I and Trent** .... From the standpoint of contents we recall that Vatican II places itself in strict continuity with the two preceding Councils and literally repeats them on decisive points."[139]

§ 128   An indirect but cogent argument confirming the 6th phase is provided by the two documents that lay down the conditions for granting the right to celebrate Mass according to the 1962 missal.

To be sure, it is an indirect argument, for the two official documents do not refer to the doctrinal force of the Council, but to the doctrinal force of the liturgical reform of 1970. However, it is notorious that such reform started mainly with the Constitution *Sacrosanctum Concilium* of Vatican II. While dealing with various aspects of liturgy in the Church, the Constitution's most important point is found in chapter II, when it establishes general norms for reforming the Ordinary of the Mass.[140] The modification of the *Ordo Missae*, which was the nucleus of Paul VI's liturgical reform, was nothing but a development and application of the norms of *Sacrosanctum Concilium*. Therefore, what is said

---

[137] PAUL VI, Letter to Msgr. Lefebvre, June 29, 1975, in Anton HOLZER, *Vatikanum II - Reformkonzil oder Konstituante einer neuen Kirche* (Basel: Sala, 1977), p. 58.

[138] JOHN PAUL II, "Letter to Cardinal Joseph Ratzinger About the Possibility of Accord With Msgr. Lefebvre," published under the title, "Lettera di Giovanni Paolo II al Cardinale Joseph Ratzinger," in *L'Osservatore Romano*, Italian edition, 4/9/1988, pp. 1, 5.

[139] J. RATZINGER, *Rapporto sulla Fede*, p. 26.

[140] SC 47-58. About the reform of the *Ordo Missae*, see Chap. IX.1.A.

about the 'doctrinal force' of the liturgical reform obviously applies to the conciliar Constitution that was its 'seed.'[141]

§ 129   The first document that permits the celebration of the Mass according to the Roman Missal of 1962 is a letter sent by the Congregation for Divine Worship to the presidents of the Bishops Conferences dated October 3, 1984 and signed respectively by Cardinal Paul Augustin Mayer, Pro-Prefect, and the Archbishop, now Cardinal, Virgilio Noè, Secretary.

As for the question of those who remain 'attached to the so-called Tridentine rite,' the document rules: "The Supreme Pontiff, wishing to be generous toward these groups, grants diocesan Bishops the faculty of using the Indult, whereby the priests and faithful who are explicitly mentioned in a petition to be presented to their Bishop may celebrate the Mass using the Roman Missal according to the edition typical of 1962, on condition that the following norms be observed: a) **That it be known publicly and without ambiguity that the said priest and faithful have nothing to do with those who cast doubt on the le-**

---

[141] a. Commenting on the approval of the Constitution *Sacrosanctum Concilium* during the second conciliar session, Fr. René LAURENTIN says: "The liturgical Constitution is part of a dynamic balance. Indeed, **it is** not a dead letter, but **a seed of reform**" (*Bilan de la deuxième session*, p. 244). Further on, he continues: **"The Constitution does not propose** new rubrics, but a doctrine, a spirit, and **a program of reforms spread out over a long term.** First stage: Missal, ritual of the sacraments and sacramentals, divine office (breviary), liturgical year all reviewed in Rome by post-conciliar commissions. Second stage: once implemented, these reforms will be applied in different parts of the Catholic world by bishops' conferences, which will add the necessary adaptations according to countries, climates, languages, mentalities, etc. .... The reforms should start 'as early as possible.' But they will not reach their term for some years" (Ibid., pp. 245f.; pp. 247-260).

b. This statement also confirms our opinion: "The extraordinary synod in homage to Vatican II, **the synod of 1985 .... also speaks of liturgical renewal as 'the most apparent fruit of the whole conciliar work'** (*Relatio finalis*, II.B.b; *Enchiridion Vaticanum* 9/1798," in Giuseppe DOSSETTI, "Vaticano II: Quale recezione," in *Il Regno*, 12/1/1991, p. 696).

c. The Holy See published (March 29, 1994) the *IV Instruction for a Correct Application of the Conciliar Constitution on the Sacred Liturgy*, whose title shows that to this day the *Sacrosanctum Concilium* continues to be the central document of the whole post-conciliar reform (G. MOCELLIN, "IV Istruzione Liturgica - 30 anni dopo pensando all'Africa," in *Il Regno*, 4/15/1994, p. 204).

gitimate doctrinal force, and correction of, the Roman Missal promulgated in 1970 by the Roman Pontiff Paul VI...[142]

The document is quite clear. Only those who accept the doctrinal principles contained in the liturgical reform of Paul VI, that is, the principles of the Constitution *Sacrosanctum Concilium* and their applications, are to benefit from the 'indult.'

Later, finding that this 'indult' was still too restrictive by virtue of the disciplinary conditions set in sections b-e of the document, which we have not transcribed, a commission of Cardinals proposed a more generous application of the 'indult,' on the sole condition that the doctrinal validity of the new liturgy be accepted. Cardinal Mayer narrates the fact: "The bishops often took into account only the first indult of October 3, 1984, which established very restrictive conditions for the celebration of Mass according to the old rite. **A commission of cardinals** assembled in December 1986 **examined this indult and found that its conditions were very restrictive. It** then **proposed that they be relaxed, keeping the recognition of the juridical and doctrinal validity of the new liturgy as the only necessary condition for someone wishing to benefit from the indult**. The *motu proprio* of July 2, 1988 adopted these suggestions, asking the bishops to be generous in the application of the indult."[143]

§ *130*

The second official document on the matter is the apostolic Letter *Ecclesia Dei*, to which Cardinal Mayer referred above. In it, as a matter of fact, John Paul II recommends this: "The will of those who feel linked to Latin liturgical tradition should be respected everywhere by means of an ample and generous application of the directives issued by the Holy See some time ago for the use of the Roman Missal according to the typical edition of 1962."[144]

The requirement remains, therefore, of accepting the 'doctrinal force' of the liturgical reform, that is, of the Constitution *Sacrosanctum Concilium* and of Vatican II.

---

[142] Congregation for Divine Worship, "Epistula - De usu Missalis Romani iuxta editionem typicam anni MCMLXII," of October 3, 1984, in *Acta Apostolicae Sedis,* Ed. Typis Polyglottis Vaticanis, vol. LXXVI, 12/1/1984, pp. 1088f.

[143] Paul Augustin MAYER, "Cardeal anti-cisma," interview to Stefano M. PACI, in *30 Dias*, June 1991, p. 60.

[144] JOHN PAUL II, Apostolic Letter *Ecclesia Dei*, July 2, 1988, in *Insegnamenti di Giovanni Paolo II*, vol. XI/3, p. 12.

7th phase   * **When, in the post-conciliar era, the progressivists have problems with their grassroots who complain about Vatican II's ambiguity, the leadership call to mind the dogmatic victories in the Council and stress the need for making them more explicit in the future.**

§ 131   Another text by the forecited author, Nicola Colaianni, corroborates what we define as the **7th phase**: "As the demand for new institutions intensified and gained urgency .... the Council appeared .... 'generic and vague' (Basset), 'with omissions and ambiguous points' (Walf), to such an extent that **in the most recent international congresses, questions were raised on whether Vatican II was still of current interest.** And even though **the timeliness of a new council, a Vatican III**[145]* **was not envisaged, it became evident that on account of the ambiguity of the conciliar texts,** when taken separately, '**the ecclesiology of Vatican II can still can be a project of current interest for the Church so long as it is estimated,** in its main lines, according to a global reading .... **and offers perspectives of development**'[146]*,"[147].

132   In order to close this topic on the pastoral and dogmatic natures of the Council, let us consider this excerpt by Cardinal Suenens that substantiates the **7th phase**: "**The invitation now is to locate Vatican II in the context of the future. For the Church is a Church that is on her way, a pilgrim Church; she never has the right to come to a full stop, and her pauses are only in preparation for new stages on her journey.** In some respects, **the Church is always 'transient.'** 'They call me a transition Pope,' John XXIII used to like to say. He added: 'It's true, but the continuity of the Church is made up of transition after transition.' **Whether we wish it or not, we are now on the way towards some Vatican III**, whose outlines are still vague and indiscernible. **This Vatican III must,** in its turn, **draw out what Vatican II contained only in germ; it must unfold what is now only potential, and make explicit its riches for the future. .... We must live the experience of Vatican II in that perspective,**

---

[145]* Congress of Notre Dame, 1977.

[146]* Congress of Bologna, 1980.

[147] N. COLAIANI, "Crítica ao Vaticano II na literatura atual," in *Concilium*, 1983/7, p. 126.

which will lead us from the present stage to the next one, from the 'already' to the 'not yet.'"[148]

Cardinal Suenens' references to the 'Pilgrim Church,' to a certain evolutionary view of the Church and to the theory of the 'already but not yet' should be kept in mind for the next Chapter.

*

§ 133   As we end this presentation of the proofs that substantiate the chronological-strategic concatenation of phases in the various usages of the Council's theological qualification, it is quite difficult not to conclude that as a whole it favors the progressivist current. In view of this fact, it is possible to conjecture that it was premeditated and executed following a certain methodology, and therefore, that it was a strategic maneuver.

*

§ 134   Was Vatican Council II pastoral? Was it dogmatic? We have seen that in the order of events it was simultaneously dogmatic and pastoral. However, the progressivists would rather have clouds of ambiguity hovering over the theological qualification of the Council. That enables them to confound possible reactions and to avoid comparisons between their doctrine and the constant and universal teaching of the ecclesiastical Magisterium.

*   *   *

---

[148] L. J. SUENENS, "Co-responsibility: Dominating Idea of the Council and its Pastoral Consequences," in V.A., *Theology of Renewal*, vol. II, p. 9.

CHAPTER VII

IS THERE A DOCTRINE
UNDERLYING THE AMBIGUITY?

§ 1   One becomes perplexed in the face of so many statements by renowned authors about the ambiguity of the Council and so many facts proving that it was indeed utilized to favor progressivism.

Would there be, in addition to the strategic reasons already presented, a more profound explanation for such a lack of precision in conciliar language?

Would there be a new doctrine that justified the introduction of this ambiguity so alien to the habits of the ecclesiastical Magisterium?

This Chapter is not intended to present a definitive answer to such questions. We attempt to do that in another place in this Collection.[1] Nevertheless, as one considers the texts below by famous authors, a certain consistency already begins to show in this confused picture.

1. A Hesitating Theology Is Supposedly Normal

§ 2   The text below by Fr. Karl Rahner gives rise to the idea that an insecure theology, subject to errors and pluralistic in its expressions, would be a normal thing: "**Present-day theology** (based on exegesis, philosophy, contemporary spiritual life) **is faced with such a large number of problems,** has such a variety

---

[1] Vol. VI, *Inveniet Fidem?*, Chaps. II, III.5, IV.2, 3; Vol. VII, *Destructio Dei*, Chaps. II.2, 3.B, III.3, IV.2.C; Vol. VII, *Fumus Satanae*, passim; Vol. IX, *Creatio*, Chaps. I, II, III, V; Vol. X, *Peccatum-Redemptio*, Chaps. V, VII, IX.

of instruments and conceptual enunciations at its disposal, **and is conscious of the ambiguity of all statements to such a point that it is no longer as easy as it used to be to oppose a real** or supposed **error with a new, positive statement immune from all confusion** and that gives all honest scholars the impression that it not only says something exact but also satisfies their own requisites. **This situation must be considered dispassionately** and clarified, for only thus can one search for a more just and efficacious behavior for the Church and her magisterium."[2]

§ 3
Not satisfied with putting forward such surprising principles, Rahner goes so far as to conclude, no less disconcertingly, that one can legitimately disagree with the centuries-old teaching of the Church: "**The situation is one of a pluralism of methods,**" he continues, "**of a scientific theological terminology, of the vastness of the theological question in face of which a theologian** on his own **can no longer be a specialist in an adequate way.** Because of this, **the theses of theologians are no longer a simple and clear yes or no to a doctrine presented in the traditional manner, formulated in an established way, but are often laid down in singular disagreement with traditional doctrine.**"[3]

§ 4
Rahner goes on to frontally combat the clarity of the theological teaching before the Council, which he brands as 'planned monolithism.' He then tries to pretend that he is opposed to excesses in theological pluralism. Nevertheless, he fails to clearly define the limits supposedly setting apart his position — which he considers to be that of Vatican II — from the excesses he seems to oppose. In his clear combat against clarity and his confused distinction about confusion, the notion prevails that theology should be always ambiguous and hesitating. Here is the text:

"**Today,** above all, **it is not the case of** simply saying the old truth, defending it in an authoritarian manner and **saying no to deviations.** It is necessary to defend this truth in such a way that it will have an effect and be accepted as true in good will and based on reality itself. To do that, it is not sufficient to appeal to the formal juridical authority of the pope and the bishops — regardless of whether this is done correctly from the formal doctrinal standpoint. Whether we like it or not, **we find ourselves in**

---

[2] Karl RAHNER, *Magistero e teologia dopo il Concilio* (Brescia: Queriniana, 1967), p. 32.

[3] Ibid., pp. 32s.

need of finding an intermediate path between a 'planned monolithism,' which made everything clear and where everything of importance could be easily and, above all, swiftly decided with clarity, even decided upon by some form of papal declaration (encyclical, papal speech, statement by the Holy Office, etc.), and a disconcerting confusion in which theologians and laity believe they may think and say anything they please in matters of faith.

"The first route .... is no longer possible. It is clear that Vatican II preferred another method: it was prudent and reserved in its dogmatic enunciations, gave a more ample space to 'dialogue' within the Church, let the diverse theological tendencies be expressed more freely, etc. It was seen that formulating a clear and binding doctrine [dogma] is not as easy as one would still have thought twenty years ago. .... The second way is a road adulterated by a peculiar Catholic conception of faith and the Church: in the Church there must be a confession of faith; in the Church there simply is no room for equally legitimate but most different, disparate, and even contradictory 'interpretations.'"[4]

§ 5   Just prior to the text quoted below, the German theologian emphatically praises Kant, German idealism, phenomenology, existentialism, and the modernist Maurice Blondel; he then returns to his apology for ambiguity: "This internal ambiguity, however, is not only a mark of modern philosophy, but also of every human work and, therefore, of philosophy in all epochs;[5] it must neither prevent us from seeing what is Christian in the historic situation of modern times nor, consequently, from understanding this situation in its essence as an element which a current theology, inasmuch as it is Christian philosophy, can no longer do without."[6]

---

[4] Ibid., pp. 24ff.

[5] It should be noted, in passing, that Rahner is laying down here a general principle: ambiguity is a characteristic of philosophy in all epochs. Now then, since Catholic philosophy — and to a paramount degree Scholastic philosophy — is known to have been always characterized by crystalline clarity, by defending ambiguity Rahner implicitly combats the philosophy of the Church and, as a consequence, theology as a whole.

[6] K. RAHNER, "Théologie et anthropologie," in V.A., Théologie d'aujourd'hui et de demain (Paris: Cerf, 1967), p. 112.

§ 6   Such principles are vehemently defended by Msgr. Luigi Sartori who, in his eagerness to praise ambiguity, boldly brands the distinction between good and evil, and truth and error as 'Manichaeism.' This amounts to a violent, albeit indirect, criticism of the whole Catholic teaching that preceded Vatican II. Here is how he puts it: "**The *ambiguity of history* does not refer only to the world. I have already repeated innumerable times, and am more and more convinced, that Manichaeism is the most dangerous, the most latent, the most persistent heresy and temptation for the faithful: that of dividing the world in two distinct parts, here and there, good and evil people, we being among the good and with the truth. On the contrary, ambiguity in history also encompasses us, the Church.**"[7]

§ 7   The way out indicated by this theologian to resolve the ambiguity of history, which supposedly also encompasses the Church, is to allow the latter to be judged by the sciences of the world. A rather curious criteria to be uttered by the president of the Italian Theological Association!

"**Then,**" Sartori goes on, "**convinced of universal ambiguity, we will discern but also let ourselves be discerned and make ourselves discerned. I want to be practical. One of the faithful, a theologian, a priest, a teacher must, for example, submit their behavior and act of faith .... to the analysis of a psychologist, a pedagogue, a sociologist, an historian. As we preach, as we make theology, as we express the Faith, how many things must be discerned, diagnosed, even through the sciences! This .... principle obliges the Church and Christians to submit themselves to the judgment of others,** rather than only laying down their own."[8]

§ 8   Supposing an ever-vacillating theology, this same criterion establishing an equivalence between modern science and matters of Faith, is also taken up by Msgr. Carlo Molari, a theologian highly regarded for his many years as a teacher in Roman universities and as a member of the Sacred Congregation for the Doctrine of the Faith. Commenting on the 'sensibility to the signs of the times' in a passage of *Gaudium et spes*, he pronounces it to be law. He then refers to the 'profound meaning' of the conciliar

---

[7] Luigi SARTORI, "Spirito Santo e storia," in V.A., *Lo Spirito Santo pegno e primizia del Regno - Atti della XIX Sessione di formazione ecumenica organizzata dal Segretariato Attività Ecumeniche, Trento* (Turin: Elle Di Ci,1982), p. 79.

[8] Ibid., pp. 79f.

term 'pastoral.' Molari says: "**The Council clearly expressed this law.** It recognized that **in order for the Church 'to understand revealed truth more deeply'** [and therefore, Molari comments, to apprehend the 'profound meaning' of its formulas] 'she has a special need for the help of those who, believers or non-believers, living in the world, are specialized in the various institutions and disciplines** and understand her profound mentality' (GS 44). **The reason for the dialogue which the Council invited believers to carry out with atheists,** Christians with followers of other religions, and Catholics with all Christians, **is not a tactical measure**, a missionary rule: **it is a requirement of faith.**"[9]

According to Molari, Catholic doctrine is, then, habitually uncertain and hesitant. In order to remedy such defects and attain truth in its 'profound meaning,' the Church must resort to dialoguing with those who are in error.[10] That is quite a singular notion of Faith to be preached by one of the best-known theologians in Italy!

*

§ 9 We call to mind that in this item we will not analyze in depth what this notion of Faith is. Before delving into a more detailed analysis, we will highlight other important characteristics mentioned by these authors.

What we want to make clear is that there are numerous doctrinal explanations for the systematic use of ambiguity. They form the basis of a philosophy and theology that is uncertain and hesitant out of principle.

*

---

[9] Carlo MOLARI, "La problematica del linguaggio teologico," in V.A., *Il linguaggio teologico oggi*, p. 89.

[10] Molari's thesis also has curious and equally grave consequences in the individual sphere: since all aspects of reality are equivalent whether expressed by science or by the Faith, it would behoove man to pick those aspects he deems most adequate to construct the edifice of his own interior thinking. This is tantamount to saying that truth becomes a subjective reality.

2. Subjacent to Ambiguity, the Doctrine of Universal Evolution

§ 10   A first impression comes to the mind of an analyst who wants to determine the doctrinal background underlying the systematic ambiguity of the Council: he notices that the Catholic Church, hitherto immutable in its doctrine and fixed in its structures, is presented as a 'Church in transition.'

Theologian Hans Küng writes: "**Just as John XXIII became a transition pope .... and Council Vatican II was a transition council, so also is the Catholic Church today a transition Church**: it is in transition from a past still not completely elapsed to a future that is just beginning to appear."[11]

§ 11   Given his often radical stands, it would not be surprising if it were only Hans Küng who made such a statement. Nevertheless, authors as important as Fr. Chenu, inspirer of the conciliar Fathers' *Message to the World* in the beginning of the Council,[12] also admit, like Küng, the same principle of transition applied to the Church and her doctrine. They even go further as they explicitate this transitional phase and link it to evolutionist principles.

From several standpoints, Fr. Chenu celebrates the introduction of the idea and the word evolution into conciliar texts.

First, from the standpoint of the formulation of the Faith: "Relative used to be a dangerous word .... up until the Council. **'Official' theology deemed the formulas expressing the faith to be immutable realities and would not even allow the word evolution, which the Council introduces, in its vocabulary**."[13]

Continuing from the point of view of dogmatic formulation, Fr. Chenu says: "That She [the Church] may be at the same time one and varied; that She may be one and multiform. For **humanity itself is in a multiform evolution. .... The dogmatic forms, which used to be considered absolute, are relative;**

---

[11] H. KÜNG, *Veracidade*, p. 112.

[12] *Jean Puyo interroge le Père Congar*, p. 128; R. LAURENTIN, *Bilan de la première session*, pp. 123f.; H. FESQUET, op. cit., p. 49.

[13] Jacques Duquesne interroge le Père Chenu, p. 47.

relative to time, places, circumstances, evolution. The same realities have different formulas."[14]

§ 12   *Second*, from the standpoint of the aim toward which the Church should tend: "**The very word evolution, obstinately under suspicion until then, was introduced three or four times, in spite of the negative reactions, into the text at critical points of** *Gaudium et spes* **as a reinforcement to the word 'history'**.... I am pleased to quote Paul VI, then still Cardinal Montini, who makes an excellent comment: '**The order toward which Christianity tends is not a static one; it is an order in permanent evolution toward a better form; it is an equilibrium in movement.**'"[15]

§ 13   *Third*, regarding the essence of evolution, which is supposedly the 'Spirit of God': "**Already chapter II [of** *Gaudium et spes*], **on describing the promotion of the common good in the human community, affirmed the presence of the Spirit in the 'evolution' of the world: 'The Spirit of God,** who, with wondrous providence, directs the course of time and renews the face of the earth, **assists at this development**' (GS 26)."[16]

§ 14   Fr. Chenu then begins to develop the inner core of the conciliar doctrine by contending that it evolves according to the 'signs of the times' that are revealed in history: "If one should qualify the Council by a main trait, I would propose to call it 'prophetic' in the full force and technical meaning of the word both in theological language and in the sociological vocabulary. A prophet is he who knows how to discern in current events that which places them in the continuity and ruptures of a history on the move. The prophet does not analyze structures and notions in their state, but in their dynamism. Thus, according to the famous formula, the future is already present. .... **The** *aggiornamento* **of which John XXIII spoke is not an updating after which one again returns to the road with definitive formulas; it is a continuous application of one's intelligence to understand the 'signs of the times' that emerge from the new values as Gospel in a world on the move.** .... Evidently, the constitution

---

[14] Marie-Dominique CHENU, Interview with the Author, Paris, February 20, 1983.

[15] *Jacques Duquesne interroge le Père Chenu*, pp. 185f.

[16] M. D. CHENU, "Les signes des temps - Reflexions théologiques," in V.A., *L'Eglise dans le monde de ce temps - Constitution pastorale 'Gaudium et spes,'* eds. Y. CONGAR - M. PEUCHMAURD (Paris: Cerf, 1967), vol. II, p. 212.

Gaudium et spes is where this prophetism is more palpable ....
And it inspires many other declarations or decrees. This is why,
gauging well the word and [applying it] in this sense, **one can say
that Vatican II is obsolete.**

**"To the extent that its basic element is prophetic, it re-
quires its own obsolescence. If it is projected** — in the proper
sense — **toward the future,** the texts take on a new density inasmuch as the future is present. Needless to say, **it is difficult to
define fidelity to the first inspiration, but it [fidelity] is the
profound law. So if I limit myself to a commentary, a dis-
course, I will be actually unfaithful.** This is why **it is normal
for those responsible at all levels in their day-to-day decisions
not always to be in agreement, as though there were a set of
norms to be applied or a dogmatic formula to be taught.** One
must undoubtedly lament deviations and ramblings, but they do
not compromise the principal character of the Council's innovations."[17]

If one were to admit Fr. Chenu's explanation and draw
only the major consequences from it, one sees that it would legitimize the abandonment of the dogmatic formulas of the past;
attachment to them would be 'infidelity;' the lack of oneness in
Church teaching would be considered normal; and a corollary
would be to deny authority — especially that of the Pope — the
competence to teach always the same thing everywhere.

Historicity applied to the dogmas of Faith and to authority
in the Church makes them relative to such an extent that one
could ask whether the concept of historicity differs from Luther's
principle of free interpretation. Since free interpretation relativizes the teaching of Catholic exegetic tradition and historicity
extends relativism to the field of exegesis in dogmatics and ecclesiastical authority, one would say that historicity differs from free
interpretation only in that it surpasses the latter in its developments, even though both begin from the same principles.

§ 15   In his explanation of the new, historic, and evolutionary
view of the universe, Fr. Chenu provides elements of an anthropology according to which man should be considered as essentially linked to the evolutionary process. These doctrines, he
claims, are the foundations of Vatican II. Fr. Chenu says: "It is
not by chance that the Christian is becoming more attentive to the
peculiar character of the economy of salvation at a moment when
man is becoming vitally aware of the historicity of his own na-

---

[17] *Jacques Duquesne interroge le Père Chenu*, pp. 191f.

ture. This is a normal convergence if it is true that faith, incarnate in the human subject, adjusts itself to man's structures and evolutions. We observe this, moreover, in the Council. **To the extent that the Council elaborated its Christological vision of a universe in movement, it experienced the need,** a need albeit inadequately satisfied, **for an anthropology.** Now, **in this 'Christian' anthropology, as it is being set forth more or less explicitly in theological statements, three attributes, three coessential attributes of man are emerging:** first, that man is by nature social; second, **that he is so linked to the universe that the very matter of the cosmos is engaged in his destiny;** and third, **that man exists in history. Let us understand this** threefold **value .... written into man's nature and in some way, too, issuing from it, as distinct from abstract analysis or anything resembling either a timeless idea or an immutable definition. Thus it is that even in its vocabulary, the Council speaks rather of the human** *condition* **than of human** *nature* **as such, by contrast with Vatican I.** Without setting aside an essentialist philosophy, **one can readily have recourse to existential analyses.**"[18]

One sees that Fr. Chenu only broaches on some central ideas of the so-called Christian anthropology, its evolutionary character, its warm reception by the Council and its relations with existentialism. But such ideas appear sufficient to confirm the impression that an evolutionary doctrine is subjacent to, and latent in, conciliar ambiguity.

16   This Item limits itself to verifying the emergence of evolutionary doctrine as one of the principal characteristics of Vatican II. An analysis of this doctrine will be made further on.[19]

17   Fr. Yves Congar, who worked on ten of the 16 schemata of Vatican II,[20] also rejoices over the introduction of the concepts

---

[18] M. D. CHENU, "The History of Salvation and the Historicity of Man in the Renewal of Theology," in V.A., *Theology of Renewal*, vol. I, pp. 163f.

[19] Vol. III, *Animus injuriandi-II*, Chap. VI; Vol. VI, *Inveniet fidem?*, Chap. IV.2; Vol. VII, *Destructio Dei*, Chap. II; Vol. IX, *Creatio*, Chaps. II, III; Vol. X, *Peccatum - Redemptio*, Chap. V.

[20] * Alain WOODROW, "A Rome: Trente théologiens du monde entier pour accomplir le Concile," in *Informations Catholiques Internationales*, 5/15/1969, p. 9.

* In a book-interview, CONGAR himself confirms: "I was pretty much involved with the preparation of most of the great conciliar texts: *Lumen*

of evolution and historicity in the Council, historicity which he links with the idea of eschatology.

"**One of the great novelties of Vatican II,** *as far as documents of the 'magisterium' are concerned,* **was the introduction of the eschatological point of view** [21] **and, therefore, also of historicity**. That was lacking, and this grave lack had to do with the predominance of the juridical aspect. **Vatican II sees the Spirit of God present in the evolution of the human community, directing the course of time** and renewing the face of the earth (GS 26)."[22]

§ 18   Consistent with his admiration for the harbingers of the *nouvelle théologie*,[23] Cardinal Wojtyla in his book, *Alle fonti del Rinnovamento*, comments on the Constitution *Gaudium et spes.* He endorses the same principles defended by Congar and Chenu, taking evolution as a doctrinal *substractum* of conciliar ecclesiology: "**The Church,** with the consciousness of the history of salvation that is her own, **goes out to meet that multiform evolution and the consciousness of today's man, which is linked to it. .... The paschal mystery of Jesus Christ is as open to escha-**

---

gentium, above all chapter II; *Gaudium et spes; Dei Verbum*, the texts on Revelation; ecumenism; religious liberty; the Declaration on relations with non-Christians; the Missions. I also worked very much with the Commission of the clergy that elaborated the text *Presbyterorum ordinis*" (*Jean Puyo interroge le Père Congar*, p. 149).

[21] About the progressivist notion of eschatology, see Vol. III, *Animus injuriandi-II*, Chap. V.2.

[22] Y. CONGAR, *Le Concile de Vatican II*, p. 170.

[23] According to Fr. Mieczyslaw MALINSKI, a friend of Msgr. Wojtyla, in a study circle held at the Polish College during the Council, he declared: "Prominent theologians like Henri de Lubac, J. Daniélou, Y. Congar, Hans Küng, R. Lombardi, K. Rahner and others, played an extraordinary role in these preparatory works [of the Council]" (*Mon ami Karol Wojtyla*, Paris: Centurion, 1980, p. 189).

Rocco BUTTIGLIONE is no less explicit in this regard: "By stating that the work of Creation is included in that of Redemption and stressing the close connection between them, Wojtyla takes a stand in favor of the *nouvelle théologie* against positions that distinguish a pure order of nature, in which man fulfills himself as a purely natural being, from an order of grace .... This was the position of 'Roman theology' and was labeled as 'rightist.' .... From this standpoint, Wojtyla is certainly an innovator and aligns himself with the *progressivist* wing of the Council" (*Il pensiero di Karol Wojtyla*, pp. 226f.).

tology (in fact, it awakens 'the desire for the future world'), **as it is to the evolution of the world, which the Council understands above all as a commitment to make the life of humanity and of men 'more humane.' Vatican II stressed the ethical meaning of evolution. .... According to the doctrine of Vatican II, the Church participates in the evolution of the world** not only because the ideal of an ever more humane world is in accordance with the Gospel, but also because the history of salvation, in which the ultimate reality is prepared, necessarily passes by the realization of this world. Furthermore, this reality, almost embryonically and in a mysterious way, is already present in the world through the Church. So **it is worthwhile**, above all, **to pay attention to** *the way in which the Church*, **according to the doctrine of the Council, participates in evolution and progress toward an ever more humane world and, therefore,** *the way that She, in her conscience, continuously overtakes this evolution by orienting herself to the ultimate reality that will also be the 'plenitude of the kingdom of God.'*

"**In many passages,** but perhaps primarily in chapters III and IV of the Constitution *Gaudium et spes* (first part), **Vatican II speaks to us about the active participation of the 'kingdom' in the evolution of the world. ....**

"*The Church, as is evident, participates in the evolution of the world also by means of her own evolution.* **Vatican II expresses a mature consciousness of this truth and makes it one of the fundamental principles of the renewal program. Here the historic consciousness of the Church is manifested in a particularly clear fashion. One may say that** *the whole conciliar conception of 'aggiornamento' (renovatio acomodata)* **expresses, above all, this consciousness. .... By emphasizing the participation of the Church in the evolution of the 'world,' even by means of her own evolution; and, moreover, by proclaiming its necessity, Vatican II takes a stand in regard to the past and,** simultaneously, **to the future.**

"**This is a particular expression of the historic consciousness of the Church, for the habitual category of history is only the past; the history of salvation, on the contrary, continuously reports to a dimension at the same time eschatological, essential, and dynamic, and has, in itself, a unique reason to face the future. It is only in the totality of these dimensions that the Church preserves a full consciousness of her own identity; in it she also finds the basis of the whole program of renewal and** *aggiornamento.* **Only on this fundamental condition can the Church participate in the evolution of the world through her own 'evolution.' One may say that this is** *the most* *profound substractum of the 'historic consciousness' of the Church."*[24]

*

§ *19*   Several characteristics appear in the texts cited in this Item 2 that point to the evolutionist conception as the foundation of conciliar doctrine.

In brief, this concept of evolution is supposed to influence the teaching of Vatican II by:

* Justifying the relativization of dogmatic formulations;

* Making the Church tend toward an order continuously in movement;

* Reflecting the very 'spirit of God.'

* Making the Church and Catholic Doctrine adapt continuously to the 'signs of the times.'

* Providing the basis for the Christological vision of a universe in movement and the 'Christian' anthropology explained by Vatican II.

* Being present in the very essence of human nature.

* Being the foundation of conciliar eschatology.

* Being the prism for understanding the new ecclesiology born out of the Council.

It is hard not to see, therefore, that the doctrinal *substractum* of conciliar ambiguity appears to be a new vision of the universe, of man, of the Church and of God Himself. We will opportunely analyze them in this Collection. Here we will limit ourselves to the finding that there is a subjacent doctrine supporting ambiguity in the conciliar documents; and that this doctrine is evolution.

*

---

[24] Karol WOJTYLA, *Alle fonti del rinnovamento - Studio sull'attuazione del Concilio Vaticano Secondo* (Vatican City: Libreria Editrice Vaticana, 1981), pp. 151-157.

3. Ecclesia semper reformanda

§ 20

The adoption of ambiguity as a norm of language starting from the principle that theology must be hesitating, uncertain, groping[25] and the notion of an evolving dogmatic teaching, modifies the very conception of the Church. If such premises were to be admitted, the Church would come to be uncertain in her teaching: now She would be right, now wrong; in order to know where truth is, She would have to consult a pluralistic array of theologians with contrasting opinions and to count on the help of other religions and the world; She would become insecure in choosing the means to fulfill her mission; She could have made mistakes and even sinned in her past, so She would have to repent and do penance; She would need to have a continuous reform in her customs and institutions.

Since the premises are absurd, so are the conclusions and consequences.

The Council is consistent in that it takes to the ultimate consequences the premises of evolutionary ambiguity and hesitation; it concludes that the Church must always subject herself to a continuing reform. In so doing, it echoes the Lutheran-flavored principle of a 'reformed Church' updated by Fr. Antonio Rosmini with the well-known expression, *Ecclesia semper reformanda.*

21

The introduction of the concept *Ecclesia semper reformanda* can be found in *Lumen gentium*: "The Church, however, clasping sinners to her bosom, at once holy and always in need of purification, follows constantly the path of penance and renewal." (LG 8)

22

The same notion is present in the Decree *Unitatis redintegratio*: "Every renewal of the Church essentially consists in an increase of fidelity to her own calling. .... Christ summons the Church, as she goes her pilgrim way, to that continual reformation of which she always has need, insofar as she is an institution of men here on earth. Consequently, if in various times and circumstances, there have been deficiencies in moral conduct or in Church discipline or even in the way that Church teaching has been formulated .... these should be set right at the opportune moment and in the proper way." (UR 6)

---

[25] "Vatican II groped. No one directed it in a somewhat systematic way," says Fr. CONGAR (*Le Concile de Vatican II*, p. 18).

§ 23   Since no one whosoever is excluded from this process of 'Church renewal,' how can it avoid being influenced by the most censurable excesses? How can a Döllinger or even a Lenin or a Marx be rejected? What are the limits to this constant reform in the Church? How could one not admit that She could not be shaken constantly and almost routinely at her very foundations?

§ 24   How can one deny the validity of the premises and the consistency of the reasoning of Hans Küng as he makes explicit the immediate consequences of the two conciliar texts cited above?

Indeed, the theologian from Tübingen writes: "**External forms and structures of the Church make difficult and,** in certain circumstances, **even impossible the realization of good intentions.**"[26]

He continues: "**Authentic reform is attentive to the creation of new structures** needed at the present time. Therefore, it is not only a simple restoration, but rather, and once again, a *renewal*. **We have already seen that this cannot be attained by an interior reform of hearts that would overlook a reform of the structures, institutions and regulations .... What becomes continuously necessary is a reform that creates situations and structures,** one that does not dissolve the essence of the Church but that replaces it and makes it appear in all its credibility. ....

"**That which men institute and constitute** in this divine institution and constitution **participates in human imperfection and sinfulness and, therefore, needs continuous reform.** But since, as we have noted, its essence and historic realization cannot be adequately separated, **there are no irreformable domains. There is no stone or place of the ecclesiastical building not in need of constant reform.** ....

"**Of the conciliar texts already cited, let us repeat only these two decisive phrases. 'Christ summons the Church, as she goes her pilgrim way, to that** *continual reformation (ad hanc perennem reformationem)* of which she always has need, insofar as she is an institution of men here on earth" (UR 6). 'The Church, at once holy and **always in need of purification** *(semper purificanda)*, **follows** *constantly the path of penance and renewal (poenitentiam et reformationem)*' (LG 8)."[27]

---

[26] Hans KÜNG, *A Igreja* (Lisbon: Moraes, 1970), vol. II, p. 118.

[27] Ibid., pp. 124f.

§ 25   Fr. Mario von Galli, SJ, of the magazine *Orientierung,* of Zurich, who followed the works of the Council as a *perito*, says this about applying the conciliar principles of reform to the liturgy: "Thanks to the Council, we have learned that the Church is a congregation in perpetual movement, in incessant transformation; and if the liturgy occupies the living nucleus of the Church, it also changes to the tune of that evolution. **It was a gross error for us to have so doggedly attached ourselves to the same forms for four centuries. We have to become accustomed to the idea that the liturgy is something that must be in constant evolution.**"[28]

§ 26   Fr. Ansgar Ahlbrecht, OSB, likens the cited excerpt from *Unitatis redintegratio* on *Ecclesia semper reformanda* to another passage about the exercise of the Pope's authority, concluding in favor of a dialogue with the Protestants, who preach such a 'reform' in the Church and combat papal authority: "In its decree on ecumenism, **Vatican Council II says that the Church needs a continual reform.** .... In the constitution on the Church, **the Church is presented less as an official society headed by the Pope than as the holy people of God, in which all authority has only a function of service. This** sacred **people** of God **appears**, in turn, **as a people filled with faults and imperfections, on pilgrimage through History, and also in the division of the Church. This guilt is confessed with frankness,** thus creating a first premise for conversation with the separated brethren."[29]

§ 27   There is but a step from admitting guilt in the Church to admitting a 'sinning Church.' Such a step is taken with ease by the well-known Jesuit authors Maurizio Flick and Zoltán Alszeghy, professors at Gregorian University, whose works are widely publicized and frequently used as textbooks by Catholic institutions at the university level. About the genesis of the concept of a 'sinning Church,' the authors state: "**The Church is weak** not only from the sociological standpoint but also from **the moral aspect** inasmuch as She fails to conform with that ideal of holiness that She must promote with her preaching and sacraments. .... **The Fathers of the Church and ecclesiastical writers before the Protestant reformation had no difficulty**

---

[28] Mario von GALLI, "La nueva liturgia," in V.A., *La reforma que llega de Roma* (Barcelona: Plaza & Janes, 1970), p. 53.

[29] Ansgar AHLBRECHT, "Dialogo con los protestantes," in V.A., *La reforma que llega de Roma*, pp. 124f.

finding, in the biblical images of Rahab, Babylon, and the harlot of the Apocalypse, the type of Church that saves albeit being herself a sinner.[30] Only when the scorching criticism of the reformers concluded that the perverted Roman Church could not be the true Church of Christ was the sanctity of the Church unilaterally emphasized and empirically demonstrated on the basis of an apologetic argumentation. Even in the nineteenth century, Rosmini was censured for speaking of the *five wounds of the Church*; it was necessary to wait until Vatican Council II for it to be again recognized that the pilgrim Church is called by Christ to a continual reformation 'of which she always has need insofar as she is an institution of men here on earth. Consequently, if in various times and circumstances there have been deficiencies in moral conduct or in Church discipline, or even in the way that Church teaching has been formulated .... these should be set right at the opportune moment and in the proper way.' (UR 6). As Rahner's analyses show,[31]* the Council, though not applying the adjective 'sinful' to the Church, in effect admits her sinful aspect."[32]

*

§ 28   One may conclude that the underlying thought that oriented the Council, besides containing an evolutionist *substratum* in its texts and indicating to a 'Copernician' transformation of the vision of the universe and man, adopts a specific concept of Church: a Church in continual reform which, in turn, presupposes or generates (depending on how you look at it) a 'sinful Church.'

*

§ 29   Even though the analysis typical of this Volume I essentially consists in demonstrating the existence of ambiguity in the Council, and it could therefore stop here, it is also opportune to ask what consequences this new concept of Church will entail.

---

[30] On the progressivist emphasis given to the 'sinful' aspect which they claim exists in the essence of the Church; on the appropriateness of the use of the metaphor of harlot to express that aspect; as well as on the studies of Patristics regarding the matter, see Vol. II, *Animus injuriandi-I*, Chap. IV; Appendix II, passim.

[31]* K. RAHNER, La Chiesa peccatrice nei decreti del Concilio Vaticano II (Rome, 1968), pp. 443-478.

[32] Maurizio FLICK - Zoltán ALSZEGHY, *Il mistero della croce - Saggio di teologia sistematica* (Brescia: Queriniana, 1978), pp. 411f.

Isn't this conciliar view of the Church disorienting for a Catholic? How can one admit that She, the light of the world, may present her truth as wavering and ambiguous? How can one imagine that She, one in her Faith, infallible in her extraordinary Magisterium, as well as, in certain conditions, in her ordinary Magisterium[33], by the special assistance of the Holy Spirit, now shows herself to be hesitating in her dogma, unsteady in her morals, fragmented by contrasting opinions? How can She assume a confused 'theological pluralism' to replace the unity and clarity of her teaching of old?

With such premises, how can She not abandon this secure assistance from the Holy Spirit to look for direction in the broken compass of other religions or the often fleeting certainties of modern sciences? How can a cry of affliction be restrained when one sees Her, most holy in her institution, structures, laws and customs, being treated as a vile sinner, given second place to heresy — as was Our Lord to Barrabas — pronounced guilty and almost forced to ask pardon for crimes She has never committed? How can one not remember the Way of the Cross and the Calvary as one sees Her, the innocent one, being led as a malefactor to the gallows where She is expected to reject her perennial mission of Queen and Mistress?

30   What an atrocious affliction! All the more so since it is confirmed by the 'clinical' analysis of great shepherds who can think of no 'medicine' for her other than perpetual adaptation.

Let us look, for example, at the testimony of Cardinal Döpfner, Moderator of the sessions of Vatican II, then Archbishop of Munich. It is a homily addressed to German Catholic politicians a few years after the Council.

"An unusual picture has now taken shape," says Döpfner. "The Church, which until today has answered everything with so much assurance, now asks questions; She who was used to sovereignly defending herself, recognizes the errors of the past; She, who conveyed an impression of solidity and cohesion (How proud we were of it!) now appears to dissolve in contrasting opinions. This disorients and disturbs many Catholic Christians. Including you, who are out there in advanced missionary posts in the world .... who saw the Church as a solid support with her de-

---

[33] On the ordinary and extraordinary Magisterium, see A. V. XAVIER DA SILVEIRA, "Qual a autoridade doutrinária dos documentos pontifícios e conciliares?," in Catolicismo, October 1967.

pendable guidelines, her cohesion, her courage with a force and clarity that were not modern. At times it will seem to you as though you have lost your support, and that is understandable: **the image of the post-conciliar Church is multi-faceted and polyvalent**."[34]

What is the solution that Cardinal Döpfner offers his perplexed audience?

"Now," he continues, "[each one] must place himself in the proper position, attain the right perspective. It is of fundamental importance to firmly believe that the Council was a unique, pentecostal event, that it carried out an authentic testimony of Christ. It is necessary to see the correlations with the whole, the relation between cause and effect starting from the fixed center, which is now seen with a new clarity. We must visualize from this center the apparently convulsive oscillations in the magnetic needle of Church life. We must commit ourselves deeply to the general lines of the Council and the balanced coordination of each of its declarations; there is need for a clarifying dialogue. Above all, we should not isolate ourselves and set ourselves apart like Thomas during Easter week .... Through cooperation, we understand better what the Church is properly aiming at, even though many forms are still imperfect and marked by experience and transition."[35]

This excerpt by the German Cardinal does not seem to provide any answer to the anguishing problems he raises: the only measures suggested are not to isolate oneself and to dialogue. So he leaves up in the air the tragic picture described above and does not say how to avoid or stop it. One is left without knowing whether or not it is a goal of the post-conciliar Church to present herself as a Church without assurance, defense, or cohesion, diluted in contrasting opinions and thus causing disorientation among the faithful.

The description by Cardinal Döpfner and his 'answer' are cited here as characteristic and symptomatic of the attitude of many Prelates faced with the same problem.

*

---

[34] Julius DÖPFNER, *La Chiesa vivente oggi*, p. 379.

[35] Ibid., pp. 379f.

§ *31*   So, in this Item, we have seen one more important consequence of ambiguity and the hesitant and evolutionist doctrine: it
is a new conception of Church, *Ecclesia semper reformanda.*

*

§ *32*   As a conclusion to this Chapter, we are led to state that
conciliar ambiguity, described in the many texts mentioned here,
finds it easy to cloak itself in a new doctrine of an evolutionist
nature, which supposes a new conception of the Church and also
of the Faith.[36]

*   *   *

---

[36] The new progressivist conception of the Faith is dealt with in Vol. VI,
Inveniet fidem? and the new vision of the Church in Vol. XI, *Ecclesia.*

CHAPTER VIII

ANOTHER SOURCE OF AMBIGUITY TENDENTIOUS OMISSIONS

§ 1   Having thus looked at several aspects of the polyvalent conciliar language, it is timely to note that there is also another type of ambiguity: tendentious omissions. It was through omissions that Vatican II introduced ambiguity into several official texts on topics that both the Magisterium and Church tradition already had unequivocally defined. Not a few authors believe that such omissions, as we shall see in this Chapter, were made intentionally to open the way for certain ideas held in high esteem by the progressivist current.

It is obviously more delicate to analyze an omission in a text than an ambiguous word that actually appears in it. In this Volume we do not intend to hold as indisputable the interpretations of Vatican II omissions emitted by the authors cited below. Nevertheless, they are well worth noting on account of their consistency with everything we have seen so far on the purpose and doctrine underlying conciliar ambiguities.

It seems indispensable, for a reader intent on forming an overall view of the question of ambiguity to know several of such omissions and the comments to which they gave rise. This is why, by way of a sampling, this Chapter focuses on them.

We will cite some of these omissions accompanied by comments of progressivist authors.

1. Virginity of Mary Most Holy

2   Negation of Our Lady's virginity is a frequent fixture in progressivist circles. Some deny it directly, others indirectly by vaguely speaking about some spiritual virginity while down-

playing bodily virginity. It is characteristic of this tendency to no longer attribute virginal conception exclusively to Our Lady.[1]

§ 3

Msgr. Gérard Philips, the primary writer of the final text of *Lumen gentium*, explains the sinuous circumlocutions he employed when dealing with the virginity of Mary during childbirth: "The conciliar text [LG 57] did not avoid the expression of the Gospel, but pointed out another fact of undeniable importance: 'The Son did not diminish her virginal integrity, but rather consecrated it.' This circumlocution is very simple, and the formula chosen is liturgical and traditional."[2]

Msgr. Philips thus justifies this circumlocution: "It is known that many questions, especially of late, have been raised about *virginitas in partu.*"[3]

Philips later explains that some bishops reacted to this and wanted the text to affirm without subterfuge the characteristic of Mary: *Virgo ante partum, in partu, et post partum.* But their reaction was not taken into account. "The Council considered that the terminology employed could suffice for that end, without entering into biological details" [sic].[4]

The official conciliar writer goes on: "One thing is certain: **the virginity in question .... is not taught as a personal privilege of Mary.**"[5]

Basing his argument vaguely on the Patristic fathers, Msgr. Philips continues his text, not cited here, trying to overestimate the spiritual aspect of virginity to the detriment of the bodily aspect, considered merely as a 'symbol.'[6]

*

---

[1] Highly expressive of this general tendency amongst progressivists is the thesis of Rahner, one of the most outstanding thinkers of the Council, which denies Our Lady's *virginitas in partu*. This thesis is analyzed in Vol. II, *Animus injuriandi-I*, Chap. VII.4.

[2] G. PHILIPS, op. cit., p. 544.

[3] Ibid.

[4] Ibid.

[5] Ibid.

[6] Ibid.

2. Original Sin

§ 4

The text below by Canon Jacques Mouroux, a theologian held in considerable renown for works written before the Council, refers to an intentional omission which, he points out, weakens the doctrine on Original Sin.

"One cannot describe the human condition without including the tragic reality of sin. One of the primitive texts[7] contained an item about original sin. Text I no longer carried any development on it. Many [conciliar] Fathers rightly considered the text to be 'exaggeratedly optimistic,' and so this tragic dimension of human condition was reintroduced.[8*] Incidentally, the Council wanted neither to add original sin to the title of chap. I, 'On the Corruption of Nature'[9*] nor to expressly mention original sin and certain doctrinal precisions [10*] since that was not required by its aim.[11*] Always pursuing its pastoral objective, it therefore limited itself, as far as this point was concerned, to the doctrinal minimum indispensable for the equilibrium of Christian truth and the clarification of man's painful condition."[12]

§ 5

Commenting on the three most important statements in *Gaudium et spes* on man's decayed condition, Mouroux points out the text's discretion in topic 18 (the mystery of death), as it mentions the sin of Adam: "Note, by the way, the text's discretion: it explicitly mentions original sin (GS 18b) without, however, making any precise comments. It says that the depth of evil

---

[7] The final text of *Gaudium et spes* approved by the conciliar Fathers on December 7, 1965, was preceded by several drafts, of which Mouroux mentions three in an abbreviated manner as Tx. I, Tx. II and Tx. III.

[8*] Rel. by Msgr. Garrone, Tx. II, p. 6.

[9*] Tx. III, p. 154.

[10*] Resuming Rm. 1:21-25 and 5:12-21.

[11*] Tx. III, 1, p. 157; 4 and 6, p. 158.

[12] Jacques MOUROUX, "Situation et signification du chapitre I (de la *Gaudium et spes*): Sur la dignité de la personne humaine," in V.A., *L'Eglise dans le monde de ce temps*, vol. I, p. 237.

harkens back to Rom 1:21-25,[13] which aims not at original sin, but rather at the behavior of sinful humanity as such."[14]

§ 6　　　　If the comment by Mouroux about *Gaudium et spes* is well-founded, as we should suppose, the way would be open for the negation of the sin of Adam and Eve and for the defense of the notion — opposed to dogma — that at its source original sin was not the sin of a couple but that of 'all humanity.'

The premise of this theory is that Adam could be a generic, cosmic reality: humanity. The designation *man* supposedly means not so much an individual, but a species. By the same token, *Christ* would also be a generic and cosmic reality. *Adam*, then, would be mankind in its initial stage; and the resurrected Christ, mankind in its final stage, representing the beginning of divinized humanity.[15]

The author says that the Council did not define whether Adam was an individual or a species. Hence doors are opened for a progressivist conception of a sin of humanity rather than the sin of a first couple. Indeed, Mouroux affirms: "The mystery of Christ and that of man finally make up only one mystery. And this is why the Council .... directly relates the mystery of the first man with that of the Word Incarnate. By saying 'Adam, the first man,' the Council repeats a biblical expression,[16]* but it does not

---

[13] Perhaps due to some reviewing oversight, Jacques Mouroux transcribes the conciliar text referring to Rom 1:21-25, whereas *Gaudium et spes* quotes Rom 5:21 and 6:23.

In fact, here is the reference to original sin: "The Christian faith teaches that bodily death, from which man would have been immune had he not sinned (Wis 1:13; 2:23-24; Rom 5:21; 6:23; Jas 1:15) will be overcome when that wholeness which he lost through his own fault will be given once again to him by his almighty and merciful Saviour." (GS 18b).

Another confusion is caused by Mouroux's statement, in the first quotation, that the "Council did not want .... to mention original sin expressly..." whereas in another quote on the same page of his book he says that the text "explicitly mentions original sin..." It is hard not to see the contradiction between the two statements.

[14] J. MOUROUX, op. cit., p. 237.

[15] This strange doctrine is broached upon in Vol. VIII, *Fumus Satanae*, Chaps. II, IV, V.4.B; Vol. X, *Peccatum - Redemptio*, Chaps. V, VI, VII, VIII.2.E, IX.2.

[16]* I Cor 15:45-47.

intend to resolve here whether Adam was an individual or a group[17*]."[18]

*

3. The Existence of Hell

§ 7   Hans Küng assembles documents of the perennial teaching of the Church on this matter and compares them to statements of Vatican II. He shows that the Council's omission about the eternal punishment of those who find themselves outside the Church, especially atheists, brings into question the very existence of Hell, which, therefore, is supposedly "an unresolved matter."

"In 1442," writes Kung, "the Council of Florence .... pronounced a whole series of human groups worthy of condemnation ....: 'The Holy Roman Church .... firmly believes, confesses and proclaims that no one outside of the Catholic Church, be he a pagan or a Jew, a non-believer or separated from its unity, takes part in life eternal, but on the contrary, falls into the eternal fire prepared by the devil and his angels unless he unites himself to her (the Catholic Church) before his death.' That which Benedict XII defined in the Constitution *Benedictus Deus* (1336) also holds true for Catholics: 'We define: Just as God universally ordered, the souls of those who die having committed a mortal sin go immediately go hell, where they are tormented by eternal punishments.' .... Instead, **Vatican Council II** (even **without revoking or** expressly **correcting the definition of Florence ....) declares that even atheists in good faith can reach eternal salvation**. With this, **the question of hell is** evidently **not resolved,** since it was not directly dealt with in Vatican Council II."[19]

[17*] Tx. III, n. 3, p. 186.

[18] J. MOUROUX, op. cit., p. 249.

[19] Hans KÜNG, *Vida Eterna?* (Madrid: Cristiandad, 1983), pp. 218f.

Küng is right in saying that Vatican II did not directly deal with Hell. The only two references made by *Lumen gentium* do not mention it by name and broach the topic only in passing:

* "But since we know neither the day nor the hour, we should follow the advice of the Lord and watch constantly so that, when the single course of our earthly life is completed (Heb 9:27), we may merit to enter with him into the marriage feast and be numbered among the blessed (Mt 25:31-46), and not, like the wicked and slothful servants (Mt 25:26),

Now then, if everyone can be saved, both those who are in the Catholic Church and those outside of her, it does not make any sense, from this progressivist perspective, for Hell to exist. This is tantamount to denying its existence. Hence one can better understand Kung's general affirmation that the 'question of hell is not resolved.'

§ 8

For his part, Fr. René Laurentin, author of a well-known chronicle of the Council, on assembling a 'list of silences' of Vatican II, comments: **"Another category of silences: those concerning disregarded sectors in which some maintain their beliefs in an archaic and somehow shameful form while others abandon them. [This is the case regarding] angels, about whom the Council said nothing, the cult of saints, or hell. The problem of hell was only materially raised and superficially resolved by adding a quote from Scripture to the *Constitution on the Church* (LG 48); nevertheless, the terrible mystery of the refusal of love and its eternal consequences should not have been placed under the table."**[20]

§ 9

Incidentally, the deliberate omission of the word Hell in the chapter of *Lumen gentium* on the eschatological origin of the Church disconcerted innumerable conciliar Fathers, some of whom expressed their perplexities in the plenary assembly. In spite of that, the final text of the document did not include it. According to a summary by Kloppenburg, several prelates intervened during the 80th General Congregation held on September 15, 1964. They expressed themselves in this way:

Cardinal Rufini, Archbishop of Palermo: "There are repetitions in the text [he gives three examples]. And **there are omissions: why does it not speak about hell?** Why is purgatory,

---

be ordered to depart into the eternal fire (Mt 25:41), into the outer darkness where 'men will weep and gnash their teeth' (Mt 22:13 and 25:30)." (LG 48c).

* The other conciliar text that deals with condemnation to Hell clears the way for the salvation of non-Christians by vaguely declaring: "But very often, deceived by the Evil One, men have become vain in their reasonings, have exchanged the truth of God for a lie and served the world rather than the Creator (Rom 1:21 and 25). Or else, living and dying in this world without God, they are exposed to ultimate despair" (LG 16).

[20] R. LAURENTIN, *Bilan de la quatrième session*, pp. 356ff.

whose existence is a dogma of faith, hardly mentioned? *Schema capitis VII iterum retractetur.*"[21]

10

Msgr. Alberto Gori, Latin Patriarch of Jerusalem: "It is certainly opportune to stress the eschatological nature of human vocation. But **n. 48** [of *Lumen gentium*] **should also remind us of hell,** of which Revelation and all of Tradition speak to us. **Such an omission on the part of a Council would be inadmissible.**"

The orator then goes on to expound the three reasons why the text must also mention hell: because it is an indisputable reality of Christian revelation; because the knowledge of this truth is of great importance for every human person; and because such a mention is especially needed at the present time: "For the quest for a better material life and hedonism destroy man's esteem for friendship with God and the sense of sin; as a consequence, the consideration of hell is cast aside as inopportune and even condemned as opposed to the present-day mentality. The preachers no longer want to talk about it. So that the conviction may prevail, among the faithful, that hell is something obsolete whose reality can be legitimately cast into doubt. **Therefore, the Council must expressly mention the doctrine on hell.**"[22]

11

Msgr. Nicodemo, Archbishop of Bari: "Also **missing** [in this chapter VII] **is a word about hell,** which is the penalty for sin. And sin is a treason against the vocation for holiness."[23]

12

Msgr. Secundo Garcia de Sierra y Méndez, Archbishop of Burgos: "What is said about Purgatory may be ecumenical, but it is little. Vague allusions are not sufficient. There are pastoral reasons for one to speak clearly. Also the fear of God must be announced to today's naturalistic man. But **Hell is not even mentioned throughout the chapter.**"[24]

---

[21] Ernesto RUFFINI, Comments on the Existence of Hell in the Conciliar Assembly, in B. KLOPPENBURG, Concílio Vaticano II, vol. IV, p. 15.

[22] Alberto GORI, Comments on the Existence of Hell in the Conciliar Assembly, p. 16.

[23] Enrico NICODEMO, Comments on the Existence of Hell in the Conciliar Assembly, p. 17.

[24] Secundo GARCIA DE SIERRA Y MENDEZ, Comments on the Existence of Hell in the Conciliar Assembly, p. 19.

§ 13   The following day, during the 81st General Congregation, Msgr. Biagio d'Agostino, Bishop of Vallo di Lucania, Italy, also criticized chapter VII's omission in regard to the question of Hell: "The naturalist and materialist mentality of our times requires that we stress the truths of the *novissimis* more. Unfortunately, current preaching deals little with them. And the present text is weak. It makes only a timid allusion to purgatory. Everyone knows the doctrine of the separated brethren on this subject. For this reason we must clearly enunciate our doctrine. And **in the whole text not a word is found about hell. Today, as we see ourselves oppressed by public and private delinquency, it is wholesome to call to mind not only the mercy, but also the justice, of the eternal Judge.**"[25]

§ 14   Therefore, it is very difficult to argue that the failure to mention Hell in *Lumen gentium* and the other conciliar documents was not deliberate.

                              *

4. Distinction Between the Church Militant and the Church Triumphant

§ 15   *Lumen gentium* mentions only once the distinction between celestial Church and terrestrial Church. Delving into this matter would have been opposed to the progressivist desire to unify the two realities. A statement by Msgr. Philips sheds light on why the distinction was enunciated only once and on the depth of the Council's thinking about the matter.

"The terminology, 'celestial Church,' 'Church on earth,' could lead us astray toward a certain dualism, as if there were two Churches, one below and another up above. Our comment deliberately avoids this language. Needless to say, there is only one Church, but the situation of its members varies. The following article (LG 50) insists on this unity, even though the terminology 'terrestrial Church,' 'celestial Church' is stained by a certain division and localization."[26]

Eliminating the distinction between the Church Triumphant and the Church Militant, which, according to Philips would have been ideal, leads to confusion and ambiguity, and casts a

---

[25] Biagio d'AGOSTINO, Comments on the Existence of Hell in the Conciliar Assembly, p. 21.

[26] G. PHILIPS, op. cit., pp. 484f.

shadow on the Holy Church's struggle on this earth, a trait indissociable from her mission.

*

5. The Roman Character of the Church

§ 16   Philips and Congar, two conciliar *periti* who worked assiduously on council documents, especially on the text of the Constitution on the Church, refer to the conscious omission of the Roman character of the Church in topic 8a.

Msgr. Philips, who wrote the final text of *Lumen gentium*, states: "We profess in the Creed [to believe in] one, holy, Catholic and apostolic Church .... Where shall we find this Church? It concretely incarnates the society governed by the Successor of Peter and the bishops in communion with him. The text does not say: the Church is the Catholic community; and it even omits the adjective, 'Roman,' which is found in the Tridentine profession of faith, because it aims to stress that which is of fundamental importance, particularly the succession beginning with Peter and the apostles."[27]

17   Fr. Congar also attests to the omission of the 'Roman' character of the Church in *Lumen gentium*: "But it remains to be known whether *Lumen gentium* strictly, that is, exclusively, identifies this Church Body of Christ with the Roman Catholic Church, as did the Encyclical *Mystici Corporis*. One can doubt this since one finds that not only the attribute 'Roman' is missing, something of little importance since there is mention of the Church 'governed by the successor of Peter and the bishops in communion with him,' but they also avoided saying that only Catholics are members of the Mystical Body."[28]

18   According to Fr. Schillebeeckx, also a conciliar *perito*, *Lumen gentium*'s omission of the Roman character of the Church also extends to the Holy Pontiff, as the document, in the above-mentioned topic 8a, emphasizes the title 'successor of Peter:' "It is typical that the *Dogmatic Constitution on the Church* completely lacks the statement that the bishop of *Rome* governs the Church .... in his capacity as Pope. Preference is given to the formal reason for his primacy, the 'successor of Peter,' so that the

---

[27] Ibid., pp. 110f.

[28] Y. CONGAR, *Le Concile de Vatican II*, p. 160.

qualification 'Roman' in the formulas 'Roman Pontiff' and 'Roman Church' only have material significance."[29]

As Congar pointed out, the omission of the Roman character of Holy Church is done to facilitate ecumenism. It favors ambiguity in determining who is a member of the 'Church of Christ.'

*

6. Survival of the Western Patriarchates

§ *19*

The existence of Patriarchs in the Church, according to a venerable tradition, is an honorific prerogative of the Seats that have been personally governed by Saint Peter. There are thus the patriarchates of Rome, Jerusalem, Antioch, and Alexandria.[30] Patriarchates also exist by special privileges granted to communities with their own history, like those of Constantinople, Venice, Lisbon, the Western Indies (Toledo), and the Eastern Indies (Goa), in addition to the Armenian, Chaldean, Copt, Melkite, and Maronite Patriarchates.[31] In the Decree *Orientalium Ecclesiarum*, even though the Eastern Patriarchs are mentioned,[32] not the least reference is made to the Patriarchs of the West. According to Philips, this was done in order to strengthen the position of the

---

[29] E. SCHILLEBEECKX, Igreja ou igrejas? in V.A., *Cinco problemas que desafiam a Igreja hoje*, p. 32.

[30] Alexandria was considered to be indirectly governed by Saint Peter, since his disciple Saint Mark had been there once. EUSEBIUS of Cesarea, *Historia eclesiastica* (Buenos Aires: Ed. Nova, 1950), lib. II, chaps. 16, 24, pp. 75, 93f.; Saint JEROME, *De viris illustribus*, XXXVI, in Jules LEBRETON, *L'Ecole chrétienne d'Alexandrie avant Origène*, in V.A., *Histoire de l'Eglise*, vol. II, p. 226; Jacques ZEILLER, *La propagation du Christianisme*, in V.A., *Histoire de l'Eglise*, vol. I, p. 283; J. Baptista PIGHI, *Institutiones Historiae ecclesiasticae* (Verome: Bibliopolae Editoris Pontificii, 1922), vol. I, p. 30.

[31] In addition to the honorific prerogatives we are stressing, some of these patriarchates also have a greater or lesser power of jurisdiction. For greater details, see Raymond VANCOURT, "Patriarcats," in DTC, vol. XI, cols. 2253-2297.

[32] OE 7-11.

Bishops Conferences. Yet it seems to point to a tendency toward extinguishing this elevated honorific prerogative.

§ 20   Gérard Philips comments on this matter: "To create a new patriarchate today, for example, for a continent other than Eurasia, would not appear to us to be a very opportune idea. Such an institution would be artificial and anachronistic .... **The honorific patriarchates have lost their meaning in the West.** On the contrary, the Bishops' Conferences .... have a great future .... Collegial solidarity will find here a vast and important field of application. **An attentive reader will not have failed to notice the silence of the conciliar text about the patriarch of the West, who is none other than the Roman Pontiff.**[33] [Those who work with] the ecumenical question strive to define this inevitable problem and to find a peaceful solution for it."[34]

*

---

[33] As one will recall, among the pretensions that brought about the Schism of the East was the demand that the Papacy and the Patriarchate of Constantinople be placed on equal footing.

Indeed, beginning with the illegal succession of Focius to the See of Constantinople (858-859), this demand grew stronger (Emile AMANN, "L'époque carolingienne," in V.A., *Histoire de l'Eglise*, vol. VI, pp. 471, 494). After his death Focius became the symbol of an imagined equality between Constantinople and Rome (Ibid., p. 501), which later fermented and helped to cause the Eastern Schism.

Ever since the Schism, one of the strongest resentments that the Eastern Orthodox has nourished against the Pope is his superiority, of divine right, over every Seat in Christendom, which cannot even be compared to the so-called orthodox, schismatic seat of Constantinople. Saint ROBERT BELLARMINE, *De Romano Pontifice*, lib. I, chap. 23; lib. II, chap. 12, in *Opera omnia*, vol. I, pp. 354f., 383; Louis BILLOT, *De Ecclesia Christi* (Rome: Aedes Universitatis Gregoriannae, 1921), q. XIV, tes. 23, p. 593; H. HURTER, *Theologiae Dogmaticae compendium* (Paris/Insbruck: Lib. Academica Wagneriana, 1883), vol. I, pp. 379f.

Therefore, the silence about the patriarchate in the West apparently is also aimed at avoiding an affirmation of the primacy of the Pope over the Patriarchate of Constantinople, considered as the *primus inter pares* of the Greek schismatic church.

[34] G. PHILIPS, op. cit., p. 277.

7. The Council's Position Regarding Freudian Psycho-analysis

§ 21   It is well to make one more observation in this Chapter on tendentious omissions, not about doctrinal points or ecclesiastical institutions that the Council left in the shadows, but about a new doctrine that it apparently wants to impose. The text of *Gaudium et spes* is laconic about modern science and, more especially, Freudian psychoanalysis, which it should have dealt with clearly. In so doing, it appears to open the gates to the doctrine of the Austrian analyst.

It is Jacques Mouroux who notes the omission and defends this opinion: "By pointing primarily to the conquest of the material world, the Council, needless to say, leaves the door open to 'human sciences,' which are increasingly important for the knowledge and equilibrium of present-day man and, therefore, for pastoral care [35*].[36] If the Council explicitly refused to consider psychoanalysis, it was undoubtedly because the question — as it was posed — did not appear to be mature and was fraught with dangerous ambiguities. But even this silence leaves the door open for prudent research afterward."[37]

§ 22   Mouroux appears to be right when he interprets the opening to culture and sciences as being, in the final analysis, an opening to Freud; in point of fact, Fr. Congar's words echo the same meaning: Ancient culture "no longer touches today's man, who seeks a different culture whose Fathers will be neither Athanasius nor Augustine but Marx, Freud, and modern technology. The Catholic Church herself is abandoning her old culture, which has been her own ever since Constantine up to Vatican II."[38]

*

[35*] GS 54, 62b.

[36] Here is the part of *Gaudium et spes* to which Mouroux refers as opening the door to psychoanalysis: "In pastoral care, sufficient use should be made not only of theological principles but also of the findings of secular sciences, especially psychology and sociology." (GS 62b)

[37] J. MOUROUX, op. cit., p. 241.

[38] Y. CONGAR, "Salvación y liberación," in V.A., *Conversaciones de Toledo - Teología de la liberación* (Burgos: Aldecoa, 1973), p. 202.

§ 23   It is not our intent to conclude that such omissions indisputably mean exactly what each author has commented on the various matters. We only affirm that these omissions are such as to give rise to these and other comments, thereby leading us to conjecture that the Council also used ambiguous omissions as a resort to favor progressivism.

*   *   *

CHAPTER IX

A DOCTRINAL CONSEQUENCE: AMBIGUITY IS FRAUGHT WITH CONCESSIONS TO THE OTHER RELIGIONS AND TO THE MODERN WORLD[1]

§ *1*
Having seen how the ambiguity in the texts and doctrine of Vatican II favors a new concept of the world, of man, and of the Church, we will now analyze how such a procedure also implies a virtual denial of the traditional missionary and militant characters of the Church.[2] Nothing could appear more consistent.

---

[1] Volume V of this Collection will study in more detail the concessions of the conciliar Church to the other religions and the modern world. This volume looks at the doctrinal underpinnings of the ecclesiastical Magisterium that condemn both types of concession and the apparent or real opposition of Vatican II to traditional Church doctrine in this matter (Vol. V, *Animus delendi-II*, Part I, Premises 1, 2; Part II, Premises 1, 2). We will not cite the pontifical condemnations here.

[2] It is necessary to distinguish two concepts of missionary Church and the missions. Until Vatican II, the goal of the missions was to convert heretics, schismatics, Jews, and pagans from the errors they professed in order to bring them into the bosom of the Church. After Vatican II, the 'missions' came to signify a movement of the Church toward the heretics, schismatics, Jews, and pagans without asking any conversion of them. What prevails is the orientation made explicit by Msgr. Louis PELATRE, apostolic Vicar of Constantinople: "Proselytism is banned" ("Islam: la paura ingiustificata," interview with Francesco STRAZZARI, in *Il Regno*, 3/15/1993, p. 147). Instead, according to this conception, it is the Church that must adapt to others.

Volume I refers to the perennial missionary character of the Church, which it deems as the exclusive fountain of all truth, that is, the one that preceded the Council and is based on the mandate of the Saviour: "Go ye into the whole world, and preach the Gospel to every creature. He

Once the Church has been denied her conditions of indefectible Mistress of the truth through the concept *Ecclesia semper reformanda*, and of perennial and exclusive custodian of the true Faith through the concept of 'sinning Church,' it becomes implicitly untenable that She continue to be militant 'against the perfidy of heretics' and missionary to become Queen of peoples and builder of cultures and civilizations.

What will follow are excerpts from the works of highly regarded commentators of the Council who clearly affirm the need, based on the premises of the Council, to abolish the defense and propagation of the Faith both with respect to the other religions and to the modern world.

1. Concessions to the Other Religions[3]

§ 2

In this Item 1, which is intended to deal with the concessions to the other religions arising from ambiguity in the conciliar texts, the subject matter is divided into two parts. *First*, we wish to focus our attention, although not exhaustively, on one of the most important and debated religious topics: the liturgical reform

---

that believeth and is baptized, shall be saved; but he that believeth not shall be condemned" (Mk 16:15-16).

On the clash between the missions' traditional character with the neomissiology *aggiornata*, see the work by Plinio CORRÊA DE OLIVEIRA, *Tribalismo indígena: ideal comuno-missionário para o Brasil no século XXI* (São Paulo: Vera Cruz, 1977).

[3] * Even though the texts of this Item deal primarily with the concessions that the Church supposedly should make to the other religions, they also contain some applications of conciliar doctrinal premises regarding the modern world and vice-versa: Some excerpts on the modern world (Item 2) also deal with concessions to the other religions. This is quite understandable, since the principles that guide both types of concession are the same. The titles presented here only aim to make it easier for the Reader to follow the matter by means of a general order that is not intended to be a definitive classification.

* Two distinct methods will be used to expound the documents corroborating Items 1 and 2. In Item 1, the subject matter is appropriate for uniform development. This is not the case with Item 2, in which the matter will be divided into segments preceded by a letter. The reason for this is that it is easy to organize a direct doctrinal exposition about concessions to the other religions. In contrast, with regard to concessions made to the world, due to their multiple consequences and the ambiguity of the word world, the exposition is indirect and multifaceted.

and the consequent reform of the Ordinary of the Mass. *Second,* we bring to the Reader's attention a certain number of testimonies by theologians with sufficient credentials to deal with the doctrinal concessions that rose from a desire to move ecumenism forward.

A. Ambiguities in the Conciliar and Post-conciliar Language Regarding the Liturgical Reform of the Holy Sacrifice of the Mass

§ *3*

    Pope Pius XII made a first attempt at liturgical reform.[4] That reform was probably a fruit of the preparatory commission that the Pontiff had established in view of a coming Council.[5]

---

[4] * "This upset of the tendencies [in the liturgy] was not made brusquely. It was prepared, stimulated for a long time, because the return to the sources in the liturgical sphere, which had been sought for more than twenty years, had already had its effect. .... Pius XII admitted and at times applied, during Holy Week, for example, the principle of an adaptation of the liturgy." These are the words of the highly regarded *perito* and conciliar chronicler Fr. René LAURENTIN (*L'Enjeu et le bilan du Concile*, vol. II, p. 80). The same author states: "The conciliar plan [regarding the liturgy] inserted itself during the long period of liturgical reform initiated by Pius XII. Concerned foremost with promoting or, better, of restoring a lively participation of the faithful in the liturgy. It followed three interrelated orientations to achieve this end: adaptation to our time, differentiation according to the needs of the people, and, finally, restoration of the powers of the Bishops in the collegial college." (Ibid., p. 23)

* Fr. Pedro ROMANO ROCHA, SJ, professor of the Pontifical Gregorian University, offers more data: "Already in 1956, the rubrics of the new *Ordo* of Holy Week mentioned the people and their intervention [in the ceremonies]." ("La principale manifestation de l'Eglise", in V. A., *Vatican II - Bilan et perspectives*, vol. II, p. 21, note 11)

* Cardinal Silvio ODDI commented: "Let us not forget it was he [Pius XII] who initiated the liturgical reform. It was he who reduced to three hours the period of obligatory fast before communion." (*Il tenero mastino di Dio*, Rome: Progetti Museali Editore, 1995, pp. 48f.)

* In the apostolic Constitution *Missale romanum*, of March 4, 1969, PAUL VI said: "Once the liturgical movement began to grow and spread among the Christian people .... it became clear that the formulas of the Roman Missal would be restored and enriched. Our predecessor Pius XII undertook such a reform." (in *Ordo Missae*, Rome: Typis Polyglottis Vaticanis, 1969, pp. 7f.)

§ 4   What is certain is that only two of the several schemata preparing for the Council remained essentially unchanged: the schema on liturgical reform and the one dealing with the communications media.[6]   The others were abrogated by John XXIII when he rejected the schema *De fontibus Revelationis*. Cardinal Suenens remodeled the schemata and gave them a new focus following his own plan of "covering the topics most dear to him."[7]

The Constitution *Sacrosanctum Concilium* was the first document to be discussed and approved by the Council (11/14/1962), promulgated by Vatican II (11/21/1963), and officially ratified and promulgated by Paul VI (12/4/1963). The Constitution substantially adopted the schema prepared by the aforementioned commission. Soon after that proceeding, the liturgical reform went into force.

a) Excerpts From *Sacrosanctum Concilium* That Open the Way for Changes in the Liturgy of the Mass

§ 5   Let us analyze some excerpts of this important conciliar document. We do not consider these excerpts to be unequivocally erroneous. Although one or the other might be so, it is not our goal to analyze them in detail. Our aim is solely to present the

---

[5] This can be inferred from the words of Fr. R. LAURENTIN: "The liturgical commission joined together specialists from around the world, including those from the Curia: men well trained in research and the study of sources, and prepared for this dialogue that was developing between Rome and the rest of the Church. This dialogue existed between the Congregation of the Rites and the promoters of the liturgical movement, which was born in Germany, Belgium, France, and other places during the last thirty years. This commission set the fundamental basis for a true reform – not without much friction and many obstacles and new starts – which make one think of Penelope and her weaving. Thus, John XIII made use of a text capable of opening in a postive and fecund way the discussion of Vatican II: It was a single text, but a text of worth." (Op. cit., vol. VI, p. 12)

Regarding the intention of Pius XII in preparing a new ecumenical Council, see Vol. IV of this Colletion, *Animus delendi*, Chap. I.1.A.

[6] R. LAURENTIN, Ibid., p. 16.

[7] Commenting the plan that he himself presented in the first session of December 4, 1962, Card. Josef SUENENS, in a work recording conciliar workings, says: "I inserted there [in the plan] the most possible themes that were dear to me." (*Souvenirs et esperances*, p. 69)

Reader with a number of passages of the said Constitution so that he is able to see that, due to their ambiguous language, many excerpts directly or indirectly open the way for the desacralization of the principal act of worship of the Catholic Church and facilitate rapprochement with the false religions. Often times, this rapprochement is done to the detriment of the orthodoxy of some of the most fundamental dogmas of the Creed.

Let us, therefore, transcribe excerpts from *Sacrosanctum Concilium*, each one preceded by a short subtitle in italics indicating its tendency toward ambiguity.

§ 6   *Adaptation to the world and to the false religions:* "The sacred Council has set out to impart an ever-increasing vigor to the Christian life of the faithful; to adapt more closely to the needs of our age those institutions which are subject to change; to foster whatever can promote union among all who believe in Christ .... Accordingly it sees particularly cogent reasons for undertaking the reform and promotion of the liturgy" (SC 1a).

§ 7   *Confusion between the various types of presence of Our Lord in the Church:* "Christ is always present in his church, especially in her liturgical celebrations. He is present in the Sacrifice of the Mass not only in the person of his minister .... but especially in the Eucharistic species. By his power he is present in the sacraments .... He is present in his word since it is he himself who speaks when the holy scriptures are read in the Church. Lastly, he is present when the Church prays and sings, for he has promised 'where two or three are gathered together in my name there am I in the midst of them' (Mt 18:20)" (SC 7a).

§ 8   *The priesthood of the faithful is placed on the same level as that of the priest:* "Mother Church earnestly desires that all the faithful should be led to that full, conscious, and active participation in liturgical celebrations which is demanded by the very nature of the liturgy, and to which the Christian people, 'a chosen race, a royal priesthood, a holy nation, a redeemed people' (1 Pet 2:9, 4-5) have a right and obligation by reason of their baptism. In the restoration and promotion of the sacred liturgy the full and active participation by all the people is the aim to be considered before all else" (SC 14a, b).

§ 9   *Desacralizing ceremonies and rendering the celebration of the Mass 'democratic':* "In this restoration both texts and rites should be drawn up so as to express more clearly the holy things which they signify. The Christian people, as far as is possible, should be able to understand them with ease and take part in them fully, actively, and as a community" (SC 21b). "With the passage of time, however, there have crept into the rites of the sacraments and sacramentals certain features which have rendered their nature and purpose far from clear to the people of today. Hence some changes are necessary to adapt them to present-day needs. For that reason the sacred Council decrees as follows concerning their revision" (SC 62).

§ 10   *Exaltation of Scripture to please Protestants:* "In order to achieve the restoration, progress, and adaptation of the sacred liturgy it is essential to promote that sweet and living love for sacred scripture to which the venerable tradition of Eastern and Western rites gives testimony" (SC 24). "In sacred celebrations a more ample, more varied, and more suitable reading from sacred scripture should be restored" (SC 35.1).

§ 11   *Rendering the liturgy less sacred and more democratic, and imitating Protestant and pentecostal customs:* "To promote active participation, the people should be encouraged to take part by means of acclamations, responses, psalms, antiphons, hymns, as well as by actions, gestures and bodily attitudes" (SC 30).

§ 12   *Indirect mention of the Protestant doctrine on the two tables:* "The Church, therefore, earnestly desires that Christ's faithful .... through a good understanding of the rites and prayers .... should take part in the sacred action, conscious of what they are doing, with devotion and full collaboration. They should be instructed by God's word, and be nourished at the table of the Lord's Body. They should give thanks to God" (SC 48). "The treasures of the Bible are to be opened up more lavishly so that a richer fare may be provided for the faithful at the table of God's word" (SC 51).

§ 13   *Rushing liturgical reform and Bishops' collegiality:* "The liturgical books are to be revised as soon as possible. Experts are to be employed on this task, and bishops from various parts of the world are to be consulted" (SC 25).

§ 14   *Attributing a messianic character to the reform:* "Zeal for the promotion and restoration of the sacred liturgy is rightly held to be a sign of the providential disposition of God in our time, and as a movement of the Holy Spirit in his Church" (SC 43).

§ 15   *Exaltation of the Bishop's power to the detriment of papal power:* "The bishop is to be considered as the High Priest of his flock from whom the life in Christ of his faithful is in some way derived and upon whom it in some way depends" (SC 41a).

§ 16   *Promoting equality among the faithful and a disdain for higher classes:* "In the liturgy .... no special exception is to be made for any private person or classes of persons whether in the ceremonies or by external display" (SC 32).

§ 17   *The priest as president of the community:* "In the liturgy God speaks to his people, and Christ is still proclaiming his Gospel. And the people reply to God both by song and prayer. Moreover the prayers addressed to God by the priest who, in the person of Christ, presides over the assembly, are said in the name of the entire holy people and of all present" (SC 33a, b).

§ 18   *Encouraging use of the vernacular:* "But since the use of the vernacular, whether in the Mass, the administration of the sacraments, or in other parts of the liturgy, may frequently be of great advantage to the people, a wider use may be made of it .... These norms being observed, it is for the competent territorial ecclesiastical authority .... to decide whether, and to what extent, the vernacular language is to be used" (SC 36-2,3).

§ 19   *Ending the primacy of the Latin Rite and establishing 'inculturation':* "Even in the liturgy the Church does not wish to impose a rigid uniformity in matters which do not involve the faith or the good of the whole community. Rather does she respect and foster the qualities and talents of the various races and nations. Anything in these people's way of life which is not indissolubly bound up with superstition and error she studies with sympathy and, if possible, preserves intact. She sometimes even admits such things into the liturgy itself" (SC 37). "In some places and circumstances .... an even more radical adaptation of the liturgy is needed .... The competent territorial ecclesiastical authority .... must .... consider which elements of traditions and cultures of individual peoples might appropriately be admitted into divine worship" (SC 40-1). "The Church, indeed, approves of all forms of true art .... and admits them into divine worship" (SC 112c). "The art of our own times from every race and country shall also be given free scope in the Church" (SC 123).

§ 20   *Opening the gates to liturgical abuse:* "The canons and ecclesiastical statutes which govern the provision of external things which pertain to sacred worship should be revised as soon as possible, together with the liturgical books .... These laws refer especially to the worthy and well-planned construction of sacred buildings, the shape and construction of altars, the nobility, placing and security of the Eucharistic tabernacle, the suitability and dignity of the baptistry, the proper ordering of sacred images, and the scheme of decoration and embellishment. Laws which seem less suited to the reformed liturgy should be amended or abolished. Those which are helpful are to be retained, or introduced if lacking. In this matter, especially as regards the material and form of sacred furnishing and vestments .... powers are given to territorial episcopal conferences to adapt such things to the needs and customs of their different regions" (SC 128a, b).

*

b) The Modifications of 1969 and the Remodeling of 1970

§ 21   To further carry out the reform of *Sacrosanctum Concilium* in 'opening up' the liturgy, Paul VI set up a new commission to reform the liturgy of the Mass: the Pontifical Commission for the Application of the Constitution on the Sacred Liturgy.[8] The commission was headed by Fr. Anibale Bugnini,[9] and included Protestant observers.[10] The fruit of these studies was the Apostolic Constitution *Missale romanum* of Paul VI, published on April 3, 1969.

---

[8] *Consilium Pontificium ad Excequendam Constitutionem de Sacra Liturgia.*

[9] Fr. Bugnini played a highly relevant role in bringing about liturgical changes in the Church. Already as far back as 1956, he was co-author of the Holy See's unofficial commentaries regarding the reform of Pius XII (A. BUGNINI - C. BRAGA, *Ordo Hedomadae Sanctae instauratus*, Rome, 1956, in P. ROMANO ROCHA, Ibid.).

Fr. Bugnini, later raised to the Episcopate, also played a key role in the preparatory phase of the schema on the liturgy. Unlike nearly all the other secretaries of preparatory commissions, his defense of the changes and the strong reactions they caused prevented him from automatically becoming the secretary of the Council's liturgical commission (R. LAURENTIN, op. cit., vol. II, pp. 23, 25; vol. VI, p. 242). However, as a manifestation of his content with Bugnini's work, Paul VI designated him secretary of the post-conciliar liturgical commission. Accordingly, the most important task of preparing the reform of the Mass was also entrusted primarily to him.

[10] On April 10, 1970, Paul VI received the commission that prepared the new *Ordo Missae*. As a picture of the audience was about to be taken, the Pontiff chose to appear at the side of the observers from "non-Catholic ecclesial communities." In the foreground, next to Paul VI, appears Max Thurian, of the community of Taizé (A. V. XAVIER DA SILVEIRA, *La nouvelle messe de Paul VI*, cover).

§ 22

This Apostolic Constitution promulgated two documents regarding the reform of the Mass: the *Institutio generalis Missalis romani* and the new *Ordo Missae*. These documents officially came into force on November 30, 1969, vested with papal authority.[11]

The *Institutio* includes 341 articles in which the new rites are minutely explained. At the same time, it establishes theoretical and practical principles for the Eucharistic celebration.[12]

The 1969 *Ordo* includes the new text of the Mass and the new rubrics for its celebration.

Paul VI declared that the promulgation of those documents had not been improvised but was rather the result of long and profound studies.[13] However, in May 1970, when the Latin edition of the new Roman Missal was published, the *Institutio* and the *Ordo* of 1969 appeared in it with numerous modifications. This is certainly surprising. In fact, the alterations of 1970 were introduced in an attempt to somehow reduce the grounds for the numerous criticisms that the ambiguities of the text and its tendency to make a rapprochement with Protestantism had provoked.

In the exposition below, we will examine whether those modifications actually attenuated the gravity of the ambiguities found in the *Institutio* and in the *Ordo Missae*.[14]

*

---

[11] Ibid., p. 12.

[12] Ibid.

[13] PAUL VI, *Missale romanum*, Typis Polyglottis Vaticanis, 1970, pp. 8f.

[14] Note that the *Institutio* of 1969 and the *Ordo Missae* of 1969 used by the author on whom we based ourselves (sections b-f) were not part of the multiple vernacular versions published, but the actual Latin text of the Apostolic Constitution in its official edition entitled *Ordo Missae* (in A. V. XAVIER DA SILVEIRA, op. cit., p. 11, note 1). The texts of 1970 quoted by the author are from the *Missale romanum*, in its official edition in Latin (Ibid., p. 13, note 9).

c) An Example of Tendentious Ambiguity: the Priestly Role of the People

§ 23   We chose one example, among many worthy of note, of instances in which the rite of the Mass was modified[15] in essential points: the role of the people in the new concept of the Mass. Although there are other points of even greater relevance, we chose this one because it can be easily understood.

The Priestly Role Attributed to the People in the *Institutio* of 1969

§ 24   According to the teaching of the Council of Trent, the priesthood "was instituted by that same Lord our Saviour, and that to the apostles and their successors in the priesthood was handed down the power of consecrating, of offering, and administering His body and blood, and also of forgiving and retaining sins, the Sacred Scriptures show and the tradition of the Catholic Church has always taught."[16]

For this reason the church teaches that the power of consecrating belongs exclusively to the priest and can in no way be attributed to the people. The reference to the 'priesthood of the faithful' that appears in Sacred Scriptures and in certain church teachings should be understood *lato sensu*. It does not indicate the power of consecrating and of forgiving sins, but only the consecration of the Catholic that proceeds from Baptism, that is, the desire of dedicating oneself to the cause of the Church and to the divine work in union with Christ.

To confuse the priesthood of the faithful people with that of the priest is to accept the thesis of Protestants, who, since the sixteenth century, have held that the celebration of the 'Lord's supper' is realized jointly by the priest and the people in equal

---

[15] About the history of the rite of the Holy Mass designated in current parlance as the 'Mass of Saint Pius V,' of its formulas and its dogmatic value that harken back at least to the time of Saint Gregory the Great, we recommend the timely and scholarly study by Remi AMELUNXEN-Paul TRINCHARD, "Historical Prelude: A Brief History of the Holy Mass from the Canonized Liturgy to the Novus Ordus English Liturgy", in P. TRINCHARD, *New Mass in Light of the Old*, Monrovia, CA: Marian Publications, 1995.

[16] DS 1764.

conditions. The pastor only presides over the assembly in the liturgical celebration as a delegate of the those assisting.

§ 25

With regard to this subject, **the *Institutio* is ambiguous. As Xavier da Silveira points out, it** "maintains some expressions found in traditional doctrine, but **introduces** along with them **notions and principles that insinuate or contain the Protestant theses**. Thus, one reads in n. 10 that the priest 'presides over the assembly representing Christ (*personam Christi gerens*),' and in n. 60 that 'the priest .... presides over the gathered assembly acting in the place of Christ (*in personam Christi praeest*).' Number 48 says that the priest 'represents Christ (*Christum Dominum repraesentans*).' As one sees, these expressions have an altogether traditional *tonus*, being even the technical terms which designate the manner by which the celebrant acts in place of Our Lord. Such expressions, however, appear in **the *Institutio*** in a context that causes a certain perplexity. **On the one hand**, it **does not say *exactly* what is meant by 'taking the place of Christ' or 'representing Him.' On the other hand**, the *Institutio* **contains numerous passages that insinuate that the celebrant is a mere president of the assembly, and that his *principal function* in the Mass consists in *representing* the faithful gathered there.**"[17]

§ 26

Such impressions, according to this same author, **open the door for an interpretation of the 'representation' of Christ in a broader sense that dilutes the specific notion of the hierarchical and visible priesthood**, in function of which the priest lends his lips and voice to Our Lord at the moment of the Consecration.

* In n. 7 of the first edition of the document, **the priest is qualified only as president of the 'assembly of the people of God.'**

* In n. 10, after the affirmation that the priest presides over the assembly, the document states that the Eucharistic prayer constitutes a 'presidential prayer.' The same article defines the 'presidential prayers' as those that "are directed to God in the name of all the holy people and of all here present."

"Undoubtedly," Xavier da Silveira observes, "there are parts of the Eucharistic prayer that are directed to God in the name of the people. But **its principal part, the Consecration, is**

---

[17] A. V. XAVIER DA SILVEIRA, op. cit., p. 31.

said exclusively by the priest in the name of Our Lord. It is impossible for a Catholic to admit any ambiguity on this point. Therefore, n. 10 of the *Institutio* is one of the most censurable of the whole document."[18]

* In n. 12, we find this affirmation: "'The *nature* of the 'presidential' parts demands that they be pronounced in a loud and clear voice, and be listened to attentively by all. Therefore, when the priest is pronouncing them, let there be no other prayers or hymns, and let the organ and any other musical instruments be silent."

"Likewise," comments the forecited author, "**the words of the Consecration should be pronounced under those conditions – which insinuates once more that, in that moment, the priest acts specifically as a delegate of the people. Furthermore, this item of the *Institutio* contains a flagrant and grave contradiction to the rubric of the traditional *Ordo,* according to which the Canon is not said in a 'loud and distinct' voice. This fact is particularly worthy of attention in view of the following anathema issued by the Council of Trent: 'If anyone says that the rite of the Roman Church whereby a part of the Canon and the words of the Consecration are pronounced in a low voice must be condemned .... let him be anathema.'[19]* By stating that the *nature* of the 'presidential' parts** (and therefore the Eucharistic prayer and the words of the Consecration) ***demand* that they be pronounced in a loud and clear voice, the *Institutio* establishes a principle valid for all times and therefore implicitly affirms that the Council of Trent erred on this point.**"[20]

* Number 271 formulates a new criticism of the traditional Mass, also based upon the false notion of the 'presidential' function of the celebrant: "'The seat of the celebrant ought to signify his function as president of the assembly and director of prayer. For this reason, its most suitable position is facing the people, in the center rear of the sanctuary.' According to the Roman *Ordo,* the priest is normally facing the altar for he is above all the one who sacrifices, who presents himself before the Eternal Father in the name of the Word Incarnate. This modification

---

[18] Ibid. p. 32.

[19]* DS 1759.

[20] A. V. XAVIER DA SILVEIRA, op. cit., pp. 32f.
Number 12 of the *Institutio* was not modified in 1970.

is based upon a notion of 'presidency' of the 'assembly' that conflicts with traditional doctrine."

§ 27

In a footnote, Xavier da Silveira makes this observation:
"We note that, according to traditional Church practice, there is
no exclusiveness in this matter. In numerous rites, for example,
the Mass is celebrated *versus populum*. **What causes perplexity
is the fact that the new *Ordo* proscribes the Mass not celebrated *versus populum* as a less adequate means since it fails
to appropriately express the priest's 'presidential function.'"**

In the Prologue of the 1970 *Institutio*

§ 28

The 1970 edition of the *Institutio* was preceded by a prologue that manifests the preoccupation of presenting principles of
Catholic doctrine that were not presented or were presented insuf-
ficiently in the *Institutio*. However, a careful study of this prologue shows that the modifications introduced did not substantially change the document of 1969.

Noteworthy articles from the prologue that are presented
with completely insufficient formulations include the following:

* Article 4, which affirms: "The nature of the ministerial
priesthood, proper to the priest – who in the place of Christ (*in
persona Christi*) offers the sacrifice and presides over the assembly of the holy people – makes itself manifest in the very form of
the rite, by means of a greater eminence of the position and function of the priest in relation to the people. The principles of this
function are expounded and explained more clearly in the thanksgiving of the Mass of the blessing of the Holy Chrism on Holy
Thursday, the day on which the institution of the priesthood is
commemorated. For this text emphasizes the conferring of the
priestly power that is realized by the imposition of hands. Enu-
merating each of its functions, it describes this same power that is
a continuation of the power of Christ, the High Priest of the New
Testament."

§ 29

This article contains some indisputable truths: that the
priest acts in the place of Christ and that the power with which he
is invested proceeds from Our Lord. However, **one** also **notes a
dangerous approximation between the 'offering of the sacrifice' and the 'presiding over the assembly of the holy people.'**
For the latter function, notes Xavier da Silveira, is "secondary,
accidental, and a simple consequence of the first. Even in the absence of an 'assembly of the holy people,' the celebrant fully
exercises his priestly function at the Mass. **The importance** thus

**given to the 'presidential' role of the priest in the Mass favors
the impression among the faithful that the sacrifice is celebrated by both them and by the priest.** .... Therefore, given the
context of the *Institution,* given the criticisms that have rightly
been made of it on this point, and given the erroneous interpretations that have arisen, **it would be suitable and even indispensable for the *Institutio,* in its corrected version, to have eliminated once and for all this very dangerous error, which completely destroys the doctrine on the Catholic priesthood. It
would be necessary to affirm not only the *ministerial* character of the priesthood but also its *hierarchical* nature, which
places it essentially above any other representation of Christ
that might exist in, or proceed from, the people."**[21]

    * Item 5 of the Prologue is even more serious than the
former, because it confirms and amplifies the tendenices manifested there. It reads: "But, alongside considerations of this nature on the ministerial priesthood, another reality of great importance is also placed in its true light, that is, the royal (*regale*)
priesthood of the faithful, whose spiritual sacrifice is insinuated
by the ministry of the priest in union with the sacrifice of Christ,
the sole Mediator. Indeed, *the celebration of the Eucharist is the
action of the whole Church;* [22]* and in this action, each one
should do only and entirely that which behooves him in view of
the position he holds in the people of God. For this reason, we
have also paid greater attention to certain aspects of the celebration that have attracted less interest over the centuries. Indeed,
this people of God, redeemed by the Blood of Christ, reunited by

---

[21] Ibid., pp. 101f.

[22]* In a footnote, the author says: "The 'celebration of the Eucharist' in
its proper sense is exclusively an action of Christ and of the priest who
represents Him at Mass. In the Encyclical *Mediator Dei,* Pius XII condemned the statement that 'the eucharistic sacrifice' is an authentic
concelebration of the priest as well as of the people present (AAS,
1947, p. 553). The faithful can and should unite with the celebrant to
offer the victim that is immolated, and in this sense the Mass really is
an action of the whole Church. But the offering made by the faithful is
essentially distinct from that of Our Lord. One may not say, in any case,
that, on account of this offering, the common faithful become authentic
'celebrants' of the Mass. There is no doubt that, analogically, the term
'celebration' can have broader meanings. But **it is not legitimate to
distort those meanings so as to insinuate that the faithful have a
function of 'celebration' properly speaking. For this reason, in the
context of item 5 of the Prologue, the expression 'the concelebration of the Eucharist is an action of the whole Church,' is ambiguous.**"

the Lord, nourished with His word; *a people called to carry to God the prayers of the whole human family*; a people that gives thanks in Christ for the mystery of salvation, *offering his sacrifice*; a people, finally, that grows in unity through communion in the Body and Blood of Christ. This people, while holy in its origin, nevertheless continuously grows in its sanctity through the same conscious, active, and fruitful participation in the Eucharistic mystery."

§ 30   Commenting upon article 5, Xavier da Silveira observes: **"When we consider carefully the terms of this item 5, we see that they clearly reaffirm the notion of the priesthood of the people,** which we previously pointed out as unacceptable. Indeed, what are these 'aspects of the celebration that have attracted less interest over the centuries'? One of them is the fact that the holy people are 'called to carry to God the prayers of the whole human family.' Another is the fact that this people, '*offering* his sacrifice, gives thanks, in Christ for the mystery of salvation.' As can be seen, **we see here the same kinds of imprecision and ambiguity that existed in the previous text of the *Institutio.*** .... Incidentally, this passage establishes a strange distinction between the 'people of God' and the 'human family.' For it says that the former, by the priestly action that it exercises in the Mass, carries to God the prayers 'of the whole human family.' **Taken in its natural sense, this expression indicates that the 'people of God' exercise, properly speaking, a priestly function of mediation between the whole human race .... and God.**

"Even more: since the phrase that follows immediately attributes to this same 'people of God' the faculty of 'offering the Sacrifice to Christ,' it appears that throughout the Mass the prayers of *all men* taken indiscriminately, that is, including non-Catholics, non-Christians, polytheists, atheists, etc., are presented to God and made agreeable to Him. **Such a conception of the Mass is all the stranger in that it agrees with a certain heterodox ecumenism that is spreading in large sectors of the Catholic public.** In view of all these dangerous ambiguities, the fears that we expressed above in regard to item 4 are aggravated in item 5 of the Prologue. Indeed, in item 5, **not only the silence about the *hierarchical character* of the priestly ministry of the celebrant, but also the absence of a clear conception of the *representation of Christ by the priest*, favor and prepare for an erroneous notion of the priesthood of the faithful."[23]**

---

[23] Ibid., pp. 102-105.

In the *Institutio* of 1970

Number 7 of the Institutio, which caused an outcry, was rewritten in the 1970 edition. It says: "In the Mass or Supper of the Lord, the people of God are united under the presidency of the priest, who acts in the place of Christ (*personam Christi gerente*) to celebrate the memorial of the Lord or the Eucharistic sacrifice. Accordingly, for this local gathering of the Holy Church, the promise of Christ, 'Wherever two or three are gathered together in My name, I am there, in the midst of them' (Mt 18:20), holds in an eminent way. Indeed, in the celebration of the Mass, in which the sacrifice of the Cross is perpetuated, Christ is really present in the very assembly gathered in His name, in the person of the minister, in His words, and moreover, substantially, and permanently under the Eucharistic species."

§ *31*   Even with this new rendering, n. 7 can still be the object of the same criticisms made about the former version. With regard to this, Xavier da Silveira makes this analysis: "In this new text, n. 7 is still susceptible to corrections almost as serious as before. .... **The gravest fault consists in affirming that it is the *people* who *celebrate* the memorial of the Lord or Eucharistic sacrifice**. Note, indeed, that the word *celebrandum* has as agent *populus Dei*. After all we have said about the gravity of this concept, we think it would be superfluous to spend more time on this point. Let us simply note that **this same concept can be found in various places in the new text of the *Institutio*. This alone would suffice to show how the document strays from the teachings of the Church**.

"Even in the new text of n. 7, one observes that the strange imprecisions about the diverse manners of 'presence' of Our Lord in the Mass continue. In fact, it is said that His presence under the Eucharistic species is 'substantial and permanent.' The expression is absolutely exact. But the [Latin] word *enim* [because] establishes an unclear and very dangerous connection between that substantial presence and the principle enunciated above: 'Where two or three are gathered together in My name, there I am in the midst of them.' What relation would there be between these two 'presences'? Would the 'communitarian' nature of the 'assembly gathered in the name of Christ' contribute to His becoming present under the Eucharistic species? Or would it cause this second presence to be more fully attained? Or does the assembled 'people of God' exercise some active function to make effective the substantial presence of Our Lord in the Eucharist? **The text allows dangerous ambiguities to remain about this point, particularly since it was said above that the 'people** of God' *celebrate* **the sacrifice**. Nor are the necessary distinctions established between the diverse modes of the non-substantial presence of Christ: that is, in the gathered assembly, in the person of the minister, and in the word of Scripture. **The fact that the assembly is mentioned before the minister is telltale since it could indicate that the presence of Our Lord in the people is, if not superior, at least more fundamental to the Eucharistic celebration than His presence in the person of the minister."[24]**

The Affinity of 'Communitarian' Liturgy with Protestantism

§ 32   To what could one liken this effort of the post-conciliar period to introduce through ambiguous formulas the notion of a priestly ministry of the faithful?

    The answer comes, a *contrario sensu,* from Luther Reed, a Lutheran pastor in the United States. Expounding on the 'communitarian' nature of the cult established by Luther, he says: "The medieval church destroyed the earlier unity and the sense of corporate worship by emphasizing the priestly class and by removing the laity from all active participation. The Reformation corrected this and duly restored the priesthood of believers and the congregational character of worship. Masses without communicants were forbidden and actual communion by the people was promoted. The use of the vernacular, together with the development of hymnody and of popular preaching, were significant factors. The worldwide liturgical movement in the Roman Church today is a belated effort to develop intelligent active lay participation in the Mass so that the people may think of themselves as 'co-celebrants' with the priest."[25]

*

d) Two Extremely Important Points

§ 34   Our concern with synthesis throughout this section does not prevent us from pointing generically to two principal points of the Mass that were modified by the *Novus Ordo*, that is to say, the Offertory and the Consecration. In these points we also note a

---

[24] Ibid., pp. 117ff.

[25] Luther REED, *The Lutheran Liturgy* (Philadelphia: Fortress Press, 1959), p. 334, in Ibid., p. 143.

tendency to accomodate the rite of the Mass to the doctrinal and liturgical desires of the Protestants.

Omissions and Tendentious Ablations in the Offertory

§ 35   How is the Offertory in the Mass of Saint Pius V understood?

The true sacrificial oblation that is made in the Mass is not in the Offertory, but in the offering that Jesus Christ, at the moment of Consecration, makes of Himself to the Most Holy Trinity. The true victim in the Sacrifice of the Mass is not the bread and wine nor the faithful there present, but Jesus Christ Himself.

The oblation that Our Lord makes of Himself is not visible to us since He does not present Himself in a manner perceptible to our senses. Thus, it is proper that there be perceptible elements that express the nature of the Sacrifice that will take place as well as the diverse oblations that will be made. This is the object of the Roman Offertory. As a consequence, during the course of the Offertory, it is stated what is the sacrificial oblation properly speaking, as well as the offering of ourselves to God. The propitiatory end of the Mass is likewise affirmed.

§ 36   The fundamental characteristics of the Offertory can, therefore, be reduced to three elements:

* The oblation of Our Lord truly takes place at the moment of the Consecration, but to make the sacrificial nature evident from the very beginning, the Roman Missal contains an ensemble of prayers that tell us who is the true Victim who will be immolated and, by way of anticipation, offers this victim to the Most Holy Trinity.

* The oblation of ourselves to God by means of Jesus Christ is symbolized by the offering of the bread and wine. Secondarily, it is symbolized by the offering of other material goods. We should note that the symbolism only becomes effective if the bread and wine, at the moment when they are placed upon the altar, are not just presented to God, but are truly offered in a sacrificial spirit. In other words, the gifts are consecrated to God.

* The Roman Offertory, through many of its prayers, clearly shows the propitiatory character of the Sacrifice.[26]

---

[26] Ibid., pp. 64ff.

§ 37   Xavier da Silveira notes this about the changes: "**These three elements have disappeared in the new Offertory, replaced by a simple 'reparation of the offerings' or 'preparation of the gifts,' which corresponds to** *a conception of the Offertory that is fundamentally different from that of Saint Pius V.* **In addition to this, various expressions of the other principles that distinguished Catholic doctrine from Protestantism were suppressed or attenuated**. The allusion to the fall of our first parents was eliminated. The invocation to Our Lady, the Angels, and the Saints disappeared. The principle that the sacrifice should be accepted by God for it to be agreeable to Him became less clear. The manifestations of humility and compunction for one's own sins were weakened, as well as the affirmation of the hierarchical priesthood of the celebrant. And there is no longer any explicit reference to the faithful departed."[27]

§ 38   Perhaps one of the most important confusions in the Offertory concerns the concept of Transubstantiation. Only an allusion to the Transubstantiation of the bread occurs, i.e.: "That this bread may become for us the bread of life." **Here also we note the presence of ambiguity, since the word of God is also the bread of life**, according to the words of Jesus Christ: "Man does not live by bread alone, but by every word that comes out of the mouth of God." (Mt 4:4) The *Mysterium fidei*, Transubstantiation, the bodily presence of Christ after the Consecration is obviously not just spiritual bread. The words 'bread of life' suggest misinterpretations such as transignification instead of Transubstantiation.

    Although we do not want to prolong the presentation of this subject beyond the indispensible necessary for this Volume, let us at least mention that there are indisputable protestantizing consequences to the elimination of the fundamental prayers of the Offertory such as the *Suscipe Sancte Pater,* the *Offerimus tibi Domini,* the *Deus qui humanae substantiae*, and the *Veni Sanctificator*.[28]

Essential Modifications of the Consecration

§ 39   There was a modification in the formula of the canon of the Mass, or the Roman canon, also now called the Eucharistic prayer. The text of the new formula tends to accommodate the

---

[27] Ibid., p. 66.

[28] Ibid., pp. 66-76.

conception of Eucharist as a simple *agape* realized by the community in commemoration of the Passion and Ressurrection of Our Lord.[29]

In the *Novus Ordo*, three new formulas of Eucharistic prayers are introduced, thus giving the celebrant a choice from four formulas. **A true canon of the Mass, that is, an exclusive rule according to which the sacrifice must be celebrated, ceases *ipso facto* to exist. The new Eucharistic prayers must desacralize the traditional Roman Canon and sound strange to pious ears even as they make, in a certain way, the central part of the Mass acceptable to Protestants.**[30] **The fact that the central part of the Mass has become less removed from Protestantism tends to create confusions that are inadmissable and extremely prejudicial to the Faith.**

The Consecratory formula has been fused into the preparatory prayer of the Consecration, *Qui pridie*, and the two together have become 'the Narration of the Institution.'[31] By this fusion, **it is implied that the Mass has been changed from a Sacrifice to merely a memorial supper.** Importantly, the form of the Consecration of the Holy Sacrifice of the Mass was definitively expressed at the dogmatic Council of Florence in 1442, reiterated at the dogmatic Council of Trent in 1545, and the *Missale romanum* was codified by Pope Saint Pius V in 1570 in the Bull *Quo primum tempore.*[32]

§ 40
The removal of the words *'mysterium fidei'* from the Consecratory formula of the wine in the *Novus Ordo* contradicts these two dogmatic councils and *Quo primum,* and could appear to be an deliberate attempt to eliminate the sacrificial nature of the Mass. This facilitates an acceptance of the *Novus Ordo* by Protestants and places grave doubts about Transubstantiation in the minds of the Catholic clergy and faithful. Doubts of this magnitude can without a question contribute

---

[29] Ibid., pp. 76-81.

[30] Ibid., pp. 81-86.

[31] Dietrich von HILDEBRAND - John McMANEMIN, "Why the Tridentine Mass?," in *Una Voce pamphlets on the Liturgy*, #2 (St. Paul: Remnant Press, n.d.).

[32] *Canons and Decrees of the Council of Trent*, translated by H. J. SCHROEDER (Rockford, Ill.: Tan Publishers, 1941); *Missale romanum*, Ex Decreto Sacrosancti Concilii Tridentini Restutum; St. PIUS V, Bull *Quo primum tempore*, of 1570.

powerfully to increase the extraordinary crisis of the Faith that is shaking large parts of the clergy.

The removal of *'Pro multis'* from the ICEL (International Committee on English in the Liturgy) version of the Consecratory formula of the wine in the *Novus Ordo* appears to contradict Sacred Scripture (Mt 26: 26-28; Mk 14: 22-24). As explained in the *Catechism of the Council of Trent*, the words 'for all' are not used because, with the miracle of Transubstantiation, the fruits of the Passion are alone spoken of and to the elect only did His Passion bring the fruit of salvation.[33] The changed Consecratory formula of the wine in the *Novus Ordo* seems undeniable. Thus, the heart of the Holy Sacrifice of the Mass has been profoundly modified by the *Novus Ordo*.

*

e) Other Topics, Not Studied Here, on the Reform of the Mass

The work by Xavier da Silveira analyzes other topics in addition to the priesthood of the faithful the Offertory, and the Consecration. His study is always punctilious and dispassionate, and its conclusions are always coherent, as the Reader can gauge from the examples cited. He covers the *Institutio* and the *Ordo* both of 1969 and of 1970.

§ *41*   For the Reader's information, we mention below some of the most important topics analyzed by the author.

In the *Institutio* of 1969

* The absence of any mention of the dogma of transubstantiation favors heresy.

* A definition of Mass, presented in n. 7, opposes that of the Council of Trent.

* The omission of the notion of propitiatory sacrifice incurs the anathema of the Council of Trent.

---

[33] *Catechism of the Council of Trent*, translated by John A. McHUGH - Charles J. CALLAN (South Bend, Ind.: Marian Publications, 1923).

* A tendency to place the 'liturgy of the Word' and the 'Eucharistic liturgy' on the same footing echoes heresies that deny the value of Tradition.

* The Mass is presented as a memorial of the Resurrection and the Ascension.[34]

In the *Ordo* of 1969

§ 42   * In the rite of communion, the general tendency is to suppress the signs that distinguished the celebrant from the assembly and to introduce prayers and symbols conducive to creating confusion between the priesthood of the celebrant and that of the faithful.[35]

In the Prologue of the *Institutio* of 1970

§ 43   * The Prologue implies that doctrinal errors in relation to Eucharistic worship no longer exist. As a consequence, one may introduce the vernacular, Communion under both species for the common faithful, new texts of prayers in the Mass, formulations adapted to modern theological language, etc.

* It repeats the tendency of the *Institutio* of 1969 to consider the action of the faithful as an essential element of the Sacrifice of the Mass.[36]

In the *Institutio* of 1970

§ 44   * The *Institutio* no longer mentions the propitiatory nature of the Sacrifice of the Mass. This is made clear only in n. 2 of the Prologue. Thus, the prior judgment about the *Institutio* prevails.

* It insists excessively upon the fact that the Eucharist commemorates the Resurrection, and thus glosses over the sacrificial and propitiatory character of the Mass.

---

[34] Ibid., pp. 16-42.

[35] Ibid., pp. 86-90.

[36] Ibid., pp. 109-113.

    * The new text, which alludes to the priestly function of the priest, absolutely fails to clarify the ambiguities about the 'celebration' of the people.[37]

In the *Ordo* of 1970

§ *45*   The new modifications introduced in the *Ordo of 1970* do not alter the criticisms made about the text of 1969.

*

f) The Ambiguities in the New Documents Contain Profound Affinities with Protestant Rites

§ *46*   We will now present some points of Protestant doctrine and rites relating to the Mass as a point of reference to analyze ambiguities in the liturgical reform.

    * For Luther and Melanchton, the Mass is no longer a sacrifice; teaching replaces sacrifice, the lectern takes the place of the altar.

    * All Christians are priests and therefore receive communion under both species.

    * Jesus Christ is not constantly present in the Eucharist. Protestants deny Transubstantiation.

    * Vernacular is introduced in worship and replaces Latin.

    * Primary importance is given to the sermon, then prayer and confession of faith, and finally, the supper.

    * Zwingli celebrated facing the assembly instead of the altar.

    * Acolytes distributed the bread to the faithful in the pews. Each took a piece of bread in his hands and put it in his own mouth.[38]

---

[37] Ibid., pp. 120ff.

[38] Ibid., pp. 130-160.

* The same heresiarch insisted that wooden chalices be used for the wine in order to reject all display of wealth.

* Luther and Melanchton were adamant about the principle of universal priesthood, thus confusing the priesthood of the priest with that of the people.

* Some parts of the Lutheran *confiteor* are said by the minister, others are said alternately by him and the people, and others said simultaneously by both the minister and the people. This also occurs in the new *Ordo Missae*.

* The pseudo-reformers confessed only to God and omitted all references to the intercession of the Virgin and the saints. The 'penitential rite' [*Confiteor*] of the new *Ordo* consists of three formulas from which the priest chooses the one he deems most appropriate. The second and third formulas contain no reference to Mary or to the saints.

* The Catholic Offertory is a legitimate and laudable 'anticipation' of the true offering of Our Lord to God the Father, which is made at the Consecration. The Lutherans reduced the Offertory to a presentation of the offerings by the people and the preparation of the bread and the wine for communion. In the *Novus Ordo*, the Offertory also appears to have taken this direction.

* As for the Canon of the Consecration of the Mass, Zwingli replaced its formula with four prayers. Luther was against its recitation in low voice.[39] In the footsteps of the two heresiarchs, the new *Ordo* also has four formulas for the canon, which is recited aloud.

*

g) Conclusions On the Protestantization of the Church Beginning with the Liturgical Reform

It is very difficult for one not to conclude that the reform of the Mass, and by extension, the liturgical reform, did not disfigure venerable characteristics of Catholic doctrine and ritual so as to bring them closer to important Protestant tenets. This conclusion inevitably arises from the exposition we have just made. It is not, however, ours alone. Let us look at the position of the late Cardinal Suenens, who had undeniable credentials to repre-

---

[39] Ibid., pp. 135-152.

sent the progressivist current, which is totally opposed to our way of thinking and judging.

In a long article published in *L'Osservatore Romano*, from which the most important excerpts are quoted in his memoirs, the Cardinal touches on the topic of the pseudo-Reformation, relating it to Vatican Council II. He says that the revolt of Luther and his cohorts was an understandable consequence of the 'evils' that supposedly afflicted Holy Church at the time. The Church allegedly erred by presenting herself as hierarchical and militant. This is what he appears to indicate by using the expressions 'abuse and juridical strictures in Latin scholastics.' In order to remedy these 'errors,' Vatican II would exercise a function of 'complementarity' by drawing closer to the heretics in many of their characteristics. Let us see what the last of the four Moderators of the Council left as record before presenting himself before God.

§ *48*

The Reformation – he says – "reacted to a large extent against abuses, juridical strictures, and Latin scholastics. As I see it, even if there had not been a decree on ecumenism in Vatican II, this Council would have remained eminently ecumenical by virtue of his very complementarity. Think about the insistence of the Council on the notions of Church and people of God, on the collegiality of Bishops and local Churches; think about the relevance given to *epiklesis*,[40] to the liturgy in a living language, to concelebration, to communion under both species, to the permanent diaconate, etc. Reinstating and re-emphasizing all this has had an effect on the present internal and ecumenical evolution in the Church. This whole contribution is laden with promise and hope."[41]

Does the ensemble of conciliar reforms analyzed here and praised by Card. Suenens mean that the Catholic Church has become entirely Protestant? This is not what he, or we, have said. But this does not lessen the gravity of the situation, since in rela-

---

[40] According to a current progressivist notion, Our Lord's presence in the Holy Mass does not take place at the moment of Consecration, in which Christ becomes really present in the Eucharistic species. Instead, it takes place during the invocation of the coming of the Holy Spirit, a part of the Mass called *epiklesis*. This is yet another confusion between the real presence and other divine presences that may occur during the Mass; it is also a virtual negation of the real presence. Furthermore, this invocation of the Holy Spirit has taken on pentecostal connotations with strong Protestant overtones.

[41] L. J. SUENENS, op. cit., p. 285.

tion to the Faith and to Sacred Liturgy, this adage prevails: *Bonum est integra causa, malum ex quocumque defectu.* Thus, the attenuating circumstance, that is, the fact that the reforms of the rite of the Mass are not entirely Protestant, could only please someone who did not truly love the Catholic Church. It would be like the situation of someone who, seeing how the insults and blows inflicted upon Our Lord Jesus Christ physically disfigured Him, were to comment, "After all, He still is not totally disfigured. Some parts in Him are still whole." Could someone who honestly thought that still deserve the honorable name of follower of Christ, of Catholic?

§ 49   Some people, nevertheless, have rejoiced at such reforms and even wish them to continue toward a full identification with Protestantism. At least, so it would appear from the words Card. Suenens attributes to Paul VI.

Narrating a visit to the Anglican cathedral in York, England, the Prelate told a theretofore unknown episode in the ecumenical relations of Paul VI. He said: "In the sacristy they showed me the chalice into which was set the ring of Cardinal Mercier given to Lord Halifax on the eve of his death. Paul VI drew inspiration from that gesture to offer an episcopal ring to Archbishop Ramsey with these words: 'This is not yet a wedding ring, but it is already an engagement ring.'"[42]

To what 'engagement' could Paul VI have alluded if not the rapprochement of the conciliar Church with Protestantism, of which Anglicanism is a denomination? If such an 'engagement' implied carrying out the change in the Church that we are now analyzing, how far will the rapprochement have gone when the 'wedding' takes place? We leave the answer for the Reader to ponder.

Once again we are clearly faced with the disastrous results produced by the ambiguities in the texts of the liturgical reform of the Constitution *Sacrosanctum Concilium* and the documents of 1969 and 1970 relating to the Mass in particular and to all acts of worship in general.

*

---

[42] Ibid., p. 171.

B. Multiple Concessions to the False Religions

§ *50*   Two pages written by Msgr. Luigi Sartori are particularly illuminating in regard to concessions by the Church to the false religions. So we do not hesitate to transcribe them here: "The pastoral character of Vatican II is further determined by the profound intention of *dialogue*. Paul VI's orientation gave this subject a greater clarity and decisiveness. **To positively mix [in the conciliar text] .... perspectives as varied as possible** has precisely this goal: on the one hand, it **enriches the doctrinal position** (and therefore the living possession of the truth) **of the interlocutor called the Catholic Church**, and on the other hand it favors dialogue with the others. The Council favors and promotes the plurality of theologies inside the Church. I would almost say it discovers their value, properly as a consequence of the external stimulus from interlocutors of the Church.

"**She is asked by the Protestants to become more sensitive and open to biblical language and that of the origin of Christianity. She is stimulated by the Jews and Muslims to return more decisively to the very origins of the history of salvation. She is called by the non-Christian religions and by the whole humanity to go beyond the letter of the Bible and fix her attention on history in general and on creation** in order to be able to speak the language of every man on this earth who has spoken, speaks, or will speak about God, himself, and the universe. .... And finally I would like to note what seems to me .... the *punctum saliens* of ecumenical dialogue in Vatican II: the updating of the *missionary* spirit for an opening and dialogue of the Church with the *world*. The insistence of Paul VI in this regard was decisive.

"Someone who reflects a little will not have difficulty discovering the progressive expansion of the ecumenical program for unity of the believers: the successive creation of the three secretariats[43] is a symbol of that. Finally, **the Council made the Church rediscover her universal mission in a perspective of openness (centrifugal and not centripetal,** one would say) and, therefore, of dialogue: **triumphant over the perils of colonialism** (which was spoken about in the Council, precisely in regard to the missions) **by means of a superior provision for 'mutual interchange'** in relations with men and the world, that is to say,

---

[43] Secretariat for the Promotion of the Unity of Christians (7/5/1960); Secretariat for Non-Christians (5/19/1964); Secretariat for Unbelievers (4/9/1965).

as she gives and receives in a spirit of humility and charity, of poverty and abundance at the same time.

"This is the dialogue which, in a certain sense, conditions all the others: from the living dialogue with brethren inside the Church to that with separated brethren, to that with all those who believe in God. Then **the *capacity to understand*** (and not just that of making oneself understood) **becomes important for the language of the Church in relation to all of humanity. Here you have a total victory [of openness] over the esoteric closedness in theological language and in the announcement of the faith.** .... I believe that the Council's effort, especially in *Gaudium et spes,* to adopt categories of thought and expression from contemporary culture to announce the faith is, therefore, of utmost importance."[44]

It is difficult not to see Msgr. Sartori's comment as a confirmation of what was said above about the new position of the Church in regard to heretics and pagans.

§ 51   Furthermore, Cardinal Suenens reveals the surreptitious meaning of a passage of the decree *Unitatis redintegratio,* which is supposed to contain the key to ecumenism: "*In the decree on ecumenism,* a small phrase was inserted, almost in passing, that must be examined in depth. Article 11 says: 'Furthermore, in ecumenical dialogue, Catholic theologians, standing fast by the teaching of the Church yet searching together with separated brethren into the divine mysteries, should do so with love for the truth, with charity and with humility. When comparing doctrines with one another, they should remember that *in* Catholic *doctrine there exists an order or 'hierarchy' of truths,* since they vary in their relation to the foundation of the Christian faith. Thus the way will be opened whereby this kind of fraternal rivalry will incite all to a deeper realization and a clearer expression of the unfathomable riches of Christ! ....

"**A precious phrase is this one that speaks of an 'hierarchy of truths.' Yes, every truth is true, but not every truth is equally central and vital to the Christian mystery.** Did the Lord perchance not say that He is 'the way, the truth and the life'? **A convergence of all Christians around the truths closer to the Lord and to the mystery of salvation,** when possible, **has a considerable importance in ecumenism.**

---

[44] L. SARTORI, "Il linguaggio del Vaticano II", in V.A., *Il linguaggio teologico oggi*, pp. 253f.

"What is central and vital in the Lord's Revelation? What is at the center of the indispensable communion of faith, preliminary to any ecumenical understanding? This question is capital: in its bosom lies all ecumenical hope. **Here also Vatican II did not say the last word, but the one it gave us is a germ of life, a grain of mustard that could become the great tree of which the Scripture speaks, where all the birds of the sky could gather."**[45]

Although he does not give explicit answers to the question he raises, Cardinal Suenens makes it clear that the foundation of ecumenism — the grain of mustard, according to him — is the notion of a 'hierarchy in truths' admitted by the conciliar Church.

The notion of 'hierarchy in truths' to which Cardinal Suenens refers is common in post-conciliar jargon. In order to explain it better, the progressivists imagine a metaphor in which the Catholic Church were higher up the mountain that leads to Christ, the other 'Christian' religions are somewhere below, those that believe in God even further below, and finally, on the base of the mountain, the atheists, who believe in nothing but vague principles. Principles are more general and encompassing to the degree that one comes down the mountain; and more specific and selective as one climbs. In this way, it would be possible to promote ecumenism with everyone starting from the general principles and one should ascend only without risking any harm to those general principles. This is the concept of 'hierarchy of truths' which the Council talks about and Cardinal Suenens has just expanded upon.

That this relativistic conception participates in religious indifferentism is a foregone conclusion.

We would like to emphasize, in accordance with the goal of this Item, that such a concept collides head-on with the Church's militancy and her missionary character.

The principle underlying the notion of a 'hierarchy of truths' is that the Catholic Church should not have a total and exclusive possession of the truth and the Faith. And consequently, she should not be the only representative of Jesus Christ.

§ *52*   Fr. Edward Schillebeeckx, the famous theologian from Nijmegen and influential conciliar *perito*, is quite straightforward

---

[45] L. J. SUENENS, "Discorso ufficiale d'apertura," in V.A., *L'avvenire della Chiesa*, pp. 50f.

as he explains the marrow of the question: "**By admitting that the other Christian communities are also Church, the Council passes judgment on the incapacity of its own Church to achieve the plenitude and unity desired by Christ. It is difficult to say that the Catholic Church is still one, Catholic, apostolic, when one says that the others are equally one, Catholic, and apostolic, albeit to a lesser degree.** Although maintaining the conviction that the Church of Christ in its apostolic plenitude is essential for salvation, **at Vatican Council II the Roman Catholic Church officially abandoned its monopoly over the Christian religion. In the conciliar documents, belonging to the Church no longer has one single meaning but an analogous meaning**. The whole problem now consists in knowing whether one should continue to see the analogy of the Church in such a way that the Roman Catholic Church is the *princeps analogatum*, whereas the other churches would be only *analogata*, called Churches only inasmuch as they approach the Roman Catholic Church. **It seems to me that it would be better to say that all the churches, and therefore also the Roman Catholic one, are *analogata* to that which in the Bible is called 'the Church of Christ.'** All of them are local churches of Christ. **The criterium of comparison is not the Roman Catholic Church as such**, but the apostolic plenitude, the plenitude of the messianic promise. **This is the perspective of Council Vatican II in the *Dogmatic Constitution on Divine Revelation*.**"[46]

The end of the Church's militant and missionary character is also subjacent, as a premise, in the author's words about the final goal of ecumenism: "**The final objective [of ecumenism] must be that all Churches recognize themselves and their own faiths in the other Churches, and not that all the other Churches return to the Catholic Church. Unity implies that the Catholic Church**, the Roman Catholic Church, see herself, beforehand, **reflected in that which we call the Protestant Church, and that the Protestant Churches plainly recognize themselves in the local Catholic Churches** without excluding all the local differences that may exist."

Here Schillebeeckx interrupts these surprising statements — though consistent from the ecumenical standpoint — to observe, in a footnote: "As I explained elsewhere, based on the recognition proclaimed by the Council of the ecclesial elements in non-Catholic Christian Churches, **we may even say that these Churches, precisely because of their character of [Protestant]**

---

[46] E. SCHILLEBEECKX, "Igreja ou igrejas?", in V.A., *Cinco problemas que desafiam a Igreja hoje*, pp. 26f.

reformation, historically have an essential function to fulfill in relation to the indefectibility of the Church in the form of a constantly renewed purification."

The author returns to his text: "Finding oneself in others is already unity. **From the moment that we understand that the differences of faith are not differences of *faith*, but only theological differences, it will become clear that the differentiation and plurality of forms can be preserved. The multiformity of the other Churches actually constitutes an enrichment for all parties**. .... Unity in the Church does not mean uniformity; there is no difficulty with admitting diverse modalities of Christian piety, to experiment with living the same fundamental reality in different thematic [doctrinal] expressions. .... This is also possible. Thus, **to the degree that study and ecumenical experience show that current divergencies are not fundamental dogmatic differences** but primarily theological differences, **we will be able to say that the various Churches together constitute only one *sacramentum mundi* and that**, in their turn, **the local Churches are signs of this great sacrament in the one Church** as the 'sacrament or sign of communion with God and of unity among all men' (LG 1)."[47]

§ 53   Fr. Hans Küng, also a *perito* of Vatican II, reinforces the statements of Schillebeeckx, basing himself on conciliar documents. He explains that the official writers wanted to leave the text ambiguous so as to foster ecumenism. He also attests to the contradictions between the attitudes of Vatican II and the perennial teaching of the Church:

"Even though some obscure points still remain, **Council Vatican II reviewed the attitude of the Catholic Church toward the other Christian Churches** in regard to very important points. 1 - **The Catholic Church used to recognize only heretics and schismatics** (whom at depth she considered to be in bad faith); **today, she addresses the remaining Christians generally as *separated brethren*. 2 - Whereas she used to recognize only isolated Christians outside the Church, today she recognizes the existence of *communities* of Christians ('*christianae communiones*', UR 1) outside the Church. 3 - She considers these communities not only as sociological quantities but as '*ecclesial communities*' or '*Churches*' ('*Ecclesia vel communitates ecclesiasticae*'; LG 15; UR 3). 4 - She also recognizes the association** of these Churches among themselves in the ecumenical movement born outside the Catholic Church and, in so doing,

---

[47] Ibid., pp. 33f.

cites the basic formula of the Ecumenical Council of Churches: 'Everywhere large numbers have felt the impulse of this grace, and among our separated brethren also there increases from day to day a movement, fostered by the grace of the Holy Spirit, for the restoration of unity among all Christians. Taking part in this movement, which is called ecumenical, are those who invoke the Triune God and confess Jesus as Lord and Saviour. They do this not merely as individuals, but also as members of the corporate groups in which they have heard the Gospel and which each regards as his Church and indeed, God's (UR 1). 5 - In this way, and notwithstanding the presence of other formulas that sound a little different, **the Catholic Church no longer identifies herself purely and simply with the Church of Christ.** At least in relation to one point, an explicit revision has been achieved: instead of the identification formula first proposed by the commission: 'The sole Church that we confess in the Creed as one, holy, Catholic and apostolic .... *is (est)* the Catholic Church, governed by the successor of Peter and by the bishops in communion with him,' this formula was admitted: '.... **subsists in** the Catholic Church' *(subsistit in)* (LG 8). **In order to justify the rejection, the first time ever, of the identification formula** (something of transcendental importance and which can give rise to grave consequences), **the commission added: 'So that this expression be in greater accord with the statement that elements of the Church also exist in other parts.'**[48]* The commission means to refer here to the 'churches or other ecclesial communities' mentioned in LG 15. **The new formula was consciously kept as vague as possible in order not to forestall a more ample theological implication,** which was absolutely necessary in so difficult a question."[49]

§ 54   In order to corroborate these explanations by renowned theologians, we would like to quote Fr. Bernard Sesboüé, a member of the International Theological Commission. By denying that the Catholic Church is the sole Church of Christ, he confirms what we have said so far about the end of the Church militant and of the missionary character of the Church. Furthermore, he attests to the influence of the Tübingen School at Vatican II, as we also said above.[50]

---

[48]* *Schema Constitutionis De Ecclesia* (Rome, 1964), pp. 15-25.

[49] H. KÜNG, *A Igreja*, vol. II, pp. 39f.

[50] Chap. VI.1.

Here are Sesboüé's words: "Fortunately, in the beginning of the nineteenth century, the romantic school of Tübingen brought a whole new stimulus to Catholic ecclesiology, whose weak propositions were becoming, it should be confessed, not very evangelical. .... **The work of Vatican II appears** then **as the conclusion of that whole germination and the definitive turnaround of the official perspectives**. .... **The Church still is not the Kingdom**, but rather the place where the latter progresses. **The Council** also **explicitly recognizes that outside the Catholic Church, there are other ecclesial communities that belong to the mystery of the Church regardless of their deficiencies. The frontiers of the Church of Christ are far from coinciding with the frontiers of the Roman Catholic Church**."[51]

§ 55

Also of interest is the testimony of Fr. Giuseppe Alberigo, a well-known professor of Church History at the University of Bologna, Secretary of the Institute for Religious Sciences of that city, journalist, director of the magazine *Cristianesimo nella Storia*, the 1960 Borgia Prize winner, and a member of the editorial staff of the magazine *Concilium*. He stresses the end to the doctrine that considers the Catholic Church as the sole Church of Christ and, consequently, the end of the era of militancy and propagation of the Faith.

Alberigo states: "After the first seven ecumenical councils, the successive general councils signaled a confirmation, from the global Christian standpoint, of a progressive reduction of Christianity to one of its constituent traditions, the primeval western tradition — Western-Roman, from Trent onward. With Vatican I, this tendency radicalized to the point that some were led to think that Catholicism had superseded its very possibility to hold councils.

"In regard to this itinerary, **Vatican II expresses an embryonic reversal of this tendency.** Indeed, although it is still a general council of the Catholic Church, posing the problem of announcing the Christian [message] to today's man and bringing the question of unity up-to-date (also with the decree, *Unitatis redintegratio*, and the presence of observers), **it explicitly raises questions that transcend the area and forces of each of the**

---

[51] Bernard SESBOÜÉ, *O Evangelho na Igreja - A tradição viva da fé* (São Paulo: Paulinas, 1977), pp. 81f.

traditional confessions and challenge all of contemporary Christianity."[52]

Alberigo goes on to criticize the 'timidity' of Vatican II and to label the part of *Lumen gentium* that still considers the constitution of the Church to be hierarchic as 'ecclesiocentric deformations': "**The** concrete **development of the works of Vatican II was only timidly consistent with such orientation**, above all to the degree that the Council concentrated on the ecclesiological question **with ecclesiocentric deformations,**[53]*** as was perhaps inevitable given its exclusive Catholic composition.**"[54]

*

§ 56   Based on the authors cited above, we conclude this Section B on concessions to the other religions by saying that the ambiguity of conciliar texts was intentional; to admit that the other religions are churches or that the Holy Spirit acts in them and that there is salvation in them is implicitly to deny the exclusivity of the true Faith and the authenticity of the Catholic Church; this is confirmed by the difference established between the Catholic Church and the 'Church of Christ.' As a direct consequence, such principles negate the militant character of the Church. She should no longer fear the onslaughts of proselytism by schismatics, heretics, and pagans, but instead approach them incautiously, in an attitude of dialogue. Finally, they deny the missionary character of the Church in the propagation of the Faith,[55] for if She is not considered the exclusive guardian of the Faith of Christ, trying to convert others would be nothing but an egocentric attitude that will soon be branded as 'spiritual colonialism.'[56]

---

[52] Giuseppe ALBERIGO, "Per un Concilio ecumenico cristiano nella prospettiva dell'unità della Chiesa," in V.A., *Verso la Chiesa del terzo millennio*, p. 63.

[53]* Chap. III of *Lumen gentium*.

[54] G. ALBERIGO, op. cit., p. 63.

[55] On the dialogue of the Church with the world, see Vol. V, *Animus delendi-II*, Part I, Chap. II.

[56] The expression is by Card. Lercaro, addressing the Brazilian Bishops gathered in Rome during the first conciliar phase (in B. KLOPPENBURG, *A eclesiologia do Vaticano II*, p. 154).

*

2. Concessions to the Modern World

§ 57
It would be well to make a few preliminary distinctions about the much-trumpeted adaptation of the Church to the world, *aggiornamento*.

A. Ambiguity in Conciliar Language Regarding the Concept of World

§ 58
The concept of *world* in Church moral teaching is not open to equivocation: the faithful are recommended to stay away from worldly things. The same does not happen in its socio-political teaching in which the word *world* can be interpreted in different ways:

§ 59
First, world can be considered the ensemble of men established as a society. In this sense, the Catholic Church is established in the world, since the ensemble of faithful is in the world. Also the State is founded in the world, of which all of its citizens make a part. Thus, in this sense, world is the place where both the Church and the State exert their influence. Therefore, the word world here has an ambivalent meaning.

§ 60
Second, world can be taken as synonymous with the temporal order, that is, the political constitution of the state. In this case, relations between the Church and the world are the same as relations between the Church and the State, and the teachings that the Magisterium has laid down during the centuries would be applied to them.

§ 61
Third, world, and especially the modern world, can be understood as 'modern civilization.' This would be that ensemble made up by the modern state born out of the French Revolution, derived from Illuminism, developed by modern philosophy and by modern science, based on Positivism and modern technology. Also, the modern world would include the egalitarian and liberal customs that were adapted in a first stage to the habits of a bourgeois consumerism, later to a proletarian communism, and today are moving swiftly toward an indigenous tribalism of a self-managing type.

Sartori also refers to the missions as 'colonialism,' § 50 above.

§ 62   When we ask ourselves which of the various meanings of
the word was adopted by the Council, we see that ambiguity prevailed also here. Even though the keynote is adaptation of the
Church to modern civilization (third meaning), the word is sometimes used to designate relations between Church and State (second meaning), or mankind as a whole (first meaning).[57]

---

[57] a. In the texts of Vatican II we find the word world used in all three
meanings:

1st meaning: "Proceeding from the love of the eternal Father, **the
Church** was founded by Christ in time and gathered into one by the
Holy Spirit. It has a saving and eschatological purpose which can be
fully attained only in the next life. But it **is now present here on earth
and is composed of men;** they, the **members of the earthly city,** are
called to form the family of the children of God even in this present
history of mankind and to increase it continually until the Lord comes ....
Thus the Church, at once 'a visible organization and a spiritual community,' **travels the same journey as all mankind and shares the
same earthly lot with the world; it is** to be **a leaven and**, as it were,
the **soul of human society** in its renewal by Christ and transformation
into the family of God" (GS 40b; PO 22b).

b. *2nd meaning:* "**All we have said up to now about the dignity of
the human person, the community of mankind, and the deep significance of human activity provides a basis for discussing the
relationship between the Church and the world and the dialogue
between them**" (GS 40a).

c. *3rd meaning:* "**The Church, moreover, acknowledges the good
to be found in the social dynamism of today, particularly progress
towards unity, healthy socialization, and civil and economic cooperation. The encouragement of unity is in harmony with the deep-
est nature of the Church's mission**, for it 'is in the nature of a sacrament — a sign and instrument — that is of communion with God and of
unity among all men.' It shows to the world that social and exterior union comes from a union of hearts and minds" (GS 42c, 23a, 34c, 54,
62b, f, g).

d. In the considerations below by Fr. Angel Antón, his letter b is close
to our 1st meaning; his letter c is not far from the 2nd meaning; his
letter a has something in common with the following Item in this Work
(Section B). His introductory remarks also confirm this Section A:

"It is necessary to indicate as the key point in *Gaudium et spes* its
concept of 'world' adopted in the preamble and abundantly described in
other passages of the Constitution. Though it is evident that the Council
tried to stress the positive aspects of the world as a work of the Creator,
Gaudium et spes left us a hardly elaborate concept of world from the
theological standpoint. Ratzinger wrote that this concept is still in its
pre-theological stage (J. Ratzinger, *Der Weltdienst der Kirche: Zehn*

Jahre nach Vaticanum II, eds. A. Bauch-A. Glasser-M. Seybold, Regensburg, 1976, p. 37), and hence it is necessary for post-conciliar theology to make it more precise.

"It is no less true that *Gaudium et spes* pointed out some positive aspects of the *polyvalent* notion of world. a) Although in the language of the Bible, whence it passed onto Christian literature, this concept has a pejorative *nuance* that comes from sin and the powers of the Evil One for working in the world, its positive aspects echoed by *Gaudium et spes* far outnumber [that nuance] as being the ensemble of God's creation renewed in Christ. b) *Gaudium et spes* also understands by 'world' the *men* who inhabit the earth, some of whom are good while others are bad in the moral and spiritual sense mentioned above, some being Christians, believers, or atheists. This does not mean that one must simply dissociate oneself from the latter. Without being of this world, the Church *lives* in the world and *for* the world. c) Finally, *Gaudium et spes* includes in the concept of world the *earthly realities* and the *temporal tasks* that man was called to carry out during his existence on earth. The realities of this world, created by God, have a certain autonomy that man must respect. By establishing the principle of distinction between the Church and human society, *Gaudium et spes* affirmed this relative autonomy of the temporal. But such a distinction does not mean that the two realities exclude all permutation and reciprocal influence. Incidentally, *Gaudium et spes* does not support the thesis that a Christian's profession of faith and his existence in the world unfold into two separate and impermeable domains" (A. ANTON, "L'ecclésiologie postconciliaire", in V.A., *Vatican II: Bilan et perspectives*, vol. I, p. 437).

e. A special excerpt of *Gaudium et spes* about the *world* calls our attention: "The Second Vatican Council .... longs to set forth the way it understands the presence and function of the Church in the world of today. Therefore, the world that the Council has in mind is the whole human family seen in the context of everything that envelopes it: it is the world as the theater of human history, bearing the marks of its travail, its triumphs and failures, the world, which in the Christian vision has been created and is sustained by the love of its maker, which has been freed from the slavery of sin by Christ, who was crucified and rose again in order to break the stranglehold of the evil one, so that it might be fashioned anew according to God's design and brought to its fulfillment" (GS 2).

Commenting on this excerpt and more generally on the position of *Gaudium et spes* toward the world, Cardinal Ratzinger calls it a 'counter-*Syllabus*,' confirming the presence of both the second and third meaning presented above. He states: **"If one is looking for a global diagnosis of the text, one could say that it (in connection with the texts on religious liberty and the world's religions) is a revision of the *Syllabus* of Pius IX, a kind of counter-*Syllabus*.** As is known, Harnack interpreted the *Syllabus* of Pius IX simply as a challenge to its century; what is true is that it drew a line of separation before the de-

An evaluation of the adaptation of the Church to the world, such as the one the Council defended, should therefore take into account the polyvalent meanings in which the word was used.

*

termining forces of the nineteenth century: the scientific and political conceptions of liberalism. In the modernist controversy, this double border was once again reinforced and fortified.

"Undoubtedly, many things have changed since then. The new ecclesiastical policy of Pius IX established a certain openness toward the liberal conception of State. In a silent but persevering combat, exegesis and Church history increasingly adopted the postulates of liberal science; on the other hand, liberalism was obliged, facing the great political upheavals of the twentieth century, to accept notable corrections. This happened because, first in central Europe, conditioned by the situation, the unilateral dependence in relation to the positions taken by the Church on the initiative of Pius IX and Pius X against the new period of history opened by the French Revolution was to a large extent corrected *via facti*; but a new, fundamental determination of relations with the world as it had been since 1789 was still lacking.

"Actually, in the countries with strong Catholic majorities, the mentality that preceded the revolution still reigned; today no one denies that for a long time this no longer corresponded to reality. Likewise, almost no one can deny that this dependence on an obsolete conception of relations between Church and State was matched by similar anachronisms in the domain of education and the attitude to be taken *vis-a-vis* the modern historic-critical method. Only a detailed research about the several ways in which the different parts of the Church welcomed the modern world could undo the complicated entanglement of causes that contributed to give shape to the pastoral constitution [*Gaudium et spes*], and only in this way could the drama of the history of its influence be clarified. Let us content ourselves here with finding that **the text plays the role of a counter-*Syllabus* to the degree that it represents an official attempt by the Church at reconciliation with the world as it became after 1789.** On the one hand, this visualization alone clarifies the ghetto complex of which we spoke in the beginning; on the other hand, it alone permits us to understand the meaning of this strange relationship of the Church with the world: **by 'world' one understands, at depth, the spirit of modern times. The group consciousness in the Church felt separated from this spirit** and looked for diaologue and cooperation with it after the hot war and the cold war [were over]" (J. RATZINGER, *Les principes de la théologie catholique - Esquisse et matériaux*, Paris: Tequi, 1985, pp. 426f.).

B. Adaptation of the Church to the World: General Considerations

§ 63   Among the great novelties of Vatican II is its opening to the modern world.

Up until that novelty was introduced, the Church had always considered the world as a territory in which good and evil disputed. Indeed, since man was conceived in the sin of our first parents, an indelible stain that affected human nature in its very origin, it would not be conceivable for society itself to escape the consequences of sin. The coming of Our Lord and Saviour Jesus Christ redeemed mankind of original sin. Nevertheless, it did not do so automatically, but in an inchoate manner. That is to say, even though Redemption was entirely accomplished by the Death and Resurrection of the Son of God, in order for the fruits of that Redemption to reach their plenitude, they require — after Baptism — the fidelity of every man to Faith and Morals within the Divine Institution that Our Lord founded.

"Only thus can those fruits expand throughout the world. Hence the divine mandate: "Go ye into the whole world, and preach the Gospel to every creature; he that believeth and is baptized shall be saved; but **he that believeth not shall be condemned**" (Mk 16:15-16). St. Matthews also puts forward the same mission entrusted to the Apostles and the Church: "All power is given to me in heaven and in earth. Going therefore, teach ye all nations: baptizing them in the name of the Father, and of the Son, and of the Holy Ghost, **teaching them to observe all things whatsoever I have commanded you**" (Mt 28:18-20). This divine mandate is also repeated in the Gospel of St. Luke: **"And thus it behooved Christ to suffer, and to rise again from the dead,** the third day; **and that penance and the remission of sins should be preached in his name, unto all nations,** beginning at Jerusalem" (Lk 24:46-47).

The premise of the divine mandate is, evidently, that the world is placed under the aegis of original sin: *"Mundus totus positus est in maligno"* (I Jn 5:19).

Therefore, the world is good only to the degree that it consciously and explicitly accepts the fruits of the Redemption of Our Divine Saviour and subjects itself to the divine mandate given to the Apostles and, consequently, to the Church.

§ 64   The acceptance of a doctrine by a group of men — society taken *in genere*, or by the world — must reflect clear attitudes that are actually expressed in the laws, customs, and institutions. A group of men, and *a fortiori* a society or the world, does not have a soul of its own to be saved or condemned. For this reason, its conformity with the true Faith must favor men, considered individually, who are susceptible of salvation or condemnation! It would not make any sense to speak of an acceptance by the world of the graces of Our Lord through the Church that would not be reflected, sooner or later, in laws, customs, and institutions.[58]

§ 65   As one seeks out the laws, customs, and institutions generated by the modern world, one sees that they are to a large extent the opposite of what was laid down as characteristic of a Catholic society. Born out of the deist philosophy of Illuminism and the Encyclopedia, synthesized in the trilogy Liberty-Equality-Fraternity and expressed in the *Declaration of the Rights of Man and of the Citizen*, it does nothing but generate laws, customs, and institutions that it proudly presents as laicist and, therefore, separate from the Church and the salvific fruits of Redemption. Moreover, this world has always struggled for the destruction of Christian Civilization shaped by evangelical principles.

The final utopia of the modern world and its agents is to establish a universal brotherhood independent of God, if not opposed to Him. Attempts at achieving this utopia were first sketched by the League of Nations, founded in 1919 with headquarters in Geneva and, after World War II, by the United Nations, headquartered in New York.

66   Hence the fact that the Church has always exercised the greatest vigilance in regard to the modern world.[59]

---

[58] True Catholic culture and civilization flourish precisely from this correspondence to grace. Prof. Plinio CORRÊA DE OLIVEIRA expounds upon this matter in his work, *Revolution and Counter-Revolution* (Part I, chap. VII.2.B): "A soul in the state of grace possesses all virtues to a greater or lesser degree. Illuminated by faith, it has the elements to form the only true vision of the universe. The fundamental element of Catholic culture is the vision of the universe elaborated according to the doctrine of the Church. .... Catholic civilization is the structuring of all human relations, of all human institutions, and of the State itself according to the doctrine of the Church".

[59] On the errors of the modern world and the condemnations it has received from the Ecclesiastical Magisterium, see the list of the main documents in Chap. I, Note 14. Also, about the Church's traditional teaching on modern errors, see Vol. V, *Animus delendi-II*, Part I, Chap. I, Premise 1.

*

C. The Church Should No Longer Orient and Influence Temporal Order, But Adapt Herself to It

§ 67   Great theologians whose thought has marked the post-conciliar period take a stand on Church-world relations by giving their doctrine on adaptation.

Hans Urs von Balthasar, the first theologian to be awarded the 'Paul VI International Prize,' was very highly praised by John Paul II when he received the prize at the Vatican Palace's Clementine Hall. The Pontiff, quoting phrases of von Balthasar called them 'grave, prophetic statements.'[60]

In his work *De l'intégration*, von Balthasar says: "It is certain that **the Church as a whole, in all of its members, but above all in its responsible hierarchy, must adapt its structures .... to the historic situation ....; but then it appears clearly that the factor of development is found first on the side of earthly history, and only in second place and by way of consequence, on the side of the Church.**"[61]

He continues: "**It is not so much the Church that develops in herself this face** [the visible face of God] **so as to adapt it to humanity; it is humanity, in its own development, that requires the Church to adapt to each human situation.**"[62]

§ 68   Fr. Chenu develops the progressivist doctrine on Church-world relations: "***Ecclesia ad extra*: with this formula one hears the announcement of the Gospel, and therefore the 'presence' of the Church *in* the world** – see the title of the new *Schema XIII* [The Church in the Modern World]. **It is not, for this reason, an extension of a previously constituted Church, nor an '*excursus*' about ecclesiastical society to affirm its rights over humanity. Here the very *nature* of the Church is what stands in question.** All the problems that She raises about herself, her

---

[60] "Giovanni Paolo II alla consegna del Premio Internazionale Paulo VI - Hans Urs von Balthasar ha messo la sua conoscenza al servizio del vero que promana da Cristo," in *L'Osservatore Romano*, 6/24/1984; Vol. II, *Animus injuriandi-I*, Chap. I.1.

[61] Hans Urs von BALTHASAR, *De l'intégration - Aspects d'une théologie de l'Histoire* (Brouges: Desclée de Brouwer, 1970), p. 136.

[62] Ibid., p. 137.

structure, her government (*ad intra*) are imposed by her reason for existence: to propagate the Word of God to men (*ad extra*) as the Mystical Body of Christ, after the Incarnation. **The Word of God and the Church** doubtlessly come from above .... nevertheless, they **are not superposed on the world, but incarnate themselves in it every day, according to the course of history that is formed gradually by successive generations.**"[63]

§ 69   Fr. Chenu points out the first part of *Gaudium et spes* as an example of Church adaptation to the world: "[At the Council] an inductive method manifested itself a little everywhere, but very particularly in this famous *Schema XIII*. It is also the first time in the history of councils that a text of this kind was preceded by a profane introductory analysis rather than a preliminary expose of Church position. **The authors of the text began by abstracting,** in a certain way, **from the problem of the Church to study the world in itself. .... The Church, officially becoming conscious of herself, obliges herself to become aware of how the world is changing. That is to say, a Church that used to rest on an established order decided that from now on she would make herself known in the movement of the world.**

In these five or six **introductory pages** to Part I **of Gaudium et spes, there are very strong statements.** For example: 'We are entitled .... to speak of a real social and cultural transformation;' **'Ours is a new age of history;'** 'We are faced with a crisis of growth that shakes the world.' I re-read all these texts complacently** as an historian as well as a theologian, not because they make an unsettling observation on novelties, but **because they go to the technical and economic roots, something the Church had never done until then. ....** In other words, **She has assumed in her behavior these realities which She neither mastered nor had to direct,** but which were her own inasmuch as they are the place in which She should utter the Word of God."[64]

70   The same new concept of Church *vis-a-vis* the world, stemming out of *Gaudium et spes*, is confirmed by Fr. Congar: **"It is not enough to see the Church and the world as two powers outside each other or placed face-to-face** (juxtaposed to each other) [sic]: **'the world' is no longer simply the power of the State, it is humanity working;** it is ready for the Church and

[63] M. D. CHENU, "La Chiesa e il mondo," in V.A., *I grandi temi del Concilio* (Rome: Paoline, 1965), p. 834.

[64] *Jacques Duquesne interroge le Père Chenu*, p. 183.

clamoring for her if the Church is understood as the one who reveals to it [the world] its own ultimate meaning. **Thus, seen in its existential and concrete condition, the world is rather part of the substance of the Church,** open to or at least ontologically or covertly oriented to her, rather than her competitor. *Gaudium et spes* often shows the world affected by the hidden presence of Christ or his Holy Spirit."[65]

§ 71   This is ratified by Fr. Leo von Geusau, founder of the Dutch Documentation Center (DOC) and later of the well-known IDOC:[66] "In the context of the Church as perfect society and its current variation expressed by the ecumenical movement, its place and implications in the world were not yet seen as a problem. Only in the last few years a growing number of thinkers attempted to formulate the question in clear and explicit terms. It is

---

[65] Y. CONGAR, "Le rôle de l'Eglise dans le monde de ce temps," in V.A., *L'Eglise dans le monde de ce temps,* vol. II, pp. 315f.

[66] The IDOC promoted a series of lectures by personalities such as Frs. Chenu, Küng, and Schillebeeckx outside of the Council's sessions. When Fr. Schillebeeckx spoke about *Schema XIII,* he was introduced by none other than Cardinal Alfrink, who congratulated DOC on the way it was carrying out its information service (H. FESQUET, op. cit., p. 425). IDOC is a huge international network, a progressivist media superpower.

Both organizations were initially denounced by the magazines *Approaches* of Scotland and *Ecclesia* of Spain as semi-clandestine organizations plotting to subvert the Church by transforming her into an atheist, desacralized, demythified, egalitarian New Church placed at the service of communism. Based on those denunciations, Prof. Plinio CORRÊA DE OLIVEIRA wrote several articles in *Folha de S. Paulo,* namely: "A propaganda progressista: um dinossauro discreto" (3/26/1969); "Artigo-bomba explode em Madrid" (5/7/1969); "Da infiltração à subversão" (5/14/1969); and "Os 'grupos proféticos' a serviço da Igreja-Nova e do comunismo" (5/21/1969). He also wrote the article, "A Igreja Católica infiltrada por adversários velados," introducing a special issue of *Catolicismo* on the subject (April/May, 1969). 170,000 copies of this issue, entitled "Grupos ocultos tramam a subversão na Igreja" were spread all over Brazil by the TFP. It was also reproduced by the magazines of the TFPs in Argentina, Chile, Colombia, Peru, and the United States.

Involved with IDOC are theologians such as Frs. Bernard Lonergan, John Courtney Murray, Gregory Baum, and Johann Baptist Metz; publishing houses like Herder & Herder, MacMillan, and Sheed and Ward; newspapers and magazines as the *National Catholic Reporter* (USA), *Informations Catholiques Internationales,* later called *Actualités Religieuses dans le monde* (France), and *Znak* (Poland).

extremely interesting and suggestive to follow a little bit the process whereby **the world — which was considered a reality
'outside' the Church — was transformed into something
which is essential to the very nature of the Church.** Perhaps
the most macroscopic example was offered to us by the history of
Vatican Council II and, above all, by the itinerary followed by the
schema on the Church and the world."[67]

§ 72   Msgr. Pierre Eyt, a member of the International Theological Commission, dean of the famous Institut Catholique of Paris
and now Archbishop of Bordeaux, was made Cardinal in 1994.
His comments on *Gaudium et spes* show a resolute and straightforward personality: "**In history,** even recent history, **there was
a great temptation to conceive the Church and the world in a
relation of opposition and reciprocal exteriority, encamped
and poised in a pathetic confrontation.** *Gaudium et spes* **was
intended to extinguish this image and make us become more
vividly aware of the convergence between the two vitally
united movements** .... Indeed, **on the one hand the world (the
whole world) is inhabited by a powerful dynamism that orients it toward the Church. On the other hand, the Church is,**
in the hands of God, **the living instrument of the passage of the
world and of every man to the Kingdom. Nothing that interests the world can be foreign to the Church.**"[68]

§ 73   Finally, Hans Küng, assuming the same doctrine, presents
as an ideal the Church as a servant of the world: "**A Church
which, in these times, forgets that she exists only for the generous service of men, her enemies, and the world, loses her
dignity, her power to convince, and her reason for existing,
because** she truly **gives up following Christ.** However, **a
Church that remains aware that it will not be she, but rather
the Kingdom of God, that will come** 'in power and majesty'
finds in her smallness her true grandeur."[69]

*

---

[67] Leo Alting von GEUSAU, "La Chiesa 'scandalo' del mondo," in V.A.,
La fine della Chiesa come società perfetta (Verona: Mondadori, 1968),
p. 157.

[68] Pierre EYT, "Igreja e mutações sócio-culturais," in V.A., *A Igreja do
futuro* (Petrópolis: Vozes, 1973), pp. 17s.

[69] H. KÜNG, *A Igreja*, vol. I, p. 144.

D. On Adapting the Church to the World: The Limits Between the Spiritual and Temporal Spheres Begin to Dissolve

§ 74
Among the most important consequences of conciliar doctrine on the adaptation of the Church to the world is the virtual disappearance of the limits between the spiritual and temporal spheres. Hence the two become mixed.

This paragraph by Leo von Geusau expresses well the consequence of this conciliar doctrine: "**After Christ the limits between the 'chosen people' and the rest of humanity became ever more vague, and it is not possible to draw a line separating the two fields.** The differences between the people of God and the rest of humanity ('the world') will never correspond to precise limits, be they geographical or moral, racial or confessional, historic or cultural. **Nor will one be able to speak any longer of a distinction between the Church and the world in terms of the redeemed and the nonredeemed, the kingdom and the darkness.**"[70]

A little later, Geusau adds: "If, therefore, **the Church exists because of the world, there must be a function related to this very world.** A majority of Protestant and Catholic theologians already agree on this, and **the second chapter of the dogmatic constitution on the Church [*Lumen gentium*] made this view its own. It no longer speaks of the 'missionary *duty*' of the Church as though it were something beyond and above her 'normal' life, but of the 'missionary *nature* of the Church,' which implies a relationship with the world that is part and parcel of the Church herself. When the Church is mentioned as the 'sacrament' of the Kingdom of God, it is understood that the Church no longer faces the world in an attitude of conquest. The Church no longer identifies with the Kingdom of God,** so that the very kingdom may be extended to the degree that the number of people who belong to the Church increases."[71]

In brief, von Geusau, whose words are cited here as an example of the general thinking of the progressivist current, draws from conciliar doctrine a consequence of such great import as to revolutionize the very concept of the Spiritual Sphere and

---

[70] L. A. von GEUSAU, op. cit., p. 178.

[71] Ibid., pp. 181f.

the Temporal Sphere. One would dissolve within the other. What will result from that? A theocratic state, a secularized Church, or absolute confusion?

*

E. Behind the Concept of Adaptation Looms the Notion of Divine Revelation in the World and in History...

§ 75   If we try to analyze in depth the underlying doctrinal perspective of the various authors cited in this Item, we will see that the change in the nature and mission of the Church is based on a new conception of Revelation. The latter would no longer be the ensemble of principles contained in the teachings and examples that Christ bequeathed to men during his life, the legacy of which the Church is the custodian and interpreter. Revelation would be the manifestation of a cosmic Christ immanent inside every man, in the ensemble of men – humanity – and in the evolution of the world through the ages, that is, history. So the world and history have immanences of revelation that the Church does not know, and they are, properly speaking, the vehicles of revelation. Hence the need for the Church to open up and constantly adapt herself to this world, to history in general, and to the cosmos, all of them mysteriously 'Christified.'[72]

Let us look at some conciliar theologians who present history as a vehicle for divine revelation.

§ 76   In his work *Level the Ramparts*, published before the Council and which later exerted considerable influence, von Balthasar preaches the self-destruction of the Church.[73] In it he comes up with a new doctrine according to which the distinction between God and the world is coming to an end. Consequently, the world has become a vehicle for revelation. Here is what 'the most cultured man of our time,' in the words of Cardinal de Lubac, wrote:[74] **"At first, the spaces of creation with its generic**

---

[72] On the 'cosmic Christ,' Vol. VI, *Inveniet fidem?*, Chap. V.6.B, D.a; Vol. VII, *Destructio Dei*, Chaps. II.2, III.3; Vol. VIII, *Fumus Satanae*, Chaps. I.3.C, II, V.3; Vol. IX, *Creatio*, Chaps. IV.3.B, V; Vol. X, *Peccatum - Redemptio*, Chaps. V.1, VII.1, VIII.2, IX.2.

[73] See overview of the destructive intentions of *Level the Ramparts* in Vol. IV, *Animus delendi-I*, Chap. II, Note 23.

[74] Hans Urs von Balthasar is "perhaps the most cultured man of his time," says Fr. Henri de LUBAC in a chapter dedicated to an apology of

revelation of God and the space of Redemption and the Church as a special guide of truth and grace .... were separate**. At least in the realm of ideas, it was possible to carefully cross the threshold. **Here also walls have crumbled; and although the order of Creation and the order of Redemption, world and Church, must always remain distinct,**[75] **we always hear as new the words of Christ who**, alpha and omega of everything created, **recapitulates in Himself everything in heaven and earth**; and who was thus destined, already before the Creation of the world, to report to the Father the world that was made through him, with him, and in him. He is not the world; but even though he is younger than that world into which he descended and from which he took his nature and being, he is at the same time older. In a mysterious sense, the world was made to his image ....

"**This high wall between God and the world was kept standing for an exceedingly long time. For this reason, anyone who wished to turn to God had to abandon the world for a time or forever. Now also this last wall is falling .... Crumbling walls can bury many things which, formerly protected by them, appeared to be alive. But in the space that is thus made, there is a more ample participation.**"[76]

§ 77   De Lubac is author of the book *Catholicisme*, which became 'the object of the worst suspicions' when it was published in 1938. He later wrote *Surnaturel*, attacking 'certain complications of modern Scholastics.'[77] That did not prevent him from being sent a letter of encouragement by Pius XII,[78] invited to par-

---

his oldest disciple, in the work *Paradoxe et mystère de l'Eglise* (Paris: Aubier-Montaigne, 1967), p. 184.

[75] Von Balthasar admits, *pro forma*, that the world and the Church 'must remain always distinct.' In this he shows less radicality than von Geusau, cited above. Nevertheless, the explanation of a world that supposedly became divinized leads, deep down, to the same consequence.

[76] Hans Urs von BALTHASAR, *Abbattere i bastioni* (Turin: Borla, 1966), pp. 115f.

[77] H. de LUBAC, *Entretien autour de Vatican II* (Paris: Cerf, 1985), pp. 10f.

[78] In an interview with Marco POLITI, the then newly designated Cardinal de LUBAC thus comments on his 'rehabilitation' by Pius XII: "Mind you that I've received from Pius XII an excellent letter; it had no shadow of a censure, it was very encouraging." "Irrequieto ma ubbidiente - La

ticipate in the Council's Preparatory Commission, named a conciliar *perito* by John XXIII, praised by Paul VI, and elevated to Cardinal by John Paul II. His opinion is regarded as one of the most authentic interpretations of the Council; and even his old work is now seen as having been a forerunning sign of the Council. This is why we quote from it.

In his book, the Jesuit says: "**God acts in history, God reveals himself through history. More, God inserts himself in history, thus giving it a 'religious consecration'** that obliges one to take it seriously. **Historical realities therefore have a depth, they must be understood from the spiritual standpoint:** *historika pneumatikos*; **and in turn, spiritual realities appear in the making and must be understood spiritually:** *pneumatika historikos* .... **if our salvation is essentially social, all of history becomes the obligatory interpreter between God and each one of us.**"[79]

§ 78   The following excerpts by Fr. Chenu make very clear the progressivist notion that divine revelation takes place uninterruptedly in history and in the world:

* "Evangelical truth will be, therefore, of a type other than metaphysical truth .... The very word 'truth' in the biblical language the exegetes have masterly analyzed, is impregnated with an original density: truth and fidelity, justice, certainty, peace, uprightness. 'Do the truth' says Saint John (Jn 3:21; 1 Jn 1:6); an unintelligible expression for a certain intellectualism. It [**the truth**] therefore does not derive from propositions placed outside of time, which we manipulate according to the structures of logic in a kind of sacred metaphysics under the custody of an authority; rather, it **proceeds from a history guided by God in facts of salvation in which he reveals himself. Revelation is the act by which God revealed himself in the course of history and continues to reveal himself, by an extension that unfolds through the centuries until the total realization fulfilled by Christ in the plenitude of time.** God speaks today in the Christian community starting from this 'Christological concentration' that the Spirit .... distributes and reveals itself in a multiplicity of signs announcing the things of the future, that is, the new order of things born out of the death and resurrection of Christ.

Chiesa e i suoi protagonisti - Henri de Lubac," in *Il Messaggero*, 2/2/1983, p. 3.

[79] H. de LUBAC, *Catholicisme - Les aspects sociaux du dogme* (Paris: Cerf, 1947), pp. 133f.

"**Time goes into the fabric of revelation. Thus, the theology deriving from this is stressed between two poles: the eternal truth of its object and the contingent situation in time. It must fulfill two fundamental conditions: provide a [new] expression to the truth of the Christian message and adapt that same expression to all situations.** The 'situation' includes the totality of the creating consciousness that man has of himself at a given moment, the synthesis of scientific, artistic, economic, political, social, or moral forms in which the conscience of a generation finds, with its own expression, the fulfillment of its hopes. From this standpoint, in the new civilization, 'secularization' as an awareness of the promotion of man and his autonomy gives the theologian an auspicious occasion for its understanding. In the final analysis, language itself .... must be a product of the community in a state of effervescence and expression of the Spirit. **By its nature, theology is**, therefore, **in faith, in a state of research**."[80]

* "The evangelical aspirations to universal brotherhood increase their theological clarity when 'neighbor' is defined in terms of a worldwide socialization. **The solidarity of the world and the diversity of its civilizations form, in the laborious creation of a 'human community,' an admirable picture and .... a challenge for the catholicity of the Church,** which has been too long confined, her theology included, to the West. **The theologian finds here something like a second inspiration of the transcendence of the Word of God. These are so many 'signs of the times' of God, spelled out in profane realities.** Does not this kind of historicity ruin the speculative construction of theology, or will it not at least reduce theology to a rather artificial superstructure? The blunders of a sort of pseudoevangelical positivism might make us fear so. But let us leave them to their failure. Let us rather observe that any articulating of a 'speculative' science on history, that is, in the present case, any constructing of a science-theology on the history of salvation, will not proceed without problems or without risk."[81]

*

---

[80] M. D. CHENU, "Omelia tenuta nel corso della celebrazione eucaristica," in V.A., *L'avvenire della Chiesa*, pp. 62f.

[81] M. D. CHENU, "The History of Salvation," in V.A., *Theology of Renewal*, vol. I, p. 163.

F. ... that Demands a New Theology

§ 79   Fr. Chenu applies these principles to a new conception of theology: "**Such, then, is the economy of revelation in the old and the new covenants: not a history in which a revelation occurred, but a history revealing itself. This introduces a serious problem for theology. It will oblige theology not to occupy itself with ontological relations and with definitions of essences, but to be primarily a reflection on a becoming,** on a plan of salvation. **It is within a history that theology encounters the problem of ontological relations. The theologian, then, in the use he makes of the documents, will have to respect both their authority and their origin, and this he cannot do except by integrating them into an historical pattern of thought, rather than using them merely as a point of departure.**"[82]

How then, should this new theology in the making be? Should theology no longer be deduced from the eternal principles contained in Revelation and in its sources, the Scriptures and Tradition, to become a continuous adaptation to history and the world, and therefore an empirical science?

§ 80   The answer is clearly given by the well-known Canadian theologian, Fr. Bernard Lonergan,[83] a professor at Rome's Pontifical Urbanian University: "**Before [the Council] .... theology was a deductive, and had become largely an empirical science. It was a deductive science in the sense that its theses were conclusions to be proven from the premises provided by Scripture and Tradition. It has become an empirical science in the sense that Scripture and Tradition now supply not premises, but data. The data has to be viewed in its historical perspective. It has to be interpreted in the light of contemporary techniques and procedures. Whereas before the step from premises to conclusions was brief, simple, and certain, today the steps from data to interpretation are long, arduous, and, at best, probable. An empirical science does not demonstrate. It accumulates information, develops understanding, masters ever more of its materials, but it does not preclude**

---

[82] Ibid., p. 159.

[83] Battista MONDIN places him among the ten greatest theologians of this century. *Os grandes teólogos do século vinte*, vol. I, pp. 269-282.

the uncovering of further relevant data, the emergence of new insights, the attainment of a more comprehensive view."[84]

In another passage, Lonergan says: **"So a contemporary Catholic theology has to be not only Catholic but also ecumenical. Its concerns must reach not only Christians but also non-Christians and atheists. It has to learn to draw not only on the modern philosophies, but also on the relatively new sciences of religion, psychology, sociology, and the new techniques of the communication arts."**[85]

§ 81

During his previously cited homily, Fr. Chenu goes back to his conception of the new theology, this time buttressing his arguments with quotes from *Gaudium et spes*. "Theology .... is oriented by its goal, that is, the daily interpretation of the Gospel. Therefore **every theological enunciation must be verified in the fact that reveals and seizes reality** (GS 3f., 10f., 22, 40, 42f. etc.) **and in the fact that efficaciously transforms reality. Conversely, the 'signs of the times' have a hermeneutic and maieutic**[86] **function to discover new aspects of the faith hitherto unrevealed or hardly revealed at all** (GS 40, 44, 62). ....

"Theology, then, be it in the Scripture, in the 'world', or in its philosophical self-interpretation, enters into a critical confrontation that prevents it from closing itself inside its problems and systems and moving only within the consecrated circle of its problems."[87]

§ 82

Journalist Fr. Bartolomeo Sorge, SJ, analyzes the failure of the modern world and the ascension of the post-modern world. Sorge claims that Vatican II had an intuition of the end of the modern world and seeks to show how conciliar guidelines suit well the new world supposedly being born. In the transition he describes, he sees above all a danger: an attempt to return to the "medieval cultural experience." As he expounds his thesis, it be-

---

[84] Bernard LONERGAN, "Theology in its New Context," in V.A., *Theology of Renewal*, vol. I, pp. 37f.

[85] Ibid., p. 41.

[86] Maieutics: Socrates' dialectic and pedagogic method of asking a great number of questions in order to form from particular and concrete cases, by way of induction, a general concept about the object in question.

[87] M. D. CHENU, "Omelia tenuta nel corso della celebrazione eucaristica," in V.A., *L'avvenire della Chiesa*, pp. 70f.

comes clear that in its adaptations to the modern world, the Conciliar Church abandoned the theological and sociological standards of the past to which, in his view, it could no longer return. A new theology, therefore, becomes imperative. As a matter of fact, Sorge says:

"No less dangerous than absence [that is, the attitude of those who defend the modern world without taking into account its crisis and replacement by the post-modern one] would be a presence conceived according to the paradigm of the 'medieval cultural experience.' The temptation is real. Indeed, some ask themselves whether restoring to man the sense of transcendence and primacy of person over structures can mean anything other than repeating the 'medieval cultural experience.' But that's not how things present themselves. The world reality is profoundly distinct. **There are acquisitions of the modern that are already irreversible, such as the pluralism of cultures and views of life or the awareness of the autonomy and the lay nature of temporal realities; they make unthinkable and impossible the homogeneity typical of 'medieval Christendom'** .... **At the same time, the Church's awareness of her nature and mission also has grown profoundly, to the point of making the medieval conception of Church-world relations an impossible proposition.**

"As for the rest, the history of the 'modern world' and its crisis should contribute to remove any doubt. **The presence of a Church, which, for an exceedingly long time remained anchored to the paradigm of the 'medieval cultural experience,' only produced an even graver rupture with the modern world. The condemnation of the 'pretended freedom of conscience' which Gregory XVI defined as a 'delirium' (*deliramentum*), the *Syllabus* of Pius IX, the antimodernism of the days of Pius X,** notwithstanding its historic justification, **did not help the 'modern world' to open itself to the whole truth, but ended by leaving it in its contradiction and crisis. For this reason, the Council,** at the dawn of the post-modern world and taking into account the changes that occurred, **characterized the Church's new attitude as one of dialogue and mediation.**"[88]

Further on, Sorge offers an outline for a new social theology: "Why should it mean a 'compromise' – as is feared – **to achieve together a society based on respect for freedom of conscience, on the principle that all men are equal and have**

---

[88] Bartolomeo SORGE, "I cristiani nel mondo postmoderno - Presenza, assenza, mediazione?," in *La Civiltà Cattolica*, 5/7/1983, p. 249.

the same human and civil rights, on the right of peoples to self-determination, on the liberty of culture and scientific research, **on the principle of tolerance and pluralism, even religious, on respect of every man, even when he errs?"**[89]

It is no wonder that Fr. Sorge, on advocating a new theological conception of the Church in consonance with the modern and post-modern worlds, combats memorable documents that represent the struggle of the Church against the French Revolution, liberalism, and modernism. Indeed, how could conciliar theology feel at ease right next to the teaching of the Magisterium that judges and condemns it? Sorge, therefore, vehemently 'anathematizes' those documents to which, incidentally, he renders an evolutionist homage.

§ 83

In this particular instance, Cardinal Ratzinger takes an analogous position. He labels as 'provisional dispositions' the antiliberal and antimodernist documents of the pontifical Magisterium. In an official pronouncement on the launching of the *Instruction on the Theologian's Ecclesial Vocation*, the Prefect of the Congregation for the Doctrine of the Faith issues this extremely grave opinion: "The text also presents the various forms of bonds that rise from the different degrees of magisterial teaching. It affirms — perhaps for the first time with this clarity — that **there are decisions of the magisterium that cannot be a last word on the matter** as such, **but are**, in a substantial fixation of the problem, **above all an expression of pastoral prudence, a kind of provisional disposition. Its nucleus remains valid, but the particulars**, which the circumstances of the times have influenced, **may need further ratifications.**

"In this regard, one may think of the declarations of Popes in the last century about religious liberty, as well as the antimodernist decisions at the beginning of this century, above all, the decisions of the biblical Commission of the time. As a cry of alarm facing hasty and superficial adaptations, they will remain fully justified. A personage such as Johann Baptist Metz said, for example, that **the Church's antimodernist decisions render the great service of preserving her from immersion in the liberal-bourgeois world. But in the details of the determinations they contain, they became obsolete** after having fulfilled their pastoral mission at the proper moment."[90]

---

[89] Ibid., p. 251.

[90] Joseph RATZINGER, "Instruction on the Theologian's Ecclesial Vocation," published with the title "Rinnovato dialogo fra Magistero e Teologia," in *L'Osservatore Romano*, 6/27/1990, p. 6.

*

§ *84*   The most important consequence of the adaptation of the Church to the world is its effect on theology. Theology used to be founded on Revelation and on the infallible teaching of the Magisterium, which scrutinized the Scriptures and Tradition, the sources of Revelation. Now God is supposedly immanent in Creation, and Revelation is to be found inside man, in the world and in history... a real 'Copernican revolution'[91] at the very foundation of the Faith.

G. Such Doctrine Also Implies the Virtual Destruction of Christendom...

§ *85*   As the reader can see, the conciliar concept of adapting the Church to the world is fraught with consequences. One of them deserves special attention as far as Church-State relations are concerned. Within the framework of the conciliar principles of adaptation and the virtual promiscuity of the spiritual and temporal spheres, the notion of Christendom appears to lose its meaning and be doomed to disappear. Indeed, Christendom has

---

[91] The expression is by Emmanuel LANNE, OSB, commenting on the conciliar concept of the local Church. "L'Eglise locale et l'Eglise universelle," in *Irenikon* (Chevetogne, Belgique, 1970) 43, p. 490, in Y. CONGAR, *Le Concile de Vatican II*, pp. 170f.

Although the metaphor was originally employed with regard to relations between the universal Church and local Churches, it later took on, by way of analogy, broader meanings such as those mentioned.

It is, for example, what Cardinal SUENENS comments on the precedence that *Lumen gentium* gives the 'people of God' in relation to the Hierarchy: "The first question: 'Church of God, what are you?' was answered with the constitution *Lumen gentium*, which is the principal text of Vatican II, the key. **It sought to give a vision of the Church that was no longer traditional, but which contained the essential, the quintessence of the essential – to such a point that it ended by deciding that the second chapter should be dedicated to the people of God.** 'Church of God, what are you?' **First of all it is the Church of the baptized. The Pope is no more baptized than you or me. And this is fundamental: to place the accent above all on that which makes us common. I believe that this is what has been called 'Copernician revolution.'** The idea is not mine, but I greatly appreciate it" ("Un nuovo battesimo per la Cristianità," interview to S. STRACCA, in *Avvenire*, 10/23/1992).

always been understood as a projection of the Catholic Church onto the temporal sphere. Christendom is established to the degree that the principles of Catholic Doctrine shape the customs, laws, and institutions in autonomous and sovereign States, which, as such, become gradually more Catholic, constituting the Temporal Kingdom of Our Lord Jesus Christ in the concert of nations.

So, in order for Christendom to exist, the Church must take upon herself the mission of expanding the principles of her doctrine so that the two Spheres are distinct from each other and the Temporal Sphere may allow itself to be docilely shaped by the wholesome action of the Church.

Now these three elements, as we have seen above, are apparently denied by the conciliar doctrine on adaptation. It is no wonder, then, that the negation of the ideal of Christendom is attributed to this doctrine.

§ 86   Speaking after the Council, Cardinal Jean Daniélou, a conciliar *perito* and a consultant to the Secretariat for Unbelievers, announces the end of Christendom: **"One of the aspects of the present crisis is that we are witnessing the end of a particular form of the incarnation of Christianity in Western culture. We refer to so-called Christendom, which started with Constantine and was the reality of the Western world until the nineteenth century,** founded on the fact that Christianity became, so to speak, the inspiration of all Western literary, philosophical, and artistic culture. It was the expression of Christianity in civilization itself. **This form today is not only going through a crisis, but its very value is ever more profoundly being cast into doubt. .... Perhaps we are entering a world in which Christianity will no longer have the same representation in culture and civilization. We will have to give up the idea of a Christian civilization and even of a Christian humanism."**[92]

§ 87   For his part, Cardinal Suenens says: **"Sociological Christianity is crumbling like a scaffold around a building. I have never attributed the same importance to scaffold and building. We must return to our roots."**[93]

§ 88

---

[92] Jean DANIELOU, "Relações entre Igreja e civilização," in V.A., *Cinco problemas que desafiam a Igreja hoje,* p. 139.

[93] L. J. SUENENS, Ibid.

Cardinal Congar says basically the same, attributing this change to the conciliar documents. He refers to Christendom generally as "relations between the spiritual and the temporal, inherited from the Middle Ages:" "**In full consonance with the dogmatic constitution *Lumen gentium*, *Gaudium et spes* profoundly changes the manner, inherited from the Middle Ages, of viewing the relationships between the spiritual and the temporal,** something that weighed on classic teaching until the preparatory theological Commission introduced chapter IX of *De Ecclesia*. **We will see that this change amounts less to a contradiction [with the past] than to an evolution [from it]: it is the problem that has changed. It has switched from the juridical and political planes to that of anthropology and personal faith. .... One may say that, with documents such as *Gaudium et spes* or the Declaration on Religious Liberty, Vatican II has definitively turned the page of the Middle Ages. Indeed, the perspectives of *Gaudium et spes* are quite different.**"[94]

§ 89

In another work, Congar takes up an analogous thesis, emphasizing that any 'nostalgia for a Christianization' must come to an end: "Some mentalities are still taken up by the nostalgia for a new baptism of Clovis .... **With the Declaration on Religious Liberty and the pastoral constitution *Gaudium et spes* on the Church in the world today** — a meaningful title! — **the Church of Vatican II has clearly placed herself in today's pluralist world and,** without denying what greatness there was, **she cut the ropes that kept her moored to the banks of the Middle Ages.**"[95]

§ 90

A similar opinion is upheld by a theologian from Louvain, Antoine Vergote, professor of psychology and philosophy at that city's university and member of various scientific associations. He expounded his theses to 223 theologians from the whole world gathered for the fifth congress of the magazine *Concilium*. From them, we chose these words: "**It is often said: Christendom died. And we are all agreed to bury it in the cultural past. No political or international institution will base its principles on Faith in God and in Jesus Christ any longer. ....**

---

[94] Y. CONGAR, "Le rôle de l'Eglise dans le monde de ce temps," in V.A., *L'Eglise dans le monde de ce temps*, vol. II, pp. 311f.

[95] Y. CONGAR, *La crisi nella Chiesa e Mons. Lefebvre*, p. 52.

The death of sociological and political Christendom has liberated man and the world to themselves."[96]

§ 91   Also Chenu, commenting on *Gaudium et spes*, appears to announce an opposition between conciliar doctrine and the concept of Christendom: "'The Church is in the world.' In *today's* world, the Council pinpoints. .... **[The Church] is 'missionary' to such a point that She is only herself** when She comes out of herself, if one may say this. **And this is so not because of an ultimately fastidious concession, but by nature**. There are no two churches, just as there are no two beliefs: the same faith is at the same time communion with Christ and witness in the world. **In contrast with a certain image of Christendom, what we have here, we believe, is not a growth due to a fervor that springs up during a second stage, when one is heavily laden with goods, as though this were a supplementary need, almost an appendage. It is only one thing.**"[97]

§ 92   As we can see, it is habitual for theologians who interpret documents of Vatican II to show the existing opposition between conciliar doctrine and the concept of Christendom. To give a few more examples, we now quote excerpts from two who hold apparently opposed positions. On the one hand, we have Gustavo Gutierrez, the controversial Peruvian priest considered the 'father' of Liberation Theology. On the other is Fr. Gustave Martelet, SJ, a disciple of Cardinal de Lubac, conciliar *perito* and professor at the Jesuit Faculties of Lyons-Fourvière, certainly a 'moderate' in comparison.

The *ardito* Gutierrez writes: "**It is classic to say that Vatican II has put an end to the mentality of Christendom**. It is time for dialogue and service to the world .... John XXIII stressed in the Council the task of opening up to the world, finding an appropriate theological language, bearing witness to a church of the poor."[98]

---

[96] Antoine VERGOTE, "La presenza della Chiesa nella società di domani - Riflessioni bibliche," in V.A., *L'avvenire della Chiesa*, pp. 163, 165.

[97] M. D. CHENU, "'Vox populi, vox Dei'. L'opinione pubblica nell'ambito del popolo di Dio," in V.A., *La fine della Chiesa come società perfetta*, pp. 222f.

[98] Gustavo GUTIERREZ, "Os pobres na Igreja," in *Concilium*, 1977/4, p. 89.

§ 93   For his part, the 'moderate' Martelet says: "**Compared to a time in which the Church could appear as the form encompassing the entire society, Christendom no longer has conditions to represent the status of the Church in our present societies.** Even more, **in the eyes of the Church herself, Christendom is not an essential ideal for her.** The Church did not wait for Vatican II to realize this and say it .... Vatican II .... should not turn back to condemn or praise a system of relations which, having played its role, should still not be discredited. Nevertheless, **the manner in which the Council defines the mission of the Church in the world visibly excludes every possible return to formulas which the development of human *and* Christian consciousness has made obsolete.**"[99]

These excerpts are quite expressive and dispense with the need for any comment.

*

H. ... and the Preaching of Socialism

§ 94   Assuming that the promiscuity between the spiritual and temporal spheres has been established, several conciliar thinkers began to present 'theologies' of socio-political realities. For this purpose, they interpret socialism at times as a temporal expression of religious principles, and at other times as a 'sign of the times' provided by the modern world to which the Church must pay heed.

§ 95   Let us see, as examples, an excerpt by Schillebeeckx in the first sense and one by Chenu in the second.

Schillebeeckx states: "**The discovery of the human being in his full secularity** .... also **characterizes the present attitude of the Church in a fundamental fashion. Today's Church**, without giving up her faith in grace and in the Kingdom of God .... **must believe in man more than ever**. When man becomes conscious of himself, we find ourselves faced with a reality that discloses its more intimate secret only through the revelation of the Kingdom of God. **Spiritual goods** .... **must be fraternally distributed among men as a sign of the return of Christ. This earthly Christian socialism, if we can so express ourselves, ... this Christian Messianism**, which as a collective force must reinforce hope in this world also in the realm of an

---

[99] Gustave MARTELET, *Deux mille ans d'Eglise en question*, p. 38.

earthly life established in justice and love, **is a sign that points to Christ not only as Head of the Church but also as Sovereign of the world** .... The humanization of the world, and in it, the humanization of man, essentially belong to the riches of Messianic goods that Christ conquered for us with the sacrifice of his life and which Christians, coheirs of Christ, must therefore fraternally share among themselves. Appreciating human value in the cultural, social and economic fields, and providing all men with the same living conditions, helping underdeveloped countries etc. are not profane, secular tasks to be fulfilled only with a Christian spirit, but they are, above all, a profound realization of the Christian consciousness of their own vocation."[100]

Alluding to Marxists, Schillebeeckx continues: "Also, **we Christians have left this Messianism too much to non-Christians, causing the most profound inspiration of Messianism to be reduced to a purely earthly messianical dynamism**."[101]

Finally, the theologian from Nijmegen concludes: "**Only if Christian lay people again bring to the world this earthly aspect of religious messianism will the Church appear to the world as a reality that speaks to hearts.**"[102]

§ 96   The following text by Chenu is parallel to the one we just cited, in which the Church appears as a transforming agent of socialism into religious messianism. Now we will see the world giving the Church the 'sign of the times' for socialization, which requires Her to reinterpret Herself.

Chenu comments on excerpts of *Gaudium et spes*: "It is not the faithful alone who in their personal lives brings light and benefit through their presence in the world .... but the Church herself as community of the Word. '**The Church** has a visible social structure which is a sign of its unity in Christ: as such, it **can be enriched and is being enriched by the evolution of social life,** not as if something were missing in the Constitution which Christ gave the Church, but **in order to understand this constitution more deeply, express it better, and adapt it more successfully to our times.**'

---

[100] E. SCHILLEBEECKX, "I laici nel popolo di Dio," in V.A., *La fine della Chiesa come società perfetta*, pp. 207f.

[101] Ibid., p. 208.

[102] Ibid.

"Such a statement by the Council (GS 44), fundamental in itself, establishes the nature, causes and criteria for a presence in the world: in this relation, **the world, 'through the evolution of social life,' and through the massive phenomenon of socialization today helps the Church in the act of evangelization.**"[103]

§ 97   According to these authors,[104] the preaching of socialism and the assimilation of socialization appear as matter-of-fact consequences of the new conciliar doctrine of adapting the Church to the modern world.

§ 98   Based on the aforementioned authors, we conclude this Item 2 on the concessions of the conciliar Church to the modern world by saying that:

* the texts of the conciliar documents are ambiguous about the concept of world;

*in the adaptation of the Church to the world, the Council appears to implicitly deny the divine mandate of Our Lord to the Church and to accept, also implicitly, the errors of the modern world;

*from every indication, the superiority of the Church is also denied and it is given that She must orient and influence the temporal sphere;

*consistent with the conciliar concept of adaptation, the limits between the spiritual and temporal spheres are diluted;

*the notion of a divine immanence in the Cosmos, manifested by divine revelation in the world and in history, appears to loom from behind the doctrine of adaptation;

*such a doctrine revolutionizes theology, which, deductive starting from Revelation, becomes inductive and departs from human and historic realities;

*important teachings of the Church's previously antiliberal and antimodernist doctrine are 'anathematized' in the name of theological adaptation;

---

[103] M. D. CHENU, op. cit., p. 223.

[104] The Reader will find analogous testimonies by other conciliar theologians in Vol. V, *Animus delendi-II*, Part I, Chap. IV.3.

* another consequence of the doctrine of adaptation is the virtual destruction of Christendom and the banishment of its ideal among men; a messianic-religious socialism is advocated for society and a secular socialization for the Church as a result of the reversibility between the two spheres.

As we see it, these are, in synthesis, the grave doctrinal concessions stemming from conciliar ambiguity in regard to adaptation to the modern world.

*

§ 99   If we add to these the conclusions reached in Item 1, we find that it is difficult to conceive a broader doctrinal panorama than the one which unfolds as we consider the concessions Vatican II made to the false religions and the modern world.

As a rule, such concessions are a direct fruit of the ambiguity in conciliar documents.

*   *   *

CHAPTER X

OTHER CONSEQUENCES: CONCILIAR AMBIGUITY PROVOKES A CRISIS OF DISCIPLINE, WHICH ALSO GENERATES A CRISIS OF FAITH AND MORALS

§ 1   As we have seen above,[1] ambiguity in conciliar texts harbored old tendencies and doctrines which, defeated at Vatican I and condemned by Saint Pius X, had still not died. As a matter of fact, in spite of some counter-measures taken in the period from Benedict XV to Pius XII, they became stronger. At Vatican II, they won.[2]

With its attitude of 'lowering the drawbridge' of the Church citadel to her enemies,[3] 'opening doors and windows for the new currents,'[4] 'leveling the ramparts' of the Holy City,[5] Vatican II inevitably gave those currents a great impetus and an unmistakable hope of imposing their designs on the whole Church.

§ 2   Furthermore, the ambiguity in the conciliar texts caused a certain reservation in conservative Catholic opinion. However hard some prelates representative of conservatism strove to pre-

---

[1] Chap. III.

[2] Chaps. IV, VI.1.

[3] Y. CONGAR, *Eglise Catholique et France moderne* (Paris: Hachette, 1978), p. 47.

[4] Ibid., p. 55.

[5] Ibid., p. 47; see also H. U. von BALTHASAR, *Abbatere i bastioni.*

sent the Council as a continuation of the ancient doctrines,[6] as time went by and the Council was applied, a large part of the faithful had a presentiment that this was not the case. The Church was faced with a reform which, considering the broad scope of the themes it covered, the importance of the changes in direction that it entailed, and its profound consequences on contemporary Catholic theological thinking, constitutes perhaps a development of unparalleled importance in ecclesiastical history.[7] The reservations of the faithful increased in greater or

---

[6] The words of Msgr. Rudolf GRABER, former Bishop of Regensburg, present a typical illustration of this: "The attribution of an anticonciliar position to the so-called 'conservatives' can be deemed an imputation that borders on bad faith. There is nothing so false as that. On the contrary, we claim an attitude of the greatest fidelity to the Council, of which we have made ourselves the defenders. What happens is that we interpret its texts just as they were written. By uniting ourselves to Pope Paul VI, we vigorously oppose the so-called 'post-conciliar mentality,' which completely ignores the 'identification of the Council, in its precepts and teachings, with the doctrine and tradition bequeathed to the Church, even if it is an extraordinary evolution' (in *Adhortatio Apostolica Petrum et Paulum*, February 22, 1967). This is the sense in which the considerations we are about to make must be interpreted. Therefore, by no means are they directed against the Council, but are meant instead as a cry of alert in the face of certain symptoms of crisis that are multiplying in an alarming fashion" (R. GRABER, *Por que a Igreja está em crise*, Rio de Janeiro: Grifo, 1971, pp. 19f.).

[7] On this matter, Prof. Plinio CORRÊA DE OLIVEIRA comments: "It is painful to say this. But, in this sense, the evidence singles out the *Second Vatican Council* as one of the greatest calamities, if not the greatest, in the history of the Church. From the Council, the *'smoke of Satan'* (*Sermon* of Paul VI on June 29, 1972) penetrated the Church in unbelievable proportions. And this smoke is spreading day by day, with the terrible force of gases in expansion. To the scandal of uncountable souls, the Mystical Body of Christ entered, as it were, a sinister process of self-destruction. History narrates the innumerable dramas the Church has suffered in the twenty centuries of her existence: oppositions that germinated outside her and tried to destroy her from outside; malignancies that formed within her, were cut off by her, and thereafter ferociously tried to destroy her from outside. When, however, has history witnessed an attempted demolition of the Church like the present one? No longer undertaken by an adversary, it was termed a *'self-destruction'* in a most lofty pronouncement having world-wide repercussion (*Allocution* of Paul VI to the Lombard Seminary on December 7, 1968). From this resulted an immense debacle for the Church and what still remains of Christian civilization. The *'Ostpolitik'* of the Vatican, for example, and the massive infiltration of communism into Catholic circles are effects of all these calamities"

lesser degrees as the fruits of the Council developed and the enthusiasm of the progressivist *arditi* augmented.

Since the Council was ambiguous, both positions — of ardent progressivists and of the cautious mass of Catholic faithful — were more or less inevitable. Such states of mind are the logical fruits of the process of the development of conciliar ambiguity. It was to be expected that the progressivist advance would become accentuated and that the reaction of the faithful against it would crystallize more and more.

Thus, what was predictable began to happen. The crisis in the Church became patent.

*

§ 3   If an analyst of public opinion were to follow in depth the acceptance of Vatican II, he could state, in round numbers and therefore in a somewhat simplified fashion, that in the post-conciliar period from 1965 to 1975 the progressivist current expanded very swiftly in the Church; from 1975 to 1985 there was a quiet but gradual increase in the reservations of the ensemble of faithful;[8] from 1985 to 1995 the Vatican leadership sought to

---

(*Revolution and Counter-Revolution,* York, Penn.: The American Society for the Defense of Tradition, Family and Property, 1993, P. III, chap. II.4.A, pp. 145, 148f.).

[8] Describing how this phenomenon of passive resistance in Catholic public opinion took place, analyzing the natural mechanism of such resistance and the role of authentic or counterfeit leadership, as well as the power and importance of these reactions, muted for the most part but often inexorable, goes beyond the scope of this Work. History will perhaps one day explain what we are just mentioning here.

As a confirmation of what the text is saying, we quote here the anguish-filled words of Fr. Gilles Pelland, SJ, describing the emptiness into which conciliar *aggiornata* preaching fell in the early 70's: "An unfortunate experiment ended up, in many cases, leading to the same 'detachment' [the '*nonchalant* disinterestedness' of modern man for Church preaching in the post-conciliar era]. After striving to 'adapt themselves' and 'become closer to the man-in-the-street' in his concerns and language, [churchmen] began to have doubts: 'Are we not simply repeating what everyone says, covering with religious names the most common merchandise, evoking 'mystery,' 'revelation,' 'tradition' to disseminate those already widely spread and often worn-out truths about liberty, dialogue, or progress? In short, are we not just present a 'moderate' view of Vatican II so as to make it accepted by those with objections and reservations.

The advance of the process set in motion by the Council was thus in a stalemate in the decade of 1975-1985.

§ 4 Even during the Sessions of Vatican II, the progressivist wing had encountered difficulties in attaining victories due to the conservative reactions of a certain number of Prelates. Much skill was required from the leadership, as we have seen,[9] to neutralize the reaction and incorporate it into the progressivist stream.

In the post-conciliar period, analogous attempts were made, although with ever greater ability, to cancel out the reaction of a large part of Catholic public opinion and foist the new theories on it.

Just as unanimity among the Prelates was sought during the Council to prevent them from offering any future reaction, a great effort has been made after the Council to avoid, as much as possible, any serious disagreements with conservative leaders of Catholic opinion, which could polarize the diffused discontent.

---

echoing others (though with a little more archaic language) without having anything to say? From this standpoint, we would not be speaking in emptiness, but of emptiness. Emptiness would not only be before us, but in us' (M. de Certeau, "La parole du croyant dans le language de l'homme," in *Esprit*, 55, 1967, pp. 463f.).

"The malaise or diffused restlessness of the faithful often won over even pastors to the degree they were closer to those whom their mission assigned them to guide .... Priests formed in a very hierarchical view of the magisterium were repeatedly told that they had to change their mentality and make the service of the Word a priority; but, at the same time, the Christian assembly melted like snow in the sun! As soon as they [the priests] had been recycled, they faced the difficult experience of the 'place of solitude,' finding themselves facing a dispersed people who expected nothing from them nor found anything 'significant' in their words .... Such a context encouraged no one to boast and cry victory! After May 1968 and during the early 70's, what was seen was, above all, a reverse triumphalism: that of bitter criticism, a 'savoring sadness.' If the Church before the Council was able to fall into triumphalism, afterward she showed herself to be restless, when not indecisive" (Gilles PELLAND, "À propos de triomphalisme," in V.A., *Vatican II: Bilan et perspectives*, vol. I, pp. 126f.).

[9] Chap. IV.

When it is not possible to avoid such disagreements, they are circumscribed as much as possible. This strategy is quite understandable from the progressivist standpoint. For if the progressivists, who hold key posts in the Church, were to react to a polarization by condemning this or that leader of the discontented faithful and thus breaking the unanimity, they would break the cohesion in the Church and in the mentality of the faithful; in the short and the long run, that could only harm them.

Should the unanimity be lost — and thus a certain mentality of consensus that goes with it and is an excellent anesthetic for deep-seated malaise and anguish — it would bring down a series of psychological barriers inherited from the past. Such barriers, which are maintained by respect to and fidelity to highly-placed authorities in the Church, prevents the faithful from asking themselves whether or not evil has also affected the highest Church echelons. Furthermore, a climate of polemics and eventual doctrinal condemnations would bring into question the 'opening' toward enemies, the *aggiornamento* with a neo-pagan world and 'dialogue' with everybody. How can one believe in 'mercy' for enemies and at the same time fulminate with condemnations of one's own children in the Church? Above all, how can ecumenism be carried out with the outlaws of yesterday while maintaining and even multiplying anathemas against the new 'outlaws'?

The loss of unanimity in the Church would also harm progressivists in the long run. Condemnations by 'moderate' or *arditi* ecclesiastical authorities against conservatives who somehow catalyzed a diffuse mentality of discontent would eventually cause the latter to withdraw into silence only to resume the fight at the first opportunity that prudence warranted, just like the liberals and modernists did *contrario sensu*, after the pontificates of Pius IX and Saint Pius X. And one can well imagine that while keeping silent for the duration of their condemnation, such conservatives would constitute a pole of attraction for the discontented 'silent majority.'

It would be impossible to prevent conservatives, convinced of their just right in spite of having been condemned, from feeling that the eighth beatitude was speaking of them: "Blessed are they that suffer persecution for justice' sake: for theirs is the kingdom of heaven" (Mt 5:10) and from remembering the Condemned One on the Cross and asking themselves:

Did He not draw all things to Himself? *"Et ego si exaltatus fuero a terra, omnia traham ad me ipsum* (Jn 12:32). *"* [10]

For these reasons — there are others we shall not expound for the sake of brevity — one sees that one of the underpinnings of post-conciliar progressivist strategy is the need for unanimity in directing Catholic public opinion.

§ 5

In order to achieve such unanimity, as was done in the Council, concessions must be made to conservative public opinion. Here, the authorities permit or promulgate a catechism with certain traditional aspects; there, they tolerate the use of Latin; elsewhere, they admit a paltry return to the Mass said *versus Deum*; further, they admonish some theology more open to Marxism or some excess of the 'homosexual ministry.' However, the concession that has caused the most pain among the progressivist 'moderates' who execute the maneuvers and that has elicited the greatest impatience among the *arditi* is the long time it has taken for the conciliar process to move forward. [11]

---

[10] "And I, if I be lifted up from the earth, will draw all things to myself".

[11] In the text we emphasized the role of ecclesiastical authorities and a certain number of concessions made to appease conservative Catholic opinion in the quest for a unanimous acceptance of the Council's application. Such factors act as anesthetics, bringing on a certain lethargy and preventing reactions. However, a relevant factor that should be emphasized, albeit in passing, is the establishment of criteriological chaos among people capable of leading some anticonciliar reaction.

Indeed, both the 'conciliar revolution' and its consequences are so vast and require so much study that practically no one has ever put together, in a clear and systematic fashion, the reasons for disagreeing with the Council so as to seriously hinder the avalanche of reforms that was unleashed upon the Church. This difficulty, which was already great among those who had reservations about the Council, increased among those who accepted in good faith the directives of ecclesiastical authorities. As a result of the Concil's contradictions with traditional Church behavior, which this great majority of Catholic opinion was accustomed to following, disorientation and perplexity took hold among them even more than among conservatives.

Thus was born criteriological chaos among the common faithful and in the conservative milieu.

The media played no small a role in the installation of chaos. In general, they reported on conciliar changes in such a way as to favor indolence and discourage reactions.

Slowness is the tribute that the discontented 'silent majority' exacts from progressivist 'moderates' as a precondition for a *modus vivendi*. Slowness is also the main cause of erosion in the enthusiasm of the *arditi* and their disciplinary protests. Failing to fully understand the advantages of the 'moderates' strategy, the *arditi* call them 'bourgeois spirits' who are 'tepid' in their progressivist fervor, 'soft' in their orientation, and so on.

§ 6   Now then, what is the so-called post-conciliar crisis?

In order to carry Catholic public opinion with them, the 'moderates' are obliged to slow down the application of conciliar reforms. This slow pace exacerbates the progressivists and leads them to revolt against the 'moderate' authorities. Some *arditi* come up with bolder doctrinal explicitations of far-reaching consequences. Now, these daring manifestations of revolt and far-flung doctrines confirm the fears of the conservative masses, which thus become even more wary and morose. This obliges the 'moderates' to make new concessions to the 'silent majority.'

If this cycle of mutual erosion is not interrupted, it will give rise to a series of reactions that may destroy the conciliar process.

This is the outline of the post-conciliar crisis.

*

§ 7   But, the Reader may ask, so far as the awakening of the 'silent majority' is concerned, how can it be explained that the reaction of the faithful only began to manifest itself in 1975? What could have prevented it from showing itself until then? What factor was eliminated which allowed it to happen?

Chaos is, therefore, an important factor in the acceptance of the 'conciliar revolution.'

While anesthesia plunges Catholic opinion into lethargy, chaos clutters its sights. A fecund reaction could rise only to the degree that both of these elements were dispelled.

Even though the phenomenon essentially consists of a crystallization against excesses, this question is *a propos*: an analysis of the situation seems to reveal that there was indeed a factor obliging Catholic opinion to accept the Council and its fruits, and that this factor ceased to have an effect.

It is useful to call to mind that also in the conciliar assembly there appears to have been some impediment that slowed the action of conservatives, rejected their presentation of the pre-conciliar schemata,[12] treated them in a pejorative fashion,[13]

---

[12] B. KLOPPENBURG, *A eclesiologia do Vaticano II*, p. 13.

[13] In the Council's *Opening Speech* JOHN XXIII reprimanded the 'prophets of doom' who saw only 'prevarications and ruins.' His censure is impregnated with that 'naive optimism' which Schillebeeckx pointed out in the Council (see the second part of this Note) that the crisis sweeping the Church and temporal society would later cause it to lose its reason for being. John XXIII said: "In the daily exercise of Our pastoral ministry, insinuations come to Our ears from souls, doubtless ardent with zeal but not endowed with a great sense of discretion and moderation. In the modern times they see nothing but prevarications and ruins; they repeat tirelessly that our time, in comparison with past ones, has become worse; and they behave as though they have learned nothing from History, which also is the mistress of truth. .... But it seems to Us that We must disagree with these prophets of doom, who are always announcing ominous developments as though the end of the world were imminent" (in B. KLOPPENBURG, *Concílio Vaticano II*, vol. II, p. 308).

According to H. FESQUET, with these words John XXIII denounced the 'integrist' tendency against which the conciliar majority would have to fight (*Le journal du Concile*, p. 27).

Two decades after the utterance of these words about conservatives, Fr. Schillebeeckx, a *perito* and aide to the Dutch episcopate during the Council, showed how the optimism of John XXIII was devoid of any foundation: "It is an irony of History that Council Vatican II accepted the 'modern era' at a moment in which 'modernity' itself came under the focus of universal criticism. .... The uneasiness and aloofness of youth toward the Council must be sought not in Church factors, but in the general change of climate in Western society. The contrast with the beginning of the Sixties, when the Council took place, could not be greater. We then had a world emerging from the chaos of the Second World War, which radiated with joy at economic development and the perspective of international peace. We find something of this 'naive optimism' even in the Pastoral Constitution *Gaudium et spes*: the role that the Church should play in this great process toward universal well-being! From the Seventies onward, the winds of austerity began to blow" (E. SCHILLEBEECKX, *Gott ist jeden* discouraged them by failing to support their initiatives,[14] fought them in public,[15] criticized them in private;[16] and so on. In the opposite direction, the same factor served to accelerate and encourage the progressivist current. This factor was the use that John XXIII and Paul VI made of their pontifical authority.

§ 8   Analogously, after the Council, the respect of the faithful for papal authority and the hierarchy's authority *in genere* prevented the 'silent majority' from showing indifference toward the Council.

Nevertheless, as the first ten years of the Council's application unfolded with ever more disconcerting changes in Church practices, the authorities gradually lost their influence. A widespread malaise took hold among the faithful that come from a heart-rendering problem of conscience: on the one hand, a filial desire to obey the Sovereign Pontiff and his hierarchical

---

Tag neu - Ein Gespräch, Mainz: Mathias Grünewald, 1984, pp. 171f., in *Orienterung*, 1/31/1985, p. 13).

[14] Chap. VI.4.B.3rd phase.

[15] Msgr. Philips comments on the attitude of Paul VI toward the debate on collegiality: "No one had any doubt about it. The argument that would dominate the last discussions about the schema on the Church would be the doctrine on the college of bishops. That was the pivotal point to which a conciliar minority obstinately clung in an attempt to defend the pontifical primacy, which they believed to be threatened, and to preserve it intact at all costs. In his inaugural speech of September 14, 1964, Pope Paul VI had to call attention to this central point, doubtless in order to reduce the resistance of the last hesitating ones" (*La Chiesa e il suo mistero nel Concilio Vaticano II*, p. 49).

[16] There is nothing more expressive in this matter than Cardinal Cicognani's letter to Msgr. Luigi Carli, Bishop of Segni, in response to the one he had sent Paul VI in the name of the Coetus Internationales Patrum. The then Cardinal Secretary of State, very likely following instructions by Paul VI, advised Bishop Carli to dissolve the Coetus. Its full text can be found in Chap. VI.4 § 99.

We must note that there is no record of any reprimand having been made to the progressivist wing, which was very well structured (as was proven by the well-documented book by Fr. Wiltgen) and counted on the invaluable support of three out of the four Cardinal-Moderators, who were openly allied with the progressivists whom Paul VI had chosen to preside over the Council (R. WILTGEN, *The Rhine Flows Into the Tiber*, pp. 82, 248).

representatives; on the other hand, the self-evidence of facts, which made resistance an imperative.

In our view, the event-symbol, not to say *princeps*, that represented the apex of this conflict took place in Brazil, and by extension, in South America.

Brazil takes great pride in having the world's largest Catholic population.[17] South America is the continent with the largest Catholic population.[18] In this country and continent is found the world's largest network of influential associations of Catholic laymen that support the traditional doctrine of the Church. These associations — the Societies for the Defense of Tradition, Family and Property — are made up of idealist men who dedicate their lives to defend Christian Civilization in the temporal sphere. Catholics who lead exemplary lives, they are models of honor, uprightness and manliness for the countries that see them in action. In their private lives they have always shown an enthusiastic devotion to the Papacy and obedience to the Hierarchy even when, at times, they were victims of misunderstandings and even persecution at the hands of ecclesiastical authorities.

It was in this network of associations that the conflict of conscience reached its highest expression. Indeed, in their struggle for the basic principles of Christian Civilization — Tradition, Family and Property — these associations played a large role in impeding the advance of communism and the wily penetration of socialism in their countries. They always founded the argumentation for their fight on the traditional principles of the social doctrine of the Church. Faced with the concessions that Paul VI was making to representatives of communism all over the world and the futility of their appeals to the Pontiff,[19] and

---

[17] 130 million Catholics.

[18] 270 million Catholics.

In a lecture to the International Policy Forum in Dallas (April 1985), Prof. Plinio CORRÊA DE OLIVEIRA spoke about "The Importance of the Religious Factor in the Direction of a Key Bloc of Countries: Latin America" (*Catolicismo*, June 1985, pp. 3-8). In it, he characterized the central role of Catholicism in the Latin American continent, destined because of its natural and human resources to become a world power in the dawn of the twenty-first century.

[19] General Introduction, Note 16.

after serious study and mature reflection, these autonomous kindred organizations decided to publicly express their fidelity to the Church and the Papacy, but also their attitude of Resistance toward the Vatican policy of detente with communist governments.

Written by the founder and president of the Brazilian TFP, Prof. Plinio Corrêa de Oliveira, and signed by all TFPs, the *Declaration of Resistance*,[20] published on April 10, 1974, was the document that in our view represented, in public opinion as a whole, the crystallization of the widespread malaise that affected the Catholic world[21] faced with the rising tide of concessions and omissions by personages of the hierarchy toward international communism. With respect but firmness, the TFPs proclaimed their position:

"The Church is not, the Church never was, the Church never will be such a prison for consciences. The bond of obedience to the successor of Peter, which we will never break, which we love in the depth of our souls, to which we give the best of our love, this bond we kiss at the very moment in which, battered by sorrow, we affirm our position. And kneeling, gazing with veneration at the figure of His Holiness Paul VI, we express to him our fidelity.

"In this filial act we say to the Pastor of Pastors: Our soul is yours, our life is yours. Order us to do whatever you wish.

---

[20] Ibid.

[21] It is well to remember that this diffused malaise with regard to the Vatican *Ostpolitik* was recorded by Plinio CORRÊA DE OLIVEIRA in a series of articles in the *Folha de S. Paulo*, one of the dailies with largest circulation in Brazil and South America, in which he stated the position of Resistance of the TFPs and reported to the Brazilian public on the widespread rejection, on a world level, of the directions of Paul VI's diplomacy. The articles were entitled: "A indispensável resistência" (4/14/1974); "Resistindo..." (4/21/1974); "Voz dos que se calam acabrunhados" (4/28/1974); "Mais um Cardeal em resistência" (5/12/1974); "A Ostpolitik do Vaticano favorece Moscou" (6/9/1974); "Casaroli: 'incorporação no contexto'" (6/30/1974); "Não conseguimos compreender" (7/7/1974); "1958-1974: que resultados?" (7/14/1974); "Détente..." (9/1/1974); "Ternuras que arrancariam lágrimas" (10/13/1974); "Conforme quer Budapest" (10/20/1974); "'Détentes' geminadas" (12/8/1974).

Only do not order us to stay idle in face of the assailing red wolf. To this, our conscience is opposed."[22]

Reactions in other continents, telltale signs of the same phenomenon, soon followed.

From this point onward, the tide of Catholic public opinion began to change. Obedience to the hierarchy and to the Pope could no longer be used as easily as in the past to hinder Catholic reaction. Mistrust legitimately generated a certain critical analysis.

Thus, excessive speed in the application of the Council caused an attitude of perplexity, if not doubt, to rise in conservative circles and in the 'silent majority' regarding certain episcopal, and even papal, documents.

It is therefore explicable for the reactions of the 'silent majority' to have begun to embarrass the progressivist current starting in 1975.

§ 9   For its part, the progressivist current was already contesting papal authority since the appearance of the Encyclical *Humanae vitae* on July 25, 1968.[23] As is known, the Encyclical condemned the use of contraceptives. It was the banner the progressivist *arditi* used to indirectly attack papal infallibility by claiming that Paul VI had erred in solving the grave problem of birth control. For them, the use of contraceptives, condemned by *Humanae vitae,* was obviously licit.[24]

---

[22] Plinio CORRÊA DE OLIVEIRA, "The Vatican Policy of Distention toward the Communist Governments - The Question for the TFP: To Take No Stand? Or to Resist?," in *Crusade for a Christian Civilization,* September 1974, p. 18.

[23] "Insegnamenti di Paolo VI, 1963 a 1970," *Encicliche,* pp. 165-186.

[24] a. Manifestations of non-conformity with *Humanae vitae* by several Bishops' Conferences (in Austria, Belgium, Brazil, Canada, France, Holland, Norway and Scotland) as well as by individual churchmen, theologians and lay people, soon became widespread.

Below are the main positions denying the Encyclical's doctrine to be infallible and attributing to the consciences of spouses the role of supreme judge to decide on the legitimacy of artificial contraception:

b. At the end of their meeting in Königstein (August 29-30, 1968), the GERMAN EPISCOPATE stated that the Encyclical's teaching is "vested with ecclesiastical authority, but is not infallible," and decided that the "shepherds shall respect, in fulfilling their pastoral ministry and particularly in administering the sacraments, the decisions taken consciously and responsibly by the faithful" ("Après l'Encyclique Humanae Vitae," *Informations Catholiques Internationales,* 9/15/1968, p. 19).

c. The BELGIAN EPISCOPATE, after a special meeting on August 23, 1968, explained: "We are not faced with an infallible declaration." They established the principle that if a person who is "competent in the subject and capable of forming a well-founded personal judgment .... after a serious examination before God, arrives in some points at different conclusions [than the Encyclical's], he has the right to follow his conviction in this matter" (Ibid., p. 20).

d. The DUTCH EPISCOPATE, in January 1969, manifested its solidarity with the "many Catholics .... who see as unjust the condemnation (of contraceptives) and criticize it with well-founded arguments" (Lucio BRUNELLI, "A pílula que dividiu a Igreja," in *30 Giorni,* July 1988, pp. 50f.).

e. The FRENCH EPISCOPATE made a statement to the same effect: "Contraception can never be a good. It is always a disorder, but not always culpable. It may happen that the spouses are faced with conflicting duties .... On this matter we shall call to mind the constant teaching of morality: if there is a conflict of duties on account of which an evil cannot be avoided no matter what decision is taken, traditional wisdom says that one should strive to determine, before God, what is the greater duty. The spouses shall decide after common reflection made with all the care required by the grandeur of the married vocation. One can never forget or despise any of the duties in conflict" ("Orientacão Pastoral de 12 de Novembro de 1968 sobre a Encíclica *Humanae vitae,*" in SEDOC, vol. I, February 1969, col. 1118, in A. V. XAVIER DA SILVEIRA, "Pode haver erro em documentos do Magistério?", in *Catolicismo,* July 1969).

f. The CNBB - NATIONAL CONFERENCE OF BISHOPS OF BRAZIL - interpreted the Encyclical in the same fashion: "Let them [the confessors and spiritual directors] strive in earnest to form in an upright manner the consciences of those who trust them, leading them to conform with the objective truth taught by the authentic Magisterium. Let those who still have not acquired a conviction about the expounded truth not be driven away from the sacraments of Confession and Communion so long as they sincerely seek to remain faithful to the love of Christ" ("Declaração da Comissão Pastoral da CNBB sobre a Encíclica *Humanae vitae,*" October 25, 1968, in SEDOC, col. 1029, Ibid.).

g. In Brazil, pronouncements to the same effect were made by Msgr. Gregório Warmeling, Bishop of Joinville, Msgr. Marcos Noronha,

§ 10   If, among conservatives, it was an excessively fast application of the Council's tenets that generated mistrust of papal

---

Bishop of Itabira and the Bishop of Novo Hamburgo, Msgr. Boaventura Kloppenburg (A. V. XAVIER DA SILVEIRA, Ibid.).

h. The Swiss-German theologian Hans KÜNG was categorical:
"Those who, after a serious and mature reflection by themselves and
their spouses and before God, reach the conclusion that in order to
keep their mutual love, to consolidate their marriage and make it a
happy one, they must act otherwise than indicated by the encyclical
are obliged to follow their own consciences as has been taught by the
popes and traditional doctrine" (*Veracidade - O futuro da Igreja*, p.
192).

i. In England, organs of the Catholic press echoed the criticisms and
dissensions of members of the clergy. Priests in the dioceses of Liver-
pool, Birmingham, Northampton, Southwark, Arundel, Brighton and
others made public statements against the Encyclical (ICI, Ibid., p.
22).

j. Meanwhile, the former Archbishop of Bombay, Msgr. Thomas
Roberts, a resident of London, deplored the 'weakness' of the Pope's
argumentation (Ibid.; L. BRUNELLI, op. cit., p. 51).

k. In the United States, the professors of theology of the Catholic
University of Washington wrote a public letter of protest in whose support they collected, in a few days, 645 signatures from theologians,
some of them famous, like the moralist Fr. Bernard Häring, CSSR (ICI,
Ibid.).

l. In South Africa, Msgr. Denis Hurley, Archbishop of Durban, stated
that the Encyclical, *Humanae vitae* "constituted one of the most arduous experiences" of his life as a Bishop (Ibid., p. 23; L. BRUNELLI,
Ibid.).

m. In this regard, Fr. CONGAR comments: "This is how the Councils
were 'welcomed,' at times with difficulty and after long vacillations. As
for *Humanae vitae*, there was a refusal, or rather a failure, to take it
into account by the mass of the faithful, who had already taken their
liberties ....; a large number of theologians and even episcopates 'welcomed' the doctrine of the Encyclical but interpreted it in such a way
that it amounted to saying: You will not sin if you don't obey it by virtue
of serious reasons weighed by a .... docile and enlightened conscience" (*Eglise Catholique et France moderne*, p. 199).

n. One sees that, parallel to the question of contraceptives, *Humanae vitae* served as a wick to explode in the Church a crisis of
contestation of pontifical authority and papal infallibility.

authority, among the progressivist *arditi* it was slowness that gave rise to revolt and rejection of pontifical authority.

This constitutes, save a better analysis, the essence of the so-called crisis of authority.

*

§ 11   The Council's 'opening' toward the other religions and the world, which brought about the relativization of the Faith and the liberalization of customs,[25] was also to cause the crisis of vocations among priests and religious and the crisis of Faith among the laity, as will be shown by some of the texts we present below.

*

§ 12   Crisis of unity, crisis of authority, crisis of vocations, crisis of Faith: these are the outlines of the present crisis in the Church, born of the ambiguity in conciliar documents.

1. Crisis of Unity in the Church

§ 13   To corroborate what we said about the crisis in the Church, we will cite Paul VI, John Paul II, and well-known magazines and authors.

§ 14   Let us first look at the eloquent testimony of Paul VI in the Allocution *Resistite fortes in fide*, of June 29, 1972.

Referring to the situation in the Church, **the Pontiff affirms he has the sensation that "through some crack the smoke of Satan has entered the temple of God. There is doubt, uncertainty, a conjunct of problems, disquiet, dissatisfaction, confrontation. One no longer trusts the Church** .... Doubt has entered into our consciences, and it has entered through windows that should be open to the light. From science, which is made to offer us truths that do not drive us away from God but make us seek Him even more and glorify Him even more intensely, has come, instead, criticism, has come doubt ....

---

[25] This conciliar 'opening,' which constituted the basis for ecumenism and secularization, will be analyzed in greater detail in Volume V of this Collection, *Animus delendi-II*.

Also in the Church this state of uncertainty reigns. It was believed that after the Council a sunny day would come in the History of the Church. On the contrary, there came a day filled with clouds, tempest, darkness, questions, uncertainty. We preach ecumenism and remove ourselves ever farther from one another. We seek to dig chasms instead of burying them."[26]

§ 15   Without mentioning the Council, John Paul II neverthe-less points out its consequences: "In fact, **one cannot deny that in many Christians the spiritual life is passing through a *moment of uncertainty* that encompasses not only moral life but also prayer and even the *theological rectitude of the faith*.** Already put to the test by a confrontation with our time, **Faith is at times disoriented by erroneous ideological addresses that are disseminated, also as a result of the crisis of obedience in relation to the Magisterium of the Church.**"[27]

§ 16   The magazine *La Civiltà Cattolica* dedicates an editorial to analyze the first 20 years of the post-conciliar era. The com-ment reveals the position of the Jesuit magazine, which, while not the same as this Work's, attests to the crisis we mention.

"At the same time, **there was not — and there is not — any lack of internal confusions and tensions, which, added to pressures, ideologies and mutations .... aggravated .... a crisis that many today see as having frightened away the great hopes for a 'springtime awakening' of religion nourished by the two Popes who wanted the Council**. We cannot fail to point out this crisis even though we are unable to go into a lengthy, meticulous and exhaustive analysis. **Not only have the conciliar documents been considered obsolete and cast aside by some, but the very 'spirit' of Vatican II was taken over and amalgamated with its 'anti-spirit' by a class of theologi-ans,** not numerous but combative, **who have taken as a pa-rameter of reflection and truth a kind of anthropological immanentism,** accepted *de facto* even when not formally enun-ciated .... Someone had the pretension .... of speaking about go-ing beyond Vatican II, not in the legitimate sense of a progres-sive maturation .... but in the unacceptable sense of the manipu-lation of defenseless Christian masses carried out in various ways .... by some theological pressure groups .... Thus, **there**

---

[26] *Insegnamenti di Paolo VI*, vol. X, pp. 707f.

[27] JOHN PAUL II, Apostolic Letter *Tertio millenio adveniente*, in *L'Osservatore Romano*, 9/14-15/1994, Supplement, n. 36.

was no lack of 'anarchical excesses,' as Cardinal H. de Lubac justly defined them .... **A distorted reading of the Council was thus proposed .... that consists of seeking contradictions in conciliar texts to tilt their balance in favor of preconceived theses that find no backing in the Council, or stating that the conciliar texts were unable to express,** for various reasons, **that which the fathers really meant to say."**[28]

The editorialist of *La Civiltà Cattolica* closes: "Concluding this quick overview, we should say that after twenty years of experience, studies and discussions, Vatican II remains little known and little understood by the majority, be it in the clergy or laity; in this regard, **people either remain obstinately closed or have indiscriminately forged ahead. On the one hand, the refusal by the integrism of traditionalists, and on the other hand, the 'para-Council' phenomenon with its clamor, have contributed to render inoperative** (when not casting them into discredit) **the seeds sown by the Council in the Church."**[29]

From the editorial of *La Civiltà Cattolica* we have retained primarily the comments confirming the existence of the post-conciliar crisis. To us its attempts to disprove those who attribute ambiguities and contradictions to Vatican II appear to be without foundation, as we have hopefully demonstrated with abundant documentation in the preceding Chapters of this Volume. Such attempts are typical of the "moderate synthesis" line of which we spoke above.[30]

§ 17   The testimony below, by Cardinal Ratzinger, also attests to the existence of the post-conciliar crisis.

"The results [of the Council] appear cruelly opposed to the expectations of everyone, beginning with those of John XXIII and later of Paul VI: a new Catholic unity was expected and, instead, we moved toward a dissension which .... seems to change from self-criticism to self-destruction. A new enthusiasm was expected, but so many people have ended in discouragement and disgust. A leap forward was

---

[28] *La Civiltà Cattolica*, Editorial: "Concilio, post-Concilio, para-Concilio," 1/5/1985, pp. 11f.

[29] Ibid., p. 13.

[30] Chap. VI.3.

expected, and instead **we are faced with a progressive process of decadence that has developed**, to a large extent, precisely **under the sign of a movement favoring the Council and, therefore, contributed toward discrediting it among many**. The balance appears to be, therefore, negative .... **it is undeniable that this period was decisively unfavorable to the Catholic Church.**"[31]

In an earlier analysis, Ratzinger had said: "**The naive optimism of the council and the self-exaltation of many who made and disseminated it justify in a disturbing way the most somber diagnoses of early churchmen about the danger of councils. Not all valid councils**, after being tested by the facts of history, **have shown themselves to be useful councils; in the final analysis, all that was left of some was a great nothing.**"[32]

And he added: "**From a global perspective, one should say that the years of euphoria [of the post-conciliar era] were followed by a phase of disillusionment and crisis.**"[33]

§ 18   Msgr. Luigi Sartori, president of the Italian Theological Association at the time, remarks: "**We live, in this period of the post-Council, in a grave crisis.** After so much fervor and enthusiasm in which everyone seemed to be in agreement, **ruptures and dilacerations now begin. Different, not to say opposed, interpretations of the Council are offered; everyone pulls to his own side. Even worse, no small parcel of responsibility for the mixups and confusions is attributed to the Council. Some go as far as to speak**, with irritation, **of 'Babel' and of the 'confusion of languages;'** and they again dream of the medieval ideal of a unity of language, for only thus — they think — can the Church still accomplish her function as *signum unitatis* amongst the peoples of the earth."[34]

---

[31] *L'Osservatore Romano*: "Il Cardinale Ratzinger: 'La fede è il bene più alto. Bisogna sempre vigilare perchè non si corrompa,'" 11/9/1984, p. 4; this article is a selection of statements by J. RATZINGER to the monthly *Jesus*.

[32] J. RATZINGER, *Zehn Jahre Vaticanum II*, Regensburg, 1976, in Rosino GIBELLINI, "Siamo d'accordo sul concilio?," in *Il Regno*, 12/15/1984, p. 545.

[33] Ibid.

[34] L. SARTORI, "Il linguaggio del Vaticano II," in V.A., *Il linguaggio teologico oggi*, p. 236.

§ 19   Soon after the Council, Fr. Leo A. von Geusau, founder of IDOC, 'prophecied' its results: **"To many it will seem as though the very supports of Christian action are falling. Many will believe they are faced with, or on the eve of, a new destruction of Jerusalem on a large scale. And it is not exaggerated to say that we are living a moment of rupture and discontinuity in the history of salvation** .... Many who think that they are Christians may find themselves in a situation in which they no longer understand what is happening; and others whom we would never expect to find in similar conditions, will appear to us as true Christians. **The crisis attacking the Church is evident .... Some go as far as to speak of 'two Churches' to express the reality of a profound and growing dislocation between the two mentalities.** All this may seem terribly sad or pessimistic. But, instead, it could turn out to be the sign of the birth of a renewed Church which, slowly, groaning, is leaving the exceedingly 'stable and safe' land of the old ecclesiastical structures to consciously take the road to the desert. There is talk of the theology of the 'Exodus' .... Maybe we will be more tranquil within a few generations, when change will have become a familiar method of advancing."[35]

§ 20   Comments on Vatican II by the former Cardinal-Archbishop of Vienna, Franz König, are not far removed from those above: "Every Council caused restlessness. It is not by chance if today there is insistence on the acceptance of Vatican II. **The conciliar Fathers spoke with great openness, causing astonishment.** The Church should open herself, *aggiornarsi*. **Have we gone too far? Have we become too liberal? One may have feared so, many had the impression they no longer found themselves facing the same Church.** Hence the arguments between right and left. So many diverse opinions."[36]

§ 21   Maurice Druon, a man of letters and member of the Académie Française, adds his voice to these testimonies.

Referring to the bewilderment of a common-sensical man watching the radicality and untimeliness that caused the

---

[35] L. A. von GEUSAU, "La Chiesa 'scandalo' del mundo," in V.A., *La fine della Chiesa come 'società perfetta'*, pp. 192f.

[36] Franz KÖNIG, "Il Concilio, sorpresa per il mondo," interview with Silvano STRACCA, in *Avvenire*, 10/16/1992.

post-conciliar crisis, he says: "Nothing, at least from the outside, threatened or attacked her [the Church] any longer. No one jested any more as priests passed by; anticlericalism was relegated to a museum of souvenirs; laicism was no longer a pretext for fights. **Never had the Church**, from the simple village pastor to the pope .... **benefited from a more secure situation, a more general respect, and such a certain prestige. Suddenly, she cracks, deteriorates, loses her roots and — one would say — is about to come crashing down on herself. Priests turn the altars around, sell Church ornaments, take the saints away; prelates change their language, shut down the organs, welcome the guitars and bless the demolishers. No rite is maintained, no rule spared. The gothic arch of dogmas is cracked. The house of the Good God opens itself to all storms**. Bewildered, we watch this internal quake...

"What is happening to the Catholic Church? Everyone asks with anxiety... Because, when an institution of this order and this grandeur was for centuries the main spiritual shield of a people and the principal moral power of a nation, she influenced everything, impregnated everything, marked everything, the ways of thinking, the references of memory, living habits, individual and collective behavior, artistic expressions, everything, including the law and the very relationships between the citizen and the State. Therefore, when the Church goes through a crisis of such an amplitude, she is not the only one at stake: it is the nation's life as a whole that is affected by this, it is the very personality of a people that can change.

"**A great need for spirituality is manifested everywhere; everywhere, anguished youths are in search of supreme values. And this is the moment the Church chooses**, by means of part of her clergy, **to humble herself inappropriately, to lavish smiles on her philosophical adversaries and to behave in everything as though she were the bearer of relative truths**. .... The Church, according to some, could not resist the rise of modernity and must radically transform herself. Attention, my priests! Everything can be modernized, except God.

"**Could it not be that this great agitation is caused simply by a weakening of the faith among those who were given the responsibility of communicating it?** I know prelates of the highest level .... who are openly restless about this crisis of faith amidst the clergy."[37]

§ 22   Speaking about the crisis in the priesthood, Msgr. Walter Kasper opines: "The crisis of the priesthood in the Catholic Church has multiple causes; it is the reflection of profound changes and great subversions in the conscience and practice of the Church .... as well as in Western society seen in its complexity. Therefore, one cannot face this problem by isolating it from its context, let alone search for any solution if it is not defined in its context. **At the depth of this crisis we undoubtedly find the accentuation of the ecclesiology of the people of God, carried out by Council Vatican II itself, which made evident the reality of the common priesthood of all the baptized and valued the specific vocation of lay Christians."[38]**

§ 23   Fr. Schillebeeckx points to a specific fruit of the spirit of the Council at the Dominican convent of Nijmegen, where he lives: **"For me**, the first evolution in religious life took place in my years of study, but **the greatest one happened after Vatican Council II, not** directly **under the influx of the council as such, but of the spirit of the council. In 1968, there was a veritable hecatomb among religious [men], a terrible decimation. In the Albertinum [convent] we were then about one hundred and ten. Half of them left the order, and this fact had an enormous repercussion on those who stayed. Many priests went to live in small communities** of seven or eight, in simple apartments. **Now we are twenty-eight in our convent."[39]**

§ 24   Gabriel Steinschulte, writing for *L'Osservatore Romano*, notes with respect to the liturgy: "In a global view of the ambience of German culture .... one finds that **the reform [of the Council] gave rise, above all, to misunderstandings, super-**

[37] Maurice DRUON, "Une Eglise que se trompe de siècle", in *Le Monde*, 8/7/1971.

[38] Walter KASPER, "É in questione la Chiesa e l'immagine di Dio," in *Il Regno*, 10/15/1993, p. 567.

[39] E. SCHILLEEBEECKX, "Dio è un dono, non una garanzia," interview with F. STRAZZARI, in *Il Regno*, 6/15/1990, p. 332.

fluous polarizations, the taking of unilateral stands, a frequent and ever more evident **dismantling of the liturgy.**"[40]

§ 25

In the same sense, Cardinal Virgilio Noé, titular Archbishop of Voncaria, Secretary of the Sacred Congregation for the Sacraments and Divine Worship, consultant to the Special Commission on the Liturgy, writes: "Also **the liturgical restoration** [in the post-conciliar period] **gave rise to fights, arguments, divisions between 'progressivists' and 'integralists.' Some left the Church because they could no longer recognize themselves in the new liturgy. Others, remaining in the Church, corrupted the liturgy with fantastic creations** and so many other facts usually qualified as 'abuses.'"[41]

§ 26

Fr. Alois Müller, professor at the Theological Faculty of Lucerne, member of the Board of Directors of the magazine *Concilium*, also points to the crisis provoked by Vatican II: "In the countries with a long Christian tradition, **the reforms of Vatican II did not bring to the Church that vital impulse that was expected. To the contrary, these reforms .... led to a breakdown of the structures and a disintegration of the ecclesial community's social fabric. For this reason, the present conscience of the Church is a conscience in crisis.**"[42]

§ 27

Although the crisis in the Church since the Council has been noticed by so many high-ranking personalities, it is nonetheless curious to note that the lamentations it has caused do not touch the marrow of the question. No question is asked about whether or not the conciliar documents, with their characteristic ambiguity, were such as to inevitably cause the crisis. Any analysis that fails to address this question appears to be *ipso facto* inefficacious.

*

---

[40] Gabriel Maria STEINSCHULTE, "Paesi di lingua tedesca - Vent'anni di riforme, prima e dopo," in *L'Osservatore Romano*, 12/14/1983, special supplement on the Constitution *Sacrosanctum Concilium*, p. IV.

[41] Virgilio NOÉ, "Il primo dono al popolo cristiano," in *L'Osservatore Romano*, 12/14/1983, special supplement on the Constitution *Sacrosanctum Concilium*, p. VIII.

[42] Alois MÜLLER, "Chiesa e riforma," in V.A., *Verso la Chiesa del terzo millennio*, pp. 137f.

2. Strategic Impasse

§ 28   For Vatican dignitaries who continue trying to impose conciliar doctrine, the crisis in the Church takes on the characteristics of a grave strategic impasse in directing Catholic opinion. Excerpts by Cardinal Julius Döpfner and Fr. Louis Boyer, and some principles of action enunciated by Fr. René Laurentin are illustrative of this impasse.

§ 29   Cardinal Döpfner, one of the Council's directors, recognizes: **"The renewal started by the Council currently finds itself in the crossfire of criticism. To some, the reform is too hesitant, to others it is too revolutionary."**[43]

§ 30   Louis Boyer, SJ, a French theologian of considerable renown, consultant to the Secretariat for Non-Christians, arrives at the same finding: **"[The Church] has been blocked by the absurd conflict .... between integralists and progressivists; her mission has been paralyzed and will continue to be as long as one does not leave this deadly circle."**[44]

§ 31   On the adaptation to modern times suggested by conciliar reforms, Laurentin puts forward general principles that foresee the strategic impasse in which high-ranking ecclesiastical authorities find themselves in this post-conciliar era. He says: "To 'act precipitously' is not, therefore, a rule of conduct, much less a panacea. Does this mean one should 'march slowly, without raising obstacles'? The answer is also no, because **in matters of reform, compromises, accommodations and half-measures are the worst things. Usually they compute the inconveniences of the** *status quo* **and of the changes without making the former comfortable or the latter advantageous. Vatican II must conquer not only the dangers of opposition and adventure, but a more redoubtable one: a certain ecclesiastical prudence which is a caricature of Christian prudence.** This false virtue is fecund with sterile but surprisingly popular proverbs: 'All that is excessive is insignificant,' for example. This formula, by Talleyrand, frontally clashes (do people think about it?) with the Gospel, Saint Paul and charity itself, whose characteristic law, according to Saint Thomas, is not that of a

---

[43] J. DÖPFNER, *La Chiesa vivente oggi*, p. 87.

[44] Louis BOYER, *A decomposição do Catolicismo*, Sampedro (Lisbon, n.d.), pp. 188f.

middle ground and does not err by excess. Christ saved us by an excess of love that confounds us."[45]

*

3. Moderates and *Arditi* Lament the Emergence of the Conservative Reaction

§ 32
Reflecting a general wariness among the faithful, the conservative reaction appeared around 1975. It is interesting to note the displeasure and concern it caused both among moderate and more fervent progressivists.

§ 33
Cardinal Roger Etchegaray, president of the Pontifical Councils for Justice and Peace and Cor Unum, although employing an accommodating language, appears displeased with the recalcitrance of innumerable people to follow conciliar reforms. As a matter of fact, on the occasion of the twentieth anniversary of Vatican II, he states: "Twenty years is little to measure the results of the Council. More than one hundred years were needed for the Council of Trent (16th century) to implement its decisions everywhere. Certainly, with the acceleration of History, changes now take place more rapidly; but **we realize that it is easier to change structures than mentalities, and religious mentalities are among the most tenacious**, understandably so, **because they touch the most profound fibers of man.**"[46]

§ 34
Msgr. Boaventura Kloppenburg, a conciliar *perito* usually presented as a moderate and even a conservative, does not hide his displeasure with the conservative reaction: "It is certain — and it is necessary to say it to those who, with pharisaic pride, proclaim themselves to be 'traditionalists' — that the Church must adapt, renew and purify herself. .... This is the tension between the dynamics of Progress and the constancy of Tradition. The equilibrium is not easy .... It requires time, serenity, maturity .... **To be hasty, raise suspicions, generalize iso-**

---

[45] R. LAURENTIN, *Bilan de la première session*, pp. 83f.

[46] Roger ETCHEGARAY, "Le Cardinal Etchegaray, Archevêque de Marseille, se souvient et balise l'avenir," in *Historia* (Paris), October 1982, p. 100.

lated cases, alarm and disturb the authorities, create a partisan climate or division, none of this will do in the historical moment we are living and will only serve to waste time and postpone (once again) the process."[47]

Kloppenburg now takes to an extreme his animadversion of conservatives: "There already are organized movements who call themselves 'traditionalist' with the end of safeguarding the patrimony of the past and openly fighting what they call 'progressivism.' **Tempers boil and there appears, more and more clearly, a spirit of fight and crusade,** of a partisan fanaticism **that blinds** and deafens **to such a point that it does not permit a sufficient serenity to see, hear and discern what is good and true** on one side and the other .... This then begins the unfortunate process of generalization by the official collectors of lamentable isolated facts. **The devil of espionage, denunciations and accusations goes into action.** 'Documents' pile up on the desks of intimidated authorities. **One would say that they are about to start the process of the Inquisition all over again.**"[48]

§ 35   Johann Baptist Metz, a political theologian and one of the disciples of Rahner who became most notorious for his radical positions, laments: "**Too quickly the faith of the reformers is cast into doubt. Too quickly the awakening of critical freedom in the Church** is denigrated as the apotheosis of incredulity. .... To any reform, to the degree that it is substantial and comes from the faith, **such an imputation** certainly **is fatal and, in the final analysis, deadly.** For this reason, it is necessary to change this." Metz goes on: "**Any reform that wants to have a possibility to advance must emerge from the dilemma in which it is found. Or will it be necessary to maintain the fatal impression that reactionary mentalities enjoy a privileged right of citizenship in the Church** and that the Christian faith can be associated to them more easily and with less problems than the disquiet of reforming positions?"[49]

Ardito Metz aligns himself with the fears of 'moderate' Kloppenburg: "Clearly, **groups that are suspicious of this**

[47] B. KLOPPENBURG, *A eclesiologia do Vaticano II*, pp. 102f.

[48] Ibid., pp. 94f.

[49] Johann Baptist METZ, *Más allá de la religión burguesa - Sobre el futuro del Cristianismo* (Salamanca: Sígueme, 1982), pp. 105s.

Council have formed again in the Church, and they want to expel from us the spirit of this Council. Again, there are veiled, very subtle forms of .... inquisition that are no more innocuous by being veiled, but are a much greater cause for concern."[50]

§ 36   Fr. Cardonnel, certainly in the *avant garde* of the French clergy, enunciates the conservative reaction as the great danger for the application of the Council: **"The greatest danger is not too much air, but on the contrary, to leave the windows ajar for a few minutes just before shutting them again in a hurry."** He adds: **"The only threat? To stick strictly to the law, to codify the spirit, to return to port, to not turn the [ship's] prow to the future, to fear to become obsolete, to want too preserve oneself. To fear becoming lost."**[51]

*

4. Inconformity of the *Arditi* With the Slowness of 'Moderate' Leaders

§ 37   Here also we present confirmations of what was said in this Chapter's introduction on the slow pace of the moderates.

§ 38   Leonardo Boff makes a general lamentation, not exclusive to the Council, about the slowness of the leadership to draw consequences from the principles they profess: "In this earnest commitment to liberation, **we** Christians **go through the bitter experience of the slowness of processes and the persistence of oppressions.**" He goes on to ask: "Shouldn't the faithful community, amid the oppressions of our people, plead like the Virgin: '**Lord**, show the power of your arm .... **overthrow the mighty from their thrones** .... fill the hungry with good things?"[52]

---

[50] Ibid., pp. 102f.

[51] Jean CARDONNEL, "Vatican II," interview with Michel DUBOST, in *Historia*, October 1982, p. 96.

[52] Leonardo BOFF, *O rosto materno de Deus - Ensaio inter-disciplinar sobre o feminino e suas formas religiosas* (Petrópolis: Vozes, 1979), p. 211.

§ 39   In a dialogue with Rahner, Metz analyzes the causes and recognizes the slowness of the institutional Church: "**There seems to be a secret correspondence between what I would call 'ideological extravagances' of current theology and a certain immobility of the institutional Church to reform herself, a reform that has certainly been proclaimed but which appears to advance very slowly.**"[53]

Metz also analyzes, in his own way, the state of mind of the Catholic 'silent majority' and blames the crisis on the moderate leaders, who carried out post-conciliar changes without sufficiently preparing the faithful as a whole. Metz accuses the leadership of a failure to communicate a 'love' of the reforms.

"**The problem of the Church of tomorrow,**" he says, "**will not be represented mainly** by intellectual critics, but instead **by the 'simple people' of the so-called 'flock of Christ,' which already appears to be profoundly disturbed**, and not foremost because of a critical theology, but rather because of the very Church institution itself. **It is the actual concrete transformations being carried out in the Church that have provoked dispersion and a crisis of identity. The so-often deplored confusion among the faithful derives .... from the fact that the faithful were exposed by the Church to a change without love, without having been given a critical understanding of the reformability of the Church.** How could the 'simple faithful' conceive the identity of the critical liberty of the one Church in her mutations? Why should they not feel deceived since they lack a mature understanding ....? **One of the causes of the ecclesiastical crisis today is not an excess of criticism but a catastrophic failure** to exercise the most fundamental critical liberty in the Church. **This failure makes the 'flock of Christ' the focus of the crisis in the Church of tomorrow. The 'silent majority' has become a very problematic question also in the Church. Let the religious identity crisis of our good mothers not be underestimated. Who, after all, will save them from a dangerous indifferentism or a skeptical resignation that cause an ever wider chasm between the ecclesiastical institution and the faithful?**"[54]

---

[53] "Karl Rahner em diálogo com Johann Baptist Metz," in V.A., *Cinco problemas que desafiam a Igreja hoje*, p. 158.

[54] J. B. METZ, "Sulla presenza della Chiesa nella società," in V.A., *L'avvenire della Chiesa*, p. 141.

§ 40   Longings for a Vatican III among many *arditi* stem from their hope to end the slow pace of the leadership.

Prof. Giuseppe Alberigo, an outstanding specialist in Church history and author of a well-known book about John XXIII, explains: "Why have a new Council properly speaking? On the one hand, the answer can be sought in the great impulse Vatican II has given all churches: it had been centuries since Catholicism in particular had seen such an intense springtime. On the other hand, it is useful to recall how **the** actual **project of the encounter of Notre Dame**[55] **and its development were situated in the final years of the pontificate of Paul VI, when not only the conciliar impulse seemed worn out but the leadership of the Church suffered an alarming paralysis. In such circumstances it seemed urgent to stimulate a reflection on the near future of the faith and the Church, placing its realization under the augur and in the framework of a new Council.**"[56]

§ 41   In the same sense, Fr. Peter Huizing, SJ, dean of the Gregorian University's Faculty of Canon Law and consultant to the Pontifical Commission for the Revision of the Code of Canon Law, writes: "**Council Vatican II did not translate its doctrine into the institutions of the Church. The statements** on the collegiality of bishops, on the responsibility of the laity, on the nature of Christian marriage, and so on, **are absolutely useless if they are not anchored in the institutions of the Church. This is the main reason for the default of Vatican II. Vatican III should fill this gap.**"[57]

§ 42   The impatient words of a Spanish missionary, Fr. Bendito Revilla Torices, reported by the press on the day we finished the first draft of this Volume, were picturesque. In an audience with John Paul II at the Vatican, he asked the latter to convene a new Ecumenical Council: "Courage, optimism, **out**

---

[55] The theological meeting promoted in 1977 by the magazine *Concilium* at the American Catholic University of Notre Dame (Chicago) under the title "Toward Vatican III."

[56] Giuseppe ALBERIGO, "Editoriale," in V.A., *Verso la Chiesa del terzo millennio*, p. 7.

[57] Peter HUIZING, "Vaticano III: una costituzione sulla Chiesa," in V.A., *Verso la Chiesa del terzo millennio*, p. 167.

with fears, ease up on the brakes and slam on the accelera-tor!"[58]

*

5. Among Progressivists, Authority Loses Credibility and Is Contested

§ 43   As we said in the introduction to this Chapter, the *arditi* also lost confidence in the authority of the Hierarchy. This weakening was manifested mainly as a loss of credibility and the most expressive fruit it generated was a denial of the authority of Rome and of the Pope. That is what can be found in the texts that follow.

§ 44   Swiss theologian Alois Müller, a member of the board of directors of *Concilium*, complains about the position of the Hierarchy, whose action, he believes, favors traditional lines and reveals that Rome has lost its authority in progressivist quarters.

"**Soon after the Council, counter-currents were formed in the Roman Curia, in some conferences of bishops and also among the grassroots, the people. First of all, they interpreted the Council only in its more traditional lines, instead of apprehending by intuition its calls for renewal. Furthermore, in later legislation they sought to moderate the impulses of the Council itself. With this march in reverse, the Curia and the Hierarchy lost their credibility among those who had committed themselves**, soul and body, **to the reform. This was the main reason for the jungle of disorderly and uncontrolled private initiatives.** These initiatives also favored an evolutionary movement in reverse, which nourished a desire to return to the old schemes even among bishops who used to favor the reform. Furthermore, the speeches of the Pope always put people on guard against 'progressivism' under the pretext of defending and favoring reform."[59]

---

[58] Benedito REVILLA TORICES, Statements to the press, "D. Aloísio quer Igreja em ação política," in *O Estado de São Paulo*, 12/6/1985.

[59] Alois MÜLLER, "Chiesa e riforma," in V.A., *Verso la Chiesa del terzo millennio*, pp. 136f.

§ 45 Hans Küng reflects well the thinking of various currents of *arditi*. He does not hesitate to blame the Pope for the faults that generated the credibility crisis of the progressivists in the Hierarchy and the Church herself: "**Behind all this**, as I see it, **[is] the fundamental shortcoming of the post-conciliar period: a lack of spiritual leadership in Rome and among the bishops**. Today we need an inspiring intellectual and spiritual authority at all levels. .... There is a dangerous abyss, now greater, now smaller, **between the bishops and a great majority of the priests in regard to the serious problems of the Church today. .... Here you have the result: a most lamentable and well-deserved damage to the credibility of the post-conciliar Church. .... In a long interview in New York .... I said this, and I and stand by it: 'The present pope [Paul VI] started out with the Catholic Church having perhaps the greatest credibility in the last five hundred years. We now arrive at the end of this pontificate and I find that the credibility of the Catholic Church is so low that we cannot explain what has happened.'"**[60]

§ 46 This attitude toward the Pope begins the period of 'respectful indifference,' which the Archbishop of Aracaju, Msgr. Cabral Duarte, with the magazine *Communio*, spoke about in the Synod of 1983. Expounding his ideas on 'Liberation Theology,' he notes the following: "**They no longer contest the Pope: they hear him, are silent, and then continue acting as before. This is the time of 'respectful indifference.' The Synod should, I believe, make a pronouncement on this urgent reconciliation of many Catholic minds with the supreme Magisterium of the Church**."[61]

§ 47 However, this 'respectful indifference' apparently supposes that the Pope approves the celebrated theological pluralism. Otherwise, brazen and aggressive contestations will arise.

Patrick Jacquemont, a French Dominican, puts forward the principle of contestation as a question: "**Should the Church not be contested when this pluralism in the language of the**

---

[60] Hans KÜNG, *O que deve permanecer na Igreja* (Petrópolis: Vozes, 1976), pp. 16f.

[61] Luciano CABRAL DUARTE, "Riconciliare le intelligenze cattoliche," in *L'Osservatore Romano*, 10/6/1983, Supplement, p. III.

faith is not recognized, when the confession of faith is wrapped in the formulation of some catechism or profession of faith?"[62]

§ 48   Upon the deposition of Msgr. Jacques Gaillot from the Diocese of Evreux because of his stands favoring homosexuals, contraceptives, the abolition of obligatory priestly celibacy and so on, commentator Jacques Duquesne, of the newspaper *La Croix*, offers his opinion on the *arditi*'s distancing from the Vatican's 'conservative' attitude: "**Many European Catholics no longer admit the imperatives of the Church**, there is much resentment against Rome, the Church is losing her social base, **we are currently living in a process I call silent schism**."[63]

§ 49   Finally, Küng also alleges the lack of greater liberalism in marital morality as a factor in the credibility crisis. Citing moralists to his liking, Küng lays down the doctrinal position that led the opposition against the Encyclical *Humanae vitae* of Paul VI:[64] "And we must hold in high esteem the theologians who prepared the moral-theological position paper for the progressivist conciliar majority, [on account of the] fact that they spoke out with extraordinary frankness about the errors of the ecclesiastical magisterium .... in regard to marital morality. '**Not a few theologians and faithful fear that a change in official doctrine could damage the confidence of Catholics in the magisterium of the Church. So they ask: how could the assistance of the Holy Spirit have permitted such an error during a series of centuries, errors with so many consequences, above all in the last centuries?** But it is almost impossible to determine *a priori* the criteria to establish whether or not the Holy Spirit could allow it. In fact, it is known that there have been errors in the declarations of the magisterium and in tradition. As for sexual relations, it should be noted that for long centuries it was taught in the Church in an almost unanimous fashion and in active concordance with the popes that the married relation is illicit if unaccompanied by an intention to procreate, or, at least, ... if it does not serve as a relief for [one of] the partners. Nevertheless, '**today this viewpoint is not shared**

---

[62] Patrick JACQUEMONT, "Igreja e contestação," in V.A., *A Igreja do futuro*, p. 38.

[63] Jacques DUQUESNE, Comments on the deposition of Msgr. Gaillot, in Any BOURRIER, "Demissão de Bispo revolta os franceses," in *Jornal do Brasil*, 1/17/1995.

[64] See Chap. X, Note 25.

by any theologian, nor does it represent an official opinion.'[65] In any case, one should not deviate from the conclusion that **only a critical reinterpretation of ecclesiastical infallibility could be able to overcome the present difficulties**," Küng concludes.[66]

§ 50   Küng's much desired 'critical reinterpretation of infallibility' finds echo in an editorial in *La Civiltà Cattolica* a few days before the beginning of the Synod of Bishops in November 1985.

One could say that in this point the 'moderates' of *La Civiltà Cattolica* join the aforementioned *arditi* to make a common front. For even though the editorial theoretically appears to obey doctrinal concerns, in fact, its publication, on the eve of a Synod being prepared to deal with the question of Pontifical Primacy, took on the character of a real political constestation. We have chosen a few excerpts: "One cannot hide the fact that **the definition of Vatican I .... has the marks of a conception of authority that no longer jibes with the theological maturity and the cultural level of the Church and society today**. This explains why a re-proposal of the doctrine of the Petrian-Roman Primacy, desired by Vatican II, was met in the Church herself by an impressive array of difficulties, intolerance, and boredom. .... **The doctrinal packaging with which *Pastor aeternus* framed the truth of the primacy of Peter and of the Bishops of Rome has a different, if not opposed, perspective than the packaging used by *Lumen gentium*, because Vatican I conceives the pope as the structural vertex and perfective causality of the visible Church-society, whereas Vatican II envisages this most high post as a sign and reality of the service of authority placed at the heart of the Church-communion**. .... After Vatican I, the aura of transcendence around the pope was strongly accentuated. The visible Chief of the Church, supreme interpreter of revelation, then appeared alone, exceedingly alone before God, committed on his conscience to decide the most serious questions for the Church and the world: a dramatic and almost unbearable effort for a human creature, capable of giving the pope's magisterium and government a *quasi* divine reverberation as a direct consequence of his

---

[65] Küng refers to the conservative minority in the Council's theological commission. The quotation inside the text was published in *Herder-Korrespondenz*, n. 21, 1967, p. 440 (*Veracidade*, pp. 136ff.).

[66] Ibid., pp. 140f.

psychological isolation with regard to other members of the Church."[67]

The editorial of the well-known Jesuit magazine, directed by Fr. Gianpaolo Salvini, goes on to introduce a subtle distinction between infallibility and 'infallibilism.' Such a distinction appears to be made, as we will see, to facilitate criticism of the traditional devotion that the faithful have always had to the sacred person of the Vicar of Christ. According to *La Civiltà Cattolica*, such devotion, which is the honor of every faithful Catholic, would amount to nothing but 'servility' and a vile, self-interested 'courtier mentality.' The magazine goes so far as to call it 'exaggerations of papalatry' and 'courtly byzantinism.'

Eschewing direct attacks on pontifical infallibility by means of this conveniently forged distinction, the editorial nevertheless indirectly criticizes the Pope as Monarch of the Church.

These are the words by *La Civiltà Cattolica*: "In the 'aura' of transcendence and sovereignty that was accentuated after the definition of Vatican I, it is necessary to emphasize, as many people say, the so-called 'infallibilism,' which is something totally different from infallibility. Indeed, as a prerogative intimately connected with the Petrian primacy, the latter is a charism which, under certain conditions, makes the Roman pontiff immune from errors; .... on the contrary, **infallibilism** expresses a maximalist mentality that **confounds infallibility with impeccability** or extends the scope of the Petrian charism beyond the confines of revelation .... Therefore, **infallibilism is a** psycho-sociological **attitude not always removed from the servility typical,** in some way, **of the courtier mentality that germinates outside of the** pure **doctrine** of the pope's personal infallibility **as an excrescence of it; and if,** at times, for contingent reasons, **it was able to play an apologetic role,** let it be said frankly that this **was the effect and cause of that ecclesiastical pyramidism that saw the exaggerations of papalatry and courtier byzantinism proliferate.**"[68]

The official magazine of the religious order that Saint Ignatius placed especially at the service of the Pope continues:

---

[67] *La Civiltà Cattolica*, Editorial: "Il ministero del Papa dopo i due Concili Vaticani," 11/2/1985, pp. 212, 215.

[68] Ibid., p. 217.

"**The papacy is called to reveal itself ever more to the Church and the peoples as a humble minister of the sole Savior**, the custodian and interpreter of his Gospel, **as a humble servant of the human conscience** .... **rejecting at the same time the human temptation of despotism and paternalism.** ..... **The new morphology of the papacy was prepared by Vatican II.** This Council did not renege the Gregorian and Tridentine theology but completed it, **grafting it on to the doctrine of the Church as a people of God and the doctrine of episcopal collegiality. With the first, it annihilated hierocracy**, showing the equal baptismal dignity of all Christians in the difference of charisms and offices; **with the second it tempered the monistic tendency inherent to the old conception of the Roman primacy**. Nonetheless, while laying the foundations for a theology of the primacy purged and exempted from pious exaggerations and mundane excesses, the Council also professes, without ambiguity, the primacy and personal infallibility of the bishop of Rome."[69]

The comments in the editorial of *La Civiltà Cattolica* are such as to 'demythify' the papal power, undermine monarchy in the Church and favor an ecclesiological conception based on the supremacy of the people, whom the Pope should serve. Save for the subleties of style, all this creates a propitious climate for the contestation of papal authority. It seems to us that the excerpts presented are a significant example of how 'moderates' such as those of *La Civiltà* indirectly help *arditi* like Küng.

*

---

[69] Ibid., pp. 218ff.

6. Crisis in the Clergy and in the Religious Orders[70]

§ 51   Ever since the Council, a crisis ravages the Catholic clergy, both secular and regular. That is what John Paul II attests to in his Closing Speech to the Synod of 1990. In fact, on delving into the causes of the 'crisis of identity in the priesthood,' he says: "**This crisis had arisen in the years immediately following the Council.** It was founded on an erroneous, sometimes voluntarily tendentious comprehension of the doctrine of the conciliar Magisterium. **Here is, undoubtedly, one of the causes of the great number of losses then suffered by the Church, losses which gravely affected pastoral service and vocations for the priesthood**, particularly missionary vocations."[71]

§ 52   Similarly grave words come from the pen of Cardinal Ratzinger: "**The crisis in today's Church is, first of all, a crisis of the priests and religious orders.** This is a tough thesis. It is a scathing *j'accuse*, although it might contain a truth. **During the shock of the post-conciliar period, the great religious orders vacillated .... suffered a heavy hemorrhage, saw the number of new vocations reduced to levels never before reached and, even today, appear shaken by an identity crisis.**"[72]

---

[70] The last two Items of this Chapter — crisis in the Clergy and crisis of faith among the faithful — might seem out of place in an ensemble dealing primarily with the disciplinary crisis. Indeed, of themselves such topics would better fit a chapter on the doctrinal or institutional reality of the Church. Nevertheless, here they will be dealt with from a specific standpoint. The crisis of adhesion to the Faith and to the institution of the priesthood undoubtedly have multiple causes with varied depths. Here we focus on only one of them, which justifies the inclusion of the said items in the sequence of the disciplinary crisis.

Once the Church's internal unity and cohesion is broken, and the power, prestige and example of the ecclesiastical authority, above all that of the Pope, are brought into question, a huge number of faithful will inevitably become disoriented and discouraged. This easily generates a crisis of faith, customs, and vocations. This is how the two following Items harmonize with the remainder of the Chapter.

[71] JOHN PAUL II, Closing Speech to the Synod of 1990, published under the title: "Grazie al Sinodo sono stati affrontati problemi cruciali che hanno sempre trovato la risposta collegiale della Chiesa," in *L'Osservatore Romano*, 10/28/1990, pp. 4f.

[72] J. RATZINGER, *Rapporto sulla Fede*, p. 55.

What the Pope and the Cardinal from the Congregation for the Doctrine of the Faith authoritatively onfirm is public and notorious. Every Catholic could give specific examples and point to this same phenomenon. The media frequently carry news items on the grave symptoms of an evil that contaminates the whole ecclesiastical body.

A. Crisis in the Secular Clergy

§ 53

Here we present an overview of the crisis by means of a collection of facts published over the years that reflect the extent and gravity of the situation generated by the Council.

The main characteristics of this post-conciliar crisis, along whose lines we have ordered the presentation below, are: abandonment of the ministry; drop in the number of vocations and consequent shortage of priests; opposition to priestly celibacy coupled with the phenomenon of married priests; the scandal of ecclesiastical concubinage; the addiction of priests to the vice of alcoholism and the perversion of homosexuality.

a) Abandonment of the Ministry, Drop in the Number of Vocations, Shortage of Priests

§ 54

Assembled in Medellin in 1968, the Latin American Bishops Council - CELAM - made these observations on the crisis of the ministry: **"Doubts arise also regarding the priestly vocation itself. Doubts caused by factors characteristic of this hour of ecclesial renewal: The growing valorization of the role of laymen** in the development of the world and the Church. .... **The superficiality with which the priesthood** itself **is personified** in routine religious functions and in a bourgeois way of life. A crisis also takes place among the priests who, either because of their age or formation, feel unable to assume the changes promoted by the Council."[73]

§ 55

Referring to the first eight years of post-conciliar era (1965-1973), Fr. Hans Küng lists some general elements on the

---

[73] CELAM, *A Igreja na atual transformação da América Latina e à luz do Concílio - Conclusões de Medellin* (Petrópolis: Vozes, 1980), p. 122.

crisis: "In the Catholic Church we are undoubtedly in a very critical phase: **Vatican II has failed in every way to solve some problems that could have been entirely solved .... Phenomena of this crisis**, especially in the Catholic Church, **are:**

"a) **The mass exodus from the ecclesiastical ministry: 22,000 to 25,000 in the last eight years.**

"b) **In ever more catastrophic proportion, the recent crisis of vocations among the new generation**, from North America to Spain.

"c) **A weakening of discipline among the faithful and churchmen**, above all with respect to Sunday worship."[74]

56

No source could be more reliable regarding the crisis of vocations in the Clergy from 1973 onward than the *Church Statistics Yearbook* for 1986, published by the Vatican's semi-official organ, *L'Osservatore Romano*. The charts presented cover **1973 to 1986**, years in which the total numbers of priests were, respectively, 433,089 and 402,886 worldwide. Summarizing the charts for the period in question, **there were:**

    * **27,366 defections;**
    * 88,751 ordinations;
    * 98,436 deaths.[75]

57

About these data, one can note the following:

    * **If we add to the defections mentioned by *L'Osservatore Romano* for the period 1973-1986 (27,366) the average estimate presented by Fr. Küng** — whom we suppose

---

[74] Hans KÜNG, *O que deve permanecer na Igreja*, pp. 15f.

[75] *L'Osservatore Romano*, "Valutazione delle linee di tendenza dell'attività pastorale della Chiesa cattolica fino al 1986," 5/30-31/1988, Supplement, pp. IIf.

Curiously, an error appears to have slipped into the statistics that *L'Osservatore Romano* presented in its charts. If the number of priests in 1973 was 433,089 and there was a *deficit* of 37,051 priests in the period 1973-1986 (27,366 defections + 9,685 representing the difference between the 98,436 priests deceased and the 88,751 ordained) the total number in 1986 should be 396,018. But *L'Osservatore* puts the 1986 figure at 402,886 — a surplus of 6,848 priests.

to be well-informed — **on the period 1962-1973 (23,500 defections), we find that since 1962, 50,866 priests are said to have
abandoned their sacred mission**.

§ 58   * Taking into account only the period 1973-1986 with
data provided by *L'Osservatore Romano*, one sees that the difference between deceased and ordained priests is 9,685. If to
this difference we add the number of defections (27,366), we
will have in this period a negative balance of 37,051 priests.[76]

§ 59   We know that in the period 1973-1986 the Catholic
population increased by about 200 million people.[77] In order to
fulfil her apostolic needs with the same level of service She had
formerly provided, the Church, which in 1973 had 433,089
priests, in 1986 should have roughly 570,000 priests. **Since in
1986 She had only 402,886, the difference is about 167,000
priests.**

§ 60   In the period 1986-1990 the world Catholic population,
which numbered 864,379,000[78] grew to 928,500,000[79], that is,
an increase of just over 64,000,000 faithful. Taking the year
1973 as a point of reference, to maintain the same proportion of
the number of priests in relation to that of faithful, there needs to
be about 612,000 priests. Now, **in 1990 the official tally of**

---

[76] Incidentally, the situation with more than just a few of those who
remained in the ranks of the Clergy is far from auspicious. See, for
example, "Les volets du presbytère sont ouverts," a work published by
the French Catholic weekly *La Vie* on the responses it received from
about 2,000 of the 29,000 priests in France: 31 percent wish to be
called by their names without the title of priest; 21 percent declare to
be favorable to the left; 44 percent have restrictions regarding Catholic
Morals; 29 percent approve the marriage of priests; 83 percent wish
married men to be ordained; and 36 percent are for the ordination of
women; and 50 percent admit to having or having had doubts about
the Faith (in L. LANGRE, "Francia - el Clero, de derechas, distinto y
levemente utopico," in *Vida Nueva,* Madrid, 11/2/1985, pp. 31f.).

[77] René LAURENTIN, "A retomada existe. Eis a prova," in *30 Giorni*
(Portuguese ed.), December 1988, p. 52.

[78] Ibid.

[79] Ufficio Centrale di Statistica della Chiesa, "La Chiesa cattolica alla
luce di alcuni fenomeni statistici dal 1978 al 1990," in *L'Osservatore
Romano*, 7/15/1992, Supplement, p. IV; *L'Osservatore Romano*,
10/17/1992, Supplement, p. II.

secular and regular priests was 403,173,[80] a difference of 208,827 priests. This amounts to a deficit of more than 50 percent.

§ 61   Recent data do not essentially change this picture. Indeed, *L'Osservatore Romano* discloses that in the year 1992 the total number of priests was 404,641. Of these, 64.2 percent were secular and 35.8 percent regular. The paper adds that in relation to the year 1978 there was a drop of 2.8 percent resulting from a small increase in the secular Clergy (0.6 percent) and a decrease of 8.3 percent in the regular Clergy. Drops were registered in Europe (9.9 percent), North America (10 percent), the Middle East (4.1 percent) and Oceania (5.6 percent), whereas Africa and Southeast Asia saw increases of 29 percent and 41 percent respectively.[81]

*

§ 62   A confirmation or update of these data in relation to the Church as a whole or to any particular country can be found in the press from various countries.

Newsweek magazine comments on the severe scarcity of priests in the United States: **The Church in the United States "is quickly losing its priests.** Since 1962, when Council Vatican II started, more than 12,000 priests have dropped out of the priesthood in the U.S., and comparatively few young men have shown up to replace them. **Two decades ago the American Church had 48,000 seminarians; at present they are less than 12,000, and probably only 60 percent will persevere until the final vows.** The average age of American priests is now 56; at the end of the century, specialists calculate, it will be 73." Now even **"homosexuals are more promptly admitted into priesthood,** as long as they are not sexually active. In the United States even **the bishops recognize that the problem of ordaining women and married men cannot be ruled out forever."**[82]

---

[80] Ibid.

[81] *L'Osservatore Romano*, "Presentato al Santo Padre l'Annuario pontificio 1994," 2/28-3/1/1994, p. 7

[82] Kenneth L. WOODWARD, "An Acute Shortage of Priests," in *Newsweek*, 4/18/1983, pp. 49f.

§ 63   In the same year 1983, *La Croix* published an analogous finding on the scarcity of priests in France: "Twenty years ago priests were still numerous in France and the seminaries teeming. In 1983 there are less priests! .... It seems to me that they don't dare tell Catholics the whole truth; that we are poorly prepared for the years 1990-2000 and that, at times, awkward solutions are improvised. .... Compared with the years 1960-1965, today there are extremely few young men in the seminaries. Nor will ordinations in the next few years be numerous."[83]

§ 64   Articles published in various issues of the magazine *30 Giorni* confirm that the crisis and the consequent shortage of priests are continuing.

In its December 1988 edition, a columnist in the magazine writes: "It will fall to historians to analyze the reasons for the blindness in the post-conciliar period. As far as the Church is concerned, it seems to me that the disorientation originates mainly in a grave crisis of identity in the clergy .... **The uniform having been dropped, commanders saw themselves without troops, and de-Christianization confirmed the preceding secularization. Traumatized by mass desertions .... and the lack of vocations, the clergy let themselves be dragged along.**"[84]

§ 65   Fr. René Laurentin, pointing out a relative increase in the number of ordinations,[85] finds that even if such a trend were to

---

[83] Jean FRECHET, "Vocations sacerdotales et sacerdoce des baptisés, lettre," in *La Croix*, Paris, 8/31/1983.

[84] Xavier TILLIETTE, "Começar de novo. Com fé," in *30 Giorni* (Portuguese ed.), December 1988, pp. 52f.

[85] a. Many see as a sign of hope a slightly higher number of admissions into secular seminaries and, as a consequence, a relatively higher number of priests ordained. An analogous phenomenon could be pointed out in relation to the regular Clergy.

However, what the figures fail to review is the origin of these new vocations. Indeed, the countries that have provided the largest number of seminarians and novices are India, Poland, some African nations (Stefano PACI, "Precisam-se vocações - Pesquisa - A crise das religiosas," in *30 Dias*, April 1990, p. 65), and, more recently, the Philippines, whereas the situation of vocations in Western European countries, which have always set the tone in the Church, remains catastrophic. Hence it could be predicted that the Church — due to the future influence of Indian and African priests — will move away from the Western cultural area, in which most of her faithful are found. Or some of those priests will be sent to Europe and the Americas, with the consequent cultural clashes that this entails. In the case of Polish priests — formed under a communist regime and usually imbued with a collaborationist mentality — one may fear they will disseminate a doctrine opposed to the regime of private property and free initiative, and favorable to socialism and communism.

Optimists about the 'recovery' in the number of vocations keep silent about such data.

b. In this sense, the words of a woman religious speaking about the difficulties experienced by novices from mission regions, appear more realistic than Fr. Laurentin's optimism. Certainly the problems she raised also apply, *mutatis mutandis*, to the recruiting of male novitiates and seminaries: "Sister Vittorina, of the Masters of Saint Dorothea (an order which opened up to missions only after the Council), faced the problem of forming novices from mission lands. It is a road that often requires a long time and the understanding of diverse cultural roots but which, in fact, brings the congregation out of 'a period of stagnation, opens new horizons, obliges one to assume change as a criterion of life'" (Miela d'ATTILIA, "Donne sulle vie della missione," in *Avvenire*, Milan, 6/16/1991).

c. This perspective is emphasized by statements of Cardinal Jaime SIN. Indeed, the Archbishop of Manila, talking about a certain proselytism without adequate criteria that some religious congregations have been carrying out in the Philippines, expounds reasons that may perhaps be valid for other countries as well: "These are the principal arguments against indiscriminate recruiting: 1) While we are pleased with the generous response of Philippine male and female vocations from the provinces, we must continue to be particularly sensitive about their true motivation. 2) In any case, the 'recruiting' of vocations, especially abroad, causes serious concerns, above all when **certain 'favors' appear to become an exchange currency for those recruited.** Vocations are gratuitous gifts, they have no price. 3) The mystery and beauty of a religious vocation have been stained by various facts over the last few years. On the one hand, we are happy with the quantitative growth, but, on the other hand, **we suffer due to the costly loss in vocation quality.** 4) **The urgency and aggressiveness that can** precisely **characterize our zeal** for the Kingdom **can become real obstacles** instead of steps in the direction of a gradual coming of the Kingdom to us. Prudence suggests that sometimes we must respect times that are not our own" ("Por algumas túnicas a mais," interview with Lucio BRUNELLI, in *30 Dias*, October 1994, p. 26).

d. The Italian press transcribes excerpts from a document that the Philippine Episcopate delivered to the Synod of 1994, denouncing the continue, it would take until the year 2000 to replenish the ranks of the Clergy to the level of 1971. Meanwhile, the Catholic population grew by 200 million new faithful in 15 years (1971-1986), a figure likely to double by the turn of the millenium.

'enticement of [female] novices' by Italian religious orders (Orazio la ROCCA, "Dalle Filippine arriva la 'tralta delle novizie,'" in *La Repubblica*, 10/3/1994).

According to the document, "in Manila alone, 87 feminine and 32 masculine congregations have been established in a few years' time. **To try to remedy their vocational crisis, such congregations are allegedly alluring young people to enter the convent, to the point of using as bait the idea of a possible transfer to Italy with better paying jobs**" (Ibid.).

"What we must safeguard," the Philippine Bishops write, "is the holiness of one's own vocation. **We are not recruiting for the army, nor are we advertising a new brand of soap**" (Ibid.). They continue: "**We must prevent a vocational problem from becoming a recruitment of .... house maids**" (Ibid.).

e. On vocations in Africa, the Bishop of Bulawayo (Zimbabwe) warned at the Synod of 1994 that "**religious vocations should not be seen as a means to gain social status and an education**" (Henry Ernest KARLEN, "Dimensione umana della formazione religiosa," in *L'Osservatore Romano*, 11/23/1994, Supplement, pp. 51f.). The Bishop of Maken (Sierra Leone) points to the same problem: "Great discernment is needed in recruiting candidates for the religious life. Because of the impoverishment in our countries, **many can be attracted to religious life in order to improve their living standards**" (George BIGUZZI, "Tenere alta la faiccola dell'evangelizzazione, della giustizia e della pace," Ibid., p. 43). The Bishop of Ndalatando (Angola) concluded his words at the same Synod by stating that "**in Angola,** the number of religious being formed is increasing, but **one senses a lack of proficient educators**" (Pedro Luis Guido SCARPA, "Formazione 'inculturata' ma esigente," Ibid., p. 46).

f. Cardinal Silvio ODDI has this to say about the East European Clergy: "With some exceptions of noble figures victimized by persecution, Christians in the East are ignorant in religious matters. They had no support from **the clergy, who were largely intimidated and inactive, if not servants to the communist** police" ("Confissões de um Cardeal," interview with Tommaso RICCI, in *30 Dias*, November 1990, p. 65).

These statements add serious qualifications to the declarations of the apologists of a 'new springtime' in religious vocations.

"The number of priests continues to drop," says Laurentin, "it went from 420,429 in 1971 to 402,886 in 1986. .... Today, however, while the overall number of priests continues to drop, the number of seminarians and ordinations is recovering some ground. The current deficit in the number of priests (obtained by comparing deaths and desertions with the number of ordinations) was 3,870. It dropped to less than 3,000 in 1978 and less than 2,000 in 1984 .... The number of desertions of priests entering the lay state (3,690 to 1,057) weighed less than deaths, since the clergy 'aged' during the years of crisis. A country such as France, where a large part of the clergy is over 60, had 761 deaths to 200 ordinations, a negative balance of almost 600, a factor that weighs on world statistics. But the general tendency has changed once again. .... It is necessary for this expansion to continue, since to return to the number of 1971 (420,000 priests), which has been forecast for the year 2000, would not be a satisfactory goal. The number of Catholic faithful increased by more than 200 million since 1970 (from 653,532,000 to 864,379,000 in 1986)."[86]

§ 66   The Eighth Synod of Bishops, held in Rome in October 1990, dealt with *The Formation of Priests in the Present Circumstances*. In regard to the topics that the issue suggests, a writer in *30 Dias* stated: "The Synod will also discuss the crisis of vocations that has dramatically reduced the ranks of Diocesan and regular clergy in the last few years. **In 1978 there were 258,541 Diocesan priests and 157,878 regular priests all over the world. In 1987, according to data from the statistics department of the Roman Curia, there were 254,281 Diocesan priests and 147,962 regular priests. In less than 10 years there was a drop of over 14,000 priests.** There is little reason for rejoicing."[87]

§ 67   The crisis is reaching such a point that the shortage of priests is felt even in the Diocese of Rome, the capital of Christianity. This finding was related by the then Vicar of Rome, **Cardinal Ugo Poletti, in a report presented at the annual**

---

[86] R. LAURENTIN, "A retomada existe. Eis a prova," in *30 Giorni* (Portuguese ed.), December 1988, pp. 51f.

[87] Lucio BRUNELLI, "Colegialidade, quanto trabalho!," in *30 Dias*, June 1989, p. 39.

meeting of Rome's priests. According to him, **the number of priests is "diminishing at a frightening pace."**[88]

*

b) Controversy About Priestly Celibacy and the Phenomenon of Married Priests[89]

§ 68   While the number of priests drops at a 'frightening pace,' a growing number of them marry, with or without Rome's permission.

In 1968, CELAM described in general terms the situation in Latin America: "In relation to priestly celibacy, a laudable deepening of the emotional value of the human person and an exacerbated eroticism in the environment, along with frequent slips in spiritual life and other causes, have opened the way to a new and varied set of problems."[90]

§ 69   In 1985, 400,000 priests carried out their ministry worldwide, while about 70,000 had left the priesthood to get married. In 1994 this latter figure has reached almost 100,000.[91]

§ 70   In various countries, some of them have been founding very active associations to have the Vatican reinstate them into the priestly ministry.

---

[88] Ugo POLETTI, Statements to the press, in *O Estado de S. Paulo*, "Faltam padres em Roma, diz Cardeal," 6/14/1989.

[89] "It is still to this same end [of combating the Catholic Religion, the divine authority of the Church and her no less venerable laws] that tends this shameful conspiracy recently formed against the sacred celibacy of the members of the Clergy. A conspiracy which counts, o sorrow! among its promoters some members of the ecclesiastical order, whom, miserably forgetting their own dignity, let themselves be vanquished and seduced by the shameful illusions and fateful attractions of voluptuousness" (PIUS IX, *Qui pluribus*, November 9, 1846, in V.A., *Recueil des allocutions*, p. 183).

[90] CELAM, op. cit., p. 122.

[91] Marisa FUMAGALLI, "Anatema del vescovo di Rimini - 'No' al raduno dei preti sposati," in *Corriere della Sera*, 8/27/1994.

In 1985 the 'universal synod of married Catholic priests and their wives' assembled in Ariccia, on the outskirts of Rome. There were 150 participants coming from 15 countries: Argentina, Austria, Belgium, Brazil, Canada, Czechoslovakia, England, France, Germany, Haiti, Spain, Switzerland, and the United States.

The 'synod' featured three discussion panels followed by lectures and testimonies. The meeting concluded that obligatory celibacy is "illegitimate from the dogmatic and juridical standpoints" and could not be imposed by a general law. The married priests also alleged that both priesthood and marriage are sacraments and, therefore, cannot be incompatible. Addressing the problem constituted by the grave shortage of priests, they made an appeal to the Bishops who were to meet at an extraordinary Synod a few months later: "We are at our posts, we are married priests. Send for us and the scarcity of priests will be resolved."[92]

The daily *La Repubblica* reported that the second meeting of married priests was organized by about twenty associations from around the world. The 'synod's secretary-general, Paolo Camellini, was reduced to the lay state during the pontificate of Paul VI "to be able to dedicate himself to married priests." He communicated that the 'synod' was being held to the Sacred Congregation for the Clergy, whose informal answer was, "You may not claim that we are officially present, but we are pleased that you can express your faith and assemble like any other Christian."[93]

It is noteworthy that, according to the same Italian daily, the conference chairman, Giovanni Gennari, a former priest who directs Vocatio, Italy's association of married priests, is a sympathizer of the Italian Communist Party. Gennari says, "Some years ago Cardinal Evaristo Arns wrote the Pope a letter in the name of other bishops asking for a reform of celibacy." **He goes on to add that the 70,000 married priests were "only the tip of a much larger iceberg."**[94]

---

[92] Georges MATTIA, "70,000 prêtres mariés en quête de légitimité," in *La Croix*, 8/27/1985.

[93] Domenico del RIO, "Sono settanta mile i sacerdoti sposati," in *La Repubblica*, 8/25/1985.

[94] Ibid.

In the following year, 1986, Vocatio organized its third national conference. In an interview with the press, Gennari said there were 8,000 married priests in Italy and a total of 50,000 in the world. He also revealed that in April of the same year the International Federation of Married Priests had been founded. This is an organization that brings together 22 groups from 16 countries.[95]

§ 71   Movements advocating the ordination of married laymen also join forces with associations of married priests to combat priestly celibacy. They enjoy important support even from people in the ecclesiastical Hierarchy. **In 1987, when American Jesuit Terence Sweeney took a poll asking 312 American Bishops and 122 Cardinals from around the world what they thought of priestly celibacy and the ordination of women, he received 144 replies from the Bishops and 10 from the Cardinals. Fifty percent of the respondents favored revising the Church's attitude regarding the two issues.[96]**

§ 72

The same article reports there were then about 80,000 married priests, with 17,000 in the United States, 7,000 in Spain and 6,000 in Brazil.

§ 73   In Brazil there are several organizations of married priests. One of them, called Rumos, also admits former seminarians. This group coordinated its members' participation in the First Latin-American Encounter of Married Priests, held in Curitiba in 1990.[97]

Another association that brings together a good number of former clergymen is the Movement of Married Priests of Brazil, created in 1972. It has 2,500 registered members. Aristides Pimentel, secretary of the movement's São Paulo Section, states that "for the most part, our associates are canonically ordained

---

[95] Giovanni GENNARI, Statements to the press, in *O Globo*, "Padres casados abrem em Roma seu congresso," 8/29/1986.

[96] Dermi AZEVEDO, "Oposição ao celibato obrigatório ganha força dentro da Igreja," in *Folha de S. Paulo*, 11/7/1988.

[97] Ibid.

former priests who carried out the ministry for periods ranging from five to 25 years."[98]

Even more examples could be cited to illustrate the growing pressures brought to bear on the Holy See to have it modify its millenary discipline on priestly celibacy.

In October 1989, the III National Encounter of Priests, promoted by the National Commission of the Clergy, an organization of the National Conference of Brazilian Bishops (CNBB), was held at Itaici with the participation of 18 Bishops and 434 priests. The meeting issued a document sent to Cardinal Silvio Oddi, Prefect of the Congregation for the Clergy, asking for the ordination of married men as a "first step toward the abolition of obligatory priestly celibacy."[99]

One year later, the Eighth Synod of Bishops was convened in Rome to study problems related to the priestly ministry. At the Synod, the president of the International Federation of Married Priests (which claims a membership of 90,000 former priests), accused the Vatican in a press interview of preventing a debate on obligatory priestly celibacy. At the same time, the Federation presented for the Synod's consideration a proposal that "celibacy not be obligatory, but the fruit of personal choice."[100]

In 1994, as Vocatio assembled in the town of Riccione, its director, Guido D'Altri, provided a more updated figure of their membership: Vocatio counts 1,000 married priests out of the 10,000 in Italy and 100,000 in the whole world. He also says there are forty associations of married priests around the world. D'Altri claims that such figures are only the tip of the iceberg, for if that many priests get married openly, how many more are clandestinely living in irregular situations?[101]

---

[98] Aristides PIMENTEL, Statements to the press, in *O Estado de S. Paulo*, "Ex-padres estão organizados," 6/15/1989.

[99] Celso FALASHI, "Ordenação de casados é defendida por padres," in *O Estado de S. Paulo*, 10/14/1989.

[100] "Celibato é discutido no Sínodo," in *O Estado de S. Paulo*, 10/3/1990.

[101] Guido d'ALTRI, Statements to the press, in M. FUMAGALLI, Ibid.; *La Repubblica*, "Preti sposati in cerca di diritto," 8/29/1994.

§ 77   The movement for abolishing priestly celibacy received important support at the Synod of 1990. In one of its sessions, Msgr. Valfredo Tepe, Bishop of Ilhéus (Brazil), looking at the question of celibacy, stated: "**The possibility of ordaining presidents of the Eucharist for the numerous communities without a shepherd should be studied with neither fear nor taboo.**" **He added there was no certainty that** "**authentically celibate vocations**" **would appear in the coming generations** and that the faithful left without a shepherd risked "falling into the hands of the sects."[102]

§ 78   At the opening of the Synod, Msgr. Aloisio Lorscheider, Archbishop of Fortaleza (Brazil), spoke in name of the American and Canadian Bishops. He proposed to upgrade the Synod from a merely consultative body to a deliberative one. Such a proposal, clearly intended to democratize the government of the Church, was interpreted as a strong impetus for the movement seeking the abolition of priestly celibacy. Italian journalist Rocco Morabito gives more details about the intervention of the Bishops who favored ending priestly celibacy: "**There are people in the Vatican who see the idea of a deliberative synod as a decisive step toward approving the abolition of priestly celibacy. For some, this would be the goal of the bishops from the United States and Canada, on whose behalf the Brazilian Cardinal spoke at the opening of the meeting**. Another important moment of the synod was the speech on Tuesday of the bishop of Ilhéus, Msgr. Valfredo Bernardo Tepe. When he said he was not afraid of taboos and defended the ordination of priests *viri probati*, he had in mind the abolition of obligatory celibacy. ....

"Repercussions of the speech by the bishop of Ilhéus were not slow in coming. **Cardinal Joseph Louis Bernardin, archbishop of Chicago, spoke of 'a celibacy that often times appears irrational.' The bishop of Stockholm, Msgr. Herbertus Brandenburg, asked for the ordination of Anglican pastors, even married ones, who have converted to Catholicism**. .... Yesterday afternoon, the auxiliary bishop of London (Canada), Frederick Bernard Henry, brought to mind recent cases of sexual abuse by some priests in his country. For the Canadian bishop, 'the sacrifice of celibacy demands a high degree of psychosexual development' that requires a 'very efficacious' formation. Frederick Henry stated that seminaries should have a program of 'psychosexual' development for future priests.

---

[102] *O Estado de S. Paulo*, Ibid.

"Msgr. Aloisio, speaking in the name of the CNBB [Brazilian Bishops Conference] and not of the American bishops, ... said that a priest cannot be separated from the church community in which he lives and whose primacy he must recognize. .... The priest's mission does not consist of carrying out actions different from those of the other faithful, but in doing the same things 'with sacrifice and the sacramental grace.'"[103]

§ 79   According to the German weekly *Quick* of April 28, 1992, **20 percent of the world's priests married during the period 1964-1992. In Germany, half of the priests oppose ecclesiastical celibacy.**[104]

*

c) The Scandal of Ecclesiastical Concubinage

§ 80   Amid the whirlpool of the current crisis in the clergy, innumerable priests scandalously resort to concubinage. The publication in 1983 of a book by Fr. Guus van Hemmert, SJ, who wrote the final version of the famous *Dutch Catechism*, brought this subject to public attention. In his work, Fr. Hemmert tells about his 'experiences' during an immoral and sacrilegious relationship. In an interview with the newspaper, *Eindhovens Dagblad*, he explained the goal of his book. *Confrontatie,* a magazine of Haarlen, Holland, reproduced his statements with an explanatory introduction: **"After the scandal that Fr. W. Berger, a well-known professor at the Catholic University of Nijmegen, caused last year by declaring he had been living in concubinage for 25 years, an even more serious case has now taken place. Fr. Guus van Hemmert has just written a book on the practice of concubinage by priests. In the work, entitled *A Manner of Being Christian*, he narrates his experiences and observations. A Jesuit for over 35 years, Fr. Hemmert wrote the final version of the** [Dutch] *New Catechism* and regularly writes articles on catechesis for dailies, weeklies and magazines. He also makes television and radio programs (including for the Catholic station) on faith and relig-

---

[103] Rocco MORABITO, "Discussão do celibato domina Sínodo," in *O Estado de S. Paulo,* 10/4/1990.

[104] *Adista,* "Un prete cattolico su cinque si sposa," 5/16/1992, p. 2.

ious movements. If Hemmert's superiors fail to punish him, the number of priests 'living with a [female partner]' will increase much more, especially among young priests.

"We reproduce here what Fr. Hemmert told the daily, *Eindhovens Dagblad*, March 5 of this year: **'I find it normal for secular priests to be able to marry**. .... At times I am astonished at seeing people so busy with Church matters adhere to concubinage with such great ease. It is possible they do so to make life a little easier. By the way, I judged this in a different light when I saw it happen with other priests. With regard to what some of them were doing, I used to think: I wouldn't do that now. As for others, [I would think], this is alright in this case. .... On some occasions (when I was with the woman), I would think: I'm a Jesuit, a free man in relation to you! But after five years of living together, I could no longer think that way. In fact, this is a marriage and it has lasted longer than many [official] marriages. .... **'In the book, I tried to show how eroticism and sexuality can be reintegrated as values**. And I am convinced that, by doing this, I am not that much out of line with ecclesiastical tradition.'"[105]

§ 81   A study carried out in Sardinia in 1987 shows that 70 percent of the Peninsula's priests live in concubinage. Italian journalist Monica Falcone reports: **"A courageous study** undertaken with modern methods and a representative sample **has proven** what popular hearsay has always taken for granted: **seventy percent of the priests have lovers**. .... One hundred priests, chosen from all regions of the island of Sardinia, agreed to undergo extensive questioning in exchange for anonymity and, probably, a certain relief to be able to reveal their situations and perhaps primarily to be able to reveal their situation. In fact, the person charged with the study, which took four years, is a former priest who recently received a dispensation to get married. He is psychoanalyst Paolo Follesa, president of Cagliari's Neo-Freudian Institute. .... Follesa was able to demonstrate what some scholars had only outlined. **In 1979, a poll taken by Catholic sociologist Silvano Burgalassi caused a veritable scandal when he revealed that one-third of Italian male religious wanted the vow of chastity to be revoked. In 1984, Fr.**

---

[105] Guus van HEMMERT, Statements to the daily *Eindhovens Dagblad*, in *Confrontatie* (Haarlem), May 1983.

Luigi Fischela consulted Italian priests and found that 53 percent of his colleagues opposed sexual abstinence."[106]

§ 82   *30 Dias* reports on statistical data provided by German theologian and psychotherapist Eugen Drewermann, professor of Systematic Theology at the Faculty of Theology of Padernborn, Germany. According to him, **6,000 out of the 18,000 Catholic priests in Germany have marital relations with a woman.**[107]

§ 83   In 1992, Msgr. Eamonn Casey, Bishop of Galway, regarded by some as the most popular Prelate in Ireland since the time of Saint Patrick, resigned his post "for personal reasons." Such reasons had to do with a report in *The Irish Times* disclosing that over the last 15 years, Msgr. Case had made regular payments to Annie Murphy. By 1990, such payments reportedly totalled $115,000. Miss Murphy, an Irish-American residing in Connecticut, told a nationwide U.S. radio station that the Bishop is the father of her son Peter, 17. The money to maintain her and her son was taken from Church funds. Since the scandal broke, private donors have been covering the $120,000 deficit, plus interest. Casey was also president of the Church-run organization Third World Development Agency.[108]

*

---

[106] Mônica FALCONE, "Pesquisa: 70% dos padres na Itália têm mulher," in *O Globo* (Rio de Janeiro), 3/22/1987.

[107] Tommaso RICCI, "Engrenagem quase perfeita," in *30 Dias*, December 1989, p. 33.

[108] Richard ERNSBERGER Jr. - Lucy HOWARD, "Ireland is Talking..." in *Newsweek*, 5/18/1992, p. 3; "Fallen from Grace," in *Time*, 5/25/1992, p. 14; "Scandalo sessuale nella cattolica Irlanda - Vescovo progressista aveva amante e figlio," in *Corriere della Sera* (Milan), 5/9/1992; "L'amica del vescovo si confessa," 5/10/1992; "Sesso, bugie e videotapes: sotto choc la cattolica Irlanda," 5/12/1992; "Il vescovo confessa la paternità e i furti," 5/13/1992; "L'amante del vescovo Casey ringrazia per la solidarietà," 5/7/1992; "Dopo lo scandalo il pentimento - Il vescovo diventa missionario," 10/19/1992.

d) Priests Succumb to the Vice of Alcoholism

§ 84   Another disastrous characteristic of the crisis affecting the clergy is the spread of alcoholism in their ranks. A report in *Folha de S. Paulo* gives a wealth of data on this topic in Brazil and other countries. The report says this vice also lures Bishops and nuns: **"Alcoholics make up about 10 percent (1,200) of a total of 12,000 Brazilian Catholic priests**, and also affects bishops and women religious. These data are furnished by the Vida Nova [New Life] community, founded in Curitiba eight years ago .... which brings together 60 alcoholic priests and nuns from all over the country .... Its director is the American priest, William Tracy. Having managed to control his own alcoholism, he sees himself as a 'hunter' of alcoholic men and women religious, whom he directs to specialized clinics. .... **The files of Vida Nova show the case of two Catholic bishops from Brazil .... who died recently from alcohol-related illnesses. In the United States, where alcoholic priests number about 3,500, a bishop was recently arrested** (and forcibly interned in a specialized clinic) **after he was caught driving while intoxicated. The problem of alcoholism in the clergy** (which also **affects about 10 percent of European priests,** mainly in Ireland, Great Britain and Scandinavian countries) has grown to such proportions that the very Code of Canon Law .... in canon 924, allows alcoholic priests to celebrate mass with grape juice instead of wine."[109]

§ 85   The magazine *30 Dias* describes a similar situation in Germany: "Alcoholism among priests: the curtain of silence that has long covered this taboo becomes ever more permeable. **The priest drunkard, who in the past was a figure in literature .... is today a cause of serious concern for Diocesan curias and religious orders in Germany**. The fact is no longer hidden or disguised as an 'accident on the job.' Diocesan personnel departments have been forced to come to grips with the fact that, **in the last few years, the number of alcoholic priests has increased significantly**. .... A drunken priest causes scandal in the community, the schools, and among the people he meets. This was demonstrated recently by Gottfried Wiesbeck, the parish priest of Dorfen, a province in northern Bavaria. .... To the bewilderment of his faithful, Wiesbeck revealed [in a sermon] that only a small part of his colleagues have no problem with the

---

[109] D. AZEVEDO, "Clero brasileiro tem 10% de alcoólatras," in *Folha de S. Paulo*, 8/14/1988.

priestly way of life. '**In no profession are there so many alcoholics as among us priests. One out of every three sporadi-
cally faces problems of this kind. One out of ten priests is an
alcoholic and needs a long treatment.**' .... The Catholic diocese of Rottenburg-Stuttgart, one of the largest in Germany,
disclosed that in 1988 it was found that 5 percent of its clergy
were affected by problems of this type. Doctors specialized in
this field put the actual percentage of affected Catholic priests at
around 10 percent. **In Germany about 2,000 priests are re-
portly alcohol-dependent. A study by the University of Han-
nover estimated that one out of ten patients interned in de-
toxication clinics is a priest or theologian.**"[110]

*

e) Homosexuality in the Clergy

§ 86   Given the gravity of the subject matter dealt with in this
letter, we believe it more appropriate to analyze it in greater detail in the *Appendix* at the end of this Volume. This has the twofold advantage of not further lengthening this Chapter and of
giving the Reader a more complete view of one of the Items
concerning the crisis in the Clergy.

*

B. Crisis of Religious Orders

§ 87   Concerning the crisis that especially affects the regular
Clergy, we found it more adequate to present a paradigmatic
example rather than make a general analysis. The example we
chose is the Society of Jesus, the Church's largest in terms of
membership, certainly one of the most powerful and, in the past,
brilliant and prestigious Orders.

---

[110] Guido HORST, "O álcool como antídoto," in *30 Dias*, April 1989,
pp. 78f.

a) A Paradigmatic Example: The Society of Jesus

On analyzing the internal situation in the Society of Jesus, we find it shaken by multiple crises. In addition to internal rivalries, one can see a crisis of vocations, of ideas, of Faith, a crisis in its relations with the Vatican, the death of its militant characteristics, and a bleak future looming in its horizon.

Three articles published by the magazine *30 Dias* provide strong indications of the Society's internal situation.[111]

Crisis of Vocations

§ 88
The articles present 1965, the year that saw the closure of the Council, as the point of reference to analyze the situation that followed. On that occasion, the Superior General of the Society was Fr. Pedro Arrupe, elected to that post during the Council.

The orientation Fr. Arrupe gave the Society, consonant with conciliar reforms, caused the number of its members to drop from 36,038 in 1965[112] to about 26,500 in 1982,[113] when he resigned. After that, under the direction of the new superior, Fr. Peter-Hans Kolvenbach, elected in 1983, that number continuously decreased. On January 1, 1988, the Society had 24,924 members, that is, 11,414 less than in 1965, what amounts to a reduction of about one third of its contingent.[114] In a press con-

---

[111] The three-part series, to which *30 Dias* gave great prominence, includes these articles:

- Lucio BRUNELLI, "O balanço de Kolvenbach: os cinco anos do Papa Negro" (November 1988, pp. 54-59);

- L. BRUNELLI, "Kolvenbach: o Papa pode contar conosco - Em primeiro plano, os jesuítas" (February 1989, pp. 6-16);

- Gérard LECLERC, "Depressão jesuítica - Europa, França" (May 1989, pp. 22-25).

[112] *30 Giorni* (Portuguese ed.), November 1988, p. 58.

[113] Ibid., February 1989, p. 16, containing a chart from which we have taken this approximate figure.

[114] Ibid., November 1988, p. 59.

ference held on March 22, 1995 during the Thirty-fourth General Congregation of the Jesuits, Fr. Kolvenbach stated that the Society then had 23,000 members.[115]

Crisis of Ideas

§ 89   The cause of such a loss was the crisis of ideas: "Shortly before May 1968, an intellectual agitation took hold in the Jesuit formation center at Fourvière, the famous school of Lyons .... The people in charge tried to control the revolt by allowing it the right to exist. But the crisis was so profound that it ended up by causing a real hemorrhage. Many years of study were sacrificed as young men dropped out en masse, intensely contesting society and the Church. The whole structure of the Society was affected by this phenomenon, which was not restricted to France. The Society's Superior General, Fr. Arrupe, convened the 32nd General Congregation .... to lay down the points of reference for an evangelizing action .... The goal of establishing social justice in the structures imposed itself as an absolute rule. Paul VI began to become concerned about the climate of doubt spreading among Jesuits and threatening their identity. Solicitude for the poor, indisputably inspired by the Gospel, has not always been free from ideological equivocations."[116]

Crisis of Faith

§ 90   Nevertheless, even more than the crisis of ideas, the Jesuits' situation stems above all from a crisis of faith.

Vatican II concepts to the effect that 'sanctity' and 'elements of salvation' supposedly exist in the other religions and in all men are indirectly targeted as having caused the Society's demise. Such notions are moderate expressions of the theory of 'anonymous Christianity,' by Fr. Karl Rahner, which claims that every man who believes in being is already a Christian, even if unknowingly.[117] *30 Dias* reported this testimony: **"Our Order,**

---

[115] Peter-Hans KOLVENBACH, "Conferencia de prensa," 3/22/1995, in *Oficina de Prensa e Información*, Congregación General 34.

[116] *30 Dias*, May 1989, p. 22.

[117] On the 'Anonymous Christianity' theory, see Vol. V, *Animus delendi-II*, Part II, Chap. III.

understood **as an official establishment, is already dead**,"
comments a young theologian who did not identify himself.
**"From this standpoint, all there is to do is to wait for its
physical disappearance**. It was killed by a diluted Rahnerism
which has spread in the last few years theories on 'anonymous
Christianity.' From this have come all the equivocations on how
social and political compromise, as well as ecumenism and inculturation, should be understood."[118]

Crisis in the Society's Relationship with the Vatican

§ *91*   Fr. Arrupe was preparing an American priest, Fr. Vincent
O'Keefe, to be his successor: "After the election of John Paul I,
[O'Keefe] deemed it well to make three requests: to abolish the
condemnation of artificial means of contraception, to allow the
ordination of women for the priesthood, and to permit the marriage of priests."[119]

          In 1981, Fr. Arrupe resigned as Superior General and
designated Fr. O'Keefe Vicar General of the Society, "indirectly
provoking the Vatican's intervention." There is little information on how such intervention took place and of what it consisted. All that is known is that Karl Rahner, "the Society's most
important theologian," defined it as "an obscure administrative
maneuver." "On September 1, 1983, the superiors of the Society
of Jesus gathered in Rome to elect their new Superior General
after two years of tenure by the 'delegate.'" The Vatican suggested three candidates. A long and agitated election was expected. To everyone's great surprise, the 220 delegates elected
St. Ignatius' 29th successor in the first round, which lasted less
than one hour. The one they chose was Fr. Kolvenbach, who
"was linked to neither the preceding guidelines nor a name
coming from the Vatican."[120]

Fundamental Changes in the Society's Profile

§ *92*   Fr. Kolvenbach's own words regarding several subjects
permit us to infer the orientation he is giving his Order.

---

[118] *30 Giorni* (Portuguese ed.), November 1988, p. 59.

[119] Ibid., p. 54.

[120] Ibid., p. 55.

As is well-known, Saint Ignatius of Loyola conceived the work he founded as an army corps. Hence he gave it a military structure, established the rigorous Jesuit obedience, and imparted the spirit of conquest that characterizes the Order's members; its very name, 'Society,' is an army term.

In relation to this military character, Fr. Kolvenbach asserts: "**Any military connotation in relation to the Society and its [Superior] General must be eliminated. .... In this process of renewal [proposed by Vatican II], a certain way of being of the Society of Jesus has died.** This explains why a theologian said in this magazine that the Society 'was dead.'"[121]

§ 93   Other characteristics clearly establish the orientation of Fr. Kolvenbach. According to his own words, a rich understanding of Our Lord Jesus Christ could be expressed by the image of a 'guru:' "We all use images to find Christ. In the *Spiritual Exercises*, Saint Ignatius explicitly resorts to the image of a medieval king in order to better understand the Eternal Father. **Even a 'guru' could be on the long list of images that Christians use to try to understand some aspect of the mysterious riches of Christ,** so long as the integrity of the Lord not be reduced to this single aspect."[122]

§ 94   On the collaboration of Jesuits with the Chinese communist regime, the Society's General explains: "As they left jail, some Jesuits reflected for a long time about China's situation and .... decided to collaborate, in some sectors, with this organization [The Patriotic Association, made up by collaborationist Catholics] approved by the communist regime."[123]

The Future That Looms in the Horizon

§ 95   Proselytism by the Society of Jesus is done today primarily in Asia, to such a point that Indian priests have become the second largest number of vocations after the Americans.[124]

---

[121] *30 Giorni* (Portuguese ed.), February 1989, pp. 14f.

[122] Ibid., p. 8.

[123] Ibid., p. 9.

[124] *30 Giorni* (Portuguese ed.), November 1988, p. 57.

In Europe, the situation is catastrophic. Only one young men entered the Society's novitiate in France in 1987. In Italy, ten joined, but the average death rate among the Jesuits in that country is thirty per year.[125] "If this pace continues," says the writer about the situation in France, "superiors will be obliged to close two convents per year."[126] "The only exception to the aridity of vocations in Europe comes from the East ...., particularly Poland and Yugoslavia."[127] "In the United States the Society lost 195 members through death or resignation. The numbers are not very encouraging, to the point that an important American Jesuit, Fr. Robert Drinan, professor of Law at Georgetown University, said this to the magazine *The Tablet* last month [October 1988]: 'What will become of the 28 faculties and universities and 42 colleges directed by Jesuits in the United States when membership drops even further? Today, these institutions are frequented by one million three hundred thousand students. Will they be forced to secularize, as happened with the 110 American faculties founded by the Methodist church?'"[128]

In 1995, during the 34th General Congregation of the Jesuits, Fr. Kolvenbach addressed the internal situation of the Society without beating around the bush: "The General Congregation has fully taken into account the reality of the numeric diminution and the progressive aging of available forces with their inevitable consequences of fatigue, loss of stability, and a fatal drop in the quality of the apostolic service to be done. This is the price we must pay for working in demanding conditions in order to continue *avant garde* apostolate and act entirely within [the guidelines of] pluralism and secularism."[129]

§ 96   As for the intellectual formation of the priests, a Jesuit linked with *30 Dias* comments: "If we observe the present situation attentively, we are impressed with the relative intel-

---

[125] Ibid., p. 59.

[126] *30 Dias*, May 1989, p. 23.

[127] *30 Giorni* (Portuguese ed.), November 1988, p. 59.

[128] Robert DRINAN, Statements on the Society of Jesus in the United States, in L. BRUNELLI, "O balanço de Kolvenbach: os cinco anos do Papa Negro", p. 59.

[129] P. H. KOLVENBACH, Ibid.

lectual sterility and theological ignorance. .... In fact, there is an emptiness."[130]

§ 97   In addition to moral crises similar to those of the secular clergy, which certainly have not spared members of the Society as well, this is the panorama that emerges regarding its internal situation since Vatican II.

§ 98   Analogous considerations could be made, *grosso modo*, about the Benedictine, Carmelite, Dominican and Franciscan Orders, as well as the innumerable Congregations that make up the bulk of men and women religious in the Holy Church.

During the Synod of 1994 about vocations for the state of perfection, expressive data came to light on the drop in their numbers. In fact, the magazine *30 Dias* **published comparative charts revealing, among the regular Clergy, a figure of 167,208 in 1970 compared to 139,258 in 1992. Among non-ordained religious, the number went from 79,408 in 1970 to 54,793 in 1992.**"[131]

§ 99   About the crisis in the regular clergy as a whole, here is what Cardinal Ratzinger has to say: "**The orders and congregations of an active life are in a grave crisis; the discovery of professionalism,** the concept of 'social assistance' that has replaced that of 'charity,' **the often indiscriminate and even enthused adaptation to new and hitherto unknown values of modern secular society, the introduction,** sometimes without a critical sense, **of psychologies and psychoanalyses of all schools into the convents: all this has brought excruciating problems of identity and has led to the loss of sufficient motivation to justify religious life for many women** .... the spiritual treatises of old have been replaced with manuals of psychoanalysis; theology has given its place to psychology, even the cheapest one. **Nearly irresistible,** furthermore, **is the fascination for things oriental** or supposed as such: **in many religious houses, both masculine and feminine, the Cross has often given its place to symbols of Asian religious traditions. In several places the devotions of old have disappeared to be replaced with the techniques of** *yoga* **or** *Zen*."[132]

---

[130] *30 Dias*, May 1989, p. 25.

[131] Andrea TORNIELLI, "O outono quente dos religiosos," in *30 Dias*, September 1994, p. 26.

[132] J. RATZINGER, *Rapporto sulla Fede*, p. 100.

§ 100   In order to have an overview of the situation in the religious Orders as an immediate consequence of the crisis in the regular clergy, it would be well to say a word about women religious *in genere*, whether belonging to feminine branches of religious Orders or Congregations.

*

b) Crisis Among Women Religious

§ 101   The data on the crisis in religious Orders deals mainly with men religious. But there are data also on women religious. We divide it here as follows: crisis of vocations, moral crisis, and feminism.

We believe the words of the Mother Superior of the Daughters of Charity, Sister Guillemin, present at the Council as an observer, are fitting to explain in depth certain causes of the crisis we are now seeing. In October 1965, speaking about "*the woman religious today*," she told how conciliar reforms placed her Congregation in a radical impasse: "The woman religious is led to change from a situation of insertion, a position of authority, to a position of collaboration; from a religious superiority complex to a sentiment of fraternity, from a human inferiority complex to a clear participation in life, from a preoccupation with moral conversion to a missionary preoccupation. One must admit that this represents a real about-face in relation to our traditional positions and means [requires] a long and persevering preparation of mentalities. One must also be aware that this will lead us to make quite serious decisions; finally, one must be convinced that to not accept this reconversion is to move in the opposite direction of the march of the world and the Church and condemn oneself to suffer the consequences."[133]

Her words reflect well the pressure undergone by women religious to accept Vatican II's *aggiornamento*.

---

[133] GUILLEMIN de la Charité, "La religieuse contemporaine," in H. FESQUET, *Le journal du Concile*, p. 1000.

Crisis of Vocations

§ 102   On this matter, Cardinal Ratzinger gives us a symptomatic and terrifying example: "**There is an updated and detailed report on the women religious of Quebec. .... As far
back as twenty years ago, in the beginning of the sixties,
Quebec had the world's highest number of women religious
per capita** in a population totaling six million. **Between 1961
and 1981, counting departures, deaths and losses in recruitment, the number of women religious fell from 46,933 to
26,294. This was a drop, therefore, of 44 percent, and [this
trend] seems unstoppable. In the same period, new vocations
diminished by 98.5 percent.** Furthermore, a large part of the
remaining 1.5 percent is made up not of young people, but of
'late vocations.'"[134]

§ 103   The magazine *Il Regno* reports a drop of more than 25
percent in the number of women religious in Italy in the period
1988-1993 alone: "**Women religious were 150,174 in 1974,
121,183 in 1988 and 111,490 in 1993. .... [This is] a massive
drop which does not show signs of abating** .... add to this nu-
merical drop, an increase in the average age. **Only 3.3 percent
of the sisters are less than 29 years old .... while 59.2 percent
of the sisters are over 60.**"[135]

However, if we take as reference the year 1966, when
there were 160,000 women religious in Italy,[136] the deficit increases to more than 30 percent.

§ 104   A reliable survey on the situation of male and female religious Orders and Congregations in the United States says:

---

[134] J. RATZINGER, op. cit., pp. 101f.

[135] Lorenzo PREZZI, "Vescovi e religiosi, profilo modesto," in *Il Regno*,
11/15/1993, p. 589.

[136] Giancarlo ROCCA, "Modelli in crisi e nuove vie," Ibid., p. 12.

In fact this journalist points out a total of 103,000 women religious in
Italy in 1992. That would mean a drop of more than 35 percent in relation to 1966. However, the figure quoted for 1992 is smaller than the
one for 1993, referred to in the news item by L. PREZZI above. So we
do not know if there was an increase in vocations between 1992 and
1993, which would seem unlikely, or whether the information from the
two journalists of *Il Regno* was contradictory.

"The thirty years that followed Vatican Council II were turbulent for Catholic religious orders in the United States. **The average age of members of many congregations rose to about 67 years, while the number of men and women religious dropped by about 45 percent among brothers and sisters and 27 percent among regular priests.**"[137]

§ 105

The data depicting the particular situations presented above are far from reassuring: "The crisis of female vocations was denounced in many reports by bishops' conferences around the world. While avoiding 'irrational alarmism,' the Vatican congregation for Catholic education recently said that the situation is very grave: there are religious families without any [new] vocation on record for the last ten years."[138]

§ 106

1994 saw the publication of impressive comparative figures on the number of women religious in the whole world: **in 1970 there were 1,003,670 women religious with perpetual or provisional vows; in 1992 that number was down to 655,031.**"[139]

Moral Crisis

§ 107

In 1985 a great scandal was caused in the United States by the publication of a book by two lesbian former nuns. The work brought to light a reality much more painful than the perversion of two sisters. Indeed, if the authors' statements are to be taken at face value, 9,000 of the 120,000 women religious in the United States are lesbian, in addition to the 51 nuns who give their testimony in the book. If 9,000 are lesbians, how many others give themselves over to debauchery without falling into this perversion against nature?

Here is the news on the launching of the book: "There can be no greater success for a book than selling out before publication. That is what happened with *Lesbian Nuns: Breaking Silence*, published this year by 'Naiad Press' in Florida .... **Written by two teachers, Nancy Manahan and Rosemary**

---

[137] David NYGREN - Miriam UKERITIS, "USA: il futuro dei religiosi," in *Il Regno*, 4/1/1993, p. 242.

[138] Bruno BARTOLONI, "La rivolta silenziosa delle suore," in *Corriere della Sera*, 6/4/1993.

[139] A. TORNIELLI, op. cit., p. 26.

Curb, former nuns and lesbians, it brings together the testimonies of 51 Catholic nuns (nine of whom still keep their vows), telling about their experiences with lesbianism. 'Naiad Press' had 125,000 copies printed. .... *The New York Times* dedicated a large article to the book, reporting that several of the ex-nuns who testify in it have stood out in the struggle for the rights of homosexuals. One of the authors says that a goal of the book is to break the taboo of lesbianism and to show that it is everywhere. .... **Putting on solemn sociological airs, Nancy Manahan says that 9,000 of the 120,000 American nuns are lesbians.**"[140]

§ 108   In the prior year, 24 American nuns had signed an advertisement published in *The New York Times* in support of abortion. According to *The Washington Times*, none of the nuns gave in to the Vatican demand that they recant. The paper also reported that their superiors supported their rebellious attitude by saying that they respected their consciences.[141]

§ 109   In May, 1992 the Gallup Institute conducted a survey — published around the middle of June — whose result showed that 45 percent of American Catholics deem homosexual relationships morally acceptable, while only 48 percent agree with traditional Catholic Doctrine on the matter.

Sister Jeannine Gramick, one of the Sisters of Notre Dame and a member of the National Coalition of American Women Religious, analyzes the result of the survey in a letter to *The New York Times* and appears to be satisfied with the erosion of morality among Catholics. "Only five years ago," she writes, "when Pope John Paul II visited the United States, *Time* magazine and The *Los Angeles Times* reported that 66 percent to 68 percent of Catholics agreed with the Catholic teaching on same-sex behavior. This 20 percent decrease in five years is as significant as the 20 percent change in favor of women's ordination in the last seven years. Most likely, the trend to accept les-

---

[140] Paulo Sérgio PINHEIRO, "A transa das freiras e outras transas," in *Folha de S. Paulo*, 6/18/1985.

[141] William F. WILLOUGHBY, "Superiors 'Honor the Conscience' of Nuns Who Signed Pro-choice ad," in *The Washington Times*, 1/11/1985.

bian and gay relationships will continue because 57 percent of those younger than 35 accept it."[142]

§ 110   In Bogota, Colombia, the women Religious of the Ado-ration — a Congregation that assists women of little virtue — walked in a parade alongside prostitutes to protest police repression against illegal pleasure houses.[143]

Feminism

§ 111   Also growing is the number of 'feminist women religious' who advocate the ordination of women. Such is the case of 120 sisters of the Daughters of Mary, Help of Christians, a Congregation founded by Saint John Bosco: **"Feminist ideas have influenced the 120 sisters gathered at a conference in this capital [Rome]. They have advocated a new theology to overthrow sexual barriers in the Church and permit women to enter the priesthood.** Promoted by the College of Educational Sciences, the conference, entitled 'Woman and Church,' was the scene of heated discussions among the Daughters of Mary, Help of Christians. The women religious of this order, founded by St. John Bosco, claim that feminist theology must overthrow the 'macho' understanding of God based on traditional 'macho' models.

"In summary, the women religious are convinced that 'the primitive Church patriarchalized the word of God, with all the consequences that followed,' including the traditional subordination of organizations of women religious to a male authority and the refusal to ordain women. According .... to the newspaper *La Repubblica*, which gave prominent coverage to the conference, the women religious insist that the priesthood 'is not a right to be claimed but a vocation that must be valued individually, without distinction of sex.'"[144]

§ 112   A demand by female Superior Generals to be represented by their own sisters at the Synod of Bishops is telltale of the trend to abolish the mediation of male superiors. A Vatican

---

[142] Jeannine GRAMICK, "Homosexuality To Be a Burning Catholic Issue" (letter of 6/24/1992), in *The New York Times*, 7/11/1992.

[143] Steve GUTKIN, "Best Little Convent in Bogota," in *Newsweek*, 10/19/1992, p. 37.

[144] *O Globo*, "Religiosas feministas lutam pelo sacerdócio," 8/7/1988.

watcher from the *Corriere della Sera* reports: "Without raising their voices, but with much determination, **the sisters asked to be heard at the bishops' synod that will address the topic of religious life next year. The World Union of [female] Superior Generals recently sent the Pope a document to request that a significant number of its delegates be present in the assembly. Soon the Union of Italian Superior Generals will make the same type of request.** .... Fifteen men religious and 15 women religious were invited to the assembly of Italian bishops to be held in Collevalenza from October 25 to 28 (1993)."[145]

§ 113   An expressive manifestation of 'religious feminism' took place on the eve of the Synod of 1994, which was discussing the institutes of religious perfection. Referring to the preparations for the meeting, a columnist of *30 Dias* says: "The most debated .... topic is certainly the one related to the role of women. In fact, **a document drafted by female religious superiors of the United States in preparation for the Synod advances a proposal that women be given more relevance in Vatican congregations so that a woman religious might also climb to the top of organizations of the Holy See."[146]

These words by an Italian journalist demonstrate the feminist impact caused by the demands of women religious: **"Salaries, powers and posts of responsibility in the Vatican Curia. This is the surprising request that a group of sister delegates officially presented yesterday to the** ongoing Vatican Synod on religious life. Without beating around the bush, the women religious surprised the roughly 250 synodal bishops by **presenting a 'contract' platform that would arouse envy in the most consummate union activist** of the CGIL. **This is the first time that expressions such as 'We ask to be admitted to decision-making posts in the congregations,' 'We want to enter the pontifical Curia with positions of responsibility' or 'We call for adequate stipends'** have been heard at the Vatican in the presence of the Pope and a ponderous array of cardinals, bishops and high-ranking pontifical prelates. **Never had similar requests been made by the silent world of women religious in the two thousand years of the history of Christianity."[147]**

---

[145] B. BARTOLONI, Ibid.

[146] A. TORNIELLI, op. cit., p. 24.

[147] Orazio la ROCCA, "Le suore a Wojtyla: 'Più soldi e potere' - Ecco le 'sindacaliste di Dio,'" in *La Repubblica*, 10/8/1994; "'Dimenticate i

Even seasoned analysts were somewhat disconcerted at the Holy See's unrestricted acceptance of the participation of women in the Synod's debates of 1994. In fact, *L'Osservatore Romano*, which publishes the minutes of the meeting, noted that women religious spoke no less than 44 times, and in some instances with far from modest considerations and requests, especially if one keeps in mind that, as far as we know, this is the first time that women religious were directly heard in a Synod. The following statements, presented in chronological order, seem worthy of note:

Sister Baril, of the Dominican Missionaries of the Adoration (Canada), claims that the Church has a 'feminine personification': "The expression 'femininity of the people of God' reveals the appropriate sense of two biblical images: that of a conjugal union symbolizing the Covenant of God with his people and that of the maternity of these people, which collaborates with God to accomplish his design of salvation. .... I stress, among others, three major meanings that derive from this symbology. First, it shows us the Church who receives her being and fecundity through Christ the redeemer. This meaning makes one understand the priority in Church life of a behavior of active welcoming, which constitutes the living faith .... Finally, speaking of ecclesial collaboration in terms of maternity, we better understand that what must be emphasized in all Church activities is, above all, the full Life offered by God to persons and communities."[148]

Sister Sumah, of the Missionaries of Our Lady of the Apostles (Ghana), asks that religious work receive financial remuneration: "**Women religious who work in the pastoral sector are often inadequately remunerated and in some places are not remunerated at all. Nevertheless, the pastoral 'worker' needs to survive. A worker**, independent of the ambit in which she works, deserves to be paid."[149]

---

beni terreni' - Il Papa contro le 'sindacaliste di Dio,'" in *La Repubblica*, 10/13/1994; Marco POLITI, "Eva sull'altare," in *La Repubblica*, 10/12/1994.

[148] Gilberte BARIL, "La femminilità del popolo di Dio e la vita consacrata femminile," in *L'Osservatore Romano*, 11/23/1994, Supplement, p. 38.

[149] Rose SUMAH, "Le religiose nelle giovani chiese," Ibid., p. 54.

Mother Sietmann, Superior General of the Missionary Sisters of the Sacred Heart of Jesus (Peru), president of the International Union of Superior Generals, emphatically advocates a determinant role of women in 'spirituality and in theology' and calls for equality with men with respect to 'planning and decisions' in all levels of the Church, including the organs of the Curia: **"We find there is an urgent need for the consecrated woman to proclaim the riches of God from her feminine perception, participating more amply and efficaciously in the sphere of spirituality and theology, in which she still has not been given due consideration nor an adequate and equivalent possibility of integration. What must be created and promoted are an attitude of discernment and a permanent dialogue between the hierarchy and the People of God, which will favor the balanced and effective presence of consecrated women in pastoral functions, works and tasks inside the Church on planning and decision-making levels, both at the local and universal levels, as well as in the official organs of the Roman Curia."**[150]

Mother Boullanger, Superior General of the Canons of Saint Augustine of the Congregation of Our Lady (Canada) and vice-president of the International Union of Superior Generals, presents a whole platform of feminist demands: **"Very often, women have the image of themselves that men have of them. It is, therefore, an image imposed from the outside**, an image that does not entirely reflect the qualities which, though not exclusively feminine, distinguish women in an outstanding way.

"Their sensibility facing the realities of creation, their innate sense of life, their capacity to listen, their respect for the person, their willingness to dialogue, allow them to establish authentic human relationships and be instruments of communion. This sensibility makes them more vulnerable to the suffering of the small, the poor. They strive to protect life, above all when it is weak and fragile. Their tenacity stands out in their quest for an organization of the world in which the poor, whoever they may be, can find their just place. Their capacity to adapt to situations and to diverse lifestyles makes them able to understand and individualize differences so that they can become instruments of evangelization according to the reality in which they find themselves. .... **All this gives their thinking a specific hue that stems from life, instead of abstract con-**

---

[150] Klara SIETMANN, "Rendere visibili i trati del volto di Dio," Ibid., p. 56.

cepts. For this reason the word of women is not always heard. .... We wish, furthermore, **that on the various levels — parochial, diocesan, national and even Vatican — a real place be given to women in the ambit of reflection, decision-making, and not only in the executive ambit, aiming at a participation and a real collaboration** [sic]."[151]

§ *114*   Mother Rochette, Superior General of the Sisters of No-tre Dame (Canada), calls for religious Institutes to be given the faculty of changing their own structures as needed: "In order to favor this prophetic action, **the Institutes must enjoy the free-dom to make adequate changes to their structures**; they have the means to discern which structures favor [people's] insertion and creativity in apostolic choices to fulfill the needs of today's world."[152]

Mother Kanongata'a, Superior General of the Sisters of Nazareth (Fuji Islands), calls for **"women to have the same opportunity as men to pursue theological studies."**[153]

Mother Bassil, Superior General of the Congregation of the Sacred Hearts of Jesus and Mary (Lebanon) makes this re-quest of the Synod: "That Islam become better known by men and women religious and that Islamic fundamentalism be under-stood as a sign of the times and an invitation to dialogue; that **Christians and Muslims build tomorrow's society to-gether."**[154]

Mother Choi, Superior General of the Olivetan Benedic-tine Sisters (Korea) presents this 'inter-religious argument': **"Can we learn any valid methods from the monastic disci-pline of Buddhism? Some sisters who practice *Zen* find it very useful for profound prayer."**[155]

---

[151] Stéphanie-Marie BOULLANGER, "La vita apostolica e la condizi-one femminile," Ibid., p. 103.

[152] Madeleine ROCHETTE, "Il ruolo profetico della vita religiosa," Ibid., p. 106.

[153] Keiti Ann KANONGATA'A, "La 'passione' per Il Regno di Dio," Ibid., p. 123.

[154] Antoinette BASSIL, "La vita religiosa femminile in Libano," Ibid., p. 124.

[155] Angela CHOI, "Profonda conversione e solida formazione," Ibid., p. 147.

Mother Carpetti, Superior General of the Sisters of Catholic Apostolate and president of the Union of Italian Superior Generals, appears to adopt feminism with no embarrassment and apply it to religious life: "The response given by the [women] religious to the *Lineamenta* and, even more, their daily life, **make it evident that in Italy there is a feminism that entails a growing maturation capable of acting generously in the construction of the new civilization of love. The emerging leaders of the feminine world are also prepared to reinterpret [religious] Consecration, evangelical counsels, community life, and the missions.**"[156]

§ 115

It is difficult for one not to be perplexed knowing that **such opinions, some of them openly revolutionary, were vented in the presence of the Pope and about 250 synodal Fathers, who gave their seal of approval, either by tacit acquiescence or explicit support, to the rise of women in the Church.**[157] Furthermore, **the Synod's** final statement, supported by all those present, **declares that "consecrated women must**

---

[156] Lilia CAPRETTI, "La vita consacrata femminile ripensata ed elaborata in Italia con riferimento alla comunione ecclesiale," Ibid., p. 151.

[157] The most significant of the various remarks by the synodal Fathers about the role of women in the Church appears to have been that of the Bishop of Owando (Congo), Msgr. Ernest KOMBO, who said: "**May He [God] inspire the prophetic behavior that would lead to designating women**, an important part of those who are consecrated, both on the numeric and qualitative planes, **to posts of responsibility, even to the highest posts in the hierarchy, such as lay cardinals**, if possible" ("Dopo aver gratuitamente ricevuto bisogna saper gratuitamente dare," Ibid., p. 86).

With regard to this possibility, "some vaticanologists commented that the proposal was not absurd" (*O Globo*, "Bispo propõe mulheres como cardeais," 10/11/1994).

Not only vaticanologists think this. In a report at the end of the Synod from one of the circles of French-speaking Bishops, Msgr. Pierre RAFFIN, Bishop of Metz, concluded with words that appear to assume the elevation of women to lay cardinalship. Indeed, he said: "The principle that should guide Church action in this field [the condition of consecrated women] is as follows: **all lay people, men and women, whether consecrated or not, should have access to all the offices and leadership levels in the Church that do not require ordination**" ("I beni dei religiozi al servizio della missione," in *L'Osservatore Romano*, 11/23/1994, Supplement, p. 158).

participate more in consultations and decision-making in the Church in situations that require it."[158]

§ 116   These are some of the major features of the crisis that rages in the secular and regular clergy, as well as among women religious.

*

7. Crisis of Faith Among the Faithful

§ 117   It does not seem superfluous to recall here the wise considerations of Pius IX in the Encyclical *Qui pluribus*, of November 9, 1846, pointing out the cause of religious crises among the faithful. Certainly the law enunciated by the Pontiff in the last century also applies as well to the present case. Addressing the Patriarchs, Primates, Archbishops and Bishops at the beginning of his pontificate, Pius IX said: "When ministers are ignorant or neglectful of their duty, then the morals of the people also immediately decline, Christian discipiline grows slack, the practice of religion is dislodged and cast aside, and every vice and corruption is easily introduced into the Church."[159]

If it is a proven law in the History of the Church that the decadence of the faithful results from bad shepherds, what should one say of a Council that so 'revolutionized' Church life?

As we said above, the opening of the Council to the world was bound to bring about a crisis of Faith among the faithful.

§ 118   On February 6, 1981, in an Allocution to the priests and religious participating in Italy's First National Conference on the topic 'Missions to the People in the Eighties,' John Paul II recognized: "**We must realistically** and with profound sensibility **admit that Christians today, in large part, feel lost, confused, perplexed, and even disillusioned**: ideas greatly contrasting with Revealed truth, which had always been taught, have been spread; **real heresies in the dogmatic and moral fields have also spread and have created doubts, confusions**

---

[158] Bishops' Synod of 1994, *Message to the People of God*, p. 163.

[159] PIUS IX, Encyclical *Qui pluribus*, November 9, 1846, in V.A., *Recueil des allocutions*, p. 189.

and rebellions; even the Liturgy has been altered; immersed in intellectual and moral 'relativism' and, thereby, in permissiveness, Christians are tempted by atheism, agnosticism, a vaguely moralistic Illuminism, **a sociological Christianity without defined dogmas and objective morals.**"[160]

119   The final document of Medellin already pointed to the crisis of Faith currently spreading so insidiously among the faithful: "**This religiosity .... in which is God's answer to all questions and needs of man, can enter into a crisis and, indeed, has begun to enter** one with the scientific knowledge of the world that surrounds us. This religiosity places the Church before the dilemma of continuing to be the universal Church or converting herself into a sect and, therefore, no longer incorporating the men who express themselves under this type of religiosity. Because she is a Church and not a sect, she must offer her message of salvation to all men, running perhaps the risk that not all will accept her in the same way and with the same intensity."[161]

120   The Jesuits of *La Civiltà Cattolica* say this: "**It is enough to read a certain Catholic literature today to feel how much bitterness and disillusionment is felt by some Catholics, even priests, in relation to the Church, the Pope, the bishops, and how dismal are their previsions about the future of the Church and of Christianity: it seems to them that the crisis which the Church is now going through is a mortal one!** From this standpoint, there is no difference between the so-called 'progressivists,' for whom the Church has already missed the train of history and has nothing left to say to the world, and the so-called 'conservatives,' for whom the Church pushed herself forward to the point of losing her own identity, almost ceasing to be the Church of Christ."[162]

121   On the crisis of faith, Msgr. Thiandoum, Cardinal-Archbishop of Dakar, offers this opinion: "**The years that followed the Council were very difficult .... The crisis of faith**

---

[160] JOHN PAUL II, Allocution to the 1st Italian National Convention for religious men and priests, February 6, 1981, in *Insegnamenti di Giovanni Paolo II*, vol. IV/1, p. 235.

[161] CELAM, *A Igreja na atual transformação da América Latina à luz do Concílio - Conclusões de Medellin*, p. 90.

[162] *La Civiltà Cattolica* - Editorial, "Testimoniare la 'gioia nella speranza,'" 4/17/1971, p. 109.

was evident. It resulted not only from social transformations, but primarily from erroneous interpretations of the Council. **Some people thought that Vatican II had changed the Church and the faith. Confusion became generalized**. In 1967, ... Paul VI decreed that this year would be the 'year of faith.' He saw that the application of Vatican II would bring problems. Two years later, he pronounced his famous 'Creed.' **People's faith was perturbed."**[163]

§ 122   In the Synod of 1994, Msgr. Foley noted, with respect to the Institutes of consecrated life: "Unfortunately, but under-standably, non-fidelity to freely engaged commitments also has a great power of communication. And **the scandal caused by depraved acts on the part of some consecrated persons and by the abandonment of their vows made many people blind and deaf to the message of the Gospel and shook the faith and fervor of many** who found in the persons dedicated to a consecrated life a source of inspiration and example according to the model of Christ."[164]

§ 123   On the post-conciliar crisis, Msgr. Graber issues this grave general assessment: "**Over the last twenty-five years we have been crossing the second Protestant and Illuminist period, accompanied by a neomodernism.**"[165]

§ 124   The diminution of the sense of God and of sin is also recorded in passing by the Synod of 1983. Summarizing its conclusions, the Secretary General of the Synod, Archbishop Jozef Tomko, later Cardinal, said: "The Fathers of the Synod have indicated the causes that provoked the diminution of the sense of sin and, consequently, of moral responsibility, above all .... **a diminution of the sense of God that necessarily leads to indifferentism, permissivess and practical materialism...**"[166]

---

[163] Hyacinthe THIANDOUM, "Paulo VI? Um Papa fiel," interview with Stefano PACI, in *30 Dias*, August/September 1992, p. 18.

[164] John Patrick FOLEY, "Formazione di base per l'uso dei mass-media nella diffusione del Vangelo," in *L'Osservatore Romano*, 11/23/1994, Supplement, pp. 24f.

[165] Rudolf GRABER, "Como no tempo de Atanásio," interview with Tommaso RICCI, in *30 Dias*, September 1990, p. 46.

[166] J. TOMKO, "Riconciliazione e penitenza," in *L'Osservatore Romano*, 12/1/1983, Supplement, p. III.

125   Msgr. Tshibangu Thsishiku, Auxiliary Bishop of Kin-
shasa and member of the Secretariat for Non-Christians, noted at
the same Synod of 1983 "a strong diminution in the practice of
the Sacrament of Reconciliation in its traditional form." As a
reason for the crisis, he pointed to the **"relativization of the
sense of sin because,** among other things, of the insufficient
explanation of **the spirit of some reforms coming out of the
principles of the Council."**[167]

126   Ecumenism has also caused the crisis in the Faith. This
becomes clear as one considers another statement by Hans
Küng, an especially meaningful testimony if one bears in mind
that the professor of Tübingen is an ecumenist *à outrance.*
"That feeling of insecurity," says Küng, **"which emotionally
insinuated itself in many Christians after the reforms put
into practice by the Church herself, was later aggravated by
even more intense contacts with the doctrine and spirituality
of other churches. In many places, therefore, ecumenism**
(oecumene) **acts as a catalyst for existing tensions."**[168]

127   For all these reasons the situation has reached such an
extreme that the people of Rome no longer identify with the
Catholic Church. Indeed, in May 1995 the Vicariate of the Holy
See was presented with a survey carried out by sociologist
Franco Garelli. In various matters of Faith — resurrection, the
existence of Heaven and Hell, the divine origin of the Church —
and Morals — homosexuality, divorce, abortion, pre-marital
relations, masturbation, most Romans have abandoned Catholic
Doctrine.[169]

        "To explain this situation," a journalist notes, "the Car-
dinal Vicar [of Rome] based himself on the words of the Pope:
'One speaks of countries in which whole groups of the baptized
have lost the living sense of the faith or no longer see themselves as members of the Church.' But these regions mentioned
by *Redemptoris missio*, Camillo Ruini points out, are no longer
distant ones: 'This is also, to a large extent, the situation of

---

[167] Tharcisse TSHIBANGU THSISHIKU, "Crisi dei confessori," in
L'Osservatore Romano, 10/5/1983, Supplement, p. II.

[168] Hans KÜNG, "Vatican III: problemi e prospettive per il futuro," in
V.A., *Verso la Chiesa del terzo millennio*, p. 88.

[169] "Roma: Cidade católica, mas nem tanto," in *O Estado de S. Paulo*,
5/11/1995; Marco POLITI, "Sesso, preghiere & aldilà," in *La Repubblica*, 5/9/1995.

Rome.' The capital of Catholicism has become 'mission territory.'"[170]

*

§ *128*   A crisis of priests and religious. A crisis of the faithful.
Would it be an exaggeration or a lack of objectivity to attribute
them to conciliar ambiguity?

Fr. Chenu himself, interviewed by Jacques Duquesne,
answers this question: *Question*: "But, in your opinion, **how
should one see this whole upheaval? Is it the fault of the fathers, the theologians, the faithful?** *Answer*: "**I see its cause in
the Council itself, in the logic of its march and its dynamism.**"[171]

About this, Chenu is entirely right. The crisis has resulted, in our view, from the necessary consequences of the ambiguity with which Council Vatican II elaborated its documents
and, later, different people interpreted them.[172] How would it be

---

[170] Roberto ZUCCOLINI, "Ruini: vero, la città è ormai diventata una
terra di missione,'" in *Corriere della Sera*, 5/12/1995.

[171] *Jacques Duquesne interroge le Pére Chenu*, p. 191.

[172] We often find mentions to the crisis that was established in the
Church since Vatican II (Item 1 of this Chapter). Less often, however,
do we find in print that which a huge number of people think but few
have the courage to write, that is, that the Council holds primary responsibility for the crisis that followed it. As an example of the latter,
we quote below the words of a Brazilian journalist with whom we do
not always agree, but who has the merit of fearlessness and clarity:

"The Council [Vatican II] – and this is hardly denied – profoundly
changed the spiritual, religious and moral life of the West and produced equally profound reverberations in the cultural sphere. What is
in question is whether the changes came for better or for worse, both
for the Church and society. Part of the answer can be anticipated by
an obvious finding: Vatican II plunged Western spirituality and morality
into an unprecedented crisis – a 'crisis' that contradicts its own definition, since the term means a violent, sudden and fleeting rupture of
equilibrium. But in the post-conciliar Church, the crisis never ends; on
the contrary, it becomes more serious every year that goes by. ....
'Many Catholics over 30 remember living in that church as if in a
spiritual fortress – comforting at times, inhibiting and even frightening
at others. But it was a secure and orderly universe, with guarantees of

possible to avoid a dilaceration in the unity of thinking in the Church when the conciliar texts were written so as to please two opposing currents? How to prevent divergence in the moral and

---

eternity for those who lived according to its rules. Now this fortress has fallen,' wrote *Time* magazine one decade after the Council. ....

"Thirty years after the beginning of the conciliar revolution, in the 'world's largest Catholic country,' Brazil, there are more evangelical ministers than Catholic priests. Every year the Church in Brazil loses more than half a million faithful, who no longer identify with her, according to data provided by the CNBB [National Conference of Brazilian Bishops]. To realize how unusual and grave the situation is, all one has to do is compare the documents of popes such as Pius IX (1846-1878), Saint Pius X (1903-1914), Pius XI (1922-1939) and Pius XII (1939-1958) with the conciliar and post-conciliar texts. There is an abyss between the theses defended by the former and the latter. Heterodoxy was raised to the position of orthodoxy. 'The promoters of error should no longer be sought among declared enemies, for they are hidden in the very bosom of the Church, thereby becoming all the more harmful to the extent they are less noticed... The enemies pose as reformers... It is in the very veins and entrails of the Church that the danger is found.' Prophetic words spoken by Saint Pius X in the encyclical *Pascendi*, written in 1907, but essentially as current as if they had been written today. ....

"Chaos is not limited to the interior of the Church, it spreads. For the Council not only turned inside out what people believe in (doctrine) and practice (worship and morality) in the Catholic sphere, but also what people believed and practiced in all of Western society, of which the Church was the spiritual center. All that was said and done until 1960, was said and done having Her as reference, be it for or against Her. Even so, in less than three decades, this point of reference was almost totally obliterated by the revolts of *aggiornamento*. Had it been attacked by its worst, declared and secular enemies, religion would not have suffered so many losses as it has sustained from the action of its own representatives, which undermined it from within.

"The council closed in 1965, with the Church abdicating her responsibilities as one who guides and orients consciences. .... Without the conciliar abdication, how could one imagine the explosion that took place at end of the 60's (May of 68, the revolution in customs, the increased use of drugs, homosexuality, violence against women and children, satanic sects, etc.)? It is no wonder that Cardinal Suenens compared Vatican II to '1789 in the Church' and the theologian, Yves Congar, to 'October 1917.' .... Thus, with the conciliar revolution, the leaders of the new Church brought down its own walls. Afterward it took only one more step for the walls of society also to crumble" (Mateus SOARES DE AZEVEDO, "O Concílio que não terminou," in *Jornal da Tarde*, 10/24/1992).

disciplinary ambits from arising from such a conflict of beliefs? Finally, how to prevent the increase of the generalized climate of chaos disorienting the faithful and causing them, in turn, to doubt the Church and the Faith?

*

§ *129*   Here we close Chapter X, considering that its title thesis has been fully demonstrated. As a result of conciliar ambiguity, a great crisis of unity and internal cohesion erupted in the Church, discrediting ecclesiastical authority, including that of the Pope. This shook the Faith of priests, religious and laity in God and in the Church.

*   *   *

CONCLUSION

As this Volume, which sought to be objective and serene, comes to a close, it has demonstrated that the Ecumenical Council of Vatican II was ambiguous in the official texts of its documents.

Two types of questions inevitably arise from this fact:

First: Whereas the Council's texts are written in a deliberately imprecise, hesitant, and provisional language that generates disparate and many times contradictory interpretations;

Whereas the doctrine that often reveals itself behind the ambiguity leads, or may lead, to a visualization that differs from traditional Catholic Doctrine;

Whereas, as a consequence of these two facts, the official line of application of the Council has produced in the Church the greatest crisis in her History, one asks:

What value should one attribute to Vatican Council II?

Are precision, clarity, and orthodoxy not characteristic of the ecclesiastical Magisterium? Are the applications of its teachings not conducive to a more fervent faith, adhesion to moral norms, and disciplinary submission?

Therefore, given the fundamental ambiguity of Vatican II, its variance on certain points with the earlier Magisterium of the Church, and the crisis it has generated, could one not advocate that it is null?

This Volume offers multiple elements for reflection about these questions. We hope that the whole Collection *Eli, Eli, lamma sabacthani?* will further contribute to their clarification. It will do this not so much through a canonical discussion on the possibility of a Council being considered null — we believe in this regard the Masters are clear and History is rich in teachings — but by presenting the facts and doctrines that characterize the Council of John XXIII and Paul VI.

Second: Since the Council's texts lend themselves as a foundation *in re* to disparate interpretations by conflicting currents, it becomes impossible, based directly on them, to know their exact meaning. Faced with this impossibility, how can one understand the thinking and the intentions of the Council?

We see no other way but an indirect one, much longer and more arduous. It is to study the spirit of the Council, the thinking of the men who designed, wrote, and applied it, as well as the fruits it has generated. By seeking in these various realms the underlying unity that defines the whole 'Vatican II phenomenon,' an interpretation that clarifies such texts becomes possible.

"Grandis enim tibi restat via," (3 Kg 19:7) said the Angel to the Prophet Elias, giving him strength to continue his arduous pilgrimage through the desert.

Encouraged by this august example and under the patronage of the Prophet, who will reenter History for the final combats of Holy Church, a simple layman could attempt to tread this road, the only one left open to him.

That is what we intend to do in the next Volumes of this Collection.

*   *   *

APPENDIX

THE CATHOLIC CHURCH
AND HOMOSEXUALITY[1]

OVERVIEW

1

In view of the scandals that have taken place in the Church this year, it occurred to us to present an overall view of homosexuality in the post-conciliar crisis in the Church.

The criteria adopted were the following: preferably to leave aside particular cases and to deal with those that reflect general situations; to give priority to news not published in our local press; and to make a summary of the locally published news so that the main points will be remembered.

1. Position of Catholic Tradition Regarding Homosexuality

Excerpts from the *Sacred Scriptures*

2

In the *Old Testament* the Scriptures refer to the vice of homosexuality with special severity:

* "And the Lord said: The cry of Sodom and Gomorrha is multiplied, and their sin is become exceedingly grievous" (Gn 18:20).

* The angels arrived at Lot's house, under the appearance of two handsome men. "But before they went to bed, the men of the city beset the house both young and old, all the people together. And they called Lot, and said to him: Where are

---

[1] The text below is transcribed from lectures given by the Author on July 12, 26, 28 and August 2, 1995, at the Auditorium of the Brazilian Society for the Defense of Tradition, Family and Property. It has been updated and slightly altered.

the men that came in to thee at night? Bring them out hither that we may know them .... And they pressed very violently upon Lot; and they were even at the point of breaking open the doors. And behold the men put out their hand, and drew in Lot unto them, and shut the door. And them that were without, they struck with blindness from the least to the greatest, so that they could not find the door" (Gn 19:4-11).

* "And they [the angels] said to Lot: .... all that are thine bring them out of this city, for we will destroy this place, because their cry [of their crimes] is grown loud before the Lord, who hath sent us to destroy them (Gn 19:12-13).

* "And they brought him forth, and set him without the city: and there they spoke to him: Save thy life; look not back, neither stay thou in all the country about, but save thyself in the mountain, lest thou be also consumed" (Gn 19:17).

* "And the Lord rained upon Sodom and Gomorrha brimstone and fire from the Lord out of heaven; and he destroyed these cities, and all the country about, and all the inhabitants of the cities, and all things that spring from the earth. And his wife looking behind her, was turned into a statue of salt. And Abraham got up early in the morning and .... looked towards Sodom and Gomorrha, and the whole land of that country, and he saw the ashes rise up from the earth as the smoke of a furnace" (Gn 19:24-28).

* "Thou shalt not lie with mankind as with womankind, because it is an abomination" (Lev 18:22).

* "Defile not yourselves with any of these things [illicit unions, child sacrifice, sodomy, and bestiality] with which all the nations have been defiled, which I will cast out before you, and with which the land is defiled; the abominations of which I will visit, that it may vomit out its inhabitants .... Beware then, lest in like manner, it vomit you also out, if you do the like things" (Lev 18:24-28).

* "If any one lie with a man as with a woman, both have committed an abomination, let them be put to death; their blood be upon them" (Lev 20:13).

* "A woman shall not be clothed with man's apparel, neither shall a man use woman's apparel: for he that doeth these things is abominable before God" (Dt 22:5).

* On the punishment that God prepared for the Jews: "And I shall give children to be their princes, and the effeminate shall rule over them .... the shew of their countenance hath answered them: and they have proclaimed abroad their sin as Sodom, and they have not hid it; woe to their souls for evils are rendered to them. .... The Lord standeth to judge the people" (Is 3:4-13).

3   In the *New Testament*, Saint Paul indignantly castigates the vice against nature:

* "Do you not err: neither fornicators, nor idolaters, nor adulterers, nor the effeminate, nor liers with mankind [sodomites] .... shall possess the kingdom of God" (1 Cor 6:9-10).

* In the *Epistle to the Romans*, the Apostle of the Gentiles threatens perverts with punishments already on this earth: "Wherefore God gave them up to the desires of their hearts, unto uncleanness, to dishonor their own bodies among themselves, who changed the truth of God into a lie and worshipped and served the creature rather than the Creator, who is blessed for ever. Amen. For this cause God delivered them up to shameful affections. For their women have changed the natural use into that use which is against nature. And, in like manner, the men also, leaving the natural use of the women, have burned in their lusts one towards another, men with men working that which is filthy, and receiving in themselves the recompense which was due to their error" (Rm 1:24-27).

How can one not relate the fulfillment of these threats to the AIDS epidemic now ravaging sodomites?

4   * Saint Peter stresses the infamy of the sin of sodomy and the chastisement God reserves for it: "For if God .... reducing the cities of the Sodomites, and of the Gomorrhites, into ashes, condemned them to be overthrown, making them an example to those that should after act wickedly, and delivered just Lot, oppressed by the injustice and lewd conversation of the wicked... [it is because] the Lord knoweth how to deliver the godly from temptation, but to reserve the unjust unto the day of judgment to be tormented" (2 Pt 2:4-9).

5   * Saint Jude is no less severe: "As Sodom and Gomorrha, and the neighboring cities, in like manner, having given themselves to fornication, and going after other flesh, were made an example, suffering the punishment of eternal fire, in

like manner these men also defile the flesh, and despise domination [of Christ], and blaspheme majesty" (Jd 7:8).[2]

Tradition of the Ecclesiastical Magisterium

§ 6

* The first statement of a Church council on homosexual practices was issued by the **Council of Elvira** (305-306). The decree excludes from communion, even *in articulo mortis*, the *stuprotores puerorum*.[3]

* The decree of the **Council of Ancira**, held in Asia Minor in 314, strongly influenced the Church of the West, and as it was often cited as an argument of authority in later declarations against homosexual practices. Canon 17 speaks about those "who .... have committed [acts of] iniquity with animals or men."[4] The Council of Ancira established for these crimes a series of punishments according to the age and state of the infractor:

"Those who have committed such crimes before age twenty, after fifteen years of penance, will be readmitted to the communion of prayer. Then, after remaining five years in that communion, let them receive the sacraments of oblation. However, let their lives be analyzed to establish how long a period of penance they should sustain in order to obtain mercy. For if they unrestrainedly gave themselves over to these crimes, let them devote more time to doing penance. However, those, aged twenty and over and married, who fall into these crimes, let

---

[2] Vague references to sodomites, without special interest for our exposition, are found in 1 Tm 1:8-10. Other references to Sodom and Gomorrha, without express mention of the vice of homosexuality: Dt 29:23; 32:32; Je 23:13-14; 49:18; 50:40; Ez 16:55-56; Mt 10:15; Rm 9:29; Apc 11:8.

[3] *Concilium Illiberitarum*, n. 71, in John McNEILL, *La Iglesia ante la homosexualidad* (Barcelona/Buenos Aires/Mexico: Grijalbo, 1979), p. 120.

[4] *Concilium Ancyrense*, 16, 17; C. H. TURNER, *Ecclesiae occidentalis monumenta iuris antiquissima*, Oxford, 1909, vol. XI, p. 19; on the influence of this Council, see *Capitulares Aquisgran*, (789), 48, Joannes Dominicus MANSI, XVIIb, col. 230; *Capitulare Caroli Magno*, 48, MANSI, XVIIb, col. 710; *Capitulare Caroli Magno et Ludovic*, 82, MANSI, XVIIb, col. 839; *Canones Isaac episcopi Lingonensis*, 4, 11, MANSI, XVIIb, col. 1259; *Concilium Parisiensi*, (829), 1, 34, MANSI, XIV, col. 560, in J. McNEILL, op. cit., p. 121.

them do penance for twenty-five years and [then] be received in the communion of prayer; and, remaining in it for five years, let them finally receive the sacraments of oblation. Moreover, if those who are married and over fifty years of age commit these crimes, let them obtain the grace of communion only at the end of their lives."[5]

7   * **Pope Saint Siricius** (384-399) issued norms for admission into the priestly state. They apply indirectly to homosexuality: "We deem it advisable to establish that, just as not everyone should be allowed to do a penance reserved for clerics, so also a layman should never be allowed to ascend to clerical honor after penance and reconciliation. Because although they have been purified of the contagion of all sins, those who formerly indulged in a multitude of vices should not receive the instruments to administer the sacraments."[6]

8   * In the opening speech of the **XVI Council of Toledo** in 693, Egica, the Gothic King of Spain, exhorts the clergy to fight against homosexual practices: "Seek .... to decisively extirpate this obscene crime committed by men who sleep with men, whose terrible conduct corrupts the grace of honest living and provokes the wrath of the Supreme Judge of heaven."[7]

9   * The most complete ensemble of norms against homosexual practices in the medieval era is composed of the canons approved at the **Council of Nablus**, assembled on January 23, 1120 under the direction of Garmund, Patriarch of Jerusalem, and Baldwin, King of the same city.[8] On that occasion, a sermon was preached in which the evils that had befallen the Kingdom of Jerusalem. Earthquakes, pests, and attacks by the Sarracens were judged as a punishment from heaven for the sins of the people. As a consequence, the Council issued twenty-five canons against the sins of the flesh, four of which related to homosexual practices. Death at the stake was decreed for those convicted of those specific crimes.

---

[5] See Council of Ancira, in St. PETER DAMIEN, *Liber gomorrhianus*, in PL 145, cols. 172ff.

[6] St. SIRICIUS, Ibid., cols. 174f.

[7] *Concilium Tolitanum*, 16, 3, MANSI, XII, col. 71, in J. McNEILL, op. cit., p. 121.

[8] *Concilium Neapolitanum* 8, MANSI, XXI, cols. 261-264, Ibid., p. 122.

§ *10*   * The **Third Council of the Lateran** (1179) establishes: "Anyone caught in the practice of the sin against nature, on account of which the wrath of God was unleashed upon the children of disobedience (Eph 5:6), if he is a cleric, let him be demoted from his state and kept in reclusion in a monastery to do penance; if he is a layman, let him be excommunicated and kept rigorously distant from the communion of the faithful."[9]

§ *11*   Such was the horror that surrounded the sin against nature that, since the late twelfth century, sodomy existed only as a secret sin, for which absolution was reserved to the Pope and, in some cases, to the Bishops.[10]

§ *12*   * Nevertheless, with the Renaissance this vice surfaced again. Homosexuality was a matter of grave concern to **Saint Pius V**. As the well-known historian von Pastor narrates, "In the first year of his pontificate, the Pope had two preponderant concerns: zeal for the Inquisition and the struggle against 'this horrendous sin whereby the justice of God caused the cities contaminated by it to be consumed in flames.' On April 1, 1566, he ordered that sodomites be turned over to the secular arm .... The various imprisonments of sodomites .... impressed Rome and frightened especially well-established people, for it was known that the Pope wanted his laws enforced even against the powerful. Indeed, to punish for vices against nature, the torment of the stake was applied throughout the pontificate of Saint Pius V .... An earlier papal Brief mandated that clerics who were guilty of that crime be stripped of all their posts, dignities, and income, and, after degradation, be handed over to the secular arm."[11]

    The Holy Inquisitor promulgated two Constitutions in which he castigates and punishes the sin against nature.

---

[9] *Concilium Lateranense can 11*, MANSI, XXII, cols. 224ff., in Fabio BERNADEI, *Chiesa e omosessualità - la ragioni di un'immutabili condanna* (Rome: Centro Culturale Lepanto, 1995), p. 13.

[10] *Synodus constitutiva Odonis episcopi Parisiensi* (1196), 4, 5 - Pope and Bishop, MANSI XXIII, col. 678; *Concilium Provinciale Fritzlar* (1287), 4 - Bishop, MANSI, XXIII, col 726; *Sancta Synodus ecclesiae Leodicae* (1287), 4 - Bishop, MANSI, XXIV, col. 891; *Concilium Ramense* (1408), MANSI, XXVI, col. 1073, in J. McNEILL, op. cit., p. 122.

[11] Ludovico von PASTOR, *Historia de los Papas* (Barcelona: Gustavo Gili, 1931), vol. XVII, pp. 299f.

In the **Constitution *Cum primum*** of April 1, 1566, Saint Pius V solemnly established: "Having set our minds to remove everything that may in some way offend the Divine Majesty, We resolve to punish, above all and without indulgence, those things which, by the authority of the Sacred Scriptures or by most grievous examples, are most repugnant to God and elicit his wrath; that is, negligence in divine worship, ruinous simony, the crime of blasphemy, and the execrable libidinous vice against nature. For which faults peoples and nations are scourged by God, according to his just condemnation, with catastrophies, wars, famine, and pests .... Let the judges know that, if even after this, our Constitution, they are negligent in punishing these crimes, they will be guilty of them at divine judgment and will also incur our indignation .... If someone commits that nefarious crime against nature that caused divine wrath to be unleashed against the children of iniquity, he will be given over to the secular arm for punishment; and if he is a cleric, he will be subject to analogous punishment after having been stripped of all his degrees [of ecclesiastical dignity]."[12]

Saint Pius V is no less rigorous in the **Constitution *Horrendum illud scelus*** of August 30, 1568. In fact, he teaches: "That horrible crime, on account of which corrupt and obscene cities were burned by virtue of divine condemnation, causes us most bitter sorrow and shocks our mind, impelling it to repress such a crime with the highest possible zeal. Quite opportunely the **Fifth Lateran Council** [1512-1517] decrees: Let any member of the clergy caught in that vice against nature .... be removed from the clerical order or forced to do penance in a monastery (chap. 4, X, V, 31).

"So that the contagion of such a grave offense may not advance with greater audacity, taking advantage of impunity, which is the greatest incitement to sin, and so as to more severely punish the clerics who are guilty of this nefarious crime and who are not frightened by the death of their souls, we determine that they should be handed over to the secular authority, which enforces civil law. Therefore, wishing to pursue with the greatest rigor that which we have decreed since the beginning of Our Pontificate, we establish that any priest or member of the clergy, either secular or regular, who commits such an execrable

---

[12] St. PIUS V, Constitution *Cum primum*, April 1, 1566, in *In Bullarium romanum* (Rome: Typographia reverendae Camerae Apostolicae, Mainardi,1738), vol. IV, chap. II, p. 284, in F. BERNABEI, op. cit., p. 14.

crime, by force of the present law be deprived of every clerical privilege, of every post, dignity and ecclesiastical benefit, and having been degraded by an ecclesiastical judge, be immediately delivered to the secular authority to be executed as mandated by law, according to the appropriate punishment for laymen plunged in this abyss."[13]

§ 13

* The **Code of Canon Law**, whose writing was undertaken at the initiative and encouragement of **Saint Pius X**, published in 1917 by his successor, **Pope Benedict XV**, says this: "So far as laymen are concerned, the sin of sodomy is punished *ipso facto* with the pain of infamy and other sanctions to be applied according to the prudent judgment of the Bishop depending on the gravity of each case (can. 2357). As for ecclesiastics and religious, if they are *clerici minoris* (that is, of a degree lower than deacon), let them be punished with various measures, proportional to the gravity of the fault, that can even include dismissal from the clerical state (can. 2358); it they are *clerici maiores* (that is, deacons, priests or Bishops), let them 'be declared infamous and suspended from every post, benefit, dignity, deprived of their eventual stipend and, in the gravest cases, let them be deposed' (can. 2359, par. 2)."[14]

*

§ 14

* **Tertullian**, the great apologist of the Church in the second century, writes: "We condemn all those who give themselves over to the excesses of luxury contrary to natural law .... and expell them from the bosom of the Church, for [such acts] are greater monstrosities than sins."[15]

§ 15

* **Saint Basil of Cesarea**, the fourth century Church Father who wrote the principal rule of the monks of the East, establishes: "The cleric or monk who molests youths or boys or is caught kissing or committing some turpitude, let him be whipped in public, deprived of his crown [tonsure] and, after having his head shaved, let his face be covered with spittle; and [let him be] bound in iron chains, condemned to six months in

---

[13] St. PIUS V, Constitution *Horrendum illud scelus*, August 30, 1568, Ibid., chap. III, p. 33.

[14] BENEDICT XV, *Code of Canon Law*, Ibid., p. 16.

[15] TERTULIAN, *De pudicitia*, IV, in J. McNEILL, op. cit., p. 134.

prison, reduced to eating rye bread once a day in the evening three times per week. After these six months living in a separate cell under the custody of a wise elder with great spiritual experience, let him be subjected to prayers, vigils, and manual work, always under the guard of two spiritual brothers, without being allowed to have any relationship .... with young people."[16]

* **Saint Augustine** is categorical in the combat of sodomy and similar vices. The great Bishop of Hippo writes: "Sins against nature, therefore, like the sin of Sodom, are abominable and deserve punishment whenever and wherever they are committed. If all nations committed them, all alike would be held guilty of the same charge in God's law, for our Maker did not prescribe that we should use each other in this way. In fact, the relationship that we ought to have with God is itself violated when our nature, of which he is Author, is desecrated by perverted lust."[17]

Further on he reiterates: "Your punishments are for the sins which men commit against themselves, because, although they sin against you, they do wrong in their own souls and their malice is self-betrayed. They corrupt and pervert their own nature, which you made and for which you shaped the rules, either by making wrong use of the things which you allow, or by becoming inflamed with passion 'to make unnatural use of things which you do not allow' (Rm 1:26)."[18]

* **Saint John Chrysosthom** denounces homosexual acts as being contrary to nature. Commenting on the *Epistle to the Romans* (1:26-27), he says that the pleasures of sodomy are an unpardonable offense to nature and are doubly destructive, since they threaten the species by deviating the sexual organs away from their primary procreative end and they sow disorder between men and women, who no longer are inclined, by physical desire, to live together and in peace.[19]

---

[16] St. BASIL OF CESAREA, in St. PETER DAMIEN, op. cit., cols. 174f.

[17] St. AUGUSTINE, *Confessions* (New York: Penguin, 1967), Book. III, chap. 8, p. 65.

[18] Ibid., p. 66.

[19] St. JOHN CHRYSOSTHOM, *In Epistulam ad Romanos IV*, in J. McNEILL, op. cit., p. 134.

The brilliant Patriarch of Constantinople employs most severe words for the vice we are analyzing. In fact, Saint John Chrysosthom argues: "All passions are dishonorable, for the soul is even more prejudiced and degraded by sin than is the body by disease; but the worst of all passions is lust between men. .... The sins against nature are more difficult and less rewarding, so much so that one cannot even say that they procure pleasure, since true pleasure is only the one according to nature. But when God abandons a man, everything is turned upside down! Therefore, not only are their passions [of the homosexuals] satanic, but their lives are diabolic. .... So I say to you that these are even worse than murderers, and that it would be better to die than to live in such dishonor. A murderer only separates the soul from the body, whereas these destroy the soul inside the body. .... There is nothing, absolutely nothing more mad or damaging than this perversity."[20]

§ 18

* **Saint Gregory the Great** delves deeper into the symbolism of the fire and brimstone that God used to punish the sodomites: "Brimstone calls to mind the foul odors of the flesh, as Sacred Scripture itself confirms when it speaks of the rain of fire and brimstone poured by the Lord upon Sodom. He had decided to punish in it the crimes of the flesh, and the very type of punishment emphasized the shame of that crime, since brimstone exhales stench and fire burns. It was, therefore, just that the sodomites, burning with perverse desires that originated from the foul odor of flesh, should perish at the same time by fire and brimstone, so that through this just chastisement they might realize the evil perpetrated under the impulse of a perverse desire."[21]

§ 19

* **Saint Peter Damien**'s *Liber gomorrhianus*, addressed to Pope Leo IX in the year 1051, is considered the principal work against homosexuality[22]. It reads: "Just as Saint Basil establishes that those who incur sins [against nature] .... should be subjected not only to a hard penance, but a public one, and Pope Siricius prohibits penitents from entering clerical orders, one can clearly deduce that he who corrupts himself with a man through

---

[20] St. JOHN CHRYSOSTHOM, *Homilia in Epistula Pauli ad Romanos*, in PG 47, cols. 360ff., in F. BERNABEI, op. cit. pp. 7f.

[21] St. GREGORY THE GREAT, *Commento morale a Giobbe* (Rome: Città Nuova, 1994), XIV, 23, vol. II, p. 371, Ibid., p. 7.

[22] J. McNEILL, op. cit., p. 123.

the ignominious squalor of a filthy union does not deserve to exercise ecclesiastical functions, since those who were formerly given to vices .... become unfit to administer the sacraments."[23]

20   * **Saint Albert the Great** gives four reasons why he considers homosexual acts as the most detestable ones: They are born from an ardent frenzy; they are repugnantly obscene; those who become addicted to it are seldom freed from that vice; they are as contagious as disease, passing quickly from one person to another.[24]

21   * **Saint Thomas Aquinas**, writing about sins against nature, explains: "However, they are called passions of ignominy because they are not worthy of being named, according to that passage in *Ephesians* (5:12): 'For the things that are done by them in secret, it is a shame even to speak of.' For if the sins of the flesh are commonly censurable because they lead man to that which is bestial in him, much more so is the sin against nature, by which man debases himself lower than even his animal nature."[25]

22   * **Saint Bonaventure**, speaking in a sermon at the church of Saint Mary of Porciuncula about the miracles that took place simultaneously with the birth of Our Lord Jesus Christ, narrates: "Seventh prodigy: All sodomites -- men and women -- died all over the earth, as Saint Jerome said in his commentary on the psalm 'The light was born for the just.' This made it clear that He was born to reform nature and promote chastity."[26]

23   * **Saint Catherine of Siena**, a religious mystic of the 14th century, relays words of Our Lord Jesus Christ about the vice against nature, which contaminated part of the clergy in her time. Referring to sacred ministers, He says: "They not only fail from resisting this frailty [of fallen human nature] .... but do

---

[23] St. PETER DAMIEN, op. cit., cols. 174f.

[24] St. ALBERT THE GREAT, *In Evangelium Lucae XVII*, 29, in J. McNEILL, op. cit., p. 141.

[25] St. THOMAS AQUINAS, *Super Epistulas Sancti Pauli Ad Romanum* I, 26, pp. 27f.

[26] St. BONAVENTURE, *Sermon XXI - In Nativitate Domini*, in *Catolicismo* (Campos/São Paulo), December 1987, p. 3; F. BERNABEI, op. cit., p. 11.

even worse as they commit the cursed sin against nature. Like the blind and stupid, having dimmed the light of their understanding, they do not recognize the disease and misery in which they find themselves. For this not only causes Me nausea, but displeases even the demons themselves, whom these miserable creatures have chosen as their lords. For Me, this sin against nature is so abominable that, for it alone, five cities were submersed, by virtue of the judgment of my divine justice, which could no longer bear them .... It is disagreeable to the demons, not because evil displeases them and they find pleasure in good, but because their nature is angelic and thus is repulsed upon seeing such an enormous sin being committed. It is true that it is the demon who hits the sinner with the poisoned arrow of lust, but when a man carries out such a sinful act, the demon leaves."[27]

§ 24   *** Saint Bernardine of Siena**, a preacher of the fifteenth century, makes an accurate psychological analysis of the consequences of the homosexual vice. The illustrious Franciscan writes: "No sin has greater power over the soul than the one of cursed sodomy, which was always detested by all those who lived according to God .... Such passion for undue forms borders on madness. This vice disturbs the intellect, breaks an elevated and generous state of soul, drags great thoughts to petty ones, makes [men] pusillanimous and irascible, obstinate and hardened, servilely soft and incapable of anything. Furthermore, the will, being agitated by the insatiable drive for pleasure, no longer follows reason, but furor .... Someone who lived practicing the vice of sodomy will suffer more pains in hell than anyone else, because this is the worst sin that there is."[28]

§ 25   *** Saint Peter Canisius**, on the sin of sodomy, says that "Those who are not ashamed of violating divine and natural law are slaves of this turpitude that can never be sufficiently execrated."[29]

---

[27] St. CATHERINE OF SIENA, *El diálogo*, in *Obras de Santa Catarina de Siena* (Madrid: BAC, 1991), p. 292.

[28] St. BERNARDINE OF SIENA, *Predica XXXIX*, in *Le prediche volgari* (Milan: Rizzoli, 1936), pp. 869ff., 915, in F. BERNABEI, op. cit., pp. 11f.

[29] St. PETER CANISIUS, *Summa doctrina christianae*, III, a, b (Cooniae, Colenium, 1557), p. 455, Ibid., p. 12.

²⁶ Prof. **Plinio Corrêa de Oliveira**, in an SBT interview about homosexuality in Brazil (not broadcast) on October 29, 1992, stated: "The sexual act exists in the natural order of things for the fecundity of the family and, through the fecundity of the family, for the expansion of mankind. The precept of Our Lord Jesus Christ to men .... is 'Multiply and fill the earth.' It is necessary, therefore, to do this and by all means to favor the fecundity of sexual intercourse, which is legitimately exercised only in matrimony. Now then, as for homosexuality, there is no matrimony, and, above all, there can be no fecundity. ...."

"For many centuries," Prof. Corrêa de Oliveira continued, "homosexuality was the object of real aversion on the part of successive generations. And this was not because of a whim .... but by virtue of the doctrinal principles I have just enunciated, which are principles of the Roman Catholic and apostolic doctrine. .... This rejection [of homosexuality] is a preservation of society against that which of itself threatens it. Everything that is alive rejects what destroys it. Thus, by a similar movement of the instinct of self-preservation, human societies modeled upon Catholic Doctrine .... have been profoundly anti-homosexual.

"*Question*: Why, in your view, are homosexuals discriminated against in Brazilian society?

"*Answer*: Brazil is a son of Portugal, and Portugal and Spain were always very strong bulwarks of the Catholic Church. We received from our Portuguese ancestors rigidity and consistency in the Catholic Faith, which modeled the customs of colonial Brazil, the United Kingdom [of Brazil and Portugal], the Brazilian Empire, and the Brazilian Republic until some time ago. Hence Catholic aversion for homosexuality impregnated our customs and constituted a tradition."

Tradition of Temporal Legislation

²⁷ * Law of December 16, 342 of **Emperors Constantius and Constant**: "When a man marries and is ready to offer himself to men in a feminine way, voluntarily ...., we order that norms be established, that the law be armed with a vengeful

sword and that these unworthy individuals .... receive the supreme punishment."[30]

* Law of August 6, 390 promulgated by the **Emperors Valentinian II, Theodosius, and Arcadius:** "All persons having the shameful custom of condemning a man's body to play the role of a woman .... (since they seem no different than women) will expiate their crime in vengeful flames."[31]

* Law of December 30, 533 of **Emperor Justinian:** "In cases of penal suits, public action will be guided by various norms, including the *Lex julia de adulteris* .... that punishes with death not only those who interfere with other people's marriages, but also those who commit acts of vile concupiscence with (other) men."[32]

* Law of the year 538 of **Emperor Justinian**: "Whereas certain men, victims of diabolical incitation, practice among themselves the most unworthy lewdness and act against nature, we exhort them to be fearful of God and the coming judgment, and abstain from such illicit and diabolical practices so that the wrath of God may not fall upon them on account of their heathen acts, and so that cities may not perish with all their inhabitants. For Sacred Scriptures tell us that similar acts of impiety caused the demise of cities with all their inhabitants .... And since such sins are the cause of famine, earthquakes, and pests, we warn men to abstain from them so as not to lose their souls. But if, after this warning of ours, it should be discovered that someone persists in such iniquity, he will be unworthy of God's mercy and deserving of the punishment established by law. Thus, we order the most illustrious Mayor of the Capital to arrest those who persist in the aforementioned illicit and impious acts .... and to inflict upon them the most severe punishments, so that the city and the State do not end by suffering on account of such iniquitous acts."[33]

---

[30] CONSTANCE - CONSTANT, *Codex Theodosii* IX; VII, 3; *Codex Justiniani* IX; IX, 31; in *The Theodosian Code* (Princeton University Press, 1952), pp. 231f., in J. McNEILL, op. cit., p. 117.

[31] VALENTINIAN II - THEODOSIUS - ARCADIUS, *Codex Theodosii* IX; VII, 6, in *The Theodosian Code*, p. 232, Ibid., pp. 117f.

[32] JUSTINIAN, *Instituta* IV; XVIII, 4, Ibid., pp. 116f.

[33] JUSTINIAN, *Codex Justiniani*, nov. 77; nov. 141, Ibid., pp. 118f.

* The influence of the Justinian Code continued for centuries. It can also be noted in Blackstone's *Comment on the Laws of England* in the nineteenth century. Blackstone states: "The crime against nature .... [must] be punished with death as required by the voice of nature and of reason, and the express law of God. We have a concrete example of this long before the Jewish diaspora in the destruction of two cities by fire from heaven; this is, therefore, not merely a special precept, but a universal norm. In the *Old Testament*, the law condemns sodomites (and possibly other homosexuals) to death as perpetrators of an abomination against the Lord, while the *New Testament* accuses them of transgressing natural law and excludes them from God's order for following the vile practices of pagans."[34]

Jurist Pietro Agostino d'Avack drafted an historic roster of laws that protected the State against the vice of homosexuality. In substantial paragraphs, d'Avack affirms: "No less severe and scathingly repressive laws against such sexual aberrations are found in the centuries following [the Roman Empire] and emanated from all civil authorities from the earliest medieval times up to the modern age. Thus, the *Lex visigothica* condemned to castration and jail those [men] 'who carnally united with men ....' and prescribed, if they were married, that their goods should be immediately inherited by their children and heirs. After the *castratio virum*, the law also prescribed capital punishment.

In turn, in the well-known collection of the *Frankish Capitularies of Ansegisius and Benedict Levite* .... those who had engaged in sexual acts with animals, who were guilty of incest, and who 'practiced copulation with men' were punished with capital punishment; if pardoned by some indult, they were obliged to subject themselves to canonical penances imposed by the Church. In the later *Capitularies of Ludovicus Pius*, while such a crime, invoking Roman legislation, was punishable with execution at the stake, this severe action was justified in the name of the 'salvation of the *rem publicam*' so that 'on account of such sins, we may not also fall with the kingdom and the glory of the whole kingdom may not perish.' ....

"During successive centuries, this lay temporal legislation was substantially unaltered and was nearly identical everywhere, whether in Italy or in the other European States, as at-

---

[34] BLACKSTONE, *Comment on the Laws of England*, London, 1826, vol. IV, p. 215, Ibid., p. 120.

tested to by the *Statutes of Bologna* in 1561, those of Ferrara in 1566, those of Milan, Rome, and [the Italian province of] Marche in the seventeenth century, the *Florentian Tires* of 1542, 1558 and 1699, the *Sicilian Pragmatics* of 1504, the *Carolingean Criminal Constitution* of Charles V, the *Theresian [Constitution]* of Marie Thérèse, the *Royal Portuguese Ordination*, the *New Spanish Recompilation,* etc. .... For their part, the *Florentian Statutes*, 'execrating the indecency of the great crime that is the sodomitic vice and wishing to extirpate it,' approved the institution of eight *officiales honestatis*, who were designated for six months specifically to repress such crime."[35]

*

2. Post-conciliar Doctrine on Homosexuality

§ *28*

The principles of adaptation of the Church to the modern world approved by the Council and the general acceptance of tolerance and mercy as remedies for evil had a special application in the case of homosexuality.

Modern psychology is divided in various currents with respect to this vice. One current believes that homosexuality results from the influence of various environmental factors — family troubles, emotional imbalance of the mother, bad example, etc. Others opine that it is due to innate factors — the simultaneous presence of masculine and feminine genes in the constitution of homosexuals, or a certain number of brain cells that determine homosexuality.

For a considerable segment of modern psychologists, homosexuality does not result from a person's concession to an unnatural tendency nor is it a moral vice; on the contrary, it is something according to nature, or pathological at most, which should be accepted as normal.

Conciliar Principles of Adaptation and Tolerance

§ *29*

With its general rule of adaptation to the modern world, the Council had to adapt to such theories. Insofar as modern

---

[35] Pietro Agostino d'AVACK, "L'omosessualità nel Diritto Canonico," in *Ulisse*, Spring of 1953, pp. 682-685, in F. BERNABEI, op. cit., pp. 21f.

psychology is concerned, it declares, in the **Constitution** *Gaudim et Spes*:

* "Advances in .... psychology and the social sciences not only lead man to greater self-awareness, but provide him with the technical means of molding the lives of whole peoples as well." (GS 5b)

* "Recent psychological advances furnish deeper insights into human behavior." (GS 54a)

* "Let the faithful incorporate the findings of new sciences and teachings and the understanding of the most recent discoveries with Christian morality and thought, so that their practice of religion and their moral behavior may keep abreast of their acquaintance with science and of the relentless progress of technology." (GS 62f)

* "In pastoral care, sufficient use should be made, not only of theological principles, but also of the findings of secular sciences, especially psychology and sociology." (GS 62b)

30   Also, with respect to tolerance for the errors and moral evils afflicting the world, **Pope John XXIII**, in the *Opening Speech* of the first session of Vatican II, declared: "The Church has always opposed these errors; many times she even condemned them with the greatest severity. In our days, however, the Spouse of Christ prefers to use more the remedy of mercy than that of severity; she deems it better to satisfy today's needs by showing the validity of her doctrine rather than by condemning errors .... Thus, the Catholic Church, raising by means of this Council the torch of religious truth, wishes to show herself the loving mother of all, benign, patient, full of mercy and kindness toward the children separated from her."[36]

Such principles led to the acceptance of modern psychology's theories about homosexuality, and also to the tolerance the Church has manifested since then toward this vice.

---

[36] JOHN XXIII, Opening Speech of Council Vatican II, October 11, 1962, in Boaventura KLOPPENBURG, *Concílio Vaticano II*, vol. II, p. 310.

Documents of the Holy See on Homosexuality

§ *31*

    As far as we can see, there are three basic documents of the Holy See on the question of homosexuality. They are all from the Congregation for the Doctrine of the Faith.

    In order to understand these documents well, it seems appropriate for us to make some preliminary observations.

    Up until Vatican Council II, the language of ecclesiastical documents was habitually clear and accessible, continuing the line of coherence of the Magisterium through the centuries. The body of doctrine thus being built constituted a supremely true, good and beautiful ensemble, a worthy reflection of Our Lord Jesus Christ, the Incarnate Wisdom.

    After Vatican II, however, ecclesiastical language often forsook such characteristics. Now more, now less, we find in it the presence of two opposing currents of thought: the traditional doctrine of the Church and progressivism. For this reason, often a text can lend itself to different and even contradictory interpretations – a lamentable but obvious fact to someone who has any experience reading post-conciliar documents.

    This fact necessitates establishing a method of analysis that permits us to confidently discern the depth of progressivist thought present in the text and the gates it thus opens for error and evil.

    The method we use is to determine that which is most unusual in each document and analyze it in order to build an overall picture.

    We know that more often than not there is a possible conservative interpretation for other excerpts of the documents. We leave this aside, for it seems to us more consonant with the spirit of Catholic vigilance to pay more attention to evil, which invades with its characteristic force of impact, rather than to good, which is often content to survive, impassive and silent, this invasion.

    Based upon these premises, therefore, we go on to analyze the three documents of the Congregation for the Doctrine of the Faith.

§ *32*

* Dated December 29, 1975, the **first document** is entitled *Declaration on Some Points of Sexual Ethics*, signed by Cardinal Franjo Seper and approved by Pope Paul VI. In our view, so far as homosexuality is concerned, the document's words tore down the barrier of horror that held back the waters of this vice against nature. In the document, Cardinal Seper says:

"In our days, in contradiction with the constant teaching of the Magisterium and the moral sense of the Christian people, there are some who, based on observations of a psychological order, go so far as to judge with indulgence, and even to completely excuse, homosexual relations among certain people.

"They make a distinction — apparently not without foundation — [between two classes of homosexuals]. On the one hand, there are those homosexuals whose tendency comes from a poor education, the lack of normal sexual development, an acquired habit, bad example, or analogous causes: for these, [homosexuality] is a transient tendency, or at least not an incurable one. On the other hand, there are those homosexuals who are definitively homosexual by force of a type of innate instinct or a pathological makeup deemed incurable.

"Now, with respect to this second category of individuals, some people conclude that their tendency is so natural that it should be viewed as justification, from their standpoint, of homosexual relationships in a sincere communion of life and love analogous to matrimony, to the degree that they feel incapable of bearing the burden of a solitary life.

"Certainly, in pastoral activity,[37] these homosexuals will be welcomed with understanding and supported in the hope that

---

[37] Not without interest are the observations by Fernand Dumont, professor of Sociological Theory at the University of Laval, Canada, on the new conception of Pastoral Theology. He says Pastoral Theology should somehow gradually replace Dogmatic Theology. This excerpt by Dumont is especially significant:

"In a Church that wishes to be both missionary and concerned with her own reform, it was inevitable that in recent decades there should have been great activity in pastoral theology. It is considered less and less as a heteroclite ensemble of practices and prescriptions on the fringe of the principal body of doctrine and has become, progressively, a comprehensive vision of the Church in its project of perpetual edification. One can even think, as we have suggested elsewhere (Fernand DUMONT, *Pour la conversion de la pensée chrétienne*, 1964, they will overcome their own personal difficulties and social non-adaptation. Their culpability shall be judged with prudence. However, no pastoral method may be employed which, by the fact that these acts are judged according to the condition of these persons, grants them a moral justification. According to the objective moral order, homosexual relations are acts deprived of their essential and indispensable end. They are condemned in Sacred Scripture as a grave depravity and therein presented as a somber consequence of a rejection of God. This judgment issued by Holy Scripture does not permit one, however, to conclude that all those who suffer this anomaly can, thereby, be held personally responsible."[38]

One sees, therefore, that Cardinal Seper distinguishes between an objective moral order — that should theoretically be respected — and a subjective moral order that should orient the pastoral action of the Church, which should accept homosexuality as a *fait accompli*. Note that on implicitly assuming the erroneous premises of modern psychology to justify Church pastoral action, Msgr. Seper provides a powerful theoretical argument opposed to objective Catholic Morals, which he sought to defend.

Further on, the Cardinal, enunciating general principles that should govern questions related to homosexuality, prematrimonial relations, and masturbation, states: "It is true that sexual faults, given their special conditions and causes, are more often committed without a full and free consent; so one should proceed with caution in every judgment to be made with respect to the subjective responsibility for such faults."[39]

---

pp. 205ss.) that .... pastoral theology is soon going to question the most profound bases of systematic theology. .... If pastoral theology and theological anthropology continue to develop along the lines indicated thus far, it is unlikely that they will limit themselves to adding new tracts to the *corpus* of theology. They will suggest new and as yet poorly defined comprehensive perspectives to all of theology, opening to the concrete historical situations of man." (F. DUMONT, "The Sociology of Religion and the Renewal of Theology," in V.A., *Theology of Renewal*, vol. II, pp. 271f.).

[38] CONGREGATION FOR THE DOCTRINE OF THE FAITH, *Declaração sobre alguns pontos de ética sexual* of December 29, 1975 (Vozes: Petrópolis, 1976), p. 11, n. 8.

[39] Ibid., p. 16, n. 10.

These were the principles that, in a certain way, legitimized and gave free rein to homosexuality in the Church. While this vice had already surfaced to the light of day on the basis of conciliar *aggiornamento*, only after the publication of this document did it feel at ease.

Ten years went by before the Holy See felt the need for a new pronouncement in face of the veritable homosexual avalanche that had fallen upon the contemporary world. However, in dealing with the topic, the point of reference was the document of 1975.[40]

33
We add here a short observation to aid in the reading of the documents below.

In them, Cardinal Ratzinger does not seem to be very precise in presenting the limits between two fundamental concepts: homosexual tendency and homosexual behavior.

According to Catholic Doctrine, any disorderly tendency, above all to a vice contrary to nature, cannot have a right of citizenship in a person's thoughts. If someone in his mind makes a concession to this tendency, he sins. This is why in the *Confiteor* one asks forgiveness for thoughts, words, and deeds. Thus, an homosexual tendency is not a sin only when it has not been given free rein by the person.

A person also sins when his external behavior is allowed to express an homosexual tendency. Indeed, we have seen excerpts from the Sacred Scriptures (Dt 22:5; Is 3:4-13) and from Saint Basil severely condemning those who behave in an homosexual fashion even though they do not practice the act.

Finally, there is the act of sodomy, which constitutes a sin that cries out to Heaven and clamors to God for vengeance.[41]

---

[40] For example: CONGREGAZIONE PER L'EDUCAZIONE CATTOLICA, *Orientamenti educativi sull'amore umano*, November 1, 1983, Poliglota Vaticana, pp. 32f., nn. 101ff.

[41] Gn 19:13; St. PIUS X, *Catecismo maior* (São Paulo: Vera Cruz, 1976), p. 174; Francisco SPIRAGO, *Catecismo católico popular* (Lisbon: União Gráfica Ed., 1951), vol. II, p. 369; F. X. SCHOUPPE, *Curso abreviado de Religião ou verdade e beleza da Religião Cristã* (Porto: Liv. Chardron, 1875), p. 296.

Now then, such clear and precise concepts of tendency, behavior and act with regard to sodomy are somewhat shuffled around in the documents we are examining.

At times, the tendency remains in the individual's thoughts, at other times it manifests itself and is confused with behavior. The concept of behavior is uncertain as well. At times, it is a public manifestation of homosexuality without practicing the act, other times it includes the act.

Perhaps this confusion can be explained as follows: since the homosexual act is indisputably sinful but the tendency is not categorically so, emphasizing the notion of tendency would be the shrewd thing to do by someone who wants to morally justify homosexual behavior.

The word tendency is also taken as synonymous with inclination, and the word behavior is replaced by homosexual practice or activity.

Having clarified these imprecisions as much as possible, we will proceed to the analysis of the document.

§ 34

* On October 1, 1986, the Congregation for the Doctrine of the Faith published its **second document** on the subject. It was called *Letter to the Bishops of the Catholic Church on Pastoral Service for Homosexual Persons*, signed by Cardinal Joseph Ratzinger and approved by Pope John Paul II. The document was prepared with the intention of repressing abuses taking place in debates about homosexuality even in Catholic ambiences,[42] as well as correcting overly benevolent interpretations of the prior document of the Holy See on homosexuals (n. 3).

Toward this purpose, Msgr. Ratzinger distinguishes between homosexual tendency and behavior:

"It is necessary to point out that the particular inclination of an homosexual person, though not a sin in itself, nevertheless constitutes a more or less strong tendency to an intrinsically evil behavior from the moral standpoint. For this reason, the very

---

[42] CONGREGAZIONE PER LA DOTTRINA DELLA FEDE, "Lettera ai Vescovi della Chiesa Cattolica sulla cura pastorale delle persone omosessuali," of October 1, 1986, in *L'Osservatore Romano*, 10/31/1986, p. 5, n. 1.

inclination should be considered as objectively disorderly" (n. 3).

Msgr. Ratzinger says that the act is intrinsically evil and that the inclination is objectively disorderly without being a sin properly speaking. This is in accordance with Catholic Doctrine.

The Cardinal also states: "Homosexual activity does not express a complementary union capable of transmitting life and, therefore, contradicts the vocation for an existence lived in that form of self-giving which, according to the Gospel, is the very essence of Christian life. This does not mean that homosexual persons are not often generous and do not give of themselves; but when they engage in homosexual activity, they reinforce in their souls a disorderly sexual inclination, itself characterized by self-complacency" (n. 7).

Thus, on affirming certain current principles of moral teaching, the Prefect of the Congregation for the Doctrine of the Faith begins to praise homosexuals — they are generous, they do give of themselves — which makes it appears as if he were seeking a right of citizenship for them.

This hypothesis is more strongly confirmed in the text below, where he writes: "It is firmly deplored that homosexual persons have been or still are the object of malevolent expressions and violent actions. Whenever such behavior takes place, it deserves to be condemned by the Shepherds of the Church. It reveals a lack of respect for others and violates the elementary principles upon which a wholesome civil conviviality is based. The dignity proper to each person must always be respected in words, actions, and laws." (n. 10)

Note that Msgr. Ratzinger advocates a legislation defending homosexuals from lack of respect or discrimination, that is, malevolent expressions, violent actions, etc.

Overall, one may say that this Instruction of the Holy See, although on one hand it condemns the sexual act as entirely evil from the moral standpoint, on the other hand defends homosexuals who openly declare themselves as such but do not practice the sexual act.

§ 35

* On July 24, 1992, *L'Osservatore Romano* published the **third document** of the same Congregation on the subject.[43] It is addressed to the Bishops of the United States but is undated. Its introduction says that the published version is a second writing carried out after consultation with the Bishops. More atypically, it says that the considerations in the document are not intended as an official instruction, but only as a resource for those who must assess legislation.

Its objective is, therefore, to orient the Bishops on what position to take regarding civil laws protecting homosexuals. That is to say, the boldest request made in the prior document becomes the premise of this one.

The document, published under the responsibility of Cardinal Ratzinger, says: "Homosexual persons, insofar as they are human persons, have the same rights as all other persons, including the right not to be treated in a way offensive to their personal dignity. Among other rights, all persons have a right to work, to be housed, etc. Nevertheless, these rights are not absolute. They can legitimately be limited by virtue of an objectively disorderly outward behavior" (n. 12).

It had earlier declared: "Taking into account the [person's] homosexual tendencies would not be discriminatory in certain cases:[44] for example, in cases regarding the custody or adoption of children or in cases regarding the choice of teachers of physical education and gymnastics and in the military service" (n. 11).

Further on, he makes a prudential warning: "To include the 'homosexual tendency' among issues over which it is illegal to discriminate can easily lead to upholding sexuality as a positive source of human rights .... To recognize homosexuality as a factor on the basis of which it is illegal to discriminate can easily, if not automatically, lead to legislative protection for, and

---

[43] CONGREGAZIONE PER LA DOTTRINA DELLA FEDE, "Alcune considerazioni concernenti la risposta a proposte di legge sulla non-discriminazione delle persone omosessuali," in *L'Osservatore Romano*, 7/24/1992, p. 4.

[44] The document presents a definition of 'tendency:' "An individual's sexual tendency generally is not noticed by others unless he publicly identifies himself as having this tendency or manifests it through some external behavior" (n. 14).

promotion of, homosexuality" (n. 13). Thus, it would not be advisable to take homosexuality as the basis for a legal right.

In its whole, the document advocates that homosexuals be given right of citizenship on the basis of human rights, but not on the basis of homosexuality. A certain contradiction remains in the concept of tendency. At times, it is taken to mean an inclination that is not manifested publicly, and at times as something that is perceived and may or may not be subject to a law.

Finally, there are two notions of discrimination against homosexuals. One is unjust, allegedly coming from a lack of respect for 'human rights.' Another is just, but it is ambiguous because it derives from the concept of 'homosexual tendency.' This just discrimination only becomes clear in the case of the examples given — the adoption of children, choosing teachers or physical educators, and in the military service.

§ 36   * A characteristic application of this ambiguity in the concept of homosexual tendency can be found in the short Allocution delivered by **Pope John Paul II** on the occasion of the approval of a marriage of homosexuals by the European Parliament. Indeed, he says: "Our thought turns toward the recent and well-known resolution approved by the European Parliament. In it, they do not simply limit themselves to the defense of persons with homosexual tendencies, refusing to allow unjust discriminations toward them. On this point, the Church is also in agreement, approves it, and makes it her own, since every human person is worthy of respect. What is morally inadmissible is the juridical approval of homosexual practice."[45]

Summarizing the concessions made, we have the following:

§ 37   * In the *first document* Cardinal Seper admits that the theories of modern psychology which claim that homosexuality is either a fruit of the ambience or part of the person's psychic makeup, but in both cases do not entail guilt, are well-founded.

---

[45] JOHN PAUL II, Allocution of the Angelus, February 20, 1994, published under the title "Con la risoluzione del Parlamento Europeo si è chiesto di legittimare un disordine morale," in *L'Osservatore Romano*, 2/21-22/1994, pp. 1, 5.

* In the name of pastoral service, he recommends that the Church's attitude toward homosexuals be one of support and understanding.

* He says that sexual faults are more easily committed without full consent and, therefore, are not sins; hence one must be prudent in passing judgment on the subjective culpability of such faults.

§ 38   * In the *second document* Cardinal Ratzinger launches an anathema, based on human rights, against those who discriminate against homosexuals by words, deeds, and laws.

§ 39   * In the *third document* Msgr. Ratzinger instructs Bishops to have legislators approve laws in favor of homosexuals based on human rights but not on homosexuality as such.

§ 40   To close this part of the exposition on conciliar and post-conciliar doctrine on homosexuality, we may say that, in addition to the numerous manifestations of tolerance toward this vice, in none of the documents quoted did the Holy See accuse homosexuality of being a vice contrary to nature, let alone call to mind that it is one of the sins that cry out to heaven and clamor to God for vengeance.

§ 41   On analogous doctrine, published under the responsibility of the U. S. National Conference of Catholic Bishops, the following documents can be consulted: Principles to Guide Confessors in Questions of Homosexuality (1973); To Live in Jesus Christ (1976); Called to Compassion and Responsibility (1989).[46]

*

3. The Homosexual Issue and the Catholic Church in the United States

§ 42   The reason we chose the United States to analyze the situation so far as this issue is concerned is that statistical data are more accessible there, probably due to the great welcome that American public opinion usually gives the publication of statistics. Perhaps people there talk more about homosexuality and there are more groups of this type of persons than in other

---

[46] *L'Osservatore Romano*, 7/11/1990, pp. 4f.

countries due to the general liberalism that characterized the formation of the United States, as well as to the characteristic of Americans to form associations more readily than other peoples.

Therefore, the overview below is not intended to classify the United States as any more or any less decadent than other countries. We simply take what is happening in the United States as an example of what is happening in the whole world.

Amplitude of the Phenomenon and Principal Movements

43   A newsletter of the Democratic Party on the 1979 political campaign in the United States (December 13, 1979), according to the book by Fr. Enrique Rueda, *The Homosexual Network,* said, "The gay vote is now so important in national [American] politics .... that no serious politician can ignore or ridicule it." The document gives the figure of 15 million homosexual Americans of voting age, an estimate confirmed by contributors to the political column of the *Washington Star*.[47]

44   A word should be said about this figure of 15 million. In the beginning of the '50s, an American biologist, Alfred Kinsey, published the result of a survey of 11,000 people on sex-related subjects. He began with the premise that, in sexual matters, people usually do not tell the truth when interviewed. So he looked for those who voluntarily wished to talk about the subject, which thus included persons primarily in marginal groups. The data collected in this study was in general use until last year. The applications of that study projected an estimated 10 percent of homosexuals in the population.[48] Today, that would mean about 25 million people.

However, in October 1994, a group of three researchers at the University of Chicago and one at New York State University published another study based on 3,500 interviews with selected people carried out by an authoritative public research institute. *Time* magazine deemed the new study provided "the first really scientific statistics in America."[49] The researchers

---

[47] Enrique RUEDA, *The Homosexual Network - Private Lives and Public Policy* (Old Greenwich, CT: Devin Adair Co., 1983), p. 134.

[48] Philip ELMER-DEWITT, "Now for the Truth About Americans and Sex," in *Time*, 10/17/1994, pp. 44, 46, 50.

[49] Ibid., p. 46.

contested the Kinsey method as being based on groups deemed atypical. But they also generally recognized, as the weak point of their research, that the sexual topic — especially homosexuality — inhibits people. One of them says: "There is probably much more homosexual activity than what people are saying."[50] They estimate the homosexual population in the United States at 2 percent, or about five million people.

On the basis of this percentage, these scholars concluded, among other things, that AIDS is not so grave as it is trumped up to be and needs to be fought only in the so-called high risk groups. This caused indignation in certain public health-related sectors. The former head of the National Commission on AIDS, for example, commenting on the study, quipped: "The message is shocking and runs against the whole history of the epidemic."[51]

One sees, therefore, that both surveys are controversial. If we want to draw an average between the two — since one claims 25 million and the other five million — we would have the 15 million mentioned by Fr. Rueda in his book.

In any case, even taking into account the most conservative estimates, a five million figure suffices to show that homosexuality has become a phenomenon of apocalyptic proportions.

§ 45   Among the principal organizations of homosexuals in the U.S. are the so-called Catholic movements: the New Ways Ministry run by a priest and a nun, and Dignity, founded by Jesuit priest John McNeill in 1971.[52] Dignity has some 100 chapters in the U.S. and Canada.[53]

Support of the Hierarchy and the Situation of Homosexuality in the American Clergy

§ 46   * The first symposium on "Homosexuality and the Catholic Church," promoted by the New Ways Ministry, whose

---

[50] Stuart MICHAELS, Statement, Ibid., p. 48.

[51] June OSBORN, Statement, Ibid., p. 49

[52] E. RUEDA, op. cit., pp. 270, 362.

[53] Ibid., p. 362.

speakers were all in favor of homosexuality, was held at the Holy Trinity Missionary Seminary at Silver Springs, Maryland, from November 20 to 22, 1981. Twenty-two religious organizations, nearly all Catholic, supported the organization of the event.[54]

* The National Conference of Catholic Bishops (NCCB) and the United States Catholic Conference (USCC), which comprises the central Church bureaucracy and is the official arm of NCBB, have supported on various occasions the movement or topic of homosexuality. Fr. Robert Nugent, director of the New Ways Ministry and one of the leaders of the homosexual movement, served as a consultant to the USCC. The NCCB's Department of Education published a document entitled "Planning for the Single Young Adult Ministry: Directives for Ministerial Outreach," a work partially written by the New Ways Ministry.[55]

* The efforts of Dignity to influence the NCCB began in 1977. The key figure of NCCB's Office of Public Affairs and Information became president of Dignity. This movement's relationships with the NCCB gradually grew more intense as time went by. Milestones in this process are: the July 1981 meeting of Dignity's president, Frank Scheuren, with the Archbishop of San Francisco, at the time, Msgr. John Quinn, president of the NCCB; another meeting with Bishop Thomas Kelly, who held an important post at the Bishops' Conference; Dignity's exchange of correspondence with the next NCCB president, Archbishop John Roach.[56] At the meeting with Msgr. Quinn, according to a Dignity newsletter, "The archbishop has requested that Dignity .... submit to him proposals that show as to how joint cooperation can be accomplished in the day-to-day pastoral ministry to our people. He expressed that this would be the beginning of an ongoing dialogue between the parties."[57]

* A booklet published by the New Ways Ministry, *Time to Speak*, presented a list of sixteen Bishops, including Cardinal Krol of Philadelphia and the then Cardinal Dearden of Detroit,

---

[54] Ibid., pp. 293ff.

[55] Ibid., pp. 306-310.

[56] Ibid., pp. 308f.

[57] Ibid., pp. 323f.

who in some way had benefited the homosexual movement.[58] Lending support to the movement, a letter from Msgr. Raymond Hunthausen, then Bishop of Seattle, stands out. It encouraged the efforts of the homosexual movement to make the state's House of Representatives approve a law granting special privileges to homosexuals. A letter from the Archbishop of Milwaukee, Msgr. Rembert Weakland, also spoke favorably about the approval of a law to protect the 'basic human rights' of homosexuals.[59] The booklet, *Time to Speak,* also contains a list of 38 Catholic associations that support homosexuals.[60]

§ 50
    * Dignity estimates that 75 percent of its meetings are held at Church properties.[61] Some homosexual parties have also taken place on Catholic premises, such as Dignity's ball, a "black and white dress" where people of the same sex dance with each other. That ball took place at Rosary Academy in Sparkill, New York on September 12, 1981. Another example was "Cabaret night," held by the same movement in the auditorium of Saint Francis School in New York City on April 7, 1982 — an Ash Wednesday.[62]

§ 51
    * The magazine *Newsweek* reports: "In one of the very few studies based on reliable data — 1,500 interviews between 1960 and 1985 — psychologist Richard Sipe of Maryland, a former priest, concludes that close to 20 percent of the 57,000 Catholic priests in the United States are homosexual and half of them are sexually active. According to Sipe, the number of homosexual priests has significantly increased since 1978; other therapists believe the real number today [1987] may be around 40 percent.[63]

§ 52
    * "The number of priests contaminated with AIDS in the United States grows daily. This disclosure was released in a documentary made by the Conference of Men Religious, an en-

---

[58] Ibid., p. 316, on which can be found the said list with the date on which each Bishop gave his support.

[59] Ibid., pp. 319f.

[60] Ibid., pp. 326f.

[61] Ibid., p. 321.

[62] Ibid., p. 329.

[63] *Newsweek* (New York), "Gays in the Clergy," 2/23/1987

tity that represents 25,000 of the 27,000 American Catholic priests. Non-official estimates put the number of homosexual priests at about 40 percent.[64]

Time magazine published statements by Fr. Robert Nugent to the effect that "a U. S. survey of vocation directors in men's religious orders showed that, from 1981 to 1985, five percent of candidates accepted for the priesthood identified themselves to the church as being homosexual in orientation.

"Perhaps the most emotional debates are those now occurring within the Roman Catholic Church. Father Andrew Greeley, the irrepressible U. S. sociologist and novelist, complained in a recent article that regard for priestly celibacy is being undermined by a 'national network' of actively homosexual clergy. 'In some dioceses, certain rectories have become lavender houses,' he grumbled. Theologian Richard McBrien, of the University of Notre Dame, contends that homosexuality is so widespread that 'heterosexual males are deciding in ever larger numbers not even to consider the priesthood.'"[65]

"Another clergyman," reports the journalist, "who is a regional director of priestly education in one of the larger men's orders, explained to *Time* the justification for his private homosexual life during recent years. 'We'll never know what is right or wrong until we open up the issue and look at people's experiences,' he said. 'I don't see any contradiction between having an intimate relationship and a total commitment to Christ.' This prominent priest said his superiors have been quietly aware of his long-running, but not live-in, relationship with a fellow gay. They expect him to be judicious, he says, not to change."[66]

* To cite a more recent case, let us look at an article printed in the Catholic newspaper, *The Wanderer* (February 23, 1995):

"Among those entering the ground floor of San Francisco's St. Mary's Cathedral on a Saturday evening, as Mass

---

[64] *Folha de S. Paulo*, "AIDS-1," 1/15/1989.

[65] Richard Nugent OSTLING, "The Battle over Gay Clergy - Demands for toleration shake many North American churches," in *Time*, 11/13/1989, pp. 44f.

[66] Ibid.

was being held above, was a tall Asian gentleman wearing a stunning scarlet cocktail dress and long spiked red high heels, arm-in-arm with two shorter men. And as Mass-goers walked out of the cathedral after the 5:30 p.m. Mass, it was hard not to notice affectionate male couples in the cathedral parking lot, hugging and kissing. And a continent and an ocean away, in Vatican offices, fax machines were buzzing as angry San Francisco Catholics informed Rome of the latest sacrilege in their city.

"Two weeks ago, on Feb. 11th, San Francisco's Catholics cathedral was the site for a major celebration of homosexual power in California. The chief political, religious, and social leaders of the homosexual rights movement in the city, state, and nation mingled with their constituents at a fund-raiser for pro-homosexual causes. The scandal and outrage .... show to what extent the American Church has bought into the homosexual agenda .... The event at St. Mary's Cathedral Conference Center was billed as a *Saints Alive* awards celebration and a celebrity auction to benefit the exclusively homosexual Metropolitan Community Church's social service programs. .... The live auction was conducted by two local gay comedians, whose patter was constant, clever, crass, and peppered with jokes about sodomy. Suzy Berger, an improvisational and stand-up comedienne, ripped off a barrage of smutty homosexual jokes, bathroom humor, asides about 'lesbian culture,' and lurid comments. .... When a painting, *Study with Fruits and Flowers*, seemed not to be getting many bids, he offered to throw in the male model with the deal. The model then turned his backside to the audience, and took a bow. The audience whooped and hollered in excitement. The more outrageous the merchandise, the cruder the MCs were, and the louder the audience. .... When two one-year scholarships to The Child Unique Montessori School did not receive many bids, the auctioneer offered to throw in one, and then two, sperm donations to lesbians who might like to have a child to use the scholarship."[67]

The "McNeil Affair"

§ 56

American Jesuit John McNeill, who holds a doctorate from the University of Louvain and is the founder of the homo-

---

[67] *The Wanderer*, "San Francisco Cathedral Is Site For 'Gay Power' Bash," 2/23/1995.

sexual movement Dignity, wrote a book making a theological defense of this vice against nature.

As far as we know, the work has become an historic milestone on the subject of homosexuality. Other than the audacity shown by a Catholic priest in publishing a book in defense of this vice, the work can be considered the strongest base for what has since been termed 'homosexual theology.'

On manifestations of support and criticism that preceded the publishing of his book, McNeill recounts: "After a long wait, a definitive and revised version of the manuscript was sent to Rome in 1975. The answer finally arrived in October. Fr. Arrupe delegated the authority to give the *imprimi potest* to the New York Provincial of the Society of Jesus. He said that he had no objection to the publication so long as certain suggestions and guidelines were followed."[68]

Soon after Fr. Arrupe made these suggestions, the Congregation for the Doctrine of the Faith published *Declaration on Certain Questions Related to Sexual Ethics*. McNeill communicated to his superiors the interpretation of the *Declaration* he had made in his book. A reply came in a letter (January 28, 1976) from the Jesuit Provincial, Fr. Eamon Taylor, stating: "In my opinion the adjustments you introduced in your manuscript, as we had agreed in a conversation on November 10, respond to the recommendations of the Superior General of September 19 and .... as a result, I am pleased to be able to grant you the *imprimi potest*, with today's date."[69]

The adjustments suggested by Fr. Arrupe and referred to by Fr. Taylor were probably rather superficial, as McNeill later writes, "I want to assure my readers that at no point was I asked to change or alter my ideas or convictions in any way to be granted official permission for publication."[70]

---

[68] J. McNEILL, op. cit., pp. 12f.

[69] Eamon TAYLOR, Letter responding to Fr. John McNeill, January 28, 1976, Ibid.

[70] Ibid.

In November 1986 — that is, ten years after the publication of the work — the news broke that Fr. John McNeill had been punished with dismissal from the Society of Jesus on account of his preaching in favor of homosexuality (Marjorie HYER, "Gay-rights Priest Faces Expulsion," in *The Washington Post*, 11/8/1986; *Jornal do Brasil*, Rio de Janeiro, 11/9/1986).

On that occasion, the press reported that already in 1977 the Vatican had revoked approval of the book, *The Church and the Homosexual* (M. HYER, Ibid.). That measure was an initiative of Cardinal Franjo Seper, then Prefect of the Congregation for the Doctrine of the Faith, who had also forbidden Fr. McNeill to speak out. After nine years of silence, the General of the Society of Jesus, Fr. Peter Hans Kolvenbach, gave Fr. McNeill the choice of ceasing his homosexual preaching and religious assistance to the movement or of quitting the ranks of the Society of Jesus. McNeill preferred to leave the Jesuit Order rather than give up his ideas (Ibid.).

The silence previously imposed on McNeill had little practical result, since the public at large was unaware of it; the priest's book continued to be sold largely in English and translated into other languages, arboring the approval of the Jesuit Provincial in New York and the good graces of Fr. Arrupe, then Superior General; for its part, the homosexual movement Dignity, which he founded, has not been hindered in its expansion.

Undoubtedly, the punishment of 1986 that dismissed the priest from the Society of Jesus is a moral and disciplinary sanction. But, from another standpoint, it is also a political disengagement from McNeill's ideas on the part of the Order. Now the priest is free to continue his work and to speak at will without compromising the Society. No word ever came out in the press about any threats by the Holy See to pronounce McNeill a heretic or excommunicate him, thus hindering his freedom of movement and expression outside the Order. On the contrary, the record shows only the surprising benevolence of New York Jesuit Provincial, Fr. David Tolan, who calls the homosexual priest "an extraordinarily good man" who "tried to stick to the letter of the law established for him" (Ibid.).

Fr. Tolan added that McNeill continues to be a priest whose situation, to be regularized, needs only for a Bishop to accept him in his Diocese.

Therefore, in practical terms, and taking into account Fr. Tolan's benevolence, one should ask whether at least several heavy-weight Jesuits granted McNeill the freedom to continue his preaching without compromising the Society of Jesus.

The Society of Jesus, *servatis servandis*, adopted a similar political procedure in relation to Fr. Urs von Balthasar, who in 1950 was also released from Jesuit obedience to be able to devote himself more fully to the foundation of his Secular Institute, the *Johannesgemeinschaft*. At the time a pioneering and audacious initiative, the institute is viewed today as one of the probable blueprints for the Church of the

In addition to denying Catholic Doctrine on homosexuality, McNeill contends that this vice should play a social role of equilibrium between a masculine culture and feminist demands.[71] In this sense, the Jesuit theologian makes his own a comment by Jung on the social 'mission' of homosexuals: "This [homosexuality] gives a great capacity for friendship, which creates bonds of admirable tenderness between men and can even rescue friendship between sexes from the limbo of the impossible. An individual can have a good taste and aesthetic sensibility nourished by the presence of a feminine vein... He often possesses a great wealth of religious sentiments, which helps lead him to practice the *ecclesia spiritualis*."[72]

Homosexuality allegedly also has a great role to play in the quest for peace, since, lacking the decisive and combative characteristics of a man, homosexuals could more easily control violence. Furthermore, because of his 'sweetness,' the homosexual is very inclined to serve others, and his 'femininity' leads him to make a contribution to humanity in the appreciation of aesthetic and religious values.[73] As he describes the role of the homosexual in the religious ambit, McNeill points to Our Lord Jesus Christ as model.[74]

The Chicago Symposium

The scandal of homosexuality in the Church took on hitherto unheard-of proportions when homosexuals assembled in

---

future... Von Balthasar himself confirms this: "The split of which I had a premonition took place in fact when I faced my duty to obey a formal order of Saint Ignatius, to abandon — much to my displeasure — my spiritual motherland, the Society of Jesus, in order to achieve a kind of prolongation of his idea in the world" (Hans Urs von BALTHASAR, "Von Balthasar: la mia opera è abbozzata più che terminata," in L'Osservatore Romano, 6/24/1984, p. 4).

Are they not using the same procedure with McNeill?

[71] J. McNEILL, op. cit. pp. 188ff., 195.

[72] Carl Gustav JUNG, The Collected Works (New York: Pantheon, 1959), vol. IX, P. I, pp. 86f., Ibid., pp. 194f.

[73] J. McNEILL, op. cit., pp. 198-204.

[74] Ibid., pp. 208f.

Chicago on March 27-29, 1992, with the support and presence of some Bishops.

The symposium was sponsored by 91 diocesan offices and religious communities. About 39 percent of the participants held leadership posts in religious Orders, parishes and other institutions; 63 percent were priests, nuns, and religious.[75]

The *Catholic News Service* distributed a press communique on the meeting entitled "Bishops Urge Less Rigid Church Attitude Toward Homosexuals." It reads: "Three Catholic bishops speaking at a forum on 'Lesbian and Gay People and Catholicism' said that they hoped pastoral leaders would adopt less rigid attitudes toward homosexual men and women. On March 26, Bishop Kenneth E. Untener of Saginaw, Mich., Bishop William A. Hughes of Covington, Ky., and auxiliary Bishop Thomas J. Gumbleton of Detroit addressed a symposium in Chicago, organized by the New Ways Ministry. The organization .... seeks understanding for and acceptance of gays and lesbians in the Catholic community. Bishop Hughes, who chaired the U. S. bishops' task force that drafted "The Many Faces of AIDS: A Gospel Response," said that .... Christians are called to be a people of compassion, aware of the difficulties and the struggles people face. He likened the church's changing pastoral approach to gays and lesbians to its experience in embracing divorcees and survivors of suicide. He said that such an outreach obviously did not endorse divorce or suicide."[76]

---

[75] Robert McCLORY, "Bishops Buck Criticism, Attend Gay Symposium in Chicago," in *The National Catholic Reporter*, 4/10/1992.

[76] Keith PICHER, "Bishops Urge Less Rigid Church Attitude Toward Homosexuals," in *Catholic News Service*, 3/31/1992.

This news release, of which we left out several paragraphs, was published by the newspaper of the Archdiocese of Chicago, *The New World*, on 4/3/1992 and by innumerable other papers in the U.S., such as *The Long Island Catholic*, 4/1/1992; *Mississippi Today*, Jackson, 4/3/1992; *The Messenger*, Belleville, 4/3/1992; *The Catholic Free Press*, Worcester, 4/3/1992; *The Catholic Review*, Baltimore, 4/8/1992; *Catholic Herald*, Milwaukee, 4/9/1992; *Catholic Courier*, Rochester, 4/9/1992; *The Monitor*, Trenton, 4/9/1992; *The Message*, Evansville, 4/10/1992; *The Catholic Sentinel*, Portland, 4/10/1992; *Catholic Telegraph*, Cincinnati, 4/10/1992; *The Florida Catholic*, Miami, 4/10/1992; *New Catholic Explorer*, Joliet, 4/10/1992; *Catholic East Texas*, Tyler, 4/10/1992; *The Green Bay Catholic Compass*, 4/10/1992; *The Catholic Post*, Peoria, 4/12/1992; *Northwest Indiana Catholic*, 4/12/1992; *The Catholic Virginian*, Richmond, 4/13/1992; *The Catholic Messenger*, Davenport, 4/16/1992; *Twin Circle*,

In a comprehensive report for *The Wanderer*, Eric Bower adds other important details:[77]

* Bishop Gumbleton was enthusiastically applauded by the 500 plus participants when he said: "I am proud to be here! Pleased to be here! And honored to be with you!" He also said: "Be patient and ready to wait until the bishops and priests show compassion, love, and care for all those in the gay community."

* Outside the main conference room, various display tables were set up featuring literature, tapes, and other information on homosexuality. A display table sponsored by Dignity also offered literature advertising the services of AGLO (Joseph Cardinal Bernardin's personally supervised Archdiocesan Gay and Lesbian Organization). The same table offered pornographic homosexual literature.

* The Bishop of Covington, Msgr. William Hughes, celebrated a strange 'mass' for the meeting's participants in the ballroom of the Westin Hotel. Coffee was served before it began. The makeshift sanctuary consisted of a platform with a stack chair and a small table on it. On the table was a punch bowl. No crucifix. The wine for 'mass' was a gallon of Gallo, served in chalices. The bread was coarse and falling in crumbs. Participants served themselves unceremoniously. After the 'mass,' wine cups, plates, and napkins were left in the ballroom.[78]

* Richard Freeman, president of the Catholic Action League, described the conference as "perhaps the most blatant and dramatic example we have yet seen of how far gone some of our bishops are and how little discipline is being exercised by the Vatican .... Our renegade bishops and Cardinal seem to fear nothing and no one, least of all God. We are moving very, very

---

4/19/1992; *The Providence Visitor*, Rhode Island, 4/23/1992; *The Saint Cloud Visitor*, 4/23/1992; *Acadiana Catholic*, Lafayette, May 1992; *Inland Catholic*, San Bernardino & Riverside Counties, May 1992.

[77] Eric BOWER, "Give Lip Service to Rome, Encourage Dissident Homosexuals," in *The Wanderer*, 4/9/1992.

[78] See also news item in *The Eternal Call*, Park Forest, Ill, Pentecost 1992.

close to a formal break with Rome and a complete disintegration of the structure of the Church in this nation."

Freeman said that it was no accident that Chicago was picked for the site of the conference. Under Cardinal Bernardin, he observed, it has become notorious for its inner-Church homosexual activism. According to a well-informed source, Cardinal Bernardin was invited to address the conference. However, perhaps because he was embroiled in a priestly pedophilia scandal,[79] he declined the invitation. But he gave it his formal blessing and singled out his three brother bishops who attended the conference for special praise.[80]

---

[79] Accused of sexually molesting a seminarian in 1975 (*Veja,* "Processado," 11/17/1993), an event that had worldwide repercussions (*Corriere della Sera,* "Ricevuto dal Papa cardinale accusato di abusi sessuali," 1/5/1994), Cardinal Joseph Bernardin was acquitted for lack of evidence (Kenneth L. WOODWARD, "Was It Real or Memories?," in *Newsweek,* 3/14/1994).

[80] a. The Vatican's reaction to these events in North America was one of extreme moderation. In July 1992, the Congregation for the Doctrine of the Faith released the document it had sent to the U.S. Bishops justifying, as we have seen, certain limitations to the civil rights of homosexuals and reaffirming principles already issued on the matter in the letter the same Congregation had sent the world Episcopate in 1986 on the subject (Congregation for the Doctrine of the Faith, "Alcune considerazioni concernenti la risposta a proposte di legge sulla non-discriminazione delle persone omosessuali," 2nd version, July 23, 1992, in *L'Osservatore Romano,* 7/24/1992).

The "Considerazioni" were published with small alterations (Ibid.), along with comments by Vatican spokesman Navarro-Valls. He said that the document "was not intended as a public and official instruction .... but to help those who have to evaluate projected bills on the matter" (Joaquim NAVARRO-VALLS, Statements to the press, in *Avvenire,* "Chiarezza, non discriminazione," 7/24/1992; "Responding to Legislative Proposals on Discriminations Against Homosexuals," in *Origins - CNS Documentary Service,* 8/6/1992, pp. 173-177).

The reaction of American Bishops to this Vatican document can be gauged by looking at this article of the *San Francisco Chronicle* entitled: "S.F. Archdiocese Opposes Vatican Letter on Gay Bias Law:" "Local Roman Catholic church leaders said yesterday that they will continue to oppose laws that discriminate against homosexuals — despite a Vatican missive declaring that gays and lesbians do not have the same civil rights as heterosexuals" (Don LATTIN, in *San Francisco Chronicle,* 7/25/1992).

Homosexuals' "Religious Orders"

58   Special mention should be made of a little publicized phenomenon, the foundation of so-called religious orders exclusively for Catholic homosexuals. Such 'orders,' described in the book, *The Homosexual Network,* still had not been recognized by the Church near the end of 1982 when it was published. Some of the main groups include the following:

59   Agape Community — a religious extension of Dignity. Its members may, if they so desire, make promises of poverty, chastity and obedience. "Lovers," says the rule, "are welcome together or without their partners .... While ideally chastity or love commitments are to be encouraged, the community is open to all who seek to be witnesses to Christ."[81]

The article goes on to say that the Holy See document "contradicts past statements by San Francisco Archbishop John Quinn. .... Quinn was on vacation yesterday .... but the Rev. Robert McElroy, the archbishop's representative on the archdiocese's Justice and Peace Commission, said, 'There is no change in the archidiocese's policy. .... But aides to several of the bishops said they doubt the Vatican document will lead to any change in their tolerance policies toward gays. 'Most of the bishops would rather just ignore this,' said one priest, a seasoned observer of the American bishops' conference" (Ibid.).

Archbishop Rembert G. Weakland of Milwaukee, a prominent leader of the Church's liberal wing, "noted that the statement carried no signature and that there was no indication that it had been seen by the Pope" (Peter STEINFELS, "Vatican Condones Gay-Rights Limits," in *The New York Times,* 7/18/1992).

b. Practical measures opposed to the Holy See's guidelines were not long in coming. As a matter of fact, a symptomatic example is the work carried out by Archbishop John Roach and the Minnesota Catholic Conference (MCC) supporting the law barring discrimination against homosexuals in employment, housing, education, and public accommodations in that state. Not only did the MCC support passage of the bill, it helped to author the bill. MCC executive director Msgr. James Habiger urged approval of the bill, stating that "the Catholic Church recognizes and affirms the human dignity and worth of gay persons and calls for the protection of their basic human rights" (James HABIGER, Argumentation in support of the law preventing discrimination of homosexuals, in Paul LIKOUDIS, "Minnesota Catholic Conference Helps Write and Pass Homosexual Rights Bill," in *The Wanderer,* 4/1/1993).

[81] E. RUEDA, op. cit., p. 350.

§ 60   Emmaus House, formerly called St. Matthew Community. Its rule says it is an entity made up primarily of Catholic homosexuals who serve the Church in a variety of ministries. Any member who wishes may make private vows of celibacy, obedience and poverty under the orientation of the spiritual director and the approval of the Diocesan Bishop.[82]

§ 61   Christian Community Association. It has several degrees of spirituality, of which the most advanced requires a monastic lifestyle. Vows of poverty, obedience, and chastity were rebaptized with the names sharing, commitment, and charity. A postulant must recite this formula: "I believe that homosexuality is a gift from God and that we have an obligation to use our gifts in the service of humanity and that this is one way in which we return our gift to God, through religious community."[83]

§ 62   Other similar organizations: Augustinians of Charity, The Order of Transformation, the Morning Star Community.[84]

*

4. The Vice of Pedophilia

§ 63   The problem of pedophilia, this moral aberration that includes cowardice, cruelty, and homosexuality, has been causing devastation in ecclesiastical circles. News items in magazines and papers portray a rising tide of scandal caused by priests who abuse children.

Some widely publicized facts permit us to gauge how deeply this moral wound has affected more than just a few ecclesiastics. It appears as another serious consequence of the liberal customs that have installed themselves in the Clergy largely due to the conciliar reforms.

§ 64   A terrible scandal broke out in the United States in 1985 when Fr. Gilbert Gauthe, of the Diocese of Lafayette, Louisiana,

---

[82] Ibid., pp. 351, 581.

[83] Ibid., p. 352.

[84] Ibid., pp. 351ff.

confessed to have sexually abused 37 boys. He was accused of 23 counts of rape, pornography, and crimes against nature.[85]

Cases of sexual abuse of children – which justly caused indignation in Catholic public opinion – tripled in a short time. The next year, 1986, a contributor to *The National Catholic Reporter* (NCR), wrote: "Since the NCR report on pedophilia cases involving Catholic priests a year ago, the number of priests accused, indicted or convicted of sexual misconduct with adolescents has more than tripled. Fr. Thomas Doyle, a Dominican who worked at the Apostolic Nunciature in Washington, speaking at a meeting of canonists in Morristown, New Jersey early this month, figured that [from 1985 to 1986] there were from 40 to 50 cases in the U.S. 'This is the most serious problem the Church has faced in the last few centuries,'" he said.[86]

Another contributor to the same paper comments: "The incendiary and painful experience [of the Diocese] of Lafayette [where Fr. Gauthe's affair took place] was a mere lightning launching a disquieting, and at times sinister light, on the problem of child abuse in the Catholic Church as a whole in the United States, and that findings on a national scale can be devastating. Many dioceses are no longer able to obtain insurance covering sexual infractions of the Clergy, and some sources indicate that penal lawsuits for sexual abuse may cost the Church one billion dollars in the next ten years – especially if preventive and corrective measures are not taken."[87]

In 1989 the United States Catholic Conference assembled for one week in Baltimore. One of the topics studied was the "pedophilia of some priests and bishops."

This topic of pedophilia, a journalist says, "is the most worrisome one: after all, 300 cases of priests who have sexually molested minors have been reported to the authorities, and the Church has had to cough up 50 million dollars in settlements with the victims in order to avoid greater scandal. .... Right at the opening of the meeting, the Catholic movement Open

---

[85] "Padre americano será julgado por tara sexual," *Zero Hora* (Porto Alegre, Brazil), 10/14/1985.

[86] Thomas DOYLE, Statements on pedophilia in the USA, in Jason BERRY, "Dioceses React to Deepening Dilemma," in *The National Catholic Reporter*, 5/30/1986.

[87] Tim McCARTHY, "Church Still on Trial in Pedophilia Crisis," Ibid.

Church, founded in Washington, accused one of the bishops present of having engaged in sexual relations with a thirteen-year-old boy seven years earlier. The victim's mother .... appeared at a press interview to confirm the accusation. A second denunciation was made by a student just over 20 years of age, who disclosed that when in high school he had had sexual relations with a priest (who's now a bishop), who paid him for it. The young man also claimed that the priest paid for several trips so they could meet in some other town. The bishops counter-attacked with a communique saying that these denunciations had already been examined by the representative of the Pope himself in the United States, Archbishop Pio Laghi, and that no solid evidence had been found."[88]

§ 67   In 1992 the number of churchmen accused of pedophilia rose to 400, and Church legal expenditures reached $400 million.[89]

Such figures keep on rising. A writer in *Newsweek* notes this about child molestation by priests: "While allegations have been lodged against an estimated 400 priests since 1982, some churchmen extrapolate that as many as 2,500 priests have molested children or teenagers."[90]

Some people claim such figures are even higher: "Precise data are lacking, but the author of a book entitled *Lead Us Not Into Temptation* estimated that from 1983 to this day, 400 priests have been sued in penal or civil courts. Richard Sipe, who left the priesthood and works as a psychotherapist at John Hopkins School of Medicine, calculated that 6 percent [that is, 3,180] of the 53,000 American priests have had sexual contacts with minors. He figured that over the last few years the Church has paid between 200 to 500 million dollars in legal fees and compensation to families. The price of silence."[91]

---

[88] José Meirelles PASSOS, "Acusações de sexo e racismo envolvem Bispos americanos," in *O Globo*, 11/7/1989.

[89] Data taken from the book of Jason BERRY entitled *Lead Us Not Into Temptation* (New York: Doubleday, 1992), in K. L. WOODWARD, "The Sins of the Fathers," in *Newsweek*, 6/1/1992, p. 57; Jemez SPRINGS, "Sins of the Fathers," in *The Economist*, 6/18/1992, p. 50.

[90] Aric PRESS, "Priests and Abuse", in *Newsweek*, 8/16/1993, p. 40.

[91] Rodolfo BRANCOLI, "Linea verde contro preti pedofili," in *Corriere della Sera*, 9/24/1992. Randall SAMBORN, "Priest Playing Hardball to Battle Abuse Charges," in *The National Law Journal*, July 1994.

Another source confirms this and adds more details: "According to a survey recently published in the American press, cases of sexual molestation occurring in American parishes over the last 20 years reportedly involve from 2,000 to 4,000 priests and about 100,000 victims, mostly women and children."[92]

A more recent publication estimates that Church expenditures for victim compensation in the U.S. have reached $650 million.[93]

In **Canada**, Fr. Denis Vadeboncoeur, pastor of St. Benedict Parish in Sainte-Foy, was accused of molesting four adolescents on counts of gross indecency, sexual aggression, and sodomy. The priest admitted his guilt.[94]

Sectors of public opinion in **Brazil** were indignant and dismayed over the scandal of Brazilian priest Frederico Cunha, found guilty of homosexuality and accused of homicide in the Island of Madeira, **Portugal**. After trying to seduce a 15-year-old boy, he threw the boy off a cliff, killing him. The priest is said to have set up a false alibi. He alleged that at the time of the crime, he was with another 19-year-old adolescent, his godson and a homosexual partner. He was condemned to 12 years in prison for homicide and another 18 months for a homosexual attempt on a minor.[95]

The April 1995 *Adista* bulletin carries this news on the Spanish Catholic Hierarchy: "**Spain** is now treading the same

---

[92] Orazio la ROCCA, "Wojtyla: 'Piango I preti tentati dai vizi del sesso,'" in *La Repubblica*, 12/22/1993; *Corriere della Sera*, "Molestie, mea culpa dei vescovi," 11/18/1994.

[93] Alessio ALTICHERI, "In Irlanda la Chiesa si scusa per pedofilia," in *Corriere della Sera*, 10/10/1995.

[94] Louise LEMIEX, "Selon un psychiatre – le père Vadeboncoeur victime d'un 'dérapage' émotionnel," in *Le Soleil* (Quebec), 8/23/1985.

[95] Cristina DURAN, "Padre brasileiro é condenado em Portugal," in *O Estado de S. Paulo*, 3/11/1993; "Padre brasileiro deve recorrer da sentença," in *O Estado de S. Paulo*, 3/22/1993; Mario PRATA, "Senhor Cunha ou Fred do caniçal?," Ibid.; *Veja*, "Pecados na sacristia," 3/17/1993, p. 83.

path taken in the United States: the scourge of sexual molestation by members of the clergy appears to be spreading like an oil slick. Two cardinals and five bishops are said to be guilty of concealing a network for corrupting minors which involves priests. There are reports of rapes and the sexual abuse of women and psychopaths. The accusation was made by writer and journalist Pepe Rodriguez, who wrote a book on the topic entitled *La vida sexual del clero*. .... The accusation, which was made as the book was launched on March 7 .... reports first and last names: Narcis Jubany, Cardinal Emeritus of Barcelona, Cardinal Ricardo Maria Carles, the present Archbishop of Barcelona, with his three auxiliary Bishops, Msgr. Carlos Soler, Msgr. Jaime Traserra, and Msgr. Juan-Enric Vives, stand accused of supporting the network. But it does not stop here: Rodriguez also made accusations against the Bishop of Cartagena, Msgr. Javier Azagra .... and denounced the Bishop of Cuenca, Msgr. José Guerra Campos, for covering up cases of sexual abuse perpetrated by a priest who was guilty, among other things, of raping a mentally handicapped person."[96]

§ 70   In **Austria,** the 'Gröer affair' was a highly publicized scandal. Here is a brief overview:

On March 26, 1995, *Profil,* a Viennese weekly with a circulation of 100,000, published the accusations of agronomic engineer Josef Hartmann, a former seminarian who had been in Hollabrunn during the time Hans Hermann Gröer was a professor there. Hartmann accused Msgr. Gröer of the crime of pedophilia between 1972 and 1976.[97] The text of the interview was said to have been sent to Msgr. Gröer three days before it was published. The Cardinal reportedly failed to answer.[98]

By April 3, the number of ex-alumni who were accusing the Cardinal of pedophilia had risen to nine. A Benedictine priest, Fr. Udo Fischer, said that in 1971 Msgr. Gröer had tried to seduce him, a fact that he had reported to the competent authorities in 1985. Nonetheless, eleven months later, Gröer was

---

[96] *Adista,* "In Spagna due cardinale e cinque vescovi accusati di silenzio sugli abusi di minori e psicolabili," 4/1/1995.

[97] "Ero seminarista, l'arcivescovo abusò di me," *Corriere della Sera,* 3/27/1995.

[98] Francesco STRAZZARI, "Di caso in caso," in *Il Regno,* Bologna, May 1995, p. 264.

designated Archbishop of Vienna.[99] In April of 1995, another newspaper, *Bild*, narrated – with details that lacked all decorum and decency - the accusations of five witnesses against the Cardinal.[100] On April 5, 1995, Cardinal Gröer was reelected to the presidency of the Austrian Bishops' Conference. One day later, Msgr. Gröer resigned the post. A public opinion poll showed that 62 percent of Austrians believed the Cardinal should relinquish all official duties,[101] and a growing number of personages suggested that he retire.[102]

On April 13, the Vatican named Msgr. Christoph Schönborn as *coadjutor*, or assistant with the right to succeed Cardinal Gröer.[103] On April 22, the news broke that several women were also accusing the Cardinal of Vienna of having molested them as children. The women claimed that he had taken them to his home on the pretext of giving spiritual direction. Theologian Adolph Holl told *Der Spiegel* that the news caused no surprise among the churchmen of Vienna, who were already aware of "Gröer's weakness for adolescents." A public opinion survey showed that 81 percent of Austrians wanted Cardinal Gröer to be removed from office.[104]

On August 1, 1995 a journalist of the *Corriere della Sera* published an article reporting that a spokesman for the Austrian homosexual movement Hosi, Kurt Krickler, said that one-fourth of all the members of the country's Bishops' Conference practiced the sin of Sodom and Gomorrha. One of the accused was Msgr. Christoph von Schönborn, whom the Pope had called to replace Cardinal Gröer when he was accused of pedophilia. "I hope to disclose it tomorrow," said Krickler. "In a press conference we will announce five names, but I still don't know which

---

[99] Vivianne SCHNITZER, "Más denuncias de homosexualidad contra el cardenal Gröer," in *El País*, 4/3/1995.

[100] "Neuen Zeugen im Sex-Skandal," *Bild*, 4/5/1995.

[101] "Vienna, il cardinale cede," *Corriere della Sera*, 4/7/1995.

[102] F. STRAZZARI, op. cit. p. 265.

[103] Celso ITIBERÊ, "Escândalos sexuais que envolvem padres põem Vaticano na defensiva," in *O Globo*, 4/14/1995; R. N. OSTLING, "An Unholy Holy Week," in *Time*, 4/24/1995.

[104] Alfredo VENTURI, "Vienna ora ripudia il Cardinale Gröer," in *Corriere della Sera*, 4/22/1995.

ones. The list is very long. We will publish names picked at random at the last moment."[105]

§ 72   Referring to the suit against Joseph Louis Cardinal Bernardin of Chicago, who was absolved because his accuser recanted, the homosexual spokesman contends: "We are not satisfied with gossip-makers. We have carefully gathered documentation and information from various sources. We are very sure of what we are saying." The reason alleged for such denunciations is to make Austrian law more tolerant of homosexuals. Although the law permits persons over 16 to have homosexual and lesbian relationships, male homosexuals believe they are being discriminated against. They take as a model an Italian law that establishes age 14 as the threshold age for any kind of sexual relationship.[106]

In fact, the next day Krickler fulfilled his promise and disclosed the names of five Bishops whom he claimed were homosexuals. Heading the list was Msgr. Christoph Schönborn, auxiliary Bishop of Vienna with right of succession, followed by Msgr. Egon Kapelari, Bishop of Klagenfurt; Msgr. Andreas Laun, Bishop of Salzburg; Msgr. Klaus Küng, titular Bishop of the Diocese of Feldkirch, and, finally, the now deceased Msgr. Leopold Ungar. Krickler claimed that he could produce three witnesses to testify against each of the Bishops, but he failed to present them. The four Prelates stated that the accusations were groundless and announced legal proceedings against Krickler.[107]

§ 73   In the beginning of July, the news broke that a petition drive with progressivist tones had attained as many as 400,000 signatures from among the Austrian population. The cause for this general indignation was the 'Gröer scandal.' And while the Cardinal was known to adhere to a Church policy called 'conservative,' some of the requests in the petition included the abolition of priestly celibacy, the ordination of women and the pos-

---

[105] Kurt KRICKLER, Statement, in Riccardo CHIABERNE, "Vienna, ricatto gay alla Chiesa," in *Corriere della Sera*, 8/1/1995.

[106] Ibid.

[107] Alfredo VENTURI, "Austria, vescovi alla gogna," in *Corriere della Sera*, 8/2/1995; *La Vanguardia*, Barcelona, "Un líder gay afirma que quatro obispos austriacos son homosexuales," 8/2/1995; *ABC*, "El Papa acepta la renuncia del Cardinal austriaco Gröer, que se retira a un convento," 8/16/1995.

sibility to veto Vatican choices for Bishops via a plebiscite.[108] The 'definitive result' of the petition was published a few days later: 505,000 signatures, including those of 1,000 Austrian priests.[109]

Such is the overview of the 'Gröer affair.' By October 13, 1994, Msgr. Gröer had already vacated his post. However, only in August 1995 was he notified that the Vatican would accept his resignation effective September 14.[110]

In **Ireland**, Cardinal Primate Cohal Daly went public to "present the humble excuses" of the Catholic Church for the long series of sexual molestation of boys by priests that had recently surfaced. Daly admitted that "these terrible violations of sacred trust" had caused "huge wounds in many boys and in their families." After a three-day meeting with the 34 Catholic Bishops of Ireland, he promised that from now on new cases will be transferred to the police, as provided by law.

"This is the most authoritative admission of the drama now undermining the confidence of the faithful in the Catholic Church, the historic mainstay of Irish society. .... According to the bishops, 1.5 percent of the clergy have been investigated for sexual abuse; sixty priests are alleged to be involved (the number rises to 100 if priests from religious orders are included). However, the question is not one of statistics, but of morals. And it is even a question of politics if one takes into account the resignation of prime-minister Albert Reynolds, who helped bring about the cease-fire in Ulster. Reynolds is said to have prevented the extradition to Ulster of a priest, Brendan Smyth, accused of continuously molesting a young man.[111]

*

---

[108] Vivianne SCHNITZER, "Amenaza de cisma en la Iglesia Católica austriaca tras el 'caso Gröer,'" in *El País*, 7/4/1995.

[109] Tito SANSA, "'Rivoluzione in Chiesa' – Referendum choc tra gli austriaci," in *La Stampa*, Turin, 7/6/1995.

[110] *ABC*, Ibid.

[111] A. ALTICHERI, "In Irlanda la Chiesa si scusa per pedofilia," in *Corriere della Sera*, 10/13/1995.

5. Ecclesiastical Homosexuality in Other Countries

§ 75   In **Brazil**, a journalist of *O Estado de S. Paulo* revealed in two reports and an interview that 15 priests had died of AIDS in the São Paulo metropolitan area from 1988 to 1993.[112] Rumor has it that the actual figure is even higher.

§ 76   To us, it seemed very significant that the Gay Group of Bahia awarded the Cardinal-Archbishop of São Paulo, Msgr. Paulo Evaristo Arns, the "rose triangle trophy" in recognition of his defense of homosexuals' rights.[113]

§ 77   Father Jacques Perotti provides some data which allows one to gauge the degree that the vice of homosexuality has been accepted in the clergy of **France**. The private secretary of the well-known Abbé Pierre says: "I am a priest and a homosexual, and I belong to a French organization called David and Jonathan, which has existed for 21 years and which brings together homosexual men and women .... It is a lay movement. Priests and women religious also take part in it. .... In the United States some studies were carried out, and they believe that between 20 to 30 percent of the priests are homosexuals. It must be similar in all countries of the world."[114]

Describing how he came to terms with his homosexuality, Perotti tells how he stopped exercising his priestly functions and was later given support to resume them: "I lived outside the Church from 1969 to 1981, working on different things just like anyone else. It was during this time that I discovered the homosexual world with its miseries, its sufferings, its hopes. Then, in 1981, I returned to see my bishop and told him: 'I return bearing in me a world I will never leave, the world of my homosexual brothers.' And he accepted me. Since I did not want to return to a parish, for that would prevent me from appearing publicly as a homosexual, and since I had known Abbé Pierre since 1954, it

---

[112] Roldão ARRUDA, "A Aids chega à Igreja," in *O Estado de S. Paulo*, 10/22/1993; "D. Angélico nega que Igreja esconda doentes," in *O Estado de S. Paulo*, 10/23/1993; "A Igreja Católica se destaca no apoio aos doentes de Aids," in *O Estado de S. Paulo*, 10/24/1993.

[113] "Grupo gay da Bahia dá troféu a D. Paulo," *O Estado de S.Paulo*, 5/25/1995.

[114] Jacques PEROTTI, "Todo amor es sagrado," interview with Maria URRUZOLA, in *El País* (Montevideo), 3/4/1994.

occurred to me that I might be able to work with him .... In 1981, I went to see him. Abbé Pierre spoke with my bishop, and ever since I have been on a mission with Abbé Pierre, to minister to him. It is a priestly mission, but I am allowed freedom of expression."[115]

Newsweek magazine adds: "Gays and the Church build bridges also in France. Jacques Perotti, a priest who left the Church when he realized it was impossible to reconcile his homosexuality with his [religious] vocation, helped found a group known as David and Jonathan, which maintains study groups, prayer meetings, and debates on the moral dilemmas faced by gays. Though the organization, with 30 centers around France and 1,500 members, is not a group officially recognized by the Church, it has frequent contacts with Catholic bishops and at times the Church lends its premises for their meetings."[116]

78 As far as the 'Gaillot affair' is concerned, *The Catholic Herald* of London published in passing this bit of news: "In the mid-eighties, [Msgr. Gaillot] admitted that he was an homosexual."[117]

79 A survey in **Holland** showed that a large number of parish priests in that country have turned away from the teaching of the Magisterium of the Church on homosexuality.

Fr. van der Ploeg writes: "In a local paper dated April 15 of last year, we found a communique entitled 'Parish Priests Reject Church Doctrine on Homosexuality.' The Union of Pastoral Agents carried out a survey among 757 pastors of the archdiocese of Utrecht to find out their opinion about 'homosexual conduct of parish priests.' Only 350 of the 750 pastors responded to the survey. Experts consider this to be a high percentage, which they deem representative of the whole. However, it should be noted that a certain number of priests may not have responded because they viewed the survey as abusive to their privacy.

---

[115] Ibid.

[116] *Newsweek*, "Gays in the Clergy," 2/23/1987.

[117] *The Catholic Herald*, London, "John Paul Meets With Gaillot," 3/10/1995.

"Of the 350 parish priests who answered the survey, 86 percent (that is, 301) are at odds with the Church position on homosexuality. As a consequence, these gentlemen place themselves outside the Church. A beautiful archdiocese, where 301 parish priests view the sin of Sodom and Gomorrha as licit and want to bring it inside the Church! Furthermore, 84 percent of the 350 (i.e., 294), believe that 'men who regularly practice homosexual relations' and who are not obliged to celibacy, may be designated pastors. And this is not in Sodom and Gomorrha, but in the archdiocese of Utrecht! How can one trust a 'parish priest' in the archdiocese of Utrecht? In Holland, the Church has become a Church in exile."[118]

A more recent survey says: "In Holland, where an open and vigorous debate has long been taking place about some of the most basic principles of Catholic doctrine, a coalition of 90 men religious formed the Work Group of Catholic Homosexual Priests. Group members have met with a delegation of bishops to discuss the gay clergy issue. Evidently, meetings have produced no substantial change in Church procedures. But the group was encouraged by the recent survey it conducted among 375 priests of the archdiocese of Utrecht: 84 percent said they had a positive opinion of homosexuality and 28 percent admitted to being homosexuals."[119]

§ 80

Telltale of the situation of some of the clergy in **Spain** are the blasphemous and arrogant statements by Fr. Emili Boils. At the IX Congress of Theology held in Madrid in September 1989, he said: "I am homosexual by nature and by the grace of God, as a believer and a religious. …. I am neither 'corrupt' nor 'scum' nor a 'shame of darkness,' nor is my sin 'nefarious,' nor does my abnormality 'cry out to heaven,' nor am I 'sick' or 'abominable.' …. I am not a Sodomite. I was not born in such an exotic place [Sodom], nor was I born more than twenty centuries ago. …. Enough of this crap! …. I am a priest because I am homosexual."[120]

---

[118] J. van der PLOEG, Survey among Utrecht parish priests, in *Katholieke Stemmen* (Tiburg), June-July 1983, pp. 275f.

[119] "Gays in the Clergy," *Newsweek*, 2/23/1987.

[120] Emili BOILS, "Declaraciones en el IX Congreso de Teología – Iglesia y derechos humanos, Evangelio y liberación," Madrid, 1990, in *Covadonga-Informa* (Madrid), May 1990, p. 8.

As far as **England** is concerned, we will delve only into the 'Hume affair,' which caused scandal in March and April of 1995. The case had two cumulative aspects: the doctrinal and the political-ecclesiastical.

From the *doctrinal standpoint,* Msgr. Basil Hume, Archbishop of Westminster and Cardinal Primate of England and Wales, released a statement to the press about homosexuality.[121] On some points, it goes even beyond the concessions to homosexuality made in the documents of the Holy See and frontally clashes with Catholic Doctrine. It says: "The Church recognizes the dignity of all people and does not define or label them in terms of their sexual orientation."[122] Further on: "The particular orientation or inclination of the homosexual person is not a moral failing .... Being a homosexual person is, then, neither morally good nor morally bad; it is homosexual genital acts that are morally wrong."[123]

On issuing this statement, the Cardinal is guilty of equivocation on some points.

First, by reducing moral culpability only to acts, Msgr. Hume appears to legitimize sinful thoughts and words, which can cause equal culpability in concessions to the vice of homosexuality or to any other vice, as Catholic Doctrine has always taught. Thus, this omission by the Cardinal can hardly sit well with Church teaching.

Second, by reducing the moral culpability of homosexuals to genital acts, Msgr. Hume appears to legitimize a series of libidinous acts between these people that can range from necking, hugging, and kissing, to acts more directly offensive to good customs such as manual or oral contact with private parts, which nonetheless are not explicitly 'genital acts.' The Primate

---

[121] Basil HUME, "A Note on the teaching of the Catholic Church concerning homosexual people," in *Briefing* (London), 3/16/1995, pp. 3ff.

[122] Ibid., p. 3, n. 4.

[123] Ibid., p. 4, n. 7.

Alhough in the beginning of the document Msgr. Hume admits the moral culpability of homosexual genital acts, later on he relativizes that judgment. He states: "Although homosexual genital acts are objectively wrong, nonetheless, the Church warns against generalizations in attributing culpability in individual cases" (Ibid., p. 5, n. 16).

of England also appears to legitimize a series of unnatural practices common to a certain type of homosexuals, such as mimicking the opposite sex in speaking, dressing, walking, and behaving in public, taking hormones to assume the characteristics of the opposite sex, and even the ever less rare practice of breast implantation or suppressing and surgically altering sex organs. Such practices appear to have been excluded from what the Cardinal considers 'genital acts' and are, therefore, indifferent, as he sees it, from the moral standpoint. This is an aberration with regard to good customs and Catholic Doctrine.

§ 84

Third: Msgr. Hume says that "the particular orientation or inclination of the homosexual person is not a moral failing." What does he mean here by particular orientation or inclination, which others call tendency? We have just seen that such an inclination cannot consist of sinful consent in the realm of thoughts, words, and deeds. Hence, for one to admit a non-condemnable tendency of this kind, one should suppose it to be repressed, without any external manifestation and without a right of citizenship even inside the person's mind. This is all the more explicable since the Church has always condemned as a sin the entertainment of thoughts of carnal desire for someone of the opposite sex, even though this relationship is according to nature. Hence homosexual thoughts and desires are all the more sinful, that is to say, morally bad. This airtight concept of the homosexual tendency is indispensable for one who honestly wishes to teach Catholic thinking. Otherwise, the tendency is given such amplitude that the moral vice of homosexuality can almost receive the right of citizenship so long as the sexual act is not directly involved. This, then, is the question to be asked: who will profit from the imprecision and ambiguity of the Cardinal Primate of England?

§ 85

Fourth: Cardinal Hume is gravely mistaken in saying that "the Church does not define or label them [people] in terms of their sexual orientation." For the sin of homosexuality, called the sin against nature, was always considered one of the sins that cry out to Heaven and clamor to God for vengeance. Hence Church teaching and customs place a deservedly infamous note on people who commit such sins.

§ 86

Fifth: The Cardinal also says that "the Church recognizes the dignity of all people." This sentence applied to homosexuals would mean that the latter have dignity insofar as they publicly manifest themselves as such, and therefore the Church respects them. Here again one finds imprecision and ambiguity in concepts. Just what is this dignity that the Church recognizes in every person? There are three types of dignity that it would be opportune to distinguish:

Ontological dignity. Every being created by God – especially angels and humans – are created to His image and, as such, should be respected. In this sense, the devil himself, despite of his antagonism toward God, continues to maintain his ontological dignity as an angel; he is an image of God and, as such, deserves respect.

Moral dignity. Superior to ontological dignity is moral dignity, since every being gifted with a will can become similar to God by adhering to good and rejecting evil. Being made to the image of God derives from ontological dignity; similarity with God derives from moral dignity. In this sense, only men who practice good have dignity, whereas those who practice evil are unworthy.

To this is added yet another characteristic of moral dignity: the internal and external practice of good. So far as the internal practice of good and evil is concerned, a person is judged only by God; so far as the external practice of good and evil goes, the person is judged by God and also by those who see him carry out his acts. Above all, he is judged by the Catholic Church, the custodian of upright morals and good customs. This is why She proposes the examples of the Saints, recognizing in them the highest moral dignity that comes from the external, constant, and heroic practice of good, and grants them the highest expression of respect by elevating them to the altars. In the opposite sense, the Church censures public and scandalous sinners and calls on her children to reject them. Obviously, such a censure can brand sinners with a note of shame and, at times, of infamy, which are consequences of their moral unworthiness.

Social dignity. Social dignity is a concept derived from the collective acceptance by a given society of the ensemble of attitudes that characterizes someone's social profile. In well-established societies, such a concept is based on natural law and natural ethics, whence it derives. According to Church doctrine, a person's social dignity is directly related to his moral dignity. That is, the Church should strive for the social body to be consonant with her morals. This or that concession to principles distinct from Catholic ones – for example, living in an ambiance of polygamy in certain African countries – can be admitted only as a lesser evil, on a provisional basis, and must cease as soon as possible.

§ 90   Given such clearly defined concepts of the notion of dignity, a question comes to the fore: in what sense could one admit Cardinal Hume's statement that "the Church recognizes the dignity of all people"? As we see it, there is only one meaning where the concept is reconcilable with Catholic Doctrine in relation to homosexuals: ontological dignity. In respect to moral dignity, homosexuals who publicly declare themselves as such are public, scandalous sinners, whose situation is aggravated even further by the fact that homosexual practice is contrary to nature. To admit self-proclaimed homosexuals as morally indifferent would be to relativize the concepts of good and evil and to subvert natural order. The same can be said in relation to social dignity.

§ 91   These are, in our view, the main equivocations and inexactitude of Cardinal Hume on establishing the premises for his document. One would say that, as a whole, these errors are apt to grant a comfortable moral and social right of citizenship to one of the worst vices ever known.

Incidentally, the English Cardinal's intent to grant moral and social citizenship to homosexuals reveals itself in other parts of his "Note." Some of the more significant texts include the following:

* "Love between two persons, whether of the same sex or of a different sex, is to be treasured and respected."[124]

* "To love another, whether of the same sex or of a different sex, is to have entered the area of the richest human experience."[125]

* "It is a fundamental human right of every person, irrespective of sexual orientation, to be treated by individuals and by society with dignity, respect, and fairness."[126]

* "Nothing in the Church's teaching can be said to support or sanction, even implicitly, the victimization of homosexual men and women."[127]

---

[124] Ibid., p. 4, n. 9.

[125] Ibid., p. 4, n. 10.

[126] Ibid., p. 4, n. 12.

[127] Ibid., p. 5, n. 15.

* "Furthermore, 'homophobia' should have no place among Catholics."[128]

Such are the advantages that the document of the Cardinal-Archbishop of Westminster procures for homosexuals that one would say his statement is intended as a writ of citizenship for homosexuality in the moral, social, and legal domains.

From the *political-ecclesiastical* standpoint, it is noteworthy that the Cardinal was pressed to go public by the homosexual group OutRage. "In January this year," says the London paper *The Daily Mail* "[Peter] Tatchell sent a letter to the Cardinal which was described as 'forceful.' .... Cardinal Hume had not intended immediate publication, *Catholic Herald* editor Christina Odone claimed, but did so only when Mr. Tatchell contacted media organizations offering the statement as a 'leaked document.' Tatchell said the statement was a direct re-

---

What does the Cardinal understand by 'victimization'? In the preceding paragraph he said: "The Church condemns violence of speech or action against homosexual people" (Ibid., p. 5, n. 14).

With respect to violent action, the Church certainly condemns taking justice into one's own hands, that is, for a private person to take on the role of judge and executioner against homosexuals. To admit such violence would be tantamount to ignoring legitimately established order and plunging society into chaos. Nonetheless, just as the Church supports equitable punishment for voluntary homicide, oppressing widows and orphans, and denying a defenseless person a just salary, so likewise She can and should support just legal measures punishing the vice of homosexuality. One can see, therefore, that Cardinal Hume generalizes excessively by failing to consider the possibility of legislation that punishes homosexuality with violent action.

As for the other types of violence condemned by the Cardinal, the question once again should be asked: Just what is 'violence of speech'? To say that homosexuality is a vice and a sin that cries out to God for vengeance? To publicly condemn such a sin? To surround it with a note of infamy? Does working to have society and the State reject homosexuals amount to 'victimizing' or exerting moral violence against them? If this hypothesis were true, the Cardinal would be condemning Catholic Doctrine. If it is a true interpretation, what Church is the Cardinal speaking of when he states that the Church condemns violence of speech against homosexuals?

[128] Ibid., p. 5, n. 15.

sponse to OutRage's demands, adding: 'When I told them I was going to publish it, they rushed out the statement themselves.' The Cardinal's office denied that the statement had been issued in a hurry."[129]

As a confirmation that the Cardinal went public out of fear that Peter Tatchell and OutRage might publish even more compromising information, we will present a summary of the facts that took place during those days in Britain to gauge the strength of the homosexuals' threats of blackmail and to see the kind of company Cardinal Hume finds himself keeping.

If we go outside the Catholic arena, we will see that already in November of 1994 OutRage had 'outed' ten Anglican bishops.[130] On March 7, the same day that the 'Hume document' came to light, the Church of Scotland assembled and issued a statement asking for more tolerance and understanding for homosexuality in line with the principles upheld by Msgr. Hume.[131]

In view of these facts, Tim Hopkins, director of a group that advocates law reform called on Cardinal Thomas Wining, head of the Catholic Church in Scotland, to express public support for the interpretations of his English colleague. Through his spokesman, Fr. Tom Connelly, Cardinal Winning said that Cardinal Hume's viewpoints "are entirely in line with the Church's general moral principles."[132] In a broadcast on BBC television the same night, Scottish bishop Derk Rawcliffe 'outed,' that is, he openly stated that he 'was always a homosexual' and advocated that a blessing be given to relationships among homosex-

---

[129] Anthony DORAN - Steve DOUGHTY, "How the gay lobby railroaded a Cardinal," in *The Daily Mail* (London), 3/8/1995; Christina FRADE, *"El sexo de los Obispos,"* in *El Mundo* (Madrid), 3/19/1995, p. 2.

[130] Greg HADFIELD, "This is just a start, say the activists," in *The Daily Mail*, 3/8/1995; Ruth GLEDHILL, "Churchmen condemn move to 'out' Hope," in *The Times*, 3/15/1995; Luca ROMANO, "Estremisti omosex minacciano di fari I nomi di prelati e deputati," in *Il Giornale*, 3/15/1995.

[131] Ray CLANCY, "Church pleads for greater tolerance of homosexuals," in *The Daily Telegraph*, 3/8/1995.

[132] Severin CARREL, "Cardinal Winning challenged to back praise for gay love," in *The Scotsman*, 3/8/1995.

ual priests.[133] On March 13, after receiving a letter from the leader of OutRage, the Anglican bishop of London, David Hope, published a letter saying he was neither heterosexual nor homosexual, since his sexuality resided in an ambiguous 'gray area.'[134] He also promised tolerance toward homosexuals. Hope condemned OutRage's campaign as "profoundly disturbing, based almost totally on rumors and unknown sources, and intimidating in nature."[135] Some people viewed his words as a semi-confession.[136]

On March 14, Hope's statement received a letter of support from 34 primates of the Anglican church assembled in Windsor. The Anglican archbishop of Canterbury, speaking in the name of the other bishops present, manifested to Hope his solidarity, "deploring this reprehensible intrusion into his private life" and manifesting his "most profound affection" and "prayerful support" for the London bishop.[137] On that same day, the Anglican bishop of Southwark, Robert Williamson, said he

---

[133] Ibid.; "Bispo anglicano admite que é homossexual," O Globo, 3/9/1995; G. HADFIELD, Ibid.; Murray WHITE, "Cardinal launches attack on homophobia," in The Catholic Herald, 3/10/1995; Rogério SIMÕES, "Bispo anglicano defende sacerdotes homossexuais," in Folha de S. Paulo, 4/9/1995.

[134] R. GLEDHILL, Ibid.; L. ROMANO, Ibid.; Allan MASSIE, "Terror tactics of the Tatchell gang," in The Daily Telegraph, 3/15/1995.

[135] David HOPE, Letter, March 3, 1995, in R. GLEDHILL, Ibid.

[136] L. ROMANO, Ibid.

[137] George CAREY, Letter of March 14, 1995, in Dan CONAGHAM, "Archbishops angry at Hope 'intrusion,'" in The Daily Telegraph, 3/15/1995.

The article by Alessio ALTICHERI, "Promosso il vescovo gay," in Corriere della Sera (4/12/1995) confirms Hope's semi-confession (Note 136) and the prestige the Anglican church sought to give him. According to Alticheri, Hope was given a promotion in the Anglican hierarchy and transferred from the London diocese to that of York, which has above it only the bishop of Canterbury. Hope's promotion was the object of new congratulations and hundreds of letters. "Many came from outside the Church, many from homosexuals, some of them really touching," said Hope, second in command of the Anglican church.

"would be happy to ordain an openly homosexual priest" living a stable relationship with someone of the same sex.[138]

On the 15th of the month, the Anglican archbishop of York, John Habgood, published in *The Times* an article stating: "The common presumption that all physical intimacy must lead to penetrative sex is unjust to those who want to enjoy some warmth of companionship, but wish to draw a line."[139]

The 34 Anglican bishops who were gathered in an international conference issued a document that said: "In the internal life of the Church, there are models of sexuality different from those recalled by traditional Christian morals; nevertheless, these experiences are marked by a genuine Christian seal."[140] In that regard, the *Corriere della Sera* comments: "A success, organizations for the defense of gay rights rejoiced .... the Anglican Church admits one can simultaneously be gay and a good Christian."[141]

Following Cardinal Hume's orientation, the group Catholic Aids Link published a 38-page booklet entitled *Positively Called*, in which it claims that "many HIV-infected clergy and religious are able not only to maintain their active ministry but .... are uniquely suited to play a special role in the Church's pastoral ministry in the HIV/AIDS epidemic."[142] "It is certainly plausible that God could call to religious or priestly life some infected with HIV', adds the report, which has the backing of the English hierarchy."[143]

---

[138] Robert WILLIAMSON, Statement to the press, in R. GLEDHILL, Ibid.; A. MASSIE, Ibid.

[139] John HABGOOD, "When sex ceases to be private," in *The Times*, 3/15/1995.

[140] 34 ANGLICAN BISHOPS, Statements, in "I gay? Bravi cristiani," in *Corriere della Sera*, 3/17/1995.

[141] *Corriere della Sera*, Ibid.

[142] CATHOLIC AIDS LINK, *Positively Called*, in Piers McGRANDLE, "Church needs HIV clergy says group", in *The Catholic Herald*, 3/17/1995.

[143] Ibid.

The journalist of *The Catholic Herald* adds: "*Positively Called*, which was culled from seminars held for those selecting candidates for the priesthood, urges the Church to act in an 'inclusive' way towards those 'who may have acquired HIV through activity not permissible under vows,' rather than treating them as 'paedophiles.'"[144] The publication, the journalist concludes, results "at least indirectly, from intense lobbying by militant homosexual group OutRage." "Peter Tatchell," the reporter continues, "claims to have written to four senior Catholic clergy and two more Anglican clergy, urging them to 'come out.'"[145]

A commentator from *Il Giornale* says Tatchell is preparing to 'out' another five Anglican bishops.[146] *The Corriere della Sera* reported these arrogant words spoken by the homosexual leader: "We will influence the future policy of the Church of England in a way that no one can imagine."[147] [148]

After his latest threats, Tatchell opened a new front of attack by sending letters to twenty members of Parliament – two of them ministers in John Major's Cabinet – suggesting that they publicly admit their homosexuality. The letters exhorted recipients to "follow the example of two MPs who admitted their homosexuality."[149]

Cardinal Hume's "Note" on homosexuality can be objectively situated within the context of this great blackmailing plot being carried out by homosexual groups against Catholic Prelates, Anglican bishops, the church of Scotland, and English cabinet ministers and members of Parliament. As a whole, the Cardinal's document is by far, in our view, the strategic piece of greatest importance and usefulness to homosexual interests in England.

---

[144] P. McGRANDLE, Ibid.

[145] Ibid.

[146] Peter TATCHELL, Statement, in Mino VIGNOLO, *Preti e politici gay dovete confessare*, in *Corriere della Sera*, 3/21/1995.

[147] L. ROMANO, Ibid.

[148] P. TATCHELL, Statement, Ibid.

[149] *O Globo*, "Grupo gay inglês ameaça revelar lista de políticos homossexuais," 3/21/1995; L. ROMANO, Ibid.; M. VIGNOLO, Ibid.

§ 93   In **Italy**, an unusual survey was carried out by German reporter Edwin Thomas of *Micromega* magazine. Every evening for several weeks, Thomas would stroll in the environs of St. Peter's Basilica. In that period, he claims to have been approached by 64 churchmen who made him homosexual propositions. Thomas says they were ecclesiastics "of all kinds, from seminarians to the secretary of a nunciature."[150]

§ 94   We cannot omit the events that occurred at the Vatican at the end of 1989 during an International Conference on AIDS promoted by the Holy See. The three-day event brought together 1,400 Bishops, theologians, scientists, and researchers from 85 countries.

     Right in the opening session, Irish priest John White stood up in Synod Hall and displayed a sign reading: "The Church has AIDS." When he was ushered out, White said, "I have AIDS and live with it every day."[151]

     Later, AIDS sufferer Peter Larking of London engaged in a heated exchange with conference organizer, Archbishop Fiorenzo Angelini, and finally stormed out.

     The following day, however, Msgr. Angelini readmitted Fr. White to the conference with a public embrace.[152] AIDS victim Larkin was also allowed to return and was even granted a brief audience with John Paul II, who told him, "I'm praying for you."[153]

*

---

[150] Edwin THOMAS, "Amori gay all'ombra del cupulone. Inchiesta di *Micromega* fra sacerdoti omosessuali," in *Adista*, 5/13/1995, pp. 8f.

[151] "Aids é debatida no Vaticano," *O Estado de S. Paulo*, 11/14/1989.

[152] Rod NORLAND, "'The Church Has AIDS' – Anger flares at a Vatican conference," in *Newsweek*, 11/27/1989, p. 55.

[153] Ibid.

Conclusion

§ 95   Nothing appeared more fitting for us to close this overall view of homosexuality than an excerpt from *Liber gomorrhianus* of Saint Peter Damien (1007-1072). The work was offered to Saint Leo IX (1002-1054), who was Pope during the years 1048-1054 as a tool to help reform customs in the clergy, a pressing issue at the time. This movement was known as the Gregorian reform, since to a large extent it was inspired by the monk Hildebrand, later Saint Gregory VII.

Saint Leo IX had glowing praise for Saint Peter Damien's book:[154]

"Leo, Bishop, servant of the servants of God, to the beloved son in Christ, Peter the hermit, the joy of eternal blessing.

"The book, beloved son, which with noble style and even more noble intention you have published …. shows with clear documents that by applying your intelligence you have attained, through pious effort, the apex of a refined purity. For you, who thus raised the arm of the spirit against the obscenity of lust, have overcome the disorder of the flesh, an execrable vice that removes people far from the Author of virtues, Who, being pure, admits nothing impure. And His inheritance will not belong to those who indulge in sordid pleasures. ….

"Most dear son, I rejoice in untold manner that you preach, by the example of your behavior, all that you have taught through the gift of oratory. Indeed, it is more holy to preach through works than words. For this reason, by doing God's work, you will obtain the palm of victory and, with God [the Father] and with the Virgin's Son, you will rejoice in the eternal mansion filled with as many rewards as the people you wrenched from the snares of the demon, and these people will serve as your retinue and, in a certain way, will crown you."[155]

---

[154] For those wishing to know more on the death of Saint Leo IX as a result of the wars he personally led against the Normans who invaded papal territories, see Emile AMANN, *Papes imperiaux et Papes romains,* in V.A., *Histoire de l'Eglise,* vol. VII, pp. 105ff.

[155] St. LEO IX, *Epistula super Librum gomorrhianum,* in PL 145, cols. 159f.

These are Saint Peter Damien's words lambasting the vice of sodomy:

"In fact, this vice is absolutely not comparable to any others, because its enormity supersedes them all. Indeed, this vice produces the death of bodies and the destruction of souls. It pollutes the flesh, extinguishes the light of reason, expels the Holy Ghost from His temple in man's heart and introduces into it the devil who is the instigator of lust; it leads into error, totally expels truth from the deceived soul, sets up traps for those who fall into it, then caps the well to prevent those who fall into it from getting out, opens the gates of hell and closes the door of heaven to them, turns a former citizen of the heavenly Jerusalem into an heir of the infernal Babylon, transforming him from a heavenly star into a straw for the eternal fire, wrenches a member away from the Church and plunges him into the voracious fire of the ardent gehena.

"This vice strives to destroy the walls of one's heavenly motherland and rebuild those of devastated Sodom. Indeed, it violates temperance, kills purity, stifles chastity, annihilates virginity – which is irrecoverable – with the sword of a most infamous union. It infects everything, stains everything, pollutes everything; it leaves nothing pure, nothing but filth. 'All things are clean to the clean', as the Apostle says, 'but to them that are defiled, and to unbelievers, nothing is clean; but both their mind and their conscience are defiled' (Tit 1:15).

"This vice expels one from the choir of the ecclesiastical host and obliges one to join the possessed and those who work in league with the devil; it separates the soul from God and links it with demons. This most pestiferous queen of the Sodomites makes those who obey her tyrannical laws repugnant to men and hateful to God; it [this sin] wages a nefarious war against God and obliges the person to enlist in the ranks of the perverse spirit; it separates him from the company of angels and deprives his soul of its nobility; it imposes on the unfortunate soul the yoke of its own domination. It tears its henchmen from the arms of virtue and exposes them as prey to the arrows of all vices. It humiliates at church, condemns at court, defiles in secret, dishonors in public, gnaws at the person's conscience like a worm and burns his flesh like fire...

"Miserable flesh burns with the fire of lust, cold intelligence trembles under the rancor of suspicion, and the unfortunate man's heart is possessed by hellish chaos, subjecting him to as many pains of conscience as he is tortured in punishment. Yes, as soon as the most venomous serpent plunges its thorns into the unfortunate soul, it is immediately deprived of its senses and memory; the edge of his intelligence is dulled, he forgets God and even himself.

"Indeed, this scourge destroys the foundations of the faith, weakens the forces of hope, dissipates the bonds of charity, annihilates justice, undermines fortitude, eliminates hope, and dulls the edge of prudence.

"And what else shall I say? It expels all the forces of virtue from the temple of the human heart and, pulling the door from its hinges, introduces into it all the barbarity of vice? ....

"In effect, the one whom .... this most atrocious beast has swallowed down its bloody throat is prevented, by the weight of his chains, to practice all good works and is precipitated into all the abysses of its uttermost wickedness. Thus, as soon as someone has fallen into this abyss of extreme perdition, he is exiled from the heavenly motherland, separated from the Body of Christ, confounded by the authority of the whole Church, condemned by the judgment of all the Holy Fathers, despised by men on earth, and reproved by the society of heavenly citizens; he creates for himself an earth of iron and a sky of bronze; on the one hand, laden with the weight of his crime, he is unable to rise; on the other hand, he is no longer able to conceal his evil in the refuge of ignorance; he cannot be happy while he lives nor have hope when he dies, because he is now obliged to suffer the ignominy of men's derision and, later, the torment of eternal condemnation."[156]

* * *

---

[156] St. Peter DAMIEN, op. cit., cols. 175ff.

BIBLIOGRAPHY

ABC - *"El Papa acepta la renuncia del Cardinal austriaco Gröer, que se retira a un convento,"* 8/16/1995. **ABBOT, Alter M. SJ** - *The Documents of Vatican II.* Herder and Herder: 1962. **ACERBI, Antonio** - *Due ecclesiologie - Ecclesiologia giuridica ed ecclesiologia di communione nella 'Lumen gentium'*, Bologna: Dehoniane, 1975. **ADAM, K.** - *Die Katholische Tübingen Schule*, in Gesammelte Aufsätze, Augsburg, 1936. **ADISTA** (Roma) - *Amori gay all'ombra del cupulone. Inchiesta di "Micromega" fra i sacerdoti omosessuali*, 5/13/1995. *Un prete cattolico su cinque si sposa*, 5/16/1992. *In Spagna due cardinale e cinque vescovi accusati di silenzio sugli abusi di minori e psicolabili*, 4/1/1995. **AGOSTINHO, Santo** - *De baptismo contra Donatistas*, in PL 43, 135, apud V. PROAÑO GIL; *Contra Julianum*, in PL 44, 662, apud C. GARCIA EXTREMEÑO; *De dono perseverantiae*, in PL 45, 1031, apud V. PROAÑO GIL; *De duabus animabus contra manichaeos*, in PL 42, 105; *Epistula 19*, apud C. a LAPIDE, *Ad Galatas*, vol. XVIII; *Epistula 19 ad Hieronymum*, apud ibidem; *Epistula 82*, in PL 33, 285f.; *De gratia Christi et peccato originali*, apud G. de PLINVAL; *Sermo 294*, in PL 38, 1346, apud V. PROAÑO GIL; *Ad Galatas*, apud ST. THOMAS AQUINAS; *Summa theologiae. Regula*, apud ST. THOMAS AQUINAS, *IV sententiarum.* **d'AGOSTINO, Biagio** - *Comentários sobre o Inferno na Aula conciliar*, apud B. KLOPPENBURG; *Concílio Vaticano II*, vol. IV. **AHLBRECHT, Ansgar** - *Dialogo con los protestantes*, in V.A., *La reforma que llega de Roma.* **ALBERIGO, Giuseppe** - Editoriale, in V.A., *Verso la Chiesa del terzo millennio; Per un Concilio ecumenico cristiano nella prospettiva dell'unità della Chiesa*, in V.A., *Verso la Chiesa del terzo millennio;* See V.A., *Conciliorum oecumenicorum decreta.* **ALSZEGHY, Zoltán** - *Sens de la Foi*, in V.A., *Vatican II: Bilan et perspectives*, vol. I; See M. FLICK. **ALTICHIERI, Alessio** - *In Irlanda la Chiesa si scusa per pedofilia*, in CORRIERE DELLA SERA, 10/10/1995; *Promosso il vescovo gay*, in CORRIERE DELLA SERA, 4/12/1995. **D'ALTRI, Guido** - *Declarações à imprensa*, **apud** M. FUMAGALLI. **AMANN, Emile** - *L'époque carolingienne*, in V.A., *Histoire de l'Église*, vol. VI. **AMELUNXEN, Remi - Paul TRINCHARD** - "Historical Prelude: A Brief History of the Holy Mass from the Canonized Liturgy to the Novus Ordus English Liturgy", in P. TRINCHARD, *New Mass in Light of the Old.* **AMERIO, Romano** - *Sob a cúpula, o vazio*, in 30 DIAS (Rome/São Paulo), January 1991. **ANTÓN, Angel** - *L'ecclésiologie postconciliaire - Les attentes, les résultats et les perspectives pour l'avenir*, in V.A., *Vatican II: Bilan et perspectives*, vol. I. **ANGLICAN BISHOP** - *Declaração coletiva*, apud CORRIERE DELLA SERA, *I gay? Bravi cristiani*, 3/17/1995. **ARAÚJO OLIVEIRA, Hermes de** - *Guerra revolucionária*, Rio de Janeiro: Biblieux, 1965. **ARRUDA, Roldão** - *A Aids chega à Igreja*, in O ESTADO DE S. PAULO (São Paulo), 10/22/1993; *D. Angélico nega que Igreja esconda doentes*, in O ESTADO DE S. PAULO, 10/23/1993; *A Igreja Católica se destaca no apoio aos doentes de Aids*, in O ESTADO DE S. PAULO, 10/24/1993. **ASSOCIAZIÓNE TEOLOGICA ITALIANA** - See V.A., *Il linguaggio teologico oggi.* **d'ATTILIA, Miela** - *Donne sulle vie della missione*, in AVVENIRE,

6/16/1991.   AUBERT, Roger - *La géographie ecclésiologique au XIXe. siècle*, in V.A., *L'ecclésiologie au XIXe. Siècle; La théologie catholique au milieu du XXe. siècle*, Tournai/Paris: Casterman, 1954; *La théologie catholique durant la première moitiè du XXe. siècle*, Tournai/Paris: Casterman, 1970, in V.A., *Bilan de la théologie du XXe. siècle*, vol. I; See V.A., *Nouvelle Histoire de l'Église.*   AVVENIRE (Milan) - *Chiarezza, non discrinazione*, 7/24/1992.   AZEVEDO, Dermi - *Clero brasileiro tem 10% de alcoólatras*, in FOLHA DE S. PAULO (São Paulo), 8/14/1988; *Oposição ao celibato obrigatório ganha força dentro da Igreja*, in FOLHA DE S. PAULO, 11/7/1988.

BACHELET, Xavier-Marie le - *Benoit XII*, in DTC, vol. XII, apud C. GARCIA EXTREMEÑO.   BALLERINI, Antonius - See J. P. GURY. BALTHASAR, Hans Urs von - *Abbatere i bastioni*, Turin: Borla, 1966; *El complejo antirromano - Integración del papado en la Iglesia universal*, Madrid: BAC, 1981; *De l'intégration - Aspects d'une theólogie de l'Histoire*, Bruges: Desclée de Brouwer, 1970; *Love alone: the way of Revelation*, London/Dublin: Sheed & Ward, 1982; *Von Balthasar: la mia opera è abbozzata più che terminata*, in L'OSSERVATORE ROMANO, 6/24/1984; BANWART, Clemens - See H. DENZINGER (1).   BARAÚNA, Guilherme - See V.A., *A Igreja do Vaticano II.*   BARBIER, Emmanuel - *Histoire du Catholicisme liberal et du Catholicisme social en France - Du Concile du Vatican à l'avènement de S. S. Benoit XV (1870-1914)*, Bordeaux: Imprimerie Y. Cadoret, 1924, 5 vols. *Les infiltrations maçoniques dans l'Église*, Paris/Brussells: Desclée de Brouwer, 1910.   BARBIERI, Raffaele - *Comentários ao Esquema XIII na Aula conciliar*, apud L. CARLI.   BARIL, Gilberte - *La femminilità del Popolo di Dio e la vita consacrata femminile*, in L'OSSERVATORE ROMANO, 23.XI.1994, supplement.   BARTOLONI, Bruno - *La rivolta silenziosa delle suore*, in CORRIERE DELLA SERA, 6/4/1993.   BARTZ, Wilhelm - *Le Magistère de l'Église d'après Scheeben*, in V.A., *L'ecclésiologie au XIXe. siècle.*   BASIL, Saint - *Adversus Eunomium*, in PG 29, 654, apud C. GARCIA EXTREMEÑO. BASSIL, Antoinette - *La vita religiosa femminile in Libano*, in L'OSSERVATORE ROMANO, 11/23/1994, supplement.   BEA, Augustin - *Comentários sobre o Esquema XIII na Aula conciliar*, apud G. CAPRILE, *Il Concilio Vaticano II*, vol. V.   BEAUVAIS, Vincent de - *Speculum quadruplex sive speculum maius*, Akademische Druck-Verlagsanstalt, Graz, 1964.   BELGIAN EPISCOPATE - *Declaração contrária a Encíclica Humanae vitae*, apud ICI, 11/15/1968.   BELLARMINE, St. Robert - See St. ROBERT BELLARMINE.   BENEDICT XII - Constitution *Benedictus Deus*, January 29, 1336, apud X. M. le BACHELET and H. KÜNG, *Vida Eterna?* BENEDICT XV – Encyclicala *Ad beatissime*, of November 1, 1914, in V.A., *Les enseignements pontificaux;* Encyclical *Soliti nos*, of March 11, 1920, in ibidem.   BERNARDINO, Angélico Sândalo - See A. SÂNDALO BERNARDINO.   BERRY, Jason - *Dioceses react to deepening dilemma*, in THE NATIONAL CATHOLIC REPORTER, Kansas City, 5/30/1986; *Lead us not into temptation*, Doubleday, 1992, apud K. L. WOODWAR, *The sins of the father.*   BETTI, Umberto - *Qualification théologique de la Constitu-*

tion, in V.A., *L'Église de Vatican II*, vol. II. **BEUMER, Johannes** - *Histoire de la théologie et des dogmes*, in V.A., *Bilan de la théologie du XXe. siècle*, vol. II. **BIGUZZI, George** - *Tenere alta la fiaccola dell'evangelizzazione, della giustizia e della pace*, in L'OSSERVATORE ROMANO, 11/23/1994, supplement. **BILD** - *Neuen Zeugen im Sex-Skandal*, 4/5/1995. **BILLOT, Louis** - *De Ecclesia Christi*, Rome: Aedes Universitatis Gregorianae, 1921. **BOFF, Leonardo** - *Igreja: Carisma e poder - Ensaio de eclesiologia militante*, Petrópolis: Vozes, 1982; *Le Ministère dans l'Église*, Paris: Cerf, 1981; *O rosto materno de Deus - Ensaio inter-disciplinar sobre o feminino e suas formas religiosas*, Petrópolis: Vozes, 1979. **BOILS, Emili** - *Declaraciones en el IX Congreso de Teología - Iglesia y derechos humanos*, Evangelio y liberación, Madrid, 1990, apud COVADONGA-INFORMA, Madrid, May 1990. **BONNET, Piero Antonio** - *Le "fidèle" récupéré comme protagoniste humain dans l'Église*, in V.A., *Vatican II: Bilan et perspectives*, vol. I. **BOULLANGER, Stéphanie-Marie** - *La vita apostolica e la condizione femminile*, in L'OSSERVATORE ROMANO, 11/23/1994, supplement. **BOURRIER, Any** - *Demissão de bispo revolta os franceses*, in JORNAL DO BRASIL, 1/17/1995. **BOUYER, Louis** - *A decomposição do Catolicismo*, Lisbon: Sampedro, n.d. **BOWER, Eric** - *Give lip service to Rome, encourage dissident homosexuals*, in THE WANDERER, 4/9/1992; *The Forum - The Wanderer Replies*, in THE WANDERER, 5/14/1992. **BOWMAN, Jim** - *The Bishops with the gays*, in COMMONWEAL, 4/24/1992. **BRAGA, C.** - See A. BUGNINI. **BRANCOLI, Rodolfo** - *Linea verde contro preti pedofili*, in CORRIERE DELLA SERA, 9/24/1992. **EBRAZILIAN EPISCOPATE** - See CNBB PASTORAL COMMISSION. **BRUNELLI (1), Lucio** - *O balanço de Kolvenbach: os cinco anos do Papa Negro*, in 30 DIAS, November 1989; *Colegialidade, quanto trabalho!*, in 30 DIAS, June 1989; *Kolvenbach: o Papa pode contar conosco - Em primeiro plano, os jesuítas*, in 30 GIORNI, (Portuguese ed.), February 1989; *1994 - Ao som de Bill e da família*, in 30 DIAS, December 1993; *A pílula que dividiu a Igreja*, in 30 GIORNI, July 1988. See J. SIN. **BRUNELLI (2), Lucio - Alfred LABHART** - See O. CULLMANN. **BUGNINI, A. - C. BRAGA** - *Ordo Hedomadae Sanctae instauratus*, Rome, 1956, in P. ROMANO ROCHA. **BULGANIN, Nikolay** - Citação sobre *guerra revolucionária*, apud H. de ARAÚJO OLIVEIRA. **BUONAIUTI, Ernesto** - *Le modernisme catholique*, Paris: Ed. Rieder, 1927. **BUTLER, Christopher Basil** - *The theology of Vatican II*, London, 1967, apud Y. CONGAR, *Le Concile Vatican II*. **BUTTIGLIONE, Rocco** - *Il pensiero di Karol Wojtyla*, Milan: Jaca Book, 1982.

CABRAL DUARTE, Luciano - *Riconciliare le intelligenze cattoliche*, in L'OSSERVATORE ROMANO, 10/6/1983, supplement. **CAMPO, Carlos del** - See P. CORRÊA DE OLIVEIRA, *A propriedade privada e a livre iniciativa no tufão agro-reformista;* See P. CORRÊA DE OLIVEIRA, *Sou católico: posso ser contra a reforma agrária?* **CANO, Melchor** - *De locis theologicis*, Rome, 1890, apud C. GARCIA EXTREMEÑO. **CAPRETTI, Lilia** - *La vita consacrata femminile ripensata ed elaborata in Italia con riferimento alla comunione ecclesiale*, in L'OSSERVATORE ROMANO,

11/23/1994, supplement. **CAPRILE, Giovanni** - *Il Concilio Vaticano II*, Rome: La Civiltà Cattolica, 1965-1969, 5 vols; Interview granted to A. SINKE GUIMARÃES, Rome, Februrary 3, 1983. **CARDONNEL, Jean** - *Vatican II*, interview with Michel DUBOST, in HISTORIA, Paris, October 1982. **CAREY, George** - *Letter*, of March 14, 1995, apud D. CONAGHAN. **CARLI, Luigi** - *Il comunismo e il Concilio Vaticano II*, in G. SCANTAMBURLO. See A. CICOGNANI. **CARREL, Severin** - *Cardinal Winning challenged to back praise for gay love*, in THE SCOTSMAN, 3/8/1995. **CARTECHINI, Sisto** - *Dall'opinione al domma*, Rome: La Civiltà Cattolica, 1953, apud A. V. XAVIER DA SILVEIRA, *Qual a autoridade doutrinária dos documentos pontifícios e conciliares?* **CASSIANO** - *De Incarnatione Christi contra Nestorium haericutum*, in PL 50, 30, apud C. GARCIA EXTREMEÑO. **CASTRO MAYER, Antonio de** - *Petição a Paulo VI, subscrita por 213 Padres conciliares, para que fizesse a condenação do marxismo e do comunismo*, in CATOLICISMO, January 1964; See P. CORRÊA DE OLIVEIRA, *Reforma agrária, questão de consciência;* See P. CORRÊA DE OLIVEIRA, *Declaração do Morro Alto*. **CATOLICISMO (Campos/São Paulo)** - *Grupos ocultos tramam a subversão na Igreja*, April-May 1969; *TFP: Em 58 dias, 1 milhão e meio de assinaturas*, August-October 1968. **CATHOLIC AIDS LINK** - *Positively called*, apud P. McGRANDLE. **THE CATHOLIC HERALD (London)** - *John Paul meets with Gaillot*, 3/10/1995. **CELAM** - See CONSELHO EPISCOPAL LATINO-AMERICANO. **CERTEAU, M. de** - *La parole du croyant dans le language de l'homme*, in ESPRIT, 55, 1967. **CHAVASSE, A.** - *L'ecclesiologie au Concile du Vatican - L'infalibilité de l'Église*, in V.A., *L'ecclésiologie au XIXe. siècle*. **CHAVES, Henrique** - *Desfazendo manobras astuciosas de Moscou, duzentos Padres conciliares pedem nova condenação do comunismo e do socialismo*, in CATOLICISMO, January 1964. **CHENU, Marie-Dominique** - *La Chiesa e il mondo*, in V.A., *I grandi temi del Concilio;* Interview granted to A. SINKE GUIMARÃES, Paris, February 20, 1983; *The history of salvation and the historicity of man in the renewal of theology*, in V.A., *Theology of renewal*, vol. I; *A Igreja dos pobres no Vaticano II*, in CONCILIUM (Nijmegen/Petrópolis), 1977; *Jacques Duquesne interroge le Père Chenu - Un théologien en liberté*, Paris: Centurion, 1975; *Omelia tenuta nel corso della celebrazione eucaristica*, in V.A., *L'avvenire della Chiesa; Les signes des temps - Reflexions théologiques*, in V.A., *L'Église dans le monde de ce temps.* '*Vox populi, vox Dei*' - *L'opinione pubblica nell'ambito del popolo di Dio*, in V.A., *La fine della Chiesa come società perfetta*. **CHIABERNE, Riccardo** - *Vienna, ricatto gay alla Chiesa*, in CORRIERE DELLA SERA, 8/1/1995. **CHOI, Angela** - *Profonda converzione e solida formazione*, in L'OSSERVATORE ROMANO, 23.XI.1994, supplemento. **CICOGNANI, Amleto** - *Carta a Luigi Carli proibindo a ação do Coetus Internationalis Patris*, apud CORRISPONDENZA ROMANA (Rome), Agenzia di informazioni per la stampa, 3/28/1990. **LA CIVILTÀ CATTOLICA (Rome)** - Editorial: *Concilio, post-Concilio, para-Concilio*, 1/5/1985; Editorial: *Il ministero del Papa dopo i due Concili vaticani*, 11/2/1985; Editoriale: *Dalla 'società perfetta' alla Chiesa 'mistero'*, 1/19/1985; Editoriale, *Testimoniare la 'gioia nella speranza'*, 4/17/1971.

CLANCY, Ray - *Church pleads for greater tolerance of homosexuals*, in THE DAILY TELEGRAPH, 3/8/1995. **CLEMENT OF ALEXANDRIA** - *Stromatum*, lib. VII, c. 17, apud LEO XIII, Encyclical *Satis cognitum*. **CLOUGH, Joy** – Forum: *Letter in defense of Cardinal Joseph Louis Bernardin*, in THE WANDERER, 5/14/1992. **COLAIANNI, Nicola** - *Crítica ao Vaticano II na literatura atual*, in CONCILIUM, July 1983. **COLOMBO, Giuseppe** - *La création*, in V.A., *Bilan de la théologie du XXe. siècle*, vol. II. **COLUNGA, Alberto** - See V.A., *Biblia Sacra juxta Vulgatam clementinam*. **COMBLIN, Joseph** - *La théologie catholique depuis la fin du pontificat de Pie XII*, in V.A., *Bilan de la théologie au XXe. siècle*, vol. I. **CO-MISSION OF STUDIES OF THE TFPs (Hispanic-American)** - *Tradición, Familia, Propiedad - Un ideal, un lema, una gesta - La Cruzada del siglo XX*, São Paulo: Artpress, 1990. **COMMISSION OF STUDIES OF THE TFP (Brazilian)** - *Meio século de epopéia anticomunista*, São Paulo: Vera Cruz, 1980; *Um homem, uma obra, uma gesta - Homenagem das TFPs a Plinio Corrêa de Oliveira*, São Paulo: Ed. Brasil de Amanhã, 1989. **CONAGHAN, Dan** - *Archbishops angry at Hope 'intrusion'*, in THE DAILY TELEGRAPH, 3/15/1995. **CONCETTI, Gino** - See P. PARENTE. **COUNCIL OF ELVIRA** - *Concilium Illiberitarum*, n. 71, apud J. McNEILL, *La Iglesia ante la homosexualidad*. **COUNCIL DE TRENT** - *Canons and Decrees of the Council of Trent*, translated by H. J. Schroeder, Rockford, Ill.: Tan Publishers, 1941; *Catechism of the Council of Trent*, translated by John A. McHugh - Charles J. Callan, South Bend, Ind.: Marian Publications, 1923. **CONGAR, Yves** - *Le Concile de Vatican II - Son Église, peuple de Dieu et Corps du Christ*, Paris: Beauchesne,1984; *La crisi nella Chiesa e Mons. Lefèbvre*, Brescia: Queriniana, 1976; *L'ecclésiologie, de la Révolution Française au Concile du Vatican, sous le signe de l'affirmation de l'autorité*, in V.A., *L'ecclésiologie au XIXe. siècle. Église Catholique et France moderne*, Paris: Hachette, 1978; Interviews granted to A. SINKE GUIMARÃES, Paris, February 16 and 19, 1983; *À guisa de conclusão*, in V.A., *A Igreja do Vaticano II. Jean Puyo interroge le Père Congar - Une vie pour la verité*, Pari: Centurion, 1975; *Ministeri e communione ecclesiale, Bologna 1973*, apud P. A. BONNET. *Un peuple messianique*, Paris: Cerf, 1975; *Le rôle de l'Église dans le monde de ce temps*, in V.A., *L'Église dans le monde de ce temps*, vol. II. *Salvación y liberación*, in V.A., *Conversaciones de Toledo;* See V.A., *L'Église dans le monde de ce temps*. **CONGREGATION FOR DIVINE WORSHIP** - *Epistula - De usu Missalis romani iuxta editionem typicam anni MCMLXII*, October 3, 1984, in ACTA APOSTOLICAE SEDIS, Ed. Typis Polyglottis Vaticanis, vol. LXXVI, 12/1/1984. **CON-GREGATION FOR THE DOCTRINE OF THE FAITH** - *Alcune considerazioni concernenti la risposta a proposte di legge sulla non-discriminazione della persone omosessuali (2nd version), July 23, 1992* in L'OSSERVATORE ROMANO, 7/24/1992; *Declaração sobre alguns pontos de ética sexual*, December 29, 1975, Petrópolis: Vozes, 1976; *Lettera della Congregazione per la Dottrina della Fede a P. Schillebeeckx*, June 13, 1984, in L'OSSERVATORE ROMANO, 1/11/1985; *Lettera ai Vescovi della Chiesa Cattolica sulla cura pastorale delle persone omosessuali*, October 1, 1986, in L'OSSERVATORE ROMANO, 10/31/1986; *Notification de la Congrégation* *pour la Doctrine de la Foi à propos du livre de L. Boff: 'Église: Charisme et pouvoir,'* in LA DOCUMENTATION CATHOLIQUE, 5/5/1985. See J. RATZINGER, *Instrução sobre a vocação eclesial do teólogo.* **CONGREGATION OF THE HOLY OFFICE, Supreme.** *Decreto contra o comunismo,* June 1, 1949. **CONGREGATION OF SEMINARIES AND UNIVERSITIES, Sacred -** *Letter to Plinio Corrêa de Oliveira about The Freedom of the Church in the Communist State. September 2, 1964.* Signed by Cardinal G. PIZZARDO and by Msgr. D. STAFFA, Prefect and Secretary of the Congregation respectively; a facsimile of the letter is found in the various editions of the work. **CONWAY, Willian -** *Comentários ao Esquema XIII na Aula conciliar,* apud L. CARLI. **CORRÊA DE OLIVEIRA, Plinio -** *Acordo com o regime comunista: para a Igreja esperança ou autodemolição?,* São Paulo: Vera Cruz, 1967; first published with the title *A liberdade da Igreja no Estado comunista,* in CATOLICISMO, August 1963. See Note 2, p. 154♦, for a list of some of the newspapers that published news items on the lauunching of this work during the Council. See also CONGREGATION OF SEMINARIES AND UNIVERSITIES, Sacred; *Artigo-bomba explode em Madrid,* in FOLHA DE S. PAULO, 5/7/1969. *Baldeação ideológica inadvertida e diálogo,* São Paulo: Vera Cruz, 1966; *No Brasil: A reforma agrária leva a miséria ao campo e à cidade - A TFP informa, analisa, alerta,* São Paulo: Vera Cruz, 1986; *Comunismo e anticomunismo na orla da última década deste milênio,* in FOLHA DE S. PAULO, 2/14/1990; *Casaroli: 'incorporação no contexto',* in FOLHA DE S. PAULO, 6/30/1974; *As CEBs... das quais muito se fala, pouco se conhece - A TFP as descreve como são* (in collaboration with G. A. SOLIMEO and L. S. SOLIMEO), São Paulo: Vera Cruz, 1982; *Conforme quer Budapeste,* in FOLHA DE S. PAULO, 10/29/1974; *Declaração do Morro Alto* (in collaboration with A. CASTRO MAYER, G. P. SIGAUD, and L. M. FREITAS), São Paulo: Vera Cruz, 1964; *Em defesa da Ação Católica,* São Paulo: Ed. Ave Maria, 1943; São Paulo: Artpress, 1983; see G. B. MONTINI, *Letter to Plinio Corrêa de Oliveira;* See B. A. MASELLA. *Détente...,* in FOLHA DE S. PAULO, 11/1/1974; *'Détentes' geminadas,* in FOLHA DE S. PAULO, 12/8/1974; *Os 'grupos proféticos' a serviço da Igreja-Nova e do comunismo,* in FOLHA DE S. PAULO, 5/21/1969; *Guerreiros da Virgem - A réplica da autenticidade - A TFP sem segredos,* São Paulo: Vera Cruz, 1985; *A Igreja ante a escalada da ameaça comunista - Apelo aos Bispos silenciosos,* São Paulo: Vera Cruz, 1976. *A Igreja Católica infiltrada por adversários velados,* in CATOLICISMO, April-May 1969; *A importância do fator religioso nos rumos de um bloco-chave de países: a América Latina,* in CATOLICISMO, June 1985. *A indispensável resistência,* in FOLHA DE S. PAULO, 4/14/1974; *Da infiltração à subversão,* in FOLHA DE S. PAULO, 5/14/1969; *A liberdade da Igreja no Estado Comunista,* see *Acordo com o regime comunista - Para a Igreja esperança ou autodemolição?; Mais um Cardeal em resistência,* in FOLHA DE S. PAULO, 5/12/1974; *1958-1974: que resultados?,* in FOLHA DE S. PAULO, 7/14/1974; *Morreu o comunismo? E o anticomunismo também?,* in CORREIO BRASILIENSE, 10/18/1989; *Não conseguimos compreender,* in FOLHA DE S. PAULO, 7/7/1974; *Nobility and Analogous Traditional Elites in the Allocutions of Pius XII.* York, PA: The American

Society for the Defense of Tradition, Family and Property, 1993; *Na "noite sandinista": o incitamento à guerrilha dirigido por sandinistas "cristãos" à esquerda católica no Brasil e na América espanhola*, in CATOLICISMO, July-August 1980; *A Ostpolitik do Vaticano favorece Moscou*, in FOLHA DE S. PAULO, 6/9/1974; *Das páginas da imprensa para as da História - I*, in FOLHA DE S. PAULO, 8/17/1968; *A política de distensão do Vaticano com os governos comunistas - Para a TFP: omitir-se ou resistir?*, in FOLHA DE S. PAULO, 4/10/1974; CATOLICISMO, April 1974. See See General Introduction, pp. 33f. ♦ for an extensive list of newspapers and magazines that published this manifesto. *Projeto de Constituição angustia o País*, in CATOLICISMO, October 1987, extra edition; *A propaganda progressista: um dinossauro discreto*, in FOLHA DE S. PAULO, 3/26/1969; *A propriedade privada e a livre iniciativa no tufão agro-reformista* (in collaboration with C. del CAMPO), São Paulo,: Vera Cruz, 1985; *Reforma agrária - Questão de consciência* (in collaboration with A. CASTRO MAYER, G. P. SIGAUD, and L. M. FREITAS), São Paulo: Vera Cruz, 1960; *Resistindo...*, in FOLHA DE S. PAULO, 4/21/1974; *Revolution and Counter-Revolution,* 3rd ed., York, PA: The American Societyfor the Defense of Tradition, Family and Property, 1993. Originally published as *Revolução e Contra-Revolução*, CATOLICISMO, April 1959; Updated in CATOLICISMO, January, 1977; and later in CATOLICISMO, August 1992; *O socialismo autogestionário: em vista do comunismo barreira ou cabeça-de-ponte?*, in FOLHA DE S. PAULO, 12/17/1981; *SOS de milhões - A mala pequena - "Tudo normal,"* in FOLHA DE S. PAULO, 11/30/1969; *Sou católico: posso ser contra a reforma agrária?* (in collaboration with C. del CAMPO), São Paulo: Vera Cruz, 1981. *Ternuras que arrancariam lágrimas*, in FOLHA DE S. PAULO, 10/13/1974. *Tribalismo indígena: ideal comuno-missionário para o Brasil no século XXI*, São Paulo: Vera Cruz, 1977; *Voz dos que se calam acabrunhados*, in FOLHA DE S. PAULO, 4/28/1974. **CORRIERE DELLA SERA (Milano)** - *L'amante del vescovo Casey ringrazia per la solidarietà*, 7/5/1992; *L'amica del vescovo si confessa*, 5/10/1992; *Dopo lo scandalo il pentimento - Il vescovo diventa missionario*, 10/19/1992; *Molestie, mea culpa dei vescovi*, 11/18./1994; *Ricevuto dal Papa cardinale accusato di abusi sessuali*, 1/5/1994; *Scandalo sessuale nella cattolica Irlanda - Vescovo progressista aveva amante e figlio*, 5/9/1992; *Sesso, bugie e videotapes: sotto choc la cattolica Irlanda*, 5/12/1992; *Il vescovo confessa la paternità e i furti*, 5/13/1992; *Vienna, il cardinale cede*, 4/7/1995. **CNBB PASTORAL COMMISSION** - *Declaração sobre a Encíclica Humanae vitae*, October 25, 1968, in SEDOC (Petrópolis), February 1969, col. 1029, apud A. V. XAVIER DA SILVEIRA, *Pode haver erro em documentos do Magistério?*. *Orientação pastoral sobre a Encíclica Humanae vitae*, November 12, 1968, in SEDOC, February 1969, col. 1118, apud ibidem. **CULLMANN, Oscar** - *O filho de Lutero e Ratzinger*, interview with L. BRUNELLI - A. LABHART, in 30 DIAS, March 1993. **CURB, Rosemary** - See N. MANAHAN.

DANIÉLOU, Jean - *Relações entre Igreja e civilização*, in V.A., *Cinco problemas que desafiam a Igreja hoje*. **DAVIS, H. F.** - *Le rôle et* *l'apostolat de la Hiérarchie et du laïcat dans la théologie de l'Église chez Newman*, in V.A., *L'ecclésiologie au XIXe. siècle*. **DELHAYE, Philippe -** *In caritate non ficta*, Louvain-la-Neuve: Centre Cerfaux-Lefort, apud E. MARIANI; *Vatican II: Autorité des textes conciliaires*, in DTC, Tables, vol. III. **DELMONT, Th. -** *Modernisme et modernistes*, Paris: P. Lethielleux, 1909. **DENIFLE-CHATELAIN -** Paris: *Chartularium Universitatis Parisiensis*, 1851, II, apud C. GARCIA EXTREMEÑO. **DENZINGER (1), Henricus - Clemens BANWART (DB) -** *Enchiridion Symbolorum definitionum declarationum*, Friburgi-Brisgoviae: Herder, 1955. Collection of the most important excerpts from documents of the Magisterium compiled by the German priest Heinrich Joseph Denzinger (1819-1883) and first published in 1854. Updated by C. BANWART between 1908 and 1921. **DENZINGER (2), Enrique - Carlos RAHNER (DR) -** *El Magisterio de la Iglesia*, Barcelona: Herder, 1963. This is the same *Enchiridion Symbolorum definitionum declarationum*, published in Spanish under another title. Updated by K. RAHNER between 1946 and 1954. **DENZINGER (3), Henricus - Adolfus SCHÖNMETZER (DS) -** *Enchiridion Symbolorum definitionum declarationum*, Friburgi-Brisgoviae: Herder, 1965 (Updated by A. SCHÖNMETZER, between 1955 and 1965). **DÖPFNER, Julius -** *La Chiesa vivente oggi*, Bari: Paoline, 1972; *Comentários sobre o Esquema XIII na Aula conciliar*, apud G. CAPRILE, *Il Concilio Vaticano II*, vol. V. **DORAN, Anthony - Steve DOUGHTY -** *How the gay lobby railroaded a Cardinal*, in THE DAILY MAIL, London, 3/8/1995. **DOSSETTI, Giuseppe -** *Vaticano II: Quale recezione*, in IL REGNO, Bologna, 12/1/1991. **DOYLE, Thomas -** *Statements about pedophilia in the USA.*, apud J. BERRY, *Dioceses react to deepening dilemma*. **LA DOCUMENTATION CATHOLIQUE (Paris) -** *Bilan du dialogue judéo-chrétien*, 1/19/1986. **DRINAN, Robert -** Comments about the state of the Society of Jesus in the USA, apud L. BRUNELLI, *O balanço de Kolvenbach*. **DRUON, Maurice -** *Une Église que se trompe de siècle*, in LE MONDE, 8/7/1971. **DUBOST, Michel -** See J. CARDON-NEL. **DULLES, Avery -** *The Church, the churches and the Catholic Church*, in T.S. 33, 1972, apud F. A. SULLIVAN; *Ecumenismo: problemi e possibilità per il futuro*, in V.A., *Verso la Chiesa del terzo millennio*. **DUMONT, Fernand -** *Pour la conversion de la pensée chrètienne*, 1964, apud *The sociology of Religion and the renewal of theology*, in V.A., *Theology of renewal*, vol. II. **DUPUY, B. D. -** *Schisme et primauté chez J. A. Möhler*, in V.A., *L'ecclésiologie au XIXe. siècle*. **DUQUESNE, Jacques -** *Comments on the deposition of Msgr. Gaillot*, apud A. BOURRIER. See M. D. CHENU, *Jacques Duquesne interroge le Père Chenu*. **DUQUOC, Christian -** *Il popolo di Dio, soggetto attivo della fede nella Chiesa*, in CONCILIUM, April 1985. **DURAN, Cristina -** *Padre brasileiro deve recorrer da sentença*, in O ESTADO DE S. PAULO, 3/22/1993; *Padre brasileiro é condenado em Portugal*, in O ESTADO DE S. PAULO, 3/11/1993. **DUTCH EPISCOPATE -** Statement. See L. BRUNELLI. *A pílula que dividiu a Igreja*.

ERNSBERGER Jr., Richard - Lucy HOWARD - *Ireland is talking...*, in NEWSWEEK, 5/18/1992. **O ESTADO DE S. PAULO (São Paulo) -** *Aids é* *debatida no Vaticano*, 6/14/1989; D. *Aloísio quer Igreja em ação política*, 7/6/1985; *Celibato é discutido no Sínodo*, 10/3/1990; *Ex-padres estão organizados*, 6/15/1989; *Faltam padres em Roma, diz Cardeal*, 6/14/1989; *Grupo gay da Bahia dá troféu a d. Paulo*, 5/25/1995; *Roma: Cidade católica, mas nem tanto*, 5/11/1995. ETCHEGARAY, Roger - *Le cardinal Etchegaray, archevêque de Marseille, se souvient et balise l'avenir*, in HISTORIA, Paris, October 1982. EUSEBIUS OF CESAREA - *História eclesiástica*, Buenos Aires: Ed. Nova, 1950. EYT, Pierre - *Igreja e mutações sócio-culturais*, in V.A., *A Igreja do futuro*.

FACUNDUS Hermianense - *Liber VII*, in PL 45, 1723. *Pro defensione trium capitulorum*, in PL 67, 687. FALASHI, Celso - *Ordenação de casados é defendida por padres*, in O ESTADO DE S. PAULO, 10/24/1989. FALCONE, Mônica - *Pesquisa: 70% dos padres na Itália têm mulher*, in O GLOBO, 3/22/1987. FEINER, Johannes - *Sem título*, in V.A., *Commentary on the documents of Vatican II*. FELICI, Pericle - *Notificações*, November 16, 1964, in V.A., *Atas do Concílio Ecumênico Vaticano II*. FESQUET, Henri - *Le journal du Concile*, Forcalquier: Robert Morel, 1966. FISCHER, E. - *Kirche und Kirchen nach dem Vatikanum II*, München, 1967, apud F. A. SULLIVAN. FLICHE, Augustin - See V.A., *Histoire de l'Église*. FLICK, Maurizio - Zoltán ALSZEGHY - *Il mistero della croce - Saggio di teologia sistematica*, Brescia: Queriniana, 1978. FOGAZZARO, Antonio - *Il santo*, Milan: n.p., 1970. FOLEY, John Patrick -. *Formazione di base per l'uso dei mass-media nella diffusione del Vangelo*, in L'OSSERVATORE ROMANO, 11/23/.1994, supplement. FOLHA DE S. PAULO (São Paulo) - *AIDS-1*, 1/15/1989. FONCK, A. Nicolas - *Moehler*, in DTC, vol. X. FORCELLA, Enzo - *Papa Wojtyla e i farmacisti*, in LA REPUBBLICA, Rome, 11/5/1990. FRADE, Christina - *El sexo de los Obispos*, in EL MUNDO, Madrid, 3/19/1995. FRANZINI, Alberto - *Tradizione e Scrittura - Il contributo del Concilio Vaticano II*, Brescia: Morcelliana, 1978. FRECHET, Jean - *Vocations sacerdotales et sacerdoce des baptisés, lettre*, in LA CROIX, 31.VIII.1983. FREEMAN, Richard - *Declarações à imprensa*, apud E. BOWER, *Give lip service to Rome, encourage dissident homosexuals*. FREITAS, Luís Mendonça de - See P. CORRÊA DE OLIVEIRA, *Reforma agrária, questão de consciência;* See P. CORRÊA DE OLIVEIRA, *Declaração do Morro Alto*. FRENCH EPISCOPATE - *Declaração contrária a Encíclica Humanae vitae*, in SEDOC, February 1969, col. 1118, apud A. V. XAVIER DA SILVEIRA, *Pode haver erro em documentos do Magistério?* FRIES, Heinrich - *C'è un magistero dei fedeli?*, in CONCILIUM, April 1986; *Église et églises*, in V.A., *Problèmes et perspectives de théologie fondamentale*, apud F. A. SULLIVAN. FRISQUE, Jean - *L'ecclésiologie au XXe. siècle*, in V.A., *Bilan de la théologie du XXe. siècle*, vol. II. FUMAGALLI, Marisa - *Anatema del vescovo di Rimini - 'No' al raduno dei preti sposati*, in CORRIERE DELLA SERA, 27.VIII.1994. FURET, François - Mona OZOUF - *Dictionnaire critique de la Révolution Française*, Paris: Flammarion, 1988, apud P. CORRÊA DE OLIVEIRA, *Nobility and Analogous Traditional Elites*.

GALLI, Mario von - *La nueva liturgia*, in V.A., *La reforma que llega de Roma*. **GARCIA EXTREMEÑO, Claudio** - *El sentido de la Fe, criterio de la Tradición*, in LA CIENCIA TOMISTA, Salamanca, July- December 1960. **GARCIA DE SIERRA Y MÉNDEZ, Secundo** - *Comentários sobre o Inferno na Aula conciliar*, apud B. KLOPPENBURG, *Concílio Vaticano II*, vol. IV. **GEISELMANN, J. R.** - *Les variations de la définition de l'Église chez J. A. Möehler*, in V.A., *L'ecclésiologie au XIXe. Siècle;* Introduction to the critical edition of *Die Einheit*, Kölh-Olten, 1956; *Der Wandel des Kirchenbewusstseins und der Kirchlichkeit in der Theologie J. A. Möhlers*, Freiburg, 1961. **GENNARI, Giovanni** - *Statement* to the press, apud O GLOBO, *Padres casados abrem em Roma seu congresso*, 8/29/1986. **GERMAN EPISCOPATE** - *Declaração contrária a Encíclica Humanae vitae*, apud ICI (Paris), 9/15/1968. **GEUSAU, Leo Alting von** - *La Chiesa, 'scandalo' del mondo*, in V.A., *La fine della Chiesa come società perfetta*. **GIBELLINI, Rosino** - *Siamo d'acordo sul concilio?*, in IL REGNO, 8/15/1984. **GLEDHILL, Ruth** - *Churchmen condemn move to 'out' Hope*, in THE TIMES, 3/15/1995. **(O) GLOBO (Rio de Janeiro)** - *Bispo anglicano admite que é homossexual*, 3/9/1995; *Bispo propõe mulheres como cardeais*, 10/11/1994; *Grupo gay inglês ameaça revelar lista de políticos homossexuais*, 3/21/1995; *Padres casados abrem em Roma seu congresso*, 8/29/1986; *Religiosas feministas lutam pelo sacerdócio*, 8/7/1988. **GONZALEZ RUIZ, Jose M.** - *Lettera aperta al Cardinal Ratzinger - Le 'verità' del Cardinale prima e dopo il S. Ufficio*, in ADISTA, 1/19-21/1987. **GORI, Alberto** - *Comentários sobre o Inferno na Aula conciliar*, apud B. KLOPPENBURG, *Concílio Vaticano II*, vol. IV. **GRABER, Rudolf** - *Athanasius und die Kirche unserer Zeit*, Abensberg: Josef Kral, 1973; *Como no tempo de Atanásio*, interview with T. RICCI, in 30 DIAS, December 1990; *Por que a Igreja está em crise*, Rio de Janeiro, Grifo, 1971. **GRAMICK, Jeannine** - *Homosexuality to be a burning catholic issue* (letter of 6/24/1992), in THE NEW YORK TIMES, 7/11/1992. **GREGÓRIO XVI** - Encyclical *Mirari vos*, of August 15, 1832, in V.A., *Les enseignements pontificaux*. **GREGORY THE GREAT, St.** - *Homilia 18 in Ezechielem*, apud C. a LAPIDE, *Ad Galatas*, vol. XVIII. **GREGORY NAZIANZENE, St.** - *Epistula 102, 2 ad Cledon*, in PG 37, 200, apud V. PROAÑO GIL. **GRILLMEIER, A.** - Untitled, in V.A., *Commentary on the documents of Vatican II. LThK*, K1, 189, apud H. WALDENFELS. **GUCHT, Robert van der** - See V.A., *Bilan de la théologie au XXe. siècle*. **GUÉRANGER, Prosper** - *L'année liturgique - Le temps de la septuagesime*, Tours: Maison Mame, 1932. **GUILLEMIN de la Charité** - *La religieuse contemporaine*, apud H. FESQUET, *Le journal du Concile*. **GUMBLETON, Thomas J.** – *Statements to the press about the homosexual conference in Chicag,* apud K. PICHER; Speech at the same conference, apud E. BOWER, *Give lip service to Rome, encourage dissident homosexuals*. **GURY, Joannes Petrus - Antonius BALLERINI** - *Compendium Theologiae Moralis*, Turin: Marietti, 1866, 2 vols., apud A. V. XAVIER DA SILVEIRA, *La nouvelle Messe*. **GUTIÉRREZ, Gustavo** - *Os pobres na Igreja*, in CONCILIUM, April 1977. **GUTKIN, Steven** - *Best little convent in Bogotá*, in NEWSWEEK, 10/19/1992.

HADFIELD, Greg - *This is just a start say the activists*, in THE DAILY MAIL, 3/8/1995. **HABGOOD, John** - *When sex ceases to be private*, in THE TIMES, 3/15/1995. **HABIGER, James** – For argumentation in support of the law preventing discrimination against homosexuals in the State of Minnesota, apud P. LIKOUDIS. **HALLEUX, A.** de - *Les principes catholiques de l'oecumenisme*, Revue Theologique de Louvain, #16, 1985, apud F. A. SULLIVAN. **HAMER, Jérôme** - **Clemente RIVA** - *La libertà religiosa nel Vaticano II*, Turin: Elle Di Ci, 1967. **HÄRING, Bernard** – Public letter in opposition to the Encyclical *Humanae vitae*, apud ICI, 9/15/1968. Statement, apud T. RICCI, *O mistério do pacto Roma-Moscou*, in 30 DIAS, October 1989; *Minha participação no Concílio Vaticano II*, in REVISTA ECLESIÁSTICA BRASILEIRA, June 1994. **HARRISON, Brian** - *Se a trompa emite um som confuso...*, in 30 GIORNI, (Portuguese edition), July 1989. **HEMMERT, Guus van** – Statements to the daily EINDHOVENS DAGBLAD, apud CONFRONTATIE, Haarlem, May 1983. **HENRY, Frederick Bernard** - *Discurso no Sínodo '90*, apud R. MORABITO. **HERMANIUK, Maxim** - *Comentários ao Esquema XIII na Aula conciliar*, apud L. CARLI. **HIANDOUM, Hyacinthe** - *Paulo VI? Um Papa fiel?*, interview with S. PACI, in 30 DIAS, August/ September 1992. **HILDEBRAND, Dietrich von** - **John McMANEMIN** - "Why the Tridentine Mass?," in *Una Voce pamphlets on the Liturgy*, St. Paul: Remnant Press, n.d. **HOLZER, Anton** - *Vatikanum II - Reformkonzil oder Konstituante einer neuen Kirche*, Saka, Basel, 1977. **HOPE, David** – Letter of March 3, 1995, apud R. GLEDHILL. **HORST, Guido** - *O álcool como antídoto*, in 30 DIAS, April 1989. **HORTAL, Jesus S.** - *Comentários ao Código de Direito Canônico*, in JOHN PAUL II, *Code of Canon Law*. **HOUTART, François** - *Les religions comme réalités sociales*, in V.A., *Bilan de la théologie du XXe. siècle*, vol. I. **HOWARD, Lucy** - See R. ERNSBERGER. **HUGUES, William A.** – Statements to the press about the homosexual conference in Chicago, apud K. PICHER. **HUME, Basil** - *A Note on the teaching of the Catholic Church concerning homosexual people*, in BRIEFING, London, 3/16/1995. **HUIZING, Peter** - *Vaticano III: una costituzione sulla Chiesa*, in V.A., *Verso la Chiesa del terzo millennio*. **HURLEY, Denis** – Statement to the press opposing the Encyclical *Humanae vitae*, apud ICI, 9/15/1968. **HURTER, H.** - *Theologiae Dogmaticae compendium*, Innsbruck/Paris: Lib. Academica Wagneriana, 1883, 3 vols. **HYER, Marjorie** - *Gay-rights Priest faces expulsion*, apud THE WASHINGTON POST, 9/8/1986; JORNAL DO BRASIL, Rio de Janeiro, 11/9/1986.

IGNATIUS DE LOYOLA, St. – Letter to D. João III, de March 15, 1545, in *Obras completas*, Madrid: BAC, 1952; *Exercícios espirituais*, apud P. H. KOLVENBACH. **INFORMATIONS CATHOLIQUES INTERNATIONALES (Paris)** - *Après l'Encyclique Humanae vitae*, 19/15/1968. **ITIBERÊ, Celso** - *Escândalos sexuais que envolvem padres põem Vaticano na defensiva*, in O GLOBO, 4/14/1995.

JACQUEMONT, Patrick - *Igreja e contestação*, in V.A., *A Igreja do futuro*. JAFFÉ-WATTENBACH - *Regesta Pontificum Romanarum*, Leipzig, 1885, apud G. de PLINVAL. JAKI, S. - *Les tendances nouvelles de l'ecclésiologie*, Rome: Herder, 1957. JEROME, St. - *Contra Vigilantium*, in PL 23, 343, apud C. GARCIA EXTREMEÑO; *De viris illustribus XXXVI*, apud J. LEBRETON. JOANNOU, Peride - See V.A., *Conciliorum oecumenicorum decreta*. JOHN XXIII - Pontifical communication extracted from conciliar debates on the Schema *De fontibus Revelationis*, in B. KLOPPENBURG, *Concílio Vaticano II*, vol. II; Opening Speech of Vatican Council II of October 11, 1962, apud B. KLOPPENBURG, *Concílio Vaticano II*, vol. II; L'OSSERVATORE ROMANO, 12.X.1962; *Discorsi, messaggi, colloqui del Santo Padre Giovanni XXIII*, Tipografia Poliglota Vaticana, 1963, vol. IV; Encyclical *Pacem in terris*, of April 11, 1963, apud K. RAHNER, *Theological reflections on the problem of secularization;* Encyclical *Mater et Magistra*, of May 15, 1961, apud ibidem; *Resposta aos votos do Cardeal Eugène Tisserant*, of December 23, 1962, in L'OSSERVATORE ROMANO, 12/24-25/1962, apud A. WENGER, *Chronique de la première session*. JOHN PAUL II - Allocution to priests and men religious participating in the First Italian National Converence on the topic *'Missions to the People in the '80s,'* of February 6, 1981, in *Insegnamenti di Giovanni Paolo II*, vol. IV/1; Apostolic Letter *Ecclesia Dei*, of July 2, 1988, in *Insegnamenti di Giovanni Paolo II*, vol. XI/3; Apostolic Letter *Tertio millenio adveniente*, in L'OSSERVATORE ROMANO, 11/14-15/1994, supplement; *Código de Direito Canônico*, São Paulo: Loyola, 1983; Apostolic Constitution Constituição *Pastor Bonus*, de June 28, 1988, in *Insegnamenti di Giovanni Paolo II*, vol. XI/2; Closing Speech of the Synod '90, published under the title *Grazie al Sinodo sono stati affrontati problemi cruciali che hanno sempre trovato la risposta collegiale della Chiesa*, in L'OSSERVATORE ROMANO, 10/28/1990; *Homilia na concelebração final da Assembléia sinodal*, in L'OSSERVATORE ROMANO, (Portuguese edition), 10/30/1987. Homily for the Mass at the conclusion of the Synod, in L'OSSERVATORE ROMANO, *Solene encerramento do Sínodo extraordinário dos Bispos*, 12/15/1985; *Giovanni Paolo II alla consegna del Premio Internazionale Paolo VI - Hans Urs von Balthasar ha messo la sua conoscenza al servizio del vero che promana da Cristo*, in L'OSSERVATORE ROMANO, 6/24/1984; See K. WOJTYLA. JUNG, Carl Gustav - *The collected works*, New York: Pantheon, 1959, apud J. McNEILL, *La Iglesia ante la homosexualidad*.

KANONGATA'A, Keiti Ann - *La 'passione' per il regno di Dio*, in L'OSSERVATORE ROMANO, 11/23/1994, supplement. KARLEN, Henry Ernest - *Dimensione umana della formazione religiosa*, in L'OSSERVATORE ROMANO, 11/23/1994, supplement. KASPER, Walter - *É in questione la Chiesa e l'immagine di Dio*, in IL REGNO, 10/15/1993 - *Espírito-Cristo-Igreja*, in V.A., *A experiência do Espírito Santo*. KLOPPENBURG, Carlos Boaventura - *Concílio Vaticano II*, Vozes, Petrópolis, 1962-1966, 5 vols. *A eclesiologia do Vaticano II*, Petrópolis: Vozes, 1971. See V.A., *Documentos do Vaticano II*. KNOWLES, M. D. - See V.A., *Nouvelle Histoire de l'Église*. KOLVEN-

BACH, Peter-Hans – Press conference of 3/22/1995, in OFICINA DE PRENSA E INFORMACIÓN, Congregación General 34; Statements about the internal situation in the Society of Jesus, in L. BRUNELLI, *Kolvenbach: o Papa pode contar conosco.* **KOMBO, Ernest** - *Dopo aver gratuitamente ricevuto bisogna saper gratuitamente dare*, in L'OSSERVATORE ROMANO, 11/23/1994, supplement. **KÖNIG, Franz** - *Il Concilio, sorpresa per il mondo*, interview with S. STRACCA, in AVVENIRE, 10/16/1992. **KRICKLER, Kurt** - Statement, apud R. CHIABERNE. **KÜNG, Hans** - *A Igreja*, Lisbon: Moraes, 1969-1970, 2 vols.; *Prêtre, pour quoi faire?* Paris: Cerf, 1971; *O que deve permanecer na Igreja*, Petrópolis: Vozes, 1976; *Vaticano III: problemi e prospettive per il futuro*, in V.A., *Verso la Chiesa del terzo millennio.* See*acidade* - *O futuro da Igreja*, São Paulo: Herder, 1969; *Vida eterna?* Madrid: Cristiandad, 1983.

LABHART, Alfred - See L. BRUNELLI (2). **LACTÂNCIO** - *Lactantii divinarum institutionum libri septem IV*, apud PIUS XI, Encyclical *Mortalium animos.* **LANDÁZURI RICKETTS, Juan** - *Comentários sobre o Esquema XIII na Aula conciliar*, apud G. CAPRILE, *Il Concilio Vaticano II*, vol. V. **LANGRE, L.** - *Francia - El Clero, de derechas, distinto y levemente utopico*, in VIDA NUEVA, Madrid, 11/2/1985. **LANNE, Emmanuel** - *L'Église locale et l'Église Universelle*, in IRÉNIKON, Chevetogne/Belgique, 43, 1970, apud Y. CONGAR, *Le Concile de Vatican II.* **LAPIDE, Cornelius a** - *Commentaria in Scripturam Sacram*, Paris: Ludovicum Vivès Ed., 1874-1877, 24 vols. **LATIN AMERICAN EPISCOPAL CONFERENCE** - *A Igreja na atual transformação da América Latina à luz do Concílio - Conclusões de Medellin*, Petrópolis: Vozes, 1980. **LATTIN, Don** - *S. F. Archdiocese opposes Vatican letter on gay bias law*, in SAN FRANCISCO CHRONICLE, 7/25/1992. **LATOURELLE, René** - *Introduction*, in V.A., *Vatican II: Bilan et perspectives*, vol. I. See V.A., *Problèmes et perspectives de théologie fondamentale.* **LAURENTIN, René** - *L'enjeu et le bilan du Concile*, Paris: Seuil, 1962-1966, 5 vols. *A retomada existe. Eis a prova*, in 30 GIORNI, (Portuguese ed.), December 1988. **LEO IX, St.** - *Epistula super Librum gomorrhianum*, in PL 145, cols. 159-160. **LEO XIII** - *Motu proprio* about Popular Catholic Action, of December 18, 1903; Encyclical *Aeterni Patris*, of August 4, 1879, Petrópolis: Vozes, 1960; Encyclical *Auspicatum concessum*, September 17, 1882, Petrópolis: Vozes, 1953; Encyclical *Diuturnum illud*, June 28, 1881, in V.A., *Les enseignements pontificaux;* Encyclical *Graves de communi*, January 18, 1901, Petrópolis: Vozes, 1956; Encyclical *Humanum genus*, April 20, 1884, Petrópolis: Vozes, 1960; Encyclical *Immortale Dei*, November 1, 1885, Petrópolis: Vozes, 1954; Encyclical *Laetitiae sanctae*, September 8, 1893, Petrópolis: Vozes, 1953; Encyclical *Libertas praestantissimum*, of June 20, 1888, in V.A., *Les enseignements pontificaux.* Encyclical *Parvenu*, of March 19, 1902, Petrópolis: Vozes, 1960; Encyclical *Quod apostolici muneris*, of December 28, 1878, in V.A., *Les enseignements pontificaux;* Encyclical *Rerum novarum*, of May 15, 1891, Petrópolis: Vozes, 1954; Encyclical *Satis cognitum*, of June 29, 1896, Petrópolis: Vozes, 1960; Encyclical *Ubi primum*, May 5, 1824, in DS 2720. **LEBRETON, Jules** - *L'École chrètienne d'Alexandrie avant*

Origène, in V.A., *Histoire de l'Église*, vol. II. **LECLERC, Gerard** - *Depressão jesuítica - Europa, França*, in 30 GIORNI, (Portuguese edition), May 1989. **LEFÈBVRE, Marcel** - *Ils l'ont decouronné - Du libéralisme à l'apostasie - La tragédie conciliaire*, Escurolles: Fideliter, 1987. See G. P. SIGAUD, *Aditamento ao Esquema XIII*. **LEMIEUX, Louise** - *Selon un psychiatre - Le père Vadeboncoeur victime d'un 'dérapage' émotionnel*, in LE SOLEIL, Québec, 8/23/1985. **LEONARDI, Claudio** - See V.A., *Conciliorum oecumenicorum decreta*. **LÉRINS, St. Vincent de.** See S. VICENTE DE LÉRINS. **LIKOUDIS, Paul** - *Minnesota Catholic Conference helps write pass homosexual rights bill*, in THE WANDERER, 4/1/1993. **LINK, Gregory** - *Declarações à imprensa*, apud E. BOWER, *Give lip service to Rome, encourage dissident homosexuals*. **LONERGAN, Bernard** - *Theology in its new context*, in V.A., *Theology of renewal*, vol. I. **LOPES, Gregório** - *Plinio Corrêa de Oliveira, um cruzado do século XX*, in CATOLICISMO, September 1985. **LÓPEZ TRUJILLO, Alfonso** - *A los veinte años del Concilio*, Departamento de Publicaciones de la Arquidiócesis de Medellín, 1985. **LORSCHEIDER, Aloisio** – Pronouncement at the Synod '90, apud R. MORABITO. **LOSADA, Joaquin** - *El posconcilio: el problema de la transformación de la Iglesia*, in V.A., *Desafios cristianos*. **LOYOLA, St. Ignatius de** - See St. IGNATIUS DE LOYOLA. **LUBAC, Henri de** - *Athéisme et sens de l'homme - Une double requête de 'Gaudium et spes,'* Paris: Cerf, 1968; *Catholicisme - Les aspects sociaux du dogme*, Paris: Cerf, 1947; *Entretien autour de Vatican II*, Paris: Cerf, 1985; *Irrequieto ma ubbidiente - La Chiesa e i suoi protagonisti - Henri de Lubac*, interview with M. POLITI, in IL MESSAGGERO, Rome, 2/2/1983; *Paradoxe et mystère de l'Église*, Paris: Aubier & Montaigne, 1967. **LUGO, J. de** - *De Fide*, apud C. GARCIA EXTREMEÑO.

MADIRAN, Jean - *Autour du Concile*, in ITINÉRAIRES, Paris, December 1962; February 1963, apud A. WENGER. **MALINSKI, Mieczslaw** - *Mon ami Karol Wojtyla*, Paris: Centurion, 1980. **MANAHAN, Nancy** - Rosemary CURB - *Breaking silence: Lesbian nuns on convent sexuality*, Naiad Press, 1985, apud P. S. PINHEIRO. **MANGENOT, Eugène** - See V.A., *Dictionnaire de Théologie Catholique*. **MANSI, Joannes Dominicus** - *Sacrorum conciliorum nova et amplissima collectio*, Venice, 1759, 31 vols., apud G. de PLINVAL. **MARIANI, Eliodoro** - *La morale cristiana di fronte ai problemi degli uomini d'oggi*, in L'OSSERVATORE ROMANO, 1/5/1984. **MARLÉ, René** - *Méthodes historiques et problemes theologiques*, in V.A., *Bilan de la théologie du XXe. siècle*, vol. II. **MARRANZINI, Alfredo** - *Introduzione*, in V.A., *Il linguaggio teologico oggi*. **MARTELET, Gustave** - *Deux mille ans d'Église en question - Crise de la foi, crise du prêtre*, Paris: Cerf, 1984. **MARTIN, Victor** - See V.A., *Histoire de l'Église*. **MASELLA, Bento Aloisi** - *Prefácio a Em defesa da Ação Católica*, see P. CORRÊA DE OLIVEIRA. **MASSIE, Allan** - *Terror tactics of the Tatchell gang*, in THE DAILY TELEGRAPH, 3/15/1995. **MATOS SOARES** - See V.A., *Bíblia Sagrada*. **MATTIA, Georges** - *70.000 prêtres mariés en quête de légitimité*, in LA CROIX, 8/27/1985. **MAYER, Antonio de Castro** - See A. CASTRO MAYER. **MAYER, Paul Augustin** - *Cardeal* *anti-cisma*, interview with S.M. PACI, in 30 DIAS, June 1991. **MAZZELLA, Camillus** - *De Religione et Ecclesia*, apud A. V. XAVIER DA SILVEIRA, *La nouvelle Messe*. **McCARTHY, Tim** - *Church still on trial in pedophilia crisis*, in THE NATIONAL CATHOLIC REPORTER, Kansas City, 5/30/1986. **McGLORY, Robert** - *Bishops buck criticism, attend Gay symposium in Chicago*, in THE NATIONAL CATHOLIC RE-PORTER, 5/10/1992. **McGRANDLE, Piers** - *Church needs HIV clergy says group*, in THE CATHOLIC HERALD, 3/17/1995. **McMANEMIN, John** - See D. von HILDEBRAND. **McNEILL, John** - *The Church and the Homo-sexual*, Kansas City: Sheed Andrews & McMeel, 1976; *La Iglesia ante la homosexualidad*, Barcelona/Buenos Aires/México: Grijalbo, 1979. **MÉGRET, Maurice** - *La guerra psicologica*, Buenos Aires: Paidós, 1959. **MESSORI, Vittorio** - See J. RATZINGER, *Rapporto sulla Fede*. **METZ, Johann Baptist** - *Diálogo com Karl Rahner*, in V.A., *Cinco problemas que desafiam a Igreja hoje. Más allá de la religión burguesa - Sobre el futuro del Cristianismo*, Salamanca: Sígueme, 1982; *Sulla presenza della Chiesa nella società*, in V.A., *L'avvenire della Chiesa*. **MIGNE, J. P.** - See V.A., *Pa-trologie Grecque-Latine;* See V.A., *Patrologie Latine*. **MINDSZENTY, József** - *Erinnerungen*, Frankfurt: Ullstein, 1974. **MOCELLIN, G.** - *IV Istruzione liturgica - 30 anni dopo pensando all'Africa*, in IL REGNO, 4/15/1994. **MÖHLER, Johann Adan** - *Unidade na Igreja ou Die Einheit in der Kirche oder das Prinzip des Katholezismus dargestellt im Geiste der Kirchenväter der drei ersten Jahrhunderte*, Tübingen, 1825, apud A. N. FONCK; LA CIVILTÀ CATTOLICA, 1/19/1985. *Simbólica ou Symbolik, oder Darstellung der dogmatischen Gegensätze der Katholiken und Protes-tanten nach ihren öffentlichen Bekenntnisschriften*, Mainz, 1832, apud A. N. FONCK; LA CIVILTÀ CATTOLICA, 1/19/1985. **MOLARI, Carlo** - *La problematica del linguaggio teologico*, in V.A., *Il linguaggio teologico oggi*. **MONDIN, Battista** - *Introduzione alla teologia*, Milan: Massimo, 1983. *Os grandes teólogos do século vinte*, São Paulo: Paulinas, 1979, 2 vols. **MONGES DE SOLESMES** - See V.A., *Les enseignements pontificaux*. **MONTINI, Giovanni Baptista** - *Carta a Plinio Corrêa de Oliveira*, of Feb-ruary 26, 1949, in P. CORRÊA DE OLIVEIRA, *Em defesa da Ação Católica* (1983 edition). See PAUL VI. **MORABITO, Rocco** - *Discussão do celibato domina Sínodo*, in O ESTADO DE S. PAULO, 10/4/1990. **MOTOLESE, Guglielmo** - *La Chiesa, compagna di viaggio dell'uomo - I grandi testimoni del Vaticano II/7*, interview with S. STRACCA, in AVVENIRE, 9/27/1992. **MOUROUX, Jacques** - *Situation et signification du chapitre I (de la Gaudium et spes): Sur la dignité de la personne humaine*, in V.A., *L'Église dans le monde de ce temps*, vol. II. **MOYNIHAN, Robert** - *A Aids cria problemas*, in 30 GIORNI, Februrary 1980. **MUCCHIELI, Roger** - *La subversión*, Paris: Bordas, 1972. **MUGGERIDGE, Anne Roche** - *The desolate city - Revolution in the Catholic Church*, San Francisco: Harper & Row, 1990. **MÜLLER, Alois** - *Chiesa e riforma*, in V.A., *Verso la Chiesa del terzo millennio*.

NATIONAL CONFERENCE OF BRAZILIAN BISHOPS - *Roma locuta - Documentário sobre o livro 'Igreja: Carisma e poder - Ensaios de eclesiolo-*

gia militante' de Frei Leonardo Boff, OFM, Petrópolis: Vozes, 1985. See CNBB PASTORAL COMMISSIONS. **NAVARRO-VALS, Joaquin** - *Declarações à imprensa*, apud AVVENIRE, *Chiarezza, non discrinazione*, 7/24/1992; *Responding to legislative proposals on discrimination against homosexual*, in ORIGINS - CNS Documentary Service, 8/6/1992. **NEW-MAN, John Henry** - *On consulting the faithful in matters of doctrine*, in THE RAMBLER, 1859, apud C. GARCIA EXTREMEÑO. **NEWSWEEK (New York)** - *Gays in the Clergy*, 2/23/1987. **NICODEMO, Enrico** - *Comentários sobre o Inferno na Aula conciliar*, apud B. KLOPPENBURG, *Concílio Vaticano II*, vol. IV. **NOÉ, Vigilio** - *Il primo dono al popolo cristiano*, in L'OSSERVATORE ROMANO, 12/14/1983, special supplement sulla Costituzione *Sacrosanctum Concilium*. **NORDLAND, Rod** - *'The Church has AIDS' - Anger flares at Vatican conference*, in NEWSWEEK, 11/27/1989. **NUBIUS** - *Instruções secretas sobre a conquista da Igreja*, apud E. BARBIER, *Les infiltrations maçoniques dans l'Église*, Paris/Brussells: Desclée de Brouwer, 1910. **NYGREN, David - Miriam UKERITIS** - *USA: il futuro dei religiosi*, in IL REGNO, 4/1/1993.

ODDI, Silvio - *Confissões de um Cardeal*, interview with T. RICCI, in 30 DIAS, November 1990; *Il tenero mastino di Dio*, Rome: Progetti Museali Editore, 1995. **OPTATUS OF MILEVIS, St.** - *Libri septem de schismate Donatistarum*, apud LEÃO XIII, Encyclical *Satis cognitum*. **L'OSSERVATORE ROMANO (Città del Vaticano)** - *Il Cardinale Ratzinger: "La fede è il bene più alto. Bisogna sempre vigilare perchè non si corrompa,"* 11/9/1984; *O Concílio é dom de Deus à Igreja e ao mundo*, 12/15/1985; *Presentato al Santo Padre l'Annuario Pontificio 1994*, 2/28/1994 - 3/1/1994. *Solene encerramento do Sínodo extraordinário dos Bispos - O Sínodo projecta o Concílio para o terceiro milênio*, 12/15/1985; *Valutazione delle linee di tendenza dell'attività pastorale della Chiesa cattolica fino al 1986*, 5/30-31/1988, supplement. **OSTLING, Richard Nugent** - *The battle over Gay clergy - Demands for toleration shake many North American churches*, in TIME, New York, 11/13/1989; *An unholy Holy week*, in TIME, 4/24/1995. **OTTAVIANI, Alfredo** - *Entrevista* a CORRIERE DELLA SERA, 10/28/1965, apud H. FESQUET, *Le journal du Concile*. **OZOUF, Mona** - See F. FURET.

PACI, Stefano - *Precisam-se vocações - Pesquisa - A crise das religiosas*, in 30 DIAS, April 1990; See P. A. MAYER, *Cardeal anti-cisma;* See F. SCHMIDBERGER; See H. THIANDOUM. **PARENTE, Pietro** - *Cristo, Maria, la Chiesa: i punti nevralgici della mia ricerca teologica*, interview with G. CONCETTI, in L'OSSERVATORE ROMANO, 12/29/1985. **PARTIDO COMUNISTA ITALIANO** - *Argumentos*, in PROPAGANDA, apud R. GRABER, *Athanasius und die Kirche unserer Zeit. Declarações sobre o diálogo com os católicos*, in PROPAGANDA, apud ibidem. **PASSOS, José Meirelles** - *Acusações de sexo e racismo envolvem Bispos americanos*, in O GLOBO, 11/7/1989. **PAUL VI** – Allocution to the students of the Lombard Seminary of December 7, 1968, in *Insegnamenti di Paolo VI*, Tipografia Poliglotta Vaticana, vol. VI; Allocution *Resistite fortes in fide*, of June 29,

1972, in *Insegnamenti di Paolo VI*, vol. X; Allocution to the Sacred College, of May 18, 1970, in *Insegnamenti di Paolo VI*, vol. VIII. Apostolic Constitution *Missale romanum*, of March 4, 1969, Typis Polyglottis Vaticanis, 1970; in *Ordo Missae;* General Audience, of January 12, 1966, in *Insegnamenti di Paolo VI*, vol. IV; Audience to the participants of the 13th Week of Pastoral Updating, of September 6, 1963, in B. KLOPPENBURG, *Concílio Vaticano II*, vol. III; Audience tot he participants of the International Thomist congress of September 12, 1970, in *Insegnamenti di Paolo VI*, vol. VIII; Brief *In Spiritu Sancto*, of December 7, 1965, in B. KLOPPENBURG, *Concílio Vaticano II*, vol. V; Opening Speech of the Second Conciliar Session, of September 29, 1963, in B. KLOPPENBURG, *Concílio Vaticano II*, vol. VIII. Encyclical *Ecclesiam suam*, of August 6, 1964, in *Insegnamenti di Paolo VI, 1963 a 1970, Encicliche*. Encyclical *Humanae vitae*, of July 25, 1968, in *Insegnamenti di Paolo VI, 1963-1970, Encicliche*. "Formulas of Promulgation of the Sixteen Conciliar Documents," in V.A., *Documentos do Vaticano II*. Encyclical *Populorum progressio*, of March 26, 1967, apud K. RAHNER, *Theological reflections on the problem of secularization. Novus ordo Missae ou Nuevas normas de la Misa - Ordenación general del Missal Romano*, Madrid: BAC, 1969; *Ordo Missae*, Rome: Typis Polyglottis Vaticanis, 1969; See G. B. MONTINI. **PEINADOR, Antonio** - *Cursus brevior Theologiae Moralis*, Madrid: Coculsa, 1946-1956, 4 vols. **PELLAND, Gilles** - *À propos de triomphalisme*, in V.A., *Vatican II: Bilan et perspectives*, vol. I. **PELÂTRE, Louis** - *Islam: la paura ingiustificata*, interview with F. STRAZZARI, in IL REGNO, 3/15/1993. **PEROTTI, Jacques** - *Todo amor es sagrado*, interview with M. URRUZOLA, in EL PAIS, Montevideo, 3/4/1994. **PEUCHMAURD, Maurice** - See V.A., *L'Église dans le monde de ce temps*. **PHILIPS, Gérard** - *La Chiesa e il suo mistero nel Concilio Vaticano II - Storia, testo e commento della Costituzione Lumen gentium*, Milan: Jaca Books, 1975; *L'Église et son mystère au deuxième concile du Vatican*, apud F. A. SULLIVAN. **P ICHER, Keith** - *Bishops urge less rigid Church attitude toward homosexuals*, in CATHOLIC NEWS SERVICE, Chicago, 3/31/1992. See a list of American newspapers that published this item in Note 1, p. 310f.◆. **PIGHI, J. Baptista** - *Institutiones Historiae ecclesiasticae*, Verona: Bibliopolae Editoris Pontificii, 1922, 3 vols. **PIMENTEL, Aristides** - *Declaração à imprensa*, apud O ESTADO DE S. PAULO, *Ex-padres estão organizados*, 6/15/1989. **PINHEIRO, Paulo Sérgio** - *A transa das freiras e outras transas*, in FOLHA DE S. PAULO, 6/18/1985. **PINSK, J.** - *La situation actuelle de la théologie catholique en Allemagne*, in V.A., *Catholicisme allemand*. **PIUS V, St.** - Bull *Quo primum tempore*, of 1570. **PIUS VI** – Allocution at the Secret Consistory, of June 17, 1793, in *Pii VI Pontificis Maximi Acta*, Rome: Typis S. Congreg. de Propaganda Fide, 1871, vol. II; Bull *Auctorem Fidei*, of August 28, 1794; Letter-Decree to the Cardinal de La Rochefoucauld and the Archbishop of Aixen-Provence, of March 10, 1791, in *Pii VI Pontificis Maximi Acta*, vol. I; Encyclical *Inscrutabile Divinae Sapientiae*, Of December 25, 1775. **PIUS IX** - Allocution *Acerbissimum*, of September 27, 1852, in V.A., *Recueil des allocutions;* Allocution *Iamdudum cernimus*, of March 18, 1861, in idem. Allocution *Maxima quidem*, of June 9, 1862, in idem; Allocution *Nemo* *vestrum*, of July 26, 1855, in idem; Allocution *Nunquam fore*, of December 15, 1856, in idem; Allocution *Singulari quadam*, of December 9, 1852, in D 1642; Allocution *Ubi primum*, of December 17, 1848, in V.A., *Recueil des allocutions;* Letter *Gravissimas inter*, of December 22, 1862, in DS 2850-2861; Letter *Multiplices inter*, of June 10, 1851, in V.A., *Recueil des allocutions;* Letter *Tuas libenter*, of December 21, 1863, in DS 2875; Encyclical *Nostis et nobiscum*, of December 8, 1849, in V.A., *Les enseignements pontificaux;* Encyclical *Quanta cura*, of December 8, 1864, in DS 2890, Petrópolis: Vozes, 1951; Encyclical *Quanto conficiamur*, of August 10, 1863, in DS 2865ff.; V.A., *Recueil des allocutions;* Encyclical *Qui pluribus*, of November 9, 1846, in DS 2785; V.A., *Recueil des allocutions,* Petrópolis: Vozes, 1960; Encyclical *Singulari quidem*, of March 17, 1856, in V.A., *Recueil des allocutions; Syllabus*, of December 8, 1864, in DS 2902, 2915-2918, 2977-2980, Petrópolis: Vozes, 1951. **PIUS X, St.** – Apostolica Letter *Notre charge apostolique*, of August 25, 1910, Petrópolis: Vozes, 1953; *Catecismo maior*, São Paulo: Vera Cruz, 1976; Encyclical *Pascendi Dominici gregis*, of September 8, 1907, Petrópolis: Vozes, 1959; *Motu proprio* about Catholic Action, in *Lettres apostoliques de S. Pie X*, Paris: Bonne Presse, 1926. **PIUS XI** – Encyclical *Divini Redemptoris*, of March 19, 1937, in DS 3773, Buenos Aires: Ed. Roma, n.d.; Encyclical *Quadragesimo anno*, of March 15, 1931, in DS 3742ff., Paris: Ed. Spes, 1954. Encyclical *Mortalium animos*, of January 6, 1928, in *Actes de S.S. Pie XI*, Paris: Bonne Presse, Paris, vol. IV. **PIUS XII** – Letter to the XLI Social Week of France, of July 14, 1954, in *Discorsi e radiomessaggi*, vol. XVI; Decree of the Supreme Congregation of the Holy Office Against Communism, of June 1, 1943; Speech to the 1st International Congress of Social Studies and the International Christian Association, of June 3, 1950, in *Discorsi e radiomessaggi*, vol. XII; Speech to the International Congress on Problems of Rural Life, of July 2, 1951, in *Discorsi e radiomessaggi*, vol. XIII; Speech to the IX International Conference of Catholic Associations, of May 7, 1949, in *Discorsi e radiomessaggi*, vol. XI; Speech to the VII Congress of the Christian Union of Corporate Heads and Mangers of Italy, of March 7, 1957, in *Discorsi e radiomessaggi*, vol. XIX; Encyclical *Humani generis*, of August 12, 1950, Petrópolis: Vozes, 1961. Encyclical *Mystici Corporis Christi*, of June 29, 1943, Petrópolis: Vozes, 1960; *Radiomensagem de Natal de 1944*, Petrópolis: Vozes, 1951; *Radiomensagem ao Katholikentag de Viena*, of September 14, 1952, in *Discorsi e radiomessaggi*, vol. XIV. **PIZZARDO, Giuseppe -** See SACRED CONGREGATION OF SEMINARIES AND UNIVERSITIES. **PLINVAL, G. de -** *Les luttes pélagiennes*, in V.A., *Histoire de l'Église*, vol. IV. **PLOEG, J. van der -** *Pesquisa entre párocos de Utrecht*, in KATHOLIEKE STEMMEN, Tilburg, June-July 1983. **POLETTI, Ugo -** *Declarações à imprensa*, apud O ESTADO DE S. PAULO, *Faltam padres em Roma, diz Cardeal*, 6/14/1989. **POLITI, Marco -** *Eva sull'altare*, in LA REPUBBLICA, 10/12/1994; *Sesso, preghiere & aldilà*, in LA REPUBBLICA, 5/9/1995; See H. de LUBAC, *Irrequieto ma ubbidiente - La Chiesa e i suoi protagonisti - Henri de Lubac*. **PRATA, Mario -** *Senhor Cunha ou Fred do caniçal?* in O ESTADO DE S. PAULO, 3/22/1993. **PRESS, Aric -** *Priests and abuse*, in NEWSWEEK, 8/16/1993. **PREZZI, Lorenzo -** *Vescovi e*

religiosi, profilo modesto, in IL REGNO, 9/15/1993. **PROAÑO GIL,**
Vicente - *Infalibilidad*, in V.A., *Gran enciclopedia*, vol. XII. **PRODI,**
Paolo - See V.A., *Conciliorum oecumenicorum decreta.* **PROENÇA SI-**
GAUD, Geraldo de - See G. P. SIGAUD. **PROSPER OF AQUITAINW,**
St. - *Liber contra Collatorem*, in PL 45, 1808. **PRZYWARA, Erich -**
Corpus Christi mysticum. Eine Bilanz, in ZEITSCHRIFT FÜR ASZESE
UND MYSTIK, 15, 1940, apud A. ACERBI. **PUYO, Jean** - See Y. CON-
GAR, *Jean Puyo interroge le Père Congar.*

QUALTER, Terence H. - *Propaganda and psychological warfare*, New
York: Random House, 1965.

RAFFIN, Pierre - *I beni dei religiosi al servizio della missione*, in
L'OSSERVATORE ROMANO, 11/23/1994, supplement.   **RAHNER, Karl**
- *Karl Rahner em diálogo com Johann Baptist Metz*, in V.A., *Cinco prob-*
lemas que desafiam a Igreja hoje;   La Chiesa peccatrice nei decreti del Con-
cilio Vaticano II, Rome, 1968, apud M. FLICK - Z. ALSZEGHY; *Magis-*
tero e teologia dopo il Concilio, Brescia: Queriniana, 1967; *Théologie et*
anthropologie, in V.A., *Théologie d'aujourd'hui et de demain;   Theological*
reflections on the problem of secularization, in V.A., *Theology of renewal*,
vol. I;   *Vaticano II: Um começo de renovação*, São Paulo: Herder, 1966;
See H. DENZINGER (2).   **RATZINGER, Joseph** - *La eclesiología del*
Vaticano, in IGLESIA-MUNDO, Madrid, October 1986;   *Ecco perché la*
fede è in crisi, interview with V. MESSORI, in JESUS (Milan), November
1984;   *Instrução sobre a vocação eclesial do teólogo*, published with the
title: *Rinnovato dialogo fra Magistero e Teologia*, in L'OSSERVATORE
ROMANO, 6/27/1990;   *La fede è il bene più alto. Bisogna sempre vigilare*
perchè non si corrompa, in L'OSSERVATORE ROMANO, 11/9/1984;   *Il*
nuovo popolo di Dio, Brescia: Queriniana, 1971, apud J. M. GONZALEZ
RUIZ;   *Um passado que não lhes diz respeito*, in 30 DIAS, January 1994;
Les principes de la Théologie Catholique - Esquisse et materiaux, Paris: Tequi, 1985; *Problemi e risultati del Concilio Vaticano II*, Brescia: Queriniana,
1967. *Rapporto sulla Fede - Vittorio Messori a colloquio con Joseph Ratz-*
inger, Rome: Paoline, 1985; *Ratzinger reafirma identidade católica*, interview with W. FALCETA, in O ESTADO DE S. PAULO, 8/29/1990; *Der*
Weltdienst der Kirche: Zehn Jahre nach Vaticanum II, Regensburg: A.
Bauch- A. Glasser- M. Seybold Ed., 1976; *Zehn Jahre Vaticanum II*, Regensburg, 1976, apud R. GIBELLINI. **LA REPUBBLICA -** *Preti sposati in*
cerca di diritto, 8/29/1994. **REED, Luther** - *The Lutheran Liturgy*, Philadelphia: Fortress Press, 1959, in A. V. XAVIER DA SILVEIRA, *La nou-*
velle Messe. **REIFFENSTUEL, Anacletus** - *Theologia Moralis*, Venice:
Bortoli, 1704, in A. V. XAVIER DA SILVEIRA, *La nouvelle Messe.* **RE-**
VILLA TORICES, Benedito – Statements to the press, apud O ESTADO
DE S. PAULO, 7/6/1985. **RICCI, Tommaso** - *A "distração" do Concílio*,
in 30 DIAS, August/September 1989;   *Engrenagem quase perfeita*, in 30
DIAS, December 1989;   *O mistério do pacto Roma-Moscou*, in 30 DIAS,
October 1989; See S. ODDI;   See R. GRABER. **RIO, Domenico del -**
Sono settanta mile i sacerdoti sposati, in LA REPUBBLICA, 8/25/1985.

RIPALDA, J. M. de - *De Fide*, apud C. GARCIA EXTREMEÑO. **RIVA, Clemente** - See J. HAMER.   **ROACH, John** - *Defesa escrita dos direitos dos homossexuais*, apud P. LIKOUDIS. **ROBERT BELLARMINE, St.** - *Disputationes de controversiis christianae Fidei adversus huius temporis haereticos* (1586-1593), Venice, 1721, apud LA CIVILTÀ CATTOLICA, Editoriale: *Dalla 'società perfetta' alla Chiesa 'mistero,'* 1/19/1985. *De Romano Pontifice*, in *Opera omnia*, Neapoli/Panormi/Paris: Pedone Lauriel, 1871, vol. I. *De Verbo Dei*, apud C. GARCIA EXTREMEÑO. **ROBERTS, Thomas** - *Declaração à imprensa* in opposition to the Encyclical *Humanae vitae*, apud ICI, 9/15/1968. **ROCCA, Giancarlo** - *Modelli in crisi e nuove vie*, in IL REGNO, 1/15/1993.   **ROCCA, Orazio la** - *Dalle Filippine arriva la 'tralta delle novizie,'* in LA REPUBBLICA, 10/3/1994; *Le suore a Wojtyla: 'Più soldi e potere'* - *Ecco le 'sindacaliste di Dio'*, in LA REPUBBLICA, 10/8/1994; *'Dimenticate i beni terrani'* - *Il Papa contro le 'sindacaliste di Dio,'* in LA REPUBBLICA, 10/13/1994; *Wojtyla: 'Piango i preti tentati dai vizi del sesso,'* in LA REPUBBLICA, 12/22/1993.   **ROCHETTE, Madeleine** - *Il ruolo profetico della vita religiosa*, in L'OSSERVATORE ROMANO, 11/23/1994, supplement. **ROGIER, L. J.** - See V.A., *Nouvelle Histoire de l'Église*.   **ROMANO, Luca** - *Estremisti omosex minacciano di fare i nomi di prelati e deputati*, in IL GIORNALE, 3/15/1995. **ROMANO ROCHA, Pedro** - "La principale manifestation de l'Eglise", in V.A., *Vatican II - Bilan et perspectives*, vol. II.   **ROUSSEAU, Olivier** - *A Constituição no quadro dos movimentos renovadores de teologia e de pastoral das últimas décadas*, in V.A., *A Igreja do Vaticano II. Les attitudes de pensée concernant l'unité chrétienne au XIXe. siècle*, in V.A., *L'ecclésiologie au XIXe. siècle*.   **RUFFINI, Ernesto** - *Comentários sobre o Esquema XIII na Aula conciliar*, apud G. CAPRILE, *Il Concilio Vaticano II*, vol. V; *Comentários sobre o Inferno na Aula conciliar*, apud B. KLOPPENBURG, *Concílio Vaticano II*, vol. IV.

SAMBORN, Randall - *Priest playing hardball to battle abuse charges*, in THE NATIONAL LAW JOURNAL, July 1994.   **SÂNDALO BERNARDINO, Angélico** - *Declarações sobre homossexualidade no Clero de São Paulo*, apud R. ARRUDA, *D. Angélico nega que Igreja esconda doentes*.   **SANSA, Tito** - *"Rivoluzione in Chiesa"* - *Referendum choc tra gli austriaci*, in LA STAMPA, Turin, 7/6/1995.   **SARTORI, Luigi** - *Il linguaggio del Vaticano II*, in V.A., *Il linguaggio teologico oggi. Spirito Santo e storia* - *Testimonianza cattolica*, in V.A., *Lo Spirito Santo pegno e primizia del regno*.   **SCANTAMBURLO, Giovanni** - *Perché il Concilio non ha condannato il comunismo*, Rome: Ed. L'Appennino, 1967.   **SCARPA, Pedro Luís Guido** - *Formazione 'inculturata' ma esigente*, in L'OSSERVATORE ROMANO, 11/23/1994, supplement. **SCHILLEBEECKX, Edward** - Statement, apud R. AMERIO. *Dio è un dono non una garanzia*, interview with F. STRAZZARI, in IL REGNO, 6/15/1990; *Fundamento da autoridade na Igreja*, in V.A., *Cinco problemas que desafiam a Igreja de hoje. Gott ist jeden Tag neu* - *Ein Gespräch*, Mainz: Matthias Grünewald, 1984, apud ORIENTIERUNG, Zürich, 1/31/1985. *I laici nel popolo di Dio*, in V.A., *La fine della Chiesa come società perfetta. Le min-*

istère dans l'Église, Paris: Cerf, 1981. *The real achievment of Vatican II*, New York: Herder & Herder, 1967, apud A. R. MUGGERIDGE. *Igreja ou igrejas?*, in V.A., *Cinco problemas que desafiam a Igreja hoje*. *Wij denken gepassioneerd en in cliche's*, in DE BAZUIN, January 1965, apud A. ACERBI. **SCHMIDBERGER, Franz** - *Mas eu respondo a König*, entrevista a S. PACCI, in 30 DIAS, November 1992. **SCHNITZER, Vivianne** - *Ameaza de cisma en la Iglesia Católia austriaca tras el "caso Gröer"*, in EL PAIS, 7/4/1995; *Más denuncias de homosexualidad contra el cardenal Gröer*, in EL PAIS, 4/3/1995. **SCHÖNMETZER, Adolfus** - See H. DENZINGER (3). **SCHOUPPE, F. X.** - *Curso abreviado de Religião ou verdade e beleza da Religião Cristã*, Porto: Liv. Chardron, 1875. **SCHWAGER, Raymund** – Interview granted to A. SINKE GUIMARÃES, Innsbruck, February 11, 1983. **SESBOÜÉ, Bernard.** *O Evangelho na Igreja - A tradição viva da fé*, São Paulo: Paulinas, 1977. **SIETMANN, Klara** - *Rendere visibili i trati del volto di Dio*, in L'OSSERVATORE RO-MANO, 11/23/1994, supplement. **SIGAUD, Geraldo de Proença** - *Aditamento ao Esquema XIII*, delivered jointly with M. LEFÈBVRE, and signed by 435 conciliar Fathers, apud L. CARLI, *Il comunismo e il Concilio Vaticano II*, 30 DIAS, August-September 1989; See P. CORRÊA DE OLIVEIRA, *Declaração do Morro Alto;* See P. CORRÊA DE OLIVEIRA, *Reforma agrária, questão de consciência.* **SILVA, José Ariovaldo da** - *O movimento litúrgico no Brasil - Estudo histórico*, Petrópolis: Voces, 1983. **SILVA HENRÍQUEZ, Raúl** - *Comentários sobre o Esquema XIII na Aula conciliar*, apud G. CAPRILE, *Il Concilio Vaticano II*, vol. V. **SIMÕES, Rogério** - *Bispo anglicano defende sacerdotes homossexuais*, in FOLHA DE S. PAULO, 4/9/1995. **SIN, Jaime** - *Por algumas túnicas a mais*, interview with L. BRUNELLI, in 30 DIAS, October 1994. **SINKE GUIMARÃES, Atila** – Interview with G. CAPRILE, Rome, February 3, 1983; Interview with M. D. CHENU, Paris, February 20, 1983; Interview with Y. CON-GAR, Paris, February 16 and 19, 1983; Interview with R. SCHWAGER, Innsbruck, February 11, 1983. **SIPE, Richard** - *A secret World: Sexuality and the Search of Celibacy*, apud THE ECONOMIST, 6/18/1992; *Estatística sobre pedofilia nos EUA*, apud R. BRANCOLI. **SIXTUS V** - Bull *Triumphantis*, 1588, apud LEO XIII, Encyclical *Aeterni Patris*. **SOARES DE AZEVEDO, Mateus** - *O Concílio que não terminou*, in JORNAL DA TARDE, 10/24/1992. **SOLIMEO, Gustavo Antonio** - See P. CORRÊA DE OLIVEIRA, *As CEBs... das quais muito se fala, pouco se conhece.* **SOLIMEO, Luís Sérgio** - See P. CORRÊA DE OLIVEIRA, *As CEBs... das quais muito se fala, pouco se conhece.* **SORGE, Bartolomeo** - *I cristiani nel mondo postmoderno - Presenza, assenza, mediazione?*, in LA CIVILTÀ CATTOLICA, 5/7/1983. **SORRENTINO, Aurelio** - *La Chiesa, compagna di viaggio dell'uomo - I grandi testimoni del Vaticano II/7*, interview with S. STRACCA, in AVVENIRE, 11/27/1992. **SOUZA LIMA, Lizânias de** - *Plinio Corrêa de Oliveira, um cruzado do século XX*, University of São Paulo, Ph.D. dissertation, 1985. **SPIRAGO, Francisco** - *Catecismo católico popular*, Lisbon: União Gráfica Ed., 1951, vol. II. **SPRINGS, Jemez** - *Sins of the fathers*, in THE ECONOMIST, London, 6/18/1992. **STAFFA, Dino** - See SACRED CONGREGATION OF SEMINARIES AND

UNIVERSITIES. **STEINFELS, Peter** - *Vatican condones gay-rights limits*, in THE NEW YORK TIMES, 7/18/1992. **STEINSCHULTE, Gabriel Maria** - *Paesi di lingua tedesca - Vent'anni di riforme, prima e dopo*, in L'OSSERVATORE ROMANO, 12/14/1983, special supplement sulla Costituzione *Sacrosanctum Concilium*. **STIMPFLE, Joseph** - *Comentários ao Esquema XIII na Aula conciliar*, apud L. CARLI. **STRACCA, Silvano** - See F. KÖNIG; See G. MOTOLESE; See A. SORRENTINO; See L. J. SUENENS, *Un nuovo battesimo per la cristinianità*. **STRAZZARI, Francesco** - *Di caso in caso*, apud IL REGNO, May 1995; See L. PELÂTRE; See E. SCHILLEBEECKX, *Dio è un dono non una garanzia*. **SUAREZ, Francisco** - *Defensio Fidei catholicae*, apud A. V. XAVIER DA SILVEIRA, *La nouvelle Messe*; apud F. X. WERNZ - P. VIDAL. *De Christo*, apud C. GARCIA EXTREMEÑO; *De Fide*, in *Opera omnia*, Paris: Vivès, 1958, vol. XII, apud A. V. XAVIER DA SILVEIRA, *La nouvelle Messe. De legibus*, in *Opera omnia*, 1956, vol. V, apud ibidem. **SUENENS, Leo Józef** - *Co-responsability: dominating idea of the Council and its pastoral consequences*, in V.A., *Theology of renewal*, vol. II. *Declaração à Rádio Vaticana*, of November 7, 1985; *Discorso ufficiale d'apertura - Alcuni compite della teologia oggi*, in V.A., *L'avvenire della Chiesa; Souvenirs et espérances*, Paris: Fayard, 1991; *Un nuovo battesimo per la Cristianità - I grandi testimoni del Vaticano II/2*, interview with S. STRACCA, in AVVENIRE, 10/23/1992. **SULLIVAN, Francis A.** - *Le sens et l'importance de la décision de Vatican II de dire, à propos de l'Église du Christ, non pas qu'elle 'est' mais qu'elle 'subsiste dans' l'Église Catholique Romaine*, in V.A., *Vatican II: Bilan et perspectives*, vol. II. **SUMAH, Rose** - *Le religiose nelle Giovani Chiese*, in L'OSSERVATORE ROMANO, 11/23/1994, supplement. **SYNOD OF BISHOPS - 1994** – *Message to the People of God*, in L'OSSERVATORE ROMANO, 9/23/1994, supplement. **SYNOD OF BISHOPS, EXTRAORDINARY – 1995** – *Message to the People of God*, in L'OSSERVATORE ROMANO, (Portuguese edition), 12/15/1985; *Relatio finalis*, in *Enchiridion Vaticanum*, 1798/9, apud G. DOSSETTI.

TANQUEREY, Adolphus - *Synopsis theologiae dogmaticae*, Tournai: Desclée, 1937, vol. I. **TATCHELL, Peter** - *Declaração*, apud M. VIGNOLO, *Preti e politici gay dovete confessare*, in CORRIERE DELLA SERA, 3/21/1995. **TAYLOR, Eamon** – Letter in response to Fr. John McNeill, of January 28, 1976, apud J. McNEILL, *La Iglesia ante la homosexualidad*. **TEPE, Valfredo** - Statements, in O ESTADO DE S. PAULO, *Celibato é discutido no Sínodo*, 10/3/1990; *Discurso no Sínodo'90*, apud R. MORABITO. **TERTULIAN** - *De praescriptionibus adversus haereticos*, in PL 2, 40, apud V. PROAÑO GIL. **THOMAS, Edwin** - *Relato*, apud ADISTA, *Amori gay all'ombra del cupulone. Inchiesta di "Micromega" fra i sacerdoti omosessuali*, 5/13/1995. **TILLIETTE, Xavier** - *Começar de novo. Com fé*, in 30 GIORNI, (Portuguese edition), December 1988. **TIME (New York)** - *The battle over gay clergy*, 10/13/1989; *Fallen from grace*, 5.25.1992. **TODARO, Margaret Patrice** - *Pastors, prophets and politicians: A study of the Brazilian Catholic Church, 1916-1945*, University of Columbia, 1971. **THOMAS AQUINAS, St.** - *Commentaria super libros* *sententiarum*, L. Lethielleux, Parisiis, 1929- 1947, 5 vols.; *Super Epistulas S. Pauli, Ad Galatas*, Turin/Rome: Marietti, 1953; *Summa theologiae*, Turin/Rome: Marietti, 1948, 4 vols. *Summa teologica*, Madrid: BAC, 1947-1960, 16 vols. **TOMKO, Jozef** - *Riconciliazione e penitenza*, in L'OSSERVATORE ROMANO, 12/1/1983, supplement. **TORNIELLI, Andrea** - *O outono quente dos religiosos*, in 30 DIAS, September 1994; *O timoneiro do Concílio*, in 30 DIAS, July 1992. **TRINCHARD, Paul** - *New Mass in Light of the Old*, Monrovia, CA: Marian Publications, 1995; See Remi AMELUNXEN. **TSHIBANGU TSHISHIKU, Tharcisse** - *Crisi dei confessori*, in L'OSSERVATORE ROMANO, 10/5/1983, supplement. **TUCCI, Roberto** - *Introduzione storico-dottrinale alla costituzione pastorale Gaudium et spes*, in *La Costituzione pastorale sulla Chiesa nel mondo contemporaneo*, Turin, 1966, apud G. CAPRILE, *Il Concilio Vaticano II*, vol. V. **TURRADO, Laurentio** - See V.A., *Biblia Sacra juxta Vulgatam clementinam*.

UFFICIO CENTRALE DI STATISTICA DELLA CHIESA - *La Chiesa cattolica alla luce di alcuni fenomeni statistici dal 1978 al 1990*, in L'OSSERVATORE ROMANO, 7/15/.1992, supplement; L'OSSERVATORE ROMANO, 10/171992, supplement. **UKERITIS, Miriam** - See D. NYGREN. **UNION OF PASTORAL AGENTS (Utrecht)** - *Párocos rejeitam doutrina da Igreja sobre homossexualismo*, apud J. van der PLOEG. **UNTENER, Kenneth** - *Declarações à imprensa a propósito de congresso homossexual em Chicago*, apud K. PICHER. **URDANOZ, Teofilo** - *Commentaire sur les 'Relecciones teologicas de Francisco Vitoria'*, apud A. V. XAVIER DA SILVEIRA, *La nouvelle Messe*. **URRUZOLA, Maria** - See J. PEROTTI.

V.A. (Various Authors)- *Atas do Concílio Ecumênico Vaticano II*, apud V.A., *Documentos do Vaticano II*. *L'avvenire della Chiesa - Il libro del Congresso* (from the journal "Concilium"), Brescia: Queriniana, 1970; *Biblia Sacra juxta Vulgatam clementinam* (logicis partitionibus aliisque subsidiis ornata a A. COLUNGA et L. TURRADO), Madrid: BAC, 1965; *Bíblia Sagrada* (translated from the *Vulgate* and annoted by MATOS SOARES), São Paulo: Paulinas, 1964; *Bilan de la théologie au XXe. siècle* (coord. R. VANDER GUCHT - H. VORGRIMLER), Tournai/Paris: Casterman, 1970, 2 vols.; *Catholicisme allemand*, Paris: Cerf, 1956; *Cinco problemas que desafiam a Igreja hoje*, , São Paulo: Herder, 1970; *Commentary on the documents of Vatican II*, Herder, 2 vols., apud F. A. SULLIVAN; *Conciliorum oecumenicorum decreta* (ed. G. ALBERIGO - P. JOANNOU - C. LEONARDI - P. PRODI), , Freiburg im Breisgau: Herder, 1962; *Conversaciones de Toledo - Teología de la liberación*, Bruges: Aldecoa, 1973; *Desafios cristianos*, Madrid: Loguez Ed., 1990; *Dictionnaire de théologie catholique - DTC* (coord. A. VACANT - E. MANGENOT), Paris: E. Librairie Letouzey & Ané, 1927- 1972, 18 vols.; *Documentos do Vaticano II - Constituições, decretos e declarações* (ed. B. KLOPPENBURG - F. VIER; Portuguese edition reviewed by the undersecretaries of the National Conference of Brazilian Bishops, Petrópolis: Vozes, 1966; *L'ecclésiologie au XIXe.*

siècle, Paris: Cerf, 1960; *L'Église dans le monde de ce temps - Constitution pastorale 'Gaudium et spes'* (eds. Y. CONGAR - M. PEUCHMAURD), Paris: Cerf, 1967, 3 vols.; *Les enseignements pontificaux - La paix intérieure des nations* (ed. MONKS DE SOLESMES), Tournai: Desclée & Cie, 1952; *A experiência do Espírito Santo*, Petrópolis: Vozes, 1979; *La fine della Chiesa come società perfetta*, Verona: Mondadori, 1968; *Gran enciclopedia*, Madrid: Ed. Rialp S/A, 1971-1976, 24 vols.; *Enciclopedia universal ilustrada europeo-americana*, Madrid/Barcelona: Espasa Calpe, 1930-1956, 70 vols., 10 appendices and 3 supplements; *I grandi temi del Concilio*, Rome: Paoline, 1965; *Histoire de l'Église depuis les origines jusqu'à nos jours* (ed. A. FLICHE - V. MARTIN), Paris: Bloud & Gay, 1946-1952, 21 vols.; *A Igreja do futuro*, Petrópolis: Vozes, 1973; *A Igreja do Vaticano II* (ed. G. BARAÚNA), Petrópolis: Vozes, 1965; *Il linguaggio teologico oggi* (ed. ASSOCIAZIÓNE TEOLOGICA ITALIANA, Milan: Àncora, 1970; *Nouvelle Histoire de l'Église* (eds. R. AUBERT - M. D. KNOWLES - L. J. ROGIER), Paris: Seuill, 1975, 5 vols.; *Patrologiae Grecquae-Latinae cursus completus ... Series Graeca* (PG), (ed. J. P. MIGNE), Paris: Migne, 1857-76, 217 vols., 4 indices; *Patrologiae Latinae cursus completus ... Series Latina* (PL), (ed. J. P. MIGNE), Paris: Migne. 1841-64, 161 vols., 1 index; *Problèmes et perspectives de théologie fondamentale* (ed. R. LATOURELLE), Paris/Tournai/Montréal: G. O'Collins Ed., 1982; *Recueil des allocutions consistoriales, encycliques et autres lettres apostoliques des Souverains Pontifes Clément XII, Benoît XIV, Pie VI, Pie VII, Léon XII, Grégoire XVI et Pie IX. Citées dans l'Encyclique et le Syllabus du 8 décembre 1864, suivi du Concordat de 1801 et de divers autres documents*, Paris: Adrien le Clere, 1865; *La reforma que llega de Roma*, Barcelona: Plaza & Janes, 1970; *Lo Spirito Santo pegno e primizia del regno - Atti della XIX sessione di formazione ecumenica organizzata dal Segretariato Attività Ecumeniche, Trento*, Turin: Elle Di Ci, 1982; *Théologie d'aujourd'hui et de demain*, Paris: Cerf, 1967; *Theology of renewal - Renewal of religious thought*, Montreal: Palm Publishers, 1968, 2 vols; *Vatican II: Bilan et perspectives, vingt-cinq ans après (1962-1987)* (ed. R. LATOURELLE), Montreal/Paris: Bellarmin-Cerf, 1988, 3 vols.; *Verso la Chiesa del terzo millennio*, Brescia: Queriniana, 1979. **VACANT, Alfred** - See V.A., *Dictionnaire de Théologie Catholique*. **VAGAGGINI, Cipriano** - *Presentazione*, in A. ACERBI. **VANCOURT, Raymond** - *Patriarcates*, in DTC, vol. XI. **VANDER GUCHT, Robert** - See V.A., *Bilan de la théologie du XXe. siècle*. **LA VANGUARDIA (Barcelona)** - *Un líder gay afirma que quatro obispos austriacos son* homosexuales, 8/2/1995. **VATICAN COUNCIL I** - *Constitutio Dogmatica de Fide catholica*, apud PIUS XII, Encyclical *Mystici Corporis Christi*. **VEJA (São Paulo)** - *Pecados na sacristia*, 3/17/1993; *Processado*, 11/17/1993. **VENTURI, Alfredo** - *Austria, vescovi alla gogna*, in CORRIERE DELLA SERA, 8/2/1995. **VERGOTE, Antoine** - *La presenza della Chiesa nella società di domani - Riflessioni bibliche*, in V.A., *L'avvenire della Chiesa*. **VERMEIL, Edmond** - *Jean-Adam Möhler et l'École Catholique de Tubingue*, Armand Colin, Paris, 1913. **VINCENT OF LÉRINS, St.** - *Commonitorium*, in PL 50, 670. **VIDAL, Pedro** - See F. X. WERNZ. **LA VIE (Paris)** - *Les volets du presbytère sont ouverts*, apud L.

LANGRE. **VIER, Frederico** - See V.A., *Documentos do Vaticano II.* **VIGNOLO, Mino** - *Preti e politici gay dovete confessare*, in CORRIERE DELLA SERA, 3/21/1995. **VITORIA, Francisco de** - *Obras de Francisco de Vitoria*, Madrid: BAC, 1960. **VORGRIMLER, Herbert** - *Dal 'sensus fidei' al 'consensus fidelium'*, in CONCILIUM, April 1986. See V.A., *Bilan de la théologie au XXe. siècle.*

WALDENFELDS, Hans - *Autorità e conoscenza*, in CONCILIUM, April 1985. **THE WANDERER (Saint Paul, Minessota)** - *The Forum - Journalistic Ethics*, 5/14/1992. **WEAKLAND, Rembert** - *Comentários à carta da Santa Sé, a qual restringe direitos civis de homossexuais*, apud P. STEINFELS. **WERNER-KÜMMEL** - *Les recherches exégétiques sur le Nouveau Testament*, in V.A., *Bilan de la théologie au XXe. siècle*, vol. II. **WENGER, Antoine** - *L'Église en son temps - Vatican II - Chronique*, Paris: Centurion, 1963-1966, 4 vols. **WERNZ, Francisco Xavier** - **Pedro VIDAL** - *Ius Canonicum*, Rome: Aedes Universitatis Gregorianae, 1927, 2 vols. **WHITE, John** - *Declarações*, apud O ESTADO DE S. PAULO, *Aids é debatida no Vaticano*, 6/14/1989. **WHITE, Murray** - *Cardinal launches attack on homophobia*, in THE CATHOLIC HERALD, 3/10/1995. **WILLEBRANDS, Jan** - *Allocution au Comité international de liaison du dialogue judéo-chrétien*, in LA DOCUMENTATION CATHOLIQUE, *Bilan du dialogue judéo-chrétien*, 1/19/1986. **WILLIANSON, Robert** – Statement to the press, apud R. GLEDHILL. **WILLOUGHBY, Willian** - *Superiors 'honor the conscience' of nuns who signed pro-choice ad*, in THE WASHINGTON TIMES, 1/11/1985. **WILTGEN, Ralph** - *The Rhine flows into the Tiber*, Devon (England): Augustine, 1978. **WOJTYLA, Karol** - *Alle fonti del rinnovamento - Studio sull'attuazione del Concilio Vaticano Secondo*, Città del Vaticano: Libreria Editrice Vaticana, 1981; See JOHN PAUL II. **WOODROW, Alain** - *A Rome: Trente théologiens du monde entier pour accomplir le Concile*, in ICI, 5/15/1969. **WOODWARD, Kenneth L.** - *An acute shortage of priests*, in NEWSWEEK, 4/18/1983; *The sins of the father*, in NEWSWEEK, 6/1/1992; *Was it real or memories?*, in NEWSWEEK, 3/14/1994.

XAVIER DA SILVEIRA, Arnaldo Vidigal. *Na nouvelle Messe de Paul VI: Qu'en penser?* Chiré-en-Montreuil: Diffusion de la Pensée Française, 1975; *Pode haver erro em documentos do Magistério?* in CATOLICISMO, July 1969; *Qual a autoridade doutrinária dos documentos pontifícios e conciliares?* in CATOLICISMO, October 1967. **YU PIN** – Commentaries on *Schema XIII* in the Conciliar Hall, apud L. CARLI. **ZEILLER, Jacques** - *La propagation du Christianisme*, in V.A., *Histoire de l'Église*, vol. I. **ZERO HORA (Porto Alegre)** - *Padre americano será julgado por tara sexual*, 10/14/1985. **ZÓZIMO, São** - Carta *Magnus pondus*, apud G. de PLINVAL; Letter *Postquam nobis*, of September 21, 417, apud ibidem; *Tractatoria*, apud ibidem. **ZUCCOLINI, Roberto** - *Ruini: 'È vero, la città è ormai diventata una terra di missione,'* in CORRIERE DELLA SERA, 5/12/1995. * * *

INDEX

134. **Thinking and intention** of the Council with regard to ambiguity: Conclusion § 3. **Transitory phase** in a process of conciliar ambiguity: Chap. II.§ 5. **Types** of ambiguity: Chap. II §§ 1-5. **Various ways** that ambiguity can be employed: Chap. II.§§ 2-5. **View of the ensemble:** Introduction to Volume I, §§1-6.

militant character: General Introduction § 20. **Negation of missionary character of**: Chap. IX.§ 1, 50-56.

CHURCH, ROMAN CHARACTER OF - In the Conciliar texts, omissions: Chap. VIII §§ 16-18.

CHURCH-STATE RELATIONS - **Adaptation** of the Church to the temporal order: Chap. IX §§ 67-73. See ADAPTATION TO THE WORLD. **Ambiguity** regarding the concept of the world: Chap. IX §§ 58-66, Note 57. **Distinction between spiritual and temporal spheres** disappears: Chap. IX § 74. **Negation of the ideal** of Christendom: Chap. IX §§ 85-93. See CHRISTENDOM.

COGNITION – Knowledge through co-naturality: General Introduction, Note 1.i

COLLECTION: ELI, ELI, LAMMA SABACTHANI? – **Audience** to whom this work is directed (Pope, bishops, theologians, laymen): General Introduction §15. **Brief history:** General Introduction, § 5, 14 §§17-29. **Certainty** of the conclusions: General Introduction, §§ 3,5. **Citations**: General information §§ 1f., 5. **Credentials** of the author: General Introduction §§ 6-13. **Criteria for analysis:** General Introduction §2. **Disposition** of the author: General Introduction § 16; clarifications: §§ 1,4. **Duty and right** to analyze the Council: General Introduction, §§ 6-11, Notes 3, 4. Clarifying Notes.§§ 1, 4. **Inspiration and orientation** given by Plinio Correa de Oliveira: Homage and Gratitude; General Introduction §§13, 17, 24. **Limits in responsibility** of the author: General information § 9; General Introduction §13. **Limits of the work:** General Introduction § 5. **Method** used: General Introduction § 3. **Official documents** that authorize a layman to analyze the Council: General Introduction §§ 8ff. **Persons** who aided in preparing and publishing the work: Homage and gratitude. **Objectives:** General Introduction §§ 1, 29. **Plan** adopted: General Introduction § 4. **Publications used** and interviews: General information § 3. **Reason for the title:** General Introduction §14. **Style** and language: General Introduction § 16. **Updating credentials** of the cited authors: General information § 7.

COLLEGIALITY - Chap. IV. § 11; Chap. VI.§ 22, 61ff., 100ff; Chap. X, Note 15.

COMMUNISM – **Adaptation** of the Church to communism: Chap. I, Note 13c. **Jesuits** who collaborate with the Chinese communist regime: Chap. X §94. **Ostpolitik**: General Introduction, Notes 16.b, Chap. X, Note 22. **Papal Documents** about communism and socialism: Chap. I, Note 14.c. **Petition at Council asking for condemnation** of communism: Chap. VI §§ 85-98. **'People of God'** and communism: Chap. I.§§ 2,4. **Pressure** on Vatican leaders to avoid condemnation of communism: Chap. VI §§ 85-98. **Satisfaction** of Italian Communist Party (IPC) with the direction taken by Vatican II: Chap. I, Note 13c.

CONCESSIONS TO THE FALSE RELLIGIONS – **Fruits:** Chap. IX.1 passim; Chap. X§11. **Judaism:** Chap. VI § 119; Chap. IX §50. **Relation to** the spirit of the Council: General Introduction, § 19, 22.

4,7; Conclusion §3. **Policy of compromise** as characteristic of the Council: Chap. III. §§ 8f. **Present-day situation:** the Council is outdated: Chap. V §§19ff. **Progressivist current:** Chap. IV §§ 3-6. **Rejection** of preparatory schemes: Chap. IV§§ 2, Note 2; Chap. VI §§ 50, 83f. **Represents end** of an era: Chap. VI§31. **Spirit** of the Council: General Introduction §§ 18-22; Conclusion §3. **Tactics:** General information §4; see Ambiguity. **Themes** of conciliar preparatory schemas: Chap. VI, Note 47. **Theological qualifications** of the Council: Chap. VI, §§33-64, 65-134. **Theological qualifications** within the context of conciliar history: Chap. VI §§35f.; **Subjects dealt with**: Chap. VI, §§ 37-48. **Titles** of the authors who wrote about the Council: General information §7. **Unity** in conciliar documents: General Introduction §§ 2f, 5.

COUNCIL, VATICAN III - Chap. V. §§11, 19, 21; Chap. VI §§ 16, 131f.; Chap. X.§ 40.

COUNCILS, HISTORY OF - Chap. VI § 35, Notes 42-45.

CRISIS, CONCILIAR - **Aspects of** the conciliar crisis in the application of Council directives: Chap. X §§ 28-31, 32-36, 37-42. **Cause of** conciliar crisis is the Council itself: Chap. X. § 128, Note 174. **Clergy and religious Orders:** Chap. X§§ 51-116. **Faith:** Chap. X §§ 117-128. **Unity:** Chap. X §§ 13-27.

CURIA, ROMAN - Reforms made by John XXIII, Paul VI, and John Paul II: General information § 6.

DEMOCRATIZATION OF CHURCH - Inter-relationship with the notion of the 'People of God': General Introduction § 23; Chap. I, § 2, Note 7.

DIALETICS, HEGELIAN - General Introduction § 23.

DIALOGUE - As a talismanic word: General Introduction § 23.

DIGNITIES - **Moral dignity**: Appendix 5 § 88. **Ontological dignity**: Appendix 5 § 87. **Social dignity:** Appendix 5 § 89.

DOCTRINE - Ways in which it can be understood: Chap. VI, Note 1.b, c.

DOGMA - Concept, according to Möhler: Chap. IV, Note 5d. Dogmatic formuations must change according to the evolution of things: Chap. VII §§ 10-14, 17.

DUTY, MORAL - That a Catholic has in relation to his Faith: General Introduction § 6; Note 3, 4.

ECUMENISM - SEE CONCESSIONS AND FALSE RELIGIONS.

ELI, ELI, LAMMA SABACTHANI? - SEE COLLECTION

ELIAS, PROPHET - Conclusion § 3

ESCHATOLOGY - Doctrine of evolution as a basis for conciliar eschatology: Chap. VII §§ 17, 19.

EVOLUTION - **Essence of,** and the 'Spirit of God': Chap. VII § 13. **Man** and evolution: Chap. VII § 15. **Natural** and **supernatural:** Chap. IV, Note 5f. **Objective** toward which the Church should tend: Chap. VII § 12. **Progressivism** and evolution: General Introduction, Note 23. **Signs of the times** and evolution: Chap. VII § 14. **Underlying conciliar ambiguity** is the doctrine of evolution: Chap. VII §§ 10-19. **Word 'evolution'** in conciliar texts: Chap. VII § 11.

EXISTENTIALISM - General Introduction § 23; Chap. VII § 5.

prevalence: General Introduction, Note 23. **Principal representatives** at the Council, Chap. IV §§ 5s; Notes 8, 9. **Radical** progressivists contest Vatican directives: Chap. X § 9, 43-50, Note 24. **Risk of fragmentation** in the unity of progressivist current of thought: General Introduction § 26. **Semi-furtive** preparations: Chap. IV, Note 7c-g. **Support** given by high Vatican authorities to its leaders: Chap. VI §§ 78-80. **Thinking** of the progressivist current: General Introduction §§ 19, 24-26. **Unity** among progressivists and their followers: General Introduction § 26. **Victory** in Vatican II: Chap. IV § 4. *SEE COUNCIL.*

PSYCHOANALYSIS, FREUDIAN – **Freudian undertones** of the new ecclesiology: General Introduction § 23. **Position of the Council:** Chap. VIII §§ 21ff. **Tolerance** in relation to Freud: Chap. VI§ 53; Appendix §§ 28ff., 37.

PSYCHOLOGY, MODERN - Doctrines regarding homosexuality: Appendix §§ 28, 37.

PSYCHOLOGICAL WAR (PSY WAR) – **Application of the expression** to conflicts that are not specifically military and to progressivist expansion: General Introduction § 23, Note 27a. **Testimony** of experts: General Introduction, Note 27b.

PUBLIC OPINION- **Aceptance of the Council** by public opinion: Chap. X §§ 3-6. **Conservative public opinion:** Chap. X § 2. **Crisis** as a phenomenon of public opinion: see *CRISIS, AMBIGUITY, SILENT MAJORITY.* **Optimism,** an erroneous position: Chap. X, Note 13. **Resistance** of Catholics to conciliar directives: Chap. X §§ 7-10.

REDEMPTION - Its fruits: Chap. IX § 64.

REFORM, LITURGICAL – Msgr. **Bugnini's role:** Chap. IV, Note 9. **Initiated by Pius XII:** Chap. IX § 3, Note 4. **Messianic character:** Chap. IX § 14. **Need for speed**: Chap. IX § 13. **Protestantization** of the Church: Chap. IX §§ 47ff. *Sacrosanctum Concilum,* **fundamental role in Council:** Chap. IX §§ 4-21. *SEE MASS, LITURGY, NEW.*

REFORM OF THE ORDO MISSAE - See *MASS.*

RESISTANCE OF THE FAITHFUL TO THE DECISIONS OF THE SUPREME ECCLESIASTICAL AUTHORITY – **Example of resistance** of two saints to a Pope: St. Augustine and St. Aurelius resist Pope Zozimus: General Introduction § 16. **Possibility of disagreement** of laity: General Introduction, Note 5b. **Rectitude** of judgment of the *sensus fidelium*: General Introduction, Note 1h. **Resistance Manifesto** to Vatican *Ostpolitik*: General Introduction, Note 16b; Chap. X § 8. **Right of Resistance** according to Church Fathers, Doctors, theologians and canonists: General Introduction, Note 3a-k.

REVELATION, CONCEPTS OF- Traditional: Chap. IX § 75. Progressivist: Chap. IX §§ 75-78.

REVOLUTION, CONCILIAR -- *COPERNICAN REVOLUTION -* Chap. VII § 28, Chap IX, § 84, Note 91.

REVOLUTION, FRENCH (FR) – **Adaptation of Church** to the errors of the FR: Chap. I § 4. **Deceptive appearance of lack of unity in FR:**

General Introduction, Note 29. **Errors** of the FR and the expression "People of God": Chap. I §§ 2, 4, Note 13a. **Pontifical documents** condemning the FR: Chap. I, Note 14a. **Doctrine** from which the modern world was born and its fruit: Chap. IX § 65.

REVOLUTION, HOMOSEXUAL - See *HOMOSEXUALITY*.

REVOLUTION, PROTESTANT – New version of free interpretation, Chap. VII § 14. See *MASS*.

RIGHT, NATURAL, that a Catholic has to expound on his Faith: General Introduction, § 6, Notes 3, 4. Example of St. Ignatius: General Introduction, § 11, Notes 10.

ROMANTICISM – Romantic school of Tübingen: Chap. IV § 3. *SEE PROGRESSIVISM, MOHLER.*

SACROSANCTUM CONCILIUM – **Adaptation of the world to false religions**: Chap. IX §§ 6,19. **Collegiality of Bishops**: Chap. IX § 13; in detriment to papal power: Chap. IX §15. **Confusion between various forms of presence** of Christ in the Church: Chap. IX § 7. **De-sacralization** of ceremonies: Chap. IX. §§ 9, 11. **Encouraging use of the venacular:** Chap. IX § 18. **Equality between the priesthood and the faithful**: Chap. IX §§ 8, 17. **Exaltation of Scriptures**, promoting social equality: Chap. IX, §16; §10. **Facilitating end of the Latin Rite:** Chap. IX § 19. **Indirect mention** of the Protestant theory of the two tables: Chap. IX § 12. **Promoting 'inculturation':** Chap.IX § 19. **Tendencies that open the doors for abuses:** Chap. IX § 20.

SCHOLASTICISM: **Benefit to Church**: Chap. 3, § 2. Disgarded in the language of Vatican II: Chap. 3, § 3. Praise of Scholasiticsm by Pope Sixtus V: Chap 3, § 2. See Thomism.

SENSUS FIDEI – Link to the *sensus fidelium*: General Introduction, Note 1c. Its signficance: General Introduction, Note 1c.

SENSUS FIDELIUM – **Amplitude and profundity** according to progressivst authors: General Introduction, Note 1k, l. **Application and limits:** General Introduction, Note 1d. **Assistance** of the Holy Ghost: General Introduction, Note 1f. **Authority**: General Introduction, Note 1f. **Concept**: General Introduction § 2; Note 1a-c. **Contemporary authors** who deal with the subject: General Introduction, Note 1g, k. **Criteria for analysis of the Council**: General Introduction, § 1. **Example in our days**: movement and school of thought of Plinio Corrêa de Oliveira: General Introduction §§12; Notes 13, 14, 15. **Historical examples:** General Introduction, Note 1g, h. **Importance** as a testimony of the indefectible Faith of the Church: General Introduction, Note 1j. **Intellectuals** who deal with the subject: General Introduction, Note 1b, d, i, j. **Link with the sense of the Faith**: General Introduction, Note 1c. **Sense** used: General Introduction, Note 1a-c, l.

SILENT MAJORITY – As a segment of public opinion: General Introduction, Note 23; Chap. 10 §§1-9. See *PUBLIC OPINION*.

SMOKE OF SATAN - Metaphor used by Paul VI describing the crisis in the Church: Introduction to Volume I § 6; Chap. X § 14.

* * *